TEACHING THE
INTEGRATED
LANGUAGE ARTS

W9-DDF-139

C. 7 pp 420-430
C. 8 up to 265
C. 13
C. 9
C. 10
C. 14

TEACHING THE INTEGRATED LANGUAGE ARTS

Process and Practice

Anthony D. Fredericks
York College of Pennsylvania

Bonnie Blake-Kline
York College of Pennsylvania

Janice V. Kristo
University of Maine

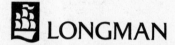

An imprint of Addison Wesley Longman, Inc.

New York • Reading, Massachusetts • Menlo Park, California • Harlow, England
Don Mills, Ontario • Sydney • Mexico City • Madrid • Amsterdam

Acquisitions Editor: Chris Jennison
Project Coordination and Text Design: York Production Services
Cover Designer: Nancy Sabato
Art Coordination: York Production Services
Electronic Production Manager: Valerie Zaborski
Manufacturing Manager: Helene G. Landers
Electronic Page Makeup: York Production Services
Printer and Binder: R. R. Donnelley & Sons Company
Cover Printer: Phoenix Color Corp.

For permission to use copyrighted material, grateful acknowledgment is made to the copyright holders on p. 503, which is hereby made part of this copyright page.

Library of Congress Cataloging-in-Publication Data

Fredericks, Anthony D.
    Teaching the integrated language arts : process and practice / by
Anthony D. Fredericks, Bonnie Blake-Kline, Janice V. Kristo.
        p.   cm.
    Includes bibliographical references and index.
    ISBN 0-673-98557-1
    1. Language arts (Elementary)—United States. 2. Language arts—Correlation with content
subjects—United States. I. Blake-Kline, Bonnie. II. Kristo, Janice V. III. Title.
LB1576.F724   1996
372.6044—dc20   95-25902
                                                                                                    CIP

Copyright © 1997 by Addison-Wesley Educational Publishers Inc.

All rights reserved. No part of this publication may be reproduced, stored in a retrieval system, or transmitted, in any form or by any means, electronic, mechanical, photocopying, recording, or otherwise, without the prior written permission of the publisher. Printed in the United States.

ISBN 0-673-98557-1

12345678910—DOC—99989796

To Cathy Swanson, whose creative energy, infectious wit,
and instructional expertise serve as models for us all!

—A.D.F.

This book is dedicated to Valerie.
May Valerie's creative spirit be released within its pages.

—B. B-K.

This book is dedicated to family, friends, teachers, and students
who encouraged and supported this endeavor, and to Ken,
who many years ago, taught me to persevere
and see a project to its completion.

. . . and to Onna, my furry friend,
who spent many hours sitting patiently
by the computer.

—J.V.K.

CONTENTS

TWO
CREATING LITERACY-RICH CLASSROOMS   165

THREE   EXTENDING LEARNING AND LITERACY   437

A Letter to Our Readers

Dear Student:

We are teachers! We have experienced the joys of reading a brand new book to our students, the thrill of watching a child "get it" during a math lesson, the excitement of bringing a science lesson to life, the fascination of creating castles with sugar cubes, and even the "delight" of having a bat zoom back and forth through our classroom. For us, teaching has been, and continues to be, a never-ending process of discovery and creativity. Indeed, we are as excited about teaching today as we were when we walked into our first classrooms, taught our first lessons, and watched our first students grow and develop in magical ways.

This book was written to communicate the joys and excitement associated with being a teacher. We believe that helping children grow as language users leads to unknown possibilities and discoveries, and to an abundance of riches for **all** youngsters. A major philosophy that undergirds this text is that children are natural learners and that teachers can share the fun and excitement of learning every day.

We think it is important at this point that you understand how this book came to be and what propelled us as we prepared the manuscript. Basically, we were driven by three highly related concepts. First, during the preparation of this manuscript, we met with teachers from throughout the country. We talked with educators from Maine to California, observed language arts lessons from Washington to Florida, and interviewed students from all points in between. What we came away with was a spirit, an energy, and an excitement that was both inspiring and motivating. We wanted to share that excitement and to present classroom vignettes from the scores of educators and students we visited throughout the United States.

Second, we were guided by a philosophy of teaching that conceives of the best teachers as those "who have as much to learn as they do to teach." Thus our emphasis throughout this text is on the "teacher as learner"—a teacher who **guides** rather than **leads**; **facilitates** rather than **assigns**; and **models** rather than **tells**. Our experiences have taught us that the most successful teachers of language arts are those who are willing to learn alongside their students—providing students with the processes and the supportive arena in which they can begin to make their own discoveries and pursue their own self-initiated investigations. As such, the focus of this text is on developing an "invitational classroom"—one in which teachers **invite** students to become active participants in the learning process and one in which students **invite** teachers to join with them as codiscoverers within an integrated language arts program.

The third factor that guided our writing was a fact known to most college students—that is, that many textbooks are lifeless, dull, and dry! We believe that if language arts is to be exciting and dynamic, then that attitude should be woven throughout every dimension of a methods text. We have worked hard to make this text a "user friendly" one—ensuring that the ideas, principles, and strategies are presented in an interesting format and in a familiar language. (In other words, we made an honest effort to stay away from an excessive amount of "professor-ese.") Although our respective philosophies are quite similar, our classroom experiences are very different. (Tony taught in suburban schools in Arizona and Pennsylvania, and urban schools in California; Bonnie taught in urban schools in Maryland; and Jan taught in suburban schools in Massachusetts, urban schools in New York, and observed rural schools in Maine.) Thus, although we have had differing classroom experiences, we wanted to demonstrate that a consistent philosophy on teaching language arts could be universally applied in a variety of school settings with an equal variety of students.

We believe that helping future educators become successful teachers of language arts means helping them to realize their own empowerment for instilling the sense of wonder, awe, mystery, and creativity usually associated with young children. Teachers need to know that language arts instruction should not be confined to the limits of a teacher's manual or a curriculum guide. Rather, it is participatory—offering unlimited opportunities to actively involve learners in a host of engaging and supportive endeavors across the curriculum. In essence, effective language arts instruction is a constant process of involvement in genuine activities for real purposes—involvement on the part of students as well as teachers.

We have designed this text as an instructional tool for future educators in a methods class and as a reference tool for teachers once they enter their own classrooms. Our emphasis throughout this book has been on practicality and utility. In our attempt to make this text as useful as possible, we have included several important features:

- **Teacher as Learner/Teacher as Researcher:** Even after more than 50 years of combined teaching experience, we still believe that we have much to learn about how kids learn and how teachers teach. We believe the asking of questions and the seeking of answers does not begin and end with a college course. Teaching is exciting for us because we continue to explore and examine its dimensions and possibilities. We hope you will join us in this constant investigation of "what can be" through the special activities we have provided at the end of each chapter. This section offers you some unique opportunities to search for instructional possibilities, both now and throughout your first few years of classroom teaching.

- **Cathy Swanson's Journal:** One way we have chosen to demonstrate the ongoing learning process of teachers is through a series of reflective journal entries tracing the year-long development of fourth-grade teacher Cathy Swanson as she examines the dynamics of teaching the integrated language arts (see the introduction to Cathy's journal near the end of Chapter 1). Cathy's journal will provide you with some insights into the decisions teachers make every day and the ways in which those decisions affect students.

- **A Community of Learners:** We believe that some of the most exciting classrooms are those that support and involve all learners. We have provided vignettes of many of those classrooms (from around the United States) throughout the chapters in this book—offering insights and models for the teachers of tomorrow. Our goal is to help prospective teachers design classroom environments that nurture and sustain the instructional opportunities for **all** youngsters.

- **Integrative Approach:** One of the major trends in elementary education is the integration of language arts throughout the entire elementary curriculum. We have tried to present language arts not as an isolated subject area but rather as a process of investigation and discovery that can be integrated throughout all subjects and certainly throughout any child's life.

- **Authentic Assessment:** We discovered that the assessment chapter in most language arts texts appeared as a final chapter. We were concerned about the implications for future teachers. We believe that assessment is not something to be considered at the conclusion of a lesson but rather something to be integrated throughout all aspects of the language arts curriculum—from beginning to end! Thus we have placed the assessment chapter in Part One of this book.

- **Literature Focus:** We believe that quality children's literature is an essential element in any language arts program and certainly in any elementary classroom. Indeed, a major focus in this text is on identifying important literature and offering engaging language arts activities that can be used with that literature. We offer prospective teachers a variety of literature choices within each chapter as well as three separate chapters on using children's literature (Chapter 10: Creating Literature-Rich Classrooms; Chapter 12: Building Reading/Writing Connections; and Chapter 14: Teaching Thematically: Integrating Language Arts Across the Curriculum).

- **What I Know: Pre-Chapter Journaling:** At the beginning of each chapter is an open-ended journaling activity. We invite you to respond to the question prior to reading the chapter. You may wish to do this in a separate journal or notebook. There are no right or wrong answers to these queries; rather we would like to have you think about how your personal experiences (your "background knowledge") are related to the concepts in each chapter. In addition, we invite you to share your responses with others in this course—noting similarities or differences in background experiences, perceptions, or interpretations.

- **Anticipatory Web:** At the beginning of each chapter is an anticipatory web. Included on the web are the major concepts and principles discussed within the chapter. You should feel free to record your background knowledge about those ideas as well as any questions you may have directly on the web. (Yes, we are encouraging you to write in your textbook.) As before, you may wish to discuss the information you have added to your web with that of others in the class. In addition, you are invited to add important data to the web after you have finished reading the chapter or discussed it in class. These webs can be valuable resources for class discussions and lesson planning.

- **For Your Journal:** We would like to invite you to maintain a personal journal throughout this course and throughout your reading of this text. Within all the chapters are one or more "For Your Journal" sections which offer you an opportunity to reflect on a particular concept, write a reaction to one or more specific questions, or investigate what is happening in elementary classrooms in local schools. These can serve as a worthwhile record of your "journey" through this text and serve as a foundation in the development of your own personal philosophy about language arts instruction.

A Final Word

We would like to leave you with a little bit of our philosophy. We hope it will provide you with some insight concerning the magnificent journey you are about to take!

A good teacher tells
   A superior teacher shows
      A great teacher involves
         A successful teacher learns.

Anthony D. Fredericks
Bonnie Blake-Kline
Janice V. Kristo

Acknowledgments

A text of this scope and magnitude is never the sole effort of the authors whose names appear on the cover. It is the result of many contributions from colleagues, teachers, students, administrators, and parents in near and far-flung places around the country. We were fortunate to have been invited into many classrooms from east to west and north to south to observe the excitement, enthusiasm, and vitality of integrated language arts programs. Countless conversations with fellow educators in large and small schools and urban, suburban, and rural districts in more than two dozen states became the foundation upon which this book was built. We are indebted to the scores of teachers and hundreds of students who allowed us to peer over their shoulders and into their academic lives during the preparation of this text.

Special appreciation goes to the reviewers of the various drafts of this manuscript whose insight and perceptive suggestions made this text a stronger contribution to the field. We are equally indebted to our sponsoring editor, Chris Jennison, whose diplomacy, support, and encouragement were unwavering. Susan Free, a project coordinator at York Production Services, deserves a standing ovation for shepherding the manuscript through the publication process and remaining a close friend at the same time. Special kudos are especially due to our undergraduate students who participated in and contributed to the philosophy and practices shared within these pages.

Tony would like to offer special recognition to Becky McCullough, Galen Guengerich, and Cathy Swanson, who endured constant observations, interviews, videotaping, and all manner of academic "snooping" in their respective classrooms during the preparation of this book. Their classrooms were not only exciting places to be, but dynamic examples of creative teaching at its best. Special merit goes to Cathy for maintaining a journal during her second year of teaching—a journal which offered some incredible insight to the teaching of the integrated language arts, the shaping of a philosophy, and the creation of a truly invitational classroom. That journal, now part of this text, illustrates the possibilities and potentialities of an "energized" curriculum and an equally "energized" teacher.

Bonnie wishes to thank her husband, Max, for being willing to forego cooked meals and a present wife throughout the long process of writing this book. Carla

Klinger served as research assistant and right arm. Her efforts, insights, and uplifting spirit are embedded within the covers of this book. Special thanks go to Heather Cahill and Gary Schubert, exemplary students who helped to inspire as well as take on an enormous workload. Along with many college students, there were several elementary students who served to inform and share the excitement of the integrated language arts. Among the many significant "informants" who helped refine the ideas for this text were Nicole Emschweiler and Meggan Caffrey. Teachers such as Joan Pison, Linda Martin, and Mary Giard contributed generously and with characteristic dedication to the profession. Finally, this project would not have been completed without the continual encouragement of department chair Brian Glandon, colleague Kathy Brace, and coauthors Tony and Jan.

Jan wishes to acknowledge Sue Russell and Amy Cates for their superb secretarial skills and encouragement to see this project through to its completion. She would also like to thank Gail Garthwait and Melissa Keenan for their understanding and knowledge of what books children like, and Judy Pusey for her expertise in working with at-risk children. Jan would also like to acknowledge the following teachers for their classroom contributions and support of this project: Adele Ames, Mary Giard, Linda Graceffa, Betty Robinson, Priscilla Sawyer, and Claire Sullivan. Also, without the enthusiastic support of colleagues such as Phyllis Brazee, Brenda Power, Rosemary Bamford, Jeff Wilhelm, and Paula Moore, a project of this magnitude is not easily accomplished.

Finally, all three authors would like to extend their warmest appreciation to the hundreds of youngsters from Maine to California and Washington to Florida who shared their excitement and enthusiasm about learning during our many visits, interviews, and observations. May this text reflect their passion for learning and their academic **joie de vivre**.

LANGUAGE, LEARNING, AND LITERACY

CHAPTER 1

LOOKING IN ON LITERACY: CHILDREN AND TEACHERS IN PARTNERSHIP

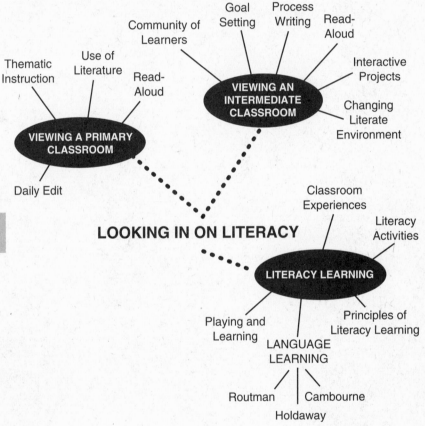

Thematic Instruction

Use of Literature

Read-Aloud

VIEWING A PRIMARY CLASSROOM

Daily Edit

Community of Learners

Goal Setting

Process Writing

Read-Aloud

VIEWING AN INTERMEDIATE CLASSROOM

Interactive Projects

Changing Literate Environment

LOOKING IN ON LITERACY

Classroom Experiences

Literacy Activities

LITERACY LEARNING

Playing and Learning

Principles of Literacy Learning

LANGUAGE LEARNING

Routman

Cambourne

Holdaway

Note to the Reader

At the beginning of each chapter in this book you will find an *anticipatory web*—a diagram that organizes and outlines the major points and data of the chapter. In addition to presenting the key points you will encounter in a visual form, the anticipatory web can also serve as a valuable study guide. We invite you to write on each web your own thoughts or background knowledge, any

What I Know: Pre-Chapter Journaling

At the beginning of each chapter is a question to which you are invited to respond. Please record your reflections, prior experiences, or knowledge about specific topics in a separate journal or notebook. There are no right or wrong answers for any of these entries; instead, you can think about how your education (past and present) has shaped or is shaping your development as a teacher. Please feel free to share your thoughts and ideas with other members of the class.

Throughout your education career (elementary school, high school, college), you have been learning many things. Some of the information you have been exposed to has been very meaningful and long-lasting; some of the information shared in your classes has been less than memorable and has been quickly forgotten. Based on your own experiences, what were some of the conditions or factors provided by your teachers that enhanced your ability to learn?

Big Ideas

This chapter will offer:

1. The guidelines and principles of effective language arts instruction.
2. The basic principles of literacy learning.
3. Three basic models of language learning.
4. The relationship between play and language learning.

ideas discussed in class, and additional information gleaned from your outside readings (there is sufficient room for you to do that). In so doing, you will be able to develop important relationships between various ideas and understand their impact on the development of a successful language arts program. Please feel free to share and compare the notes on your chapter webs with those of other class members and to consult those notes as part of classroom discussions.

LOOKING IN ON A PRIMARY CLASSROOM

The first graders in Becky McCullough's room were filled with excitement and anticipation as they raced into the classroom one warm spring day. The tape recorder in the corner was playing Japanese music ("Favorite Songs of Japanese Children"), and the room was brimming with Japanese and Chinese symbols, banners, books, and posters. It was evident that a new thematic unit was about to begin, and Becky's students could hardly wait for the school day to start.

On the chalkboard was the "Daily Edit"—a sentence filled with several intentional errors for students to copy into their journals and correct. Today's sentence was:

what do you remember about chinese new year

Students stuffed homework papers into their desks, took out their journals, and began to work.

"Thank you for getting started so quickly on your Daily Edit, Lisa," Becky says. "I see that Ashley's started on her Daily Edit, too."

After students have worked for several minutes, they all turn their eyes to the front of the room as Becky gives each of several students an opportunity to come to the chalkboard and correct one error on the Daily Edit.

Michael takes a piece of chalk and changes the "c" in "chinese" to a capital letter.

"Michael, why did you do that?" Becky inquires.

"Because it's a proper noun and all proper nouns need capital letters," Michael replies.

"How many agree or disagree with Michael? Put your thumbs up if you agree or your thumbs down if you disagree," Becky says. All the students put their thumbs up and Becky asks Cole to come to the board to make a correction. Cole places a question mark at the end of the sentence.

"Why did you put that end mark there, Cole?" Becky asks.

"Because it's a question," Cole replies.

"What hint gave you a clue that it was a question?"

"The sentence started with the word 'what,'" Cole replies.

The Daily Edit continues for several more minutes with other students making corrections and the class participating in verifying answers and supporting students who aren't quite sure of their responses.

After the Daily Edit, Becky asks students to brainstorm for words or ideas about what they remembered about Chinese New Year (a previous lesson conducted earlier in the school year). Words such as "dances," "dragon," "Chinese," "food," "clothing," "firecrackers," "feasts," "red envelopes," and "parade" are written on the board and combined into a semantic web (see Figure 1.1).

The web is left on the board as the children gather in the back of the classroom to listen to Becky read a new book.

"I see that Michael, Cole, Matt, and Kelly are ready to read," she says.

"As you may have guessed, we are starting a new unit today on China. We're going to travel back to China, a country we studied earlier this year, and also look at two other Asian countries. To begin our unit, I'd like to share a book entitled *Chinese Mother Goose Rhymes*" [edited by Robert Wyndham, Cleveland: World Publishing, 1968].

Becky reads several rhymes to the students and then rolls out a map of the world to indicate the origin of the stories. She also points out the other two countries (Japan and Korea) they will be studying during the course of the unit.

Afterward, she reads to the class the Caldecott Award–winning book *Lon Po Po* (by Ed Young, New York: Scholastic, 1989), a Chinese version of Little Red Riding Hood. Periodically throughout the reading, Becky stops and asks the students to make some predictions.

"Carter, what do you think might happen next in the story?"

"I think the wolf will eat the kids," Carter replies.

"Let's have a 'Kids' Court.' How many of you think the kids will be eaten by the wolf?" Becky asks. "Raise your hands."

The children all raise their hands.

"It seems as though everyone agrees with your prediction, Carter. Let's find out."

Becky continues reading the book, occasionally assisting the students' interpretation and appreciation of the story by referring to the more familiar Little Red Riding Hood.

After finishing *Lon Po Po,* Becky divides the class into three groups. One group is provided with directions for a game of Chinese hopscotch, and another plays the Chinese version of "Paper, Scissors, Rock." A third group works together to compare Lon Po Po with Little Red Riding Hood by completing a Venn diagram—two or more interlocking circles illustrating the similarities and differences between two or more concepts, books, or items. (Figure 1.2 illustrates a Venn diagram completed by one of the groups.) Student groups engage in each activity for approximately ten minutes; they then switch to another activity and then a final activity until each group has completed all three activities.

The remainder of the day is spent sharing more books related to China. Becky reads several of them to her students and suggests that students choose books to read independently and to share them in group discussions or "Literature Circles." The atmosphere is always supportive and students are provided with several opportunities to share their reflections on certain books and to extend their reading into creative projects such as wall murals, posters, dioramas, journal entries, and group skits.

After lunch, a demonstration of tae kwan do is presented to all the first-grade classes by members of a local martial arts studio. The students are enthralled, particularly when one of the smallest girls is able to break a board with one well-placed kick. Later in the afternoon, a parent who has traveled extensively throughout China and Japan brings in slides of some of her visits and shares some of her interpretations with students. Students are told they can write about those experiences in their own journals.

As a final activity for the day, all the first-grade classes gather together to listen to one of the teachers read "Sadako and the Thousand Paper Cranes" (by Eleanor Coerr, NY: Putnam, 1977). Afterward, students participate in an origami activity, creating their own paper cranes, which are eventually displayed throughout the first-grade hallway.

FIGURE 1.1   A Semantic Web

FIGURE 1.2

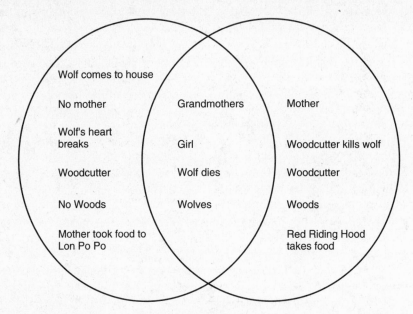

Venn diagram comparing *Lon Po Po* (left) and *Little Red Riding Hood* (right). Common elements to both stories are listed in the middle.

The day ends with the students gathering on the carpet in the rear of their own classroom to listen to Becky read *The Paper Crane* (by Molly Bang, New York: Greenwillow, 1985). As students prepare to leave for the day, Becky hands each of them a strip of paper and asks them to write down one important thing they learned during the day. These ideas are posted on the bulletin board beside the door. Becky asks students to share one or more of any of those items with their parents when they arrive home. (The next day those items will be reviewed with students as one of the initiating activities.)

And so, the children, filled with the same level of boundless energy and enthusiasm that they began the day with, stream out the door and into waiting buses. It has been a day overflowing with wonder and excitement for Becky and her students, a day that signals the start of some dynamic new explorations and adventures.

LOOKING IN ON AN INTERMEDIATE CLASSROOM

A visitor to Galen Guengerich's fifth-grade classroom is immediately struck by the high level of activity in the room, the active engagement of every student, and the incredible amount of sharing and support that takes place. Of no less importance is the student work hanging from every available space throughout the room. Wires are strung across the ceiling from which student-created books, papers, and posters are hung. The walls are covered with an assortment of student murals, timeline, and miniature dioramas. Tables overflow with triaramas (see Box 1.1), three-dimensional displays, art projects, and other creative enterprises. The initial impression is that the room will soon explode from the sheer volume of student work that fills every nook and cranny of available display space. It is quickly evident that students take an enormous amount of pride in displaying and sharing their work with others. The visitor hardly has a chance to take in the spectacle before one or more students quickly usher him or her to several examples of students' work—work representative of all students. Indeed, there is an intense spirit of sharing that pervades the room—students sharing their own work as well as the work of their classmates. In a very real sense, this is a "community of learners."

Galen begins each day by reading to his fifth graders. In most cases he chooses a picture book (see Chapter 10), which allows him to complete the book in one reading, demonstrate the relationships that exists between the illustrations and the text, discuss the development of characters, and provide students with several interactive opportunities that ensure success right from the start of the day.

After the initial reading, Galen talks with the entire class about their daily goals—what each of them would like to accomplish during the course of the day. He tries to meet with several students individually and assist them in establishing appropriate goals. These goals are shared with the whole class and are added to each student's individual journal. If a particular student has difficulty in developing an appropriate set of goals, other class members pitch in and work with that student to generate a set of daily goals.

After the goal-setting process, individual students begin to work on an assortment of self-directed writing tasks. Galen works primarily as a facilitator for these tasks, assisting students when necessary or when asked but not imposing himself on any single student. Students can choose to work on a variety of tasks: their individual journals (writing about recent events or matters of personal concern); working folders (a collection of recent work which can be evaluated by Galen or other students in the class); permanent folders (a collection of each student's best work—work indicative of the student's progress through the year); a "Field Notes" book (a collection of observations, reminiscences, background knowledge, and important facts related to various areas of study; this serves as a prewriting collection of ideas which may eventually find their way into the "Permanent Folder"); or a class writing activity in which small groups of students work together to pursue a writing task related to a particular piece of literature. (One of the group writing activities Galen's students participate in regularly is the creation of "Big Books" which are donated to some of the lower grades in the school on a regular basis.)

After approximately one hour of writing, students gather in the back of the room as Galen begins the daily reading of a popular novel. The choice of books ranges from those familiar to students to new selections recommended by the school librarian or professional resources. Typically, Galen will select a book tied into one of the content areas (science or social studies) and which can be expanded into a wealth of thematic activities (see Chapter 14), allowing students to initiate and follow through on their own self-discovery projects. For example, during a unit on the Civil War, Galen might read *Across Five Aprils* by Irene Hunt (Chicago: Follett, 1964) to students; for a unit on the American frontier, *Caddie Woodlawn* by Carol Brink (NY: Macmillan, 1973) might be the novel of choice.

After the reading, students are invited to participate in a number of interactive projects related to science and/or social studies. For example, in a unit on explorers students might create their own "Explorer's Diary" as though they actually traveled with a particular explorer. They may create a diorama of a North American site visited by an explorer, or a mural of selected events in an explorer's life. To help tie science into the unit, Galen may encourage his students to look at environmental conditions at the time of the explorers and relate those to current conditions. Small groups of students may look at the geological features of a region and compare those with the geology of their section of the country. Every attempt is made to help students see the relationships that exist between and among subject areas through a

TRIARAMAS

Triaramas can be used to effectively "show off" student work in a classroom. Appropriate for display tables, they can also be stapled to the bulletin board or hung with string from the ceiling.

Triaramas can be constructed from photocopy or construction paper, or oak tag. (The sturdier the paper, the sturdier the display.) After students have constructed a triarama, they can place a three-dimensional display inside the shell. Possibilities for display include an illustration of the setting from a favorite book, a clay model of a story character, a model of an important landmark in a piece of literature, or other object(s) deemed important by students.

1. Fold a square piece of paper diagonally both ways.

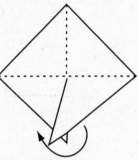

3. Fold 1/2 of cut section under the other cut section.

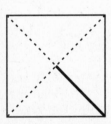

2. Using scissors, make a cut halfway up one fold.

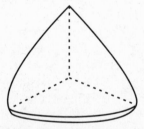

4. Attach together with glue or staples to form a half shell.

variety of interactive and mutually supportive projects.

The next part of the school day is devoted to math. While Galen attempts to coordinate math concepts into the themes he shares with his students, he freely admits that is not always possible. He does, however, provide numerous opportunities for his students to see the relationships that can and do exist between math concepts and the "real world." One of the ways Galen does that is through a "Math Log"—a collection of summary paragraphs that students write upon completion of each math lesson. The logs provide students with an opportunity to summarize what they have learned and to use writing as a vehicle for sharing that information with others. (Students will peruse each other's logs and assist in the development of appropriate summary statements.)

The afternoon is taken up by a selection of content-related projects pertaining to literature studies and writing activities. Typically, these involve extensions or continuations of activities begun earlier in the day or earlier in the unit. A typical activity is the "Literature Circle"—a group project involving a small group of students that selects an appropriate work of literature (in collaboration with Galen) and works together in reading it, generating and responding to self-initiated questions, maintaining a log of extending activities related to the book, developing story maps, or creating special murals for the school library. Five separate groups of students may each be working on a different book selected from the scores of books Galen has displayed around the classroom.

Galen believes that his classroom should be a *family* of learners—everyone working together to help each other succeed in all tasks (academic, personal, social). Galen sees his role as that of a guide, facilitating the learning process but not directing it. In fact, it is not unusual to hear him say quite frequently, "I don't know, let's find out together!" Such statements indicate that Galen is as much a learner as are his students. When asked about his philosophy of teaching, Galen is quick to point out that his philosophy (even after 15 years of teaching) is still in a state of evolution. "I should be learning along with the kids, my knowledge should never be stagnant or should never be forced on my students. When we all learn together we all grow together. I've probably learned more from kids than I have from any textbook or curriculum guide," he says proudly.

Galen designates his classroom as a "changing literate environment"—one filled with an abundance of books from the school library as well as the local public library. The books change every month—offering his students an abundance of literature, both traditional and new, in a variety of genres. In so doing, Galen is able to surround his students with an environment that grows *and* changes—much as he wishes his students will do.

One thing clearly evident in Galen's classroom is the responsibility students assume for their own learning. Galen believes that students can learn as much from each other as they can from the teacher, and his job is to provide them with learning opportunities and extensions that transcend textbooks and lesson plans and open up doors and expand learning horizons. This is quite evident, even to the casual observer, as students are actively engaged in a host of facilitative activities, enthusiastic about what they are learning, and supportive of each other in, not only obtaining knowledge, but using that knowledge in productive ways. This is even more evident when students are heard to say "This is *my* classroom" as opposed to "This is Mr. Guengerich's classroom." Indeed, there is a feeling of both pride and ownership by students of what they are learning and how they are learning it.

Both Becky and Galen have created classrooms that are "invitational" in nature. That is, students are invited to share in the act of learning; they are active participants in all classroom activities and are supportive of the overall "environment of learners." Also, both Becky and Galen act more as facilitators of learning rather than as dispensers of knowledge. For them, teaching is an active and dynamic process that involves students in a host of stimulating, encouraging, and meaningful engagements. So too, is the literacy instruction woven into almost all dimensions of the school day—providing youngsters with rich experiences in learning about and using their developing literacy in a variety of endeavors. In short, these two classrooms encourage, support, and promote literacy learning. Let's stop for a moment and take a look at a definition:

> **Literacy:** The ability to use the language arts (reading, writing, speaking, listening) in ways that are intrinsically meaningful to the individual and are communicative in nature.

Let's reflect again on some of the events that took place in Becky's and Galen's classrooms. There, students were engaged in a variety of language arts: reading books that they had selected on their own, listening to adults read stories and books to them, conversing with each other about literature, writing and sharing ideas. In other words, Becky and Galen offered their students engaging opportunities to use all of the language arts—reading, writing, listening, and speaking—in a coordinated and integrated fashion that provided real meaning for children.

Students also have a host of opportunities to interact with each other and to use their communicative abilities. Sharing and cooperation are emphasized and valued; they form the structure upon which students will experience success, not only in language arts activities but in all subject areas. During this learning process, students are "recruited" as coteachers, thereby discovering that knowledge does not only reside in a teacher's manual or in the teacher's head.

When we think about helping students develop or grow into literacy, it is important to remember that reading, writing, speaking, and listening do not develop as separate components and should not be taught as separate subjects (Cooper, 1993). In fact, all aspects of literacy develop simultaneously and interactively (Freeman and Hatch, 1989; Galda et al., 1993). Indeed, we must keep in mind a key factor as we assist children in literacy development: *Children learn to read, write, speak, and listen when they are provided with meaningful and authentic opportunities to use those language arts in integrated and sustained endeavors.*

THE CONDITIONS OF LITERACY LEARNING

Let's reflect again upon the two classrooms presented earlier. Although one was a first-grade classroom and the other a fifth-grade classroom, there were five conditions in each that "cut across" grade levels and promoted literacy learning for all students, five conditions that are appropriate for any elementary classroom and any teacher seeking to stimulate literacy development.

Condition 1 Students are actively involved in their own learning. The emphasis should be on helping students assume a sense of responsibility for their own learning process. It can be an intimidating task for some teachers to provide the framework in which students can begin to "take charge" of some of the learning in a classroom. However, when an "invitational environment" is created, students become eager and willing to participate. In the process that evolves, students are not "told" what to do but rather learn to contribute to the dynamic milieu of the classroom, to the interaction between teachers and students and between students and students. The decisions and input of the entire group are actively solicited and acted upon.

Condition 2 Students are given a sense of ownership in their own learning. One of the terms you will often hear in education circles is "empowerment." To us, that term implies that students are provided with meaningful opportunities to be active participants in the learning process. They achieve that sense because their input and suggestions are solicited and valued. The teacher is not "in control" of the classroom, rather the classroom is one in which the teacher and students work together for the common good. For example, some teachers feel as though they need to cover their bulletin boards with an array of colorful posters and designs. The hidden message to students may be "these are *my* bulletin boards, not yours!" In a classroom "owned" by students, on the other hand, pupil's ideas for bulletin boards are solicited and acted upon, not just by the teacher, but by everyone in the classroom community.

Condition 3 *Learning is holistic.* As we indicated above, children do not learn any of the language arts independently from any of the others. What is clear from the research (Galda et al., 1993) and from our own observations in hundreds of classrooms is that learning to read supports learning to write, speak, and listen; learning to speak supports learning to listen, read, and write; and so on. When we talk about the integrated language arts we are talking about learning that is holistic and complete. We are not emphasizing a discrete set of activities that will help students master a particular writing skill (ending each sentence with a punctuation mark, for example), but rather meaningful endeavors that offer multiple opportunities to use skills in a variety of learning activities. *Isolation of skills is deemphasized; integration of skills is emphasized.*

Condition 4 *Students are given choices.* This principle relates to our belief that students need to develop a sense of self-responsibility in all their academic endeavors. In too many classrooms, all the decisions and choices are made by teachers—which means that the primary objective of students is to complete the "academic chores" selected by the teacher. Students who complete those chores according to standards determined by the teacher are those who get the highest grades; those who don't, don't. Self-selection is an important aspect in the literacy education of any child. We believe that when children are provided with opportunities to make their own choices and to follow through on those choices (sometimes referred to as "risk taking"), then they are making an *investment of self*—a contribution of their personality, scholastic attributes, and intellectual power, all of which forms the foundation for individual motivation and personally meaningful discoveries.

Condition 5 *The teacher is a colearner.* One of the most powerful tools teachers have at their disposal is that of modeling. That is, teachers should be willing to "practice what they preach." If we believe that it is valuable to students to have quiet opportunities to read books, then we should demonstrate that by taking time ourselves to quietly read a book during part of the school day. If we believe that students should write in a journal on a daily basis, then we, too, should write in a personal journal on a daily basis. In many ways, we should be willing and eager to demonstrate the attributes and activities of literacy to our students regularly. We also need to be comfortable in demonstrating to students that learning does not end when school is completed, that there are many things for us to learn throughout our lifetimes. Subscribing to professional journals, attending workshops and conferences, and interacting with other teachers are indicative of the lifelong learning we wish to impart to our students. Join hands with your students too and make new discoveries throughout any subject area. Most important, however, is: learn to feel comfortable saying to your students "I don't know, why don't we find out together!"

LANGUAGE LEARNING

Have you ever ridden a bicycle? Do you remember the first time you tried to do it? You may have fumbled with the pedals, fallen over on the ground, or become very frustrated at your efforts. Learning how to ride a bike takes practice and, perhaps, someone to assist you in mastering a proper technique. That individual may have helped you maintain your balance, shown you how to pedal and steer at the same time, and how to keep the entire process going continuously. At times, that person may have run alongside you to assist in the learning process.

In many ways, learning how to ride a bicycle is similar to learning language. Few of us are perfect language users the first time we try to say a sentence or write a story. We need to be surrounded by lots of oral language (for example) in order to understand the dynamics of speaking. We need to be surrounded by lots of books in order to understand the dynamics of reading. And, we need to be surrounded by lots of writing examples in order to understand the dynamics of writing. Children need to have valid opportunities to practice language in order to become language users.

We present here three models of language learning that we have found to be particularly instructive for developing a philosophy of language arts instruction and for the design and development of a personal language arts program.

Routman's Model for Language Learning

Regie Routman, a 20-year veteran of the classroom, has written a pivotal book entitled *Invitations: Changing as Teachers and Learners K-12* (Portsmouth, NH: Heinemann, 1994). Routman outlines her beliefs about literacy learning, stating that much of her learning has come not from formal courses but rather from her experiences with children and the wide variety of books she reads regularly. What is impressive about her philosophy is that it is one in a state of metamorphosis— changing and evolving through different stages as she adds to her knowledge base, refines old ideas, modifies new ones, and works to achieve a balance between what students are capable of doing and can be doing in a supportive classroom environment.

Routman's philosophy is predicated on eight "standards" or beliefs about how children learn. Those standards have come from the work of

many educators, but have been primarily influenced by the work of three individuals: Don Holdaway in New Zealand (1979), Brian Cambourne in Australia (1987, 1991), and Kenneth Goodman (1986) in the United States.

The following are Routman's beliefs about language learning, along with our annotations. We hope these provide you with some "food for thought" as you seek to establish your own beliefs about how children learn to become literate.

1. *Literacy acquisition is a natural process.* Children are exposed to language at a very early age. (Some contend that children are introduced to language in the womb.) They hear people using language as part of everyday experiences and interactions. Language is "understood" by children as a natural, normal part of everyday life.

2. *The conditions for becoming oral language users are the same for becoming readers and writers.* Oral language is a way in which humans share information with other humans. Writing and reading are means whereby information is shared by literate people. The form and substance may be different but the fact that writing and speaking are expressive language arts and reading and listening are receptive language arts demonstrates the relationships that exist.

3. *Young children enter school with much knowledge about literacy.* Many children have been read to by their parents and other caregivers from early in their lives. They have seen and heard humans communicating with each other. They have been provided with opportunities to communicate with others in their environment, and they have seen the power that a few words can convey. While children may not be able to describe what they know about literacy, they are fully aware of its social significance and its "power" in their lives.

4. *Becoming a reader and becoming a writer are closely related.* Many of the same

processes writers use in their work are similar to the processes readers use in their work. Language is used, manipulated, interpreted, integrated into background knowledge, and summarized in both reading and writing. As a result, teachers often talk about the reading/writing connection—a connection that is both natural and powerful at the same time.

5. *Optimal literacy environments promote risk taking and trust.* As we will discuss throughout this book, it is vital that students feel "comfortable" in the classroom—that is, that they are encouraged to discover new ideas and are supported in their efforts to do so. Walking a tightrope across Niagara Falls would be a scary proposition for most of us simply because of the realization that there is no support for us other than one thin piece of material. Yet, if we were playing on an athletic team we would know that there were one or more coaches as well as teammates there to offer not only encouragement but support as well. Hence, most us would probably feel more comfortable playing basketball than we would walking on a rope 500 feet above a waterfall. So it is in the classroom. Students must know that they can take chances, but also that there is someone there who will "catch" them if they fall.

6. *Becoming literate is a social act and a search for meaning.* Literacy is achieved through interaction with other literate individuals. As we socialize with other people, we are adding to our storehouse of knowledge as well as underscoring the communicative acts that allow us to obtain and use that knowledge. We also have a basic drive to understand the knowledge presented to us. (Have you ever been reading a newspaper article and realized halfway through it that you didn't understand what the writer was saying? Undoubtedly, you probably went back a few paragraphs to reread some information again in an attempt to understand and clarify certain information.)

7. *Literacy development is continuous.* There is no absolute point at which we become totally literate. We add to our literacy base through additional conversation, reading, writing, and acts of listening. So it is with children who discover that there is much to discover both in and out of the classroom. Children also learn that the discovery process is enhanced and facilitated through acts of language use. In other words, language becomes the vehicle that drives learning.

8. *Genuine literacy acts are authentic and meaningful.* Giving students a batch of workbook pages simply because a teacher's manual states that they must complete those sheets at a specific point in the textbook is not authentic learning. At best, it is artificial and emphasizes the belief that *all* children are developmentally ready for a specific task or skill at the same point in their individual learning continuums. Real learning, on the other hand, values the individual differences of children and builds upon those differences to create a classroom climate that respects and encourages each child's personal involvement. Each act of learning must be intrinsically meaningful and purposeful for children or it is an act without meaning or purpose.

Holdaway's Developmental Model for Language Learning

Don Holdaway, an educator from New Zealand, has observed the ways in which children all over the world acquire language. He has been primarily concerned with the means whereby children acquire oral language skills. His discoveries not only have been intuitively correct but have had far-reaching implications for helping children, no matter what their native language, learn spoken language.

Holdaway's work has also had a significant impact on what teachers can and should do in the classroom. As a result of his investigations, he created a simple model for learning language that has had enormous implications in the classroom (1979). Holdaway's model is composed of four separate yet highly interrelated components:

1. *Demonstrations.* Many of the tasks we learn come about because we have watched someone else do them. We watch a quarterback throw a football and we try to "copy" that style of throwing; we see someone cast a fishing line into a river or lake and we attempt to emulate those movements; or we hear someone sing a song with a distinctive style and we try to copy that individual. So it is with children. When they have opportunities to see and hear how language is used by those around them, they are provided with models they can copy, emulate, or duplicate. Listening to language in use is the first prerequisite to becoming a language user.

2. *Participation.* Children are *invited* to use language—to manipulate it, massage it, or play with it. The object is not to have children become accomplished users of language immediately, just as you would find it difficult to throw a football 75 yards the first time you tried. A collaboration is necessary between the "expert" (teacher) and the "novice" (learner) to build confidence and a willingness to continue the learning process.

3. *Practice.* This is the stage in which learners begin to develop a sense of independence in any learning activity. They have seen an activity demonstrated and have been provided with opportunities to participate in the activity; now they are encouraged to practice the activity on their own. It is at this stage that learners begin to achieve a sense of independence and self-control—particularly when they know that there is support and encouragement from the demonstrator or teacher. Self-direction and self-regulation are established, and learners begin to develop a feeling of worth in their individual learning processes.

4. *Performance.* At this stage, learners achieve a level of competence that allows them to become "demonstrators" for others. Learners are accomplished and competent in their abilities and are sufficiently competent to share what they have learned with others. In so doing, learners receive feedback—usually positive—and approval for their accomplishments.

Cambourne's Model for Language Learning

Brian Cambourne, an Australian researcher, has spent hundreds of hours observing children and how they learn—particularly how they learn language. His discoveries have led to the creation of a model of language learning that has had enormous implications and possibilities for all teachers—particularly teachers of the language arts.

The key features of Cambourne's model can be briefly summarized: (1) it provides teachers with a developmental model of learning (as opposed to an absolute model); (2) it is learner-based, rather than teacher-directed; and (3) it has implications for all curricular areas, not just language arts. These features provide the foundations for what is called whole language instruction (see Chapter 2).

Cambourne's model, sometimes referred to as "The Conditions of Natural Language Learning," is based on a critical factor in the educative process; that is, the primary responsibility of teachers is to create stimulating environments that foster learning. In other words, teachers do not just teach; instead, they are facilitators of learning. While you may argue that there is little difference between your role as a teacher and your role as a facilitator, the contrast is enormous, particularly in terms of how children can become comfortable with language and its uses.

Cambourne's model includes the following conditions:

1. *Immersion.* Children need to be surrounded by books and literature of every genre. So too must they have open opportunities to use

those books in a variety of activities and projects.

2. *Demonstration.* Children are provided with sufficient opportunities to "see" how "experts" use and manipulate language. While teachers often serve as reading and writing models for their students, children can also benefit from seeing older students and other "language masters" use reading and writing in their daily lives. Reading aloud to children, writing in a journal, quietly reading a piece of literature, and talking about the things "going on in one's head" while reading are all important demonstrations for children.

3. *Engagement.* Children are encouraged and supported in their efforts to try new materials, processes, activities, or experiments. Their desire to learn is supported by others; in other words, they are motivated to *want* to try new things and feel sufficiently confident that there will be some measure of success for their efforts. Engagement is always accompanied by immersion and demonstration.

4. *Expectation.* Children need to know that they have the support and encouragement of others. At the same time, teachers must convey the attitude that students can succeed, learning will occur, and progress will be made. The emphasis is on what children can do rather than on the errors or mistakes that are always a natural byproduct of the learning process. Remember the first time you tried to ride a bicycle? Somebody was probably there to help you out, and that individual fully expected you to eventually ride that bike successfully. Sure, you probably fell down and skinned your knees a few times, but you always received the support of that person to get back up on the bicycle and try again. It was that person's *expectations* that contributed to your eventual success in learning to ride the bicycle. The same processes applied when you were learning to walk and certainly when you were learning to drive. So too

do those expectations need to be part of the dynamics of the language arts curriculum as well as the entire classroom.

5. *Responsibility.* Children need to develop a sense of responsibility for their own learning. That responsibility does not come easily and needs to be shared by both teachers and students. Teachers must be willing to *demonstrate* responsibility for students and to offer opportunities for students to begin taking on responsible acts on their own. Classrooms in which all of the decisions and all of the directions are mandated by the teacher are classrooms in which students are teacher-dependent learners rather than independent thinkers. Children become responsible when they are given choices—choices on which books to read; choices on what piece of writing they will edit and publish; choices on how to respond to a piece of literature; and choices on the duration of a specific book-related activity. That sense of responsibility also develops when children know they are supported in their decision making.

6. *Employment.* When children are provided with realistic opportunities to read books, they have realistic opportunities to become accomplished readers. When they have realistic opportunities to write, they have realistic opportunities to become writers. Using language in meaningful contexts is an important part of the learning process.

For too many children language learning revolves around artificial practice: workbook pages, photocopied skill sheets, and commercial tests requiring single right answers. If children are to become accomplished readers, they need to become involved in reading real books. So too do they need time to pursue those learning opportunities—extended time that allows for sufficient practice and sufficient occasions to use what they have learned in a realistic arena.

7. *Approximation*. How did you learn how to talk? We doubt that you were able to recite the Gettysburg Address during your first year of life. Undoubtedly, you began to babble and chatter some type of incomprehensible language (incomprehensible to everyone except your parents) beginning with one- or two-syllable "words" (e.g., "Da da," "Ma ma"). Later, you learned to put two or more words together to form some sort of makeshift sentence (e.g., "Me go," "Dog woof"). Still later, you learned to put more words together into comprehensible units and began communicating with others outside your immediate family. In short, you learned to talk through a series of approximations. In other words, part of the individual language learning of all of us came about through a series of approximations. The implications are that all approximations of language use need to be supported and rewarded by teachers—for it is through that process that success is built and language becomes a valuable tool for additional learning.

8. *Response*. Children need to receive feedback about their learning—particularly about their language learning. As a student, you know the value of receiving some type of evaluation about papers you have written or tests you have taken. Whether that assessment is positive or negative, you still need to receive it. Response implies that children are provided with verbal and nonverbal information about their progress and that such data are critical to students' continuing advancement in learning about and using language.

Playing and Learning

With these models of language learning in mind, let's look at another "learning" situation in which students frequently participate. In fact, it would be best to complete the "For Your Journal" activity on this page (if possible) before reading further in the text.

After completing the "For Your Journal" activity, you will probably have noted several events taking place. Here are some of the things we think you may have observed as you watched a group of youngsters engaged in free play:

1. *Children were interacting and socializing with each other.* Most kids were playing with other kids. They were talking and conversing, pushing and pulling, helping (and perhaps hindering)—

B O X
12

FOR YOUR JOURNAL

With a classmate, visit a local playground area or park. Locate a group of young children playing together in a designated play area (with a seesaw, teeter-totter, jungle gym, slides, etc.). If possible, try to locate a group of kids who are playing with a minimum of adult supervision. Observe the group for approximately one hour and record some of the activities individuals participate in as well as some of the interactions that take place between group members. Later compare notes with your classmate to arrive at a consensus about the activities you observed. What were some of the interactions that took place? How similar or different is the playground environment from the environment of a classroom? What did you observe that might be useful in terms of the design or dynamics of an elementary classroom? If possible, visit the same play area at a later date and observe a different group of youngsters at play. How are they similar to or different from the activities of the first group?

but they were all involved in a variety of social activities. Perhaps there were a few kids who were quite content to play on their own, while others were engaged in "team" or group activities (e.g., pushing each other on the swings, taking turns on the sliding board, building sand castles together). Whether pursuing solitary or group activities, all of the children were aware of the other children in the vicinity and either acknowledged their presence by playing with them or glancing at them occasionally.

2. *Children were pursuing enjoyable activities.* Children participated in activities that were fun or stimulating (physically or intellectually). You probably observed children participating in a variety of activities—each of which was enjoyable and pleasurable. Youngsters who started activities and found them to be too challenging moved on to other activities that gave them some sense of pleasure and accomplishment.

3. *Children were making decisions.* Kids made decisions as to what kinds of activities they wanted to pursue, who they wanted to be with them, the time limits for selected activities, and how the activities were to be accomplished (or if an activity was to be successfully completed at all). What was evident was that children had the freedom to make some decisions (for reasons of safety, some decisions may have been made by parents or other caregivers). Youngsters also had the opportunity to follow through on the decisions they did make and perhaps determine if their decision was an appropriate one or not.

4. *Children engaged in some challenging activities.* You may have noted that certain children were taking risks on some of the playground equipment (e.g., climbing to the top of the jungle gym, seeing how high they could swing on the swing set, etc.). Some children may have been encouraging other children to take risks, too ("Come on, you can do it!"). You may have observed several children trying something for the first time, discovering that they like it, and then doing that particu-

lar activity for an extended period of time. In effect, a lot of experimenting was taking place on the playground.

5. *Children participated in a variety of self-initiated activities.* Children were able to select activities that met their personal needs or were in accordance with what they considered to be fun. If there was little parental intervention, you probably noted that different kids were engaged in different activities. In other words, not all the children were participating in the same activity or playing on the same piece of apparatus. They could choose what they wanted and the period of time they wanted to participate.

6. *Children were communicating with each other.* Kids were talking with each other, giving directions, and shouting commands ("Hey, look at me!"). There was a great deal of discussion taking place—some positive discussions and perhaps even some negative discussions. Nevertheless, the area was infused with the chatter and banter of kids communicating with each other.

7. *Children were supportive and cooperative with each other.* You may have noticed that kids were assisting other kids with some of the activities and games. Some were pushing brothers or sisters on the swings, others were helping to keep the merry-go-round in motion, others may have been "catching" kids as they came down the sliding board. For the most part, children realized that for certain activities to take place they must be done with the support and cooperation of each other. True, there may have been squabbles and arguments about who was "supposed to" do the pushing on the merry-go-round, but that was also part of the realization that kids needed other kids in order for the entire process to work.

8. *Children engaged in a variety of independent and group activities.* Some children may have participated entirely in activities

involving other kids, others may have played by themselves the entire time, while other children may have gone from group activities to an independent activity and back again. What was evident was that individual children had certain "styles" of playing—some more comfortable by themselves, some playing with other kids, and some who needed both.

9. *Children were confident and competent in activities that were meaningful for them.* Activities that provided certain youngsters with a great deal of pleasure were also activities in which those children participated freely. For example, a child building a sand castle might include roads and bridges for cars and trucks. The utility of the roads was important and meaningful for that child because they had a specific purpose. The child determined what that purpose was, provided for that purpose, and achieved a level of self-satisfaction and "comfortableness" in completing the task.

10. *Children were emotionally involved in activities.* You probably noted that some children were laughing and giggling as they participated in selected activities. Others were chattering incessantly, talking back and forth among each other. Smiles and laughter, and perhaps, even some tears and crying were evident as kids interacted with each other and participated in any number of activities.

As you might guess, we believe that play is as normal and natural part of each child's development as is learning. In fact, many of the same types of experiences children participate in prior to entering school are also experiences they can participate in when in a more formal learning environment—the classroom. Unfortunately, some youngsters are not allowed to "play with learning" once they enter school; for them, learning becomes routine, systematized, and overly formalized.

Are we suggesting that there is a blame here? Absolutely not! What we are suggesting is that many of the learning experiences that are normally and naturally part of a child's discovery of the world during the first five or six years of life can also be part of the dynamics of the classroom as well. Learning is a natural and normal process of the human species and nowhere is this more succinctly demonstrated than when kids are allowed to participate in activities that are meaningful to them (e.g., games and activities on the playground or in the park). So too can this "learning continuum" be part of your classroom—providing kids with opportunities and support for learning about themselves and their environment.

We believe an integrated approach to language arts instruction holds the potential for enhancing your students' learning opportunities and maximizing your own teaching opportunities. We do not presume to say that the implementation and maintenance of a language arts curriculum will be an easy task. It *will* be a challenge but it will also have a significant impact on your ability to transmit the excitement of learning and language arts to your students. So too will it have an impact on your student's competence in and attitude toward education long after they leave your classroom. It will undoubtedly become exciting for you as you, too, change your concepts, ideas, feelings, and beliefs about the teaching of language arts.

As we close this first chapter, we suggest that you reread the lists of Holdaway, Routman, and Camborne presented earlier. Are your educational experiences similar to those identified in any or all of those lists? Most important, how will your past experiences shape or define your own philosophy about the teaching of language arts? At this stage of your professional training, we would like to invite you to consider the effects of your experiences as a former elementary student on your development as a future elementary teacher. Just as important, what is your model of literacy learning and how will that model change and grow throughout your professional career? We invite you to write the responses to these questions in a journal and to share them with your classmates and colleagues.

CATHY SWANSON'S JOURNAL

An Introduction to Cathy's Journal

If you are like most prospective teachers, you are probably apprehensive about the next few years. You may be worried about getting a job after you graduate, whether you'll be an effective classroom teacher, or whether you've chosen the "right" profession. We, too, experienced those same concerns as we started our teaching careers. It seemed like there was so much to know and so many responsibilities to consider. Yet, as we began working with children, we discovered that teaching was much more than writing behavioral objectives, memorizing lists of facts and figures, or taking a teacher exam. We found out, as you will, that teaching is as much an art as it is a science and that how we perceived teaching was as important as what we did when teaching.

*   With that in mind, we'd like to tell you about a friend of ours—Cathy Swanson. Cathy was an elementary education major at Kutztown University in Kutztown, Pennsylvania. Bright, energetic, and creative, she was entering the teaching profession because she wanted to stimulate the natural curiosity of children and utilize her innate talents to promote learning as an active and engaging process. During her student teaching semester and shortly before she began sending out applications to various school districts, Cathy sat down to write out her educational philosophy. Writing a philosophy allowed her to assess her personal strengths as a teacher and provide her with a course for her future. Defining her philosophy allowed Cathy to key into the personal attributes and attitudes she wanted to share with children. In short, she gave herself a direction and a goal to strive for during those first critical years of her teaching career.*

*   We believe that Cathy's philosophical statement says a lot not only about her but also about her approach to teaching. We would like to share Cathy's statement with you and ask that you consider it as one teacher's philosophical orientation to language arts instruction. What is important here is that Cathy has a clearly articulated philosophy that provides the basis for her decision making and what she does with her students throughout the school day. We invite you to think about how your developing philosophy of teaching, particularly your philosophy of teaching language arts, compares or contrasts with Cathy's philosophy. In other words, what will you bring to your classroom that will ensure your success as a teacher of language arts and your students' success as learners and users of language arts? Of course, we do not expect you to "adopt" Cathy's philosophy; rather, we hope that you will be aware of your own developing philosophy throughout this course.*

A PHILOSOPHY OF EDUCATION

Like most teachers, Cathy's philosophy is ever evolving, as she interacts with students and acquires new information. Cathy would be one of the first to tell you that she has grown and developed in a multitude of ways during her teaching career. Yet, before she began her first year of teaching, Cathy conveyed her philosophy of teaching to us this way:

> *Lao-Tse once described an effective leader as one who imparts to his charges the feeling, "We did it ourselves!" So it is in the realm of teaching and learning.*
>
> *An effective educator does not simply disseminate facts and figures, but acts as a catalyst, teaching (by example) a love for learning. By providing provocative questions rather than patent answers, children are led to discover knowledge; thus they become active participants in the learning process rather than passive receptors.*
>
> *To be a successful "catalyst" requires a great deal. As a doctor selects the appropriate tool to execute a surgical procedure or an artist the correct brush to express a desired gesture, a teacher must have the knowledge and creativity to utilize a plethora of tools.*
>
> *In order to meet the individual needs of students, an educator must skillfully incorporate visual, aural, and tactile activities via a variety of teaching strategies. However, even the wisest tactical decisions are rendered ineffective unless a climate of love, excitement, humor, and mutual respect is engendered.*
>
> *To provide an environment that fosters both intellectual and emotional growth is a responsibility of the greatest magnitude. The reward, however, is of equal proportion if one is truly committed to leading children to love learning, life, and to say, "We did it ourselves!"*

Cathy is now a very successful elementary teacher at Lower Salford Elementary School in Harleysville, Pennsylvania. Her classroom is filled with the love, excitement, humor, and mutual respect she subscribes to in her educational philosophy. She is enthusiastic about teaching and her students are enthusiastic about learning. But, more important is the fact that Cathy is as much a learner as she is a teacher. Not only does she serve as a positive role model for her students; so too does she constantly seek new ideas and strategies for inclusion in her daily plans. We believe that it is teachers who have clearly defined and articulated the philosophies that guide their decisions, that set the standards for what education should be—and more specifically, for what good teachers can do!

In order to help you understand and appreciate the constant need for teachers to become learners along with their students, we would like to offer you a glimpse into Cathy's development as a teacher. During Cathy's second year of teaching (her first year as a full-time fourth-grade teacher), we asked her to maintain a diary of her thoughts, perceptions, ruminations, and considerations throughout the entire school year. We believe this process of journaling can be an important part in the growth of any teacher and offers some valuable insights into the developmental stages that novice (and experienced) teachers undergo in their individual learning experiences. We hope that this will serve as a model for the kind of journaling you will do throughout your teaching career.

So that you will understand the ongoing process of learning in a teacher's career, we will offer glimpses into Cathy's journal at the end of each chapter. The selected entries will chronicle the events in Cathy's classroom and her thoughts about them. We invite you to be a part of Cathy's self-initiated learning process and to read about the successes (and challenges) that are integral to everyday classroom teaching.

Cathy will reveal an incredible journey of self-discovery, one that challenged her thinking, fortified her beliefs, and strengthened her philosophy about how children learn and specifically, how they learn the language arts. At the conclusion of this course, take a moment to reread Cathy's philosophy (on page 20) and compare it with your own developing philosophy on the teaching of the integrated language arts. We hope that you will consider Cathy as one of the instructors for your course and will join with her as she celebrates her own learning, just as she celebrates the learning of her students.

❧ *August 20*

I've been asked, "Where did you get your education?"—as though in the past tense, already completed!

"Kutztown University," I'd answer. Indeed, I'm grateful for the experience I had at Kutztown, especially for the inspiration and support I received from two professors in particular, Drs. Liddicoat and Smith. But my REAL education began last September when I found myself staring back at 28 fifth graders! Nothing can prepare a new teacher for that moment.

So here I am again; anxious for school to begin, but also very nervous. What will *fourth graders* be like? As this is only my second year of teaching, I don't really have a frame of reference for this age group. I want to keep expectations high, but what is realistic? What will they enjoy? What will engage them most? How much abstract thinking are they capable of? Will I be able to

accommodate the range of learning styles of these 20 kids?

It's easy to become overwhelmed, as a new teacher, with all the questions, all the self-imposed expectations. One thing that's not easy (at least for me) is to remember to share those fears, that sense of being overwhelmed, with someone supportive. I have found that even the most experienced teachers have some of the same questions each September.

Pennsylvania has a state-mandated mentoring program. This was a life-saver for me! It empowered me to ask questions and seek advice without feeling like I was constantly imposing on another already busy staff member. My mentor, Betty, allayed many fears for me, offered assurances, and gave me more encouragement than I could ever ask for. People like this can change your whole experience as a novice in education.

❧ August 31

I was thrilled to find out I will have a class of only 20 students! When the bulk of your teaching is assigning worksheets and administering multiple-choice tests, the difference between 20 and 30 students isn't significant. But when you are committed to whole learning and all that is required by that commitment, the difference is tremendous.

One of the biggest challenges in a whole learning environment is management. Providing time for writing conferences, book conferences, project conferences, sharing time and hands-on exploration isn't easy. And just when you think you've gotten a good system together, the need to be flexible and respective of the children's interests will change your time frame. Teaching would be a train conductor's nightmare!

❧ September 3

O ne of the first things I've been impressed with at Lower Salford Elementary School is the sense of community here!

Before school starts, the "Back-to-School Extravaganza" is held. Parents and children attend this evening picnic to meet their new teachers, play games, see old friends after the summer, and eat!

What a wonderful way to remove some of that "first day of school" anxiety and to build a positive rapport with your new class! Additionally, I appreciated meeting parents before conference time and in such a casual, warm atmosphere. (I also think that students, wondering if they would be stuck with a witch for the year, were at least somewhat relieved!)

I also valued observing the students in such a natural setting. I noted who seemed shy, who seemed verbal and confident, etc. I was even able to determine who would "rescue" me when we played "Goldmine" [a language arts game]; these kids, of course, earned straight A's for the year!

TEACHER AS LEARNER/TEACHER AS RESEARCHER

Framing the Question

We believe that learning to become a teacher does not begin and end with the courses you take in college, the textbooks you study, or your student-teaching experience. It has been our experience that the best teachers are those who continue to ask questions and continue to seek answers. Indeed, we would argue that much of our "knowledge" about teaching has come from our own classrooms and our own students.

We hope that when you finish this book and this course, you will continue to ask questions. We have found that good teaching is not the accumulation of miscellaneous data or the memorization of new strategies or techniques. Good teaching, for us, is an active search for new opportunities to make learning "come alive" for our students. For that reason, we ask questions—many of them—simply because we realize that there is much to wonder about and much to learn.

We hope that you will be able to take an active role in searching for the answers to your own questions. We hope that you will query your former professors, your friends and colleagues, and your own students. Equally important, we hope you will initiate some research in your own classroom—examining, exploring, and investigating the dynamics of learning and the potentialities of teaching. We hope you will continue to explore the "possibilities" of instruction, rather than the "absolutes." Continuing your education throughout your career may be one of the most significant factors in your success as a teacher.

Just as the scientist begins by posing a question, out of which a design of study will emerge, so it is with the teacher-researcher. The first step of the journey leading to classroom research is the same for every teacher. It begins with a question.

As you extend your personal learning beyond your textbooks and college courses, and embark upon creating new knowledge and insights into what is going on in your own classroom, you may be surprised to discover that the first step in being a teacher researcher is the hardest. Framing the question to guide your own classroom research is the key to successful discoveries.

You might begin to frame your question by considering the answers to some other questions:

- What intrigues you in a classroom?
- What do you wonder about?
- What puzzles you?
- How can you provide for the learning needs of all children?
- What do you need to change?

You might begin by brainstorming some answers, the goal being to identify as many answers as possible without judging or censoring any of them.

The following questions can assist you in establishing appropriate guidelines for classroom exploration:

- Is the question open-ended (as opposed to a yes/no question)?
- Does the question allow for several possibilities?
- Does the question allow sufficient time for its investigation?
- Is the question narrowed to a specific area of investigation without being too detailed?
- Can the question be modified or altered as new information is discovered?
- Will the question intrigue and excite you enough to pursue an answer?
- Will the question impact on childrens' literacy development and/or your growth as a teacher?

Journal Reflections

Select one or more of the questions below that interest you and respond in your journal or notebook.

1. What were some of the questions Cathy Swanson asked at the beginning of the year? Based on her initial journal entries how might she begin searching for answers to her self-initiated questions?

2. Write a paragraph on your philosophy of teaching language arts. With which of the individuals mentioned in this chapter would you agree most? With which would you differ most?

3. Make a list of your personal attributes that will contribute to your success as a language arts teacher. How do your attributes compare with the attributes of your classmates?

4. Design your own question.
   ✓ What is a question you have about the chapter?
   ✓ How will you pursue the answer to that question?
   ✓ Respond in your journal.

REFERENCES AND SUGGESTED READINGS

Au, K. *Literacy Instruction in Multicultural Settings.* Fort Worth, TX: Harcourt Brace Jovanovich, 1993.

Barell, J. *Teaching for Thoughtfulness: Classroom Strategies to Enhance Intellectual Development.* White Plains, NY: Longman, 1991.

Borich, G. D. *Effective Teaching Methods.* Columbus, OH: Merrill, 1988.

Cambourne, B. "Helping Students Seek the Patterns Which Connect: A View of Literacy Education from Down Under." In K. S. Goodman, L. B. Bridges, and Y. M. Goodman, eds., *The Whole Language Catalog.* Santa Rosa, CA: American School Publishers, 1991.

Cambourne, B., and Turbill, J. *Coping with Chaos.* Portsmouth, NH: Heinemann, 1987.

Cooper, J. D. *Literacy: Helping Children Construct Meaning.* Boston: Houghton Mifflin, 1993.

Galda, L., Cullinan, B. E., and Strickland, D. S. *Language, Literacy, and the Child.* Fort Worth, TX: Harcourt Brace Jovanovich, 1993.

Goodman, K. *What's Whole in Whole Language.* Portsmouth, NH: Heinemann, 1986.

Goodman, K. S., Bridges, L. B., and Goodman, Y. M. *The Whole Language Catalog.* Santa Rosa, CA: American School Publishers, 1991.

Holdaway, D. *The Foundations of Literacy.* Portsmouth, NH: Heinemann, 1979.

Johnson, T. D., and Loius, D. R. *Literacy Through Literature.* Portsmouth, NH: Heinemann, 1987.

Monson, R. J., and Pahl, M. M. "Charting a New Course with Whole Language." *Educational Leadership* (March 1991): 51–53.

Rasinski, T. V., and Fredericks, A. D. "School Sharing Literacy: Guiding Principles and Practices for Parent Involvement." *The Reading Teacher* 41, no. 5 (1988): 508–512.

Rasinski, T. V., and Fredericks, A. D. (1988). "Beyond Parents and Into the Community." *The Reading Teacher* 44, no. 9 (1991): 698–699.

Routman, R. *Transitions: From Literature to Literacy.* Portsmouth, NH: Heinemann, 1988.

Routman, R. *Invitations: Changing as Teachers and Learners, K-12.* Portsmouth, NH: Heinemann, 1991.

Salinger, T. *Models of Literacy Instruction.* New York: Macmillan, 1993.

Sumner, D., ed. *Into Teachers Hands.* Peterborough, NH: Society for Developmental Education, 1992.

Weaver, C. *Understanding Whole Language: Principles and Practices.* Portsmouth, NH: Heinemann, 1990.

CHAPTER 2

LITERACY LEARNING: CHANGING PERSPECTIVES

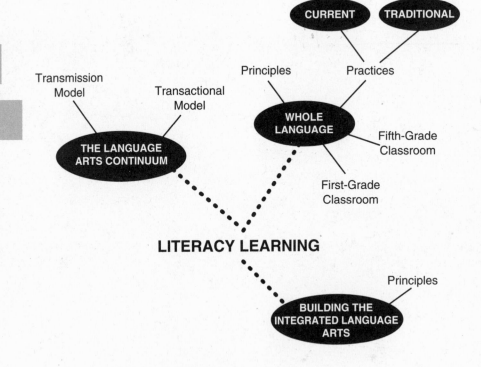

Note to the Reader

Please feel free to add your own ideas (your background knowledge) or ideas from the chapter to this web (yes, we are encouraging you to write in this book). We invite you to "fill in" the webs preceding each chapter. The webs can thus serve as appropriate study guides or in-class discussion tools.

What I Know: Pre-Chapter Journaling

Think back to your years as a student in elementary school. Try to imagine some of the lessons, activities, or instruction you received while in school, particularly the ways in which your teachers taught you to read and write. What were some of the things your teachers did that were a *positive* influence on your growth as a reader and writer? (If you wish, you may want to share your recollections with other members of the class.)

Big Ideas

This chapter will offer:

1. The interrelationships that exist between reading, writing, listening, and speaking.
2. Beliefs held by whole language teachers and the principles of whole language instruction.
3. The roles of students and teachers in an integrated language arts curriculum.
4. Principles of an integrated language arts program.

CONSTRUCTING THE LANGUAGE ARTS CONTINUUM

At this point in your teacher preparation program, you may have heard terms such as *literature-based reading programs, whole language, integrated language arts, emergent literacy, thematic teaching,* or *language across the curriculum.* This terminology suggests that teaching and learning are in a state of flux, that they may be quite different from the types of experiences you had when you were in elementary school. In fact, we would like you to take a few moments to think back to your years in elementary school. Select a favorite grade or favorite teacher and create a mental picture of the events and circumstances of that classroom. What was it about that environment that made learning an enjoyable experience? Was it the teacher? Was it the design or layout of the room? Was it the friends you had that year? Was it a very special event that happened that year? Or, was there a combination of factors that made that year a memorable one?

While it may be difficult to remember *all* the specific things your teacher did that year, we would like you to consider (in general) how your teacher might have taught you and your classmates. What were some of the materials, activities, and events that were part of each day's instruction in that grade? Why was learning fun that year? In fact, how do you think your teacher taught? What did you learn as a learner? Please take a few moments to write a few statements (in your journal) about those experiences.

The statements you wrote can be indicators of your former teacher's philosophy about classroom instruction. For example, if you decide that your teacher took a more skills-oriented approach to teaching, then she or he tended toward a *transmission (or traditional) model* of instruction. On the other hand, your former teacher's philosophy may have reflected a *transactional (or whole language) model* of instruction. In fact, your own philosophy about the teaching of language arts

will reflect elements of one model more than the other. Let's take a look at these two models in closer detail.

Transmission Model Often referred to as a skills approach to learning, the transmission model places a great deal of responsibility on the teacher for giving students the skills they need to successfully complete a task. By definition, the teacher transmits information to the student who, presumably, is able to combine that information with previously learned data in order to "solve" or complete an educational task (circling words on a workbook page, for example). The intent of the transmission model is for students to master a set of component skills so that they might be able to put them together into a recognizable pattern or sequence.

The distinguishing feature of the transmission model is that learning is "broken down" into a sequence of skills to be mastered by the student. The logic is that students should master simple tasks before moving on to more complex activities. For example, in reading instruction, skills begin with letter discrimination and move on to letter names, letter sounds, sight words, and then sentences made up of combinations of known words (Au, 1993). It seems reasonable to expect that the mastery of simple skills form the foundation for instruction in more complex skills. Extending that thinking further would imply that students are "ready" to learn words only after they have effectively learned the names and sounds of letters. The implication of the transmission model is that knowledge is transmitted by a teacher or passively absorbed by a learner (Weaver, 1990).

Transactional Model In a transactional model the responsibility for learning shifts from the teacher to the student; that is, students become more actively engaged in their own learning and play a greater role in the discovery process. At the heart of this model is the notion that learners must actively construct their own understandings (Au, 1993). Instead of the teacher "giving" everything to the student, the teacher and student work together in a spirit of mutual cooperation and support that provides a structure for learning and a foundation for independence. Teachers are doing more than just teaching; they are guiding, facilitating, and supporting the literacy development of their students—development that begins with what the child knows and proceeds through activities that are purposeful and self-directed. One of the chief roles of the teacher in a transactional classroom is to work with students to create a "community of learners."

In a transactional model, children are provided with opportunities to interact with their environment. They are provided with a multitude of activities that demonstrate the use and utility of language in a variety of contexts. For example, reading to children has been posited as one of the most engaging of all literacy activities. Among other things, it demonstrates the vitality of language, the ways in which people share ideas, the imagination and creativity that can result through a combination of words, sentences, and ideas, and the enjoyment of places and people far removed from the classroom. In short, reading aloud surrounds children with functional and meaningful language—language that is both powerful and instructive.

What children learn is that language is used to convey ideas and thoughts and that it is "organized" in a utilitarian manner. Most importantly, children learn that they, too, can convey and share those same ideas and ideals, not necessary because they know the letters and sounds of words, but more so because they were surrounded by words that were intrinsically meaningful for them. Language in action, language in use is how we typically define the transactional model of literacy learning. It also forms the basis for the "whole language" philosophy as well as serves as the impetus for the integrated language arts.

Two Teaching Models

In more traditional classrooms most of the responsibility for the scope and structure of instruc-

tion rests with the teacher. If your teachers embraced a transmission model of teaching, you may remember filling in blanks on a series of workbook pages as part of a reading lesson, writing an essay on "What I did on my summer vacation" on the first day of school, or memorizing a list of 20 spelling words for a weekly spelling test given on Friday mornings. These experiences were product-oriented; that is, the emphasis was placed on obtaining a high grade or successfully mastering isolated bits of information.

In a transactional classroom, however, there is an assumption of responsibility on the part of students for some of the direction and depth of learning activities. The implication is that teachers release instructional responsibilities to their students. Students learn to become more independent learners simply because they are given opportunities to "take charge" of what and how they learn. What results is a fuller appreciation by students of their role as active participants in the learning process—particularly in the processes of literacy learning.

Kathy Au (1993) states that "through involvement in the full processes of literacy, and *with the assistance of teachers* [emphasis ours], students gradually construct their own understandings of the hows and whys of reading and writing. In this sense, they learn to read by reading, and to write by writing." That learning process is both natural and expected, simply because students are involved as *invited* decision makers in their own literacy growth and development. The emphasis is more on the *processes* rather than the *products* of learning. Transactional classrooms assist children in taking an active role in their own learning, helping them develop and follow through on self-initiated discoveries, and presenting language learning holistically, rather than as a series of fragmented elements.

We do not want to give the impression that you must be *either* a transmission teacher or a transactional teacher. Few teachers are strictly one or the other. It is important to know that as a teacher, your instructional philosophy will tend to embody the components of one model more than the other, but, as you grow and learn, you will continue to move back and forth along a *transmission/transactional continuum.* You will discover, however, that after your first few years of teaching, your teaching philosophy and classroom practices may emphasize one model more than the other.

Currently, there is an exciting revolution in language arts instruction—a "reform movement" suggesting that many teachers are thinking (and rethinking) about the way they teach and the way children learn. It also means that teachers are taking a serious look at the policies and practices of the past, asking questions about the materials and methodologies that facilitate literacy learning, and assessing their own roles in the learning environment. What is clear is that this "self-discovery" process means that teachers are examining, taking risks, and becoming learners alongside their students.

As teachers, our own philosophy of teaching has allowed us to move up or down the transmission/transaction continuum line according to our ongoing education, the journals we read, the conferences we attend, the colleagues with whom we talk, and the discoveries we make in our classrooms.

We believe that good teachers are on a continuous journey—making new discoveries, learning new information, and participating in new activities. Their journeys will take them several steps in one direction and a few steps in another. What will become clear is the fact that that teaching philosophy, while evolving, will serve as a critical foundation for success in the classroom.

The factors most evident in transmission and transactional classrooms are summarized in Table 2.1. Note the items in the transactional column of the table that would be embodied in the literacy

TABLE 2.1 Transmission vs. Transactional Literacy Models: Classroom Organization and Management

Transmission	Transactional
Emphasis on the development of skills	Emphasis on the processes of learning
Instruction moves from the parts to the whole	Instruction moves from the whole to the parts
Individualistic learning	Learning in a social context
Competitive	Cooperative
Teaching focused on the forms or skills of literacy	Teaching focused on the functions and utility of literacy
Teacher-directed	Student-centered
Skills taught in a set sequence to all children	Skills determined by the needs of children
Teacher-set goals	Student-initiated goals
Selection of all instructional materials by teacher	Student–self-selection emphasized
Focus on the products of thinking	Focus on the processes of thinking
Textual materials can have only one interpretation	Interpretation is a dynamic interaction between reader and text
No emphasis on differing backgrounds and experience	Prior knowledge of students is assessed, respected, and built upon
Instruction reflects the values of the cultural mainstream	Instruction emphasizes cultural diversity (Au, 1993)
Teacher monitors learning	Students monitor themselves
Evaluation is standardized and teacher controlled	Students are actively involved in self-assessment
Language arts taught as a separate subject	Language arts integrated into all subject areas and instructional activities
Teacher provides all instruction	Teacher is a co-learner

learning models of Holdaway, Routman, and Cambourne.

Where are you on the transmission/transactional continuum? Where will you be in five years? In ten years? In 20 years? What you will certainly discover is that your placement along that continuum will change as your career as a teacher progresses. If you have come from traditional classrooms in your elementary and secondary experiences, then you may find yourself starting your teaching career more at the transmission end of the continuum. If your education was more transactional in nature, then your initial experiences as a classroom teacher may be positioned at the other end of the continuum.

Our personal views of literacy instruction are transactional in nature. We submit that students learn to value, appreciate, and productively use their literacy skills when provided with an educational environment that supports, encourages, and stimulates literacy in all dimensions of education. Surrounding students with authentic literacy experiences and a supportive learning environment provides them with opportunities and a "level of comfortableness" to use their developing language arts in meaningful constructs. When students understand the interrelationships, interdependencies, and integrated nature of language arts throughout their classroom experiences *as well as* personal experiences outside the classroom, then their learning becomes functional and meaningful. The language arts become a tool for learning as well as a tool for immense personal satisfaction for every student.

Perhaps you are now wondering where the topic of the integrated language arts fits into the continuum. The remainder of this chapter will outline and illustrate this concept in greater detail; but it is important at this point to turn to the related concept of whole language, a philosophy from which we draw strategies for teaching the integrated language arts (Morrow et al., 1993). In short, whole language provides us with the philosophical underpinnings upon which the methodologies and practices of the integrated language arts are based. Please note that whole language is not a program or a method of teaching; it is a philosophical orientation about how children learn. Teachers who embrace that orientation can choose the integrated language arts as a method of promoting those concepts.

Let's take a look at *whole language* in more detail and, later, how the *integrated language arts* promotes this philosophy of teaching and learning.

WHOLE LANGUAGE/ WHOLE LEARNING

"Reading is the funnest thing that ever happened to me!" exclaims Josh, a first grader.

"I've read 20 books so far, and it's not even December!" remarks Cherise, a sixth grader.

"I've published four books this year. They're all part of a series on the Flying Turtles," third grader Jamie proudly responds.

"Our class went on a field trip to visit another fifth-grade class to talk to all the kids and the fifth-grade teachers about how we do share circle as part of our writer's workshop," notes fifth grader Audrey.

"I like how our teacher does her own writing during our writer's workshop. She writes some really neat poetry. You should see all the rough drafts she has to do!" says Sean, a fourth grader.

"I've written a report on dinosaurs and I know more about them than even my teacher," exclaims first grader Timothy.

"I like the way our teacher makes us think about our goals for reading and writing. I never had to do that before. It's hard work, but I know I'm becoming better at it," comments sixth grader Cassandra. "I never knew I could write poetry, but I'm doing it, and it's great." (Cassandra has been labeled learning disabled for most of her school years.)

"I like how Mrs. Robinson gives us loads of time to read and write. It takes awhile to write a really good story!" notes Katie, a sixth grader.

It is an obvious point that these students are excited about their reading and writing accomplishments. They all consider themselves to be readers and writers, whether they're first graders or sixth graders, or labeled as gifted or learning disabled. There is also a real sense of ownership over what they can do. These children are in classroom environments where teachers encourage them to take risks in their learning, to try out new ways of thinking, new ways of writing. They are encouraged to become more powerful in their reading by doing just that—reading, reading, and more reading!

What follows is a list of important whole language principles and practices and how these differ from more traditional classroom practices. One of the features that makes whole language unique is that the principles listed below are not age or grade specific. You will find these principles demonstrated by whole language teachers in kindergartens as well as in eighth-grade classrooms. They are the principles that we have observed in many different whole language classrooms. They are also based on discussions with teachers across the country and have been drawn from the literature on whole language teaching and learning.

Whole Language Principles

Principle 1 Whole language teachers are lifelong learners and demonstrate the importance of their own learning in the classroom. Whole language teachers are not passive; they are *actively engaged* with children throughout the day. Whole language teachers are not ashamed to admit that they may not have an answer to a child's question. They view learning as a collaborative enterprise. They see themselves as a vital part of the learning community. Whole language teachers have a positive self-concept about their own learning; they do not see their learning as being complete.

Whole language teachers are readers and writers. They understand that to become more skilled they, too, need to practice the crafts of reading and writing both inside the classroom as well as outside. They want children to see them as learners—as readers, writers, and inquirers about the world. Instead of giving children answers to all their questions, whole language teachers enjoy working through solutions to problems or questions. For example, in response to a child who wants to find out why it gets darker earlier in the evening as fall and winter approaches, a whole language teacher would help the child find some sources that would answer the question.

Whole language teachers are also active in their profession. As lifelong learners, they attend conferences and workshops to learn, grow, and network with other teachers. They subscribe to professional journals to keep abreast of new developments in literacy learning and teaching.

Whole language teachers are actively engaged with their students' learning. They are not assigners of work; they work *with* children. They demonstrate what students will learn and use stimulating and enriching materials such as children's literature. They ask students to do a lot of reading and writing rather than fill-in-the-blank worksheet activities.

Traditional Practice You might be asking yourself, shouldn't all teachers exhibit this kind of enthusiasm for learning? Most teachers do want to learn new things, and they want students to become excited about learning. However, it is whole language teachers who consciously *show* students that they are active learners; they are not afraid to show their vulnerable side and to say "I don't know the answer, but let's take time to find it together."

In traditional classrooms many children find that they are engaged in more seatwork completing worksheets than actively engaged in reading and writing. Some traditional teachers are proud to say that the methods they used 25 years ago are just as good for today's children. Can you imagine going to a doctor who hadn't changed her practices in the last 25 years?

Principle 2 Whole *language teachers believe in the classroom as a democracy. They encourage children to work in collaboration with each other.* Whole language teachers believe in establishing a classroom learning community. They build a climate of trust, support, risk taking, and learning in the classroom community. They talk *with* (not to) students. They have high regard for each student and value diversity. When there are challenges during the day, the teacher gathers students together to talk things through and come to decisions as a group.

For instance, during a writer's workshop, a teacher notices that children are working on their writing but that their voice levels are reaching a high point. Some students who need a more quiet environment for writing seem frustrated. Rather than "shoulder the problem" herself, the teacher gathers all the students together. "How did writing workshop go today?" Some students comment, "Fine; it was great." But, many remark that the noise level got too high. The teacher asks students for suggestions, writes them on chart paper, and asks students which ones they can commit themselves to putting into action. As a group they decide that it might help the classroom environment if soft music is played on a tape recorder. If students can no longer hear the

music, the teacher will signal them by shutting off the lights. Students and teacher will gather again the next day to talk about how this new procedure works.

Whole language teachers want to establish the notion that everyone is in the classroom to support each other as learners. They encourage students to work together on projects, meet in small groups to read a book in common, write to each other in their journals about reactions to books, help one another come up with topics for writing, and listen to drafts of writing. Teachers encourage students to choose a buddy to listen to each other read. They value the fact that students of all abilities, not just the teacher, can help each other learn and grow. Whole language teachers help children form collaborative working groups. These groups change during the year, so that students have an opportunity to work with *everyone* in the classroom.

Whole language teachers also welcome parents as part of the classroom learning community. They are encouraged to come in to classrooms to listen to children read, to help them publish their books, to read aloud to them, and to make presentations as guest speakers, etc.

Traditional Practice Students in traditional classrooms often do not have many opportunities to work together. In fact, some students consider it cheating to help each other. Many traditional teachers value quiet classrooms. Students speak when spoken to. When there are so many strict rules, one begins to see how students break the rules.

The teacher is the "boss" in these classrooms. In fact, in visiting one classroom, there was a placard on the teacher's desk that read, "I'M THE BOSS AROUND HERE!" There is only one teacher, and he or she makes all the decisions about learning and classroom decorum.

Principle 3 Whole *language teachers are "kid-watchers"; they observe, listen, and learn from* *children. Children are "informants" demonstrating to teachers what they know and what their strengths are as learners.* Kid-watching is a term first coined by Yetta Goodman (1978). Goodman believes in the knowledge teachers have about their own students and views kid-watching as an informal way to learn and understand what learners can do. Many whole language teachers believe that formal tests to find out what students know only give limited information. Whole language teachers believe in ongoing assessment—observing students during reading and writing, taking anecdotal records, using checklists, and carefully attending to what children do when they read "real" books and work through the writing process. They glean more valuable information in this manner, rather than relying on test scores and unit tests.

Notice that the focus of the whole language teacher is on what students "can do" rather than on all the things they cannot do—on strengths rather than weaknesses. This is not to say that whole language teachers do not help students deal with areas of weakness. They give balance to both; they take a "reading" of students and flex to their needs. For example, inside student writing folders there may be a form that declares what student writers feel they can do well in writing (demonstrated by their actual writing pieces) and things they need to work on in writing. This "can do" attitude gives students a feeling of empowerment and instills in them the belief that they are accomplishing something in school and are successful.

Many children in our schools carry only failure around with them. They may have been retained in a grade or their teachers may have never pointed out anything valuable or good that they had to offer. Whole language teachers believe in getting a multidimensional view of every child; to do this they gather many pieces of information. They feel this is necessary to be able to talk about the progress of the child. They are teachers who believe that a string of grades in a rank book from

worksheets will not give an accurate picture of what a child can do.

Students also have a responsibility to gather a multitude of information. Many teachers use a portfolio approach to assessment. Students gather samples of their work for the portfolio. Also included might be samples of their goals as learners and lists of what they feel they have accomplished as readers and writers. (See Chapter 4 for more information on kid-watching techniques and Chapter 11 for more information on the writing process and writer's workshops.)

Traditional Practice In more traditional classrooms, there is a greater emphasis on both test taking and test results. In such contexts, students have to prove on paper-and-pencil quizzes and unit tests how much they remember. Teachers seldom collect any other information about students on an ongoing basis.

Principle 4 Whole language teachers plan experiences for students that are authentic. Whole language teachers are not assigners of busywork for children. They believe in planning authentic learning experiences—experiences that are meaningfully connected with each child's life as a learner. Children in whole language classrooms learn to take responsibility for their learning: how to set learning goals for themselves and how to read and write for their own purposes; how to learn strategies, not isolated skill work, and how to become more powerful readers and writers. Their teachers believe in working with students' writing to determine needs rather than following a language arts textbook page by page. They believe in the values of using children's literature in helping children become powerful readers.

Traditional Practice The primary sources of reading material in traditional classrooms are the textbook and associated worksheets and/or workbook pages. Usually there is a separate textbook for reading, language arts, math, science, and social studies. When "graduates" of traditional classroom teaching are asked about the reading and writing they have done in school, many say that their "real" or authentic reading and writing was done outside of the classroom. Some enjoyed writing poetry or short stories for the children's section of their local newspaper or for children's magazines.

Principle 5 Whole language teachers believe that children learn best in an environment that supports risk taking. They believe that learners need to take risks in order to learn and grow. Whole language teachers work hard to establish a classroom climate that welcomes learners. For example, it is next to impossible for writers in a hostile environment to want to risk writing words they do not know how to spell. If their first draft of writing has to be submitted to the teacher for a grade, they are usually cautious about using words they don't know how to spell. Their penmanship has to be neat and their grammar correct on the first draft! How many students are going to risk trying anything new?

If writers are going to experiment with their writing, teacher comments need to be genuinely supportive of all stages of a writer's development. Writers need to know they can share their work with a class audience and be rewarded for it in terms of supportive and helpful comments from both their teacher and peers. Writers also need to be challenged to try forms of writing they may not be used to—from poetry to play scripts to chapter stories.

Readers, too, need lots of opportunities to experiment with broadening their reading tastes by trying an endless list of genres: poetry, historical fiction, biography, myths, fables, folktales, legends, fantasy, realistic fiction, picture books, and nonfiction to name but a few.

Students in whole language classrooms learn how to formulate questions about what they want to learn. For example, a teacher planning a unit on mammals might use a variety of strategies to find out what children know about mammals. Her planning is not done in a vacuum. She follows the lead of her students. What do my students know about mammals? What do they want to learn? How can I expand and enrich their learning? How can my students develop ownership over their learning?

Traditional Practice The seat of power in the traditional classroom is the teacher, the person who makes all decisions about learning. Children's interests are something they pursue on their own free time, outside of school. There is a need to "cover" the curriculum, rather than using more concentrated time for children to really get into a topic. To read books on mammals, for example, takes a far bigger investment of time and energy than for children to just read the chapter from the textbook. To write about a topic, in some depth, takes far more time, energy, and a commitment to gathering resources than filling in the blanks on a plethora of worksheets.

Principle 6 Whole language teachers commit large blocks of time for reading and writing. Whole language teachers believe that the process of learning is, in many cases, far more meaningful than the product. For example, whole language teachers teach writing as a *process.* Students in these classrooms learn how to identify their topic for writing. They consider other audiences for their writing, other than the teacher. They decide on the form the writing will take—a poem, a song, a persuasive piece, a letter, a story, etc. They write drafts of the piece and discuss these drafts with other students. They revise and edit their work, until at the end of the process they have created a final draft (the cosmetics of writing—penmanship, spelling, grammar, paragraphing, usage, etc.—receive attention at this point).

Writers learn about new strategies to become better at their craft through the vehicle of mini-lessons. Teachers look at student writing carefully. What strengths do the writers demonstrate in their writing? Where do they need help next? For example, a teacher might see that many students are using dialogue in their stories but need help with using this device effectively. This is the opportune time for a minilesson on how other writers use dialogue in their writing. The teacher might gather good examples of this technique in other student writing and examples of how authors of children's literature incorporate dialogue in their writing.

Teachers also take time during writer's workshop to work on their own writing. This demonstrates to children that teachers also need to work on improving their skills as well. This all takes time! Many teachers use about an hour a day for writer's workshop. (See Chapter 11 for more information on writing process and the writer's workshop.)

Students in whole language classrooms also use the language arts (writing, reading, listening, and speaking) all day long. Children begin to view the language arts not as a subject but as the tools for learning about the world—through math, science, and social studies. Children in the primary grades through middle school are formulating their own questions to topics and doing extensive writing to answer their questions. (See Chapter 14 for more information on designing integrated units.)

Traditional Practice Students in traditional classrooms have far less time for reading and writing. Typically, reading is taught by dividing the classroom into three reading groups—a low group, a middle group, and a high-ability group. Students read from basal reading textbooks containing short stories, poems, and plays. Sometimes the language is controlled in these selections. Words are used in the selection that have been previously taught, and words that the publisher believes will be new to students are taught prior to reading the selection. After the lesson, students return to their seats to complete worksheets and/or workbook pages. Sometimes when students complete these assignments, there might be time to choose a book from the library to read. In these kinds of classrooms poorer readers are often kept at a disadvantage because there just is no time to get to do the "real thing"—read books. They are too busy filling in all the blanks on the workbook pages. Most often children are asked to read a book *outside* of school and write a book report.

Children in more traditional programs write from topics that are mostly decided by the teacher. Often a first draft of writing is the final draft. In these classrooms writing is *assigned not taught,* as in process writing classrooms.

The curriculum is determined by the textbook in these classrooms, whether it be in reading, math, social studies, or science. The typical student reads a chapter from science or social studies but is not actively engaged in learning how to make inquiries about topics, or taught how to think like scientists and historians.

Principle 7 *Whole language teachers believe in keeping language whole.* Whole language teachers do not believe that children should wait to become readers and writers. They believe that reading and writing are developmental processes. Children come to school from a wide variety of experiential backgrounds. While some children have been read to from birth and have interacted with a caring and loving family, other children are not as fortunate. However, primary teachers welcome *all* children into the literacy community of the classroom. They read aloud from high-quality children's literature and begin by having children read books with predictable language (books with language that repeats or rhymes and is easy to read). Teachers help children understand that reading is a meaning-making process. They use predictable language to help students learn how language works in print and how to develop strategies for words that they do not know.

From the beginning of school, children write their names and begin writing stories. Teachers also view spelling as a developmental process. They know children will grow as writers and readers because they will be practicing every day. Teachers learn what children can do when they are immersed in print.

Traditional Practice   More traditional teachers view young children as getting ready to be readers and writers. Instruction focuses on the skills of becoming readers and writers. Reading is usually taught from a skills perspective, meaning that children are taught such skills as letters and letter names removed from the context of whole stories. Many children in these kinds of programs do not see reading as a meaning-making process.

Young children in these programs are not viewed as writers. The viewpoint in traditional programs is one in which children need to master skills before they can actually write stories. Children in these programs learn early to spell only the words they can write correctly. They focus on how neat their papers look. They wait for the teacher to tell them what to write about. The focus in this kind of program is out of balance. There is too much emphasis on the mechanics of writing rather than on the content of the writing. (See Chapter 6 for a more in depth look at what children can do at this early stage of literacy development.)

Principle 8   *Whole language teachers view the use of literature as the "backbone" of the curriculum.* Whole language teachers believe that readers of all ages need to read "real" books rather than textbooks. They open the keys of the magic kingdom of reading by having a well-stocked classroom library, reading aloud to stu-

dents, and building a strong reading program that brings children and books together. Children learn how to make choices about what to read and have ample time to read, not short snippets of stories in basal reading texts, but reading long and short books cover to cover. Children learn about the world by reading widely across the curriculum, which means they read real books in social studies and science, not just textbooks.

Whole language teachers also believe that there are connections between reading and writing. Young writers need the "fuel" of good literature for inspiration to write their own stories. (See Chapter 12 for ways to incorporate literature into the writing program.)

Traditional Practice   Children in traditional programs are rarely asked to read beyond the textbook. Teachers may read aloud to them but they do not make the connections needed to see reading and writing as processes that develop and strengthen each other. Literature is viewed as an "extra," not the very "heart" of a literacy curriculum.

Principle 9   *Whole language teachers believe in integrating the language arts across the curriculum.* The language arts (reading, writing, listening, and speaking) are not a subject to be studied in whole language classrooms; they are rather the thread that binds the curriculum together. Children in these classrooms see that they read and write, talk and listen to each other all through the day, whether it be in science, math, or social studies. For example, children working on their research reports on birds of the southwest read widely to answer their questions. Teachers help students to apply what they know from writer's workshop to writing their research reports.

Traditional Practice   Curriculum in traditional classrooms is defined by subject areas and text-

TABLE 2.2 Best Practice in Teaching Reading

Increase	Decrease
Reading aloud to students	Exclusive stress on whole class or reading-group activities
Time for independent reading	
Children's choice of their own reading materials	Teacher selection of all reading materials for individuals and groups
Exposing children to a wide and rich range of literature	Relying on selections in basal reader
Teaching modeling and discussing his/her own reading processes	Teacher keeping her own reading tastes and habits private
Primary instructional emphasis on comprehension	Primary instructional emphasis on reading subskills such as phonics, word analysis, syllabication
Teaching reading as a process: —Use strategies that activate prior knowledge —Help students make and test predictions —Structure help during reading —Provide after-reading applications	Teaching reading as a single, one-step act —Solitary seatwork
	Grouping by reading level
Social, collaborative activities with much discussion and interaction	Round-robin oral reading
Grouping by interests or book choices	Teaching isolated skills in phonics workbooks or drills
Silent reading followed by discussion	
	Little or no chance to write
Teaching skills in the context of whole and meaningful of literature	Punishing pre-conventional spelling in students' early writings
Writing before and after reading	Segregation of reading to reading time
Encouraging invented spelling in children's early writings	
Use of reading in content fields (e.g., historical novels in social studies)	Evaluation focused on individual, low-level subskills
Evaluation that focuses on holistic, higher-order thinking processes	Measuring the success of the reading program only by test scores
Measuring success of reading program by students' reading habits, attitudes, and comprehension	

Source: S. Zemelman, H. Daniels, and A. Hyde, *Best Practice.* (Portsmouth, NH: Heinemann, 1993), p. 45.

books. Children, unfortunately, see clear demarcations between subject areas—now we're doing social studies or science; that means reading the textbook and worksheets. Students don't see connections between and among curricular areas. Everything is done by the clock—first reading, then spelling, math comes next, and if there's time maybe science or social studies.

Now let's turn to a summary of best practices. Zemelman, Daniels, and Hyde (1993) include summary charts of "Best Practice in Teaching Reading" and "Best Practice in Teaching Writing." Do you see connections between our listing of whole language principles and the recommendations of national curriculum reports?

TABLE 2.2 *Continued*

Increase	Decrease
Student ownership and responsibility by: —helping students choose their own topics and goals for improvement —using brief teacher-student conferences —teaching students to review their own progress	Teacher control of decision-making by: —teacher deciding on all writing topics —suggestions for improvement dictated by teacher —learning objectives determined by teacher alone —instruction given as whole-class activity
Class time spent on writing whole, original pieces through: —establishing real purposes for writing, and students' involvement in the task —instruction in, and support for, all stages of writing process —pre-writing, drafting, revising, editing	Time spent on isolated drills on "subskills" of grammar, vocabulary, spelling, paragraphing, penmanship, etc. Writing assignments given briefly, with no context or purpose, completed in one step
Teacher modeling writing—drafting, revising, share—as a fellow author, and as demonstrator or processes	Teacher talks about writing but never writes or shares own work
Learning of grammar and mechanics in context, at the editing stage, and as items are needed	Isolated grammar lessons, given in order to determine by textbook, before writing is begun
Writing for real audiences, publishing for the class and for wider communities	Assignments read only by teacher
Making the classroom a supportive setting for shared learning, using: —active exchange and valuing of students' ideas —collaborative small group work —conferences and peer critiquing that give responsibility for improvement to authors	Devaluation of students' ideas through: —students viewed as lacking knowledge and language abilities —sense of class as competing individuals —work with fellow students viewed as cheating, disruptive
Writing across the curriculum as a tool for learning	Writing taught only during "language arts" periods—i.e., infrequently
Constructive and efficient evaluation that involves: —brief informal oral responses as students work —thorough grading of just a few of student-selected, polished pieces —focus on a few errors at a time —cumulative view of growth and self-evaluation —encouragement of risk-taking and honest expression	Evaluation as negative burden for teacher and student by: —marking all papers heavily for all errors, making teacher a bottleneck —teacher editing paper, and only after completed, rather than student making improvements —grading seen as punitive, focused on errors, not growth

BEGINNING THE SCHOOL YEAR IN A WHOLE LANGUAGE CLASSROOM

It is the first day of school, and there is a scurry of activity as 25 new fifth graders enter Betty Robinson's classroom.[1] Student desks have been arranged in groups of four or five with the students' names already on the desks. Children find themselves sitting with peers that they may not have even talked to on the playground. Betty explains that these are cooperative learning groups, and that every six weeks they will rotate areas so that all students will have worked with each other in the class sometime during the year.

Betty believes that there are many reasons that make this kind of arrangement important.

She believes it is crucial for students to have an opportunity to work and learn from each

[1]Betty will be discussed in scenarios in several other chapters. Because she changed grade levels a year after we first observed her, you will later read that Betty is a sixth-grade teacher. We believe Betty is an outstanding teacher and wanted to share what she has accomplished in both a fifth- and sixth-grade classroom.

other. As students get older, they tend to form cliques and may socialize and choose to work on projects with just a few of their friends. Since her class represents a wide spectrum of ability and social levels, she wants her students to begin gaining the benefits of working with each other. Betty establishes the groundwork for this to happen by organizing students into these groupings on the first day.

In-School Family Betty talks with students about their class being an in-school family. Just as they have a family outside of school that works, cares, and helps each other, they also have an in-school family who will do the same for each other. They each have unique capabilities and strengths, as well as areas they need to work on through the year. She explains that she wants everyone to succeed and wants to build an atmosphere of mutual respect, kindness, and caring.

From day one, Betty begins to build a climate of trust and cooperation. She realizes that her writing and reading workshop, research writing in science and social studies, and math curriculum requires her students to take risks and to challenge themselves. Betty also understands that it is often difficult to do this if learners come to school apprehensive to try new things and afraid that they will be all alone if they do not understand something. She wants to build the notion that there are 26 teachers in this class, including herself. All are there to support each other's growth and development over the school year.

Listening and Learning from Each Other Betty sits comfortably on a stool at the front of the room and talks about some of the interesting and also "ho-hum" kinds of things she did during the summer. She also relates how scary first days of school are for her even though she has been teaching for over 15 years. She then asks students about how their summers went. First only a few students speak up, then more and more tell about some of the ordinary things they did and about

some of the places they visited. Betty easily joins in the laughter as Annie relates an escapade of dropping two cones of ice cream, one right after another, and the local dog gobbling them up before she had a chance to return to the ice cream shop to say she dropped them!

After all the storytelling, Betty asks if anyone remembers what someone else said during all of this conversation. Timmy speaks up and says, "I remember that Jason said he went to visit his grandparents."

"Annie lost her ice cream!!" chime Susan and Beth in unison.

Betty Robinson says, "I remember Tony saying that he had the kind of summer I did, not doing too much, just staying around the house trying to keep cool!"

Betty explains that the reason she asked everyone to try and recall what others had said was because being a good listener is going to be very much valued in the upcoming year. They will be doing a lot of talking in their reading and writing workshops, so it will be very important to focus their attention on what others say.

The kind of sharing that you just read about is very common in Betty's classroom. In most classrooms, students direct their comments only to the teacher. It is almost as if no one else is in the room except for the student doing the talking and the teacher. Again, Betty wants to emphasize the importance of being a class family where everyone engages in conversation, listens to one another, and gives feedback.

Betty also encourages students to look at one another, not just at her, when they talk in class. Again, most teacher–student conversations go one way—from teacher to student or from student to teacher. This is because students look to the teacher for feedback and are not used to carrying on a conversation with many others within the classroom context.

Notice, too, that we use the term conversation. The atmosphere in Betty's room is relaxed and comfortable, one in which Betty freely talks about what she did during the summer, becoming a participant rather just an observer of student interaction.

This kind of informal storytelling also proves to later connect with ways Betty talks about topic development in the writing process; EVERYONE HAS A STORY TO TELL!!

Designing Classroom Rules for Living Together

Betty believes that it is crucial to begin the year with a set of expectations that are designed together as a classroom family. In fact, this is one of the first tasks that her students will work on in cooperation with each other. The assignment for each group is to arrive at a set of rules or ways the class can work together efficiently, effectively, and in a caring and humane way. There is a hum in the room as students in each group talk through rules they feel are important for the whole class to consider. Betty also asks that each group appoint a scribe to take notes and a spokesperson.

Establishing classroom rules with the class is not a new idea, but the manner in which Betty goes about it is worth noting. Betty's procedure aligns with her philosophical belief about providing students with as many opportunities as possible to help them see themselves as decision makers and to hold them responsible for their actions. Also by having students discuss rules within the groups, everyone in the class has an opportunity to become involved, not just a few students as would have happened if Betty had done this as a whole class discussion.

Betty also takes this activity as an opportunity to observe how students interact with each other during this small group activity.

- Who seems to be doing the most talking?
- Is turn-taking evident?
- Does everyone seem engaged in this activity?
- Does everyone have a chance to contribute?
- How do students decide who will emerge as scribe and spokesperson?

After the discussion, Betty asks students for feedback on how well the groups worked, as well as discussing some of the kinds of interactions she observed. She will not name names but will give students feedback such as, "I noticed that this group appeared to work well this morning. I observed how each member contributed some ideas." Or, "This group got right down to business. I saw how they began to talk right away about some rules that seemed to work well in the past."

After much talk and debate during the whole group share (especially about stating rules in a positive way, rather than saying "what we shouldn't do"), the class decided on the following "Rules to Live By":

1. Be kind to each other.
2. Try to always be helpful and patient when others need help.
3. It's important to take turns and not have one person always be the leader.
4. We need to be considerate of each other.
5. When the class gets too loud when everyone is talking, Mrs. Robinson will give us a signal to keep the "buzz" down!

Betty asked for a volunteer to record the final list and to post it in the classroom where everyone could see it. She also said that, periodically, they would review the list to see if any changes needed to be made. This is just one more indication that the class is valued as a family, and important decisions affecting everyone need to be discussed and determined by the group. With just this one activity, students feel a sense of ownership over their destinities, plus they get to know each other as participants in the process of establishing an effective work environment. Betty also realizes that these rules will serve the group well as they begin to work in small groups for science lab projects, figuring out math problems, as well as during the writing and reading workshops.

Another interesting insight into giving students responsibilities is through the customary daily flag salute. Typically, every morning in most public school classrooms, students all rise to salute the flag. Either the teacher leads the group or a student is assigned the responsibility. When we observed Betty over the course of a year, we noticed that right from the start, she waited until someone started the salute. Then it was determined by the students that each member would rotate this duty. The next day students seemed to forget, and everyone stood looking at each other. Betty didn't say a word. After what seemed to be at least a very long minute, someone finally started. It is often so difficult for teachers not to say something, but Betty is a master at controlling herself! She waited and the salute to the flag began, without her saying a word. It was a memorable moment, and from that day on the salute began right away!

You may be thinking that all of this seems to take so much time. Isn't it a lot easier for the teacher just to be in charge and get these little management things done quickly and efficiently? Betty is absolutely convinced that all of these moments when children learn to take initiative and responsibility pay big dividends with everything else they do the rest of the day. For instance, when you later read about how she establishes the reading and writing workshops and the amount of student responsibility needed during these times of the day, it would be difficult to all of a sudden "switch gears" so to speak and say to students, "Well I was in charge of everything all day, now it's your turn to act responsibly." So, again, everything that is done all day long follows Betty's strong philosophical beliefs that children need to learn how to think and act independently and responsibly, whether it be in establishing rules, deciding who is going to begin the flag salute, or how they will leave the room to go to recess or lunch.

Taking a Break for Storytelling Another strong feature of Betty's classroom is the storytelling time. Her class takes a 20-minute break for a healthy snack, and while eating they enjoy tapes of storytellers or songs. Her students are not scheduled for a morning recess so, instead, this becomes a valuable break in the morning for everyone. Betty not only uses this time to reinforce bringing in healthy snacks, but children also enjoy the tapes. In order to broaden her children's range of experiences hearing literature presented by a diversity of voices, she chose a variety of recordings by well-known storytellers from across the United States. Children hear not only a wide range of stories and songs but also an array of dialects. The stories and songs provide more "fuel" for her writers in terms of potential topics they might like to adapt for their own stories. Annie, one of her most enthusiastic writers, so enjoyed hearing different dialects that she offered to help her classmates incorporate dialect into their own writing. She posted a notice on the bulletin board offering her services for five cents. This money was added to the pool for field trips!

In discussing the stories, Betty invites students to also think about how the storyteller presented the story, the choice of words, how the story began and unfolded, and the way the storyteller captured their attention and made them want to hear more. Another intention was to help her students see connections between the storyteller's weaving of a tale and how they, as writers, make some of the same decisions as they write their own stories. Some students want to pursue reading the actual story they heard on tape. This was the case with Tom and John who so enjoyed hearing Edgar Allan Poe's "The Pit and the Pendulum," that they wanted to read the story themselves. As observers, we thought that this story was very complex and that students "wouldn't get it," but to our surprise students had a wonderful time discussing it after hearing the tape. So much for making assumptions about what children will or will not understand.

Literature: The Thread that Weaves the Curriculum Together Literature in the form of real books is the "backbone" of the curriculum in this classroom. No basal readers can be found. Every day Betty reads aloud to children during a reading workshop, at which time students self-select from the many paperback and hardcover books in the classroom library. Betty is a reader and so collecting books for the classroom library is not a chore but an avocation! She supplements the collection from the school and public library. Betty is very aware of her student's reading interests from having them complete an interest inventory, but she also is aware that they need to broaden and expand their reading tastes. So, the classroom library includes a wide assortment of books: poetry, picture books, historical fiction, biography, contemporary fiction, traditional literature (myths, fables, legends, and folktales), fantasy, and nonfiction titles.

Students spend about an hour reading and recording responses and reflections about what they read in their literature logs. Betty also offers the possibility for small groups of three or four to read a book in common. During the reading workshop, then, you'll find both individual students and small groups reading from "real" books, not textbooks. Betty meets with individual students and small groups both during their reading and at the completion of a book. Students select from a wide range of response opportunities or ways to help make the book more memorable. In consultation with Betty, two or three students may work on a response as a team. No book report forms in this classroom! For example, children may decide on a wide range of writing opportunities such as writing a sequel or prequel to the book, journal entries from the point of view of a main character, and rewriting a segment of the book in play format to be used later as a reader's theatre presentation. For reader's theatre, three or four students will take roles and practice their lines again and again. They focus on producing a clear and stumble-free reading, as well as using their voices to interpret characters in the way they imagined they would talk. The final production is performed for the class using only minimal props. Lines are not memorized so that students use their scripts for the production. Reader's theatre is such a fabulous way to "perform" stories without the threat of having to memorize lines. So

even for the shyest student, dramatic performance is within reach.

Other popular response opportunities are other forms of drama such as a puppet theater and interviewing characters as if they were on television. Art opportunities are also a favorite. Students enjoy designing murals or maps, preparing television scripts and illustrations that use a roll of paper, dowel rod, and a cardboard cut-out television set, working with slides, dioramas, or shadowboxes, and experimenting with different media such as pastel chalks, watercolors, and charcoal. Some students even prepare a food that would have been a favorite of a main character. This is particularly fun and challenging as it relates to historical fiction. Students sometimes have to pore over old cookbooks and think through how to translate recipes for today's cooking, as well as preparing them in the most authentic way possible.

The most wonderful moments occur when students give a synopsis of a book and share their project with other members of the class. They talk about their choice of response and the process they went through to complete it. (After sharing they field questions from Betty and the group.) This sharing opportunity is a valuable time to learn about new books and ways to respond to them.

Students can also use literature to explore topics of interest and for thematic units. They do have science and social studies textbooks, but these are used as starting points and for reference. Students quickly learn that textbooks are of necessity limited in scope and present only the bare essentials on any topic.

Betty uses a research process whereby students select a topic and brainstorm questions they have about it. They also think of a product (chart, poster, model, etc.) to accompany their written report. In summary, children are reading and writing for different purpose throughout the day.

Betty believes in the power of reading aloud to students everyday. She chooses books wisely and carefully based not only on student interest but how these books might give students another "window" in which to examine the craft of good writing. For example, she might choose a picture book to read aloud because the author tells a great story and the illustrations are ones her students will surely appreciate. Some favorite picture book authors and illustrators are Chris Van Allsburg, Mitsumasa Anno, David Macaulay, Maurice Sendak, Anthony Browne, and Nancy Willard. Lots of rich conversation abounds after reading aloud a book by one of these author/ illustrators. Betty's questions focus on the interplay between pictures and text and how the words capture the imagination and tell a good story. Children then naturally want to try their hand at creating their own picture books or applying the illustrator's technique to their own writing.

Betty also reads aloud poetry (sometimes several times a day) and chapter books. Again, she makes wise choices. She reads the book first carefully assessing whether students will enjoy the content but also looking for reading and writing connections. She knows that literature is her most powerful vehicle in providing inspiration for her community of writers. For example, she may observe that her writers are having a difficult job with beginning their own stories in an exciting and powerful way. So, her read aloud choices might be ones in which the authors do a particularly fine job with capturing the attention right from the start.

Betty believes in the power of a good book to turn around the most reluctant readers, some of them falsely proud of never reading an entire book, and to further strengthen her most enthusiastic readers to expand and extend their reading. With pride Betty says that by December the class, as a whole, has read over 100 books. She quite honestly believes that her students would not have read so many books on their own if their reading time in school was predominantly from a basal reader.

Betty has clearly made the decision to look for ways that her readers can talk in authentic ways about books together. She avoids question-answer cycles where the teacher follows a basal script. She begins with asking students about their initial reactions to a book, either on a one-to-one basis or with a small group reading a book in common. Betty read Peterson and Eeds' book, *Grand Conversations: Literature Groups in Action* (1990) to help her with ways to guide children to discover and talk about their personal reactions to a book. She uses their personal responses as a basis for further conversations about plot, character, setting, point of view, and mood.

Betty doesn't hesitate to add her own reflections as a reader, thus providing a model for students. She might initiate this by talking about the part she loved the most, how a part of the book reminded her of a personal experience, and how surprised she was when a character acted in a particular way.

Betty also uses questions from "The Tell Me Framework" from Aidan Chamber's, *Booktalk* (1985). "The Tell Me Framework" offers open-ended questions such as the following: When you first saw the book, even before you read it, what kind of book did you think it was going to be?; Tell me about anything that particularly caught your attention; What will you tell your friends about it?; Tell me about the parts you liked the most; Tell me about the parts you didn't like; Was there anything that puzzled you?

Chambers suggests that teachers avoid asking "Why" as a follow-up to how a student responds. He claims that this question invites a defensive posture and tends to "box in the reader." Instead, he suggests that teachers use the phrase, "Tell me more about how you're thinking." Try this yourself sometime; it takes a great deal of practice because it seems that we, as teachers, were born asking the "Why" question.

The tell-me framework also works well with different kinds of text. You might try these questions with short stories or even textbook materials.

Betty has also abandoned the traditional book report format, which is usually so prevalent at her grade level. Students have honestly remarked that the usual book report format—writing a summary, listing major characters, identifying the theme, and giving an evaluation—is so easy to do. Most information can be found in the book "blurp," which means that actually reading the book is unnecessary! Developing more challenging responses to the book through writing, drama, and artwork, as described earlier, gives students more choices and ownership over how they wish to personally respond to what they read.

Writing and Reading Workshop Betty's writing workshop has long been one of the strongest features of her program. Her reading of the works of Graves (1976), Atwell (1987), Calkins (1986, 1990), and Wilde (1993) have led her to think of writing as not only a critical component of the language arts but a significant portion of what students do all day. Students explore what they know and how they think from their writing—writing in their current events reaction journals, writing to explain mathematical principles and terms, writing on self-selected topics in the writer's workshop, writing to discover answers to questions from thematic studies.

Betty is an active participant during writer's workshop. She helps students with strategies to identify topics they care about. All the way through the writing process she is there to offer assistance without taking over a student's writing. (See Chapter 11 for an in-depth description of the writer's workshop in Betty's classroom.)

Long ago Betty came to the conclusion that if she truly wanted her students to become more powerful and expert readers at the fifth- and sixth-grade levels then she had to let go of the basal. The fifth and sixth grades are such crucial years for readers. Some students reach the fifth grade never having read a book! Knowing this, Betty wanted to energize her readers.

Betty has a class notebook in which students record each book read. She is amazed at the volume of reading *all* students do throughout the year. If their reading was limited to a basal, they would have read only several hundred pages or so! Students learn how to make their own self-selections. Betty does many booktalks, telling a little about a particular book—enough to make students want to read more. Children record reactions to what they read in a log. When students have completed a book, each of them has a conference with Betty. She keeps a large loose-leaf notebook with pages for each child. She asks the students what genre or type of book they read. They give her a summary of the book, which leads to a discussion of the plot, characters, setting, and theme of the book. Next, she asks the students to read aloud a section from the book. She listens carefully for the strategies they use if they come to a word that is unfamiliar. Do they use the context (or other words to help identify the unknown word)? Do they say a word that makes sense in the passage? To what extent do they use their knowledge of sounds and letters (phonics) to help figure out a word? At the end of the conference, Betty talks with each student about what response might make the book memorable. Such responses range from writing (e.g., write a script for one of the chapters to dramatize, write diary entries from the point of view of one of the characters, write a new ending to the book, write a letter to the author) to art work (e.g., design a diorama or shadowbox of a favorite scene, make clay models, paint a watercolor of the setting). (See Chapter 10 for additional book response suggestions.)

Betty has an incredible mix of students—from students who have been labeled gifted to those designated as learning disabled. Yet when you observe her reading and writing workshops in action, you cannot detect these differences. *Everyone* is engaged in reading a book and writing. Betty does not believe in having children who have had trouble with learning spend this period doing isolated skill work. She believes that these children have had enough of this kind of classroom work and fill-

IDEA BOX

Children's literature is the vehicle which "drives" the whole language classroom. The infusion of good books and good literature into the elementary curriculum holds the promise of exposing students to values, cultures, concepts, and ideas they might not normally encounter in traditional textbook approaches.

What follows is an assembly of whole language activities developed across the curriculum for a single book, *Dear Mr. Henshaw* by Beverly Cleary. Note how all of the language arts (reading, writing, listening, and speaking) have been integrated throughout these activities. We do not suggest, however, that you would want to use *all* of these activities with any single class or any single student; what is important is that you and your students have a variety of meaningful activities from which you can choose. Equally important is the fact that students should be invited to contribute their ideas and suggestions for exploration and discovery. When students have sincere opportunities to invest in their own learning, then that learning will be intrinsically more valuable and enduring for them. Consider the following suggestions as possibilities to be used with a single book—possibilities that place a value on integrating the language arts throughout all aspects of the elementary curriculum.

TO OUR READERS: We invite you to read *Dear Mr. Henshaw* by Beverly Cleary and add your own suggestions or write your own ideas in the spaces at the end. We encourage you to share your activities with others in the class.

Dear Mr. Henshaw
Beverly Cleary
New York: Morrow, 1983

Summary

Over a period of time, Leigh Botts writes to his favorite book author. Leigh's letters are filled with questions and advice as well as a lot of revealing information about his life, his thoughts, and his feelings about his mother and father.

- Invite students to read other books by Beverly Cleary. There are many, but here are a few to start with: *Henry and Beezus* (New York: Morrow, 1952); *Mitch and Amy* (New York: Morrow, 1967); *Ramona the Pest* (New York: Morrow, 1968); and *Ramona Quimby, Age 8* (New York: Morrow, 1981).
- Encourage students to read about the life and writings of Beverly Cleary. Your school or local librarian will be able to supply several references. One particularly useful source is the author's autobiography, *A Girl from Yamhill* (New York: Morrow, 1988).
- Invite students to put together a guidebook entitled "How to Become a Better Writer." Encourage them to interview adults, teachers, businesspeople, reporters, and other children in the community about the tips and strategies that help people write. The information the students collect can be assembled into a booklet to be distributed to other classes.

in-the blank worksheets. What they have not had enough of is actual time reading "real" books and writing. They have been turned off to reading, writing, and anything that is academically related.

Betty has great success with these students by treating them as she would her most gifted students. In traditional classrooms, it is the gifted students and developmentally "on track" children who usually get to do the "real stuff." In Betty's classes, all children read children's literature and are engaged in the writer's workshop. This is not to say that Betty lets "at-risk" students drift aimlessly. For example, she helps them choose books that they can feel successful reading, and no

- Invite students to set up a pen pal network with students from another school. Contact colleagues in other schools or contact the education department of a local college and ask for the names of former students who have secured teaching positions in other parts of the state. Contact these individuals and invite their class to correspond with the students in your class and vice versa. Encourage students to keep the letters flowing throughout the year (and beyond!).
- Invite students to watch the development and growth of butterflies. Nasco (901 Janesville Ave., Fort Atkinson, WI 53538 [800-558-9595]) produces the *Butterfly Garden,* which can be ordered through their catalog or can be found in many toy/hobby stores. Students can observe and record the growth of butterflies from cocoons to adults.
- Encourage students to assemble an oversize collage of pictures of trucks and the trucking industry. Using pictures from old magazines as well as information and brochures collected from local trucking firms, students can create an informative collage for posting in the classroom or on a wall of the school.
- Invite students to compute the number of miles from Leigh's home in Pacific Grove, California, to some of the other cities mentioned in the book (e.g., Bakersfield, California; Taft, California; Albuquerque, New Mexico; Hermiston, Oregon). Later, encourage students to figure out the number of miles between each of those cities

and their own school. These figures can be posted on a large classroom map of the United States.
- Invite students to check their local library for recordings or songs dealing with trucks or truck drivers (country & western songs might be a logical place to begin). Encourage students to put together a listing or series of recordings of trucking songs to share with classmates.
- Encourage students to obtain travel and tourist information about California. They can write to Office of Tourism, Box 189, Sacramento, CA 95812-0189. After the material arrives, invite the students to arrange it into an attractive display.
- Invite students to put together a large mural on the history of transportation. Teams of students can be encouraged to gather the necessary research for one aspect of transportation (i.e., land, air, sea travel). Information, pictures, brochures, photos, and the like can be included in the mural.
- _____
- _____
- _____

SOURCE: Adapted from *The Integrated Curriculum: Books for Reluctant Readers, Grades 2–5* by Anthony D. Fredericks (Englewood, CO: Teacher Ideas Press, 1992). Used by permission.

stigma is attached to reading shorter novels or picture books. She might conference with them several times during the course of the book, rather than only at the end of the book.

Some of her students show great artistic strengths, others demonstrate a keen ability in writing, and still others like to put together models and are more mechanically gifted. Because this classroom is a learning community—an in-school family where members help support each other—it is not unusual for a child labeled as "learning disabled" to be working side by side with one who is "gifted" as an art consultant for a project related to a book.

Betty is continually amazed at what her students can do with their writing. She marvels at the connections they make with their reading. For example, as a follow-up to a book Betty reads aloud to the class, she invites discussion about the author's craft. What did you like about this author's writing? How did the author pull us in right at the beginning of the book? What did you think of the dialogue in this section of the book, etc.? Betty talks with students about ways they might incorporate some of these writing techniques into their own pieces. Some of her students remark that this is the first time they have been given enough TIME to work and talk about their writing. It is almost as if Betty has given them a gift—the gift of time and support to grow as readers and writers.

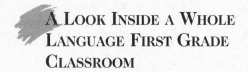

A LOOK INSIDE A WHOLE LANGUAGE FIRST GRADE CLASSROOM

A Morning Filled with Literacy Events

Now let's visit the first grade classroom of Mary Giard. While observing what happens as students walk into the classroom, we see a bustle of activity—taking off coats and putting lunch boxes away. Children talk to each other, and a group of eager students cluster around Mary to inform her of the growth of the radish and carrot plants that are growing in the corner. "Did you see how much they've grown, Ms. G., overnight?" Mary is attentive to each child—she always maintains eye contact with the speaker. She laughs at Todd's comment that maybe Garfield, the guinea pig, is really Bunnicula in disguise! "Some morning we'll walk in and all the plants will have turned white and droopy, just like in the book *Bunnicula!*" Mary had recently read aloud Deborah and James Howe's *Bunnicula* (1983), the humorous fantasy about a rabbit that appears to be a vampire who drains plants of their juices!

Before the morning meeting each child signs in on an attendance sheet. Even though Mary makes a mental note of who is present each morning, every child has the responsibility to write his or her name on a dated attendance sheet. Children drift over to the message board for their daily written morning message from Mary. Children also are invited to write messages to each other and tack them to the message board, which they eagerly do!

As children gather on the rug, Mary asks which children borrowed book bags and who would like to share what they read last night. The book bag program has been a great hit in this room. Mary bought enough burlap book bags for each member of the class. Each bag is filled with an assortment of children's literature or children's magazines. She uses a luggage tag attached to each bag to note what books or magazines children will find. For example, one bag has four folktales from Africa, another bag has several *Ranger Rick* and *National Geographic World* magazines, and yet another is filled with the beautiful picture books by Barbara Cooney. Children can sign out a bag every night and share the books with family members. Mary believes that it is vital to have a home–school partnership because it allows parents to share a time at night to read with their children. Mary discovered that sometimes the book bag is the only way books are brought into the home.

After the book bag share, Mary asks who took Bat Bear home for the night. "Bat Bear" is the name chosen by students for the stuffed bear that makes "home visits." Children sign out the bear and a cloth-covered journal. That night the child will write about the adventures Bat Bear had at their house. In the morning the child shares the journal entry with an appreciative audience. So, right from the beginning of the school day, children are engaged as readers and writers in authentic ways!

Mary believes that *all* of her students are readers and writers. Some children who have been told that they can't read are shown that they indeed can read their name and many of the labels for objects around the room. They know how to read signs they see, like "walk" at an intersection on the way to school. They all know the sign for MacDonald's and can identify their favorite cereal boxes and other foods. Some of Mary's children coming to first grade are already avid readers, ready to read short chapter books. However, as in Betty's classroom, all children are members of the literacy club (Smith, 1988). Mary believes in the social aspect of reading and values children helping each other as readers and writers.

When children come into the classroom in the morning they are not greeted with worksheets to keep them quiet while the teacher takes attendance and lunch counts. Instead, the children are involved in interesting reading and writing morning routines. From the first day of school, children sign the attendance sheet. Mary keeps these dated attendance sheets to share the growth in the writing of their names with the children and their parents. Children also read and write messages from the message board. Mary believes in engaging children in informal reading and writing events throughout the day. She is an avid kid-watcher, noticing the reactions of children at the message board. Which children consistently write messages to her and their classmates? Which children borrow book bags? Which students want to take home Bat Bear and write in the journal? Mary writes short notes about each child's extent of involvement with these literacy experiences. Even these very incidental reading and writing activities are, in fact, not so incidental. They inform Mary in *big* ways about how children interact with print on a daily basis.

Notice, too, how Mary spends time with children in the morning. She is not busily preparing for the day; she did this before children came into the room. First thing in the morning is the time to listen and learn what children say to her. What have they noticed on the way to school? What do children have to share with her? What children may have had a particularly bad night at home or had something wonderful happen?

Reading and Writing Workshop

After the early morning activities, Mary begins with a reading and writing workshop. She usually begins each workshop time with a mini-lesson focusing on helping children learn new strategies as readers and writers. For example, in reading, she will choose a children's book that is highly predictable, meaning that the language of the book is easy to read because of a repetition of words or lines of print, a good picture-text match, rhyming words, and so forth. She reads the book aloud, and after several repeated readings the children join in with the reading. On subsequent days, Mary plans other activities using the language of the book. For example, she will write the text of the story on chart paper and ask children to be word detectives and circle some aspect of the language they notice. For instance, one child will go to the chart and circle all the capital letters, another will underline all the marks of punctuation; another child may circle all the rhyming and compound words, and so on. Children inform Mary about what features of the text they notice. She then plans other ways for children to interact with the text, such as providing each child with a booklet of the story and inviting students to illustrate each page. On another day, students dictate another story patterned after the one they have been reading together during the week.

After this group lesson, children are ready to disperse to read their self-selected books on their own or to sit with a buddy and share the story aloud. Those who choose to read to a buddy use a clipboard with a running list of strategies to use with unknown words. For example, give the reader a hint, the reader sounds out the word, the reader uses the picture to help figure out the word, the reader uses other words in the sentence (context) to figure out the word, and so on. After the reading, the child is asked by the buddy to retell the story. The buddy writes several comments about the reader's retelling. Mary initially designed this buddy reading sheet, but children wanted to add to it because they used more strategies than what Mary had initially listed on the sheet!

Mary uses a "status of the class" form to record what each child is committed to doing during this time before they leave the rug. The "status of the class" form includes each child's name on the left side of the page and the days of the week at the top. Mary simply writes several notes about what each child says he or she will do during this time.

During the writer's workshop Mary will again start with a minilesson focusing on some strategy to use in writing. Mary knows what to do for each minilesson because she has looked carefully at what her young writers can do. Writing minilessons might focus on the following: using capital letters, knowing when to use periods and other marks of punctuation, incorporating dialogue in stories, coming up with topics, and so forth. Again, she uses a status-of-the-class recordkeeping procedure so that she knows what each child is committed to doing during writer's workshop. For more information on early reading and writing, see Chapter 6 on "Emergent Literacy" and Chapter 11 on "Inviting Children to Become Writers."

Readers and writers in Mary's class are decision-makers about their learning. She has high, but not unrealistic, expectations for her students. Notice how children took the initiative to add more strategies to the buddy reading checklist. Mary meets with students after the workshop time to discuss how things went. What went well? What can be improved? This is when she learned that the buddy reading checklist needed revising. The next day students used the revised copy, titled as such.

Mary's language style with her first graders is conversational in tone. In fact, if you walked by her classroom and did not see the size of the children, you might think that she was teaching a much higher grade level. She never uses condescending or a sing-songy tone with children, as many teachers of primary children do. She uses authentic language about literacy learning with them. For example, when she talks about kinds of books to read (i.e., poetry, fantasy, realistic fiction, etc.) she uses the term "genre." Children understand the differences between types of literature; for example, how realistic fic-

tion differs from fantasy. Mary capitalizes on the fact that young children are excited about learning and enjoy big words! Just think about how young children love learning about dinosaurs and being able to say all of those big dinosaur names!

She believes in children taking responsibility for their learning. She helps them do this, as Betty Robinson does. We can say that Mary offers a kind of scaffolding (Vygotsky, 1979) or support for their learning. She offers just the right amount of guidance and support without taking over the child's learning.

Mary believes that students need to think about goals for their reading and writing. Questions such as, "What can I do well?" and "What do I need to work on?" are helpful. Again, Mary meets on the rug with students in a circle. She prefers to do a lot of her teaching and talking with students when they are gathered on the rug because it brings her in closer contact with the children. She asks students how they go about deciding what book to read. Mary has observed that some children have a particularly difficult time deciding on which book to select for reader's workshop. She asks that everybody contribute an idea. Mary records all contributions on chart paper, including her own idea about choosing books to read. Mary's contribution sends the message that she, too, is a reader and needs to make good choices for herself. If a child does not have a contribution, she very kindly says that she'll ask later. It is all right for a student to even repeat a recommendation made previously. Mary clearly values each student's contribution. This is different from what happens in many classrooms. Ordinarily, only several students respond and others are left out of the discussion.

Mary also believes in empowering her young readers. She tries to tap what they understand about themselves as readers. Being able to articulate what you understand about your own learning is called "metacognitive behavior." We learned how Mary does this as she asks readers how they go about choosing books to read. Here are other questions she uses to invite children to talk about themselves as readers.

What do you notice about me as a reader?

What do you notice about each other as readers?

What reading strategies work best for you?

What do you need to do to become a better reader?

What might be the advantage of keeping a list of the books you have read? How would it help the class?

How does reading aloud help you as a reader?

Why is retelling a story important?

When you are finished with this book, what are you going to do next?

What are your reading goals?

Do you believe that the more you read, the better you become?

Why do we read everyday?

If you are reading aloud with a buddy, how does it help that person? How can your buddy help you? How can you become a better buddy reader?

Take a look at this poem (or story). What discoveries can you make about the text?

Source: J. V. Kristo "Reading Aloud in a Primary Classroom: Reaching and Teaching Young Readers," in K. E. Holland, R. A. Hungerford, and S. B. Ernst (eds.), *Journeying: Children Responding to Literature.* Portsmouth, NH: Heinemann, 1993, p. 67.

Mary also demonstrates that she is a writer. She often writes about her classroom for professional publications. Since she is writing about her students, she shares her rough drafts and conferences with the group about reactions to the ways she has described what they do in reading and writing. Children think it is great fun to see all of Mary's rough drafts and enjoy making recommendations.

Mary takes a bit of time during each writing workshop to work on her own writing. She does not always work on pieces for professional publications; sometimes she writes poetry or works on another form of writing. She believes in doing her own writing, not only because it is a powerful demonstration of the teacher as writer but because it also helps her to appreciate the struggles children have with their own writing.

In Mary's class, as in Betty's, children vary in ability. Sandy, a rather immature first grader, was labeled early as severely learning disabled with a low I.Q. The child was targeted to go to special education for language arts. However, Mary made a case for the child to remain in the room during this time because of the rich literacy experiences Sandy would miss if she left. It was a wonderful sight to observe Sandy engaged with her own writing for 45 minutes everyday. She struggled with spelling all the words she wanted to use in her writing, but she persevered until she was satisfied with her piece.

Engaging Literature Together

Mary loves books! She is an avid reader of children's books and purchases many for the classroom. Like Betty, Mary has selections from all genres (i.e., poetry, picture books, traditional literature, fantasy, etc.). Early in the year children help to organize the classroom library by browsing through all the books and categorizing them according to type. For example, children placed all the fairy tales together, and the books by Barbara Cooney and Ezra Jack Keats were organized as a set, as were all the books about the solar system and dinosaurs.

Mary does not use a basal reading text; instead, she uses only children's literature. She believes strongly in providing the best books for children to read. Her school has a well-stocked school library and media center. She borrows books from the center, but firmly believes that books need to be in the classroom where children have easy access to them.

Children in Mary's room read all day: they read stories together, and Mary reads aloud several times daily. The children learn about the world around them from books, not textbooks. She designs thematic units around interests, such as mammals, dinosaurs, the solar system, etc. (see Chapter 14). Children formulate questions they have about the topic and read books to find answers to their questions. Mary also believes, as Betty does, that good books are the fuel that keeps the writing engine working. Children need to read and be acquainted with the style and language choices of published authors. Mary shares that to become good authors, writers have to read a lot, and they do in this classroom!

Early in Mary's career she taught middle school students who had reading difficulties. She learned from this experience how little success these students had with reading from a textbook and workbook program. She wanted to turn students on to the pleasures of reading. Her middle school students groaned every time they had to read from the textbook and viewed the reading as work. Reading was something they claimed never to do on their own. Mary turned to the use of literature to spark the interest of these students. She read aloud to them, and before long students read from their own self-selected books. Mary vowed that if she ever taught first graders, she would only use actual books so that children would get hooked on books at an early age. And, of course, this is what happened!

Mary is also convinced of the power behind sharing books aloud with children. After lunch, Mary reads aloud for sometimes up to 45 minutes. She chooses books that delight her, as she knows the enthusiasm will rub off on the students. Mary loves *The Lion, the Witch, and the Wardrobe* written by C. S. Lewis and illustrated by Michael Hague (1988). This particular edition is beautifully illustrated. *The Lion, the Witch, and the Wardrobe* is typically used with much older students, but Mary loves it, and so do the children.

They even understand the symbolism in the book and beg her to read other titles in the series. Mary knows the books she chooses for reading aloud and thus is able to maintain a lot of eye contact with her students. Her read-alouds are engaging and fun! Children love to interact with her during this time as well.

Experiencing the World Around Us

Mary believes in enriching her students' experiences as much as possible. She knows that the more children experience the world around them, the more they bring to their reading. Mary opens the world of great music and artists to her first graders. Every month she features a different composer and artist. For example, children hear the music of Debussy, Chopin, and Beethoven. Mary shares books written for children about great artists. They learn about the lives of Van Gogh, Matisse, and Georgia O'Keefe. They see illustrations of the artist's work and learn to appreciate art and music that they might not have seen until they were much older, if at all. Mary invites children to try painting their own works in the style of the artist they are studying. Then Mary mounts their work and makes a gallery of their art outside of the classroom. Whenever she displays work, she also has children dictate a message about what they have done. This message is posted on the wall near the children's work so that everyone passing by will know of the students' accomplishments.

Mary also plans a field trip for children to attend the symphony. Again, this is an experience that many of these children would never otherwise have. Parents also join the group trip. Mary values her close relationship with parents. Many volunteer in the classroom to hear children read and to help publish the children's writing in book form. Sometimes there might be several moms and dads in the classroom at one time. Parents understand Mary's program and rejoice at the progress their children make with reading and writing.

Mary enjoys designing opportunities for children to explore the neighborhood in new ways, as well as attending cultural events. She believes that all of these opportunities contribute to the children's growth as readers and writers. Children want to read books about music and orchestras. They "find" topics for writing as they observe their neighborhood in new ways.

Mary also tries to bring the world of the community inside the classroom with parents not only helping children with reading and writing but also by sharing what they do for work, special interests and hobbies they have, places they've visited, and so on. Whenever possible, Mary arranges for children's authors and illustrators to visit. There is nothing quite as exciting as to see an admired author or illustrator in the classroom! Without a doubt, Mary's classroom is an exciting and enriching place to be a reader and writer!

What Beliefs Do Betty and Mary Share About Literacy Learning and Teaching?

1. Instead of using textbooks, they believe in using children's literature to help students become more powerful readers and writers.
2. Children are involved in authentic learning experiences that integrate the language arts—reading, writing, speaking, and listening.
3. Students formulate their own questions to guide their exploration of topics. They use a variety of print and non-print resources to help them answer questions.
4. Mary and Betty use a process approach to writing so that students experience selecting topics, writing drafts, conferencing, and sharing their writing.
5. Betty and Mary believe in establishing a democratic classroom where children participate in decision making.
6. They believe in establishing a climate of trust and support for learners to take risks and accept challenges to their own learning.
7. Mary and Betty believe in being active participants in the learning community of their classrooms. They demonstrate their own enthusiasm and interest for learning, as well as

in the development of their own literacy. Children view these teachers as readers and writers because they see them reading and writing everyday.

8. Betty and Mary believe in keeping language whole and teaching students not skills but rather strategies to become better readers and writers. Betty and Mary design authentic learning experiences for their students.
9. They are kid-watchers: Betty and Mary allow students to inform them in different ways about what they know. They do not rely on test scores to define what they do with children in the classroom.
10. Both Betty and Mary are professionally active. They read journals and books about literacy learning. They both attend and participate as speakers at conferences and workshops. There is always something new to learn! (See the list of References and Suggested Readings at the end of this chapter for resources to further explore whole language in the classroom.)

BUILDING THE INTEGRATED LANGUAGE ARTS

As we stated earlier, the integrated language arts is a method of teaching that is based on the philosophy of whole language. The design of a successful and effective language arts curriculum requires an investment of both students and teachers. With that in mind, we invite you to study Table 2.3 as a set of conditions that distinguish and establish the integrated language arts classroom.

PRINCIPLES OF AN INTEGRATED LANGUAGE ARTS PROGRAM

The development and maintenance of an integrated language arts curriculum depends upon

TABLE 2.3 An Integrated Language Arts Classroom

What Children Do	What Teachers Do
✓ Children are invited to "try out" new ideas and learn from the results of their "tests."	✓ Teachers are co-learners—working in collaboration with students.
✓ Children are encouraged to become self-reliant and responsible learners.	✓ Teachers encourage students to take risks and to solve self-initiated problems.
✓ Children's oral and written language reflect approximations rather than absolutes.	✓ Teachers provide demonstrations of language and its various uses.
✓ Children use meaningful language to make sense of the world around them.	✓ Teachers offer integrative opportunities for students to use all the language arts in a host of learning environments.
✓ Children use authentic language—language that is holistic and authentic.	✓ Teachers focus on the approximations of language learning and assess accordingly.
✓ Children use all the language arts in all their learning activities and projects.	✓ Teachers provide children with an abundance of choices and a support system through which students can follow through on their individual choices.
✓ Children have a sense of "ownership" in what they do and what they learn.	✓ Teachers promote students' ownership of the learning environment.
✓ Children have choices and opportunities to follow through on those choices.	✓ Teachers provide regular and constant feedback to students throughout all learning activities.
✓ Children work in collaboration with other students and in tandem with the teacher.	✓ Teachers design opportunities in which students can self-regulate and monitor their own progress.
✓ Children can monitor and regulate their own learning as a result of feedback from peers and adults.	✓ Teachers design learning opportunities in which all the language arts are used across the curriculum.
✓ Children can use all the language arts in authentic explorations across the curriculum.	✓ Teachers provide systemic and sustained opportunities for students to explore topics in detail.
✓ Children have ample time to examine and explore meaningful topics.	✓ Teachers are learners.
✓ Children initiate their own questions and pursue answers to those inquiries.	
✓ Children are invited to contribute to their own language learning and that of their peers.	

Source: Adapted from C. C. Pappas, B. Z. Kiefer, and L. S. Levstik. *An Integrated Language Perspective in the Elementary School.* (White Plains, NY: Longman, 1990.)

several assumptions about the learning (and *teaching*) of children. What we find so interesting about these assumptions is their similarity to the literacy-models presented in Chapter 1 by Cambourne, Holdaway, and Routman. That should not be surprising, but rather should reflect a conscious desire on the part of teachers to extend the theories and research of language learning into practical classroom practices. It is important to keep in mind that a successful integrated language arts program is founded on a strong structure of relevant research and personal beliefs.

The principles of language arts instruction presented below (adapted from Galda et al., 1993; Block, 1993; and Tchudi, 1994) are valuable in helping youngsters achieve a measure of success in all their languaging activities. These features can also be important in planning meaningful and relevant activities for students within the framework of the total curriculum. The emphasis is on interactive or transactional teaching where students begin to develop the abilities and habits that will allow them to learn how to learn. In short, these features of an integrated language arts program emphasize the active engagement of students in their own learning.

Principle 1   Process is emphasized over product. The acts of creation and expression are considered to be of greater significance in the development of appropriate languaging skills than are the final products that result from those acts. We do not mean to suggest that products are unimportant; only that when they are deemed of greater significance than the processes that produced them are children less likely to appreciate and learn from all the dynamics of language. For example, students who are learning English as a second language may be hesitant to participate in class discussions if they know that the emphasis is on correct pronunciation and proper grammatical format.

Principle 2   Strategies are stressed rather than skills. Too often, children perceive learning as a simple accumulation of dozens (perhaps hundreds) of skills. Mastery of a collection of skills is frequently perceived as mastery of a specific subject. In language arts, however, the emphasis should be on helping students learn the strategies that will help them in a multitude of language opportunities. Strategies are more universal than skills and place a premium on literacy in use. For example, learning to correctly punctuate sentences is often presented as an appropriate language arts skill. Knowing when to use a period, question mark, or exclamation point is only valuable, however, in the context of writing a complete story. Isolated from the story, those skills have little meaning or relevance; in the context of a story they are purposeful and comprehensible.

Principle 3   Whole texts rather than language fragments are used for instruction. Exposure to complete stories, books, or poems is important in the developing language skills of children. Students need to see how all the parts work together in the development of personal enjoyment and satisfaction for a piece of work. Filling in blank lines on a worksheet or underlining words out of context on a workbook page signals to children that language is merely the mastery of its parts, rather than an appreciation of how those parts work together to create a rich and complete story.

Principle 4   Every attempt is made to integrate the language arts as much as possible. Children who are provided with active opportunities to participate in the expressive language arts (writing, speaking) are also enhancing and further developing their appreciation of the interpretive language arts (reading, listening). In short, as students develop higher levels of mastery in one language art, they are also enhancing the development of other language arts as well. The language arts are not separate or divorced from each other. They are interrelated and dependent on each other in facilitating an individual's overall language development.

> In an integrated language arts curriculum, reading instruction is nestled among instruction in writing and oral language, resulting in greater command of all these language tools than is possible when they are taught in isolation.... Children must *read* about what they hear and talk about; they must *write* about what they read and hear and talk about; they must *talk* about what they read and write and hear. (Searfoss, 1989)

One way of illustrating the interrelationships that exist between the four language modes is graphically detailed in Figure 2.1. The emphasis here is on stories—and how children use all the language arts to enjoy, appreciate, and learn from stories. Although we have separated the four language modes into individual groupings, it is important to remember that they each impact on the other and are not learned independently from each other.

FIGURE 2.1 How the Language Modes Are Used in Learning About Stories

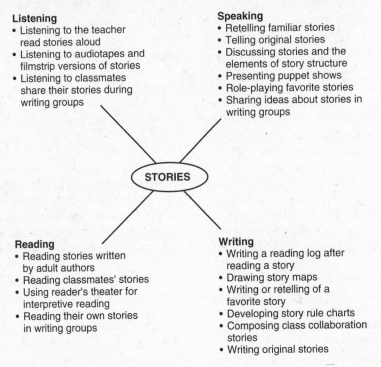

Listening
- Listening to the teacher read stories aloud
- Listening to audiotapes and filmstrip versions of stories
- Listening to classmates share their stories during writing groups

Speaking
- Retelling familiar stories
- Telling original stories
- Discussing stories and the elements of story structure
- Presenting puppet shows
- Role-playing favorite stories
- Sharing ideas about stories in writing groups

STORIES

Reading
- Reading stories written by adult authors
- Reading classmates' stories
- Using reader's theater for interpretive reading
- Reading their own stories in writing groups

Writing
- Writing a reading log after reading a story
- Drawing story maps
- Writing or retelling of a favorite story
- Developing story rule charts
- Composing class collaboration stories
- Writing original stories

Source: Gail E. Tompkins and Kenneth Hoskisson, *Language Arts: Content and Teaching Strategies.* (New York: Merrill, 1991), p. 24.

Although Figure 2.1 isolates each of the language arts, you will note that they are all supportive of and essential to the use of language. That is to say, use of one language skill is dependent upon and critical to use of the other language skills.

Principle 5 *The integrated language arts integrates language and language use into every curricular area.* The integrated language arts helps youngsters build bridges and establish connections between subject areas. Learning is seen less as a memorization of disjointed facts and more of an interrelationship of ideas bound by a common concept—the language arts. It is through the language arts that children can learn about the world around them and take their place as givers and receivers of worldly information.

Principle 6 *Numerous multilevel activities are offered daily.* Providing an abundance of engaging and mutually satisfying activities that encourage children to stretch to the limits of their abilities (and beyond) can be the hallmark of an effective language arts program. "Teaching to the mean"—the traditional practice of providing the same instruction in the same way to all students in a classroom—may be counterproductive to the individual needs of students. Specifically, having a gifted student, a non–English-speaking student, and a learning disabled student all do the same activity in the same way is counterproductive to their specific instructional needs.

Principle 7 *Learners are helped to recognize the function and purpose of learning activities either because they are self-initiated or because they are embedded within a purposeful context.* One important factor often surfaces in well-designed language arts programs: Children will tend to do their best in activities that have personal meaning for them or in activities that they have selected or designed. Doing an activity simply because "the teacher told me to" often has negative consequences for children. In those settings children see the classroom as one in which the teacher has all the answers and where students simply complete exercises to determine the answers to the teacher's questions. As indicated above, the emphasis is on the products, not the processes, of learning.

Principle 8 *The integrated language arts program integrates students' interests and needs with the aims of the curriculum.* Children are provided with authentic opportunities to contribute to their own learning through meaningful language activities. An integrated approach accommodates students of varying abilities and needs and provides learning experiences that are relevant, developmental, and specific. Students can make an "investment of self" in the day-to-day affairs of the classroom and reap the benefits of a personal curriculum.

Principle 9 *Opportunities for social interaction are planned for and encouraged rather than avoided.* Learning occurs when students are given an appropriate level of instruction and instructional support. That support comes most naturally in a community of learners—from other students who are also engaged in the learning process and who offer support and encouragement for the learning efforts of all. Learning is a social process that encourages deliberation, cooperation, and collective wisdom. When children are provided with an atmosphere that is supportive and stimulating, they can utilize all the language skills in a stimulative social context that is mutually reinforcing and strengthening.

Principle 10 *Learning activities are planned to foster experimentation, invention, and discovery.* One of the most valuable skills we can assist our students in attaining is that of risk taking. We learn when we are given opportunities to take risks and make mistakes—and when we are supported in those efforts. When children know they have something "to fall back on" then they may be encouraged to try new activities or pursue new types of learning. Students who are stimulated to ask their own question and inspired to pursue the answers to those questions are those who achieve high levels of independence in all learning activities.

Principle 11 *Teachers are supportive and facilitative, rather than dictatorial.* Teachers of the integrated language arts are willing to work alongside their students, encouraging them to pursue a host of investigative learning opportunities. These teachers realize that they are not repositories of information, but rather models of learning who promote high-level thinking and deeper examination of ideas and concepts meaningful to students.

Principle 12 *Learners are taught strategies and are encouraged to self-monitor their own learning.* One of the fundamental goals of any learning situation should be to assist children in evaluating their own progress. When students are provided with opportunities to reflect and react to what and how they are learning, they are developing a sense of "control" over that process. In a larger sense, children become independent learners when they feel "comfortable," not only with what is being learned but also with how that learning is being gauged.

Principle 13 *Students will engage in real-world activities.* It is doubtful that many students will spend some or all of their lives circling words on a sheet of paper or underlining the verbs on a business document. What they will do is read different types of literature, write letters and manuscripts for others to read, communicate with friends and family members, and listen to news broadcasts and public speakers. The value of an integrated language arts program lies in providing youngsters with the skills and strategies they will need long after they leave your classroom.

CATHY SWANSON'S JOURNAL

✤ September 13

As I talked with the class today, I realized that everyone has experienced Writing Workshop a bit differently. Most seemed familiar with the steps I had used last year: prewriting, drafting, conferencing, revising, editing, and publishing. The kids expressed a few other ideas that seemed to be generally agreed upon:

- That they liked to write
- That they loved their published books
- That sometimes they didn't feel like doing a prewrite; they had an idea and just wanted to go with it
- That they hated to revise more than once (Greg [one of Cathy's students] shared that he had written a story in third grade that he really loved but hated it in the end because he had to revise it seven times!)

- That sometimes it seems to take a long time from the time they start till their story is complete

I have been mulling over some approaches to process writing this year, thinking about what to incorporate and how to do it. I've been giving thought to having the kids keep a Writer's Notebook. This would fall somewhere between daily journals and finished pieces; a collection of personal anecdotes, photographs with captions, poems, whatever! They would not contain anything like a problem of the day or a daily edit like their journals might, and they could be used at their discretion when they are in between stories or need a break.

Considering that I feel the kids need a fresh start with writing—just something different for a while—I think I'll start with these.

✤ September 14

I've caught snippets of conversation recently about books published last year. The children are so proud of these books; we decided to make a place in the reading corner for books by "Local Authors." Within a few days this bin was full! They love to read each other's work—and it is a nice option for SSR [Sustained Silent Reading—a scheduled quiet independent reading time during the school day] when they're in between books.

✤ September 21

The first novel we're reading this year is *Dear Mr. Henshaw* by Beverly Cleary (New York: Dell, 1983). [This book is about Leigh Botts, a boy who, through the years, corresponds with his favorite book author—Mr. Henshaw.] It's a great book to read in conjunction with the Pacific region (the story takes place in Northern California), but I've chosen to use it now to reaffirm some ideas about writing.

1. Written correspondence has great power; a whole relationship develops and changes through the course of writing letters.
2. Writing is an acceptable alternative to television (Leigh's [the major character in the book] TV broke and his mother didn't get it repaired, so he started writing in his journal).
3. What improves writing is *more* writing.

4. Writing is personal and can provide a safe haven for emotions.
5. Writing about WHAT YOU KNOW makes for meaningful, authentic writing; even though Leigh didn't win first prize in the writing contest, the author [Mr. Henshaw—the person with whom Leigh is corresponding] admired his piece because Leigh chose to write about something that was important to him.

As we discuss the steps of the writing process, I want to reinforce these ideas by examining Leigh's growth as a writer.

✤ *September 23*

One of the powerful things about *Dear Mr. Henshaw* is Cleary's ability to speak for children of this age and illustrate their responses to adults in a very realistic way. I think that is what has helped the class to really see this story through Leigh's eyes and to empathize with him.

All children have a grandmother who always pinches their cheek, a neighbor who remarks on how much they have grown, etc. The class almost cringes when they read about Leigh's dad always saying, "Keep your nose clean, kid." They are also clearly able to feel Leigh's disappointment when his father constantly breaks promises.

The book has been a point of departure for discussion in other arenas as well. Leigh's parents are divorced. The kids have openly related personal experiences and feelings about living through my parents' divorce as well (students don't readily picture their teachers as having ever been children); with the close of the conversation came a pregnant pause—one that seemed to say, "Wow, we forgot that we experience things outside of our class, that we don't know everything there is to know about Stephanie [a student in the class] for example." This seemed to be one of those moments that helps foster a sense of community, a sense of respect for each other.

The other arena that has surfaced through this book is personal knowledge of the trucking industry! Like Leigh, Travis's and Josh's [students in the class] fathers have been truck drivers. Josh shares very openly in class and has done so since the beginning of the year. But Travis is much more reserved; this was a new opportunity for him to share with confidence about something he has a personal investment in. He has shared stories about riding with his dad, and how hard it can be to have your dad gone for a week at a time!

Discussions like these reinforce my belief in using "real" books; this is how bridges are built, how meaning is made, how kids become owners of their own learning.

✤ *October 1*

One of the most exciting things to happen to this class has been to correspond with the students at York College [preservice teachers in a language arts course were paired with Cathy's students as part of a pen pal program during the fall semester]. Most of the kids have had pen pals before; several have overseas pen pals with whom they are still in touch. But I have never seen greater enthusiasm than when I told everyone the first letters had arrived and were in the mailboxes! They literally tore into their letters as if they were Christmas presents!

Some [college] pen pals sent pictures, some sent little gifts like pencils or stickers. The room was just buzzing with conversations about what they read. Billy [one of Cathy's students] was in stitches because he thought his pen pal, Dorothy, was 55 years old. (Bill did not know that the apostrophe-like marks above the fives indicated her height!) The idea of a 55-year old college student is a funny notion to a nine-year-old—especially to Bill!

After passing around (and showing off, really!) the letters and pictures, it was time for lunch. As Elena [one of Cathy's students] watched the other fourth graders file by on their way to the cafeteria, she repeatedly and very smugly told every fifth person or so, "We have pen pals who go to college, you know. . . ." At that point, I knew this venture would be a success!

TEACHER AS LEARNER/TEACHER AS RESEARCHER

Journaling

When you were young, did you ever keep a diary—recording your thoughts, activities, and predictions for the future? Many people have kept diaries and are often amazed at the information recorded in these journals and the thoughts they were thinking at certain stages in their lives. If you've ever kept a diary or had an opportunity to observe the diary of someone else, you know how one's ideas and perceptions can change over time and how that record preserves memories that may otherwise be forgotten.

We, too, keep diaries. However, we refer to our diaries as "journals" and the process of recording information in those journals as "journaling." Journaling provides us with an opportunity to record our thoughts and observations during a class or immediately at the conclusion of a class. While the ideas are "fresh in our minds" we can preserve them and ponder their significance at a later time. Journaling also provides us with opportunities to make notations about successful (or unsuccessful) classroom procedures, the progress of selected individuals in a class, and our level of motivation for selected activities. Journaling is a way of maintaining our observations and providing us with a record of students' academic and social development.

We have found, throughout our teaching careers, that journaling is one of the easiest and most productive ways of conducting research in the classroom. This is especially true if we record observations and notes while an activity is taking place or immediately after a sequence of projects. Later, in reviewing these notes we can reflect on the impact of classroom procedures on selected individuals or the entire class. Equally important, we have some background data that will allow us to make changes or develop new procedures that might not otherwise be possible if we were to rely solely on our memories.

Our friend Cathy Swanson is also a believer in journaling. You've read portions of her second year journal so far and noted some of the challenges, musings, and insights with which she has dealt. What you will discover, as you continue to read her journal, is that it provides her with solid information on which to base educational decisions for individuals and the class as a whole.

We encourage you to engage in journaling, too. This process can have some far-reaching implications for the success of your students and the impact of your instruction on those students. As a research tool, a journal is a quick and easy way to record events and to begin developing plans and strategies based on those events. Indeed, we may even argue that it can be the most powerful research tool at your disposal.

We urge you to carefully read Cathy's journal entries as they appear at the end of each chapter in this book. Note how Cathy is able to make decisions and modify her thinking as a result of this journaling process. We trust that this ongoing assessment and discovery approach to classroom research will become a valuable part of your growth as a teacher, too.

Journal Reflections

Select one or more of the questions below that interest you and respond in your journal.

1. What are some of the decisions Cathy had to make with regard to her classroom writing program? How are those decisions similar to or different from the decisions made by a more experienced teacher? How are Cathy's decisions similar to or different from the decisions you will need to make about your classroom writing program during your first year of teaching?

2. Given your style of learning, would you be "comfortable" as a student in a whole language classroom? Please defend your position. To what extent is your position similar to most of the other students taking this course?

3. How have your views about the teaching of language arts changed as a result of reading the first two chapters of this book? Have your views changed dramatically, slightly, or not at all? To what would you attribute any significant changes?

4. Design your own question.
   ✓ What is a question you have about the chapter?
   ✓ How will you pursue the answer to that question?
   ✓ Respond in your journal.

REFERENCES AND SUGGESTED READINGS

Anderson, R. C., Elfrieda, H. H., Scott, J. A., and Wilkinson, I. A. G. *Becoming a Nation of Readers: The Report of the Commission on Reading.* Washington, National Institute of Education, 1985.

Atwell, N. *In the Middle: Writing, Reading, and Learning with Adolescents.* Portsmouth, NH: Heinemann, 1987.

Au, K. *Literacy Instruction in Multicultural Settings.* Fort Worth, TX: Harcourt Brace Jovanovich, 1993.

Block, C. C. *Teaching the Language Arts.* Boston: Allyn and Bacon, 1993.

Borich, G. D. *Effective Teaching Methods.* Columbus, OH: Merrill, 1988.

Brown, H., and Mathie, V. *Inside Whole Language: A Classroom View.* Portsmouth, NH: Heinemann, 1991.

Bybee, R., et al. *Science and Technology Education for the Elementary Years: Frameworks for Curriculum and Instruction.* Andover, MA: National Center for Improving Science Education, 1989.

Bybee, R., et al. *Science and Technology Education for the Middle Years: Frameworks for Curriculum and Instruction.* Andover, MA: National Center for Improving Science Education, 1991.

Calkins, L. *The Art of Teaching Writing.* Portsmouth, NH: Heinemann, 1986.

Calkins, L. *Living Between the Lines.* Portsmouth, NH: Heinemann, 1990.

Cazden, C. B. "Classroom Discourse." In M. C. Wittrock ed., *Handbook of Research on Teaching,* 3rd ed., 432–463. New York: Macmillan.

Chambers, A. *Booktalk.* New York: Harper & Row, 1985.

Clay, M. *Reading: The Patterning of Complex Behavior.* Aukland, New Zealand: Heinemann, 1972.

Cordeiro, P. *Whole Learning: Whole Language and Content in the Upper Elementary Grades.* Katonah, NY: Richard C. Owens Publishers, 1992.

Cox, C., and Zarrillo, J. *Teaching Reading with Children's Literature.* New York: Merrill, 1993.

Dehaven, E. *Teaching the Language Arts.* Glenview, IL: Scott, Foresman, 1988.

Dewey, J. *The Child and the Curriculum and the School and Society.* Chicago: University of Chicago Press, 1943.

Doake, D. *Reading Begins at Birth.* New York: Scholastic, 1988.

Duckwood, E. *The Having of Wonderful Ideas.* New York: Teachers College Press, 1987.

Edelsky, C., Altwerger, B., and Flores, B. *Whole Language: What's the Difference?* Portsmouth, NH: Heinemann, 1991.

Fredericks, A. D. *The Integrated Curriculum: Books for Reluctant Readers.* Englewood, CO: Teacher Ideas Press, 1992.

Galda, L., Cullinan, B. E., and Strickland, D. S. *Language, Literacy, and the Child.* New York: Harcourt Brace Jovanovich, 1993.

Golub, J. Introduction. In J. Golub, ed., *Focus on Collaborative Learning* (Classroom Practices in Teaching English, 1988), 1–2. Urbana, IL: National Council of Teachers of English, 1988.

Goodman, K. *What's Whole in Whole Language?* Portsmouth, NH: Heinemann, 1986.

Goodman, K. S., Bird, L. B., and Goodman, Y. M. *The Whole Language Catalog.* New York: American School Publishers, 1981.

Goodman, K. S., Bird, L. B., and Goodman, Y. M. *The Whole Language Catalog Supplement on Authentic Assessment.* New York: Macmillan/McGraw Hill, 1992.

Goodman, Y. M. "Kid-Watching: An Alternative to Testing." *National Elementary Principal,* (1978): 41–45.

Goodman, Y. M. "Roots of the Whole Language Movement." *The Elementary School Journal,* (1989): 113–127.

Goodman, Y. M., Hood, W. J., and Goodman, K. S. *Organizing for Whole Language.* Portsmouth, NH: Heinemann, 1991.

Graves, D. H. *Writing: Teachers and Children at Work.* Portsmouth, NH: Heinemann, 1976.

Graves, D. H. *Discover Your Own Learning.* Portsmouth, NH: Heinemann, 1990.

Graves, D. H. *Build a Literate Classroom.* Portsmouth, NH: Heinemann, 1991.

Hagerty, P. *Readers' Workshop: Real Reading.* New York: Scholastic, 1992.

Halliday, M. A. K. *Learning How to Mean.* New York: Elsevier North-Holland, 1975.

Harste, J. C. *Policy Guidelines for Reading: Connecting Research and Practice.* Urbana, IL: National Council of Teachers of English, 1989.

Harste, J. C., Short, K. G., and Burke, C. *Creating Classrooms for Authors: The Reading-Writing Connection.* Portsmouth, NH: Heinemann, 1988.

Health, S. B. "Research Currents: A Lot of Talk About Nothing." *Language Arts* 60 (1983): 999–1007.

Hillocks, G. *Research on Written Composition.* Urbana, IL: National Council of Teachers of English, 1986.

Holdaway, D. *Foundations of Literacy.* Sydney, Australia: Ashton-Scholastic, 1979.

Holland, K. E., Hungerford, R. A., and Ernst, S. B., eds. *Journeying: Children Responding to Literature.* Portsmouth, NH: Heinemann, 1993.

Hornsby, D., Parry, J., and Sukarna, D. *Teach on-Teaching Strategies for Reading and Writing Workshops.* Portsmouth, NH: Heinemann, 1992.

Karelitz, E. *The Author's Chair and Beyond.* Portsmouth, NH: Heinemann, 1993.

Kauchak, D., and Eggen, P. *Learning and Teaching Research-Based Methods.* Boston: Allyn and Bacon, 1989.

Loban, W. *Language Development: Kindergarten Through Grade Twelve.* Urbana, IL: National Council of Teachers of English, 1976.

Lundsteen, S. *Language Arts: A Problem-Solving Approach.* New York: Harper & Row, 1989.

Lytle, S. L., and Botel, M. *The Pennsylvania Framework for Reading, Writing and Talking Across the Curriculum.* Harrisburg, PA: Pennsylvania Department of Education, 1990.

Mason, J., and Au, K. *Reading Instruction for Today.* Glenview, IL: Scott, Foresman, 1990.

Mills, H., and Clyde, J. A., eds. *Portraits of Whole Language Classrooms: Learning for All Ages.* Portsmouth, NH: Heinemann, 1990.

Moffett, J., and Wagner, B. J. *Student-Centered Language Arts, K-12,* 4th ed. Portsmouth, NH: Heinemann, 1991.

Morrow, L. M., Smith, J. K., and Wilkinson, L. C. *Integrated Language Arts: Controversy to Consensus.* Boston: Allyn and Bacon, 1993.

National Council of Teachers of Mathematics. *Curriculum and Evaluation Standards for School Mathematics.* Reston, VA: Commission on Standards for School Mathematics, 1989.

Newkirk, T. *Listening In: Children Talk About Books (and Other Things).* Portsmouth, NH: Heinemann, 1992.

Norton, D. *The Effective Teaching of Language Arts.* Columbus, OH: Merrill, 1989.

Piaget, J. *The Psychology of Intelligence.* Paterson, NJ: Littlefield, Adams, 1969.

Piaget, J. *The Development of Thought: Equilibration of Cognitive Structures.* New York: Viking Press, 1975.

Pigdon, K., and Woolley, M. *The Big Picture: Integrating Children's Learning.* Portsmouth, NH: Heinemann, 1993.

Position Statements on Preschool and Elementary Level Science Education and Science Education for Middle and Junior High Students. Washington: National Science Teachers Association, 1985.

Power, B. M., and Hubbard, R. *Literacy in Process: The Heinemann Reader.* Portsmouth, NH: Heinemann, 1990.

Read, C. *Children's Categorization of Speech Sounds in English* (Research Rep. No. 17) Urbana, IL: National Council of Teachers of English, 1975.

Rief, L. *Seeking Diversity: Language Arts with Adolescents.* Portsmouth, NH: Heinemann, 1991.

Rosenblatt, L. *Literature Through Exploration,* 4th ed. New York: Modern Language Association, 1938.

Routman, R. *Invitations: Changing as Teachers and Learners K-12.* Portsmouth, NH: Heinemann, 1991.

Sampson, M. R. *The Pursuit of Literacy: Early Reading and Writing.* Dubuque, IA: Kendall/Hunt, 1986.

Science for All Americans: A Project 2061 Report on Literacy Goals in Science, Mathematics, and Technology. Washington: American Association for the Advancement of Science, 1989.

Searfoss, L. "Integrated Language Arts: Is It Whole Language?" *California Reader* 22 (1989): 1–5.

Short, K. G., and Pierce, K. M. *Talking About Books: Creating Literature Communities.* Portsmouth, NH: Heinemann, 1990.

Sims, R. "Reading Literature Aloud." In B. E. Cullinan and C. W. Carmichael, eds., *Literature and Young Children,* 108–119. Urbana, IL: National Council of Teachers of English, 1977.

Smith, F. "The Language Arts and the Learner's Mind." *Language Arts* 56 (1979): 118–125.

Smith, F. *Joining the Literacy Club.* Portsmouth, NH: Heinemann, 1988.

Smith, F., and Goodman, K. "On the Psycholinguistic Method of Teaching Reading," *Elementary School Journal* (1971): 177–181.

"Social Studies for Early Childhood and Elementary School Children Preparing for the 21st Century: A Report from the NCSS Task Force on Early Childhood/Elementary Social Studies." *Social Education* (January 1989).

Statements on Preschool and Elementary Level Science Education and Science Education for Middle and Junior High Students. Washington: National Science Teachers Association, 1985.

Stauffer, R. *Directing the Reading-Thinking Process.* New York: Harper & Row, 1975.

Taylor-Heald, G. *The Administrator's Guide to Whole Language.* Katonah, NY: Richard C. Owen Publishers, 1989.

Tchudi, S. *Integrated Language Arts in the Elementary School.* Belmont, CA: Wadsworth, 1994.

Templeton, S. *Teaching the Integrated Language Arts.* Boston: Houghton Mifflin, 1991.

Tompkins, G. E., and Hoskisson, K. *Language Arts: Content and Teaching Strategies.* New York: Merrill, 1991.

The Tool Kit. Washington: National Council for the Social Studies, 1988.

Trelease, J. *The New Read Aloud Handbook.* New York: Penguin, 1989.

Vygotsky, L. S. *The Development of High Psychological Processes.* Cambridge: Harvard University Press, 1979.

Warner, S. A. *Teaching.* New York: Simon & Schuster, 1963.

Wason, E. L. *Start with a Story: Literature and Learning in Your Classroom.* Portsmouth, NH: Heinemann, 1991.

Watson, D., Burke, C., and Harste, J. *Whole Language: Inquiring Voices.* Ontario: Scholastic, 1989.

Weaver, C. *Understanding Whole Language: From Principles to Practice.* Portsmouth, NH: Heinemann, 1990.

Wilde, J. *A Door Opens: Writing in Fifth Grade.* Portsmouth, NH: Heinemann, 1993.

Wilson, L. *An Integrated Approach to Learning.* Portsmouth, NH: Heinemann, 1993.

Zemelman, S., Daniels, H., and Hyde, A. *Best Practice: New Standards for Teaching and Learning in America's Schools.* Portsmouth, NH: Heinemann, 1993.

CHAPTER 3

CREATING CLASSROOM ENVIRONMENTS FOR LITERACY LEARNING

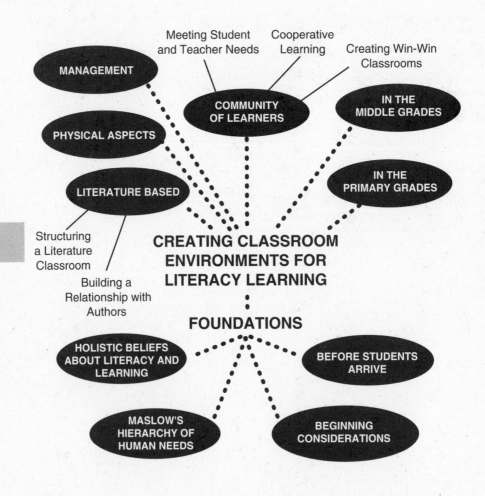

MANAGEMENT

Meeting Student and Teacher Needs

Cooperative Learning

Creating Win-Win Classrooms

PHYSICAL ASPECTS

COMMUNITY OF LEARNERS

IN THE MIDDLE GRADES

LITERATURE BASED

IN THE PRIMARY GRADES

Structuring a Literature Classroom

Building a Relationship with Authors

CREATING CLASSROOM ENVIRONMENTS FOR LITERACY LEARNING

FOUNDATIONS

HOLISTIC BELIEFS ABOUT LITERACY AND LEARNING

BEFORE STUDENTS ARRIVE

MASLOW'S HIERARCHY OF HUMAN NEEDS

BEGINNING CONSIDERATIONS

What I Know: Pre-Chapter Journaling

Close your eyes and think back to a classroom you can remember from elementary or middle school. Picture what it looked like, the physical arrangement of the room, what you and your classmates were doing while your teacher was instructing you. What did the class look like when learning was occurring? What were the sounds you most often heard while you were working? Can you recall anything else from your earlier classroom memories? After you have created a clear image in your mind, sketch out what you "saw" with your mind's eye.

Big Ideas

This chapter will offer:

1. Holistic beliefs about literacy and learning.
2. Suggestions for how to begin creating classroom environments for literacy learning—from the classrooms of real teachers.
3. An explanation of the relationship between Maslow's hierarchy of human needs and the creation of classrooms where the needs of both teachers and learners are met.
4. The processes for the design of whole language classrooms.
5. The practices that lead to the development of a community of learners.
6. The physical and philosophical elements necessary in a whole language classroom.

On March 18, Erin Wade, an eight-year-old girl, published a book entitled *Interesting Animals*. It is a factual text, comprised of chapters, a table of contents, and an index. In general terms her book may be described as a report of fascinating facts about animals; however, within the text she employed a range of writing styles and authoring devices that make her book especially interesting to read. In Erin's classroom there are many factual texts. Her teacher has shared many "chapter books" with the students in Erin's class (students refer to these as "true books"), and they are readily available to the students for reading and reference.

When interviewed about this piece of writing, Erin offered these comments about the sources of her ideas and the decisions she made throughout the writing process:

> Well, to begin with, I like animals. But what got me really interested in them was when our class did a research project on animals. My group studied about cats. I had seen kittens born before, when my cat had kittens, but I did not know how kittens know when it is time to be born until I read it in *How Kittens Grow* (by Millicent E. Selsam). Then I read *The Amazing Book of Animals* (by Hilda Simon) and learned that pet cats are related to wild cats and that there are so many kinds of cats—even cats with no hair, that I next got interested in reading about dogs. We have two dogs at home, and John's group was studying dogs. First I looked at the pictures of all the different kinds of dogs that there were and drew pictures of my favorite ones. Then I asked John's group if they had any books about dogs with interesting information like how kittens know how to be born, and Tim Bradshaw gave me the book *The Language of Animals*. That book told about how dogs have special ways of being able to smell things that people can't and how they are used to sniff out things that criminals hide from the police. Well that got me thinking that every animal has interesting facts about them and that is how the idea for my book got started. I had written one chapter book before about the Mario Brothers, but I wanted to write a chapter book that had facts in it.

> . . . . I wrote this to tell my classmates some true things about animals.

> . . . . I'm going to try to get real pictures instead of drawing them myself because it will be more real like the book. I'm not telling a story about animals. Besides, I can't draw some of the animals I wrote about very good.

> I'm going to look in magazines, like *National Geographic* and ask Mrs. Delph, our librarian for some too. I used questions at the beginning of each chapter so somebody could know if they knew the facts or not. That way, they would know whether they wanted to read the book or not.

It is apparent that Erin has developed a keen sense of audience. She is aware that readers may use factual texts for a range of purposes and in doing so use them differently from other books.

> I've got a Table of Contents because some people might not want to read all the book, just one section. For instance they might just want to look up Gorillas. Or, they could use the Index. Sometimes indexes don't have the exact name that is in the book. So gorillas might be under Jungle Animals. The index tells you what page to go to, and how many pages of information there are.

Erin's reporting of some of the considerations she made in writing *Interesting Animals* highlights her developing understanding of the purposes of writing, how she selected information, her sense of audience, her choice of genre, the organization of her text, and how she used different literature models throughout the development of her book.

This interview with Erin reveals a great deal, not only about Erin—which is always the case when we take the time to talk to children about what they are doing—but also about Erin's teacher, and what it is that she values in her students and in her classroom.

The conscious decisions that teachers make in establishing learning environments for children convey unconscious beliefs about what they deem important in the learning process. The classrooms that teachers construct provide clues about how they believe literacy, in all its forms, is nourished and maintained. Teachers' perceived notions of student–teacher relationships are revealed by the physical and psychological environments they create. The remainder of this chapter will offer insights into creating learning environments where holistic (comprehensive, integrative) views of literacy acquisition and development are advanced.

Creating a Classroom for Literacy Learning

Beginnings can be difficult. For some, they constitute openings for anxiety and self-doubt. Few of us can proceed boldly into unknown territory without some feelings of trepidation. And thus it will always be for new teachers who first take on the challenge and responsibility of their own classrooms. Fortunately, such journeys are not unchartered ones. Teachers who desire to create classrooms that focus on the development of literacy can be assured of the companionship of other teachers who generously share their classroom experiences in books, relevant for the novice as well as for experienced teachers (Routman 1988, 1994; Atwell, 1987; Butler and Turbill, 1984; Newman, 1985).

Teachers speak to other teachers in voices that cut to the heart of whole language teaching. The redesign of traditional elementary classrooms has rekindled the enthusiasm of legions of teachers who have practiced their craft for many years and is currently adding to the excitement of those entering the profession. The difference between teachers who are eager to get to work each morning and those who dread facing another school day is largely dependent upon whether what they are doing is congruent with what they value. Succinctly stated, teachers who believe in what they are doing thrive on being classroom teachers. Those who do not passionately believe in what they are doing can eventually become physically and spiritually diminished by teaching.

Thus a discussion about creating environments for literacy learning must necessarily begin with the system of beliefs that undergirds classroom decision making. We are aware that this is probably not the place where you, as a developing teacher want to begin. What probably interests you more, at this point, is learning precisely *how* to do it. Unfortunately, there is no single formula for the creation of classrooms where holistic beliefs of language and learning prevail. There are reasonable suggestions for getting started in building an integrated, whole language classroom. There is, however, no short cut to first determining if whole language teaching is for you.

Let's begin with an analogy to convey the significance of what we are attempting to illustrate here. Recently, some friends of ours decided to build a new house; they obtained some architectural plans, which they had seen in a publication entitled, *House Planners*. By ordering the plans from the publisher, they were able to save the cost of an architect but were still able to utilize expert design specifications for their home. A general contractor was hired to execute the construction, and ten months later our friends took possession of their dream home. The family was delighted to be in a house of such fine quality—until the first severe storm hit—leveling the new house. As everyone would painfully discover, the plans they had secured were intended for a desert terrain—not a building lot on a piece of ocean-front property! The "fit" between the house construction and the property was incompatible, resulting in disastrous consequences.

And so it will be when you become a classroom teacher; an examination of the "fit" between the philosophical foundation you possess and the classroom you wish to "construct" will be a necessary part of your teaching strategy.

Building a Firm Foundation

What then constitutes a firm foundation for building an effective whole language classroom? Why are some teachers able to receive such satisfaction from their teaching while others become quickly disillusioned and ultimately abandon whole language teaching as something that "simply doesn't work"? Again, as is often expressed throughout this text, teacher beliefs are at the core of what distinguishes teachers who thrive in whole language classrooms from those who become disillusioned. The decisions that classroom teachers make are neither random nor accidental. They are firmly rooted in the beliefs they hold about the nature of teaching and learning.

Let's return again to Erin, the eight-year-old author with whom we began this chapter. At this point, it might help our understanding of the classroom context out of which Erin emerged to hear something from Erin's teacher, Sandy Fox.

Influencing Factors

We asked Sandy to reflect upon some of the factors that influenced the decisions she made regarding the creation of her classroom.

She was eager to share information with us, explaining that at the outset she did not start out the school year hoping to "create a whole language classroom." When asked where she would place herself along the continuum of teaching philosophies, she felt she would most likely be in the vicinity of teachers who call themselves "whole language teachers." However, she said that this was usually not a conscious consideration. What she was conscious of at the beginning of every school year was the sea of young faces looking back at her, each child arriving with a unique set of experiences, talents, expectations, and fears. She says that she never fails to think about *The Teacher from the Black Lagoon* by Mike Thaler (New York: Scholastic, 1989), and she is certain that along with whatever other fears her students may bring with them, each is thinking that this is the year that they are certainly going to meet their own "teacher from the black lagoon." Consequently, for each of the past three years, she has read this book aloud to her students. It is her way of acknowledging that she understands that "beginnings" are scary—whether they relate to the first day of school, the first trip to the dentist, or writing something for public consumption for the first time.

Sandy stressed that in the creation of her classroom she is guided not so much by what she has read about whole language instruction, but by what she has come to know about children and the nature of learning through her own observations. To be sure, she is fortified on an ongoing basis by subscribing to six professional journals each month. What she knows squarely from experience, however, is that each class of students will be different, that what worked for her in previous years may not work with this particular class, or the one that will follow. In addition, she knows that she is not the same person that she was at the start of the previous school year, or the year before that.

As we listened to Sandy over a period of several days, it was apparent that what we were hearing emanated from a philosophy that has *evolved* over the course of her teacher preparation and classroom experiences, and is, at this very moment, continuing to evolve with the acquisition of new information, additional experiences, and the lessons learned from every child.

Sandy describes the immeasurable importance of having a personal set of beliefs about how teaching and learning works: "Knowing what I believe and acting on it, makes me an effective teacher. Being open to conflicting opinions and new ways of doing things helps me to test my beliefs and keeps me growing as a teacher. Without a doubt though, the best and most important lessons I have learned have come directly from my students. If I can just remember to stay quiet long enough, and keep my eyes and ears open, they usually tell me what it is I need to know and what I ought to do next."

Beginning Considerations

Sandy reflected upon her considerations at the beginning of the academic year. Among the "givens" are the physical aspects of her classroom and the other teachers with whom she works most closely. The physical arrangements are dictated by the open layout of the school where Sandy teaches. The teaching space allocated to Sandy lacks walls and barriers between her teaching area and the areas of the teachers beside her.

It might be noted here, that the teachers on either side of Sandy do not share similar teaching philosophies. Since Sandy's style of teaching calls for an abundance of active student involvement and "hands-on" activities, this was an area for elaborate negotiation for all concerned. Embedded within Sandy's philosophy is the belief that children are served best by teachers who employ their "authentic teaching selves." Sandy thus believed that her colleagues should be able to teach in accord with their beliefs. Such divergent styles often necessitated some skillful juggling acts to balance the activity and noise level sometimes required by Sandy's students with the needs for quiet and inactivity required by the other teachers.

Sandy spent a great deal of time during the beginning days of school trying to come up with mutually satisfying solutions with the teachers who would be the most affected. Among their decisions was the establishment of certain "quiet" times throughout the day. Knowing this ahead of time enabled Sandy to acquaint her students with the rationale of these rules and necessary regimen that would enable classes to work harmoniously with each other.

This system has also allowed Sandy to achieve two essential goals that she has for all of her students. The first is that the educational objectives in the classroom should mirror what students will need to be successful citizens in our pluralistic, multicultural society: a regard for differences, a respect for others, and a willingness to compromise. The second objective is to ensure that portions of every school day are allocated to free-choice, independent, silent reading and writing. In this matter Sandy had to compromise—she would not have the liberty to schedule these activities at the times throughout the day that she felt were most appropriate. Sandy was also aware that this would serve as an opportunity to show children how to feel good about themselves by showing respect and consideration for others.

Sandy was faced with more difficult problems regarding the physical aspects of her classroom: the lack of wall space, cupboards, and bulletin boards. She had nowhere to display student work, fasten shelves to contain books, and in general, store all of the "stuff" necessary to a busy classroom. To solve this problem, she turned to her educational journals, where she came across the name and address of a company that supplied sturdy and inexpensive building materials with which children could easily erect bookcases, storage bins, worktables, and movable walls. Originally, Sandy thought about planning a fundraiser to raise the money needed to purchase the materials but she admits that she "selfishly" decided to donate her own money to this project, when it became apparent how easily the furniture pieces could be broken down and moved to another location if she were to transfer to another school.

This construction project resulted in many wonderful art, mathematics, and problem-solving activities as Sandy and her students planned and then built their learning space together. Another benefit of this project was that it highlighted certain talents and abilities of her students. As it turned out, students who were the least capable academically were the real "stars" when it came to building furniture and thus won membership into groups from which they might otherwise have been excluded. Reflecting upon this further, Sandy said that she realized how many times an apparent disappointment or inconvenience can often serve as a dramatic opportunity to come up with alternatives that would never have been considered. It is "half glass full" vs. viewing the glass "half empty" that seems to distinguish teachers who make their teaching lives work for themselves and their students.

Fostering Group Interaction

Sandy revealed that at the beginning of the school year she probably sacrifices quite a bit of what would customarily be referred to as "instructional time" in order to mutually establish ground rules for working effectively with others. For Sandy, establishing effective group process skills is the best use of instructional time she can make. Greater time for instruction is gained later when students have internalized the procedures for optimizing the benefits of learning through group process.

Sandy begins by grouping her students in pairs. Students soon learn that communication is furthered when they make eye contact with one another, listen attentively, and respond first to their partners' statements or ideas before advancing their own. A great deal of time is given over to practicing the various roles of group membership. Eventually the size of groups is expanded as the needs of students and the events of learning dictate. The rules are worked out by Sandy and her students and displayed for students to use as a reference throughout the year. When new guidelines are found to be necessary, they are collectively worded and posted along with the others. Following group activities, Sandy and her students frequently gather together to reflect on the effectiveness of the group process itself. By the beginning of November, it is unusual that any time is required to tend to the mechanics of group process, although constant discussion about the things that worked especially well continues.

Devotion to positive and productive group interaction is fundamental to the success of this teacher's classroom. One of the biggest benefits of effective group process, according to Sandy, is that it enables her to engage in uninterrupted, one-on-one contact with students, while productive learning episodes are still occurring for the remainder of her students.

Providing Students Choices in Organizing the Classroom

Sandy's comments below reveal an implicit view about some of the conditions of learning which foster literacy in her classroom and the importance of students and teachers designing their classrooms together. In setting up her room she emphasizes student selection of reading material and student management of how those materials will be organized and displayed in the classroom.

At the beginning of the year I decided that I wanted our classroom to be a poetry classroom, so I organized a large poetry section in the room with a display of poems for the children to choose and read. I also photocopied a collection of my favorite poems and put them into folders for the children to choose and read. Next, we decided to have display areas for other genres of children's literature. We experimented with several ways of organizing the books in our classroom so students could locate books easily and quickly. What I discovered was that the organization of books in a classroom changes throughout the school year as books are added, as children publish more of their own works, as themes change, etc. The important thing here is to always have children be part of the decision-making process concerning the organization and display of books in the classroom. Not only do they become genuine resources to children in performing their own work, but it becomes an excellent means for students to really understand different genres and become familiar with authors. In the lower grades, children need to have book covers showing rather than the spines to assist students in making their selections. As students get older and have had more opportunity to locate materials in the library and have acquired familiarity with the Dewey decimal system, this is no longer necessary except to highlight new inclusions to the class library. By the end of third grade I recommend organizing and displaying books by their spines, according to a coding system developed by the class, which is compatible with the type of organization they will encounter in the school and community libraries.

Crates work especially well in my classroom because books can be assembled according to all types of categories, labeled, and circulated around the classroom very easily. Groups working together on a project can readily pick up a crate of books, all of which relate to their topics of exploration. When crating books, I am careful to have a rich mix of reading levels and always make certain that there are a number of easy-to-read and picture books among the collection.

I make certain that there are empty crates available in the classroom so that student groups can assemble their own collections and label the crates accordingly, so others may have informed access to them.

I encourage students to choose their own books, and we talk about what constitutes good and poor selections. I stress to students that there are no non-readers in my classroom. Some students choose thick books because they think that is the grown-up thing to do. However, when they find that they can't share the contents of the book with a friend they realize that it is better to select a book they can read, rather than choosing a book based on size. I deliberately select from among the easier-to-read books in our classroom, for my own personal reading, during silent reading time. When students observe me reading the so-called simple books and observe my being able to discuss a lot of information from them, they soon begin to look for ones that are more appropriate to their interests and ones they will enjoy.

I also model the five finger method for selecting books. In doing so, I show students how to read the text and when they come to a word they don't know, to hold down one finger. If they run out of fingers on one hand, on any page, then the book is probably too difficult for them to read. Some children will still use this, but I find it preferable to get them to read the first page and ask them to tell me what they thought the text was about so far and what they guess what the rest of the book might be about. If they are unable to do this, then they should probably make another selection. After several weeks of doing this, children assume this procedure and now question themselves after a page of text.

NEEDS OF STUDENTS AND TEACHERS

Creating an effective classroom means being aware of the human dynamics involved. Teaching is, arguably, one of the most complex of human encounters, regardless of the philosophy that drives the decisions teachers make. It may be,

argued, however, that creating a classroom which places the needs of children at its center presents particular challenges. Abraham Maslow advances a view of human motivation that offers some insight into why this might be true.

According to Maslow (1970), human beings are motivated to meet certain physiological and emotional needs. He has organized these according to categories that are sequential and hierarchical in nature (see Figure 3.1). At the lower levels of Maslow's hierarchy are "deficiency needs"— basic needs that humans require for physical and psychological well-being.

Deficiency needs must be at least partially satisfied before individuals can be motivated to pursue satisfaction of higher level needs, which are called "growth needs." Growth needs refer to transcending basic needs and achieving one's full potential in life.

When teachers and students engage with one another throughout the school day, they are all experiencing and attempting to satisfy inner needs. We see only the external evidence of this ongoing dynamic through observable behaviors of the individuals involved. Although the external behaviors may be very apparent, the internal needs that teachers and students are attempting to satisfy are not so evident. Much of what is labeled as a breakdown in successful management of classroom interaction is actually the result of a clash among individuals in terms of the needs they are attempting to fulfill. In fact, much dissatisfaction could be avoided if teachers and students could wear signs saying "I just need to be noticed right now," or "I'm feeling inadequate as a teacher when I cannot get everyone's attention and this chips away at my feelings of self esteem."

As human beings, we have needs that change from moment to moment and from situation to situation. Different people have different needs. For some, the need for shelter or for food is more important than for others. Each of us has experienced the need for a drink of water when we've been very thirsty. When that need for a drink diminishes, after consuming a liter of soda, other needs will

FIGURE 3.1   Maslow's Hierarchy of Needs

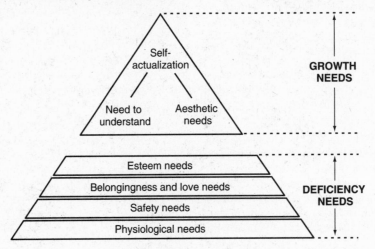

Source: L. A. Lefton, *Psychology,* 4th ed., (Needham Heights, MA: Allyn and Bacon, 1991, 406.

predominate. An appreciation for the motivating power attached to the fulfillment of inner needs can be the beginning of a satisfying relationship between students and teachers. Yet, when we ask both teachers and students what needs must be met for them inside the classroom, we discover that their needs differ dramatically from each other.

As we work with teachers throughout the country, we pose two questions concerning what is important to them in teaching. Among new and experienced teachers alike, similar responses appear on their lists to the two questions we ask. Here are some typical responses to the first question we ask teachers: *"What is important to you to have as a part of each teaching day?"*

Teacher Responses

1. Success
2. Achievement of my goals
3. Recognition of my efforts
4. Respect from my coworkers and my students
5. A sense of completion
6. Humor
7. New learning
8. Appreciation of my hard work
9. A sense that I did something better this day than I did the day before
10. Choice in what I do

Teachers offer similar responses to the second question: *"What needs must be fulfilled in order to achieve and maintain satisfaction with your teaching role?"*

Teacher Responses

1. A sense of continued growth
2. Colleagues who inspire me to try new things and to be my best
3. Opportunity for professional advancement
4. A working environment that is aesthetically pleasing to me
5. Recognition as having made a positive contribution to my profession
6. Recognition from parents and students that I have made a difference in the lives of the children I have taught
7. Attainment of an advanced degree

Refer back to Figure 3.1 and determine where the needs expressed by teachers would be classified.

There may not be complete agreement as to the exact category into which each teacher response falls, but a pattern of the responses among teachers becomes apparent (see Figure 3.2). We see that teachers are motivated primarily by what Maslow classifies as growth needs. In order to feel satisfied at the end of each school day, fulfillment of needs pertaining to *self actualization, the need to understand,* and *aesthetic needs* predominate among classroom teachers. Among the deficiency needs, only needs pertaining to self-esteem appear often on the lists of classroom teachers.

Since teachers and students share the same environment an average of six hours a day, 180 days a year, we decided to ask students a question similar to those that we asked teachers: *"Tell us what is important to you, that makes you want to come to school each day?"* The most typical responses given by students, which differ markedly from those given by teachers, were as follows:

Student Responses

1. All of my friends want to play with me
2. My sister lets me walk with her and her friends so I don't have to walk to school alone
3. Good lunch in the cafeteria
4. When we've been good and the teacher gives us snack time
5. Recess, and I get picked for the winning team
6. When I get 100's on my papers
7. When "so-and-so" is absent/doesn't pick on me
8. When our regular teacher is there
9. I get to work with "so-and-so"
10. We don't get any homework so I can play with my friends
11. The teacher doesn't yell/punish us

Figure 3.3 illustrates a pattern of student responses revealing that teachers and students are simultaneously pursuing fulfillment of needs that

FIGURE 3.2   Teacher Responses

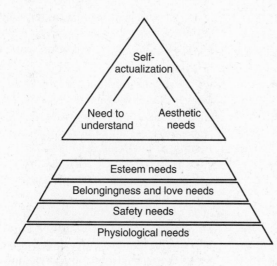

Growth Needs

Question 1
Self-actualization: 1, 2, 5, 9, 10
Need to understand: 7
Aesthetic needs: 6

Question 2
Self-actualization: 1, 2, 3, 7
Need to understand: 0
Aesthetic needs: 4

Deficiency Needs

Question 1
Esteem needs: 3, 4
Belongingness and love needs: 0
Safety needs: 0
Physiological needs: 0

Question 2
Esteem needs: 5
Belongingness and love needs: 0
Safety needs: 0
Physiological needs: 0

Classification of typical teacher responses to the questions asked by authors: Question #1 "What is important to you to have as a part of each teaching day?" and Question #2 "What needs must be fulfilled in order to achieve and maintain satisfaction with your teaching role?" Numbers refer to actual teacher responses.

FIGURE 3.3   Student Responses

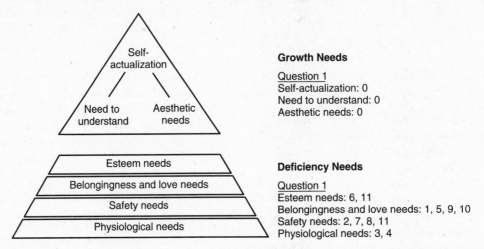

Classification of student responses to the question: "Tell us what is important to you; what makes you want to come to school each day?" The numbers refer to the actual student responses (see previous page).

do not readily complement each other. In traditional classrooms, whoever is "in control" of the classroom—teacher or students—will most likely have their needs met. What is created in this paradigm are "win-lose" classrooms, where the majority of needs of one group get met at the expense of the other. Conflict is inevitable, and both teaching and learning are impeded.

In effective classrooms, teachers strive to create learning environments that are "win-win," where the needs of both teachers and students are met. "Win-Win" classrooms are often the result of implementing Cooperative Learning.

COOPERATIVE LEARNING

Cooperative learning is an essential ingredient for teachers who share the notion that both literacy and learning should be seen as cooperative ventures. Studies have shown that student performance is enhanced with group acceptance, social goal setting, group problem-solving, and a sense of trust (D. W. Johnson and R. T. Johnson, 1986). Learning environments should provide abundant

opportunities for practicing respect, trust, and cooperation. The process of reading represents an act of cooperation. As readers, we respect and trust writers, even feel empathy toward them—at least for as long as they communicate well and accurately with us and for as long as they fulfill our purpose for reading. The process of writing represents the same act of cooperation, trust, and respect. To communicate in *any* way is to cooperate (May, 1994). Engaging students in cooperative learning, then, is important in establishing the right mind-set for children to actually experience reading and writing as collaborative acts.

Looking back at Maslow's Hierarchy of Needs and at the statements students gave in Figure 3.3, we see that all of the responses fall within the area of meeting deficiency needs, and in particular, those needs that pertain to attaining a sense of *"belonging."* Students do not satisfy such needs by working in isolation. They require activities that provide high levels of interaction.

Traditional wisdom has guided educators to create competitive learning environments, reflecting the conviction that competition is a necessary condition for learner motivation to take place. Johnson and Johnson (1989) have summarized more than 300 studies that reveal the merits of cooperative learning over learning that fosters competition between students. Johnson and Johnson report that in addition to learning more, students who learned in groups did better on higher-level reasoning, critical thinking, and transferring knowledge to their personal lives.

Whole language classrooms, where students work cooperatively toward common goals and where collaboration between learners is fostered, are noticeably different from other classrooms. The first thing that visitors notice is the students. The sounds heard upon entering are students' voices. Students are actively engaged in helping one another in the learning process. Active, interactive, and supportive student exchanges can be observed everywhere.

Cooperative Roles

Unfortunately, American society provides few models for students to gain skill in working cooperatively. It takes time and frequent teacher modeling in the beginning to create a community of learners who can work effectively in cooperative groups. Most teachers find it helpful to clearly delineate the individual roles for each group member, along with plenty of opportunity to practice the behaviors and language associated with each of the roles. For example, teacher modeling of each of the roles presented in Table 3.1 can provide practice and feedback for group members. Such whole group reflection and discussion might be a regular feature for the first two or three months of school. Eventually students can suggest their own roles, appropriate for their learning goals.

A Cooperative Learning Strategy: Think-Pair-Share

Think-pair-share is a strategy developed to encourage student participation in the classroom. Students are taught to use a new response cycle in answering questions. The technique is simple to learn and is applicable across all grade levels,

disciplines, and group sizes. In some cases students can facilitate the process themselves.

The components of think-pair-share are as follows:

- Students *listen* while the teacher poses a question.
- Students are given time in which to *think* of a response.
- Students are sometimes cued to *pair* with a neighbor and discuss their responses.
- Students are invited to *share* their responses with the whole group.

A time limit is set for each step in the process. Many teachers use cueing devices such as bells, pointers, hand signals, or cubes to move students through the cycle. Students may be asked to write or web (diagram) their responses while in the think and/or pair mode(s).

Benefits to Students   Students have time to think through responses to questions mentally, and sometimes verbally with another student, before being asked to answer them publicly. All students have an opportunity to share their thinking with at least one other student, thereby increasing their sense of involvement, acceptance, and peer support.

Benefits to Teachers   Students have been found to spend more time on task and to listen more to each other when engaged in think-pair-share activities. Many more students raise their hands to respond after rehearsing in pairs. Students may have better recall due to increased "wait time," and the quality of responses is improved.

Like students, teachers also have more time to think when using think-pair-share. They can concentrate on asking higher-order questions, observing student reactions, and listening to student responses. Class discussion can be a much more relaxing experience for both teachers and students.

TABLE 3.1 The Language of Group Membership

Praiser

"Thanks for sharing that with us."

"That was a helpful suggestion."

"A great idea!"

Questioner

"What do you think about this one. . . ?"

"Let's discuss that idea. . . "

"Does anyone have an idea?"

Organizer

"What material do we need?"

"I'll get that."

"I'll make sure we're ready."

"Remember to bring in _____."

Summarizer

"You said. . . "

"What I heard you say is. . . "

"I heard you say something different than. . . "

"Your idea goes along with _____'s."

Participation Expert

"We haven't heard from _____."

"Everyone needs to respond."

"_____, what do you think?"

"Take a minute to think about what you want to say."

Observer

"This is what I saw. . . "

"I heard _____ speak five times."

"How many responses did our group make?"

"One of the things I noticed was. . . "

Law Enforcer

"What is the problem we are facing?"

"How can we solve this?"

"Can we find a better way to discuss this?"

"What is stopping us from making progress here?"

Note: Cooperative Learning is aided by clearly defining students' roles within the group and typical responses associated with each of the roles.

BUILDING A COMMUNITY OF LEARNERS

Effective group membership is essential to establishing positive learning environments where collaboration, meaningful student interaction, and class cohesion are valued. Group process refers to the ways that the students work together toward commonly held goals in the classroom. Creating a sense of "community" and placing children at the center of all decision making are necessary for effective group process to evolve. Galen Guengerich, introduced in Chapter 1, is in many ways the quintessential child-centered teacher, placing students at the vortex of all that goes on in his classroom. According to Galen, *group process* embodies the concept of *community building:*

> Community building is a basic ingredient to a successful whole language classroom. A true whole language setting will need to have strong peer relationships for writing workshop, cooperative learning, and group decision making.

This extraordinary teacher has given considerable thought and research to what a sense of community means and how a feeling of community is formed in the classroom. His understanding of the essence of community building was achieved by focusing intently upon a fifth-grade student named Randy. Through insights derived from the anecdotal records he maintained on Randy, Galen identifies four prominent areas that depict the essence of the term "community of learners." Here is what Galen believes:

1. *A community of learners celebrates student events and accomplishments.* A highlight of the day is students spending time discussing their own personal lives at the start of each day. In this format, students readily share events, personal likes and dislikes, or difficulties they may have faced. Community begins to actively happen as students empathize with others or celebrate their accomplishments.

2. *A community of learners provides success for all.* A parent can frequently tell a teacher about the best way his or her child learns. Our tendency is to continue to see children as identical or very similar in how we learn. It is easy to be less flexible when evaluations occur. A community-centered classroom will consider individual strengths, weaknesses, and student learning styles.

   "A great deal of time in my classroom is devoted to team learning. One way Randy helps with this is through peer tutoring. I have found that the level of learning is higher when children of similar learning styles assist one another. Community building is a natural result of students being responsible to each other."

3. *A community of learners celebrates humor.* A sense a humor walks hand-in-hand with community. Students often are not sure how to react to a humorous response when a more businesslike interaction is what they have experienced in classrooms. Students are able to soon understand that they can have fun and laugh while they learn. They are also able to experience a sense of personal appreciation for their own well-being when a teacher is able to joke with them.

   "Randy was not sure how to respond to classroom humor. At the start of the year, time was set aside to briefly share jokes, usually during transition from one activity to another. Soon Randy had his own joke book and was sharing one-liners. Reticent learners become more comfortable with speaking through the medium of humor."

4. *A community of learners has a fair, purposeful classroom structure.* Students respond to a classroom structure that is fair and under-

standing. Discipline may play a major role in how students perceive their classroom structure. Unfortunately, teachers often rely on discipline as a central component of the learning process.

"Discipline may ruin the sense of community and fairness in the "blink of an eye" if it is administered hastily or without reason. On the other hand, discipline can be a fantastic learning tool where guidance is carefully given and the child's mistake is eased by the teacher. This can only happen if the teacher truly cares for the child."

In Galen's quest to ensure that he is creating and maintaining a "functional classroom community of learners," he shares these suggestions with new teachers:

1. Spend time at the beginning of the year talking about guidelines students find in their own homes. Draw parallels from the home as a learning environment to being a family of learners in school. Invite students to write in their journals what the expectations will be in order to be a successful class family member. As a concluding activity, encourage students to develop a class motto which depicts the kind of class they want to be. This year our class motto was, "As a class we have decided to be a family of learners."

2. Each student needs to have a sense of belonging as a family member. On the first day of school, student-made photo albums from previous classes are looked at by all the new class members. From this they are able to see that they will be remembered for many years to come.

   A culminating activity in June is to make the class photo albums for the next generations of class members. I like to call the albums my "Hall of Fame." Each child is given a 5 × 7 photograph. Next to the picture, students write about themselves. Below the picture, students write about what they will be doing 25 years

later. A pop-up of themselves is included on each page. The pages are then glued together and a cover added. Parents and students love to come back to school and look at the book.

3. Each class wishes to know what their new teacher will be like. At the end of each year, I have each class member write a letter to the owner of the desk for next year. In the letter, each child is to write about what it means to be a community of learners in the classroom. The new students love reading the letters from the previous years. In addition, expectations for the next year are quietly transferred from one set of students to another.

4. Graduating from high school is indeed a milestone. I think that elementary school teachers need to have a way to connect with the lives of the students they had in class. At the end of fifth grade, I have students write a letter to themselves that will be sent to their homes when they complete high school. Students give themselves advice, congratulations, set goals and talk about how the world has changed from being a fifth grader to a high school student. A self-addressed envelope is written. Along with the letters, I keep a class list to call or send cards to them as they move through the school system.

   When they graduate, I write a note on the bottom of each letter that they wrote to themselves and send the letters, seven years later.

Finally, Galen encourages all teachers to plan for and work toward creating a community of learners by remembering to do the following:

1. *Take time for student interaction.* Student interaction and sharing enhances instructional time. It prepares students to function more effectively as a body of learners. As teachers we must recognize the importance of these dynamics and find ways to celebrate student life. Not to do so is to say that we are preparing students for life rather than recognizing their own lives today!

2. *Recognize learning styles.* Each child is unique. All of us recognize this. We need to go beyond lip service and be willing to actively use other teaching and evaluation styles. This will yield a higher degree of success and a more accurate evaluation of their learning.

3. *Celebrate the moment.* Each day, each moment is to be cherished. If this is always kept in the forefront, discipline and structure will be centered around the students and their perspectives, not the teachers.

Galen concludes by saying, "Each day that I go to the door and greet the children as they come bursting into my room, I no longer hear individual conversations, I hear a community being built."

Creating a Love of Books

Creating an environment for literacy learning is about creating a love affair. According to fourth-grade teacher Anne Burns, "Quite simply and fundamentally, the role of the teacher is to broker a love affair between children and books!" When you conceive of your role as teacher in that way, you plan differently for students. The question always in the back of your mind should be, "Will this activity, assignment, task, etc., further or thwart my students' love affair with literature?" If the answer is "thwart," then clearly the plan has to be changed. Such questions can serve as a good "litmus test" for teachers to use for all learning activities they plan for youngsters.

For Anne, the idea of creating a love affair between her students and books came from a passage she had read long ago from Alfred North Whitehead's *The Aims of Education,* written in 1929. She does not remember Whitehead's exact words but one particular idea remains clear: At whatever age students begin their "formal learning," they should begin to learn playfully, almost romantically, with wonderful teachers who make it exciting and interesting.

It helps to have some organizing principle in your mind to provide a focus for your decision making. For one of the authors of this book, the only maxim she could recall from her educational psychology classes as a beginning teacher was, "Begin them [students] where they are, and take them as far as you can, in the time you have been given with them." When you think about that statement, it is a galvanizing message, which covers a myriad of educationally sound teaching practices. It infers the need to look closely at each child and to individualize instruction in a manner that will assist each student to reach his or her potential during that school year.

So what is inferred by viewing the role of teacher as one of creating a love affair between students and books? Well, for one, it probably rules out many of the things teachers have traditionally done to turn students off to reading—even those students who may claim that they like to read outside of school. To many students, "reading" is at the bottom of the list of subjects they like in school. That is certainly no basis for the creation of a love affair. We tend to love those things that make us feel good about ourselves, that bring us pleasure, that meet our personal needs. Creating a whole language classroom for literacy learning, then, should reflect teaching and learning episodes which realize these things in the lives of children, as they relate to books and other literary events throughout their school days.

Structuring a Literate Classroom

In his book *Build a Literate Classroom* (1991), Donald Graves cautions teachers not to interpret the natural process of acquiring literacy with the need to create classrooms, where reading and writing will just "naturally" develop. Literacy development as a natural act does not eliminate the need for reliable teacher leadership and careful attention to structure and classroom routines. Graves paints a grim picture of what a misinterpretation of a natural learning environment would mean:

> A natural environment would mean letting you and the children occupy a room where there was little definition to either territory or process. If you imagine a classroom in which a laissez-faire mood exists, I see the children reading and writing when they want, about what they want, and completing products as they please. They discuss the work of others, either punishing or applauding. A natural environment, without any structure, allows each child's notion of territory and ownership to compete for center stage. The richness of the many cultures and family traditions represented in the classroom is then lost. (Graves, 1993, p. 33)

Only through careful design and structure can teachers nurture the natural tendency of young children to explore communicating with each other through reading and writing. Immersion alone (refer to Brian Cambourne's Seven Conditions of Literacy Learning, Chapter 1) will not ensure that children's natural urge to express themselves will be realized. Two elements which teachers need to deliberately tend to are *time* and *choice*. In classrooms where students clearly understand how to successfully manage time and choice, optimal conditions for learning are possible.

Children come from vastly different home environments which contribute to the complexity of issues relevant to how time and choice are naturally exercised in the classroom. Certain parenting practices encourage students to use time wisely and complete tasks before engaging in play. There is an established rhythm within the home where certain events occur at certain times of the day and evening. Routines in these homes are well established. Mealtimes, bedtime, family time, and free time are subject to regularly scheduled hours of the day. Children are assigned regular chores and are required to carry them out without being told. There are consistent and known consequences attached to not fulfilling one's responsibilities within the household. Children who have experienced backgrounds of this kind enter a new grade, with a new teacher, anticipating that

there will be rules to keep and a rhythm to the classroom which must be learned and followed in order to be successful there.

Conversely, there will be other children who come from environments where the rules change from moment to moment and where nothing is constant. Behaviors which are permitted today may become incidents for severe punishment tomorrow. Not only are expectations in general inconsistent, they vary from individual to individual within the family constellations of such children. Time, within these families, is both used and valued differently. With no specified times allotted to certain activities, effective management of time has little opportunity to develop. In addition, time is not a highly valued attribute of daily life in these families. Opportunities for children to exercise choices are often exercised capriciously as well. Parents who are forced to work long hours and are absent from home for long periods of time often must abdicate some of their parental authority and offer children abundant choice over what they will do and when they will do it. Chances for parents to model good choice making and effective use of time are not very often present. Consequently, children arrive at school lacking the skills for making choices and structuring time wisely. If one views the class as an extended family, even the awareness of these elements as being useful to working together productively, is missing.

The cultural diversity which marks many of our public schools compounds the issues of time and choice. Although every culture has a means of documenting time, the importance given to things like "being on time," "being aware of the passage of time," and what constitutes "good use of time" may differ remarkably from culture to culture.

Setting your students up for success, then, requires that you overtly deal with the elements of time and choice in your classroom. Making your students conscious of these elements requires much time and energy during the first few weeks of school. Avoiding it, however, will probably take even greater time away from teaching and learning throughout the entire school year. The key to orchestrating dimensions of time and choice in the classroom is structure. It requires teachers to assume leadership in their classrooms. It runs contrary to the notion that a child-centered, integrated classroom is run by children. Rather, it is the child-centered teacher who models appropriate behavior, establishes acceptable parameters in the classroom, and ensures the stability and predictability of the learning environment where learners feel safe enough to risk changing and growing.

Teacher as leader and provider of class structure is in no way an attempt to condone or encourage a return to authoritarianism. But children need to experience the safety and security of knowing that someone is in charge and that there are clear boundaries for functioning successfully in this learning environment. Part of exercising good leadership in the classroom is to know how and when to delegate responsibility to students. Delegating responsibility is at the heart of the structured classroom. In a class where children are free to engage their curiosities for sustained periods of time and where teachers can realize uninterrupted time to work intensively with students who need assistance, learners must know how to operate without the immediate attention of the teacher. Donald Graves quotes a teacher who delegates wisely by continually asking herself the question, "Let's see, what am I doing that the children ought to be able to handle?" He continues to quote her by stating, "I want children to need me *less* so that I can choose more effective moments for real teaching."

Creating an Environment for Literacy

The foundations of literacy are not created in a vacuum; they are always embedded within some context. When youngsters first utter sounds that are recognizable as the sounds of human speech, the response they receive from their environment has profound consequences upon whether they will seek to reproduce the sounds, continue to play with other sounds, or cease experimenting with sounds altogether. The context we create within our classrooms where literacy is to occur, then, is of utmost significance, from the physical arrangement of the room to its contents, and the important human dynamics that emotionally connect children and teachers with one another.

Linda Martin is a talented first-grade teacher who knows the importance of creating environments in which the love of literacy can happen. For Linda, the creation of her community of learners begins long before students ever enter her classroom for the first time. From the time she establishes closure with the class that has just moved on and has resolved the sense of loss associated with passing them on to their next teacher, Linda is already thinking about her new students and begins to make plans for early contact with them over the summer vacation.

Like Linda, many teachers recognize the importance of connecting with their students *before* they actually enter the classroom. Communication with their new teacher, prior to the start of school, begins to establish a mindset within children that "This is going to be a good year." The attitude that a child walks into—in *any* teaching model, is a key element in establishing early rapport with youngsters and beginning to create a learning environment which furthers literacy development.

For Linda, this takes the form of sending a personal letter to each child in her class, as well as to each parent. She uses a word processor, which helps her to save considerable time in generating letters to many individuals. Since many youngsters may have parents who have divorced and entered into new marriages, it may mean sending as many as five letters per child. Since each child is a product of, and influenced by, each parent and stepparent, acquiring information from all of those close to the child provides a fuller view of the perceptions, expectations, and unique qualities of each child. Figures 3.4 and 3.5 show examples of letters that Linda has written.

The value of this early communication becomes apparent when you read the replies from parents. Figure 3.6 presents a letter from the stepmother of a student named Robert. The information contained in this letter will help Linda to make his initial time in her classroom successful for him.

Linda learns that Robert has experienced more disruption in his life than most six-year-olds and that it is often difficult for him to remain focused on what he is doing. Linda sees implications here for where she seats him in her classroom and the types of activities she will plan for him. She will want to be especially sensitive to Robert's natural interests and strengths. Linda wants all her students to encounter early success in her classroom, but she knows that this might be especially crucial for Robert. Helping Robert to feel safe and secure in this new

FIGURE 3.4 Letter to a New Student from Teacher

```
                    LINDA J. MARTIN
                     FIRST GRADE
              SEVEN VALLEYS ELEMENTARY CENTER


                 The first day of school.
               Now I know that butterflies
                   Can be in bellies.


Dear Krystal,

  Welcome to first grade. I'm sure you are excited and maybe a little nervous.
I am too. I always get butterflies the first day of school. I have so many new
people to meet and so many new things to do. Every year I end up loving the
first day - but every year I still get butterflies in my belly.

  We will begin our year by talking and writing stories about what we think
first grade will be like. I would like you to talk with someone at home about
what you hope will happen this year. What do you want to learn? What kind of
things do you hope we do? Is there anything you are nervous about? Think and
talk about this with someone and we will share and write together at school.

  Orientation will be Tuesday, August 31 at 3 pm. I hope you can come. I look
forward to meeting you.

  You are beginning a happy and important time of your life. I am pleased to
be sharing this time you.

  I'll see you soon.

                                        Your friend and teacher,



                                        Linda J. Martin
```

FIGURE 3.5   Letter to Parent

```
Linda J. Martin
First Grade
Seven Valleys Elementary Center

Dear Ms. Lahr,

  As we begin a new school year, it is always important to me that I get to
know my new students as quickly and as well as possible. You can help me get
to know your child. Would you please take a few minutes to write an informal
letter of introduction for Krystal. I would like to know Krystal through
your eyes. What are your expectations for the coming year? What are your
concerns? What experiences has Krystal had that you think I should know about?
What makes Krystal a special person? You may write a few sentences, a few
paragraphs or a few pages. I will be delighted to read every word.

  You may bring your letter of introduction to school for the orientation on
August 31, or send it along with Krystal on September 1.

  Thank you for your time and consideration. I look forward to working with
you this year.

                                    Sincerely,


                                    Linda J. Martin
```

classroom will thus be essential. She already begins to write down notes about ways that she might do this.

A very different picture is painted in a letter written by the father of Eric in Figure 3.7.

Figure 3.8 shows the letter dictated by Eric to his father. Both letters provide Linda with some

wonderful insight into Eric's expectations about the new school year. She has already jotted down some ideas:

Must remember to clarify how we are going to handle homework this year on the very first day. I think I will use the "Pass" system that I read about in *Teach-*

FIGURE 3.6 Letter from Robert's Stepmother

> Dear Mrs. Martin,
> Hi, I am Roberts Stepmother. Robert has been with myself and his father since he was 2 years old. His father and I have custody of him. Robert gets to see his mother every other weekend. Robert has just started seeing his mother since school let out and last year. Robert likes setting and reading. Robert likes working one on one. Robert likes to talk about things such as fishing, toys he has and things he has done around the house.
> Robert gets really mad if he can't figure things out the first or second time he has a tendancy of giving up to soon. Last year Robert was having trouble concentrating and doing his work. So his teacher and I set up a reward system then that seemed to help, hopefully we will not have to do that this year.
> Robert usually waits til the last minute to say he has to use the bathroom so I *just* wanted to let you know. Thats about it I guess.
>
>   Sincerely yours,
>   Mrs. Amy Taylor

ing K-8 last month. That may take the scare out of homework for Eric and others who have similar fears.

Remember to tell Eric on the first day about the field trip we have planned to the Hanover Dairy.

The summer correspondence between Linda Martin and her students has begun to create the type of environment where literacy development can flourish.

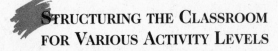

STRUCTURING THE CLASSROOM FOR VARIOUS ACTIVITY LEVELS

As teachers develop more interactive and stimulating approaches to literacy learning they face a new question: "How do I organize the room so that the liveliness works *for* learning and not *against* it?"

Effective integration of the language arts, throughout the school day, requires the creation of areas where children can congregate, to interact, and to collaborate on projects that are meaningful to them.

There is no singular physical arrangement or structure that can guarantee a successful classroom, but some arrangements lend themselves better than others to active, meaningful, student involvement, while fostering a learning environment that encourages self-regulation and organized movement. The

FIGURE 3.7   Letter from Eric's Father

> This is to introduce Eric Ryan Blevins.
>
> Eric is a happy, well-adjusted young man who enjoys riding his bike and playing soccer on the Spring Grove League. His team name is "The Blast".
>
> He also enjoys fishing with Dad.
>
> Eric had Mrs. Marburg last year, who suggested we have him tested for ADD, and even though he tested positive (slightly) he does have an above average I.Q. Therefore, you will be receiving a Rx for Ridilen for Eric with the dosage to be given (1 tablet at noon).
>
> Eric can be very strong about his convictions which is sometimes hard to deal with, but he usually does try VERY hard to please.
>
> We hope that you and Eric can develope a close relationship as he does have a tendancy to get very close to his teachers.
>
> Please do not hesitate to let us know if there are any problems during the year so we can make efforts to correct them ASAP.
>
> Thank you
> Ed Blevins

creation of distinct areas or centers, designed for specific learning activities and having similar noise level requirements, constitutes a room arrangement that furthers those behaviors. Here are some suggestions for specific activity centers:

Activity Centers

- *The conference center:* It is here that students, teachers, and volunteers come together to discuss books, articles, and one another's writing. Although the conference center generally is not a quiet area, the noise level here should be under control.
- *The library:* This is where copies of novels, magazines, nonfiction reference books, and published works by members of the class are stored. The noise level in this area is quite low.
- *The publishing center:* When students complete a work, they take it to the publishing center, which is well stocked with a variety of papers, pens, markers and other art supplies, and binding materials. The noise level in the publishing center can be high.
- *Author's corner:* Readings to the class by students, guests, and the teacher all take place here. This area—in which the noise level is focused—should be provided with comfortable seating for all students.
- *The reading center:* Often located next to the classroom library, the reading center is

FIGURE 3.8 Eric's Dictated Letter

> Eric's Ideas About School
>
> Eric says that he is not afraid of anything at school. Just a "Little Nervous" about having homework every night.
>
> Eric hopes that he will get to go on some field trips this year.
> He says he hopes to learn how to tell time.
>
> He is also looking forward to making some new friends.
>
> Eric

where students can relax (e.g., sitting on pillows or in comfortable chairs) while reading to themselves.

- *The writing center:* This is an area where students can write without having their concentration disturbed by distractions from other parts of the classroom. The writing center may be nothing more than the students' regular desks. The noise level will vary here, depending upon the nature of the writing projects. Both independent as well as small-group writing teams need to be accommodated for within the classroom.

(Modified from: *The Whole Language Companion,* published by Scott, Foresman and Company, Glenview, IL. [1991] David Clark Yeager.)

Things to Consider

There are several things to consider when planning a whole language classroom environment:

- Work space for each student (tables or desks arranged in clusters)
- Storage place (desk, cubbie, supply box, etc.) assigned to each student to store supplies in
- Open space where entire class can gather on floor close to the teacher for group activities
- Chalkboard (at group work space) large enough for group brainstorming, recording, and modeled writing
- Teacher's personal area where teaching resources, records, etc. are housed (file cabinet, storage closet)
- Area for students' backpacks, coats, etc. (closet, hooks)
- Storage area for paper (lined writing paper, plain unlined paper, extra paper from prior lessons)
- Word bank area (large chart paper) displayed low enough for students to read and make additions

- Science observation area located away from individual work space
- Art area with organized supplies (media, stencils, art tools) and art instruction books
- Feature author bulletin board with space for storage of collection of author's works
- Physical education equipment storage
- Listening area
- Computer area
- Speaking platform
- Big book storage (rack on wall or large laundry basket)
- Stand for pocket charts
- Large bulletin board, wall space, or clothesline
- Bulletin board for class information
- Message bulletin board near entrance to classroom
- Drama Center or Reader's Theatre Center with simple costumes and props
- Student responsibility (job) bulletin board
- Student of the week (VIP) bulletin board

Middle and upper-grade students will benefit from having access to word processors and electric typewriters when they reach the "publish" stage of the writing process. Figures 3.9 and 3.10 present sample classroom arrangements that take into account many of the considerations cited above.

Three overriding principles should be kept in mind when making decisions about the physical environment in a whole-language classroom:

- The classroom should show students models of good language.
- The classroom should stimulate students to use language.
- The classroom should offer opportunities for students to experiment with language.

Managing Materials

Distribution of materials is a major consideration in a classroom where numerous learning activities are going on simultaneously. The creation of a decentralized pattern for distribution of materials can prohibit impediments to the smooth operation of the classroom. Interrelated materials can

be placed around the room, based on their role in stimulating learning, as opposed to simply grouping items by similarity. For example, science trade books on rocks and minerals, tools for identification and testing, a variety of sample rocks, and materials for recording and illustrating can be displayed together, thus creating a higher level of complexity and promoting independent involvement. Decentralization also reduces congestion in areas of the classroom as well as the transition time and spillage and breakage of materials, thereby alleviating unwanted behaviors. Altering just this one organizational aspect of the classroom can often transform unacceptable student behaviors into highly acceptable ones.

The classroom design in Figure 3.11 shows how writing tools and reference materials (dictionaries, encyclopedias, word lists, charts, etc.) are located in several work areas around the room, therefore dramatically reducing the need for students to traverse the classroom to obtain what they may need to work on individual and group projects.

This chapter presented the basic elements of creating classroom environments where literacy learning is allowed to flourish. Most important is that a classroom emanate from a set of teacher beliefs about how teaching and learning occur. Each teacher decision should support those beliefs. Literacy development is furthered where these classroom practices are in evidence:

- Time devoted at the very beginning to fostering group interaction and establishing class rules, thus creating more time for instruction and learning to take place throughout the remainder of the school year.
- Student responsibility for the organization and management of books and other materials in the classroom is emphasized.
- Learning environments which recognize that teacher and student needs may differ and strive to meet the needs of both.
- Many opportunities for cooperative learning and feedback to take place.

FIGURE 3.9 Sample Classroom Arrangement

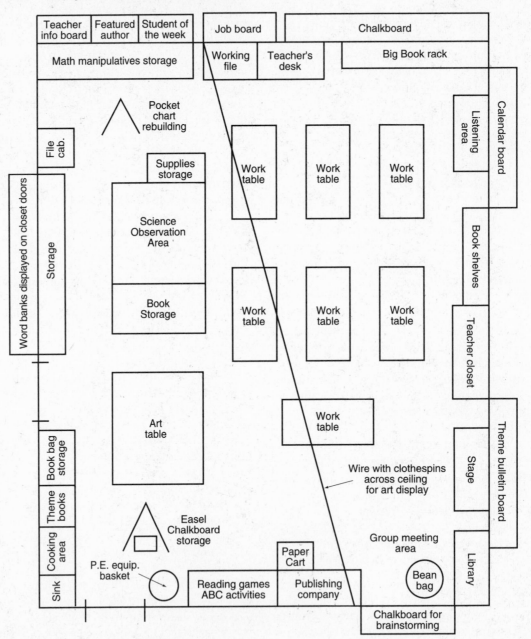

- Establishing a "Community of Learners" where every member is both teacher and learner.
- Physical organization of classrooms that foster appropriate behavior by separating cen-

ters of high activity from centers requiring quiet concentration and solitude.
- Decentralized placement of reference and resource materials, throughout the classroom,

FIGURE 3.10 Classroom Floor Plan

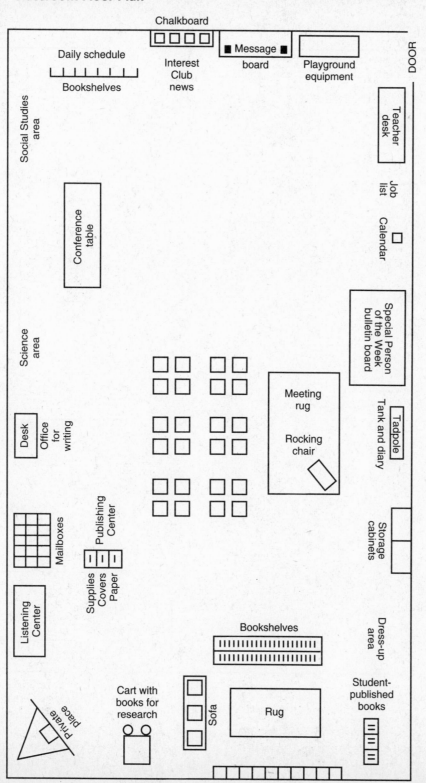

FIGURE 3.11 Room Design

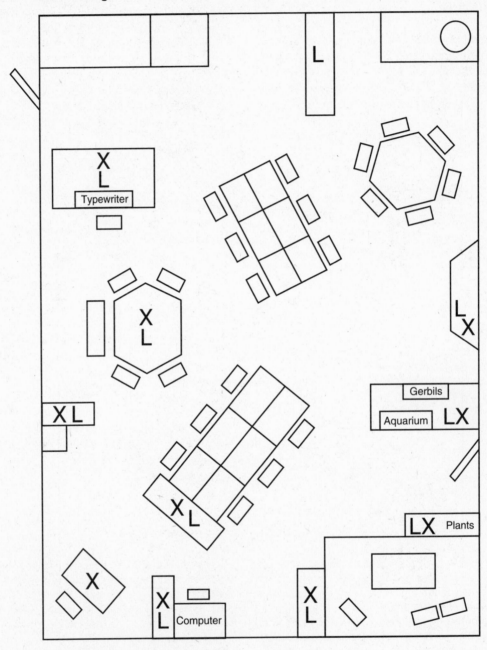

X = Writing materials and tools
L = References (dictionary, encyclopedias, word lists, charts, etc.)

to support numerous activities occurring simultaneously.

Becoming a whole language teacher is no easy journey. There is no blueprint, or formula for success. There are few shortcuts and no ready solutions, and each teacher's route is slightly different. There is no best course to take or classroom to visit to get all the answers. There is not even a commonly accepted definition—for whole language is a philosophy—a way of thinking. Becoming a whole language teacher is more about learning than it is about teaching. It is more about asking questions than it is about finding answers. Most of all, it is about making a profound philosophical shift in beliefs about learning and teaching.

CATHY SWANSON'S JOURNAL

✤ October 9

One of my goals this year is to help the kids develop a sense of ownership, with their work, their portfolios, etc. We took some time last week to decorate portfolio folders. We also discussed what could go into their portfolios and why it was important that they select some of the contents. I also created a short form, intended to reveal the student's reason for choosing the piece.

This week the students chose a piece of writing to include. Their written explanations were not what I expected. This is one of those times when I'm not yet sure if my expectations are too high, if I didn't model what I expected, or if I just need to return them and share that their explanations are not complete enough to give the reader a clear picture . . . (or do I just need to be patient and watch them grow in the process?).

✤ October 12

We met with our kindergarten buddies today! We plan to meet every Wednesday morning for about 30 minutes or so.

Today's activities were centered around getting to know one another. The children interviewed each other about general likes and dislikes, favorite foods, favorite books, etc. The K-buddies then selected books they wanted the fourth-grade buddies to read to them.

Toward the end of our time together, I read Steven Kellogg's *Best Friends* to the entire group. By this time, some of the kindergarten girls were already snuggled upon their buddy's lap . . . I love to watch this rapport develop! I think it is especially nice for children with no siblings, and for those fourth graders who are the youngest in their families and don't know what it's like to care for someone younger.

A secret handshake, mutually agreed upon, signified the end of our first session together.

Today the kids enacted telephone conversations they had written between Leigh [a character in *Dear Mr. Henshaw* by Beverly Cleary] and his father. Many were filled with inferences and clever nuances, revealing the level of involvement with the book and the awareness they have of the personalities of the characters. Two groups actually brought in telephones!

Most at least included references to that now-famous line, "Keep your nose clean, Kid!" Bandit [Leigh's dog] was usually mentioned as well. Although they were really well presented overall, I wish I had either modeled one such conversation myself, or had selected one strong pair to model first; some dialogues were well written but were lost in the "acting." One or two pairs wrote pieces that could have been more replete and might have been had they been aware of my expectations for them. (I'm learning that fourth graders are much more literal than fifth graders; they really need modeling!)

This kind of activity is really an effective (and fun) way to integrate the language arts! The children *read* and respond to the book, *write* their dialogues together, present (*speak*) them to an audience who *listens* to them and then comments on their effectiveness/authenticity. Even those most reticent to speak become more willing as a sense of safety within the classroom is developed.

After obtaining fall writing samples, I conferenced with the kids about their pieces, asking them what they thought were their strengths and what they might want to improve in their writing. I was surprised at how closely their evaluations matched mine; they are very insightful about their work, especially if they are asked about it *before* any teacher evaluation is shared!

I shared with them my evaluation, then asked them to think about setting goals for improvement. Billy (my wonderful mentor) created a "Goal-Setting Page" that he shared with me. The children completed these, we conferenced again, and the signed goal sheets went into the writing folders to be examined at the end of each marking period.

What I need to do to make this evaluation more effective is to rewrite what each of McCaig's levels indicates in terms the kids can understand. This should be posted in the Writing Center as well as kept in their folders for reference. It would then be more clear what they need to work on to attain the next level of competence.

Today we were discussing how the life of the Amish differed from our own. We created a Venn diagram, of sorts, on the board and listed what would be the same and what would be different. This led to a great discussion on what one does when there is no television—a thought that seemed unfathomable to many! Eyes widened as we listed all the appliances/gadgets/toys that would not be a part of their lives were they a member of this religious order.

Many decided Esther's life would be boring, although Caitlin pointed out that "you can't miss what you don't know." She added that she could even understand how they might feel a bit afraid of electricity.

For homework tonight, the students will be creating a double bar graph comparing the number of hours they eat, sleep, play, watch TV, spend quiet time (including reading), and attend school with the number of hours Esther might do the same. I'm curious to see the how these kids spend their time and what their reaction is to seeing that reality on paper!

TEACHER AS LEARNER/TEACHER AS RESEARCHER

Sociograms

A sociogram is a useful tool in gathering information you may need about the social dynamics in the classroom. Information is obtained from the children themselves, in response to questions you pose to them that reveal how they regard other members of the class and their relationship to them. Children's selections of other children in the class are then quantified and organized in a chart form that gives a visible "picture" of the social dynamics in and outside of the classroom, relevant to the question(s) asked. The sociogram is especially useful when it is important to know who is perceived to possess the most power in the classroom; who is regarded as the isolate (the child not chosen by others); what strong bonds of friendship exist in the classroom, etc. The following are examples of the kinds of research questions that might be suitable for sociograms:

How does the presence of resource personnel in the classroom affect the attitudes of students toward their peers who receive one-on-one help?

How does grouping students according to mutual interests change students, perceptions of peers?

What attributes are important to students in selecting reading buddies?

Creation of sociograms begins with developing one to three questions (more than this gets confusing) to ask each class member, based upon your research question. It is best to devise questions that students can answer by selecting the name or names of classmates. For example:

If you could pick anyone in the class to work with on your next research project, whom would it be?

If I assign you a journal buddy, someone who you will correspond with for one whole month in your personal journals, who would you like me to pair you with?

If we rearrange the room so that everyone's desk is next to one other person, what one person in the class would you like to be seated next to?

Students are requested to give a first, second, and third choice for each question. For children in the primary grades, this information is best collected individually, at a table or other location out of earshot of other students. For children whose age or ability permits them to write the first, second, and third choices of their classmates on a piece of paper, this can be done with the entire class or in smaller groups of students. For each child, whether your data are collected individually or with a larger group, you need to record (a) the name of the child responding to the question, and (b) the first, second, and third classmate selection for each question answered.

Once the questions have been asked of each student and their responses recorded, the numbers are tallied and a sociogram constructed. For example, suppose you wanted to explore the impact of team sports on students' perceptions of one another in other areas of the curriculum. You might ask students the following questions:

If you were told you were going to be team captain next week, what member of the class would you select to be on your team first? Second? Third?

If you could work with anyone in class on a research project, who would it be? Who would you pick next? Who would be your third choice?

For each student response given, a point value is assigned: 3 points for first choice, 2 points for second choice, and 1 point for third choice. A scoresheet can be constructed to record and tally points. A chart can then be constructed to visually present the patterns of student selections: which children are selected most often (referred to in the sociogram as "stars"), which segmented groupings appear in the class (referred to as "cleavages"), which children select each other ("mutual choices"), and which children are not selected by any other member of the class (referred to as "isolates"). An interpretation of Figure 3.12 shows that:

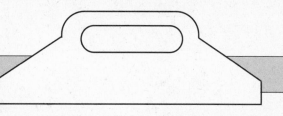

A. Josh is one of the stars. He was the first choice of Paul, Alin, and Hannah. He was chosen by 3 students out of 5.

B. Andy is the isolate in this group of students. He was not selected by anyone.

C. No cleavages or subgroups are represented.

FIGURE 3.12   Students Answer the Question "Who would you like to work with on a research project?"

	Josh	Paul	Aline	Andy	Hannah			⟶
Josh		3	2		1			
Paul	3		1		2			
Aline	3	1			2			
Abdul		1	2		3			
Hannah	3	2	1					

First choice = 3 pts.   Second choice = 2 pts.   Third choice = 1 pt.

Stars	**Mid-range**	**Low-range**	**Isolates**
Hannah (8,4)*	Aline (6,4)		Andy
Josh (9,3)	Paul (6,4)		

* First number represents point total for first, second, and third selections; second number represents the number of classmates who chose this individual.

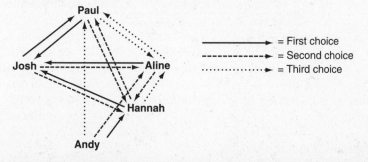

Journal Reflections

Select one or more of the questions below that interest you and respond in your journal.

1. Cathy's journal entries in early to mid-October already indicate the development of a "community of learners." What are some activities or procedures Cathy has implemented to foster the advancement of the classroom community?

2. The concept of a community of learners is essential in the creation of a child-centered classroom. What are some of the ways that you will establish a sense of community and cooperation in your classroom?

3. At the beginning of this chapter, you were asked to recall a classroom from your own elementary or middle school experience and to draw it. Now that you have acquired new ideas to consider in setting up your classroom, design the classroom as you would create it if you were going to begin your teaching career today.

4. Design your own question:
   ✓ What is a question you have about the chapter?
   ✓ How will you pursue the answer to that question?
   ✓ Respond in your journal.

REFERENCES AND SUGGESTED READINGS

Atwell, N. *In the Middle. Writing, Reading, and Learning with Adolescents.* Portsmouth, NH: Boynton/Cook, 1987.

Butler, A., and Turnbull, J. *Towards a Reading-Writing Classroom.* Portsmouth, NH: Heinemann, 1984.

Cambourne, B., and Turnbull, J. *Coping With Chaos.* Portsmouth, NH: Heinemann, 1991.

Chambers, A. *Booktalk.* New York: Harper & Row, 1985.

Crafton, L. K. *Whole Language: Getting Started . . . Moving Forward.* New York: Richard C. Owen, 1991.

DeFord, D. E. "Validating the Construct of Theoretical Orientation in Reading Instruction." *Reading Research Quarterly* 20 (spring 1985): 351–367.

Goodman, K. *What's Whole in Whole Language?* New York: Scholastic, 1986.

Graves, D. H. *Writing: Teachers and Children at Work.* Exeter, NH: Heinemann, 1993.

Heller, M. F. *Reading-Writing Connections: From Theory to Practice.* White Plains, NY: Longman, 1991.

Johnson, D. W., and Johnson R. T. *Cooperation and Competition: Theory and Research Evidence.* Edina, MN: Interaction, 1989.

Johnson, D. W., Johnson, R. T., et al. *Circles of Learning.* Englewood Cliffs, NJ: Prentice Hall, 1986.

Maslow, A. H. *Motivation and Personality* 2nd ed. New York: Harper & Row, 1970.

May, F. *Reading as Communication.* New York: Macmillan, 1994.

McDermott, C. "Creating Communication." *Book Links* (September 1993): 23–25. Booklist Publications (American Library Association) Chicago, IL.

Newman, J. *Whole Language: Theory in Use.* Portsmouth, NH: Heinemann, 1985.

Peterson, R., and Eeds, M. *Grand Conversations: Literature Groups in Action.* New York: Scholastic, 1990.

Reutzel, D. R., and Cooter, R. B. *Teaching Children to Read: From Basals to Books.* New York: Macmillan, 1992.

Routman, R. *Transitions: From Literature to Literacy.* Portsmouth, NH: Heinemann, 1988.

Routman, R. *Invitations—Changing as Teachers and Learners K–12.* Portsmouth, NH: Heinemann, 1994.

Yeager, D. C. *The Whole Language Companion.* Glenview, IL: Scott, Foresman & Company, 1991.

Whitehead, A. N. *The Aims of Education and Other Essays.* New York: The Macmillan Company, 1929.

Zemelman, S., Daniels, H., and Hyde, A. *Best Practice: New Standards for Teaching and Learning in America's Schools.* Portsmouth, NH: Heinemann, 1993.

CHAPTER 4

AUTHENTIC ASSESSMENT

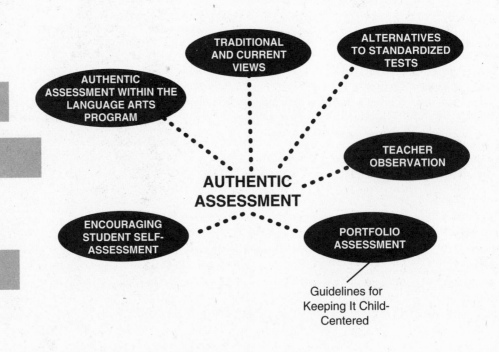

TRADITIONAL AND CURRENT VIEWS

ALTERNATIVES TO STANDARDIZED TESTS

AUTHENTIC ASSESSMENT WITHIN THE LANGUAGE ARTS PROGRAM

TEACHER OBSERVATION

AUTHENTIC ASSESSMENT

ENCOURAGING STUDENT SELF-ASSESSMENT

PORTFOLIO ASSESSMENT

Guidelines for Keeping It Child-Centered

What I Know: Pre-Chapter Journaling

Think back to the many tests you have taken throughout your school career—and especially during your elementary and middle school years. What do you recall most vividly about your experiences with tests during that time? Reflect upon some of those memories prior to reading this chapter.

Big Ideas

This chapter will offer:

1. A comparison between traditional and current views of assessment.
2. Alternatives to traditional assessment of student progress.
3. An introduction to portfolio assessment and its place within the integrated language arts curriculum; the mechanics for establishing portfolios in your classroom.
4. Techniques for encouraging student self-assessment.
5. The elements of authentic assessment within the language arts program.

Teachers whose beliefs place children squarely at the center of their instructional programs face some difficult decisions when it comes to assessing and evaluating student performance. Methods of assessment that have traditionally measured student achievement and progress no longer seem appropriate. Perhaps the best way to build an understanding of this assessment quandary is to look at the profiles of four elementary students. Imagine that you are the classroom teacher, to whom each of these four students has been assigned. Consider how you would begin a language arts instruction program that would accommodate the needs of these four youngsters. As you read the descriptions of the four students, keep in mind the fact that assessment of students' needs and abilities is *implied* any time that we make initial instructional decisions about students.

After you have considered how *you* would begin instruction for the four youngsters described, compare your approach with that of their *real* teacher—Jed Jackson. We will share with you the basis upon which Jed makes his initial decisions about the students in his class. Then, before we begin to explore assessment and evaluation more fully in this chapter, we will share the actions of two other teachers whose approach is very different from that of Mr. Jackson. You'll want to remember your initial impressions of these teachers when you meet them again later in this chapter.

ASSESSMENT VS. EVALUATION

One note of clarification: For purposes of this chapter, we have elected to use the term *assessment* rather than *evaluation*. In our minds, assessment is more consistent with the notions we have regarding the appraisal of student performance. We consider assessment to be an important and ongoing part of the instructional process. Evaluation, on the other hand, connotes an "endpoint judgment" regarding student achievement that seems somewhat static and lacking in movement "toward something." The use of assessment suggests "glimpses" of students' behaviors over time as they strive toward the attainment of personal goals in reading, writing, and the other language arts.

Profiles of Four Children

José   Eight-year-old José is one of 11 children. He has an insatiable appetite for books, especially books about adventure and super heros. But the subject doesn't really matter. If a book is there, he will read it. There are no books in José's house, except those he has brought home. He has reread some books so many times that he has them memorized; so José spends a lot of time at the local library, six blocks away from where he lives. His father calls him "lazy" because he is the only family member over five years of age who is not doing something to bring money into the household. When asked how he became so interested in books, he says, "I don't know; I just always liked them."

When the school counselor is asked the same question, she confides that the only time José feels safe is when his head is buried in a book. "Somehow he discovered early that when he was reading, being scared about what would cause his father to go into a rage and start beating up on his mother and his smaller brothers and sisters seemed to disappear," she discloses. Whenever he is asked to tell about what he is currently reading, however, he says, "I don't know." José wants to be a doctor when he grows up.

Jasmine   Jasmine is nine years old, in the fourth grade, and does not like books at all. She says that reading is "Boring!" and that she would rather be outside playing with her friends. Besides, she wants to own a beauty shop someday, like her Aunt Ethel, and she does not see any reason to go to school all of her life. Aunt Ethel stopped going to school in the fourth grade and is the richest relative in the family.

Jasmine likes it when her teacher reads books to the class, but she hates it when she has to read on her own. Usually Jasmine's teacher assigns workbook pages for students to do after they have completed their reading. Jasmine never does them—not because she can't but because she thinks workbook pages are "stupid." She recalls reading a book she really liked (although she does not remember the title or the author of the book). The story was about a bunch of kids who run away and live in a boxcar. She is worried about her new teacher and wonders if she will be made to sit by herself again this year away from all her friends.

Tyrone Eight-year-old Tyrone has an imagination bigger than he is. Although he is small for his age, his ideas are boundless. By his own count, he has written 180 stories last year; one of them was a chapter book with 23 chapters in it. The person he admires most is Stephen King, and he wants to be just like him when he grows up. Tyrone likes school, but he says his teachers never give him enough time to write. He finds the stories written by his classmates to be more interesting than those he has to read during reading class. He is anxious to begin this new school year because he has heard that the new school he will be attending has a Publishing Center, where the works of young authors get typed, bound, and placed in the library for other students to read. He hopes that his teacher will like what he writes this year.

Latisha Nine-year-old Latisha does not want to go back to school. To go back means leaving the safety of her home and running the risk of being attacked again on the way to school. She has had a good summer, most of it spent in front of the television, taking care of four younger siblings while her mother works. When Latisha is in school, she worries about her brothers and sisters being home alone. She says that she likes school and that it is not hard for her, but she has trouble concentrating on what the teacher is saying. Recess and lunchtime are the most difficult; no one wants to play with her or sit next to her in the cafeteria.

Four children's profiles—each of whom is remarkably different from the other. There is José, who despite being an avid reader, is unable to talk about what he has read. Then there is Jasmine, who appears to be José's polar opposite. She hates all books! Tyrone, the future "Stephen King," can't contain his inner drive to write. Tyrone's reading skills are behind those of his classmates, but his imaginative writings seem to compensate for that and have made him somewhat of a local hero to his peers. Then there is Latisha, who seems to be especially bright, but is unable to express it in class because of her preoccupation with things at home.

The four children presented here have apparently very different needs. With José, trust seems to be an issue. Because he is distrustful of the adults in his life, he is unwilling to share what he knows, for he cannot trust the reactions of those close to him. It is easier to say "I don't know" than to risk the wrath of an adult. For Jasmine, the issue is about relevance. She has some very practical and clear goals for herself—one being owning her own beauty shop—and fails to see how what goes on in school relates to any of them. For Tyrone, goals are clear—he *knows* he will be a famous writer some day—but the day-to-day assignments he receives from his teachers in language arts do not interest him. For Latisha, her attention is focused upon problems at home, a need that cannot be easily addressed in the classroom.

Teacher—Jed Jackson

Jose, Jasmine, Tyrone, and Latisha have been assigned to the classroom of Jed Jackson for the upcoming school year. As summer vacation is coming to an end for each of these youngsters, Jed Jackson is making use of the remaining days of his summer. As he has done for each of the previous eight years, Jed spends several weeks making preparations for the upcoming school year. Prior to meeting with his students, he has already spent hours preparing his classroom for their arrival. Jed now turns his attention to making some preliminary teaching decisions.

Jed is in the process of forming his reading groups and discovers that José, Tyrone, Jasmine, and Latisha will be in the same group, since their ability levels appear to be similar. He bases his decision to group these children together, on two measures, which have provided the basis for the school's grouping policy for years. First, he checks the scores these students received on a standardized test called the Stanford Achievement Test. Jed discovers that the four students scored at the second-grade reading level; these are among the lowest scores of all his students. He thus concludes that they will be in his lower reading group. The second measure that Jed consults is the written report issued by each child's teacher from the previous year. According to these, Jose, Jasmine, Tyrone, and Latisha had completed the second-grade reader from the basal program (see Chapter 8 for information about basal programs) and had received grades of U (unsatisfactory) or S– (less than satisfactory grades) in reading on their report cards.

Teachers—Jan Lin/Faye Lundrum

In the same city there are two other teachers preparing for the opening day of school. The manner in which they spend the remaining days of summer differs considerably from Jed's. First-grade teacher Jane Yin is sitting on a beanbag chair in her classroom, reading *The Sea Breeze Hotel,* a book by Marcia Vaughan and Patricia Mullins—one of more than 200 books on her summer reading list. As soon as Jane finishes the book, she will decide the most appropriate basket to house it temporarily, until her new crop of students comes and can share in the task of organizing the 436 books she has carted into her classroom over the past couple of weeks. Before she leaves for the day, she places an enlarged copy of

the book, *Brown Bear Brown Bear, What Do You See?* by Bill Martin on an easel in the front of the room.

In another school, fourth-grade teacher Faye Lundrum is similarly caught up in a virtual sea of books, which she has collected over the past two years. Surveying them for samples of various reading levels, genres, authors, subjects, and illustrators, Faye plans to use these books as a means of finding out the competencies her new students have acquired as readers.

ASSESSMENT

Three teachers, each preparing in his or her own way for the opening day of school and an incoming group of new students. Of the myriad things a teacher must accomplish before students actually walk into the classroom, decisions regarding where and how to begin instruction in the language arts is perhaps the most challenging.

Grouping for reading instruction has traditionally been accomplished at the conclusion of the academic year, based upon previous teachers' judgments and test results on standardized reading tests. This had been the policy in Jed Jackson's school since he arrived, and this procedure feels very comfortable to him.

Jan Lin and Faye Lundrum had each previously begun the school year in a manner identical to Mr. Jackson's—until about three years ago, when they began to question some of the time-honored practices they were using that just did not seem to "fit" any longer with the goals they had for their students. What began as vague inner conflicts later emerged as realizations that the beliefs they held regarding the natural acquisition of language and learning were in direct conflict with the means by which they were making decisions about students and their abilities.

Cambourne and Turbill (1990) have captured the conflict felt by these two teachers:

Teachers who decide to implement a whole-language philosophy share a common experience: the methods of assessment that they have traditionally been expected to use in their language programs no longer seem to be appropriate. Teachers who try to apply traditional assessment procedures to whole-language contexts typically express uneasiness about what they are trying to do.

We believe that this uneasiness is a consequence of the fact that thinking about educational assessment has not kept pace with thinking about language and learning. (p. 337)

The term *assessment* has been synonymous with testing for many years. Consequently, you might have had a slight wrenching in your stomach when you first encountered the title of this chapter. That is a feeling that many of us associate with all such terms—assessment, evaluation, testing, etc.—that connote judgment of our performance by others. All of us probably have personal horror stories associated with being judged by someone in a position of authority, where the consequences of that judgment have been less than we had hoped for, and in some instances, perhaps even harmful.

By some estimates, most students will take nearly 2,500 tests, quizzes, and exams during their school years (grades 1–12). For the most part, those measurement devices are designed to determine how much students know about a particular topic—or perhaps, more appropriately, how much they have crammed into their heads the night before an exam. Sound familiar? What should be evident is the fact that assessment is very much a part of the learning cycle; and although it is not always an exciting one, it is a necessary one.

We contend, however, that assessment does not have to be the dull, dry, pedantic "monster" it is often perceived to be by both students and teachers alike. It is an integral part of teaching for any teacher seeking to promote a dynamic and engaging classroom.

One of the reasons that the term assessment has been a negatively loaded one for most of us is that it has usually revealed our shortcomings and has been associated with advancing our feelings of inadequacy, especially as our shortcomings were made public and/or compared with the accomplishments of others. Very rarely have the terms evaluation, assessment, or testing been associated with good feelings and personal empowerment. All too often, they have been end points of our personal efforts and have visibly flagged our coming up short of a mark that had been set for us by others.

We wish to make an important point here—that *effective assessment is a continuous process.* It is not simply something that is done at the conclusion of a lesson or unit. Effective assessment is integrated into every aspect of the language arts curriculum, providing both teachers and students with relevant and useful data to gauge progress and determine the effectiveness of materials and procedures.

The negative associations that have traditionally been linked to assessment and evaluation measures do not have to persist. Assessment does not have to be viewed as synonymous with testing. There are more constructive ways of defining and implementing the concept of assessment, ways that are especially compatible with current thinking about language and learning.

Education at a Turning Point

You are entering the field of education at a very interesting time. There are many reasons for this, not the least of which is related to what is happening in the area of educational assessment. Assuming that you are a couple of years away from stepping into your own classroom, you will be facing your first class of students at a time when two powerful trends seem to be on a collision course. On the one hand, there are the policy makers and community members who are calling for greater accountability on the part of educators; on the other hand, there are the teachers, principals, administrators, and theoreticians who are increasingly concerned with school restructuring, teacher empowerment, and integrated curricular approaches, making education more meaningful and exciting for students. As one group calls for the use of more objective measures of documenting learning outcomes, those working most closely with learners are expressing a desire to utilize more "authentic" strategies for marking student progress and pointing the directions for educational reform. Although the end goal for these respective groups may be the same, the routes for getting there appear to be at odds.

TRADITIONAL PURPOSES OF CLASSROOM ASSESSMENT

Traditionally, assessment has sought to serve two purpose in education:

1. To guide instructional decisions
2. To ensure accountability

Unfortunately, most of our assessment measures are still designed largely for the purpose of ensuring accountability as opposed to making informed instructional decisions. Measures of assessment for the purposes of accountability focus upon the outcomes of student learning. Assessment measures administered primarily to demonstrate level of competence attained by students offers little guidance by which teachers can make improved instructional decisions, because they are not connected to the educational process. For example, if students score low on a particular measure of achievement, how do teachers determine what is responsible for the low score, and more importantly, what can they do to enable students to experience greater suc-

cess? If teachers do not know what is responsible for disappointing student learning outcomes, then it will be difficult to identify procedures that will lead to improved outcomes. On the other hand, assessment that is linked to instructional episodes provides teachers with information about students that can directly guide the moment-to-moment decisions they make regarding the students in their classrooms.

Pedagogical Assessment

There are massive efforts within the U.S. school system to reform public education. But if the goal of these reform efforts is to improve the quality of education, then assessment of educational outcomes needs to be linked to the educational process. The emphasis upon assessment measures, inextricably linked to the instructional process, has spawned a new term: *pedagogical assessment,* an assessment that is designed to teach as well as to test. In the process of linking testing with instruction, the role of the teacher has become more central to the assessment process than ever before. No longer is the teacher merely a reporter or conveyer of test results. The roles of both teachers and students have been greatly expanded with the shift from formal assessment procedures to pedagogical assessment.

Institutional Assessment vs. Pedagogical Assessment

Institutional, or traditional, assessment, follows a scientific model in which improvement is accomplished through a step by step procedure. Traditionally, assessment is achieved by initially collecting and analyzing data, followed by making a diagnosis of the problem, leading to making the improvements and/or indicated changes, and then, ideally, retesting to see if changes have been effective. Each step in the scientific model is separate and distinct. In keeping with scientific form, the scientist (or teacher in this case), does not contaminate the assessment data by mixing actions of making improvements while assessing the quality of instruction as it currently exists. In pedagogical assessment, however, assessment and improvement are simultaneous and continuous. With the advent of pedagogical assessment, new requirements and conditions for teachers have come into existence. No longer is the main role of the classroom teacher to administer and evaluate student performance following instructional episodes. The integration of assessment and instruction, then, mandates a new breed of teacher. What is necessitated is a classroom teacher who is not only expert at delivering instruction, but is an astute "kidwatcher" as well (Y. Goodman, 1978). Teachers, employing pedagogical assessment, note when students are not "getting it," and intervene by experimenting to see what they can do to improve learning. A more appropriate metaphor for teacher, as "pedagogical assessor," might be a prize fighter, who instinctively reads the behavior of the other person in the ring and appropriately bobs and weaves in reaction to the other's actions. The traditional metaphor associated with the assessment role of classroom teachers has been one of a judge, sitting on the bench in juvenile court.

CURRENT CHANGES IN VIEWING ASSESSMENT

Literate behavior reflects both the *processes of learning* as well as the *products of knowledge;* thus assessment strategies must involve both. In the area of reading, however, assessment has often been limited to tests of decoding (figuring out unknown words by breaking them down into their component parts), knowledge of sight vocabulary (immediate recognition of words in isolation), and comprehension of brief story passages.

Viewing Assessment Holistically

Current views of assessment encompass a more holistic perspective. Teachers who hold such views regard assessment as a strategic means to determine what each student has learned, to build student self-esteem, to improve instruction, and to examine the processes by which individual students learn. Three guidelines are consistent with a holistic view of assessment and learning as a process:

1. Assessment should be child-centered and classroom-based.
2. Assessment should be viewed as an ongoing, natural part of daily instruction.
3. Assessment should emphasize student strengths: what students know, what they do, and how they have grown as learners.

Valencia (1990) has delineated four criteria that should be part of all assessment procedures.

1. Effective assessment is a continuous, ongoing process. In other words, it is much more than assessing the outcomes of learning; rather it is a way of gauging learning over time. Learning and evaluating are thus never completed, they are always evolving and developing.
2. A variety of assessment tools are necessary to provide the most accurate assessment of students' learning and progress. Dependence on one type of tool to the exclusion of others deprives students of valuable learning opportunities and denies teachers a well-rounded view of students' growth.
3. Assessment must be a collaborative activity between teachers and students. In short, students must be able to assume an active role in assessment so that they can begin to develop individual responsibilities for development and self-monitoring in the language arts. It is vitally important that means and methods be

provided that allow children the opportunity to objectively and subjectively measure their learning and to work along with teachers in making pedagogical decisions within all aspects of the curriculum.

4. Assessment needs to be authentic—that is, it must be based on the natural activities and processes in the classroom as well as at home. For example, relying solely on formalized testing procedures may send a signal to children that education is simply a search for "right answers." If teachers wish to portray learning as the processing and discovery of new information on a continuous basis, then they also need to give attention to evaluative measures that subscribe to that approach. Focusing exclusively on students' knowledge of skills (as may be presented with multiple choice tests, for example) may be counterproductive to their understanding of the language arts as a process.

THE DIFFERENCE BETWEEN AUTHENTIC AND PERFORMANCE ASSESSMENT

The terms *authentic assessment* and *performance assessment* are relatively new to the evaluation literature and are often used interchangeably. Although authentic assessment is a type of performance assessment, the two terms are not synonymous. The focus of this chapter is upon authentic measures of assessing student progress.

If you relate the notion of authenticity to your own life, you are probably keenly aware of when you are behaving in ways that are less than authentic. Whenever you are acting from a motivational base that is not from within, in order to please another person or to meet someone's expectations, you are not behaving authentically. The circumstances are similar when applied to youngsters in a classroom setting. Whenever students are performing for others, not for their own

purposes, they are behaving in ways that are distinct from what is genuine, natural, and/or self-motivated. Authenticity thus ceases to be present. With that somewhat sketchy distinction in mind, read the following assessment situations to see if you can begin to apply this distinction to language arts assessment:

Situation A: At the conclusion of each academic year, the local school district assesses the writing ability of each third-, fifth-, and seventh-grade student. The testing is spread over a four-day period, intended to parallel the sequence described in the "writing-as-a-process" instructional model. Teachers follow a strict script to direct students through each step of the writing process. On day one, students are provided with a topic and told to do some prewriting for 30 minutes or so. On day two, students produce a rough draft. Day three is devoted to revision and editing. On the fourth day, students are instructed to do their final copying and proofreading.

Situation B: In a neighboring district, at the same time of the year, students are similarly being assessed on their writing. In this case, however, the circumstances are different. Students schedule a conference with teachers for the purpose of selecting several pieces of writing to go into folders, showing growth in writing development since the last marking period from among the writings they have worked on throughout that period of time. The students have already selected the samples of their writing that they think best represent their writing abilities and the things about which they are most proud. Together with their teachers, they will decide which pieces will go into their folders and the reasons for their selections.

In both situations, performance assessments were made of students engaged in some aspect of the writing process. Were you able to see a clear distinction, however, between the two in terms of one being more "authentic" than the other? In Situation A, students were complying with the expressed wishes (instructions) of an authority figure, not for their own purposes. The context was a contrived one. In real life, individuals seldom write under the conditions imposed during a standardized direct writing assessment. So although Situation A represents a "performance-based assessment," it is not an "authentic assessment."

There are several reasons why Situation B is an example of authentic assessment:

1. It constitutes a naturally occurring event in the life of the classroom.
2. Both students and teachers are conferring about *real* writings that the students developed over time, under *real* conditions.
3. The interaction between teachers and students is a natural one. There is give and take on both sides. Everyone gets to talk and everyone learns how to listen to others.
4. The writing selection is assessed in the *process* of the young author reflecting and discussing the piece. Thus the intentions of the authors become clear as do the circumstances under which the writings were developed.
5. Performance is assessed in a context more like that encountered in real life.

What makes these situations examples of performance assessments is that they both seek to examine some type of performance in students, in this case performance in writing. Meyers (1992) discusses both kinds of assessment:

> Performance assessment refers to the kind of student response to be examined; authentic assessment refers to the context in which that response is performed. While not all performance assessments are authentic, it is difficult to imagine an authentic assessment that would not also be a performance assessment. (p. 40)

Performance assessment (also referred to as performance-based assessment) requires students to perform a task rather than simply answer questions. In Situation A, the task required was to produce a piece of writing. Each area of the elementary curriculum has its own types of tasks from which performance assessments can be created. The key to whether a task is a suitable one for a performance assessment is whether or not it is an important task in its own right. For instance, writing a cohesive paragraph is, arguably, important for students to be able to do. Circling consonants in a paragraph, however, is of questionable value in the real world and would probably not be considered a valid assessment.

The Context of Assessment

Authentic assessment means that evaluation of language learning can occur only during situations where children are actually engaged in language activity. The context in which assessment should take place is the context where living, learning, and language are occurring—*when* they are actually occurring. Teachers who truly believe that language and learning are *processes* must observe and interact with children when they are meaningfully engaged in the process of learning through language activity. The learning environment must be rich with opportunities and experiences that allow for observations to occur.

Revisiting Two Teachers

Let's revisit Jan Lin and Faye Lundrum, the two teachers who were introduced earlier in this chapter. They are about to begin the first day with their new class of students.

Jan Lin has already met her new group of first graders out on the playground and has warmly greeted each of them by name. She is already beginning to closely observe each of her new students to collect some first impressions. She has already noticed who made eye contact with her when she walked out to greet her students on the playground. She has noted the body language individual students displayed as they walked into the school—suggesting how they generally feel when venturing into unknown territory. She also observed that some students seemed to interact effortlessly with others, and some held back in order to size up the safety of this new situation. Mrs. Lin notes where the eyes of the children focus as they first enter the room and what things in the room the children seem to resonate to and which things go unnoticed. She has already logged in her mind the frail young girl who has not yet visually taken in any of her new environment and for the time being seems content to gaze down at the bow on her seemingly brand-new sash.

Jan invites the children to sit wherever they feel comfortable this morning—and watches closely as they make their selections. The furniture in Jan's classroom is deliberately arranged to create various-sized groupings, and she has made certain that there are at least three desks that are situated off by themselves. The initial selections that children make regarding their places in the room reveal a great deal. These first observations of new students are always sources of fascination for Jan Lin.

Jan is particularly intrigued this morning by one young lady who has now sought out five different locations in the room and cannot seem to decide upon one. She looks at Jan now as though to say, "Help me. Please tell me where I should sit." Jan is very conscious of first interactions of this type. She knows that among her primary goals is to foster the maximum amount of independence in these youngsters and yet have them feel safe and secure in this new environment. So she is deliberate in withholding any suggestion to her new student as to where she could sit—despite the child's silent pleas for her new teacher to come to her aid. Instead, she offers a reassuring look that seems to say, "Keep looking, I have faith in you that you will select a good spot for yourself in this classroom."

It is only 15 minutes into the first day of school, and Jan Lin is well into the assessment process. Already, she is aware of the wide range of linguistic abilities from listening to children informally interact with one another. Jan records these observations on a clipboard to which is attached a sheet of adhesive labels where she jots down her notations. Later, she will date them and organize them on notebook pages designated for each student.

When Jan directs students to gather around her at the back of the room, she continues her careful observations. It is here that she will read aloud to them for the first of many, many times—this time from Bill Martin's book, *Brown Bear Brown Bear.* . . . From the moment she draws their attention to the book and tells them that she is going to read to them, she is making mental notes:

Who has apparently been read to before?
Who already knows the story of Brown Bear? (She knows that this particular book is a very popular one with kindergarten teachers.)
Who is excited by the prospect of having a book read to them?
Who does not appear to care? Who cannot focus long enough upon the book to be either excited or disappointed? And which of her new students is just too reticent to show any emotion?

By 9:30 a.m., evidence of authentic assessment has been clearly established. As soon as she has an opportunity, Jan wants to jot down some of the things she has noticed about several children. Later, when her students are drawing a picture of something related to *Brown Bear,* she writes in a notebook:

9/3: John J. was familiar with the book and began to recite the text before I even had a chance to begin. Appears to be excited about being read to; I wonder if he is as enthused about his own personal involvement with books?

9/3: Cheryl H. did not enter into choral reading or discussion at any time. This may be uncertainty about this new situation she finds herself in. I will have to watch her closely this week; perhaps someone-on-one time with her would be helpful. Check w/ last year's teacher to see if this is normal for Cheryl.

9/3: Rashid M. familiar with author, Bill Martin.

Teacher Observation As An Assessment Tool

On the other side of town, Faye Lundrum is off to a different beginning with her students, yet her purposes are very much the same as Jan Lin's. Faye has orchestrated a literacy activity that will present her new students with an opportunity to demonstrate some of their attitudes, ideas, and skills related to reading. The day before, she carefully scanned her collection of books and selected a variety of books representing different genres and reading levels. Now students have already gathered in pairs on a large carpet. Each learner pair, including Faye and her partner, has a book in front of them.

They listen attentively as Faye announces that they are going to have a "book-tasting party." There are cheers! She gives each team a piece of paper and instructs them to "taste" a book in front of them and to rate it from one to five according to how well they like it. In all, her students will "taste" 10 to 15 books. Sixty seconds is allotted for each "tasting" and the book is then passed along to the next learner pair.

This activity is just one of the ways that Faye encourages her students to begin thinking about the books that they might want to read this year. In the process, she can assess the kinds of books her students enjoy reading and the authors that will be favored this year. She is also able to observe a great deal about the techniques her students use to make decisions about books, what her students know about surveying a piece of unfamiliar text, and how individuals interact with one another. As soon as the "book tasting" has concluded and the results are tallied, Faye jots down some observations about individual youngsters:

9/3: Joey S. shows broad familiarity with books. Applied no surveying skills to books which were unfamiliar to him.

9/3: Lisa A. was paired with Rosa A. today and accepted Rosa's rating of the books each time. I did not observe her taking any active role in this activity. (I don't know if this is revealing something about Lisa's overall reticence or just about this particular partner relationship.) I will have to observe her working with other members of the class.

Overall, Faye was able to observe, and verify through a follow-up discussion with her students, that they were aware of the strategies of surveying and scanning but that they do not equally and consistently apply the strategies for their own purposes in selecting books to read. She noted to herself that she wants to plan more opportunities for students to employ surveying skills and to become more aware of how she uses these techniques in her own reading so that she can share that with them.

From the moment their students arrived, teachers Jan Lin and Faye Lundrum have been actively involved in applying authentic assessment in their classrooms. In a very brief period of time, these teacher have collected an abundance of information on their students, which will provide the navigational guideposts to chart the beginnings of the ten-month journey they are about to embark upon with their students. You may already have noticed that not a single test has been administered, yet many of the interests, abilities, and learning needs of students are already apparent to these teachers. What may not be easily recognizable to the casual observer is the fact that serious and systematic assessment has been an ongoing and important element in both of these classrooms. This powerful and effective form of assessment is called *teacher observation,* a technique that is gaining among researchers and other professionals despite some lingering mistrust of classroom observation as a valid and reliable means of assessment (Genishi, 1985).

We are not referring here to the casual observation of children. Effective observational assessment requires skilled observers who possess in-depth knowledge of the developmental characteristics of children, the acquisition of language development, and the nature of learning itself. Teacher observation not only requires great skill on the part of teachers but necessitates constancy as well. By this, we mean that observational information is not a one-time occurrence. Collecting data on children needs to occur over time and must take place across numerous and varied settings. Bill Harp (1993) reiterates this message and suggests where teachers need to focus their observation:

> The power of using observations to evaluate a child is directly related to the amount of observation used to form the evaluation. Too few observations are just as dangerous as one-time testing to evaluate a child's language development. A good kid watcher is always looking for what the child can do. The total language development picture the teacher is attempting to build is based on what he or she has observed the child do, not on what he or she has not seen. (p. 78)

Teacher observation is one important aspect of authentic assessment. Equally important in authentic assessment is the opportunity provided to students to reflect upon their own growth and performance in the classroom. One powerful tool for motivating students to reflect upon their own growth as learners is through the use of portfolio assessment.

PORTFOLIO ASSESSMENT

Most professional artists have portfolios—collections of their best work that can be shown to galleries and art dealers. A portfolio is a coordinated assembly of past and present work, providing the viewer with a definitive and representational look at the depth and breadth of an artist's work.

Portfolios can also be used in the language arts to exhibit the talents and skills of individual students and to demonstrate their growth and progress. A *portfolio assessment* can be described as the accurate and systematic assembly of a student's work and academic development.

Researchers have developed their own definitions of portfolio assessment. Sheila Valencia (1990) defines portfolio assessment as "a philosophy that honors both the process and the products of learning as well as the active participation of the teacher and the students in their own evaluation and growth" (p. 340). Portfolio assessment relies on samples or evidence of student work to illustrate strengths and needs as well as the processes or strategies the student used. Students are involved in self-evaluation as they reflect on their learning by revisiting their portfolios. Teachers work with students to highlight students' strengths and needs while guiding them toward their goals.

Types of Portfolios

There are three basic types of portfolio designs to consider—and myriad teacher and student variations to meet the unique needs of classrooms and individual students (Tierney, 1991). Well-rounded portfolios often include elements from all three designs in order to be useful throughout the elementary curriculum:

1. *Showcase:* The showcase portfolio focuses on works selected primarily by students themselves. Students are thus given opportunities to choose their favorite and most representative pieces of work for inclusion into their portfolios.
2. *Descriptive:* The descriptive portfolio includes many works chosen by the classroom teacher. Student work may represent selections determined by either the classroom teacher or the student and measured against standards that have been collaboratively established by teacher, student, peers, and family members.
3. *Evaluative:* The evaluative portfolio is often considered to be a more directed type of portfolio and is more indicative of a quantitative approach to assessment than are the other two types. Materials in these portfolios may include unit tests from commercial reading

TABLE 4.1 Reasons Why Portfolios Help Students

1. They allow students to make a meaningful collection of their work.
2. They reflect strengths and needs.
3. They help students set personal goals.
4. They help students see their own progress over time.
5. They help students think about ideas presented in their work.
6. They represent a variety of work.
7. They illustrate the effort each student puts forth.
8. They help students understand their versatility as readers and writers.
9. They help students feel ownership.
10. They help students discover personal relevance in their work.

Source: Adapted from Valencia (1990).

programs, knowledge of content-area subjects, and spelling quizzes (Tierney, 1991).

Teacher philosophies, learner goals, and district-wide and school-wide expectations will all contribute to the relative weight given to these three basic portfolio designs.

Portfolio Contents

A portfolio can be a simple file folder or it can be a series of containers placed around the room, each container serving a particular function. There are no exact requirements for the contents of student portfolios, but here are some suggestions from teachers who use portfolios as a major

component in monitoring and assessing student performance:

1. *Examples of the student's work in progress.* Each piece is stamped with a "work in progress" notation (rubber stamps can be made up at most stationery stores or local printing firms) and included in a separate file folder.
2. *Dated progress notes written by the teacher.* These can include brief observational notes by the teacher or evaluative checklists prepared during a selected period of time.
3. *Dated progress notes written by the student.* Self-evaluative questionnaires, checklists, and narrative summaries might be included.

TABLE 4.2 Reasons Why Teachers Should Use Portfolios

1. They show respect for a student's work.
2. They facilitate discussion that reflects student strengths, versatility, interests, and efforts.
3. They show student development over time.
4. They establish a safe place to store collections that support student interests, decision making, and collaboration.
5. They invite parents to be involved.
6. They include students' explanations for the reasons for including particular works.
7. They reflect updates at regular intervals.
8. They showcase work for parents and peers.

Source: Adapted from Valencia (1990).

4. *Dated progress notes written by the parent(s).* Well-rounded portfolios also include notes and narratives solicited from parents regularly throughout the school year.

5. *Work samples selected by the teacher.* Teachers may wish to choose work that best represents a student's progress over selected periods of time.

6. *Student-selected work samples.* Students are encouraged to include work that they are especially proud of and that they feel is illustrative of their progress.

7. *Self-evaluation forms completed by students.* A student or teacher can create evaluation forms that become part of the portfolio.

8. *Anecdotal and observational records.* These are usually collected on students by the teacher, but items from peers and family members can also be included. Chronological samplings are most useful in charting student progress.

9. *Photographs/illustrations of student work or projects.* A camera, loaded with film, can be kept in the classroom at all times in order to take photographs of student works, plays, projects, special events, etc. These can be included in a portfolio.

10. *Audio or video tapes of student work.* Students may wish to record speeches, dramatic presentations, or choral readings to demonstrate their progress in oral reading activities.

11. *Experiments, project logs, content-area literature logs.* As students conduct scientific experiments or observations, they can record their predictions and discoveries in a logbook or journal. Selected samples can be included in a portfolio.

12. *Written work of any kind.* It is not necessary (nor is it practical) to place everything students have written in portfolios, but a representative sampling of students' works should be included.

13. *Lists of literature read and book projects completed.* Students may keep a running record of individual genres and numbers of books read, and a listing or brief descriptions of any accompanying activities.

14. *Reading response logs.* Students record their thoughts and perceptions of books they have read and include these notations as part of their portfolios.

15. *Writing samples.* Representative writing samples, across the curriculum, can be included in the portfolio. It is important to date writing samples and have them organized chronologically to demonstrate student progress.

16. *Conference records.* Any teacher/student conference notes can be considered for inclusion in a portfolio. Notes prepared by the teacher, as well as those penned by the student, would be equally important.

17. *Checklists, questionnaires, and survey forms.* Data recorded by the teacher, the student, or any other member of the class can be important elements in a portfolio.

The major criterion for including items in a portfolio is that they be representative samples of a student's work over time and that their selection be the result of a joint decision between teacher and student. It is crucial that "ownership" of the portfolio remain with the student.

What to Consider When Implementing Portfolios

There are many things to consider when instituting the use of portfolios. In *Portfolio Assessment: Getting Started* (1992), Allan DeFina lists several suggestions for implementing a portfolio approach. First, teachers should explain the methods, strategies, results, and implications to administrators and colleagues and to parents through newsletters or meetings. Students should also be introduced to portfolios and made partners in the process from the very beginning.

DeFina's suggests a "phase-in schedule" of implementing portfolio use. For instance, teachers should begin gathering student work gradually. They should discuss their reasons for the selections with students and invite their input, even if they see pieces of their work differently. The point of discussion at this point is to help students develop a criteria range for selecting work for portfolios that is meaningful for them. Gradually more and more of the responsibility for portfolio development, management, and evaluation can be given to students as they become ready to assume it. Students and teachers may wish to brainstorm a list of possible artifacts to include, keeping in mind the goals students wish to fulfill.

DeFina cautions that one of the most difficult aspects of portfolio use is matching portfolio assessment to district- or school-wide grading policies. The teacher implementing this method needs to consider alternative measures for most effectively reporting student progress in the classroom. Some teachers have experimented with supplementary forms, and some school districts have developed new report cards which reflect alternative assessments.

Prior to implementing portfolios with a class of students, teachers might begin by developing their own portfolios. In this way, teachers will better understand the difficulties their students will face in determining contents, setting goals, and self-evaluating (Graves and Sunstein, 1992). By beginning slowly and learning about portfolio use together, students and teachers will have greater appreciation and respect for the value of their portfolios.

Management of Portfolios

Utilizing portfolios as a learning strategy and assessment tool will require that teachers and students have additional time to get organized. Teachers must consider how their classroom environments will be altered by portfolios. Robert J. Tierney, coauthor of *Portfolio Assessment in the Reading-Writing Classroom* (1991), conducted a two-year study of teachers using portfolios. The study revealed that time management involves refocusing, setting new priorities, and using classroom time in different ways (p. 7) and that stu-

dents need time to conference with peers and the teacher, to visit their portfolios, to self-evaluate, and to select materials. Teachers will also need to schedule time for planning, conferencing, evaluating, and record-keeping. Initially, portfolio development is very time consuming for the classroom teacher. Eventually, however, the goal is to enable students to assume greater responsibility for the creation and maintenance of their own portfolios. Teachers may also want to train aides or parents to help with portfolio activities such as conferencing and goal setting. As students become increasingly familiar with the use of portfolios in their classroom, even these activities can be conducted with peers, thus reducing the dependency upon the teacher and classroom aides.

Techniques for Encouraging Student Ownership and Self-Evaluation

Student ownership and self-evaluative behaviors do not automatically accrue with the adoption of portfolios in the classroom. Teachers need to take deliberate action to encourage these behaviors in their students. Let's consider some of the ways that teachers have successfully encouraged students to assume greater ownership for assessing and evaluating their own work in the language arts.

Cora Five, a fifth-grade teacher from Scarsdale, New York, employs a technique adapted from one that was taught to her by Donald Graves (Five, 1993, pp. 48–51). Before the end of each grading period, Five hands out a batch of self-sticking notes to each student. The purpose of the notes is to encourage self-reflection on pieces of writing produced throughout the grading period. Five instructs her students to "spread out all of their writing" and "to choose one or two pieces with great leading lines and label those pieces with self-sticking notes." (Self-sticking notes have become such a common part of contemporary living that there is a comfort level associated with them that is not always present with ready-made "forms" designed to record students' judgments of their works.)

The technique described by Five can be used in all areas of the curriculum to foster responsibility-taking and self-assessment on the part of students. Teachers of younger students could certainly use this technique, but more modeling and group selection would be required before students would be able to engage in this type of decision making independently. The following are suggestions for additional categories by which students could categorize and reflect upon their written works (adapted from Five, 1993, p. 48):

Writings I learned something from
Great endings
Writings with lots of details
Still needs some work
My best effort
Favorite adaptation from another author's writing
Was (were) fun to work on
Most enjoyed by peers
Includes scientific facts
Weirdest
Funniest
Hardest to write
Good character development
Good use of quotations

The same technique can be used to encourage student self-reflection about books read, or listened to, which could be used for future writings. A set of index cards can be used for each book, containing the information shown in Figure 4.1. They can then be categorized and labelled as such:

Contains story starter ideas
Good examples of dialogue
Authors employ story twists
Great story endings
Good chapter lead-ins
Contains interesting character descriptions

In the process of making such value judgments, students develop increased feelings of self-worth and confidence. Hansen (1992) stresses the particular benefit that portfolios offer inner-city youth when she wrote about the experiences of students and adults involved in a Literacy Portfolios Project: "Many of the students in these inner-city schools think, 'I'm nobody.' Later, with a self-created literacy portfolio in hand, they say, 'This is me. I exist'" (p. 605).

The role that a literacy portfolio can play in affirming a child's existence is illustrated by the story of Lawrence, a ten-year-old boy from Newark, New Jersey. Lawrence was barely passing the third grade, for his second time around, when a group of education majors from the local college visited his classroom. Prior to observing the students, the college guests were provided with a "preview" of the students they would be observing from their teacher, a veteran of 18 years of inner-city teaching. They learned that the particular class of students they would be seeing had several "tough cookies" and that the "toughest" was, indeed, a freckled-faced little guy by the name of Lawrence. It became apparent from this teacher's description that Lawrence was at the lowest end of the ladder academically but numerically led the other members of his class, by far, in misdemeanors and misdeeds. To substantiate this last claim to Lawrence's fame, the teacher regaled them with several of his most notable "misdeeds." Finally, she shared with the group that she was using portfolios as one means of assessing her students this year.

Provided with the information supplied them by this teacher, the college students were anxious to learn more about the use of portfolios and what portfolio assessment could reveal about student's abilities. They thought that they were also prepared for Lawrence! But nothing that they had heard from this experienced teacher had prepared them for the contents of Lawrence's portfolio. Surely, they concluded, there must be two Lawrence's in this class! But, alas, there was only one—the writer responsible for these two small pieces of writing, contained in his portfolio:

Peace is something you need to have in your life. If you don't have it your life is worthless and means nothing.

The second piece reflected the sadness he felt over a student in his classroom who was unjustly accused of stealing.

> Nathan did not come back to school for six days and said nothing to anybody. I wanted to let him know that he still had friends. At lunch I sat next to him. I told Ronnie to shut up and wanted to hit him.

The writings in Lawrence's portfolio revealed a person markedly different from the description the visitors had received from his teacher. Later, when students reflected upon the classroom observation with their college instructor, they talked about Lawrence, the "social activist," the "champion of the downtrodden." It seemed obvious to the visitors that day that ten-year-old Lawrence had found his voice through writing.

The story of Lawrence supports Hansen's observation that literacy portfolios just might provide greater insight into who children really are more than their outward behaviors. This story also underscores the need for you as a teacher to look well beyond the surface behaviors of students. Students' writings yearn for readers to beckon to their calls of "Here I am!" to see not only the conventions of print but the real persons residing within. For every piece of writing you will receive from a student, keep in mind that you will have in your hand a piece of that child's being. How you treat such writings will provide youngsters with potent messages about themselves. Lawrence's teacher failed to notice the real child, the noble and admirable part of his being.

What lesson can we draw from this incident relevant to responsibility taking? Lawrence *was* taking responsibility for himself in this classroom. In fact, he was assuming responsibility for one of the most basic of human needs—the need for

FIGURE 4.1 Writing Helpers

TITLE:

AUTHOR:

GENRE:

TYPE:

SAMPLE:

PAGE(S) WHERE AUTHOR USES THIS:

recognition. The fact that he was receiving recognition in this class for behavior that added little to his sense of worth in the classroom was of lesser consequence than the fact that he *was* being noticed.

Virtually every interaction students have with their portfolios will likely become self-evaluative. Students may organize, arrange, and select arti-facts, plan future work, or share their work with others. Other possible reflective activities include rereading previous writings, revising writings, or determining topics of interest to pursue. Prepared charts and forms can be used by beginning teachers seeking to find ways to encourage self-reflection in students. Figure 4.2 presents an example that can serve as a starting point for students.

FIGURE 4.2   Portfolio Progress Sheet

Name: _____   Date: _____

Some things I have learned since the last "visit" to my portfolio include:

_____

_____

_____

My favorite entry is: _____

Because: _____

_____

My work shows that I have: _____

_____

_____

But, I still need to: _____

_____

I want to learn more about: _____

_____

_____

Here are some additional items I'd like to include in my portfolio before my next "visit":

_____

_____

_____

Advantages to Using Portfolios

Portfolios provide teachers, students, administrators, and parents with a concrete representation of student growth over a designated period of time. They also offer a forum to discuss that growth as well as procedures and processes that might stimulate further growth. Although portfolios are useful in parent–teacher conferences, they are even more beneficial in teacher–student conferences. Portfolios personalize the evaluation process, making it dynamic and relevant to the lives of children and useful in the planning and design of relevant lessons.

Despite the numerous concerns and time-consuming planning activities teachers associate with the use of portfolios, the benefits can be great. Teachers who use portfolios as primary sources for monitoring students' development in the language arts usually cite the following advantages:

- Students are encouraged to take more responsibility for their own learning.
- Students learn to set their own goals.
- Students are aided in discovering and defining themselves as readers and writers.
- Students become more aware of their strengths in reading and writing.

Note that each of the advantages is phrased in terms of how portfolio assessment benefits students, not teachers—although it was the teachers who were reporting the benefits.

The fact that teachers frame the advantages derived from portfolios in terms of benefits to students carries with it the implication that portfolios can be viewed as a child-centered form of alternative assessment and that child-centeredness is a core component of a whole language philosophy. Let's take a final look at the guidelines for establishing a child-centered approach to portfolio assessment in the classroom, presented in Table 4.3.

Setting Learning Goals

Student reflection leads naturally to students setting their own goals for learning. By reflecting on their previous accomplishments and struggles, students are able to see areas that need refining or further exploration (Graves and Sunstein, 1992).

Based on the type of portfolio and the depth of students' self-evaluations, many different learning goals are possible. Linda Crafton (1991) shares some of the goals that a group of elementary students in the Chicago area had after reflecting upon entries they had made in their journals:

Draw more pictures to go with my writing.
Say more than one thing about my topic.
Find new ways to start my journal entries.

TABLE 4.3   Guidelines for a Child-Centered Approach to Portfolio Assessment

- Teacher and students both add materials to the portfolio.
- Students are viewed as the owners of the portfolios.
- Conference notes and reflections of both the teacher and the student are kept in the portfolio.
- Students are encouraged to set criteria and categorize the contents of their portfolios.
- Portfolios need to reflect a wide range of student work, not only that which the teacher or student decides is the best.
- Portfolios are kept in an area where they are readily accessible to students.
- Students are free to peruse their portfolios at any time.
- Students' input is solicited by the teacher prior to parent conference time regarding portfolio contents they would especially like shared with parents.

Older students may have goals such as trying new writing styles, reading in other genres, or considering audience when writing. Teachers may assist students in generating goals during portfolio conferences. This collaborative goal setting may also represent a verbal contract between teacher and student. Reflecting upon their work and setting personal goals allows students to become responsible for the outcomes of their own learning.

A CHILD'S PORTFOLIO

We have presented here what the recognized "experts" in the field have stated about portfolios. We have scoured through the professional literature and have interviewed dozens of classroom teachers and administrators. It seems to us, however, that we need to hear from a real expert, someone on the receiving end of this alternative form of assessment. So before we conclude this chapter, we would like to present the wisdom of such an expert: nine-year-old Nicole, a student from the third-grade classroom of teacher Joan Pison. We are indebted to Joan and Nicole, for permitting us the opportunity to view portfolios from a child's perspective. Nicole satisfied our curiosities about the significance that the use of portfolios can have to a student and informed us about things we would not have discovered from reading the professional literature alone.

We learned from Nicole exactly how the students in this third-grade classroom select and manage their portfolio collections. The plastic crates containing the portfolios are conveniently located in the classroom where children have open and easy access to them. They are free to add works to their personal portfolio collection, but no piece of writing or other work can be placed into the portfolio without an accompanying form explaining the reasons why the student elected to place it there. At the con-

clusion of each marking period, the portfolios are subjected to a "purging process" (or "purging party," as the children refer to it). Together with Joan they decide what selections of student works should be purged and taken home, which pieces of work are still representative of current performance and, thus, should remain, and which ones should be transferred to another folder that serves as a guide to students in setting new goals for the upcoming marking period. Joan has found it useful to color code each of the teacher–student comment sheets which accompany portfolio selections to clearly designate the marking period for which it was intended. Anything on blue paper, for instance, is immediately recognizable as a September-November selection. Yellow designates inclusions from mid-November through mid-February. Although students know they must date each piece of work that goes into their portfolios, the presence of color-coded items makes growth over time all that much more evident to students, the teacher, parents, and visitors to the classroom.

Understanding better how portfolios are organized and managed within this particular classroom, Nicole then proceeded to "walk" us through her personal portfolio.

Item 1: Parent Response Sheet for Portfolio Review Nicole explained to us that this form (Figure 4.3) was completed by her mother, following parent and grandparent visitation day, at which time children share selections from their portfolios with family members. According to Nicole, "With the help of our teacher, Miss Pison, we get to organize the stuff in our portfolios ahead of time and she gives us time to practice explaining why things were selected to go into our portfolios."

Nicole's response sheet consists of two things that her mother really liked from the portfolio and one wish she would like for Nicole this year.

FIGURE 4.3   Parent Response Sheet For Portfolio Review

PORTFOLIO REVIEW

Date _____

Name _____

Two Stars

> Nicole's book report on Dr. Seuss with her art project was very "eye catching"
>
> Nicole's computer seal project was very neat and filled with interesting facts - Good job!
> * Two stars *

One Wish

> I wish Nicole will always _love_ to read and write stories with enthusiasm!

Comments written by Mother and Grandmother following Grandparent Visitation Day.

FIGURE 4.4   End of Making Period Review Form

One thing I like...	One thing I need to do better...
I Like how I read or books in my reading log.	write.
One thing my parent(s) would really like about my work...	One thing my teacher would notice about my work is...
how well I right in my journal,	How good I am in discussion.

Form used by students at the end of each marking period to review their selected works.

Item 2: "One thing I. . . ." "At the end of each marking period we look over everything that we have selected to go into our folders and we complete this form. One thing I liked was that I had 3 pages of books that I read in my Reading Log." (A sample of Nicole's log can be seen in Figure 4.5.)

Item 3: Reading Log "This is where we record all of the books we have read during this school year. We have to be sure we mark the date when we read each book, and Miss Pison asks us to rate

how we felt about the book. A smiley face means we liked it a lot; a straight face means it was just o.k., and a frowning face means we didn't like the book. We also tell when we finished reading the book. I liked just about every one I read so far, except one."

Item 4: Literature Discussion Forms and Group Matrix "Every week we meet with our discussion groups to talk about the books we are reading. We talk about what we are reading and then we fill out a Literature Discussion paper

FIGURE 4.5

BOOKS I'VE READ

Name: Nikki

Title/Author	Date Started	Date Finished	Rating
Clifford's BirThDay ParTy	10-26	10-29	☺
How The Grinch STole Christmas	12-16	12-18	☺
ArThur's ChrisTmas	12-16	12-16	☺
Our Hobbies	12-16	12-16	☺
HoliDays Around world	12-20	12-20	☺
Cam Jansen and THe mysTery	12-20	12-21	☺
if you made a million	1-3	1-3	☺
The village of round and Square houses	1-3	1-4	☺
The real moTher Goose	1-24	1-25	☺

Books read by Nicole between September and January as recorded in her Reading Log.

FIGURE 4.6 Literature Circles Reflection Sheet

Name Nicole Date 2/16

Title of book discussed Superfudge

Literature Discussion

1. How much did you participate in the discussion today?

about the right amount too much not at all (too little)

2. What was an important contribution you made to the discussion?

I sat and listend not saying a word exept for one questioN and telling about my book.

3. What was an important idea expressed by someone else in the group during the discussion? (Identify the person and tell what he or she said).

Christina, she read a part in her book, She told alot, and when she read she used expretion.

One of the forms used during Literature Circles which encourages students to reflect upon their contribution to the literature discussion.

FIGURE 4.7 Group Matrix Form

Date 2/22

Group Discussion

Selection

Children in group

Strategies:	Brett (Goosebumps (+) Say Cheese + Die)	Nicole (Superfudge (+) Judy Blume)	Christina (Arthur's (E) Valentine)	Joanna (The Three Bears (✓))	Robert (Valentine's Day (E))			
Makes predictions	~	~	~	~	~			
Adds to group's discussion	+	-	+	+	+			
Uses high level thinking	✓	✓	+	✓	✓			
Is able to retell	✓	✓	+	✓	+			
Has background knowledge	~	~	~	~	~			

CODE: D = dependent
S = somewhat independent
I = independent

Student feedback form used by Joan Pison during Literature Circles.

(Figure 4.6). This tells us how we did in the group, what important contribution each one made to the discussion. Then we tell one important thing a member of our group said.

"The Group Matrix (Figure 4.7) has the name of each person in our group and when Miss Pison listens to us in our discussion groups, she fills out this form. She also writes the names of the books we are reading. She listens if we 'Make predictions'; 'Add to group's discussion'; 'Use high level thinking'; 'Can retell the story'; and 'Has background knowledge.' A plus means that they did a really good job in any one of those areas during the discussion. A blank box means

FIGURE 4.8 Feelings About Reading

Name: _Nicole_

Date: _9 - 2_

1. **How do you feel when your teacher reads a story to you?**

2. **How do you feel when someone gives you a book for a present?**

3. **How do you feel about reading books for fun at home?**

4. **How do you feel when you read to your teacher?**

5. **How do you feel about how well you read?**

Form used by Joan Pison to monitor students' feelings about reading over the course of the school year.

FIGURE 4.9

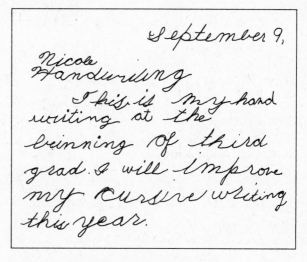

Nicole's September handwriting sample.

she did not hear us doing any of them; and a minus means that we did not do so good on that one. Sometimes we write that as one of our goals for next week. When we have a conference with Miss Pison, she discusses these sheets with us."

Item 5: Feelings About Reading "The Feelings About Reading form tells our teacher how we feel about reading. This one is from September. We did not do one of these in February, but Miss Pison says that we will do another one for our port-

folio at the end of the year. That tells her if our feelings have changed about reading."

Item 6: Handwriting Samples (Figure 4.9) "This shows how I wrote my handwriting at the beginning of the year. I did this one in September.
"We haven't done ours for February yet."

Item 7: My Garfield Story (Figure 4.10) "This is a page from the story I wrote about Garfield, my favorite cat, as President. I selected this to go into my portfolio because I put effort into it and because it was the first time I used humor in my writing. I used "Turkey" in two ways to give readers a laugh.

As we have seen through this portfolio, Nicole takes a lot of pride in the work she has included there. Not only is she deeply involved in her individual assessment process, she also realizes that assessment is a natural process of learning about her growth in all the language arts. It is far easier to determine how Nicole has progressed with these examples than it might be through more traditional forms of *evaluation*, which focus on end results rather than on the continuing process of learning.

FIGURE 4.10 Student Criteria for Portfolio Selections

Date _4/9_

This project is about _Gafied Experes as Presnit_

I want to include it in my portfolio because _I did a great job in putting efort into it. I Put facts and fumm & things_

GARFIELD'S EXPERIENCE AS PRESIDENT

Hi! I am President Garfield. I am going to tell you about my life. I am not allowed to be president for more then four years. Doesn't that stink? Well, I have 3 million people working for me. I love it! My favorite place is Turkey, I shot one yesterday, it was good! I also like to go to Italy. I eat a lot of lasagna there. I make $200,000 a year-it's great! I also have work, like bring the taxes down to zip! I have to keep the world peaceful, safe, happy, clean and find homes for the homeless. Well, that about wraps things up. That is all about my life!

Nicole's reasons for including her Garfield piece in her portfolio.

CATHY SWANSON'S JOURNAL

October 27

There is a healthy respect for humor and fun in this school, this has been engendered by our wise principal, Dr. Garis. What happened today made me reflect on what little appreciation there was for laughter in the course of my elementary experience, and how grateful I am that these students know something different.

Lynn Derstine has four rats in her kindergarten classroom. She claims that they are quite gentle and that the kids love them. (I do too, as long as they are in *her* classroom which is at the *other* end of the building!!) Somehow, Calvin the Rat, sleeping peacefully in his carrying case, ended up in a picnic basket on the desk of our reading specialist, Ruby. From there the rodent traveled to the principal's office, the guidance office, and eventually landed on my desk!

I discovered Calvin when we returned from lunch. The kids, of course, were fascinated with him and wanted to keep him for awhile. We decided, in the spirit of the whole affair, to keep him and to send K-3 a ran-

som note. We composed the letter together, deciding that if Lynn's class wanted their beloved Calvin back, they would have to visit our room and sing three songs.

Mara delivered the note which was in the hands of the stuffed mouse that lives in our reading corner! A response followed indicating the terms were acceptable, and within the hour 25 kindergartners, a harpsichord, student teacher Wendy, and Lynn knocked at our door.

The songs were wonderful and the fourth graders complimented the little ones on their performance (they knew how scary it must be for them!) They also assured the class that good ol' Calvin was well-cared for during his stay. The event ended as our class sang "Hit the Road, Rat" (more commonly known as "Hit the Road, Jack") and Calvin and company returned to their classroom.

These happenings are certainly not everyday occurrences. But the freedom to react spontaneously, in good nature, is a blessing and fosters warmth and sense of community among the children.

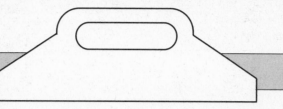

TEACHER AS LEARNER/TEACHER AS RESEARCHER

Anecotal Records

11/24: Joseph needed to spell the word "father" to go into his new story. After three unsuccessful attempts, he set out to find a book that he remembered seeing the words written in.

Joseph's teacher may not have realized the milestone that Joseph had just experienced if she did not have notations similar to this one from earlier in the year:

9/15: During individual conference time today, Joseph requested help with the spelling of six words.

Anecdotal records are one of the most versatile forms of record keeping on students. Collecting anecdotal evidence requires no special materials or training. A piece of paper, a pencil, and a keen eye for kidwatching are all that is needed to begin compiling anecdotal information. Compared to other forms of collecting observational data on students, anecdotal notes are used by virtually all teachers at some point over the course of a school year. Anytime written notations are made, where a student is identified and behavior is described, an anecdotal notation has been made. One teacher has described an anecdotal record as enabling her to "see" a child when that child is no longer in front of her.

The same attributes that contribute to the simplicity of compiling anecdotal records are at the same time responsible for their shortfalls. Although it is simple to record a single anecdote on a child, the goal of collecting anecdotal evidence is to make "consistent" (i.e., frequent) notations, "over time," and across a broad spectrum of circumstances, in order to compile an accurate picture of a child's overall abilities and needs. Our human tendency is to document in writing those slices of learner behavior that have impressed us in some way. This means that we are more likely to note student behaviors that may deviate from the norm, or may even irritate us in some way, which may not be representative of all that a child "contributes" to the classroom—and may divert us from looking at the "growth" that a child is making before our very eyes. Anecdotal records should provide us with a clearer picture of student performance and progress "throughout" the school year.

We have to be constantly vigilant to recognize our own biases as they influence the selection of behaviors we choose to record about a child. Anecdotal evidence, collected wisely, can be a powerful instrument for informing parents of their child's progress and for enabling teachers to recognize learning milestones when they occur in the classroom.

The letters in the word "anecdotal" can serve as a mnemonic (memory) device to help you remember some guidelines for furthering your own research and learning to use the anecdotal method of data collection:

- **A:** Involve another person, or persons, in collecting anecdotal records, if at all possible. Parents, volunteers, or other teachers can be asked to help.
- **N:** Note the circumstances in which the behavior transpired as well as the behavior itself. For instance:

  12–13: While working in a group with Allen, Jody, Zach, and Beth, Tommy volunteered to be the scribe and constructed a job list of what each person had to do on the science project.

- **E:** Every behavior is worth noting, because seeing patterns of behaviors over time is more important than any individual behavior or incident.
- **C:** Collect anecdotal evidence at consistent time intervals so that a clear and accurate picture of the child's

performance begins to emerge.

- **D:** Describe the behavior. Be careful not to judge the behavior in the anecdotal notation.
- **O:** Objectivity is the key to useful anecdotal records.
- **T:** Take notes in as many different situations, throughout all areas of the curriculum.
- **A:** Allow another person, whose judgment you trust, to occasionally view anecdotal records and see what patterns, relationships, and observations he or she may make. Often, a fresh perspective, devoid of some of the biases we use to filter our interpretations of observations we have made, will open our eyes to a child's strengths and abilities that we had failed to recognize ourselves.
- **L:** Let children in on what you are recording about them (unless, of course, you perceive the information to be destructive in any way to their self-esteem or confidence). You can derive important insights by inviting children to reflect upon the anecdotal evidence of their performance in your classroom. Keep in mind that most of your learning will come from "looking" and from "listening" to your students.

Journal Reflections

Select one or more of the questions below that interest you and respond in your journal.

1. Cathy's journal entry for October 27 reveals a very magical experience——certainly one that cannot be designed beforehand or included in a lesson plan. How will you foster and support those kinds of spontaneous events in your future classroom or school?

2. As a prospective teacher, with what aspects of assessment are you most comfortable? With what aspects are you least comfortable? Explain your reasons.

3. Imagine yourself in your first teaching assignment: You have not read the records of your new students from the previous year. What type of information would you like to gather about them in the first few days of school? How will you go about collecting the data?

4. Design your own question.
   ✓ What is a question you have about the chapter?
   ✓ How will you pursue the answer to that question?
   ✓ Respond in your journal.

REFERENCES AND SUGGESTED READINGS

Cambourne, B., and Turnbill J. "Assessment in Whole Language Classrooms: Theory into Practice." *The Elementary School Journal* 90, no. 3 (1990): 337–349.

Crafton, L. *Whole Language: Getting Started . . . Moving Forward.* New York: Richard C. Owen, 1991.

Crafton, L. "Whole Language: Getting Started . . . Moving Forward." Paper presented at Educator's Source Conference, Lancaster, Pennsylvania, December 12, 1992.

DeFina, A. A. *Portfolio Assessment: Getting Started.* New York: Scholastic, 1992.

Farr, R. "Current Issues in Alternative Assessment." Proceedings of a National Symposium cohosted by Phi Delta Kappa and ERIC/RCS held in Bloomington, Indiana, August 27, 1990: 3–17.

Five, C. "Tracking Writing and Reading Progress." *Learning,* (February 1993): 48–51.

Flesch, R. *Why Can't Johnny Read?* New York: Harper, 1955.

Fredericks, A. "Whole Language and Literature: Creative Ideas for Your Classroom." Booklet prepared for seminars held by the Institute for Educational Development, Medina, Washington.

Genishi, C., and Dyson, A. *Early Language Assessment.* Norwood, NJ: Ablex, 1985.

Goodman, Y. M. "Kidwatching: An Alternative to Testing." *National Elementary Principal,* (1978): 41–45.

Graves, D. H., and Sunstein, B. S., ed. *Portfolio Portraits.* Portsmouth NH: Heinemann, 1992.

Greenwood, S., and Smith, G. "Assessment in Whole Language Classrooms." Paper presented at Lehigh University, July 12 and 13, 1992. Workshop on Whole Language: Philosophy Implementation and Evaluation. Office of Continuing, Distance, and Summer Studies.

Hagerty, P. *Reader's Workshop: Real Reading.* Ontario, Canada: Scholastic Canada, 1993.

Hansen, J. "Literacy Portfolios Emerge." *The Reading Teacher* 45, no. 8. (1992): 604–607.

Harp, B. *Assessment and Evaluation in Whole Language Programs.* Norwood, M: Christopher-Gordon, 1993.

Hymes, D. L. "The Changing Face of Testing and Assessment: Problems and Solutions." *AASA Critical Issues Report.* Washington, DC: American Association of School Administrators, 1991.

Johnston, P. H. *Constructive Evaluation of Literature Activity,* New York: Longman, 1992.

Lamme, L. L., and Hysmith, C. "One School's Adventure into Portfolio Assessment." *Language Arts,* 68 (1991): 629–640.

Meyers, C. A. "What's the Difference Between Authentic and Performance Assessment?" *Educational Leadership* (May 1992): 39–40.

National Association of Elementary Principals. "Looking At How Well Our Students Read." (July 1991).

National Commission on Excellence in Education. *A Nation at Risk.* 1983. U.S. Dept. of Education, Washington, DC.

Smith, C. "Setting the Future Agenda." Proceedings of a National Symposium cohosted by Phi Delta Kappa and ERIC/RCS held in Bloomington, Indiana, August 27, 1990: 229–234.

Tierney, R. J., Carter, M. A., and Desai, L. E. *Portfolio Assessment in the Reading-Writing Classroom.* Norwood, MA: Christopher-Gordon, 1991.

Valencia, S. W., and Peters, C. W. "You Can't Have Authentic Assessment Without Authentic Content." *The Reading Teacher* 44, no. 8 (1991): 590–602.

Valencia, S. W. "A Portfolio Approach to Classroom Reading Assessment: The Whys, Whats, and Hows." *The Reading Teacher,* 43, no. 4 (1990): 338–340.

Valencia, S. W., and Paris, S. G. "Portfolio Assessment for Young Readers." *The Reading Teacher,* 44, no. 9 (1991): 680–681.

Yancey, K. B., ed. *Portfolios in the Writing Classroom.* Urbana, IL: National Council of Teachers of English, 1992.

MEETING THE CHALLENGES OF DIVERSITY

Contributions
Approach

Additive
Approach

**LEVELS OF
INTEGRATION**

Transformation
Approach

**MULTICULTURAL
LITERATURE
STUDY MODEL**

MODELS

Decision Making
and Social Action
Approach

Benefits — **MULTICULTURAL
LITERATURE**

Selecting Multicultural
Literature

Concerns and
Issues

Programs

Principles

**DIVERSITY IN THE
CLASSROOM**

**TEACHING BILINGUAL
STUDENTS**

Unit
Outlines

**MEETING THE CHALLENGES
OF DIVERSITY**

Monolingual
Teachers

**TEACHING GIFTED
STUDENTS**

Identification

Public Law
94–142

Instruction

Models

**TEACHING
STUDENTS WITH
SPECIAL NEEDS**

**TEACHING
AT-RISK STUDENTS**

Principles and
Practices

Learning
Disabilities

Inclusion

Principles

What I Know: Pre-Chapter Journaling

One of the questions classroom teachers are asking quite frequently these days is "How do I provide for the wide diversity of students in my classroom?" Unquestionably, you too will be teaching youngsters with different languages, customs, traditions, and religious practices. With that in mind, what are some special elements of *your* culture, heritage, traditions, or religion that make you unique?

Big Ideas

This chapter will offer:

1. The challenges and promises of a diverse and eclectic classroom.
2. The value of multicultural literature within the elementary classroom.
3. Some of the principles of bilingual education.
4. Definitions of "mainstreaming" and "inclusion" and their implications for the regular classroom teacher.
5. Some strategies for teaching students with learning disabilities.
6. The nature of at-risk learners and appropriate instructional strategies.
7. Identification of, and instruction for, gifted students.

Unquestionably, your future classroom will have a wide diversity of children exhibiting various talents, skills, emotions, languages, and perceptions. You may feel overwhelmed by the differences in your classroom, sometimes feeling as though you have to create 25 or 30 different curricula in five different subject areas in order to just begin teaching all your pupils.

Although all this diversity may, on the surface, seem overwhelming to you, it need not be. We believe it offers some unique opportunities for every class you teach.

1. Children will grow up and live in a pluralistic society. The attitudes and experiences they have in your classroom and the classrooms of your colleagues will help shape and determine their perceptions and interactions with their fellow human beings.
2. All children, no matter what their physical, emotional, or educational limitations, bring unique and distinctive talents to the classroom setting. A learning disabled student can also be one who scuba dives for a hobby or collects butterflies. The astute teacher will be one who takes advantage of those skills and talents so that they can be appreciated and enjoyed by all students in the classroom.
3. It is of particular importance to note that children are probably more alike than they are unalike. Although we may tend to focus on a single disability, skill, or handicap, those same youngsters watch TV programs other members of their peer group watch, they enjoy observing the same sporting events their classmates observe, and they eat pizza, ice cream, and peanut butter sandwiches—just like everyone else in the class. Indeed, one of your greatest challenges will be to see past the one or two "limitations" of particular students and work with the commonalities that all students have with their classmates.
4. It will be important to keep in mind the fact that you are teaching children more than you are teaching language arts. In other words,

you need to be cognizant of each student in your classroom and how you can provide for his or her instructional needs in an encouraging and stimulating environment. Language arts becomes one of the "tools" at your disposal that allow you to individualize instruction. In short, your language arts program should be built around the educational needs of students, not around a textbook or curriculum guide.

5. When working with students, you are not alone. Often there are specialists, clinicians, and other experts in the school who can be part of a "team approach" to the education of the children in your classroom. Included on the team may be special education teachers, diagnosticians, parents, social workers, representatives from community agencies, administrators, and other teachers. By working in concert and sharing ideas among all interested parties, a purposeful and practical education plan can be provided for each child.
6. Learners are not independent of each other (Borich, 1988). For example, a gifted student can also be physically handicapped; a learning disabled student can also be gifted; and a physically handicapped child can also be a non–English-speaking student. In fact, it can be argued that each of us has a unique set of limitations and complementary strengths. So, too, do our students. Capitalizing on the strengths each student brings to your classroom will be a teaching talent worth developing.

Isolating students solely because of a limitation or disability does more harm than good. Assigning a label of "learning disabled" or "culturally deprived" may be detrimental when it is done for the convenience of the educator and when it isolates the student from the mainstream of the class. It is important to note that when individuals are grouped according to one common characteristic, they will differ on many other characteristics that also affect their behavior. Sometimes the variation in the behavior occurring *within* a group of learners may be greater than the variation found *between* groups of learners (Borich, 1988). In other words, *integrating* students (and taking advantage of that combined pool of talents) is far more advantageous than *isolating* students (and reducing the "people resources" at your disposal).

This chapter will focus on some issues and concerns facing a teacher of the integrated language arts. We offer these ideas in the hope that you will begin to appreciate the wide diversity of youngsters in your classroom, the talents and abilities they bring to any lesson, and ways in which *all* students can be sensitized to the unique capacities and potential of every person. The "salad bowl" we call the elementary classroom is a microcosm of our larger society and offers unique learning opportunities that will last far beyond any curriculum guide or subject area textbook.

CELEBRATING MULTICULTURAL LITERATURE

Multicultural literature is essential for most classrooms today—particularly given the infusion of peoples from many countries and differing lifestyles into classrooms across the country. Including multicultural literature throughout a language arts or entire elementary curriculum holds the promise of extending all students' cultural awareness while at the same time expanding their appreciation of good books in a variety of genres.

We are not suggesting, however, that multicultural literature be used only by students who come from a country other than the United States, speak a language other than English, or have a cultural background or heritage different from "standard" American. Nor are we suggesting that multicultural literature be a small part of the language arts curriculum—something done for a few weeks during the school year and then "left behind" while students pursue other topics and other interests. The real value of multicultural literature for students lies in the fact that it can be infused—not *forced*—throughout all aspects of a language arts curriculum, naturally integrated into a plethora of activities and strategies throughout the school year.

Several educators have noted the benefits of using multicultural literature with elementary students, among them:

1. Using traditional folklore from various cultural sources helps students develop awareness of different language and cultural backgrounds (Piper, 1986).
2. Multicultural literature helps students grow in understanding themselves as well as others (Tway, 1989).
3. Through carefully selected and shared literature, students learn to understand and to appreciate a literary heritage that comes from many diverse backgrounds (Norton, 1990).
4. When students of diverse backgrounds read literature that highlights the experiences of their own cultural group, they learn to feel pride in their own identity and heritage (Harris, 1992).
5. Students develop social sensitivity to the needs of others and realize that people have similarities as well as differences (Norton, 1990).
6. All students, whether of mainstream or diverse backgrounds, learn from multicultural literature about the diversity and complexity of American society and can develop tolerance and appreciation for those of other cultural groups (Walker-Dalhouse, 1992).
7. Through multicultural literature, all students can gain a more complete and balanced view of the historical forces that have shaped American society and of the contributions of people from different cultural groups (Au, 1993).
8. Multicultural literature helps students expand their understanding of geography and natural

history, increase their understanding of historical and sociological change, broaden their appreciation for literary techniques used by authors from different cultural backgrounds, and improve their reading, writing, and thinking abilities (Norton, 1990).

9. Students can explore the concept of social justice through multicultural literature, which can be used to introduce key issues through well-drawn characters, authentic situations, and compelling stories (Au, 1993).

What is clear from the research is the compelling need not only to expose children to the wealth and variety of multicultural literature (no matter what their cultural or ethnic heritage) but also to infuse that literature naturally throughout the elementary curriculum. Teachers intent on exposing their students to the variety of literature available, and certainly the variety of multicultural literature, will want to be cognizant of the fact that the impact of that literature will be achieved only if it has been woven throughout the language arts and not "added on" to the curriculum. In short, multicultural literature achieves its greatest significance when it is considered as essential to all parts of the instructional experience and not as an adjunct to the language arts curriculum.

MODELS FOR TEACHING MULTICULTURAL LITERATURE

Multicultural Literature Study Model

Norton (1990) offers a sequential model for the introduction and study of multicultural literature in the elementary or middle school classroom. Its emphasis is on literature written specifically for children and adolescents, which is introduced to youngsters in a series of increasingly complex and related steps. The emphasis in this model is on helping children move from a simple awareness of a cultural or ethnic group to an investigation of specific literature written by members of that particular group.

Norton's model is significant because it provides youngsters with a complete and intensive study of a single cultural or ethnic group. That study, accomplished through a variety of literature choices (fiction and nonfiction), offers students more than a simple glimpse into a cultural/ethnic group. It provides an elaborate and diverse immersion in the customs, traditions, and heritage of that group that would ordinarily be unavailable in social studies textbooks. For example, five phases have been identified in this model:

1. A broad and general awareness of folktales, fables, myths, and legends from one cultural group (e.g., Native Americans, African Americans);

2. A "narrowing" of literature to those folktales, fables, myths, and legends of one or two tribal or cultural arenas (e.g., Native American legends from the Plains Indians; Black folktales from the southern United States);

3. Analysis of autobiographies, biographies, and informational literature from an earlier time in history;

4. Analysis of historical fiction; and

5. Analysis of contemporary realistic fiction, poetry, and biography written for children by authors whose work represents that cultural group (Norton, 1990).

Table 5.1 presents the five phases of this model along with some suggested literature for a unit on Native Americans. Note that these stages are related—each stage being dependent on the stage(s) that precede(s) it.

This model is significant because it provides a systematic introduction to and analysis of both traditional and contemporary literature of a specific culture. Students obtain a well-rounded approach to the use of multicultural literature which can last throughout the school year and well beyond single lessons.

Levels of Integration Model

Rasinski and Padak (1990) outline a sequence of four approaches to the teaching of multicultural literature, arranged in a hierarchy that moves from simple (familiarity with a cultural or ethnic group) to complex (taking action to solve important social problems):

1. Contributions approach
2. Additive approach
3. Transformation approach
4. Decision making and social action approach

TABLE 5.1   Sequence for Multicultural Literature Study (Native Americans)

Phases	Focus	Selected Literature
1. Traditional Literature	Identify distinctions among folk-tales, fables, myths, and legends. Identify ancient stories that have commonalities. Identify types of stories that dominate the subject.	• J. Monroe, and R. Williamson, *They Dance in the Sky: Native American Star Myths* (Boston: Houghton Mifflin, 1987). • E. Cleaver, *The Enchanted Caribou* (New York: Atheneum, 1985). • P. Gobel, *Buffalo Woman* (Scarsdale, NY: Bradbury, 1984).
2. Traditional tales from one area	Analyze traditional myths and other story types. Analyze and identify values, beliefs, and themes in the traditional tales of one region.	• O. Baker, *Where the Buffaloes Begin* (New York: Warne, 1981). • P. Gobel, *Star Boy* (Scarsdale, NY: Bradbury, 1983). • J. Bierhorst, *The Ring in the Prairie: A Shawnee Legend* (New York: Dial, 1970).
3. Autobiographies, biographies, and historical nonfiction	Analyze values, beliefs, and themes identified in traditional literature. Compare information in historical documents with autobiographies and biographies.	• D. N. Morrison, *Chief Sarah: Sarah Winnemucca's Fight for Indian Rights* (New York: Atheneum, 1980). • A. Marrin, *War Clouds in the West: Indians and Calvarymen* (New York: Atheneum, 1984). • R. Freedman, *Buffalo Hunt* (New York: Holiday, 1988).
4. Historical fiction	Evaluate according to authenticity of settings, conflicts, language, and traditional beliefs. Search for role of traditional literature. Compare with nonfictional autobiographies.	• F. Mowat, *Lost in the Barrens* (Toronto: McClelland and Stewart, 1966/1984). • S. O'Dell, *Sing Down the Moon* (Boston: Houghton Mifflin, 1970). • E. G. Speare, *The Sign of the Beaver* (Boston: Houghton Mifflin, 1983).
5. Contemporary fiction, biography, and poetry	Analyze the inclusion of any beliefs identified in traditional literature. Analyze characterization and conflicts. Analyze themes and look for threads across literature.	• J. Highwater, *Moonsong Lullaby* (New York: Lothrop, 1981). • V. D. H. Sneve, *When Thunder Spoke* (New York: Holiday, 1974). • J. Highwater, *The Ceremony of Innocence* (New York: Harper & Row, 1985).

Source: Adapted from Norton (1990), pp. 31–35.

Based on the work of James Banks (1989), this hierarchy may be viewed as moving from least important to most important along the following continuum:

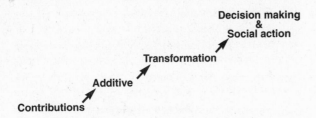

The Contributions Approach   This approach is used quite frequently in many classrooms to introduce special holidays (Cinco de Mayo) or important historical figures (Martin Luther King, Jr.) through a collection of relevant literature. The advantage here is that this approach offers youngsters an introduction, through literature, to customs, traditions, celebrations, and heritages without a major shift in the direction of the overall curriculum. As you might expect, there is a down side: Youngsters may be provided with only a superficial exposure to specific cultures or ethnic groups. Nevertheless, it can be an important place to start introducing students to a variety of multicultural and multiethnic literature (Cox and Zarrillo, 1993).

The Additive Approach   As in the contributions approach, the additive approach provides youngsters with exposure to quality literature without significantly altering the language arts curriculum. In this approach, however, a book or unit is added to the core curriculum, instead of being treated separately, as in the contributions approach (Au, 1993). For example, during a unit on African folklore a teacher may introduce students to *The Village of Round and Square Houses* by Ann Grifalconi (Boston: Little, Brown, 1986)—a story that describes a village in Central Africa in which the women live in round houses and the men in square houses and explains how those living arrangements came to be. Literature at this level adds cultural content, concepts, and themes, but it is not woven throughout the curriculum (Cox and Zarrillo, 1993).

The Transformation Approach   This approach requires a change in the basic language arts curriculum so as to promote the study of concepts, events, and issues from the perspectives of subordinate as well as dominant groups (Au, 1993). It is a balanced approach to historical and cultural events in that both sides of an issue are presented for discussion and reflection. For example, a book such as *The Matchlock Gun* by W. D. Edmonds (New York: Dodd, Mead, 1941), which presents an Anglo view of Native Americans as attacking savages, could be contrasted with a book such as *The Valley of the Shadow* by J. Hickman (New York: Macmillan, 1974), which recounts a massacre of Native Americans by Anglo settlers. An advantage of this approach is that children are exposed to two differing points of views about a singular topic and can be led into comparative discussions (and an appreciation for a different point of view) on important issues.

The Decision Making and Social Action Approach   This approach builds on the transformation approach and encourages youngsters to make some choices and decisions about significant issues. It melds the problem solving approach with children's literature in the classroom. Basically, children identify important social issues, gather information, clarify their values and assumptions, arrive at decisions, and take action to address the issues (Au, 1993). For example, students might gain a different perspective on World War II when they begin reading and discussing books written from a Japanese perspective: *Journey to Topaz* by Yoshiko Uchida (New York: Scribner's, 1971) and *The Journey* by Sheila Hamanaka (New York: Orchard, 1990) describe the interment of Japanese Americans during the war; *Hiroshima No Pika* by Toshi Maruki (New York: Lothrop, 1980) recounts the dropping of the atomic bomb through the eyes of a seven-year-old child. After reading selected books, discussing the issues, and participating in relevant activities, children may be encouraged to design action plans or a social agenda for presentation to parents, administrators, or community agencies (i.e., letters to the editor, community bulletin boards, newspaper inserts, essays contributed to children's magazine, etc.).

Selecting Multicultural Literature

There is a variety of resources from which you can select appropriate multicultural literature for your classroom. The implication is that not all literature that purports to be "multicultural" or "cultural" in nature is relevant for classroom use. In fact, there are far too many books that lack any cultural accuracy and, thus, should not be considered for classroom use.

Yokota (1993) provides a list of five key points that can serve as guidelines for any teacher wishing to use quality multicultural literature. Her points are summarized below:

1. *Cultural accuracy, both of detail and of larger issues.* Cultural accuracy means that issues are represented in ways that reflect the values and beliefs of the culture. This factor serves as the "umbrella" criterion; that is, it takes precedence over all other criteria. Included are richness of cultural details, authentic dialogue and relationships, in-depth treatment of cultural issues, and the inclusion of members of minority groups for a purpose.
2. *Rich in cultural details.* If readers are to gain a sense of the culture they are reading about, it is essential that details from the culture be included throughout the text. Details offer readers perceptive insights into the everyday lives of people of a specific culture and offer glimpses of factors that affect those lives.
3. *Authentic dialogue and relationships.* The dialogue used in a book must be an accurate and up-to-date representation of the speech habits and patterns of a specific group of peo-

ple. Too often, characters in so-called "cultural" literature selections use Anglo speech patterns significantly different from the speech patterns of the people portrayed in the accompanying illustrations.
4. *In-depth treatment of cultural issues.* Every culture has issues that are specific to it. It is vital that these issues be realistically portrayed so that readers can obtain authentic insights into the culture. For example, religion is a significant element in many Hispanic cultures, more so than in Anglo culture. A book about a Mexican-American family, for example, might have significant references to religious life.
5. *Inclusion of members of a "minority" group for a purpose.* Using minority figures in order to complete a "quota" of multicultural individuals detracts from the impact of the story. Characters should be regarded as distinct individuals whose lives are rooted in their culture—no matter how minor their role in the story.

The criteria above can help teachers in determining the appropriateness of specific pieces of literature for a true multicultural perspective. Tway (1989) suggests several criteria to be used in judging a book's usefulness for raising awareness of other cultures and differences.

1. An authentic cultural and historical perspective should be reflected.
2. Individual differences among people, despite a common heritage, should be shown.
3. Characters should hold positions in society apart from their heritage, and because of their abilities.
4. The story should evolve from the plot and character development rather than preexisting conceptions of a group.
5. White middle-class characters should not always set the norm; minorities should not always be victims.
6. Books set in urban areas should show a range of heritages, and characters should be three-dimensional and not stereotyped.

7. Differences in language or dialect should be authentic, and not demeaning.

Selecting Books For too many years, books about specific cultural groups were rife with stereotypes and inaccurate depictions. Literature often portrayed some peoples as living in very quaint communities, working at menial occupations, lacking in social skills, or engaging in less than desirable pursuits. Children often came away with a distorted view of cultural groups (when they were mentioned) or no view at all, since far too many children's books dealt primarily with white, Anglo-Saxon, Protestant characters in middle-class situations.

Fortunately, there is a great deal of children's literature written and published today that can assist youngsters in developing a unique perspective about their own cultural identity as well as gain an appreciation about the cultures and traditions of others. Here are some questions (from Latimer, 1972; Norton, 1993; Council on Interracial Books for Children, 1977) to consider in the selection of literature about cultural groups:

Do characters conform to old stereotypes?
Do characters have exaggerated features or do they look natural?
Do the characters represent unique individuals or are they merely representative of a group?
Does the clothing or behavior perpetuate stereotypes?
Is the presentation balanced or are the characters glorified or glamorized?
Does the author have a patronizing tone?
Is any dialogue true and authentic or is it merely an example of substandard English?
How accurate are any historical or biographical facts? Have they been altered to perpetuate stereotypes?
Does the book show the characteristics and accomplishments of characters in a realistic and authentic fashion?

Are the characters portrayed as individuals with their own thoughts, emotions, and philosophies?
Does the author use offensive or degrading vocabulary to describe characters?
Are the illustrations realistic and authentic?
Are problems handled realistically or superficially?
Is the language free of derogatory terminology?
Are any dialects used as a natural part of the story?
Does the book rectify historical distortions and omissions?
Are the characters respected for themselves, or must they display outstanding abilities to gain approval?
Does the author provide role models for girls other than subservient females?

Teaching Bilingual Students

The term *bilingual* refers to an individual's ability to speak his or her native language as well as English. Some estimates indicate that approximately 10 percent of the school-age population in this country speak languages other than English as their primary language (Baca and Cervantes, 1984). Obviously, not all the children in our classrooms are able to speak English as their second language. They may be recent arrivals to this country, they may use their native language exclusively at home, or they may not understand some of the patterns and grammar of English sufficiently to speak it with any degree of competence. In reality, many of these students are limited English proficient (LEP), which means that they may range from being unable to express themselves at all in English, either orally or in writing, to being marginally proficient in English (Borich, 1988).

When we discuss bilingual education, we are speaking of the need to provide youngsters with instruction in two different languages. Here is an excellent definition:

The term *bilingual education* refers to a mix of instruction through the medium of two languages. This means teaching skills and words in English as well as in another language, which in the United States is predominately Spanish. The primary goal of bilingual education is not to teach English as a second language, but to teach concepts, knowledge, and skills through the language the learner knows best and then to reinforce this information through the second language, in which the learner is less proficient. (Borich, 1988)

Bilingual Programs

There are several different types of bilingual programs available in schools around the country. The U.S. General Accounting Office (1987) has categorized bilingual programs as follows:

- *English as a Second Language (ESL):* Programs of bilingual education in which instruction is based on a special curriculum that typically involves little or no use of the native language and is usually taught only during certain periods of the school day.
- *Immersion:* General term for an approach to bilingual instruction not involving the child's native language. Two variations of immersion are structured immersion and submersion.
  Structured immersion: Programs of bilingual education in which teaching is in English but with several special features: (1) the teacher understands the native language, and (2) knowledge of English is not assumed.
  Submersion: Programs in which students whose proficiency in English is limited are placed in ordinary classrooms in which English is the language of instruction. They are given no special program to help them overcome their language problems.
- *Sheltered English:* Programs that use a simplified vocabulary and sentence structure to teach school subjects to students who lack sufficient English-language skills.
- *Transitional bilingual:* Programs of bilingual education with emphasis on the development of English-language skills in order to enable students whose proficiency in English is limited to shift to an all-English program of instruction.

Bilingual Education

Freeman and Freeman (1992) state that much of our traditional orientation to bilingual education has been based on some assumptions about the role of language arts instruction in the education of second language learners. The Freemans present a convincing argument for the fact that these assumptions serve to limit the potential of bilingual learners. Indeed, they reason, these assumptions may be a limiting factor in assisting ESL students in achieving appropriate levels of literacy. Let's take a look at some of those assumptions:

1. Learning proceeds from part to whole; i.e., for students whose native language is not English, it is necessary for them to learn (memorize) the individual elements of English in order to master the language.
2. Lessons should be teacher-centered because learning is the transfer of knowledge from the teacher to the student. In other words, the teacher needs to "control" the rate and intensity of second-language learning so that it is systematic and orderly.
3. Lessons should prepare students to function in society after schooling. After all, school is but one element in a child's life—he or she must be able to "deal with" the outside world with minimal language difficulties.
4. Learning takes place as individuals practice skills and form habits. Learning must be individually tailored to each second-language learner in the classroom through the use of workbook activities and appropriate skill sheets.
5. In a second language, oral language acquisition precedes the development of literacy. For example, students must be exposed to the

oral patterns of language *before* they are able to handle written language.

6. Learning should take place in English to facilitate the acquisition of English. The child's native language should be sublimated to the learning of English, since the child will be expected to function or communicate in English outside the classroom.

7. The learning potential of bilingual students is limited. Because second language learners are not familiar with the customs and conventions of native English speakers, their ability to learn English is restricted.

As you think about these assumptions, it should become evident that some "artificial barriers" have been placed in the path of second-language learners. The list above represents the ways in which many teachers have approached bilingual education in the past—a series of precepts we believe may be more limiting than stimulating. Implicit in those beliefs is the presumption that bilingual learners bring literacy limitations to the elementary classroom—limitations suggesting that they need a differentiated language arts curriculum (i.e., that they cannot participate in, or benefit from, the "regular" language arts program).

Unfortunately, these preconceptions and biases persist in many schools and classrooms. In contrast, Freeman and Freeman (1992), who have observed scores of bilingual classrooms around the country, have found that when classroom teachers use the principles of an integrated language arts perspective (as opposed to the assumptions above) with bilingual learners they discover higher levels of success and higher levels of literacy learning. The Freemans (1992) have taken those assumptions and presented seven principles that all teachers need to consider when working with bilingual learners.

1. *Lessons should proceed from whole to part.* It is important for second-language learners to see the big picture. Concepts are developed when they are able to start with the general ideas and fill in "gaps" with specific details. It is vital that bilingual learners understand where they are going as they learn their new language.

Instructional Strategies/Activities

- Shared book experience
- Reading to children
- Language experience
- Listening to tape-recorded stories and songs
- Students reading to students

2. *Lessons should be learner-centered because learning is the active construction of knowledge by students.* As you will discover throughout this text, children learn to become literate when instructional lessons begin with what students know (background knowledge) and build on their interests. In other words, learning is not the simple transmission of knowledge, but rather the *construction* of knowledge based upon what learners bring to any learning situation.

Instructional Strategies/Activities

- Publication of a classroom newspaper
- Journal writing
- Self-initiated questions
- Interactive brainstorming
- Bringing in native language literature to share

3. *Lessons should have meaning and purpose for students now.* It is vital that students not only know why they are learning something, but are also able to see some immediate relevance and applicability of that material to their daily lives. Learning should proceed from present needs to future needs.

Instructional Strategies/Activities

- Student to student letters; pen pals
- Invented spelling; invented grammar (see Chapter 13)
- Survival words, phrases

- Semantic webbing of vocabulary
- Thematic units (see section in this chapter on multicultural literature; see also Chapter 14)
- Daily journaling

4. *Lessons should engage groups of students in social interactions.* Collaborative work can be a powerful stimulus to learning. When children have opportunities to interact with each other—sharing ideas and concepts—then learning becomes a social function . . . a function of support and camaraderie. Group work does enhance individual achievement.

Instructional Strategies/Activities

- Cooperative learning
- Small group and large group work
- Language experience
- Simulations
- Group problem solving
- Pen pal letters
- Long-distance book exchanges
- Cross-age tutoring

5. *Lessons should develop both oral and written language.* True literacy learning comes about when children are immersed in all the dimensions of language (see Chapter 1). Consequently, the development of oral and written language can happen simultaneously (each supporting the other) when students are provided with realistic opportunities to use those language arts in a productive learning environment.

Instructional Strategies/Activities

- Language experience
- Modeled writing
- Content area reading and writing
- Word sorts
- Environmental print (menus, labels, billboards, etc.)
- Tape-recorded books

6. *Learning should take place in the first language to build concepts and facilitate the acquisition of English.* While we will agree that this will be a most difficult principle for you to embrace, particularly if you do not speak the native language(s) of your students (see below), we submit that acquisition of English occurs when youngsters are encouraged to build concepts in their first language. Recognition and *appreciation* of students' native language enhances their learning of the English language.

Instructional Strategies/Activities

- Oral presentations
- Native language books (commercial and student-created)
- Teacher presentation of instruction in the native language
- Classroom aids who speak the native language
- Concepts taught in the first language followed by concepts taught in English
- Valuing students' language and culture (e.g., learning students' languages, learning about students' cultures, hiring bilingual staff, allowing students to speak their primary language)

7. *Lessons that show faith in the learner and expand students' potential.* When teachers develop and plan activities that demonstrate a faith in the second-language learner's potential, they are offering a valuable framework for that child to become literate. This requires realistic, meaningful, and authentic lessons that support literacy learning for all students regardless of culture or language.

Instructional Strategies/Activities

- Sustained silent reading
- Individualized reading

- Shared book experience
- Alternative grouping patterns
- Portfolio assessment (see Chapter 4)

As you review these seven elements, you may note several similarities between this list and Brian Cambourne's conditions of language learning, which were presented in Chapter 1. Indeed, many of the elements of an effective bilingual program are parallel to the elements of literacy learning in any classroom. Let's take a look, once again, at the conditions of learning as advocated by Cambourne (1987) particularly as those conditions apply to bilingual students.

1. *Immersion:* Bilingual learners need to be immersed in a wide range of texts.
2. *Demonstration:* Bilingual learners benefit from explanations and models that allow them to see how texts are constructed.
3. *Expectation:* Bilingual learners are influenced by the expectations of their teacher (as well as of their classmates).
4. *Responsibility:* Bilingual learners develop language proficiency when allowed to make decisions about their language learning.
5. *Employment:* Bilingual learners need time and opportunity to practice and use their developing language skills.
6. *Approximation:* Bilingual learners learn language through many trial-and-error opportunities, not by memorizing "correct" English.
7. *Engagement:* Bilingual learners participate actively in the affairs of the language arts curriculum as well as in the "life" of the classroom environment.

Monolingual Teachers and Bilingual Students

At this point you may be asking yourself, "How will I be able to teach the bilingual students in my classroom if I don't speak their language?" The question is a good one but should not be one of undue concern. There are a variety of integrated language arts strategies and techniques you can employ in your classroom that will facilitate the literacy development of students whose native language is other than English, while yours may be strictly English. The ideas presented in Table 5.2, from Freeman and Freeman (1991), have been used by teachers in many different areas of the country and are effective in supporting the development of both English and the primary language(s) of students.

It should be evident that second-language learning is in many ways similar to first-language learning and that it is developmental in nature. We hope that the suggestions presented here provide you with effective methods and techniques by which you can offer your non–English-speaking students meaningful and relevant literacy experiences. The implication is that there are abundant resources at your disposal that can be utilized in helping your students achieve appropriate levels of language proficiency—even though you, as their teacher, may not be facile or conversant in their language.

PROVIDING FOR STUDENTS WITH SPECIAL NEEDS

For many years, teachers and administrators tried to provide for children with "special needs" by removing them from the regular classroom and putting them in isolated classrooms staffed by one or more specialists. For example, children with learning disabilities were all grouped together and provided with instructional procedures and materials that could be similar to or completely different from those used in the regular classrooms. This "pull-out" or tutorial approach to education was deemed educationally sound because the special needs of the students could be met on an individual basis.

However, as Wang (1986) notes, this practice may not be in the best interests of students:

The widely used "pull-out" approach—removing students with special learning needs from regular classes—has been the predominant strategy for structuring programs to improve the educational attainment of students with special learning needs. Although well intentioned, the pull-out approach neglects the larger problem: regular classroom learning environments have failed to accommodate the educational needs of many students. The pull-out approach is driven by the fallacy that poor school adjustment and performance are attributable solely to characteristics of the student rather than to the quality of the learning environment. (Wang et al., 1986, p. 26)

Public Law 94–142

One of the landmark pieces of legislation passed in recent years was Public Law 94–142, which was enacted in 1975 (and reauthorized in 1986 as Public Law 99–457). (It was also reauthorized in 1990 at which time a regular education initiative was added.) This legislation mandates that children be placed in "the least restrictive environment." Although it is up to each state as to how those four words will be interpreted, they usually imply that students (those with physical, emotional, social, and learning disabilities) will be educated in the same classrooms and with the same curriculum as their peers, except when special aids, devices, or services are required and are not available in the regular classroom.

According to the Education for All Handicapped Children Act (Sect. 619), students with special needs are to be *mainstreamed,* that is they are to be *placed into classes where they can receive the best education possible in the least*

TABLE 5.2   Ten Tips for Monolingual Teachers

1. Arrange for bilingual aides or parent volunteers to read literature written in the primary language to the students and then to discuss what they have read.

2. Plan for older students who speak the first language of the children to come to class regularly to read to or with the younger students and to act as peer tutors. For example, sixth-grade students might come to a first-grade class two or three mornings a week to share reading. This often proves beneficial to the older students as well as the younger students. Younger students can choose books to read to older students on certain days.

3. Set up a system of pen-pal letters written in the primary language between students of different classes or different schools.

4. Have students who are bilingual pair up with classmates who share the same primary language but are less proficient in English. This buddy system is particularly helpful for introducing new students to class routines.

5. Invite bilingual storytellers to come to the class and tell stories that would be familiar to all the students. Using context clues, these storytellers can convey familiar stories in languages other than English. Other well-known stories such as "Cinderella" have their counterparts (and origins) in non-English languages.

6. Build a classroom library of books in languages other than English. This is essential for primary language literacy development. At times, teachers within a school may want to pool these resources.

7. Encourage journal writing in the first language. A bilingual aide or parent volunteer can read and respond to journal entries. Give students a choice of languages to read and write in.

8. To increase the primary language resources in classrooms, publish books in languages other than English. Allow bilingual students to share their stories with classmates.

9. Look around the room at the "environmental print." Include signs in the first language as well as articles and stories in English about the countries the students come from.

10. Have students engage in oral activities such as "show-and-tell" (see Chapter 7) using their first language as they explain objects or events from their homelands.

Source: From Y. Freeman and D. Freeman (1991), p. 90.

IDEA BOX

The following resources are all excellent books which can assist you in designing an effective language arts program for non-English speaking students. Consider them as potential resources for your professional library.

Cummins, J. *Empowering Minority Students.* Sacramento, CA: California Association for Bilingual Education (CABE), 1989.

Edelsky, C. *Writing in a Bilingual Program: Había Una Vez.* Norwood, NJ: Ablex Publishing Co, 1986.

Enright, D. S., and McCloskey, M. L. *Integrating English: Developing English Language and Literacy in the Multilingual Classroom.* Reading, MA: Addison-Wesley, 1988.

Goodman, K., Goodman, Y., and Flores, B. *Reading in the Bilingual Classroom: Literacy and Biliteracy.* Silver Spring, MD: National Clearinghouse for Bilingual Education, 1979.

Nevarez, S., Mirales, R., and Ramirez, N. *Experiences with Literature: A Thematic Whole Language Model for the K–3 Bilingual Classroom.* Reading, MA: Addison-Wesley, 1990.

Willig, A. C., and Greenberg, H. F., ed. *Bilingualism and Learning Disabilities: Policy and Practice for Teachers and Administrators.* New York: American Library Publishing Co., 1986.

An additional organization which can provide you with a wealth of additional resources including: an information exchange, selected publications, a quarterly journal, and a newsletter which includes articles, job listings, book reviews, and conference information—all vital in helping you design an effective language arts curricula—is:

Teachers of English to Speakers of Other Languages (TESOL)
1600 Cameron Street
Suite 300
Alexandria, VA 22314
(703) 836-0774

---

restrictive environment. Mainstreaming is elaborated further:

- *Zero reject:* All children who qualify for special services must receive them. There can be no waiting lists.
- *Nondiscriminatory evaluation:* Children must receive individual evaluation, and the evaluation must consider the child's unique cultural and linguistic background. In some cases this means that the child must be evaluated in his or her native language. Each child must be reevaluated every three years.
- *Parent participation:* Parents must consent to evaluations, approve the special education placement, and participate in designing the child's individual education program.
- *Individualized education program:* An individualized education program (IEP), which includes the child's current performance and yearly goals, must be developed for the child.
- *Due process:* The family has the right to disagree with the decisions concerning their child. They may have the child evaluated by a professional outside the school or seek legal help to settle their dispute.

A key provision of Public Law 94–142 is that an individualized education program (often referred to as an IEP) must be developed for every youngster with special needs (i.e. special learning disability, giftedness). This plan is written in consultation with the necessary administrators, teachers, special education specialists, school counselors, and parents. It outlines the specific learning objectives for a child and how they will be carried out over the course of the school year. Each IEP is reviewed and updated (as needed) on an annual basis. An IEP must have the following for each child:

(A) a statement of the present levels of educational performance of such child; (B) a statement of annual goals, including short-term instructional objectives; (C) a statement of the specific educational services to be provided to each child, and the extent to which such child will be able to participate in regular educational programs; (D) the projected date for initiation and anticipated duration of such services, and appropriate objective criteria and evaluation procedures and schedules for determining, on at least an annual basis, whether instructional objectives are being met; and any assistive devices needed. (Public Law 94-142, 1975, Sect. 4, a, 19)

It is quite common, therefore, to find many classrooms with children of all ability levels working and learning together. To assist classroom teachers in providing the best possible environment for all students, consultants or special education specialists frequently work with teachers in providing materials, techniques, and accomodations useful in teaching students with special needs. Some schools may have a special room in which students with special needs can receive individual learning programs tailored to their special learning disabilities or abilities for part of the day, with the rest of the day spent in the regular classroom. Children who exhibit severe handicaps that preclude their performance in a normal classroom environment may be placed in resource rooms on a full-time basis—although this is the exception rather than the rule.

BOX 5.2

IDEA BOX

You may wish to obtain information and resources from a regional Bilingual Education Multifunctional Support Center. Here are just a few of the several around the country. Check your college or local public library for the addresses of others.

Bilingual Education Training and Technical
   Assistance Network (BETTA)
University of Texas, El Paso
College of Education
El Paso, TX 79968

Georgetown University Bilingual Education
   Service Center (GUBESC)
Georgetown University

2139 Wisconsin Ave. NW
Suite 100
Washington, DC 20007

Bilingual Education South Eastern Support
   Center (BESES)
Florida International University
Tamiami Campus, TRM-03
Miami, FL 33199

Bilingual Education Multifunctional Support
   Center
School of Education
California State University
5151 State University Drive
Los Angeles, CA 90032

We certainly subscribe to the notion that children with special needs, whenever and wherever possible, should be included in all activities and functions of the regular classroom. To do so, is to offer students of all abilities, talents, and skills those learning opportunities that can only accrue between and among different individuals and would not be possible in the truly homogeneous classroom.

Some Principles and Practices

You will undoubtedly have a diversity of children in your room—representing a variety of talents and abilities. With that in mind, we would like to suggest some generalized strategies for you to consider as you work with mainstreamed students throughout the language arts curriculum.

1. Be aware of the fact that mainstreamed students may not wish to be "singled out" for any special treatment. To do so may identify their specific learning disability or ability for other students and cause them to receive some form of attention they may not be able to handle. It is not necessary to "highlight" mainstreamed students in the classroom, and it may even be counterproductive to do so. Homework assignments, classroom behavior, participation in activities, and academic achievement should coincide with a child's ability and capability; however, teachers should not grant privileges to these students solely because of the disabilities (Pasch et al., 1991).

2. Ensure that your attitude and responses to mainstreamed students are identical to those of "regular" students. If you value the diversity of students in your classroom, then it is likely that you will achieve success in mainstreaming. All students should be viewed as contributing students. Teachers who have successful experiences with mainstreaming are those who see *all* children as individuals, get to know their strengths and weaknesses,
and attempt to meet their individual needs (Jacobson and Bergman, 1991).

3. Plan for longer periods of time for learning. Mainstreamed students may require extended periods of time to master a concept or to learn a specific skill. Information may need to be repeated several times and reinforced many ways.

4. Encourage all students to "tap into" their background knowledge and prior experiences. As we have indicated in previous chapters, that information forms a foundation from which new learning can emanate. This is even more important with mainstreamed students who often require concrete experiences upon which to base new concepts. Helping students relate what they are going to learn with what they already know can be one of the most significant features of any successful language arts lesson.

5. Do not fall into the trap of focusing on the weaknesses of mainstreamed youngsters. It is vitally important that you be aware of and seek to identify the individual strengths of every mainstreamed student in your room.

6. Be fair and consistent with praise, punishment, assignments, and granting of privileges (Pasch et al., 1991). In so doing you help students understand that grading, evaluation, and assessment are based on identifiable objectives in accordance with individual potential. In short, evaluation is not capricious and haphazard; it should focus not on the limitations of students but rather on their expectations.

7. Provide significant opportunities for students of all abilities to learn from each other. Structure a variety of learning activities in which students can teach other students in cooperative learning groups or other informal situations. Expand and extend the plethora of talents each student brings to your classroom.

8. Do not make inappropriate assumptions based on students' physical disabilities. Do not assume that a student who is confined to

a wheelchair is an unhappy child. Do not assume that children with disabilities are disabled in all areas or are less mature than those without disabilities (Biklen and Bogdan, 1977). For example, it would be inappropriate to treat hearing-impaired children as though they were mentally incompetent.

THE TREND TOWARD INCLUSION

Rusty McManus is an active, jovial, and energetic fourth grader in Sarah Jenko's class in a suburban school district on the outskirts of Denver. He makes friends easily and is always in the company of one or more classmates during any learning activity or lesson. He is an eager participant and has a particular fondness for math and science activities.

Rusty also has cerebral palsy, is mute, and needs a wheelchair to get around the classroom. He participates in class discussions using a "talking light" in which he moves an infrared beam attached to his head and points to keys on a computer keyboard. The computer then voices his thoughts and with the assistance of his instructional aide, Mrs. Kreger, Rusty learns alongside his classmates.

"I really enjoy having Rusty in my class," says classmate Sepea Washington. "I think we all can help him learn, and besides, he's fun to be with."

"I feel comfortable with Rusty in the class," states Michael DeForest, another classmate. "When I first met him, I thought he would have lots of trouble in the class. Since then, he's really done a lot."

It is evident that the tolerance, understanding, and kindness displayed by students in Sarah's classroom are an important factor in Rusty's acceptance into the learning environment. It is equally apparent that Rusty presents Sarah and the other students with some fascinating challenges in helping him become a functioning member of the class. But as one observer remarked after watching this class for an entire day, "This is a true 'Community of Learners'—everyone is working together in a true spirit of cooperation and collegial support."

We have addressed the notion of mainstreaming as a way of providing educational services for youngsters of varying mental or physical handicaps. The trend in recent years, however, has been to include all children, no matter what their handicaps, in most, if not all, the academic and social affairs of the classroom. This trend, referred to as *inclusion,* is slightly different from the concept of *mainstreaming.* For example, *mainstreaming* typically means that children with special needs should spend at least some of their time in classes with the regular school-age population while also receiving instruction in differentiated classes specifically tailored for their disability. *Inclusion* means that significant efforts are made to include youngsters with special needs in regular classrooms to the fullest extent possible. This trend also means the following:

1. Each child is provided with the most appropriate education in the least restrictive environment.
2. Most attention is given to the educational needs of children rather than to their clinical or diagnostic performance levels.
3. Alternatives are sought within the educational program of the regular classroom to better serve students with special needs.
4. Special education programs are unified with general education programs for the educational benefit of special-needs children (Petty et al., 1994).

Many teachers, although faced with the unique challenges presented by students with special needs, embrace the concept of inclusion. Their experience has been that these students benefit everyone—that there is a tremendous amount to be gained by having these students in the regular classroom. Youngsters with special needs illustrate that there are different ways to communicate and build a true *community* in the classroom, just as there is in the world outside the classroom.

Students with Learning Disabilities

Students with learning disabilities are those who demonstrate a significant discrepancy between academic achievement and intellectual abilities, which is not the result of some other handicap. Such discrepancies are found in one or more of the areas of oral expression, listening comprehension, written expression, basic reading skills, reading comprehension, mathematical calculation, mathematics reasoning, or spelling (Borich, 1988). It is not uncommon for teachers to encounter, and have to deal with, learning disabilities more frequently than any of the other impairments mentioned previously (Jacobson and Bergman, 1991).

A learning disability can also be defined as follows:

> A disorder in one or more of the basic psychological processes involved in understanding or in using language spoken or written, which may manifest itself in an imperfect ability to listen, think, speak, read, write, spell, or to do mathematical calculations. The term includes such conditions as perceptual handicaps, brain injury, minimal brain dysfunction, dyslexia, and developmental aphasia. The term does not include children who have learning problems which are primarily the result of visual, hearing, or motor handicaps, or mental retardation, or emotional disturbance, or of environmental, cultural, or economic disadvantage. (*Federal Register*, 1977, p. 789)

The following list presents some of the common indicators of students with learning disabilities. Please keep in mind that these traits are usually not isolated ones but rather appear in varying degrees and varying amounts in most students with learning disabilities. We are well aware of the fact that the disadvantage of a list such as this will be to isolate factors that typically appear in combination with other factors.

In fact, it is quite rare to find any two youngsters with learning disabilities who exhibit the same traits in the same amounts at the same time. So, for the time being, look at this compendium as a series of "markers" that are not mutually exclusive but rather may be intertwined in varying degrees (adapted from Fredericks and Cheesebrough, 1993; Tompkins and Hoskisson, 1991; and Smith, 1990). The child with learning disabilities:

is disorganized
is easily distracted
moves constantly
has poor listening skills
has trouble following directions
has poor verbal expression for his or her age
in inconsistent in behavior and work
confuses left and right
loses place when reading and repeats words
has difficulty with tasks employing paper and pencil
has poor auditory memory, both short-term and long-term
has a low tolerance level and a high frustration level
has a poor self-esteem
finds it difficult, if not impossible, to stay on task for extended periods of time
does not read fluently
uses immature speech and language
displays exceptional ability in the arts, sports, science, and verbalization
has coordination problems with both large and small muscle groups
displays inflexibility of thought; "stands by his or her guns"; is difficult to persuade otherwise

Again, we are not suggesting that all students with learning disabilities exhibit all of the characteristics; neither are we implying that the manifestation of one or more of these traits indicates a learning disability in any youngster. As a classroom teacher you will need to be aware of the interrelationships between and among several of these factors before referring a child for appropriate testing or evaluation. You should, however, be aware that the factors listed should be observed carefully over an extended period of time for any individual.

Instructional Implications   Youngsters with learning disabilities will present you with some unique and distinctive challenges throughout your teaching career. They will not only demand more of your time and patience but they will also require specialized instructional strategies in a structured environment that supports and enhances their learning potential. It is important to keep in mind the fact that students with learning disabilities are *not* students who are incapacitated or unable to learn—they need differentiated instruction tailored to their distinctive learning abilities. Listed below are a selection of appropriate strategies that have been proven successful in educating students with learning disabilities (adapted from Fredericks and Cheesebrough, 1993; Ford and Ohlhausen, 1988; Tompkins and Hoskisson, 1991; Routman, 1991; and Zucker, 1993). Knowing the learning needs of each of your students with learning disabilities will help you in selecting the strategies below (singly and in combination) most appropriate for your classroom.

- Provide instruction orally for students with reading disabilities. Tests and reading materials may be presented in an oral format so that the assessment is not unduly influenced by lack of reading ability.
- Provide students with frequent progress checks. Let them know how well they are doing, how they are progressing toward an individual or class goal, and what they can do to quickly correct any discrepancies.
- Provide immediate feedback. It is important for students with learning disabilities to quickly see the relationship between what

was taught and what was learned. Handing a test back several days after it was completed may be counterproductive for a student with a learning disability.

- Try to keep activities concise and short. Long projects are particularly frustrating for a child with a learning disability.
- Offer students a multisensory approach to learning. Take advantage of all the senses in helping students learn. If you tend to be a verbal learner, you are probably a verbal teacher. Be aware of your own learning and teaching styles and compensate for them (whenever necessary).
- Provide students with concrete objects and events—items they can touch, hear, smell, etc., and that will make learning a true hands-on experience. This will help those youngsters who have difficulty learning abstract terms and concepts.
- Make sure you provide specific praising comments that link an activity directly with some recognition and sincere praise. For example, say "I was particularly pleased by the way in which you organized the rock collection for Karin and Miranda" instead of just saying, "You did well" or "I like your work."
- When necessary, repeat instructions or offer information in both written and verbal formats. Again, it is vitally necessary that children utilize as many of their sensory modalities as possible.
- Provide meaningful learning opportunities through the use of thematic units or thematic teaching (see Chapter 14). Thematic units allow teachers to include a host of "hands-on" activities under a common "umbrella."
- Invite students to create a "Words I Can Write" notebook—a list of words they frequently encounter or use in both reading and writing. Adding to this list helps build self-esteem and serves as a record of progress.
- Whenever possible, use a variety of oral language experiences. For most students with

learning disabilities, oral skills will exceed writing or reading skills. Help students capitalize on that ability.

- Use predictable books. The regular pattern and sequencing of language helps children experience success in reading.
- Encourage students to engage in regular sustained silent reading (SSR) activities along with other students in the classroom. Be sure that books at a variety of reading levels are made available for all students.
- To facilitate writing development, allow students to use a word processor whenever possible. Seeing how a word processor does all the hard work of checking spelling and grammar can be a positive aid in the reading/writing development of learning disabled youngsters.
- Provide students with wordless picture books and invite them to create original stories for those books. Stories can be dictated to you or to students who can transcribe or record the stories on cassette tape for others to listen to and enjoy.
- Provide students with a series of open-ended projects—projects that require several students (of varying abilities) to tackle together and that demand differing levels of input or achievement. A classroom newspaper and a dramatic presentation are two examples of this type of activity.
- Plan group writing activities that allow children of all abilities to contribute to the final project. A bulletin board display, letter to the editor, small group journal, or diary would all be appropriate.
- Implement a cross-grade arrangement with a group of younger students. Encourage children with learning disabilities to practice the oral reading of a book or story that can be shared with a lower grade. These types of projects are always beneficial in terms of self-concept and attention.
- Experiment with repeated readings—that is, reading the same story or book several times.

One very beneficial technique is to tape record a book each time you read one to the class. Students can later listen to you "read" the story over again, as many times as they wish.

- Encourage cooperative learning activities when possible. Invite students of varying abilities to work together on a specific project or toward a common goal. Create an atmosphere in which a true "community of learners" is facilitated and enhanced.
- Provide regular opportunities for youngsters to engage in paired reading experiences. One student reads to another for a predetermined length of time; then roles are switched and the second student reads to the first. Make the assignment of student pairs a random choice so that all students may participate equally and without regard for ability level or friendships.

TEACHING AT-RISK STUDENTS

"At-risk" students are those who are in danger of "failing" the education system due to any number of reasons—reasons including, but not limited to, poor attendance, social or emotional difficulties, low achievement, behavior problems, limited language proficiency, limited intellectual abilities, or any combination of these factors. This is not to suggest, however, that these youngsters cannot be taught or cannot achieve a measure of academic achievement in the integrated language arts program. It does mean, however, that there is a significant portion of the school-age population who present teachers with challenges that must be addressed.

Unfortunately, it is quite easy to "label" academically challenged students and to provide instruction that is considerably different from the "average" or "above-average" students in a classroom. Our experience has been that at-risk youngsters have traditionally received a curriculum that is fragmented, skill-oriented, and divorced from the natural processes of learning (see Chapter 1). Too often, at-risk students have been provided independent curricula in reading, writing, listening, and speaking—the result being an instructional program that obscures the natural relationships that can and do exist between and among the literacy areas (Allington, 1994).

This fragmented and incoherent curriculum creates a literacy learning environment that is difficult and overly challenging for at-risk youngsters. It also presents a clash of philosophies since these students are typically engaged in a "skill and drill" program that assists them in mastering discrete elements of the language arts (this is usually done in a "pull out" program separate from the regular classroom) and a classroom curriculum that offers opportunities to read whole texts and participate in interactive activities. It has been these children—those experiencing the most difficulty making sense of the instruction they received—who have been asked to exhibit the greatest flexibility and to integrate the largest amount of diverse instruction into some coherent whole (McGill-Franzen and Allington, 1991).

Teachers who support an integrated language arts philosophy for *all* students are discovering that at-risk youngsters are offered more opportunities to become successful users of language than would be the case in fragmented programs. Students are able to see the connections between language elements because they deal with language holistically. Important, too, is the fact that the at-risk youngster is not isolated from the "community of learners" in the classroom by having to attend a class in another room or visit a specialist in another building. The integrated language arts classroom becomes supportive of the literacy development of *all* students—irrespective of the challenges they may bring or the skills they may offer.

Selected Teaching Strategies

The following strategies for at-risk youngsters have been proven to offer students meaningful,

authentic, and comprehensible opportunities to become language learners. Culled from a variety of sources (Fredericks, 1992; Routman, 1991; Galda, Cullinan and Strickland, 1993), they focus on important considerations in the design and structure of any language arts program. It is important to keep in mind that these strategies are important to use with all students but that they have particular significance for at-risk youngsters.

Giving Students Choices   At-risk students often have few opportunities to make their own decisions—decisions that will affect their enjoyment or use of all the language arts. Students who are provided with opportunities to make choices are students who are more self-assured and competent. When students feel some control over their literacy growth, they will want to invest more of themselves in that development

Here are some suggestions that give students opportunities to make their own choices:

- Allow students to select books they want to read. Do not make all their choices for them.
- Establish specific times to spend in silent reading. Allow students to select their own reading materials at this time and to interact with those materials in pleasurable and productive ways. A plethora of paperback books, an abundant and rich classroom library, and access to the school library can all be sources of reading materials.
- Provide opportunities for at-risk students to make decisions and to take responsibility for their own progress. Encourage them to ask their own questions, integrate their background knowledge and experiences, select their own books, design their own activities, and establish their own goals and objectives. In so doing, you can help students become less "teacher dependent" and more independent.

Allowing Students to Self-Monitor   Responsible learning occurs when students have opportunities to establish, monitor, and assess individual goals, and to make decisions on how they can become more actively involved in the learning process. Competent students do this quite naturally—often without thinking. That may be because they have assumed a measure of independence or because they are more internally motivated than at-risk youngsters.

At-risk students wear many monikers—yet it is important to note that their drive or level of motivation is often dependent on what others say or how others react to their academic performance. In short, at-risk students have a tendency to be "teacher dependent" rather than "student independent." Helping students achieve a level of independence and self-assurance can lead to higher levels of motivation and a more positive self-concept.

Allowing Students to Self-Assess   One very productive method teachers can use to help students assume a measure of responsibility is to have them engage in some self-assessment procedures. In so doing, students can begin to take control over their literacy progress and can become more independent. When independence is fostered, then reluctance to learn is diminished.

The following procedures can be used to help students engage in a process of self-assessment. Note that many of these can be implemented into a wide variety of classroom activities and can be used for specific individuals as well as small and large groups.

- Provide opportunities for students to establish their own goals for a lesson. Afterward, encourage them to decide if those goals were attained.
- Stimulate the development of student-generated questions instead of relying on textual questions.
- Model your own metacognitive processes as you share information with students.
- Provide opportunities for students to explain the reasons why they understood or did not understand parts of a lesson.

- Frequently allow students to evaluate their own predictions, purposes, and questions. The intent is not to validate "right answers" but rather to illustrate literacy as an active and constructive process.
- Allow students to state their own expectations or criteria for assignments.
- Encourage students to reflect on their errors and what they can do to learn from them.
- Help students assume responsibility for their own learning through activities in which they set, monitor, and assess their personal goals.
- Provide a variety of self-correcting assignments within each unit of study.

Using the Child's Language   In a subsequent chapter (Chapter 6), you will learn about the language experience approach (LEA) to learning. This strategy uses the language of the child as an important instructional aid. Children are encouraged to talk about things that are important to them, and that language is written down and used as textual material for lessons that follow. Skills, when necessary, come from the language the child has generated and which has intrinsic, personal meaning for that individual. The advantages of LEA are many, but this strategy holds particular significance for the at-risk learner because it places a value on what the child knows and can create.

Using Predictable Literature   Predictable literature is literature in which a pattern of words or phrases is easily discernible by the reader (or listener). In Chapter 10 you will learn about the significance of predictable literature in the integrated language arts program. Suffice it to say, these materials offer at-risk youngsters a level of "comfortableness" and familiarity that breeds success and ensures their active engagement in the learning process. Teachers have reported high levels of motivation, initiative, and interest on the part of students using predictable materials because literacy achievement is enhanced exponentially.

Repeated Readings   Reading a selection over and over again increases fluency, building confidence and enabling the student to focus on comprehension (Routman, 1991). Another advantage of repeated readings for an at-risk youngster is that familiarity with a text allows the student to utilize other language arts in extending activities and meaningful projects. Students also get a "feel" for the pattern, rhythm, and pacing of language "in action." As such, they develop an appreciation for the utility of language throughout all curricular areas.

Essential to the academic success of at-risk students is their inclusion in all the literacy activities of the classroom. The Community of Learners is enhanced considerably when every youngster is valued for what he or she can and does contribute to the class. At-risk students present unique challenges for the teacher of language arts, but they are also important members of the family of learners in any classroom.

Teaching Gifted Students

"The time has come," the Walrus said,
*   "To talk of many things:*
Of shoes—and ships—and sealing-wax—
*   Of cabbages—and kings—*
And why the sea is boiling hot—
*   And whether pigs have wings."*

—Lewis Carroll

Gifted students present a unique challenge to elementary teachers. They are often the first ones to complete an assignment or those who continually ask for more creative and interesting work. What those students frequently demand are ideas and materials that are not only challenging, but relevant as well. What they need are exciting activities and energizing projects that offer a creative

curriculum within the framework of the regular language arts program.

It has been estimated that between 3 percent and 5 percent of the students in this country are gifted. If that figure is true, then it is quite likely that you will have one or more gifted youngsters in your classroom each year. As with "special needs" students, gifted pupils will present you with challenges that may be unimaginable at this time. Suffice it to say at this point—they are not easier to teach than the learning disabled or "average" students; rather, they not only have more demands, but demand more of your time and energy.

Identification of Gifted Students

Gifted students come in all shapes and sizes. Let's take a look at one definition:

> . . . children capable of high performance, including those with demonstrated achievements or ability in any one of more of these areas—general intellectual ability, specific academic aptitude, creative or productive thinking, leadership ability, visual or performing arts, or psychomotor ability. (Sisk, n.d.)

Table 5.3 lists several other characteristics of gifted students. As in the case of learning disabled students, giftedness usually means a combination of factors in varying degrees and amounts, and no two gifted youngsters are exactly alike. Each has his or her own combination of distinctive characteristics.

Table 5.4 is an observational checklist teachers can use to help identify gifted students, particularly those students for whom a differentiated curriculum may need to be provided.

Models for Gifted Programs

Just as gifted students come in all shapes and sizes, so too do programs for gifted students. Here is just a sampling of some of the instructional options:

TABLE 5.3 Characteristics of Gifted Students

1. A high level of curiosity. Gifted children will examine, probe, poke, and look at everything in their path (and off the beaten path, too).
2. A well-developed imagination. Is prone to daydream and think of things that have never been thought before.
3. Often gives uncommon responses to common queries.
4. Can remember and retain a great deal of information. Can also retrieve that information easily and readily.
5. Not only pose original solutions to common problems, but can also pose original problems, too. Instead of asking, "Why is the sky blue?" a gifted child might ask, "What are the long range effects of a depleted ozone layer on the agricultural production of Third World countries?"
6. Ability to concentrate on a problem or issue for extended periods of time.
7. Can see and understand the various relationships between seemingly dissimilar things. For example, when asked to state the similarity between a dictionary and a rubber band a gifted student might reply, "The rubber band stretches, and the dictionary stretches a person's mind."
8. Gifted students are capable of comprehending complex concepts. They can deal with abstract relationships at high levels of cognition.
9. They can organize themselves and devise a sequential "plan of attack" for tackling most any problem. They can understand where to start as well as how to proceed toward a potential solution.
10. Gifted students are academically "energized." That is, they are excited about learning new facts and concepts and pursue learning tasks with a vengeance.
11. They are often independent learners—needing only a task (usually in the form of a problem) and a place to pursue that task to begin working. By nature they tend to be self-directed and exhibit an internal locus of control.

1. *The self-contained classroom.* One teacher of the gifted (often assisted by an aide) provides all the instruction. Students are removed from their regular classrooms and scheduled for the "gifted" room for various periods of time throughout the school day. Coursework may be devoted to single subjects (i.e. language arts) or may be cross-curricular. Assignment is usually for the entire school year. Often referred to as a "pull-out" program, this model is used by about 70 percent of the school districts in the country.
2. *"Enrichment" model.* Special projects and activities are provided for gifted students in the regular classroom. About two-thirds of the school districts in the country use this model.
3. *Combination model.* Nearly 25 percent of the school districts use a combination approach—students are "pulled out" for part of the day and are also provided with special projects in the regular classroom.
4. *Team teaching.* Two teachers, one classroom teacher and one teacher of the gifted, pool their resources and teaching strengths. Such a program provides for flexibility, individualization, and opportunities for large-group instruction.
5. *The integrated full-day program.* Pupils from different classrooms are "pulled out" for the whole day and given special or accelerated instruction by a teacher of gifted students.
6. *The departmental model.* In this model, which is popular at the junior high school level, students receive instruction in subjects from different teachers in different rooms.
7. *A regular classroom teacher assisted by a "gifted" aide.* The classroom teacher provides instruction to all the youngsters in the class. An aide supplements the instruction for gifted students with additional projects and activities.
8. *A district-wide center for gifted students.* Often referred to as a "magnet school," this model is usually offered in larger school districts. Students from various schools in the

district are bussed to a special school building to receive specialized instruction.

9. *Revolving door identification and programming model.* Renzulli et al. (1981) have identified a new concept for the education of gifted students. In this model, special programs are made available to a relatively large percentage of the student population (usually 15% to 25%)

TABLE 5.4 Observation Checklist for Gifted Students

Name: _____ Grade: _____

Date: _____

	Seldom	Sometimes	Consistently
1. Works well independently; requires little direction.	_____	_____	_____
2. Observes, explores, and investigates; asks thoughtful, searching questions.	_____	_____	_____
3. Analyzes a situation or problem in great depth and offers a variety of solutions and ideas.	_____	_____	_____
4. Masters and recalls factual information quickly.	_____	_____	_____
5. Concentrates for a long period of time when challenged and interested.	_____	_____	_____
6. Thinks logically; applies understanding in new situations.	_____	_____	_____
7. Generates unusual, unique, or clever responses; demonstrates creative thinking.	_____	_____	_____
8. Gives evidence of abstract, critical, and creative thinking; probes beyond the literal interpretation.	_____	_____	_____
9. Utilizes an advanced or extensive vocabulary for age/grade level.	_____	_____	_____
10. Attempts to understand difficult material by separating it into its component parts.	_____	_____	_____
11. Strives to improve and refine efforts by seeking suggestions; is self-evaluative.	_____	_____	_____
12. Develops new ideas or solutions when needed; is able to organize and bring structure to situations and ideas.	_____	_____	_____
13. Demonstrates special expertise in oral/written skills.	_____	_____	_____
14. Is an avid reader.	_____	_____	_____

BOX
5.3

FOR YOUR JOURNAL

Visit several elementary schools in your local area. Ask the principals and teachers about some of the provisions made for gifted youngsters. What special programs are in place for language arts? How much time do gifted students get to spend in long-term projects? Who is responsible for teaching or monitoring the gifted program? How does the gifted program differ from the regular classroom program? What implications are there for your future classroom or school?

known as a "talent pool" for short periods of time. Different levels of enrichment programs are then proposed for students: the first level is designed to capitalize on the existing interests in the talent pool and to promote new ones (Type I enrichment); the next level is designed to develop a wide variety of thinking processes and research skills (Type II enrichment). Eventually the most successful students in Type I and Type II programs go on to more creative work (Type III enrichment).

Instruction for Gifted Students

"Hey, Miss Ancona, did you know that Dr. Suess had his first book rejected by more than two dozen publishers?"

"I bet you don't know when the next lunar eclipse is going to occur?"

"Can I write to the Department of Commerce to get some statistics on the trucking industry in this country?"

"Can I do a report on some of the psychological interpretations of *Where the Wild Things Are?*"

"Hey, when are we going to do some real reading in this class?"

If there's one constant about gifted students it's the fact that they're full of questions—and full of answers. They're also imbued with a sense of inquisitiveness rivaling the best thinkers and philosophers of this country. Providing for their instructional needs is not an easy task and will certainly extend you to the full limits of your own creativity. Nevertheless, here are some instructional strategies for you to keep in mind.

1. Allow gifted students to design and follow through on self-initiated projects. Have them pursue questions of their own choosing.
2. Provide gifted students with lots of open-ended activities—activities for which there are no right or wrong answers or any preconceived notions. These can be initiated through open-ended questions (i.e. "How do different authors write their books?", "Why are there so many books about the environment?").
3. Keep the emphasis on divergent thinking—helping gifted students focus on many possibilities rather than any set of predetermined answers.
4. Provide opportunities for gifted youngsters to engage in active problem solving. Be sure the problems assigned are not those for which you have already established appropriate answers, but rather those that will allow gifted students to arrive at their own conclusions.
5. Encourage gifted students to take on leadership roles that enhance the language arts program. Developing a slide program which illustrates the life of a well-known author, making a videotape of students' reactions to the latest Caldecott winner, and sharing a collection of books on a specific topic are examples of appropriate activities.
6. Allow students to talk with writers, other language arts teachers, and people in the com-

TABLE 5.5   Five "Golden Rules" for Gifted Students

1. Gifted students should be involved in a facilitative learning process. They should be encouraged to plan and select assignments that meet their individual needs and interests. In turn, these self-directed explorations will lead to greater personal involvement and participation.

2. Gifted students should learn to assume more responsibility for their own learning. In doing so, they gain a greater awareness of their own abilities, develop a sense of self-direction, and improve their self-esteem.

3. Students must be exposed to a wide range of materials, assignments, and experiences—all designed to stimulate reading explorations above and beyond the textbook.

4. Divergent thinking skills need to be emphasized in concert with creative endeavors. Pupils should be encouraged to both process and interpret information. As a result, they will come to appreciate language arts as a multifaceted subject.

5. Students must be able to explore the language arts beyond the walls of the classroom. By using their skills in practical and meaningful pursuits, they will gain a heightened awareness of their own competencies.

munity involved in literacy-related occupations (librarians, professors, archivists, etc.) on a regular basis.

7. Put gifted students in charge of portions of the language arts program that require regular attention. For example, have them organize the classroom library so it is readily available for all students, monitor literature journals, or work on the details associated with field trips.

8. Provide numerous opportunities for gifted youngsters to read extensively about subjects that interest them. Work closely with the school and local librarian to select and provide trade books in keeping with students' interests.

9. Provide numerous long-term and extended activities that allow gifted students to engage in a learning project over an extended period of time.

CATHY SWANSON'S JOURNAL

November 11

Today was Plain Day! Sharon and I planned a day of celebration after our classes finished reading the book *Plain Girl* by Virginia Sorensen. We divided the students so that half would be "plain" children and half would be "fancy." I made caps and aprons for the plain girls and black hats for the plain boys. We also made fresh apple pies and played jacks (both activities taken from the book). As we wove in and out of the conversations these "plain and fancy" children were having, they shared their opinions about the book, its characters, its plot and resolution. We also held a Reader's Theatre—an absolute favorite in Sharon's class. The fact that Stephen could be nominated for a Tony Award has contributed to this activity's status! He played a remarkable Don (Esther's brother who leaves his people to see what life outside the Amish is like), complete with a pseudo-Pennsylvania Dutch accent!

Teaching can be a very isolated profession. A typical elementary school day does not allow for a great deal of interaction with other adults; most of the time is spent alone in the classroom with the kids.

It's important to share ideas, debate, laugh, commiserate with others on staff. A commitment has to be made to make time for this if one is to grow professionally (and maintain sanity!).

Feeling as though I would make better use of my time if I worked through lunch, I stopped going to the faculty room. I'd grab some crackers or an apple and headed right back to the room. What I accomplished in that time did not make up for what I missed.

Sharon reminded me today of the importance of being with other adults, of all the informal sharing that can occur. While I've been so busy trying to foster a sense of community in my classroom, I'd forgotten to maintain my membership in the community outside of it. Thanks, Sharon!

Last year I initiated a read-and-review club called the R.A.T. (Read and Tell) Club. The purpose of this club is to (1) motivate the kids to read, and (2) help to develop a collection of book reviews that they could refer to when looking for a good book. Since it was my first year in teaching, it helped me to very quickly get an idea of what kids this age like to read.

Along the perimeter of the membership cards I made were the abbreviations of the months. For every month a member reviewed at least 3 books they would get their card punched. Anyone with every month punched at the end of the year received a free book.

The reviews were pretty brief; they required a summary, title and author, genre, and a rating of 4, 3, or 2 stars standing for Excellent, Good, or Fair respectively. By June, we had a nice collection of about 150 reviews. These were written on 5 × 8 index cards and housed in a file card box in the Reading Center.

I kept those cards and incorporated them into our Reading Center in fourth grade. They serve as both a good resource and as good examples of what a review should be like. Although initial response was enthusiastic, this class didn't seem as motivated by this idea as my class did last year. Perhaps publishing a quarterly newsletter from the club to all the kids in fourth grade would keep their interest level up.

TEACHER AS LEARNER/TEACHER AS RESEARCHER

Field Notes

One of the most common ways you can collect information on your students is through the use of field notes—notes recording information or situations in your classroom as they are happening, rather than hours or days later when your memory of selected events may have faded. Field notes should be taken in an unobtrusive manner, and they should not detract your instruction or monitoring of student events and from the learning taking place.

Field notes can be as extensive as long paragraphs about selected individuals or as brief as a series of code words and symbols designating selected actions by members of the class. It may be important to share with your students the reasons why you take notes in class and how those notes are used to improve the instruction you provide. You may wish to share selected examples of your notes with students to remove some of the mystery from this ethnographic process.

Of course, we are not suggesting that you take notes throughout the entire day or on every student in the class. You may wish to designate isolated students for observation or a specific area of the curriculum for investigation. In deciding on what to observe and what to record you may wish to keep the following points in mind:

Who or what is to be observed?
What is the context of the observation?
What is being done (curricular or social)?
Why is it being done (curricular or social)?
Is the behavior isolated or consistent over time?
Am I discovering answers to preformatted questions?

As indicated above, it may be necessary to invent your own note-taking system or code. If so, plan to take time immediately after students have left for the day or during some other quiet time to review the notes and indicate any patterns or traits. It would be equally important to date your notes so that you may be able to track the development of behaviors. As such, field notes can then be shared with parents and administrators.

Journal Reflections

Select one or more of the questions below that interest you and respond in your journal.

1. Cathy's journal entry for November 23 indicates a very startling discovery. Why is that discovery so important in Cathy's growth as a teacher and how might it affect the students in her classroom?

2. Work with a classmate and list all the benefits that learning disabled students should derive from an integrated language arts program. How should they be involved? What should they get out of that program?

3. Design a language arts lesson with a multicultural emphasis. What types of projects or activities would be appropriate for all students—particularly for those students who have had limited exposure to different cultures and/or traditions?

4. Design your own question.
   ✓ What is a question you have about the chapter?
   ✓ How will you pursue the answer to that question?
   ✓ Respond in your journal.

REFERENCES AND SUGGESTED READINGS

Allington, R. L. "Reducing the Risk: Integrated Language Arts in Restructured Elementary Schools." In L. M. Morrow, J. K. Smith, and L. C. Wilkinson, eds. *Integrated Language Arts: Controversy to Consensus,* 193–213. Boston: Allyn and Bacon, 1994.

Au, K. *Literacy Instruction in Multicultural Settings.* Fort Worth, TX: Harcourt Brace Jovanovich, 1993.

Baca, L. M., and Cervantes, H. T. *The Bilingual Special Education Interface.* Santa Clara, CA: Times Mirror/Mosby, 1984.

Baltimore County Public Schools. *Summary Sheet for the Identification of Talented Students in Reading/Mathematics.* Towson, MD: Baltimore County Public Schools, no date.

Banks, J. "Integrating the Curriculum with Ethnic Content: Approaches and Guidelines." In J. A. Banks and C. A. M. Banks, eds. *Multicultural Education: Issues and Perspectives,* 189–207. Boston: Allyn and Bacon, 1989.

Borich, G. D. *Effective Teaching Methods.* Columbus, OH: Merrill Publishing Co., 1988.

Council on Interracial Books for Children. "Criteria for Analyzing Books on Asian Americans." In *Cultural Conformity in Books for Children.* Metuchen, NJ: Scarecrow, 1977.

Cox, C., and Zarrillo, J. *Teaching Reading with Children's Literature.* New York: Macmillan, 1993.

Federal Register, vol. 42. (August 23 1977). Washington: Department of Health, Education, and Welfare.

Flores, B. "Language Interference of Influence: Toward a Theory of Hispanic Bilingualism." Ph.D. diss. University of Arizona, 1982.

Ford, M., and Ohlhausen, M. "Helping Disabled Readers in the Regular Classroom." *The Reading Teacher* (October 1988): 18–22.

Fredericks, A. *The Gifted Reader Handbook.* Glenview, IL: Scott, Foresman, 1988.

Fredericks, A. *The Integrated Curriculum: Books for Reluctant Readers, Grades 2–5.* Englewood, CO: Teacher Ideas Press, 1992.

Fredericks, A., and Cheesebrough, D. *Science for All Children: Elementary School Methods.* New York: HarperCollins, 1993.

Freeman, Y., and Freeman, D. "Ten Tips for Monolingual Teachers of Bilingual Students." In K. Goodman, L. Bird, and Y. Goodman, eds. *The Whole Language Catalog,* 90. Santa Rosa, CA: American School Publishers, 1991.

Freeman, Y., and Freeman, D. *Whole Language for Second Language Learners.* Portsmouth, NH: Heinemann, 1992.

Galda, L., Cullinan, B. E., and Strickland, D. S. *Language, Literacy and the Child.* Fort Worth, TX: Harcourt Brace Jovanovich, 1993.

Gega, P. C. *Science in Elementary Education.* New York: Macmillan, 1990.

Gonzolas, P. C. "Beginning English Reading for ESL Students." *The Reading Teacher* 35 (1981): 154–162.

Harris, V. J. "Multiethnic Children's Literature." In K. D. Wood and A. Moss, eds. *Exploring Literature in the Classroom: Content and Methods.* Norwood, MA: Christopher-Gordon, 1992.

Jacobson, W. J., and Bergman, A. B. *Science for Children: A Book for Teachers.* Englewood Cliffs, NJ: Prentice Hall, 1991.

Latimer, B. *Starting Out Right—Choosing Books About Black People for Young Children.* Madison: Wisconsin Department of Public Instruction Bulletin Number 2314, 1972.

McGill-Franzen, A., and Allington, R. L. "Every Child's Right: Literacy." *The Reading Teacher* 45(1), (1991): 86–90.

Norton, D. "Teaching Multicultural Literature in the Reading Curriculum." *The Reading Teacher* 44, no. 1 (September 1990): 28–40.

Norton, D. *The Effective Teaching of Language Arts.* New York: Merrill, 1993.

Pasch, M., Sparks-Langer, G., Gardner, T. G., Starko, A. J. and Moody, C. D. *Teaching as Decision Making.* White Plains, NY: Longman, 1991.

Penfield, J. "ESL: The Regular Classroom Teacher's Perspective." *TESOL Quarterly* 21, no. 1 (1987): 21–39.

Pennsylvania State Education Association. *Common Questions about Inclusion.* Harrisburg, PA: No date.

Petty, W., Petty, D., and Salzer, R. *Experiences in Language: Tools and Techniques for Language Arts Methods.* Boston: Allyn and Bacon, 1994.

Piper, D. "Language Growth in the Multiethnic Classroom." *Language Arts* 63 (1986): 23–36.

Public Law 94–142, *The Education for All Handicapped Children Act,* 20 U.S.C. 1401 et seq., 89 Stat. 773 (November 29, 1975).

Rasinski, T., and Padak, N. "Multicultural Learning Through Children's Literature." *Language Arts* 67, no. 6 (1990): 576–580.

Renzulli, J., Reis, S. M., and Smith, L. H. *The Revolving Door Identification Model.* Mansfield Center, CT: Creative Learning Press, 1981.

Routman, R. *Invitations: Changing as Teachers and Learners.* Portsmouth, NH: Heinemann, 1991.

Sisk, D. *What If Your Child Is Gifted?* Washington: Office of the Gifted and Talented, no date.

Smith, S. "The Masks Students Wear." In K. Freiberg, ed. *Educating Exceptional Children,* 68–71. Guilford, CT: Dushkin Publishing, 1990.

Thompson, A. "If I Remember Everything." In *Watching Ants.* Ventura, CA: National/State Leadership Training Institute on the Gifted and Talented, 1990.

Tompkins, G., and Hoskisson, K. *Language Arts: Content and Teaching Strategies.* New York: Macmillan, 1991.

Tway, E. "Dimensions of Multicultural Literature for Children." In M. K. Rudman, ed. *Children's Literature: Resource for the Classroom.* Norwood, MA: Christopher-Gordon, 1989.

U.S. General Accounting Office. *Bilingual Education: A New Look at the Research Evidence.* Gaithersburg, MD: GAO/PEMD-87-12BR, 1987.

Waggoner, D., and O'Malley, J. "Teachers of Limited English Proficient Children in the United States." *NABE Journal* 9, no. 3 (1985): 25–42.

Walker-Dalhouse, D. "Using African-American Literature to Increase Ethnic Understanding." *The Reading Teacher* 45, no. 6 (1992): 416–422.

Wang, M. C., Reynolds, M. C., and Walberg, H. J. "Rethinking Special Education." *Educational Leadership* 44, no. 1 (September 1986): 26.

Yokota, J. "Issues in Selecting Multicultural Children's Literature." *Language Arts* 70, no. 3 (1993): 156–167.

Zucker, C. "Using Whole Language with Students Who Have Language and Learning Disabilities." *The Reading Teacher* (May 1993): 660–670.

Creating Literacy-Rich Classrooms

6

EMERGENT LITERACY

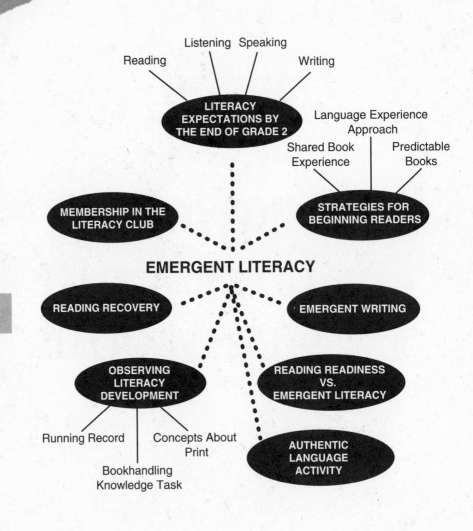

Reading Listening Speaking Writing

LITERACY EXPECTATIONS BY THE END OF GRADE 2

Language Experience Approach

Shared Book Experience

Predictable Books

STRATEGIES FOR BEGINNING READERS

MEMBERSHIP IN THE LITERACY CLUB

EMERGENT LITERACY

READING RECOVERY

EMERGENT WRITING

OBSERVING LITERACY DEVELOPMENT

READING READINESS VS. EMERGENT LITERACY

Running Record Concepts About Print

Bookhandling Knowledge Task

AUTHENTIC LANGUAGE ACTIVITY

What I Know: Pre-Chapter Journaling

Reach into your "memory bank" and think about the first one or two times someone read a book to you (if you can't remember, create a mental image of what that event might have been like). Describe that event in as much detail as possible in your journal.

Big Ideas

This chapter will offer:

1. The essential elements of emergent literacy.
2. Information on the "Literacy Club" and how youngsters become members.
3. Background on the literacy development of young children.
4. Shared book experiences in the classroom.
5. The use of the language experience approach in developing literacy.
6. Characteristics of emergent writers.
7. Expectations for second graders in listening, speaking, reading, and writing.
8. Early intervention for at-risk learners: Reading Recovery.
9. Assessment measures that evaluate what children know about literacy.

When Paul Bissex decided that he wanted some privacy, away from the bustle of family activity, he confidently posted the sign

DO NAT DSTRUB—GNYS AT WRK

on his bedroom door. His parents smiled as they quietly walked past his bedroom door, trying to honor his request and respect his privacy (Bissex, 1980).

Obviously, at the tender age of five and a half, Paul considers himself a writer. The reactions of his parents to his posted message not only affirms that fact but underscores for Paul the *power* associated with being a writer! His parents, on the other hand, are convinced that their son is indeed a genius, and they are oblivious to the four spelling errors in his message.

When Katelyn was 13 months old, she was sitting at a restaurant with her parents and was given a placemat with a cow pictured on it. Under the picture was written, "Rutters Family Restaurant." She pointed to the picture and made the sound that a cow makes: "Moo." She then pointed to the words under the picture and said, "Cow."

At age two, Katelyn was examining a carton of milk at the breakfast table on which the word "milk" was printed and recognized the K and L because they belonged in her name. Puzzled, she looked up at her mother and asked, "What are they doing at the breakfast table?"

At the age of three, Katelyn discovered some spotted cows while on a family vacation, after seeing the movie *101 Dalmations*. Later, while reflecting back upon her sighting of the spotted cows, Katelyn drew the picture shown in Figure 6.1 and exclaimed, "Those must be Dalmation cows!"

Also when she was three, Katelyn clearly identified the color that she was using while making scribbles on a piece of paper with a red crayon (see Figure 6.2). After labeling the color crayon, Katelyn appeared to go back and circle the letter attempts she made with which she was most satisfied and crossed out those that did not meet her specifications.

By this time she was requesting that certain books be read aloud to her over and over again. Sometimes she would read along and sometimes she would just look at the illustrations, seemingly caught up in the rhythm and language of the story. At three and a half, one of her favorite stories was *Goodnight Moon*, by Margaret Wise Brown, which she could recite by heart. Figure 6.3 presents Katelyn's depiction of the bear in *Goodnight Moon*. Alongside the picture is the "text" she included to retell the story. Figure 6.4 is a self-portrait of a decidedly happy Katelyn just three days before she was to begin school.

It is apparent that Paul and Katelyn have acquired a great deal of knowledge about literacy. As they act upon and interact with their respective environments, they are trying to construct *meaning* out of their young lives. The connections they make are not always accurate, but they often re-

FIGURE 6.1

Katelyn's drawing of a "Dalmation Cow"—age 3.

FIGURE 6.2

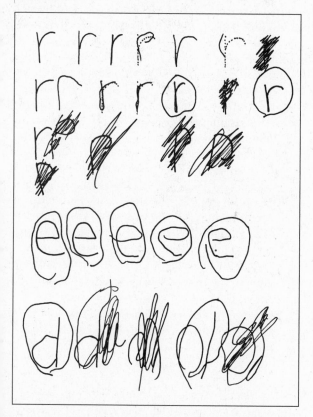

Katelyn, at age 3, identified the color of the crayon she was using (red). She then circled the best letters and crossed out the ones that did not fit her expectations.

- They are writers.
- Writing is a form of communication.
- Writing can be used to satisfy personal goals and to persuade others.
- Whatever they experience, they can talk about; whatever they can talk about, they can write down; whatever they can write down, they and others can read back.
- Reading is an enjoyable activity, and it can be enjoyed for its own sake, much like playing ball, helping parents prepare a meal, going to the park, etc.
- Reading and writing are means of connecting with significant others.
- Events can be recorded for processing later.
- Language and literacy are useful in making sense of their worlds.

FIGURE 6.3

Picture with the text of *Goodnight Moon* by Margaret Wise Brown, drawn by Katelyn at age 3½.

veal masterful competence at drawing conclusions that are temporarily useful to them in seeking to make sense of the things around them. As their acquisition of information expands, so does the accuracy and reliability of the connections they make. As much as "dalmation cows" are a real feature of Katelyn's world, so is the unfolding world of literacy. As these youngsters strive to make sense of their worlds and to communicate their needs and wishes to others, they are discovering reading and writing as dramatically effective tools. Let's identify just a few of the things about literacy which Paul and Katelyn seem to have discovered:

FIGURE 6.4

Katelyn's September self portrait—age 5.

Pretty impressive learnings, wouldn't you agree? Certainly neither Paul nor Katelyn could have expressed these understandings about literacy in the same manner as we listed them, but if we were to observe a consistent collection of behavioral portraits like those described above, we would be forced to conclude that these concepts about literacy have been internalized for both of these children. And you might note that they did not have to go to school to learn any of them. Merely interacting with their environment, in which literacy was a *natural* part, these children discovered, in meaningful and joyful ways, some of the most profound concepts about being alive and becoming literate.

What you have witnessed through these brief vignettes are aspects of the journeys taken by two young children toward becoming fully literate in our society. They are actually very far along in their journeys, but by many standards, they might be referred to as "nonreaders," or "illiterate" at this stage. But just look at how much they know about reading and writing already. In addition to the major concepts just cited, the informed observer would make the following points:

- They have acquired much of the vocabulary and most of the structures of the language that form the basis for all reading and writing.
- They recognize certain words in print by sight beginning with their own names and the names of the members of their families, colors, etc.
- They know that letters represent sounds.
- They know that letters can be strung together to make words that are equivalent to words spoken in the English language. (Bilingual children make the same discoveries in more than one language.)

As effective users of language, and written language in particular, it is evident that Katelyn and Paul are active members of the *literacy club*. This term—coined originally by Frank Smith in his book, *Reading Without Nonsense (1985)*—conveys the idea of being part of an exclusive club comprised of written language users. It is a very powerful message to share with children in your classroom as they voyage along with you, toward their full realization of literacy. According to Smith, "Children can join the literacy club with a single unqualified reciprocal act of affiliation. There are no dues to be paid, no entry standards to be met. A mutual acknowledgment of acceptance into a group of people who use written language is all that is required" (124). For beginning members, "errors are expected, not frowned upon or punished as undesirable behavior. . . . Children learn to identify themselves as members of the literacy club. They see themselves as readers and writers" (125). It is apparent that

Katelyn and Paul are already official members. They "own" their status as writers and, thus, are fully qualified for membership. Not all children, however, have emerged from backgrounds that have supported their literacy development. For those children especially, becoming members of the literacy club can be a powerful, motivational vehicle for wanting to embark upon the journey into literacy.

It is significant to note that this chapter on emergent literacy opened with a quotation from a young child—a child who has not yet entered school. This should implant in the minds of our readers that children do not come into our

FIGURE 6.5

PLEASE, MOM AND DAD . . .

MY HANDS ARE SMALL - I DON'T MEAN TO SPILL MY MILK.

MY LEGS ARE SHORT - PLEASE SLOW DOWN SO I CAN KEEP UP WITH YOU.

DON'T SLAP MY HANDS WHEN I TOUCH SOMETHING BREAKABLE AND PRETTY - I DON'T UNDERSTAND.

PLEASE LOOK AT ME WHEN I TALK TO YOU - IT LETS ME KNOW YOU ARE REALLY LISTENING.

MY FEELINGS ARE TENDER - DON'T NAG ME ALL DAY - LET ME MAKE MISTAKES WITHOUT FEELING STUPID.

DON'T EXPECT THE BED I MAKE OR THE PICTURE I DRAW TO BE PERFECT - JUST LOVE ME FOR TRYING.

REMEMBER I AM A CHILD NOT A SMALL ADULT - SOMETIMES I DON'T UNDERSTAND WHAT YOU ARE SAYING.

I LOVE YOU SO MUCH - PLEASE LOVE ME JUST FOR BEING ME - NOT JUST FOR THE THINGS I CAN DO.

The words to a poem that a young child might write to adults, reminding them that he is more than a small adult.

BOX
6.1

EMERGING AND EXTENDING LITERACY

In *Becoming a Nation of Readers,* the Commission on Reading divided reading development into two stages: emerging literacy and extending literacy. They may be defined as follows:

Emerging Literacy: During this phase, children take the important first steps in learning to read. Their readiness for reading depends on their ability to speak and listen, to experience, understand, and talk about things, events, and ideas in their world. During the emerging literacy stage, which usually encompasses kindergarten and first grade, students are taught to read to a fair level of fluency.

Extending Literacy: During the phase of extending literacy, children still have a great deal to learn about reading, even though they have developed the ability to decode words fluently and can understand simple, well-written stories. The focus of instruction at this stage of development shifts to teaching children how to use reading as a tool for understanding and mastering other subject areas.

Source: Anderson (1985) p. 61.

---

kindergartens and first-grade classrooms as empty slates awaiting some learned adult to unfold the secrets of literacy to them. In actuality, the foundations of literacy have been laid long before children enter school. For five to six years, children have been observing and using language—the very basis of literate behavior.

The term *emergent literacy* encompasses the idea that reading and writing development evolve from birth and continue until the time when children read and write in conventional ways (Teale, 1987). Emergent literacy follows a natural progression to the next phase of development, called *extending literacy.* These two stages are described in Box 6.1.

The importance of early integration of the reading process with the writing process is essential in developing early concepts about literacy. The merging of these two processes is enhanced when the children are exposed to a print rich environment beginning at an early age.

The language arts are rooted in childrens' experiences from which individual background knowledge emerges. Individual background knowledge about books is what the child brings from stories, first read aloud to him, and later to those he reads and writes for himself. It is from these early experiences that concepts are formed. Verbal interaction with a peer or an adult about an experience will enhance the memory of a concept. For example, if a child has been to the beach, some kind of feeling or emotion has been attached to the experience. The child has experienced excitement by jumping into the waves and being carried back to the shore. This experience could later be used to write a story. The child could then "read" the story. This is a firsthand illustration of the connection between reading and writing. Meaning is attached to the activity as a child relives his experience each time he looks at his picture and reads the text. This reinforces the concept that visual symbols have meaning attached to them. This is the emergence of comprehension skills (see Chapter 8).

This notion of literacy development emerging early in the life of the young child, and gradually developing over time, is in marked contrast with an earlier theory that viewed children as reaching a "coming of age" when they would be ready for formal instruction in reading and writing to commence, usually around the age of six and a half.

The term used to describe this view is *reading readiness*. According to such theories, the literacy abilities of Paul and Katelyn would be largely unappreciated as benchmarks of emerging literate behaviors.

LITERACY DEVELOPMENT IN YOUNG CHILDREN

All teachers who envision themselves working with young children will want to identify those principles that will provide the basis for advancing young children's abilities and love for literacy. The recommendations prepared by the Early Childhood and Literacy Development Committee of the International Reading Association are presented in Table 6.1 on page 174. Let's take a look at how a teacher can implement and enact some of those recommendations.

Building Instruction on What a Child Already Knows

In creating learning environments to foster literacy development in young children, whether in the classroom or at home, two overriding principles should remain at the forefront. First, young learners should be involved in real reading, and real writing, in contexts that are authentic. Second, instruction should respond to what the child already knows and needs to know about reading and writing.

One of your ongoing jobs as a teacher will be to *authentically* build upon what children already know. *Inauthentic* language activity results anytime we ask students to engage in tasks which lack a genuine context and meaning. (See Table 6.2 for examples.)

The Shared Book Experience

The very earliest memories that most children have of stories is being read to by someone in their lives who matters to them. Often it occurred just prior to bedtime, and the surroundings and associations recalled from these early times conjure up an array of positive feelings. The shared book experience is a method of immersing young children into good literature in a manner not unlike bedtime story conditions.

The shared book experience is typically conducted with an entire class. An oversized book called a *Big Book* is used, constructed so that the entire class can view the text and enjoy the illustrations at the same time. Likening the shared book experience to the familiar bedtime story situation, Butler and Turbill (1987) have identified the following elements, which you might try to replicate when you conduct shared book experiences with your students:

- The stories are shared in a warm, supportive environment.
- The child often chooses the story to be read.
- The adult reads the story to the child.
- Adult and child together interact with the printed page.
- The child freely participates in the reading of the story in any way he or she wishes.
- The focus is purely on relaxed enjoyment and following the story line.
- There is no expectation that the child will exhibit any "reading-like" behavior, although, if this does happen, the adult expresses delight and the child receives strong, positive, encouraging response.
- There are no obligatory follow-up tasks.
- Later on, the child often "pretend reads" the story to a teddy or a doll, or to self.
- Favorite stories are read over and over again.

Were you thinking about Brian Cambourne's eight conditions for learning (see Chapter 1) as you read through this list? If you go back over the list, you should be able to identify all eight. This is why this method is so highly recommended for instructing beginning readers. Another advantage of this method is that it accomodates all levels of book and print awareness on the part of students.

TABLE 6.1 Literacy Development and Pre-First Grade

Recommendations

1. Build instruction on what the child already knows about oral language, reading, and writing. Focus on meaningful experiences and meaningful language rather than merely on isolated skill development.

2. Respect the language the child brings to school and use it as a base for language and literacy activities.

3. Ensure feelings of success for all children, helping them see themselves as people who can enjoy exploring oral and written language.

4. Provide reading experiences as an integrated part of the broader communication process, which includes speaking, listening, and writing, as well as other communication systems such as art, math, and music.

5. Encourage risk taking in first attempts at reading and writing and accept what appear to be errors as part of children's natural patterns of growth and development.

6. Encourage children's first attempts at writing without concern for the proper formation of letters or correct conventional spelling.

7. Use materials for instruction that are familiar, such as well-known stories, because they provide the child with a sense of control and confidence.

8. Present a model for students to emulate. In the classroom, teachers should use language appropriately, listen and respond to children's talk, and engage in their own reading and writing.

9. Take time regularly to read to children from a wide variety of poetry, fiction, and nonfiction.

10. Provide time regularly for children's independent reading and writing.

11. Foster children's affective and cognitive development by providing opportunities to communicate what they know, think, and feel.

12. Use evaluative procedures that are developmentally and culturally appropriate for the children being assessed. The selection of evaluative measures should be based on the objectives of the instructional program and should consider each child's total development and its effect on reading performance.

13. Make parents aware of the reasons for a total language program at school and provide them with ideas for activities to carry out at home.

14. Alert parents to the limitations of formal assessments and standardized tests of pre-first graders' reading and writing skills.

15. Encourage children to be active participants in the learning process rather than passive recipients of knowledge, by using activities that allow for experimentation with talking, listening, writing, and reading.

Source: Literacy Development and Pre-First Grade. A joint statement of concerns about present practices in pre-first grade reading instruction and recommendations for improvement. Prepared by the Early Childhood and Literacy Development Committee of the International Reading Association, 1994.

Students sitting side by side might have had considerably different exposures to books prior to coming to school. Some may already be able to read with some degree of independence; others may not even be certain which direction a reader begins to read a book. Right from the start then, with the shared book experience, children inexperienced with printed matter have the opportunity to feel as successful as their more advantaged counterparts, after several repetitions of the story, while they follow along as the teacher reads aloud.

Students are also witness to some of the skilled reading behaviors on the part of their peers.

SUGGESTED PROCEDURES

There are many ways of conducting a shared book experience. At the outset you might be more comfortable with a step-by-step procedure to follow, but eventually when you become more at ease and realize the fun that you and your students can have with this method, you can become as innovative and as responsive to your students as you want. To get you started, here is a suggested procedure for implementing the shared book experience. As you read through the steps, note how you can use a story to teach a great deal about reading and writing while having an enjoyable experience with your students.

1. *In-depth introduction:* Draw the students' attention to the words and illustrations on the cover. Encourage students to make predictions about the story based on the cover illustrations and the title. Record the predictions that then become the purpose for reading. Name the author and illustrator. Point out the copyright date. Read the dedication aloud.
2. *First reading:* Read the book to the students in an enthusiastic, dramatic manner without interruptions. After the first reading, encourage the students to discuss their reactions and compare their earlier predictions with the actual events of the story read.
3. *Repeated readings:* This step of the shared reading experience may occur over a time span of several sessions. Repeated readings provide you with opportunities to observe students:
   - Understanding the story
   - Interpreting illustrations
   - Recognizing words and phrases
   - Self-correcting errors
   - Monitoring comprehension
   - Drawing on background knowledge
   - Participating in discussion

At appropriate times during the repeated readings, the following activities may be highlighted:
   - Underscore the text with your finger or a pointer to reinforce the sound-symbol correspondence.

TABLE 6.2   Authentic vs. Inauthentic Language Activities

Authentic Language Activities	Inauthentic Language Activities
• Talk about a picture and construct a web of words that emerge from the language used by students to describe the picture.	• Color the vowels in a list of words.
• Write an original sentence to describe a picture or an event experienced by the children.	• Make words in a list plural.
• Respond to a story in a manner of the child's choosing to share with a friend.	• Circle a clown's face that is different from others in a line.
• Discuss a story, or Read Aloud, from the point of view of the someone other than the main character. Draw a picture of a scene as seen from that person (or animal's point of view).	• Choose the correct word to complete a sentence from among four choices.
• Ask students to circle the words in their writing where they are unsure of the spelling and want assistance from peer or teacher.	• Match the rhyming words.
• Web out what is already known about the subject of the story.	• Read the story to answer the teacher's (publisher's) questions.
• Identify two or three questions that you think might either can be found in the story or that you would like to have answered.	• Exchange papers with your neighbor and place a check beside each incorrect response.
• Draw a circle around the answers you wrote in which you have the greatest degree of confidence.	

- Stop frequently for discussion and clarification; students may ask questions and comment about each page.
- Encourage students to read along.
- Use what is referred to as "oral cloze" by pausing before predictable words or phrases and encouraging students to verbally fill in the word or phrase.
- Call attention to selected characteristics of books and conventions of print which may include these:

Words
Sentences
Spaces
Page turning
Left to right, top to bottom
Correspondence between print and
the spoken word
Punctuation marks
Capital letters
Lowercase letters

4. *Exploration:* Provide time for students to engage in a variety of experiences and activities that will integrate listening, speaking, reading, and writing. Identify opportunities to integrate other subjects, like science or math, with the reading. Such activities are not viewed as extras or fillers; rather these are to be used to connect learning and make learning more meaningful to the young child.

Applying the Shared Reading Experience   The shared book experience is an excellent strategy for developing young children's emerging concepts about written language. It fits our guideline of using real literature, in an authentic setting, and promotes the integration of all the language arts. In addition, it provides opportunities for students to begin to develop basic reading skills as well as to observe the teacher and their peers employing strategies that independent readers use to make sense of text, such as prediction, applying background knowledge, monitoring comprehension throughout the text, etc.

Let's look at an actual shared reading experience, an in-depth first reading of *The Three Billy Goats Gruff*:

1. Introduce *The Three Billy Goats Gruff* by reading the title; discuss the hillside scene on the front cover.
2. Identify the illustrator, Otto S. Svend. (Typically the author would be identified but since the story is based on a classic folktale, the identity of the author is unknown.)
3. Record students' predictions about the story. These may be recorded using a web (see the example in Figure 6.6).
4. Read and discuss the story, checking the student's predictions.
5. Invite students to read along as the story is read the second time. Students may join in on repeated phrases, such as "trip-trap" and "green, green grass." During repeated readings and exploration, refer to the lists in the next section for examples of activities/experiences that may be used.

Repeated Readings   With each repeated readings, students' individual readings will become closer and closer to the fluency and expression associated with mature readers. Thus the shared book experience is a success-oriented model for emerging readers. Eventually, after several repeated readings, the text will become familiar to your students, and you can use this text to instruct students in the conventions of print and/or create brief minilessons according to student needs.

Predictable Books

A major reason why the shared book experience is highly recommended for emerging readers is the built-in success factor—a factor that is maximized if teachers select books containing predictable text. In predictable books, children can anticipate or predict what is coming because of the books' highly patterned structures. It allows children to use their familiarity with the predictable patterns in our English language, such as "Once upon a _____, or "And they all lived _____

FIGURE 6.6

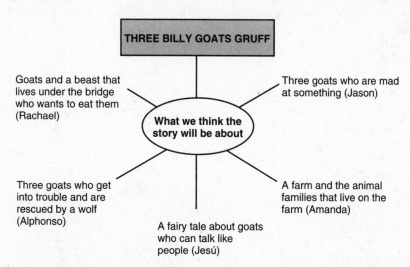

Web, recorded by teacher, based upon the predictions children made for *The Three Billy Goats Gruff*.

_____ _____." Children who have had previous experiences with having been read to know immediately, from known language patterns contained in books, how to fill in the missing words. Books fit into the "predictable" category on the basis of containing highly patterned language, rhyme, repetitive phrases, and predictable plots. One of the most frequently used predictable books, and usually one of the first ones used to introduce children to the predictable patterns contained in text, is *Brown Bear, Brown Bear, What Do You See?* Published in 1967, its author, Bill Martin Jr., is credited with establishing the genre of predictable books (Strickland and Morrow, 1989). Below is a selected list of predictable books that would be suitable selections for shared book experiences with emerging readers.

BOOKS FOR BEGINNING READERS

Ahlberg, J., and Ahlberg, A. *Each Peach Pear Plum.* New York: Scholastic, 1985.

Brown, M. W. *Goodnight Moon.* New York: Harper and Row, 1984.

Martin, B. Jr. *Brown Bear, Brown Bear, What Do You See?* Toronto: Holt, Reinhart and Winston, 1967.

Martin, B. Jr. *Fire! Fire! Said Mrs. McGuire.* Toronto: Holt, Reinhart and Winston, 1982.

Martin, B. Jr. *Monday, Monday, I Like Monday.* Toronto: Holt, Reinhart and Winston, 1983.

Melser, J., and Cowley, J. *Grandpa, Grandpa.* San Diego: The Wright Group, 1987.

Melser, J., and Cowley, J. *Hairy Bear.* San Diego: The Wright Group, 1987.

Melser, J., and Cowley, J. *Yes Ma'am.* San Diego: The Wright Group, 1987.

Parkes, B. *Who's in the Shed?* Crystal Lake, IL: Rigby Education, 1986.

Parkes, B., and Smith, J., retold by. *The Three Little Pigs.* Crystal Lake, IL: Rigby Education, 1986.

Sendak, M. *Chicken Soup with Rice: A Book of Months.* New York: Scholastic, 1986.

Wells, R. *Noisy Nora.* New York: Scholastic, 1987.

BOOKS USING RHYME

Gardner, M., et al., illustrators. *Time for a Rhyme.* Crystal Lake, IL: Rigby Education, 1987.

Glusac, R. et al., illustrators. *Time for a Number Rhyme.* Crystal Lake, IL: Rigby Education, 1987.

Melser, J., and Cowley, J. *Boo-hoo.* San Diego: The Wright Group, 1987.

Melser, J., and Cowley, J. *Obadiah.* San Diego: The Wright Group, 1987.

Melser, J., and Cowley, J. *Poor Old Polly.* San Diego: The Wright Group, 1987.

Melser, J., and Cowley, J. *Woosh!* San Diego: The Wright Group, 1987.

Smith, J., and Parkes, B. *Gobble Gobble Glup Glup.* Crystal Lake, IL: Rigby Education, 1986.

BOOKS USING REPETITION

Carle, E. *The Very Hungry Caterpillar.* New York: Scholastic, 1987.

Cowley, J. *Meanies.* San Diego: The Wright Group, 1987.

Galdone, P. *The Little Red Hen.* Boston: Houghton Mifflin, 1981.

Galdone, P. *The Three Billy Goats Gruff.* Boston: Houghton Mifflin, 1981.

Hutchins, P. *The Doorbell Rang.* New York: Scholastic, 1987.

Krauss, R. *The Carrot Seed.* New York: Scholastic, 1984.

Melser, J., and Cowley, J. *The Big Toe.* San Diego: The Wright Group, 1987.

Melser, J., and Cowley, J. *In a Dark Dark Wood.* San Diego: The Wright Group, 1987.

Melser, J., and Cowley, J. *Lazy Mary.* San Diego: The Wright Group, 1987.

Melser, J., and Cowley, J. *One Cold Wet Night.* San Diego: The Wright Group, 1987.

Parkes, B., and Smith, J., retold by. *The Gingerbread Man.* Crystal Lake, IL: Rigby Education, 1986.

Parkes, B., and Smith, J., retold by. *The Enormous Watermelon.* Crystal Lake, IL: Rigby Education, 1986.

Parkes, B., and Smith, J., retold by. *The Little Red Hen.* Crystal Lake, IL: Rigby Education, 1985.

Parkes, B., and Smith, J., retold by. *The Three Little Pigs.* Crystal Lake, IL: Rigby Education, 1985.

Slobodkina, E. *Caps for Sale.* New York: Scholastic, 1984.

Smith, J., and Parkes, B., retold by. *The Three Billy Goats Gruff.* Crystal Lake, IL: Rigby Education, 1986.

BOOKS WITH PREDICTABILITY AND HIGH-INTEREST THEMES

Bridwell, N. *Clifford's Family.* New York: Scholastic, 1985.

Hutchins, P. *Rosie's Walk.* New York: Scholastic, 1987.

Keats, E. J. *The Snowy Day.* New York: Scholastic, 1987.

Rose, G. *Trouble in the Ark.* New York: Scholastic, 1984.

BOOKS FOR GRADE 2

Hoberman, M. A. *A House Is a House for Me.* New York: Scholastic, 1986.

Odgers, S. F. *Elizabeth.* Crystal Lake, IL: Rigby Education, 1988.

Ormondroyd, E. *Theodore.* Boston: Houghton Mifflin, 1984.

Parkes, B., and Smith, J., retold by. *The Hobyahs.* Crystal Lake, IL: Rigby Education, 1988.

Parkes, B. *McBungle's African Safari.* Crystal Lake, IL: Rigby Education, 1988.

Parkes, B., and Smith, J., retold by. *The Musicians of Bremen.* Crystal Lake, IL: Rigby Education, 1988.

BOOKS FOR GRADE 3

Butler, A., compiled by. *Shuffle Shuffle Rhyme Chime.* Crystal Lake, IL: Rigby Education, 1988.

Odgers, S. F. *How to Handle a Vivid Imagination.* Crystal Lake, IL: Rigby Education, 1987.

THE LANGUAGE EXPERIENCE APPROACH

Another approach to developing literacy at this emergent stage of development is the *language experience approach.* Viewed in its broadest context, anytime that children have the opportunity to talk about their experiences and have them written down, either by themselves or by someone else so that they can read it back, they have engaged in what is referred to as a language experience approach (L.E.A.).

The language experience approach facilitates reading by ensuring a perfect match between the oral language of children and the written material they read. It promotes a holistic view of reading in that students actually get to experience how thought, speech, reading, writing, and listening are all connected. It is one of the best ways to ensure success on the part of the young learner, since the easiest text to read should come from the child's own language. It is an approach to early literacy acquisition that has been used by primary teachers for a very long time (Allen, 1976) and is currently experiencing a resurgence in popularity with the advent of the whole language movement in this country.

For children who come from homes deprived of print materials and few opportunities to experiment with print, the language experience approach helps them to realize that (1) what they experience they can talk about; (2) what they can talk about they can write; and (3) what they can write can be read by themselves and others. L.E.A. is also an excellent technique for students for whom English is a second language, since the text is an exact replica of the youngster's oral speech.

Stories generated as a language experience can be composed by large or small groups of students or by individual students. The procedure used is basically the same, regardless of group size.

Procedures for Conducting a Language Experience Story

Step 1: Stimulus   The stimulus is whatever constitutes an experience that prompts discussion and generates oral language, which will eventually be recorded. Examples of a stimulus could be inviting the curator from the local zoo to visit the classroom with one of the zoo animals, or cooking up a recipe and recording the steps in the process. The stimulus can take advantage of a naturally occurring event that the students collectively experienced and prompted lively discussion—for example an uproar in the cafeteria or a fire drill that kept everyone outside in the pouring rain for 45 minutes. A favorite stimulus with whole language advocates is kicked off with a good piece of children's literature.

Step 2: Discussion   The richer the discussion, the richer the written product will be. This step is an excellent and natural way for youngsters to develop their oral language skills. It permits them to hear how others express the same event they have just experienced. The attempt here is to get everyone to participate.

Step 3: Dictation/Writing of the Story   This is the step where the story actually gets recorded. With older students, a computer can be used and they can each generate a story that may proceed through the entire writing process. With emergent readers and writers, however, the teacher may act as scribe and model all the conventions of good writing, such as capitalization, proper punctuation, spelling, and grammar, or children can be encouraged to use their temporary spelling to write their own stories. It is recommended that teachers try to preserve the children's oral language as much as possible. Grammatical errors and lack of proper sentence structure, for example, can be opportunities for minilessons later on. Teachers should pause occasionally during dictation to comment on the conventions of print.

Step 4: Reading   Actually, this step should should occur simultaneously with Step 3. Teachers will want to have students reread a story often as it progresses. As they read, the teacher makes a sweeping motion from left to right, with his or her hand, to guide students' oral rereading. By the time the story is completed, it should be familiar text to almost every student. The goal is to promote fluent oral reading here and to encourage children to experience themselves as capable readers. Like the shared book experience, it is an instructional model with a built-in success factor for students; hence, it is an excellent approach for fixing positive attitudes toward reading in emerging readers.

Step 5: Follow-Up Activities (a) *Word banks or key words.* Children are encouraged to select words that are important to them in some way and words they want to use in their personal writing. These words can then become *key words* and form part of a permanent file called a *word bank,* which students can consult when composing their own pieces. The key word method is a strategy based on the work of Sylvia Ashton-Warner (1965) and works especially well with the language experience approach, although it can be used with any approach to reading and across all subject areas. Words can then be stored in a box or written on cards that are then placed on a ring. Plastic baggies can also store words by categories. Once word banks are established, they can be used for a multitude of purposes: developing sight words, parts of speech, categorization, spelling, etc.

(b) *Class books.* The individual stories by youngsters can be combined and bound into a class book. These books can then become important contributions to the classroom library and can be shared with other classes.

(c) *Illustrations.* A fun and motivating strategy for getting youngsters into the writing process is to ask them to illustrate an experience and then to add a sentence under their drawing.

Using the Language Experience Approach to Access Students' Writing Development

The language experience approach accommodates for a wide range of writing abilities and can be used to assess writing development. Three students—Nicky, Russell, and Amanda—are each developing a story to go into a class book, following a reading and discussion of *Ira Sleeps Over* by Bernard Waber. While Nicky (Figure 6.7) will only risk writing his own name at this point, he relies solely on his drawing to express his ideas. Later, before the individual stories were put together into a class book, Nicky asked his teacher to write down his ideas under the picture as he dictated them to her. Another stage is illustrated by the work of Russell (see Figure 6.8). Russell indicates the letters that are needed to complete the words in his text by using dashes. Figure 6.9 shows the beginning of Amanda's story which demonstrates a much more advanced stage of writing and the elements of conventional writing. Amanda has done something else here worthy of note. Several days ago, her classroom teacher taught a minilesson on making images in students' minds before beginning to actually write their stories. She modeled this strategy for organizing writing and encouraged her students to get the pictures in their heads down on paper before beginning to write their stories. Amanda's teacher has evidence for her portfolio of Amanda's first attempt at applying this strategy to her writing.

FIGURE 6.7

Nicky relies on his drawing to express his response to the book *Ira Sleeps Over* by Bernard Waber.

FIGURE 6.8

Russell reveals his knowledge that letters are missing by inserting dashes for the missing letters.

FIGURE 6.9

Amanda has accomplished conventional writing here. She first organizes her ideas by drawing pictures of what she wants to write in response to *Ira Sleeps Over*.

READING RECOVERY: A PRIMARY INTERVENTION

Although we believe firmly that every child can become a reader, we recognize that all readers do not start out equally, nor do they advance at the same rate. Like the young lion in Robert Kraus's *Leo the Late Bloomer,* some learners take a little longer to "bloom" than others. Traditionally, students who failed to keep pace with their peers were placed in a reading group for slow readers or assigned to a special intervention program, which often lasted throughout a child's elementary schooling. Today an exciting early intervention program is spreading through the United States called *Reading Recovery.* It provides a second chance at literacy for "at-risk" first graders in an individually supported learning environment. In 30 minutes of daily, intense, one-on-one instruction, Reading Recovery teachers help low-achieving six-year-olds develop the strategies that good readers employ. During lessons that focus on individual strengths, a child is taught to learn about literacy. Reading and writing abilities are developed within lessons that use natural language and predictable texts rather than isolated drills on skills. Writing is an extension of the text or based on a child's experience. The aim of the program is to enable these students to make accelerated progress and to be able to read and write at an "average level" in their classroom within 12 to 20 weeks (Clay, 1994). Children are selected for the program who have been in school for one year and are performing in the lowest 20 percent of the first-grade class.

The instructional procedures used in the Reading Recovery program are based upon field research done by Dr. Marie Clay in New Zealand and upon research that identified teaching procedures that accelerated the progress of "at-risk" readers. The focus of instruction is upon the development of strategies that will enable children to become competent readers. During every lesson, students read five or six real books that rep-

resent a balance between familiar and new texts. The students also compose a one- or two-sentence story every day to provide opportunities to discover links between messages in oral and printed language. Reading Recovery is explicitly based upon a constructionist theory of learning—that is, the child is seen as actively constructing knowledge while being supported in learning by a highly trained teacher.

Longitudinal studies conducted in New Zealand and in the United States have shown that 85 percent of the children who have completed a Reading Recovery program have become independent readers. In addition, investigators have reported that Reading Recovery was more effective than either conventional remedial techniques or programs that used one-to-one tutoring but lacked the extensive teacher training done in the Reading Recovery program.

The teacher-training model in Reading Recovery is a year-long certification program combining theory and practice. Although only teachers certified as Reading Recovery specialists are able to teach in the program, some elements can be implemented by regular classroom teachers. For instance, any teacher can benefit from incorporating the specific verbal responses taught to teachers in the Reading Recovery program. In Table 6.3, three areas of teacher response illustrate the support that teachers can give to youngsters who are struggling to become independent readers.

The responses listed under the heading *Teacher Praise* go beyond merely praising the efforts of the child. Instead, they provide the learner with specific and immediate feedback concerning the behavior that prompted the teacher praise. Researchers have shown us that the chances of students repeating desirable behaviors, following responses of general or vague praise—for example, saying only "Good for you" or "Nice job!"—are equal to providing no praise at all. The more specific the teacher feedback, the greater the likelihood that learners will exercise the praised behavior.

TABLE 6.3   Specific Teacher Language to Reinforce Strategies that Good Readers Employ

Teacher Praise	Teacher Language After an Error	Teacher Language at Difficulty
I'm glad you stopped.	Look at the picture to help yourself.	Get your mouth ready to say it.
Good, you found the hard part.	Are you right? Check that again.	Try that again and think what would make sense.
I like the way you worked out the hard part.	Start that sentence again.	Try that again and think what would sound right.
I like the way you fixed that.	You said _____. Does that make sense?	Try that again and think what would look right.
I like the way you tried to help yourself.	You said _____.	Look at the picture to help yourself.
Good for you. I saw you checking the word with the picture to see if you were right.	Does that sound right? You said _____.	Start that sentence again.
I noticed you tried _____ when you had trouble.	Does that look right?	Skip that word and go on.
Good for you. That's what good readers do.	Try that again and think what would make sense.	Now what do you think it is?
I like the way you're thinking.	Try that again and think what would sound right.	Read it with your finger. Could it be _____?
	Try that again and think what would look right.	[Insert possible words.]
	There's something not quite right.	How do you know?
	You need to check that again.	What can you do to help yourself?
	Can you find the tricky part?	What do you see about this word that you already know?
	What can you do to help yourself?	How did your reading sound?
	Read it with your finger. Did that match?	
	Were there enough words? Did you run out?	
	If that word was _____, what would you expect to see at the beginning?	
	If that word was _____, what would you expect to see at the end?	
	It could be _____, but look at _____.	

Source: Adapted from Clay, Marie M. *Reading Recovery: A Guidebook for Teachers in Training.* Portsmouth, NH: Heinemann, 1994.

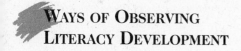

WAYS OF OBSERVING LITERACY DEVELOPMENT

Hopefully by this time you have acquired an appreciation for the vast amount of knowledge about language and literacy that young children bring with them when they first enter school. It becomes your role, then, to build upon the knowledge that they already have and to guide their individual journeys as mature users of language of the "literacy club." This requires that you provide young students with abundant opportunities in print-rich environments where you can observe them as they are authentically engaged in the stages of literacy development. Much of what you will discover will come from simple kid-watching—observing students as they interact with print in your classroom. In addition, however, there are assessment measures you might find useful in collecting information in a more deliberate fashion. Each of the measures discussed below is designed to obtain information on children engaged in the acts of literacy. They are based upon the assumption that information collected in the most desirable manner must conform with certain requirements:

- Observing precisely what children are saying and doing
- Engaging children in tasks that closely resemble the learning tasks of the classroom
- Focusing upon what the child knows versus what the child does not know
- Discovering what reading, writing, listening, and speaking behaviors children are ready to be taught, through an analysis of performance, not from assessment material that is distinct from real engagements with literacy.

With these requirements in mind, we have selected two informal assessments to share with you: (1) Concepts About Print and (2) the Running Record.

Concepts About Print

The background and experiences that students have had with books are indicators of future success in the school environment as well as keys to planning instruction for children. The Concepts About Print tests were originally introduced by Marie Clay in the 1970s and were entitled *Sand* (Clay, 1972) and *Stones* (Clay, 1979). Since that time, there have been several adaptations of the Concepts About Print tests. These methods of assessment focus on directionality, use or understanding of terminology such as page, letter, word, and concepts regarding the source of the language. They show the familiarity children have with books, their knowledge about the function of print in books, and their use of language related to print in books.

Bookhandling Knowledge Task This process begins with presenting a student with a book and explaining that you would like to read the book together. The following general guidelines will help in the selection of a book and getting started:

1. Select a picture book that is suitable for reading to a young child, but do not choose one that is so familiar that the child has the text memorized.
2. Select a book that has a title page containing the title of the book and the author's name.
3. Carefully select a book with pages that have clear, bold print and many pictures throughout. If possible, there should be a page with print on one side and a picture on the other.
4. If you are right-handed, sit with the student on your left side; reverse this position if you are left-handed.
5. Once a sufficient comfort level has been established between you and the student, you can proceed to guide the child's responses according to these instructions:
   a. Show book; cover title with your hand. "Do you know what this is called?"
   b. Present book wrong way up and back toward student. "Can you show me the front of this book? Take the book and open it so that we can read it together."
   c. "Can you read any of this to me?" Pause and encourage the child to read any known parts of the book to you.

d. If student does not read the book (or after the student completes reading), continue. "I'm going to read you this story. Can you show me where I should start reading?" Read to the bottom of the page.

e. Turn to the next page. "Show me the top of this page. Show me the bottom of this page."

f. Read the page, after saying to the child, "You point to the story while I read it."

g. Read to the middle of the story. Somewhere in the middle ask, "Can you show me where I am?"

h. Read to the end of the story, then close the book and pass it on to the student. "Show me the name of the book or the name of the story." Leave the book with the child. "Show me the beginning of the story. Show me the end of the story."

i. Explore comprehension. "Tell me something about the story."

j. To observe if the youngster has letter and word concepts, use two pieces of small light cards that the child can hold and slide easily over the line of text to block out words and letters. To start, lay the cards on the page but leave all print exposed. Read the first sentence on the page and ask the youngster to place one card where he thinks you began reading and the other card where you stopped. If the child is unable to do this, demonstrate the movement of the cards. Then say, "Now, can you show me a letter—just one letter? Can you tell me what that letter is called? Can you show me any other letter? Do you know that letter's name?" Then say, "Now use the cards to show me just one word." Wait for response. "Can you show me two words, using the cards?"

The information that can be obtained through this method will reveal a great deal about a child's previous experiences with books and printed text. Once you become accustomed to the types of questions you can ask of youngsters, you can adapt this procedure to almost any piece of written text.

For a more formal approach, you may want to use the *Sand* and *Stones* books developed by Marie Clay. Specific directions for these are presented in her book *The Early Detection of Reading Difficulties* (1991).

Running Records

A Running Record is a graphic record of a child's oral reading. It is constructed by simply recording the child's reading behavior on a blank sheet of paper, using a simple coding system. For instance, each word read correctly by the child is recorded by a "✓" on the paper.

The Running Record is a useful and versatile method of obtaining information on children's competence over print. Again, it was Marie Clay (1991) who devised this insightful approach to observing how individual students are making sense of text. Perhaps the most appealing attribute of the Running Record is that it combines readily with what whole language teachers are already doing in their classrooms and requires little or no effort on the part of teachers.

For children, reading aloud is a means of sharing enjoyment of books with their teacher (as well as their peers). For teachers, it is a means whereby they can monitor a child's development as a reader. The Running Record can provide a system for maximizing this process and acquiring visual glimpses of what children are thinking and doing as they are reading. By systemizing these observations, teachers are able to determine what strengths children already have as readers and what

FIGURE 6.10

Name: Heather

Book Title: Little Bear

Level: 18   Date: 7/22

A running record of Heather's first grade oral reading of *Little Bear* by Else Holmelund Minarik.

strategies could help them develop into more effective readers.

A Running Record can be taken anytime that a teacher listens to a child read aloud from a text that presents a degree of challenge. It does not require any special materials or vast amount of training on the part of teachers. It can be done on any piece of paper and used with any reading material. Essentially, what the teacher does is to make a visual representation of exactly what the child did when reading aloud, through the use of the systematic markings of the "running record." These markings can then be analyzed so that the teacher can plan future instruction that will *specifically* help that student to move forward as a reader. Figure 6.10 shows an example of a completed Running Record. Because of the versatility

of this method it should be noted, however, that the end product will differ somewhat from teacher to teacher.

Standard Marking for Recording The Running Record shown in Figure 6.10 was recorded while Heather, a first-grader, read aloud from a book entitled *Little Bear*. In order for Heather's teacher to preserve her oral reading in visual form, she had to learn a few standard markings. With practice, these markings become automatic, making running records easy to administer; thus running records are a practical means of observing a child's reading development over time.

- A stroke indicates a word read correctly:

  ✓ ✓ ✓

- A substitute word is written above the word in the text:

  coming
  ―――――
  come

- An omission is marked with a circle:

- A self-correction is marked by the letters SC:

  wanted
  ―――――――
  went | SC

- If a word is pronounced by the teacher, it is coded with the letter T, for Teacher Pronounced.

Miscue Analysis Revealed by Running Record
Categorizing and counting the actual miscues

(words read which deviate from the actual text) made by Heather leads to a "picture" of the reading strategies she employs regularly, sometimes, and seldom. Such cueing systems can be classified according to meaning (semantic) cues, sentence grammar (syntax), and the visual cues from the letters and words (graphophonics). (The cueing systems will be fully explained in Chapter 8.) The small grid in the upper right-hand corner in Figure 6.10 reveals the number of reading cues used by Heather, in each category.

Meaning Cues	Semantic Cues	Visual Similarities
⊤⊦⊦⊦⊦ l	l	⊤⊦⊦⊦⊦ l

According to the Running Record, Heather employs meaning, or semantic cues and those dealing with visual similarities, or graphophonic cues, in equal amounts (six each). There was only one indication in this particular reading where Heather's miscue demonstrated her use of syntax, or sentence structure cues.

By comparing the number of total errors a child makes when reading orally with the number of actual words read (i.e., "running words"), the level of difficulty of the text can be determined. If there is more than 10 percent of error recorded, then the text would be rated as too difficult for the reader. If you were Heather's teacher, you would only begin to see her as the unique reader that she is by looking at *each* miscue and asking yourself, "What was she doing to make her say that?" "Was she distracted by the visual cues of the unfamiliar word?" "Did she check the word to determine if it made sense?" Your students will develop strategies that they believe will help them to become proficient readers. Through careful analysis of Running Records, you will be provided with a window to view exactly what reading strategies your stu-dents are employing and which ones you will want to model for them.

Literacy Expectations

No two children will ever learn exactly alike in your classroom, or will they achieve in exactly the same proportions or grow at the same rate of speed. While acknowledging the existence of such diversity among your students we can nevertheless expect, with proper nourishment and access to opportunities, that children in the primary grades should achieve certain abilities in the four areas of the language arts: listening, speaking, reading, and writing. As you consider the type of learning environment you want to create for your students and the kinds of opportunities you wish to orchestrate for them, it might be helpful to have some guideposts to follow. We'll bring this chapter to a close, then, by sharing a set of expectations that primary teachers in one school district hold for all of their students in each of the language arts by the time they emerge from the second grade. We believe these to be reasonable guideposts for all primary teachers.

These guidelines, presented in Table 6.4, should not be regarded as checklists with the listed items viewed as being acquired in a particular order. It is our intention that the abilities described will develop within contexts that are meaningful and developmentally appropriate.

We hope that as you continue to interact with emergent readers and writers you will have a renewed sense of appreciation for the amazing linguistic competence they have acquired at such an early age. It reflects an insatiable desire to learn and to communicate effectively with others. Most of what we have to do as educators is to build upon this rich and resourceful foundation by immersing young children in meaningful activity that will sustain their excitement and enthusiasm for achieving full literacy—in all its forms.

TABLE 6.4 Expectations for Students Who Have Completed Grade 2

Speaking

1. Develops a vocabulary that enables the student to describe, reason, explain, and use qualitative works.
   • Labels classroom and environmental objects
   • Describes events or objects
   • Relates experiences to others
   • Tells familiar stories in correct sequence
   • Memorizes and recites nursery rhymes, poems, or short passages
   • Dictates sentences, stories, and books for transcription
2. Uses appropriate speaking behavior in a classroom assembly or informal situation.
   • Gives others a chance to talk
   • Respects opinions and rights of others
   • Avoids interrupting
   • Sticks to the topic being discussed
3. Forms ideas through impromptu talk, using incomplete and tentative structures if necessary.
4. Discusses topics and issues that are personally significant.
5. Participates in creative oral activities: puppetry, informal choral speaking, charades, role playing, character roles using appropriate voices, plays, and assuming the role of narrator.

Listening

1. Appreciates and responds to children's stories, rhyme, poetry, riddles, jokes, music, and rhythm patterns.
2. Is able to connect prior knowledge with new information he/she is hearing in order to listen with understanding.
3. Understands that language has a variety of patterns, rhymes, sounds, and rhythms.
   • Hears differences in environmental sounds, letter sounds, and words
   • Hears rhyming words

Writing

I. Interest
1. Develop a sense of "I *am* a writer."
2. Writes every day.
3. Makes hypotheses about language and language use in writing.
4. Uses written language to explore ideas and feelings.
5. Appreciates the purpose for writing.
6. Seeks response to own writing.
7. Shares writing with others.

II. Awareness of self as a writer
1. Creates stories or poems using known patterns ("patterning" of stories, songs, poems, etc.).
2. Contributes to group or class stories, poems, songs, plays.
3. Writes to clarify own thoughts.
4. Writes to share ideas and feelings with others through stories, letters, poems, messages, invitations, advertisements, reports, and plays.
5. Seeks opinion of others when revising.
6. Seeks opinion of others in proofreading.

Reading

I. Interest
1. Uses reading as a source of personal enrichment and pleasure:
   a. Looks to books for enjoyment, to satisfy curiosity, and to gain information.
   b. Reads daily from a variety of reading materials of student's own choice—(poetry, fiction, folk literature, animal stories, realistic fiction, informational books).
   c. Understands and responds in personal ways to the ideas, attitudes, and feelings expressed in various reading materials.

II. Book knowledge
1. Can identify and use book terms: page, author, illustration, page number, title page.
2. Begins to be aware of classification of books.
3. Can locate particular books by author.
4. Begins to recognize literary forms (i.e., the differences in form of drama, poetry, and prose).
5. Uses personal and picture dictionaries to locate words when needed for reading and writing.

TABLE 6.4   *Continued*

Writing *(continued)*	**Reading** *(continued)*

Writing *(continued)*

7. Writes for variety of purposes and audiences.
   a. Uses brainstorming, group or class discussions, exploratory writing, personal experience, and incidental reading to generate ideas for writing.
   b. Writes extensively using a variety of forms. Writes for various purposes, including stories, captions, poems, reports, notes and letters, and lists.
   c. Uses writing as a means of developing personal awareness through keeping journals and writing stories based on personal experiences, using both inverted and conventional spelling.
   d. Is able to write for several different audiences, including the teacher and the principal, peers, and family.
   e. Understands the author's purpose in writing and that authors have various purposes.
   f. Respects audience by revising to ensure
      • Message is clearly stated
      • Supporting details are relevant
      • Clear pattern of organization is used.
   g. Respects audience by proofreading to ensure
      • Presentation is legible.
      • Conventions of spelling and punctuation are used at the appropriate level.
   h. Begins to develop an understanding and appreciation of the elements of a story in own writing and writing of others.

III. Skills and strategies
1. Identifies and limits a topic with some assistance from class discussion or teacher suggestions and selects material appropriate to the subject, purpose, and audience from ideas generated during prewriting.
2. Develops a story line to include a sense of sequence and logic that enables individual progress from isolated phrases and sentences to the coherence of a paragraph.
3. Uses functional spelling in writing.
   • Demonstrates a knowledge of the patterns of spelling words.
   • Spells accurately in writing words found on high frequency word list for grade 2.
   • Uses simple dictionary as an aid to spelling accurately.
   • In writing and discussion of writing begins to demonstrate use of possessive forms, contractions, and singular and plural forms.
   • Uses contractions as a shortened form of two words in own writing.
4. Shows awareness that conventions of print are designed to help the reader understand what is written.

Reading *(continued)*

III. Strategies
1. Brings meaning (background knowledge to get meaning from print) using the cueing systems in conjunction with one another.
   a. Pragmatic—able to adjust strategies to situation.
   b. Semantic—able to use background knowledge with surrounding text; e.g., "The day after Monday is _____."
   c. Syntactic—able to use intuitive knowledge of word order to predict the kind of word that belongs in a particular place in a sentence; e.g., "The day after Monday _____ Tuesday."
   d. Visual/phonic—able to use pictures, punctuation, sight vocabulary, and sound/symbol relationships. "The day after Monday is" T_____y."
2. Begins to understand reading is a predictive process:
   a. Makes predictions about meaning while monitoring print:
      • When reading, can fill in a missing word or phrase and can do this because he/she understands the story and how language is used.
      • Uses expanding awareness of sound/symbol correspondence.
   b. Self-corrects when something does not make sense. Specifically when
      • Something does not sound like language, by using intuitive knowledge of patterns of language.
      • Something does not make sense, by using previous knowledge about content.
      • Something does not look right, by using knowledge or graphophones.
      • The number of words read does not match number of printed words.
3. When reading and coming to a word he/she does not know,
   • Will return to beginning of sentence or phrase and try again.
   • Will look at pictures in a story.
   • Uses dictionary or other support clues to help to understand the word.
   • Will read ahead to find other clues.
4. Continues to expand word recognition skills in context of reading.
   • Shows instant recognition of words that occur frequently in general reading material using sight words, structural analysis, and knowledge of phonics.
5. On being questioned about a story, makes comparisons, shows cause and effect, and begins to make inferences.

TABLE 6.4 *Continued*

Writing *(continued)*	Reading *(continued)*

5. Uses capitalization in writing.
  • Proper nouns
  • Beginning of a sentence
  • The word "I"
  • Titles
  • Days of week
6. In own writing demonstrates use of
  • Period at end of sentence
  • Question marks
  • Apostrophe in contractions
7. Prints legibly with ease; is in the beginning stages of developing cursive writing.
	6. Reads critically: begins to judge literary quality of a story or poem, e.g., great or boring; begins to appreciate the visual images words can create and their sound value; identifies words that express a mood.
	7 Begins to develop an appreciation of story:
	  a. Is developing an understanding of the elements of a story (plot, characters).
	  b. Distinguishes between fiction and nonfiction.

As we reflect upon the important contributions that teachers, along with parents, play in encouraging emergent readers and writers, we want to remain alert to the continuing lessons young children have to teach us in our understanding of literacy development. Because we took the time to listen and to observe children acting naturally, we no longer regard kindergarten and the other primary grades as places where children come to "get ready" to read and write.

CATHY SWANSON'S JOURNAL

≈ December 18

The whole idea of Kidsville is terrific! Most classrooms have selected a particular business (or theme) for the year. There are two banks, a farm, a curiosity shop, a country store, and a television station just to name a few! Dr. Garis's office is known as "City Hall" and the janitors' office as "The Scrub Club."

All the hallways have been named (Literary Lane, Main St., Magical Blvd., Kinder Way, etc.) and there is a mail system that collects and circulates kid-to-kid correspondence every Wednesday.

Our business happens to be an art gallery, *Gallery 44*. I firmly believe that the arts should be part and parcel of any classroom and not just relegated to the forty minutes a week that the special teachers are allotted. Art is a reflection of culture and can teach us about history, regional characteristics, ideas and society's response to them—many things!

Since we are studying Pennsylvania, our first exhibit features a collection of work by Pennsylvania artists including: the Wyeths, Edward Hicks (his painting, *The Peaceable Kingdom,* portrays William Penn), impressionist Mary Cassatt, and sculptor Alexander Calder (who was born in PA, although I'm not sure he claims to be a native artist!). We also featured watercolors by Judy Alderfer (our school's terrific secretary) and, of course, the work of the "Artists in Residence" of Gallery 44!

The planning and implementing of this exhibit was absolutely a cooperative/collaborative effort. In a brainstorming session, the kids determined that, according to what they knew from books and personal experience, a gallery should have:

Ropes to keep visitors back from the work

Guided tours

Business cards

Security guards and an admission desk

A banner to hang outside the gallery announcing the current exhibit

And a gift shop!

Having tables rather than desks certainly came in handy for this venture! We removed many of the chairs, moved the tables to the perimeter of the room. White sheets loaned or donated by parents draped the tables, and prints signed out from the Art Room were positioned on easels. K.T. came up with a slogan for the gallery and our business cards—"Art from the Heart."

Of course, everything had to be labeled, so there was lots of print throughout the exhibit. A sign-up sheet was posted in the office and within two days we booked 17 tours! This truly indicates the supportive atmosphere found in this school; it's just before the holiday!

The "Artists in Residence" exhibit featured "pseudo-copper" busts of their favorite book characters. These were made from papier maché, sprayed with metallic paint, and mounted on paper-covered oatmeal containers that served as bases. They were wonderful and included such well-loved characters

as the Fox from Roald Dahl's *Fantastic Mr. Fox,* Captain Nemo from Jules Verne's *Twenty Thousand Leagues Under the Sea,* Alex Frankovich from *Skinnybones* by Barbara Park, and Dylan from *Dylan's Day Out* by Peter Catalanotto. A few children chose to "sculpt" their favorite authors; Meg honored Mr. Dahl in her piece and Billy created a very recognizable likeness of Shel Silverstein. (Bill has performed the poem "Sick" more times than he has eaten breakfast!)

A collaborative mobile created by the students emulated Calder's work. It consisted of holiday words of cut paper letters hanging vertically from ceiling to floor. Once it was balanced (which was no small feat!) it awed the children as it moved slowly and gracefully with the circulation of the air.

Everyone had a job. Some presented information about the artist at their station, some spoke about their sculptors, some escorted the classes to the gallery. For children in K-2, we presented an abbreviated program. The kids suggested giving them something to look for when they visited the gallery—like "what we do when we read," they said!

And, of course, there was the gift shop. This idea came from students who had Mrs. Krupp in third grade. They had organized a museum and had invited other classes in, offering little items they made for sale. They wanted to do the same with the gallery, so we made greeting cards and post cards to sell for a nickel or a dime. Optical illusions drawn on graph paper and colored with marker turned into bookmarks that sold out!

Many ideas and "teachable moments" were generated by the gift shop. Discussions about retailing, pricing, organizing and displaying merchandise arose very naturally. "What happens to the profits?" was asked by several kids. Although having a pizza party would have been the preferable answer, they understood when I told them that profits must usually be put back in the business; in our case that means more supplies for our next exhibit, perhaps.

This whole project has grown in snowball fashion; Ruby suggested the town theme, interested teachers took the idea and developed their own themes, and the kids became invested in their own ways as well. The possibilities expand exponentially at each level when someone is willing to sow the seeds!

✤ January 5

Last year, the fifth graders at Franconia had a goal: to read at least 4,000 pages during the year. Students who reached their goal were invited to an end-of-the-year sleep-over in the school (although I think "sleep-over" is a misnomer!).

I wondered if this would make slow or reluctant readers the target of negative, competitive remarks, but that wasn't the case. The kids were more concerned with their own progress, or talked about the top readers and how many pages they had read. The star of the year read over 34,000 pages. Jessica could read *Gone with the Wind* from cover to cover in about 12.6 minutes, I think!)

Anyway, I decided to try this in my fourth grade class. We were starting in January, however, so we made the goal 2,000 pages by June. The kids turned in reading slips signed by parents and Mrs. Schroth (homeroom mother extraordinare) faithfully tallied the pages. Response was slow in the beginning, but once I required reading slips as daily homework, the kids began to realize how much they really did read and that this was not an intangible goal!

✤ January 7

In any reading I've done about process writing, the value of peer response is emphasized. That has always made sense to me, but it has also raised a few concerns.

I remember attending critique sessions in Art classes at Kutztown University. It wasn't always easy to open yourself up to the criticism of others—especially when you were very proud of your work. It really demanded maturity to both listen to and offer criticism.

If, at this stage of the game, our goal is to promote fluency and a love for writing, then aren't we playing with fire when the kids put themselves and their work on the line, seeking their peers' criticism? Is it too much to expect that they listen to the comments of others and take it in stride?

My current position is "yes" and "no" (aaah, so decisive!). While I do agree that the kids benefit from the dialogue that occurs among their peers, I feel strongly that they need to be guided in how to deliver that dialogue sensitively. Kids can be brutally honest and, without intending harm, can stifle another's creative urge.

I hadn't really given my class any guidelines to follow; when we shared as a class, I merely tried to temper the sharper comments and reshape them in a more positive light. Then Ruby used something with my class I really liked.

When sharing writing, you need to:

1. Put your own writing on the floor in front of you.
2. Listen very carefully until the author is finished.
3. Respond first by saying "I heard . . . "
4. Respond by saying "I liked. . . "

This format gave the kids structure and kept the responses positive. I still wondered, however, how to help them deliver suggestions in a way that a sensitive writer could tolerate. Telling someone they *should* do something carries a different meaning than if they say "you *could* do thus and so." The connotation was apparent to me, but would a nine-year-old hear the difference? I decided to try it out.

During our next sharing circle, Steph shared her piece and Katie responded using *should.* I asked her to rephrase using *could* instead. Liz said by using *could* it sounded like the author still had a choice and that the suggestion wasn't necessarily the right way, just another way. We incorporated that rule as the fifth rule of the sharing circle.

TEACHER AS LEARNER/TEACHER AS RESEARCHER

In Another Classroom

For the first two years of her career, Roberta McEnroe has taught fourth grade in San Antonio, Texas. An ardent supporter of the integrated language arts, Roberta has eagerly sought ways in which her students could assume active roles in the learning process. During her preservice training in college, Roberta had been introduced to thematic teaching and the use of thematic units throughout the elementary curriculum (see Chapter 14). Roberta knew that the strength of this approach to language arts instruction lay in the active utilization of children's literature across the curriculum.

However, Roberta was having difficulty introducing her students to a literature-rich science program. For many of her students, science was perceived as the simple memorization of facts and figures, the completion of "standardized" experiments, and the reading of a boring textbook. For the most part, Roberta's students perceived science as a textbook-oriented subject with few opportunities to become actively engaged.

Roberta saw the need to change the science curriculum and to change her students' perceptions of science. Her initial research question was "How can I use children's literature as a vehicle for maximizing positive attitudes toward science?" As part of her research, she decided to visit the classrooms of two of her fourth-grade colleagues—Dushane Thompson and Sonya Martinez. She made arrangements with her building principal to observe their classrooms during the afternoon on four consecutive days (the principal had a substitute teacher "cover" Roberta's class during her observations). In addition, both Dushane and Sonya allowed Roberta to interview students about their perceptions of science and their involvement in the literature that Dushane and Sonya provided in class.

Roberta's research into the uses of literature throughout the science curriculum was centered on her observation of other classes. As a novice teacher, she took advantage of an opportunity to see her more experienced colleagues in action and to observe the ways in which they structured and tailored their science curriculum. Although Roberta had been exposed to thematic teaching in her undergraduate years, this was a real opportunity to see it used by two of her grade-level colleagues. Just as important was the opportunity to interview the students in those two classes and obtain their perspectives and opinions about this instructional approach. What Roberta discovered was that there was a wide variety of literature that would allow her to expand and enlarge the science program and offer students opportunities to explore areas of interest beyond the topics offered in the science textbook.

Roberta's research was based on her realization that she needed to broaden her base of experiences and gather data from individuals in similar situations. Equally significant was the fact that Roberta included students from other classes in her data gathering. She wanted to know how a literature-based approach to science instruction affected the cognitive and affective development of students. Gathering that information firsthand from students proved to be the most useful data of all. The comments from Dushane's and Sonya's students helped Roberta redesign her science program into a "user-friendly" form—one that was student-oriented and student-driven.

As a beginning teacher, it will be constructive for you to take advantage of the expertise and experiences of your colleagues. Equally significant will be the perceptions, thoughts, and comments of students (other than your own) who experience that instruction and philosophy of teaching. Tapping resources outside your classroom, yet within your building, can yield valuable data unavailable from any other source. Indeed, it can prove to be one of the most important data collection techniques you use during your first few years of teaching.

Journal Reflections

Select one or more of the questions below that interest you and respond in your journal.

1. Cathy Swanson is a strong believer in integrating the arts throughout the elementary curriculum. In so doing, she is able to expose kids to aspects of the outside world they might not normally experience while, at the same time, fostering a sense of community. What do you think might be some of the challenges involved in developing an "arts-centered language arts curriculum?"

2. Interview several parents of primary level (Grades K–3) students. What do they feel their role is in promoting the literacy development of their children?

3. If you were a kindergarten teacher, what are some of the literacy activities you would want to initiate during the first few weeks of school? What activities or projects would you want to introduce to your new students that would emphasize their unique language skills?

4. Design your own question.
   ✓ What is a question you have about the chapter?
   ✓ How will you pursue the answer to that question?
   ✓ Respond in your journal.

REFERENCES AND SUGGESTED READINGS

Allen, R. V. *Language Experiences in Communication.* Boston: Houghton-Mifflin, 1976.

Anderson, R., Hiebert, E., Scott, J., and Wilkinson, I. *Becoming a Nation of Readers: The Report of the Commission on Reading.* Champaign, IL: Center for the Study of Reading, 1985.

Ashton-Warner, S. *Teacher.* New York: Simon and Schuster, 1965.

Barrs, M., Ellis, S., Hester, H., and Thomas, A. *The Primary Language Record: Handbook for Teachers.* London: Webber Row Center for Language in Primary Education, 1989.

Bissex, G. L. *GNYS AT WRK: A Child Learns to Write and Read.* Cambridge: Harvard University Press, 1980.

Butler, A., and Turbill, J. *Toward a Reading-Writing Classroom.* Portsmouth, NH: Heinemann Ed. Books, 1987.

Cassady, J. K. "Beginning Reading with Big Books." *Childhood Education,* (fall 1988): 18–23.

Clay, M. M. *The Early Detection of Reading Difficulties,* 3rd ed. Portsmouth, NH: Heinemann, 1991.

Clay, M. M. *Reading Recovery: A Guidebook for Teachers in Training.* Portsmouth, NH: Heinemann, 1994.

Clay, M. M. *Sand: The Concepts About Print.* Portsmouth, NH: Heinemann, 1972.

Clay, M. M. *Stones: The Concepts About Print.* Portsmouth, NH: Heinemann, 1979.

Clay, M. M. *What Did I write?* Portsmouth, NH: Heinemann, 1984.

Cochran, J. M. "The Best of Worlds." *Instructor* 98, no. 9 (May 1989): 38–41.

DeFord, D. E., Lyons, C. A., and Pinnell, G. S. eds. *Bridges to Literacy: Learning from Reading Recovery.* Portsmouth, NH: Heinemann, 1991.

Fields, M. V. *Let's Begin Reading Right: A Developmental Approach to Beginning Literacy.* Columbus: Merrill, 1987.

Galda, L., Cullinan, B. E., and Strickland, D. S. *Language, Literacy and The Child.* Fort Worth: Harcourt Brace Jovanovich, 1993.

Gentry, R. "An Analysis of the Developmental Spellings in Gnys at Wrk." *The Reading Teacher* 36, (1982): 192–200.

Graves, D. H. *Build a Literate Classroom: The Reading/Writing Teacher's Companion.* Portsmouth, NH: Heinemann, 1991.

Heald-Taylor, G. "How to Use Predictable Books for K–2 Language Arts Instruction." *The Reading Teacher* 40 (May 1987): 656–661.

Holdaway, D. *The Foundations of Literacy.* New York: Ashton-Scholastic, 1979.

Hudson-Ross, S., Cleary, L., and Casey, M. M. *Children's Voices: Children Talk About Literacy.* Portsmouth, NH: Heinemann, 1993.

International Reading Association. *Early Childhood and Literacy Development Committee.* "Literacy Development and Pre-First Grade." Published by IRA. Newark, Delaware.

Kristo, J. V. "Reading Aloud in a Primary Classroom: Reaching and Teaching Young Readers." In K. Holland, R. Hungerford, and S. Ernst, eds. *Journeying: Children Responding to Literature,* 54–71. Portsmouth, NH: Heinemann, 1993.

Lynch, P. *Using Big Books and Predictable Books.* Toronto: Scholastic, 1986.

Mavogenes, N. "Helping Parents Help Their Children Become Literate." *Young Children* (May 1990): 4–8.

Minarik, E. H. *Little Bear.* New York: Harper & Row, 1957.

Moffett, J. *Detecting Growth in Language.* Portsmouth, NH: Boynton/Cook, 1984.

Moll, L. C., ed. *Vygotsky and Education.* New York: Cambridge University Press, 1993.

Moore, S. A., and Moore, D. W. "Beginning to Read." *The Reading Teacher* 43, no. 9 (May 1990): 678.

Morrow, L. M., and Rand, M. K. "Promoting Literacy During Play by Designing Early Childhood Classroom Environments." *The Reading Teacher* 44, no. 6 (1991): 396–403.

Pinnell, G. S. "Success for Low Achievers Through Reading Recovery." *Educational Leadership* (September 1990): 17–21.

Raymond, C. "New Study Reveals Pitfalls in Pushing Children to Succeed Academically in Preschool Years." *The Chronicle of Higher Education* 36, no. 9 (1989): A4–A11.

Roser, N. L. "Helping Your Child Become a Reader." Parent Booklet Number 161. Published by the International Reading Association, Newark, Delaware, 1989.

Routman, R. *Transitions.* New Hampshire: Heinemann Educational Books, 1988.

Searcy, B. "Getting Children into the Literacy Club—And Keeping Them There." *Childhood Education* (winter 1988): 74–77.

Smith, F. *Reading Without Nonsense.* New York: Teachers College Press, 1985.

Smith, M. L. "Cubbies, Coloring, and Computers." *Childhood Education* 67, no. 5 (1991): 317–18.

Strickland, D. S. "Some Tips for Using Big Books." *The Reading Teacher* 43, no. 4 (January 1990): 342–343.

Strickland, D. S., and Morrow, L. M. "Sharing Big Books." *The Reading Teacher* 41 (May 1988): 966–968.

Strickland, D. S., and Morrow, L. M. *Emerging Literacy: Young Children Learn to Read and Write.* International Reading Association, Newark, DE, 1989.

Suizby, E. "Children's Emergent Reading of Favorite Storybooks." *Reading Research Quarterly* 20 (1985): 458–481.

Teale, W. H. "Emergent Literacy: Reading and Writing Development in Early Childhood." In J. Readence and S. Baldwin, eds. *Research in Literacy: Merging Perspectives,* 45–74. Rochester, NY: National Reading Conference, 1987.

Trelease, J. "Read Me A Story." *Parents* 662 (1991): 106–110.

DEVELOPING LISTENING AND ORAL LANGUAGE ABILITIES

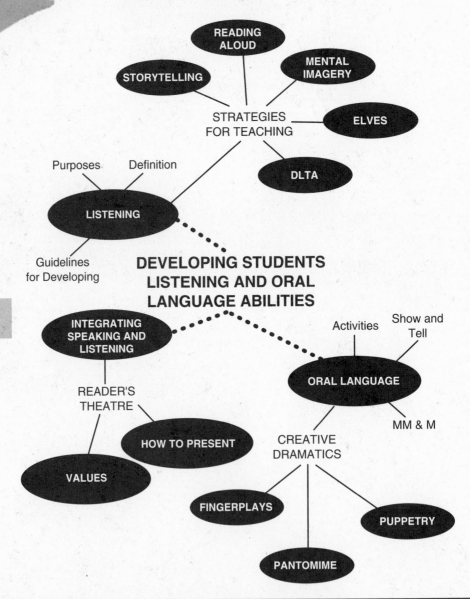

READING ALOUD

STORYTELLING

MENTAL IMAGERY

STRATEGIES FOR TEACHING

ELVES

Purposes   Definition

DLTA

LISTENING

Guidelines for Developing

DEVELOPING STUDENTS LISTENING AND ORAL LANGUAGE ABILITIES

INTEGRATING SPEAKING AND LISTENING

Activities   Show and Tell

ORAL LANGUAGE

READER'S THEATRE

MM & M

HOW TO PRESENT

CREATIVE DRAMATICS

VALUES

FINGERPLAYS

PUPPETRY

PANTOMIME

What I Know: Pre-Chapter Journaling

Throughout our lives we spend a lot of time listening. We listen to music, television programs, and even the lectures in our college courses. It seems as though much of the information we need is the result of how well we listen. With that in mind, how should we teach the skills of listening to youngsters—particularly in an integrated language arts curriculum?

Big Ideas

This chapter will offer:

1. The various purposes of listening.
2. Strategies teachers can use to teach listening.
3. Various types of speaking activities.
4. Teaching strategies which stimulate oral language development.
5. The role of storytelling in the elementary classroom.
6. Ways to integrate listening and speaking in the classroom.

Long slivers of morning light cascade down off the mountain peaks and find their way through the venetian blinds in Tonya Pierce's third-grade classroom. The shimmering rays slowly dance across the walls—walls that are covered with a rich array of student writings, posters, three-dimensional book characters, dioramas, mobiles, and other assorted works. Books and literature of every variety spill off shelves and countertops and collect in plastic trays and discarded dishwasher racks. Cardboard displays, puppet theaters, and a two-passenger rocket ship are scattered around the perimeter of the room. Wires zigzagging across the ceiling hold student murals about pioneer life on the central plains, posters of rain forest habitats in Brazil, mobiles of East African recipes, and an ever-growing collection of favorite adjectives discovered in books. There is evidence of student work in every available space of the room—publicly displayed and publicly celebrated. It is a room engaging and inviting—filled with new discoveries and a profusion of possibilities.

This morning students are assembled in various ad hoc groups around the room reading and sharing a variety of literature related to an introductory geography unit on regions of the United States. Previously, Tonya has described books such as *As the Crow Flies* by Gail Hartman, *Gila Monsters Meet You at the Airport* by Marjorie Sharmot, *Geography From A to Z* by Jack Knowlton, *Let's Visit the United States* by David Gantz, and *Erie Canal* by Peter Spier. Students quickly divide into interest groups to begin reading their selected books. For each book, students are invited to record the book's factual information and its relationship to a specific geographic region. Student chatter echoes throughout the room as ideas are shared, discussed, and recorded on assorted index cards. Students listen carefully as each member of a group presents the data collected from his or her book. The information is discussed in terms of the general topic, index cards are exchanged back and forth, and decisions are made as to how the necessary data could be recorded in the group's geography journal. Later, the information will be shared in a large class forum "run" by two of the members of the class. The resulting collection of information will be recorded on a large sheet of newsprint in the form of a semantic web. As additional information is accumulated throughout the unit it, too, will be added to the web. Students will have opportunities throughout the day to reassemble in other groups to use the data for reader's theatre scripts, self-initiated videotapes to be shared with other classes, a tape recording, and a skit to be shared with the first graders down the hall.

The quiet cacophony that pervades Tonya's classroom throughout the day is evidence that students are taking an active role in their own learning. They are engaged and engrossed in working with each other, supporting the learning of their classmates, and participating in interactive projects that demand cooperation and collaboration. Tonya believes that her students grow in each of the language arts when they are provided with authentic opportunities to use *all* the language arts in realistic academic pursuits. Tonya has designed her curriculum so that her students can participate cooperatively in a host of learning endeavors—sharing information, discussing ideas, considering different points of view, and debating possibilities. Students are active listeners and active speakers; they participate in a support system in which each student's opinions are valued and recognized. Most important, each student is offered an abundance of opportunities to share ideas and to receive feedback on his or her contributions to the class. Not only is there a decided impact on each student's developing self-concept; so too, is Tonya's class strengthening as a true "Community of Learners."

Tonya integrates all the language arts into every topic she shares with her students. She also plans time when she can offer her students direct instruction in how they can use the language arts as learning tools within each of those subject areas. Time is allocated throughout the school year on the strategies and techniques that will assist students in becoming better readers, writers, listeners, and speakers. In this chapter we consider two of the language arts: listening and speaking.

LISTENING

As we begin this section we'd like to invite you to take a few moments and write your own definition of *listening*. Please keep in mind that there are no right or wrong responses. After you have written a definition, we encourage you to share your interpretation with other members of the class. How did your definition compare with other members of the class? Did you happen to note any similarities? Or were there some major differences in your respective interpretations?

Interestingly enough, your personal philosophy about the role of listening in the classroom will have a significant impact on your teaching effectiveness. Let's see if we can make this point through the use of some statistics. In most traditional classrooms, approximately 80 percent of the instructional time is taken up by "teacher talk" (time when the teacher is doing all the talking). Stated another way, most of the school day is based on the teacher lecturing, giving instructions or directions, reminding, disciplining, or telling.

Researchers such as Lundsteen (1989) have found that students typically spend about 50 percent of their classroom time listening. Other data suggests that only about 25 percent of a ten-minute speech is processed by students (De Haven, 1988) and that students learn approximately 20 percent of what they hear. According to Stother (1987), teachers expect children to listen 60 percent of the day, and half of that time listening to the teacher. What surfaces from this research is a need to provide youngsters with systematic and sustained instruction in listening and learning to listen. In a society in which children are bombarded by a constant array of verbal information, the ability to listen selectively and effectively is critical.

At this stage, we wish to make a distinction between the terms *listening* and *hearing*. Hearing is the ability of an individual to take in the sounds of language or the sounds of his or her environment. This implies that there are many different types of sounds and that the "hearer" is able to distinguish one sound from another (often referred to as auditory discrimination). A toddler, for example can distinguish the word "Mommy" from the word "cookie"; an older child can distinguish the sound *sh* from the sound *ch*. Hearing is when a listener takes in sounds and differentiates one sound (or a combination of sounds) from other sounds. It does not necessarily imply that the individual was able to understand or comprehend those sounds . . . that is where listening comes in.

Listening can be defined as "the process by which spoken language is converted to meaning in the mind" (Lundsteen, 1989). Listening is a constructive process; that is, the listener takes in information auditorily and combines that data with personal experiences, background knowledge, expectation, attitude and mood, and familiar patterns to "assemble" meaningful language. The implication is that while students may all hear the same thing in a classroom, they each interpret that information in a slightly different way. In other words, each student listens in a way that is different from every other student.

Suffice it to say, listening is much more complex than hearing. Listening involves hearing, but it also involves *thinking* as well as *comprehension*. That is to say that we must not only be able to hear the sounds of language, but also be able to do something with (or process) those sounds in order for listening to occur. Unfortunately, that is not as easy as it sounds—the reason being that listeners understand twice as fast as speakers can talk (Block, 1993). Because people understand speech much more rapidly than they hear it, they tend to only half-engage their mental capacity to comprehend what they hear (Block, 1993). Even as you sit in your language arts course (or science course, or social studies course), you are only listening (*hearing* + *thinking* + *comprehending*) to about 50 percent of what your instructor(s) presents.

At this point you may be asking, "If listening is so important, why don't we just teach it to kids?" We wish it was as easy as that. Unfortunately, teachers have not traditionally taught youngsters how to listen. Whereas the average child will have received approximately 1,274 hours of reading instruction by the time he or she graduates from high school, that same individual will have received less than six hours of listening instruction during this same period (Burley-Allen, 1982). Unfortunately, too many teachers in the past equated hearing with listening (Do you remember a teacher saying to you "You never listen!"; or "Just listen and you'll know what to do."; or "Listen up!"?). Even more telling is the fact that listening is not systematically taught to youngsters simply because systematic teaching strategies are not normally part of the education of preservice teachers. Swanson (1986) discovered in an analysis of nine preservice language arts texts that only 12 percent of those texts was devoted to methods of developing listening skills. Another survey of elementary teachers enrolled in a graduate class indicated that only 17 percent of them recalled receiving any instruction in listening education in their language arts methods courses (Tompkins, Smith and Friend, 1984).

Typically, listening is practiced, not taught, in schools. Having children listen to an audiotape at a listening center, respond to a seemingly endless array of classroom questions, or recite poetry are examples of listening being practiced—processes not necessarily the result of listening being taught. What is clearly evident from our experiences in classrooms, as well as those of our colleagues, is that listening, just like any other skill, is something that must be taught systematically to youngsters throughout the elementary grades.

Funk and Funk (1989), in a review of research on developing listening abilities, offer the following guidelines for classroom teachers:

1. Teachers and students should state the purpose for listening. Students should be given specific purposes for each listening experience. They should approach listening differently depending on the purpose—for example, listening for a main idea, differentiating fact from opinion, or visualizing and responding to vivid language in a literature selection or to pleasing passages in music.
2. Teachers and students should set the stage for listening. This requires a classroom atmosphere conducive to listening for the intended purpose. Teachers may need to provide interesting lead-up activities as well as create the atmosphere.
3. Follow-up activities should be used to help achieve listening goals and encourage students to apply their new information and techniques. Art projects, writing assignments, library research, and choral arrangements are a few possibilities.
4. Teachers should use instructional techniques that promote and develop positive listening habits. The techniques should include many different types of listening experiences—for example, listening to and responding to stories, poetry, and music. Critical analysis can be fostered by having students listen to determine a speaker's intention or bias. Students should be involved in strategies that improve listening comprehension as well as reading comprehension.

In a related review of listening comprehension research, Pearson and Fielding (1982) offer the following conclusions about listening instruction:

1. Direct teaching of listening strategies appears to help children become more conscious of their listening habits than do more incidental approaches.
2. Listening training in the same skills typically taught during reading comprehension tends to improve listening comprehension.

3. Active verbal responses on the part of students during and following listening enhance listening comprehension.
4. *Listening to literature tends to improve listening comprehension* [emphasis added].
5. Instruction directed toward writing or reading comprehension may also improve listening comprehension.

These conclusions suggest that listening instruction does not need to be "divorced" from the other language arts in order to be taught. In fact, when listening instruction is interwoven with the other language arts it demonstrates certain points:

1. There are different purposes for listening just as there are different purposes for reading, writing, and speaking.
2. Listening provides opportunities for students to *do* something with what they hear.
3. Listening is much more than memorizing what a speaker says or recording everything a speaker utters.
4. Some information is much more important (or useful) than other types of information.
5. Listening is not necessarily related to intelligence.
6. Listening ability can be improved and enhanced when taught integratively.

Purposes for Listening

Wolvin and Coakley (1979, 1985) have defined five specific types of listening: discriminative, comprehensive, critical, appreciative, and therapeutic.

1. *Discriminative listening.* This refers to a person's ability to distinguish between sounds (see above). For example, most of us learn to distinguish between several sounds in the English language as we learn how to read. (We know that the sound of a "c" is different from the sound of an "m"; thus the be-ginning of the word "carrot" will sound different than the beginning of the word "mustard.") Being able to distinguish between sounds is but one skill children use in the reading process.
2. *Comprehensive listening.* Listening to a message in order to understand it is an example of comprehensive listening. Not only do students need to know why a speaker is presenting information, but they also need to be able to organize or arrange that information in a framework that facilitates comprehension. Knowing what a speaker meant, rather than just what a speaker has said, is involved in comprehensive listening.
3. *Critical listening.* Understanding a message is the essence of comprehensive listening; evaluating and judging the worthiness of that message is involved in critical listening. When we listen to a political speech, for example, we often judge the appropriateness of the speaker or candidate based on our evaluation of what he or she said. We listen critically to determine if the speaker's views are consistent with our views. If they are, then we are likely to vote for that individual; if they are not, then we may vote for someone else.
4. *Appreciative listening.* Listening to stories read aloud remains one of the most significant and pleasurable classroom activities. Most of us can remember sitting on a classroom rug or at our desks listening to a teacher read a continuing story from a favorite book or retelling a folktale or legend. Listening to stories enhances our appreciation of story composition as well as the magic of a well-told tale. Reading aloud and storytelling are powerful elements in any language arts program and should be staples of the daily activities of the classroom.
5. *Therapeutic listening.* When people listen to a speaker talk through a common problem or life crisis, they are providing a sympathetic audience for the speaker. Part of the allure of television talk shows lies in the fact that the

audience can relate to problems expressed by the guests on a particular show. By recognizing that the guests are articulating problems or conditions familiar to the listeners, then the listeners feel reassured in their quest for potential solutions to their (similar) problems. Therapeutic listening also allows the speaker to verbalize feelings and emotions to a receptive and sympathetic audience—hence its appeal as a standard counseling technique.

STRATEGIES FOR TEACHING LISTENING

In this book we will focus on instructional strategies designed to enhance three purposes for listening: comprehensive listening, critical listening, and appreciative listening. We are not suggesting that these purposes are mutually exclusive from each other or that they should be divorced from the other language arts in order to be taught effectively. Our point is simply that listening is seldom taught in most elementary classrooms; rather teachers mistakenly assume that children, by the time they arrive in elementary classrooms, have adequate and sufficient listening strategies with which to process most of the verbal information shared in school. Unfortunately, as we indicated above, nothing could be further from the truth. Listening is an active processing of language that can be systematically presented and taught to children within the context of the other language arts.

Another concern is the fact that most children tend to listen for only one purpose: that is, to try and remember everything the speaker presents. Unfortunately, given the limits of short-term memory, this single-minded purpose makes listening a somewhat frustrating experience for many students. (For example, do you remember everything your instructor told you in the class previous to this one?) It is important, therefore,

that youngsters be offered an array of listening strategies and instructional techniques designed to improve their listening abilities as well as to integrate those abilities with the other language arts.

Let's now take a look at some strategies and techniques designed to assist children in developing their listening abilities in meaningful and purposeful situations. You should note that these suggestions do not concentrate exclusively on the development of listening skills; they also include the integration of other language arts. This "marriage" is both intentional and deliberate: students' listening abilities will improve when presented in context with other language skills. Isolated listening lessons may be counterproductive to the development of a truly integrative approach to language arts.

Storytelling

The magic of storytelling has been a tradition of every culture and civilization since the dawn of language. It binds human beings and celebrates their heritage as no other language art can. It is part of the human experience because it underscores the values and experiences we cherish as well as those we seek to share with each other. Nowhere is this more necessary than in today's classroom. Young children who have been bombarded with visual messages (i.e., television) since birth, still relish and appreciate the power and majesty of a story well-told. Even adults, in their hustle and bustle lifestyles, always enjoy the magic of a story or the enchantment of a storyteller. Perhaps it is a natural part of who we are, that stories command our attention and help us appreciate the values, ideas, and traditions we hold dear. So too should students have those same experiences and those same pleasures (Fredericks, 1993).

One of the most valuable activities teachers do in the integrated language arts classroom is to share stories with their students on a regular (i.e., daily) basis (see Chapter 1). Not only does this storytelling experience provide students with a positive role model; so too does it demonstrate ways in which stories can be interpreted and shared with others. Students' imaginations are stimulated and their creativity is enhanced when they become active listeners *and* active speakers.

Storytelling not only enhances children's listening comprehension but facilitates their appreciation of a variety of stories. The inclusion of daily periods of storytelling can enhance the development and appreciation of all the language arts, not just listening. It is a magical time of the day because it conveys the forms and structures of language, the various interpretations of literature, and the literacy traditions of different peoples and cultures (Templeton, 1991). Just as important is the fact that it helps build and solidify communicative bonds between teacher and students in a meaningful and pleasurable arena.

You may wish to consider the following guidelines as you begin your "career" as a classroom storyteller:

1. It is important that you select a story *you* enjoy. Your enthusiasm will rub off on your students!
2. Practice a story several times before sharing it with your students. The object is not to memorize a story, but rather to develop a flow or "patter" that will keep the story moving along.
3. Consider using one or more simple props with which you can animate the story. These may include puppets (discussed later in this chapter), plastic figures, costumes, pictures or illustrations, or other appropriate artifacts.
4. Involve your audience whenever possible. Students can repeat a phrase, clap their hands rhythmically at appropriate points in the story, or perform some sort of physical action.
5. When appropriate, dramatize a story by changing the tone of your voice, moving across the "staging" area, or using necessary hand or body gestures.

When storytelling is made a regular part of the language arts program, children learn to listen. Storytelling serves as a natural vehicle for developing appreciative and comprehensive listening skills; it also offers a host of opportunities which encourage the development of a "community of learners." Most important, however, is that children discover the power of storytelling as a vehicle for communicating with others and as a meaningful "languaging" activity.

Students as Storytellers   One of the magical consequences of regular storytelling times in the classroom is that children begin to understand that storytelling is a natural act of communication. Witness the excitement of primary level students returning from a trip or holiday vacation as they eagerly share their stories with the teacher or other members of the class. Here, the energy level is at an all time high as family episodes, shared tales, and personal experiences are shared back and forth. Indeed, youngsters soon learn that we are all storytellers—that we all have something to share.

When children are provided with regular opportunities in the classroom to become storytellers, they will develop a personal stake in the literature shared and cultivate personal interpretations of that literature—interpretations that lead to higher levels of appreciation and comprehension. When offered opportunities to practice and perform stories for their classmates, children are not only provided with a chance to dramatize familiar or traditional tales but also become involved in a number of languaging activities. Youngsters learn to listen to their classmates and appreciate various interpretations of stories.

It is important for students to understand that memorizing is *not* a necessary ingredient in effective storytelling. However, children should be aware of some strategies that will make the storytelling experience pleasurable for both themselves and their audience. The following are some suggested storytelling preparations (note the similarities between these and the suggestions offered for teachers above):

1. Invite students to select a story that will interest them and their audience. Their enthusiasm for a story is important in helping the audience enjoy the story, too.
2. Encourage students to practice a story several times before presenting it to a group. Invite them to learn all they can about the characters, settings, and events within the story.
3. Students may wish to consider how they might animate the story. Hand gestures, facial expressions, or body movements are all appropriate for spicing up a story.
4. Encourage students to practice different accents, voice inflections (angry, sad, joyous), and loud and soft speech patterns (as necessary) to help make characters come alive as well as add drama to the presentation. (This is an opportunity for kids to "ham" it up!)
5. Students may wish to consider the use of simple puppets as a way to animate the story. Individual puppets can be made for selected characters or "generic" puppets can be made and used in a variety of storytelling presentations.
6. Invite students to promote their storytelling time. Children may wish to create announcements, advertisements, or proclamations about an upcoming storytelling time or special story/book. "Advertisements" can be posted in the classroom, throughout the halls, or in a school newspaper.
7. Children may wish to consider the use of simple props (other than puppets) to use during the telling of a story—for example, a paper boat for a sea story, a magnifying glass or camera for a mystery story, or a paper flower for a springtime story.
8. After the telling of a story, invite the storyteller to discuss the story with class members. Students may wish to discuss their favorite parts, what they liked most about the main character, or how they might prepare a sequel for the story.

Storytelling, whether presented by a teacher or a student, is a natural facilitator of all the language arts. It enhances the listening comprehension and appreciation of youngsters, it magnifies the role of reading and literature throughout the entire curriculum, it serves as a vital foundation for promoting the writing process, and it offers innumerable opportunities for children to use their speaking abilities in personally satisfying ways.

Reading Aloud to Students

Stimulating imaginations, enhancing listening skills, and introducing children to a variety of literature can all be facilitated when you read aloud to students—particularly when this sharing activity is made a regular and featured part of every school day. Traditionally, the reading of books to students begins in the primary grades. Unfortunately, some teachers believe that when children learn to read on their own then the need to be read to diminishes. Nothing could be farther from the truth. Our own experiences as classroom teachers have taught us that children of all ages (and even most adults) enjoy listening to someone read aloud from a new or familiar book. Reading aloud makes language active—it stimulates creativity, it develops an appreciation for the wide variety of literature that children can begin reading on their own, it assists children in the development of vivid mental pictures, and it promotes an easy and natural enjoyment of stories.

As you might suspect, there are many benefits associated with the "read aloud" experience. These include the following (adapted from Kimmel and Segel, 1983; Sims, 1977; and Trelease, 1989):

1. Reading aloud stimulates children's interest in books and literature. Old "classics" as well as new tales broaden students' exposure to a variety of literature.
2. Students' reading interests are broadened and enlarged when teachers utilize read-aloud literature from several areas.
3. Students are introduced to the patterns of language including sentence structure, se-

quence, and the development of story themes.

4. Children are provided access to books that may be beyond their independent reading level or too difficult for them to read on their own.
5. Reading aloud helps develop a community of learners within the classroom.
6. Reading books from many different sources helps children expand their backgrounds of experience—an important element in reading comprehension development (see Chapter 9).
7. When teachers read books to their students, they are serving as positive reading models. Students see the pleasure, enjoyment, and excitement of reading demonstrated by an accomplished reader.
8. Reading aloud enhances the development of appreciative, comprehensive, and critical listening skills in a variety of informal contexts.
9. Reading aloud provides a host of pleasurable sharing experiences and facilitates teacher-student communication.

Here are some guidelines (Templeton, 1991; adapted from Trelease, 1989) that will make the read-aloud experience enjoyable and gratifying for you and your students:

1. Before reading a book to your students, take time to read or skim the story beforehand. This will give you a sense of the story necessary for an effective reading.
2. Select a book you enjoy as well as a book your students will enjoy as well.
3. Make reading aloud a daily part of your classroom schedule. When possible, include more than one read-aloud session each day. Consider the beginning of the school day, immediately after a recess or gym period, after lunch, or just before students are dismissed at the end of the day.
4. Sit so that you are positioned in front of the students. This allows for appropriate voice projection and permits all students an oppor-

tunity to listen. Also, if you wish to show illustrations in the book, all students will be able to see them.
5. Emphasize to students that the read-aloud time is solely for the purpose of listening to a book read aloud. It should not be an opportunity for students to complete homework assignments or converse with their classmates.
6. Be cognizant of the pace of your reading. Provide opportunities for students to create "pictures" in their minds—mental imagery is a positive factor in children's enjoyment of reading as well as in the development of reading comprehension strategies. It may be necessary to "slow down" your reading to allow students to develop appropriate images.
7. When reading longer books or chapter books (books with several chapters), plan to stop at a suspenseful or climatic point. Students will be eager to resume the reading at the next read-aloud session.
8. Give students the option of sharing or discussing the story afterward. This is not a time for "testing" how well students listened to the story or what they remembered from the story; rather it can be an opportunity to compare individual impressions or interpretations. Obviously, the discussion should be relaxed and informal.
9. Begin your read-aloud sessions with short stories and books and gradually progress to longer readings. Be mindful of your students' attention spans and adjust the reading time accordingly.
10. Don't impose your own interpretations of a book on your students. Read-aloud time is a time for the sharing of good literature in a relaxing environment, not a time for formal reading lessons.

Elves—A Read-Aloud Strategy Levesque (1989) describes ELVES, a five-part read-aloud strategy, designed to develop listening comprehension through a planned sequence of activities:

1. **Excite:** Focus the discussion on listeners' experiences, the literary elements within the story, and predictions about the story.
2. **Listen:** Have students listen to verify predictions and to comprehend other story elements.
3. **Visualize:** Ask listeners to share their mental images.
4. **Extend:** Have students gain new understandings by relating previous knowledge and new knowledge.
5. **Savor:** Have students reflect on the story, verbalize their responses, and become involved with follow-up activities, such as writing or reader's theatre.

The following example illustrates how ELVES could be used with *The Village of Round and Square Houses* by Ann Grifalconi (Boston: Little, Brown, 1986):

1. *Excite:* Begin the discussion by posing questions that will help students relate their own experiences to various elements within the book. For example, you might ask, "Have you ever had your grandparents over to your house for a family celebration?" or "How is your house similar to or different from other houses in your neighborhood?" Pose questions which stimulate students to make predictions about the story. For example, "Why do you think there might be a village in Africa with two different kinds of houses?", "Who might live in the square houses?", "Who might live in the round houses?", and "How did this tradition come to be?"
2. *Listen:* Read the book to your students and invite them to listen so that they can determine if their earlier predictions match the information in the story. Encourage students to listen for descriptive language or sentences that are especially memorable. These may include, "Then she would sit alone in the moonlight, looking up at the dark slope of Naka Mountain, rising high above. . . ." (p. 9, un-

numbered). As you read, encourage students to create mental images of the scenes in the book and of how the characters were acting within each scene.

3. *Visualize:* Encourage students to describe their mental images. What are some of the pictures they have created in their minds as they were listening to the book? For example, when they heard "'Suddenly, the black night was split open like a coconut! And a great white burst of light rose like the sun'" (p. 14, unnumbered), what was the image in their heads? Invite students to describe their images as though they were watching a motion picture.
4. *Extend:* Invite students to participate in a discussion in which they can begin making connections between their background knowledge and any new information they heard in the book. You may wish to have students think about how changes (in the setting, characters, or point of view) might alter the story. For example, "How would the story change if it were told from the point of view of an adult rather than the young girl?" or "What might have changed if the story took place in an urban area rather than a rural region of Central Africa?"
5. *Savor:* Invite students to extend the story through a variety of other language arts activities. For example, students could write an imaginary letter to the narrator of the story about how much they appreciate her tale; they could create an original and/or imaginative story about some of the architecture in their town and how it came to be designed in the way it was; they could develop a reader's theatre production of the story for presentation to another class; or they could compare this African tale with other tales they could read, such as *Mufaro's Beautiful Daughters* by John Steptoe (New York: Lothrop, Lee and Shepard, 1987); *Why Mosquitoes Buzz in People's Ears* by Verna Aardema (New York: Dial, 1975); *Tower to Heaven* by Ruby Dee (New York: Henry Holt, 1991); *Darkness and*

the *Butterfly* by Ann Grifalconi (Boston: Little, Brown, 1987); *Beat the Story-Drum* by Ashley Bryan (New York: Atheneum, 1980); or *Bringing the Rain to Kapiti Plain* by Verna Aardema (New York: Dial, 1981).

Directed Listening-Thinking Activity (DLTA)

Another powerful activity which assists youngsters in the improvement of their listening abilities is the Directed Listening-Thinking Activity (DLTA). Patterned after Russell Stauffer's (1975) *Directed Reading-Thinking Activity,* the DLTA provides children opportunities to relate "new" experiences (learned through listening) with "old" experiences (those which reside in the child's memory bank or schema). The DLTA helps students understand the relationships that can and should exist between what they already know and what they can know. In other words, they learn to use their background knowledge as a foundation for new "learnings."

One distinctive element about the DLTA is that it not only facilitates listening comprehension, but also aids in the development of appropriate reading comprehension abilities. Many of the same processes used in listening are also utilized in reading (making the DLTA an appropriate integrated language arts instructional strategy). As you will note below, the emphasis is on the processes of discovery rather than the final products generated as a result of those processes.

The following list of steps illustrates one way in which DLTA can be introduced and used with your students. Be mindful of the fact that modifications may need to be made according to individual learning styles, ability levels, and difficulty of the material.

1. Obtain a book or story appropriate to the interest level of your students.
2. Show the cover illustration and read the title to your students. Ask them, "What do you think this story might be about?" Record several responses on the chalkboard.

3. Read the story to a predetermined stopping point (e.g. a "break" in the action, a climatic point, a change in the setting). Query students on whether their initial predictions matched with the events of the story (e.g., "How did our original ideas about the story match with what we learned in the first part of the story?"). Ask students to determine if any changes in the initial predictions need to be made as a result of reading the first part of the book.
4. After discussing the first part of the story, ask students to generate predictions about the next part of the story (e.g., "What do you think is going to happen?", "Why do you believe as you do?"). Encourage children to listen to validate their original predictions or formulate new predictions.
5. Continue reading and encouraging students to make predictions throughout the remainder of the story. At the end of the story, ask students to determine how closely their original predictions matched the events of the story. By listening to the story as it unfolded, how were students' preconceptions altered and what new predictions were made?
6. Discuss with students the relationships between their backgrounds of experiences and the information learned through listening. Can they devise a semantic web which illustrates those relationships?

The DLTA has proven itself to be an effective instructional tool in a variety of classrooms. It's strength lies in the fact that students *actively participate* in the dynamics of good listening and are able to apply those dynamics in realistic listening situations. Of no less importance is the fact that DLTAs provide additional language arts opportunities for extending and elaborating the learning experiences of youngsters.

Final Thoughts

Stimulating the listening development of children in your classroom is an important and viable goal.

As youngsters improve their listening abilities (particularly when those abilities are enhanced within the context of the other language arts), they will be able to develop a support structure that both enhances and stimulates those abilities. However, as we indicated previously, when listening instruction is divorced from the other language arts its effectiveness diminishes. In other words, do not plan to teach isolated listening lessons, but rather include, incorporate, and integrate listening into all of your other language arts activities. Students' listening comprehension will be strengthened as will their reading, writing, and speaking comprehension.

ORAL LANGUAGE

It could be rightfully argued that of all the language arts, speaking (or oral language) is the one language mode in which children are most fluent. For many children, the early years of their lives—from birth to age five—have been surrounded with language (being read to, listening to adults, watching TV, etc.). Those language experiences have provided youngsters with the foundational support upon which their primary expressive language art (speaking) rests. Indeed, even before children learn to read and write, they learn to talk and communicate with those around them.

So too do children learn that speaking is a way of satisfying their immediate needs (hunger, thirst, etc.) as well as their secondary needs (entertainment, clothing, etc.). Most children discover that speaking is not only a method of communicating with others, but also a way in which they can express their emotions and desires. Indeed, there is a convincing body of research suggesting that adequate speaking opportunities, both in and out of the classroom, form the foundation upon which successful learning rests (Cazden, 1986; Golub, 1988; Heath, 1983; Tompkins and Hoskisson, 1991).

Since this text is concerned with an integrative approach to the teaching and learning of language arts, it may be of some interest to know that students who have less well-developed oral abilities will have limited reading, writing, and overall scholastic success (Loban, 1976; Sampson, 1986). This relationship exists due to several interrelated factors:

1. Oral language development forms the foundation upon which successful reading and writing experiences rest.
2. When youngsters are encouraged to use and practice their oral language skills, their vocabulary development improves concomitantly.
3. Systematic instruction in developing oral language abilities enhances personal feelings of self-worth and facilitates individual self-concepts.
4. Regular opportunities to participate in oral language activities demonstrate the "active" nature of language as a tool to communicate and a tool to comprehend.
5. Through speaking, children are engaged in positive languaging opportunities that enhance, stimulate, and encourage the development of and "comfortableness" with all the language arts.

It is important to note that facility in speaking also translates into facility in reading, writing, and listening skills. A more integrative approach to the development of oral language abilities can eventually translate into greater familiarity with and competence in the other language arts. To this end, it becomes important for teachers to provide sufficient opportunities throughout the entire language arts curriculum (indeed, the entire elementary curriculum) in each of the following four speaking areas (adapted from Tompkins and Hoskisson, 1991):

1. *Informal talk activities:* Planned opportunities for students to engage in the exchange of information need to be woven throughout the school day. These may include various ex-

changes of data including spontaneous conversations as well as organized discussions (on specific topics) between teacher and students and students and students. Obviously, both speaking *and* listening skills are enhanced and facilitated at the same time during these opportunities.

2. *Interpretive talk activities:* These opportunities allow both teacher and students to take previously created material (books, stories, etc.) and recreate it into another format. For example, after a book such as *East of the Sun and West of the Moon* by Mercer Mayer (New York: Macmillan, 1980) has been read to the class, students may wish to rewrite a portion of the story and develop it into a reader's theatre presentation. While the basic plot would be preserved, students would have the freedom to interpret the story line in a variety of ways.

3. *Formal talk activities:* In these instances, individual students research, assemble, and present information to their classmates. These presentations are formal and are usually scheduled as part of a lesson in social studies or science, for example. Examples of these activities include debates, oral reports, and interviews.

4. *Dramatic activities:* Drama provides a medium for students to use language, both verbal and nonverbal, in a meaningful context (Tompkins and Hoskisson, 1991). These are engaging opportunities for children to put language "into action." Youngsters have opportunities not only to interact with their classmates but also to interpret, reconfigure, redesign, and evaluate all of the language arts. Drama has a positive effect on elementary students' oral language development as well as their literacy learning (Kardash and Wright, 1987; Wagner, 1988).

The following are several examples of speaking activities which can assist children in developing and improving their oral language abilities.

Note that many of them utilize other language modes besides just speaking. Obviously, that is intentional, not only because speaking ability is facilitated when combined with listening, reading, and writing activities, but also because systematic inclusion of active speaking opportunities will have a positive effect on students' developing self-concepts.

Show and Tell (Share Time)

One of the staples of most primary classrooms is the "show and tell" time scheduled for each week. Typically, children are each asked to bring in an item or object of interest, stand before the other members of the class, and explain or describe the item for all to enjoy. Obviously, the emphasis is on providing an opportunity for children to utilize their speaking abilities in a worthwhile context, while enhancing their developing self-concepts at the same time.

Unfortunately, it has been our experience that show and tell dissolves into an activity we refer to as "bring and brag." This is when children bring larger or more expensive items from home to try and "outdo" their classmates. This happens quite frequently after holiday celebrations or birthdays. Too often, this simple activity is transformed into the process of seeing who gets the biggest and most expensive presents. Those youngsters who come from impoverished backgrounds or families lacking in financial resources frequently get the message that they are "not as good" as their classmates because they cannot bring high-priced objects to show off.

Instead of telling your students to each bring in something for show and tell, it would be more appropriate to link the sharing experience to a concept or lesson in the classroom. This not only provides direction and structure for the presentations but also helps demonstrate relationships that can exist between home and classroom environments. For example, if you and your students were studying the first five ordinal numbers as part of a math lesson, it would be appropriate to ask students to each bring in an object (magazine picture, photograph, illustration, etc.) that has one or more of the ordinal numbers portrayed on it. Students would each be asked to describe their objects and the various ways in which those ordinals numbers are represented. On the other hand, if an upcoming lesson is to deal with the three types of rocks (sedimentary, igneous, metamorphic), you can ask each student bring in a rock or two from their neighborhood to present to their classmates. Or, if you are talking about the primary colors, you might have each of your students bring in different colored objects as indicated in the web shown in Figure 7.1. You can place the words "Primary Colors" in the middle of the chalkboard and the names of the three colors around the sides. Invite students to brainstorm for items in their homes that might have one or more of the primary colors. List the names of those items on the web. Then, invite students to each bring in one item that was listed or a colored item not on the original web. Such a procedure downplays or eliminates the competitive atmosphere that often develops when children are given "free rein" about what to bring in to share with the class. This activity has the added advantage of "marrying" the show-and-tell experience with an element of classroom instruction. The result is a more meaningful extension of that lesson or experience than would otherwise be present.

You may wish to work with your students in establishing some "ground rules" for your show-and-tell experiences. Table 7.1 presents some ideas we have found to be especially appropriate. Feel free to modify or adopt these according to the individual dynamics of your classroom.

Show and tell offers students unique opportunities to participate in informal sharing experiences that facilitate the development of speaking skills while strengthening self-confidence and self-esteem. Another advantage of show and tell is that it offers fuel for a host of writing topics.

We also wish to emphasize that show and tell is not restricted to the primary grades; it can be used as a stimulus for a host of curricular tasks at any grade level. Intermediate-level students can actively participate in this experience and demonstrate the relationships that exist between classroom "learnings" and the "outside world." Teachers, too, should actively participate in this experience—modeling the behaviors and conversations that can naturally develop as a result of this sharing process. When this technique is used on a regular basis, you will discover a plethora of interactive possibilities that extend across all the language arts.

FIGURE 7.1 A Color Web for Show and Tell

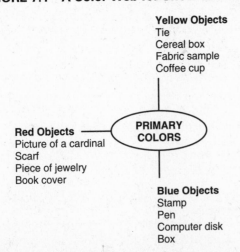

Yellow Objects
Tie
Cereal box
Fabric sample
Coffee cup

Red Objects
Picture of a cardinal
Scarf
Piece of jewelry
Book cover

PRIMARY COLORS

Blue Objects
Stamp
Pen
Computer disk
Box

Metacognitive Modeling and Monitoring (MM & M)

Effective speaking is more than an individual standing before a group of people and talking for a given period of time. It presupposes that there is a message to be shared between two or more individuals and that that message will be comprehended by all parties involved. This applies to all of the informal speaking situations (as indicated above) as well as all formal applications.

In order to help youngsters understand the value of speaking, it is often appropriate for them to "see" inside the mind of a speaker as he or she goes through the speaking process. In essence the teacher serves as a model of efficient speaking, demonstrating for students the thought processes and mental activities used while speaking. When students are made aware of the thought processes speakers use (inside their heads) then they can emulate those strategies for themselves. MM & M (Fredericks, 1992) gives students an insight into the mind and demonstrates processes that can go on inside their head as they speak.

In this strategy, the teacher selects a reading passage and begins to "think out loud"—verbalizing what is going on inside his or her head while speaking. Since students cannot observe the thinking process firsthand, the verbalization allows them to get a sense of good thinking as practiced by an accomplished speaker. Since you serve as the most significant role model for students in all their academic endeavors, your "talking while speaking" gives them some first-hand experiences with speaking as a thinking process—processes they can begin to incorporate into their schema.

Mason and Au (1990) have outlined a five-stage process of how MM & M can work. Initially, you will want to select a piece of textual material that is short and contains some obvious points of difficulty (vocabulary, sequence of events, ambi-guities, etc.). Read this passage aloud to students, stopping at selected points and verbalizing the thought processes you are using to work through any difficulties. This verbalization is essential, in that it provides a viable model for students to "copy." Here are examples of the five steps:

1. *Make predictions.* (Demonstrate the importance of making hypotheses.)

   "From this title, I predict that this story will be about a missing ring and a haunted house."

   "In the next chapter, I think we'll find out how the two twins were able to sail to the other side of the lake."

   "I think this next part will describe what the thief took from the dresser drawer."

2. *Describe your mental images.* (Show how mental pictures are formed in your head as you read.)

   "I can see a picture of an old man walking down a country lane with his dog at his side."

   "I'm getting a picture in my mind of a sparsely furnished apartment with very small rooms."

TABLE 7.1 Suggestions for Show and Tell

1. Students can select an item that will interest their classmates and that is related to a lesson or concept presented in class.

2. Each presenter can prepare two or three questions to ask the audience about the item shared or the sharing experience itself.

3. Members of the audience can ask the presenter questions about what was shared.

4. Members of the audience can describe what they enjoyed about each classmate's presentation ("I really liked it when you told us. . . .", "I liked the part about. . . .").

5. Teachers can ask open-ended questions which will assist a student in elaborating upon his or her presentation.

6. Teachers can become passive members of the audience, stimulating (not dominating) the conversation whenever necessary.

7. Occasionally plan some modeling times in which you demonstrate the behaviors expected of student sharers. In other words, you can take on the role of a student sharer and invite class members to interact with you in ways similar to how they would interact with a classmate.

8. Provide an opportunity for students to develop a listening or critique guide for show and tell. It will be important for student sharers to receive feedback about the quality of their presentations.

Source: Adapted from Block (1993).

"The picture I have in my mind is that of a very short girl with curly red hair and a face full of freckles."

3. *Share an analogy.* (Show how the information in the text may be related to something in one's background knowledge.)

"This is like the time I had to take my daughter to the hospital in the middle of the night."

"This is similar to the time I first learned to ski in Colorado and kept falling down all the time."

"This seems to be like the day we had to take our family dog to the vet's to be put to sleep."

4. *Verbalize a confusing point.* (Show how you keep track of your level of comprehension as you read.)

"I'm not sure what is happening here."

"This is turning out a little differently than I expected."

"I think I don't understand."

5. *Demonstrate "fix-up" strategies.* (Let students see how you repair any comprehension problems.)

"I think I need to reread this part of the story."

"Maybe this word is explained later in the story."

"Now that part about the fishing rod makes sense to me."

These five steps can and should be modeled for students in several different kinds of reading material. As you read and model, allow students opportunities to interject their thoughts about what may be going on in their heads as they listen to the selection. Your goal, obviously, will be to have students internalize these processes and be able to do them on their own in all kinds of speaking situations. Here are some alternate approaches to MM & M:

A. Have students practice the procedure with a partner. One student reads a passage out loud to another and verbalizes some of the thinking taking place in his or her head as they read. The partner records those thought processes and discusses them with the reader upon completion of the story.

B. Students can read a passage into a tape recorder. Afterward, they can play the recording and stop at selected points and tell a partner about some of the thinking that was taking place when dealing with the text at that spot.

C. Bring in other adults to the classroom to model their thinking behavior as they speak. The principal, secretary, custodian, librarian, superintendent, and other school-related personnel can all be "shown" as positive speaking models for students. Be sure to provide a brief "in-service" on MM & M for each person prior to the presentation.

D. Invite students from grades higher than yours to visit the classroom and read selected passages to your students. Ask them to model their thinking as they speak.

E. Designate a student "Speaker of the Day" who selects a passage to share with other students and demonstrates the MM & M procedure. This daily events designates every student as a model for all the other students and validates the utility of this strategy.

CREATIVE DRAMATICS

Probably no other area of language arts instruction stimulates children's imaginations and language abilities as much as the various forms of drama (Norton, 1989). From the time children begin learning the value and power of language, they participate in a number of drama activities.

Playing house, putting on mother's or father's clothes, playing doctor, talking with an imaginary friend are all examples of creative dramatics. What is clearly evident is that drama is a natural and normal part of children's lives—so too can it be a natural and normal part of classroom dynamics.

Drama provides opportunities for students to be creative, inventive, and imaginative. There are no limits to the ways in which thoughts, ideas, or concepts can be presented and interpreted when drama is made a regular and vital part of daily classroom activities. Not only does it demonstrate the utility of language, language in action, but it also provides innumerable opportunities for children to interact on a personal level that fosters cooperation and deemphasizes competition. Drama has enormous power as an instructional technique because it involves both logical (left-brain) and creative (right-brain) thinking; it requires active experience; and it integrates the four language modes (Tompkins and Hoskisson, 1991).

Of no less importance is the fact that "drama has a positive effect on personal attitudes often associated with language growth: self-confidence, self-concept, self-actualization, empathy, helping behavior, and cooperation" (Wagner, 1988, p. 48). The implication is that when teachers employ creative dramatics as a permanent element of the language arts curriculum, they are not only facilitating the development of all the language arts but also having an impact on the development of each child's sense of self-worth and identity. This, in turn, becomes a self-perpetuating cycle in which children are increasingly reinforced through a regular routine of productive and worthwhile dramatic activities.

According to Tompkins and Hoskisson (1991) there are four types of creative dramatics appropriate for use in the classroom. These include:

1. *Dramatic play:* These are the spontaneous, informal, and unrehearsed make-believe activities children tend to engage in on a regular basis. Turning blocks of wood into race cars or a piece of cloth into a wedding dress are examples of dramatic play.

2. *Informal drama:* Like dramatic play, informal drama is unrehearsed, spontaneous, and playful. Informal drama typically occurs when students dramatize a story they have read collectively or engage in some role-playing activities.

3. *Interpretive drama:* Interpretive drama is somewhat more formal than the two types of drama mentioned above. It usually involves an interpretation of some form of literature and includes rehearsals and a standard method of presentation. Examples may include reader's theatre or student storytelling episodes.

4. *Theatrical productions:* These are the most formalized type of dramatic presentations. Typically, students memorize a script, don appropriate costumes, and make a standardized presentation to another group of students. Students are assigned parts, and practices ensure that a polished presentation is the result. Interestingly, Stewig (1983) and Wagner (1976) caution that these types of productions may be inappropriate for the elementary grades; the emphasis during these years should be on informal dramatic presentations.

The following sections discuss examples of creative dramatics appropriate for use in any elementary classroom.

Puppetry

Puppetry has been a traditional form of creative dramatics for hundreds of years. Not only do puppets allow children to animate a specific story, but they also provide opportunities for the audience to become personally involved in the story through the actions and reactions of selected characters. Puppets are also a good way of stimulating imagination and enhancing the expressive arts. Creating puppets, too, allows children to express themselves in an imaginative way and to use all the language arts in demonstrating their creativity.

Puppets are particularly appropriate as an aid in stimulating speaking abilities. A puppet can become an "alter ego" for a child afraid to stand in front of his or her peers, a child with a speech problem, a shy or reluctant individual, or a youngster learning English for the first time. By manipulating a puppet, a child is presented with innumerable opportunities for self-expression in an atmosphere of support and encouragement.

Puppets, particularly when they are created by children, allow students to utilize their creative talents in tandem with their expressive abilities. There is no need to create elaborate puppets or purchase expensive commercial puppets. In fact, children discover that the puppets they create themselves are more useful and dynamic than costly puppets in toy stores and hobby shops.

An additional benefit of puppets as an aid in the language arts is that they can be used to introduce a grammatical element such as quotation marks or adjectives, for example ("Clarence the Clown presents the parts of speech") in addition to serving as familiar characters in story retellings or discussions.

Figure 7.2 presents some simple designs that you and your students can use to design appropriate storytelling puppets. These puppets can be kept in a convenient location in the classroom and used periodically to "characterize" a story, enhance an oral report, or illuminate conversations between two or more characters in a book. Puppet "shows" can range from very elaborate affairs with colorful stages and props to very simple presentations using one or two child-crafted puppets.

To be successful, children need sustained and regular opportunities to engage in puppetry activities. The many benefits of puppets and puppetry ensure that when they are included systematically throughout the language arts curriculum children's imaginations, creative spirit, interpretive abilities, and social skills will be enhanced considerably.

Pantomime

Pantomime is another popular storytelling technique that has been around for hundreds of years. The presenter shares a story with the audience through gestures, facial expressions, and body movements, but without the use of words. This is interpretive storytelling—the individual rendition of a tale in a creative format.

Norton (1989) outlines several descriptions of pantomime activities appropriate for use with elementary children. Some of these are briefly summarized in Table 7.2 on page 219.

Fingerplays

Fingerplays are brief presentations using the hands and fingers to illustrate the rendition of a story. Usually, fingerplays involve all members of the class, but can be effectively presented with two or more individual students standing in front of an audience.

A fingerplay includes a planned sequence of finger and hand movements designed to animate a story. Here is an example of two fingerplays (adapted from Bauer, 1977):

RHYME	MOTIONS
An elephant goes like this and that	(stamp feet)
He's terrible big	(raise arms)
And he's terrible fat	(spread arms)
He has no fingers	(wiggle fingers)
He has no toes	(touch toes)
But goodness gracious, what a nose!	(draw hands out indicating long curly trunk)
I'm a little bunny	(make a fist)
With nose so funny	(wiggle thumb)
This is my home in the ground	(opposite hand on hip)
When a noise I hear	(put hand to ear)
I perk up my ears	(put two fingers of fist up)
And jump into the ground	(put fist into "hole" of arm)

FIGURE 7.2

(a) Stick Puppet:
Use a stick, tongue depressor, or dowel. Glue a picture drawn by the student on the end.

(e) Paper Plate Puppet:
Glue a paper plate to a large stick or dowel. Add facial features using markers or crayons.

(b) Egg Head Puppet:
Poke a hole in each end of an uncooked egg and drain the contents. Enlarge a hole to fit on a child's finger and add facial features with markers and other art materials.

(f) Paper Bag Puppet:
The fold of the paper bag becomes the puppet's mouth. A face can be painted on the bag. Yarn and other materials can be used to decorate the bag.

(c) Finger Puppet:
Cut the "fingers" of a glove or old pair of mittens. Use yarn, buttons, sequins, and other art materials to create a face on each "finger."

(g) Spoon Puppet:
Wrap some material around a large serving spoon. Glue handmade eyes, nose, and mouth on the back of the spoon.

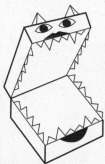

(d) Cereal Box Puppet:
Cut a small cereal box in half on three sides. The uncut side becomes the "mouth" of the puppet. Decorate with art materials.

(h) Sock Puppet:
Glue pieces of fabric, yarn, buttons, sequins, and other art materials to a sock. Colored markers can also be used.

FIGURE 7.2 *Continued*

(i) Flyswatter Puppet:
Glue cotton, yarn, paper features, buttons, etc. to the flat side of a flyswatter to create a character's head.

(m) Bottle Brush Puppet:
Flatten an old bottle brush. Glue on plastic or felt eyes and paper pieces for the facial features.

(j) Photo Puppet:
Have students use school photos and glue them to the ends of tongue depressors. Each student's face can become a character in a story.

(n) Meat Tray Puppet:
Cut a Styrofoam© meat tray into the head of a character. Glue yarn for the hair and buttons and other art materials for the facial features.

(k) Coat Hanger Puppet:
Bend a wire coat hanger into a circle shape (the hook is bent to form a handle). Slip a nylon over the circle and tie to the base of the handle. Decorate the "face" with paper pieces, yarn, buttons, etc.

(l) Cup Puppet:
Stick a dowel into the center of a Styrofoam© cup. Decorate the "head" with various art materials.

(o) Pop-up Puppet:
Place a dowel in the center of a Styrofoam© ball. Cover a tin can (both ends cut out) with an old sock. Slip the ball into the top of the sock and tie it. Put facial features on the sock for the head. Children will be able to pop the head in and out of the can.

INTEGRATING SPEAKING AND LISTENING

It should be evident in the examples and activities above that it is difficult at best to separate listening from speaking, speaking from listening, or either one of those two language modes from the other language arts. Clearly, each language art supports and is "wrapped around" elements of the other language arts. To attempt to design an activity that focuses on a single language skill would be nearly impossible, if not counterproductive. As we have implied earlier, instruction in the language arts involves and necessitates instruction in an integrative environment.

One integrative activity that has clearly demonstrated the interrelationships that naturally exist between the language arts *and* facilitates comprehension of an integrative approach to language learning is Reader's Theatre.

Reader's Theatre

Reader's theatre is a storytelling device that stimulates the imagination and promotes *all* of the language arts. Simply stated, it is an oral interpretation of a piece of literature read in a dramatic style. But its value (see below) goes far beyond that simple definition. It is an act of involvement, an opportunity to share, a time to creatively interact with others, and a personal interpretation of what can be or could be (Fredericks, 1993). Here's another definition of reader's theatre:

Reader's Theatre is an interpretive reading activity for all the children in the classroom. Readers bring characters to life through their voices and gestures. Listeners are captivated by the vitalized stories and complete the activity by imagining the details of scene and action.... Used in the classroom, Reader's Theatre becomes an integrated language event centering upon oral interpretation of literature. The children adapt and present the material of their choice. A story, a poem, a scene from a play, even a song lyric, provide the ingredients for the script. As a thinking, reading, writing, speaking and listening experience, Reader's Theatre makes a unique contribution to our language arts curriculum. (Sloyer, 1982, p. 3)

TABLE 7.2 Selected Pantomime Activities for Elementary Students

- *The glob:* This is a good way to "stretch" the creative muscles and stimulate the imagination. Students "toss" a pretend glob back and forth among themselves. Each student perceives the glob in a different way. For some it can be hot, for others it can be sticky, still others can perceive the glob as heavy. This activity is useful in learning about the imaginative powers of selected students.

- *Pantomime games:* Each student demonstrates an occupation, sport, or popular game for others in the class. Students attempt to guess the sport or occupation being pantomimed through a series of questions that can only be answered with *yes* or *no* responses.

- *People machine:* Students combine to create a familiar or original machine. Each student in a group takes on the role of a machine part (e.g., gear, wheel, crank) and the entire group works together to portray the selected machine.

- *Imitation game:* In this activity one student performs a pantomime that uses large body motions (fixing a bicycle, delivering newspapers, skiing, etc.). Individual students are selected from the audience—each attempting to replicate the motions exactly like the original student.

- *Slow motion:* Individual students each duplicate the motions of a popular activity (e.g., playing baseball, doing a homework assignment, cleaning their room), but in slow motion. This activity usually engenders a lot of laughter and much creativity.

- *Narration:* Whenever you present a familiar or popular story to the class, invite individual members to pantomime the roles of selected characters during the presentation. This is an excellent activity to use with stories with which some members of the class may already be familiar.

Reader's theatre helps students understand and appreciate the richness of language, the ways in which to interpret that language, and how language can be a powerful vehicle for the comprehension and appreciation of different forms of literature. Reader's theatre provides numerous opportunities for youngsters to make stories and literature come alive and pulsate with their own unique brand of interpretation and vision. In so doing, literature becomes personal and reflective—and students have a plethora of opportunities to be authentic "users" of language.

Reader's theatre is a way to interpret literature without the constraints of skills, memorization, or artificial structures (e.g., lots of props, costumes, elaborate staging). Reader's theatre allows students to breathe life and substance into literature—an interpretation that is neither right nor wrong, since it will be colored by students' unique perspectives, experiences, and vision. It is, in fact, the reader's interpretation of a piece of literature or a familiar story that is most valuable. Table 7.3 illustrates some of the values of readers theatre as a viable language arts activity.

Presenting a reader's theatre script need not be an elaborate or extensive production. As students become more familiar and polished, they will be able to suggest a multitude of presentation possibilities for future scripts. It is important to help students assume a measure of self-initiated responsibility in the delivery of any reader's theatre. In so doing, you will be helping to ensure their personal engagement and active participation in this most valuable of language arts activities (Fredericks, 1993).

TABLE 7.3 The Values of Reader's Theatre

1. Reader's theatre stimulates curiosity and enthusiasm for different forms of literature.
2. It allows students many different interpretations of the same story—facilitating the development of critical and creative thinking.
3. It supports a whole language philosophy of instruction and allows children to become responsible learners who seek out answers to their own self-initiated inquiries.
4. Since it is the performance that drives reader's theatre, children are given more opportunities to invest themselves and their personalities in the production.
5. Students are given numerous opportunities to learn about the major features of children's literature—plot, theme, setting, point of view, and characterization.
6. Reader's theatre is a participatory event. The characters as well as the audience are all intimately involved in the design, structure, and delivery of the story.
7. It is informal and relaxed; it does not require elaborate props, scenery, or costumes.
8. It stimulates the imagination and the creation of visual images.
9. It enhances the development of cooperative learning strategies. It requires youngsters to work together toward a common goal and supports their efforts in doing so.
10. It is valuable for non–English-speaking students or non-fluent readers (see Chapter 5). It provides them with positive models of language usage and interpretation. It also allows them to see "language in action" and the various ways in which language can be used.
11. Teachers have also discovered that readers theatre is an excellent way in which to enhance the development of communication skills such as voice projection, intonation, inflection, and pronunciation skills.
12. The development and enhancement of self-concept is facilitated.
13. Students are active participants in the interpretation and delivery of a story; as such, they develop thinking skills that are divergent rather than convergent, and interpretive skills that are supported rather than directed.
14. When students are provided with opportunities to write and/or script their own reader's theatre, then their writing abilities are supported and encouraged.

Source: Adapted from Fredericks (1993).

IDEA BOX

Here are some reader's theatre resources and scripts you may wish to obtain for use in your classroom:

Barchers, S. *Readers Theatre for Beginning Readers.* Englewood, CO: Teacher Ideas Press, 1993.

Coger, L. I. and White, M. R. *Readers Theatre Handbook: A Dramatic Approach to Literature.* Glenview, IL: Scott, Foresman, 1982.

Fredericks, A. D. *Frantic Frogs and Other Frankly Fractured Folktales for Readers Theatre.* Englewood, CO: Teacher Ideas Press, 1993.

Laughlin, M. K., Black, P. T., and Latrobe, K. H. *Social Studies Readers Theatre for Children.* Englewood, CO: Teacher Ideas Press, 1991.

Laughlin, M. K. and Latrobe, K. H. *Readers Theatre for Children.* Englewood, CO: Teacher Ideas Press, 1990.

CATHY SWANSON'S JOURNAL

✤ *January 13*

With each novel we read, I require the children to keep a response log. What I've used so far has simply been a booklet with each page having lines for writing and space for drawing, and a copy of the book jacket on the front.

The children came to fourth grade well aware of what might be a good response to a book. They remembered prompts their third-grade teachers had posted to get them started (a great idea—I'll have to make a chart for our room, too!). These included:

I liked . . .

I didn't like . . .

I didn't understand when . . .

A funny thing happened when. . . , etc.

Using these logs allows for flexibility; the book might make a connection for one child in one vein that another child would not respond to at all. I also like to use the logs as "catch-alls," a place to respond to a class discussion when we run out of time and someone didn't get to share. Of course, the children critique the book as well, supporting what they liked and/or didn't like about it. Additionally, they are valuable tools for assessing comprehension.

✤ *January 18*

Several of us have formed a professional colloquium for the purpose of reading and discussing *Interwoven Conversations* by Judith Newman.

The book is primarily Newman's conversational reflections about teaching as she lives it. The readers are given insight into how to be flexible, yet give structure to a class, how to put learning in the hands of the students,

how to gently lead from behind. Although the students in Newman's workshop are primarily teachers, the ideas presented are certainly transferrable to the elementary domain. What is most refreshing about this colloquium is the opportunity it provides to share ideas on a higher, more philosophical level. This kind of experience always translates into motivation in my own teaching.

✻ January 20

Whatever we read, we try to read as writers. Conventions such as alliteration or similes might be noted, or someone may note a "cliff-hanger," descriptive language, the effective use of humor and the like. Once the kids begin assuming this focus, they become very sensitive to it and it seems to come very easily to them.

Today we were talking about ways to start a story and that it can be really hard to think of a good beginning. I asked everyone to get either a book they were currently reading, or to grab one from the Reading Corner. We turned to the first few lines of the books and took turns sharing how the authors began. The kids were able to recognize some common techniques, like describing a specific moment or beginning with an exclamatory statement. Nik even recognized the use of onomatopoeia.

I was surprised at the enthusiasm with which they analyzed the authors' works; they almost had a sense of ownership about them—or perhaps it was a sense of camaraderie with the writers.

✻ January 21

It might be January, but the sun was shining and a warm ocean breeze swept through the hallway today, Beach Day!

Every hour the kids "head for the beach" (a.k.a. the hallway) to read for fifteen minutes. Sponsored by the Communication Arts committee, this event has become a real hit!

Everyone brings towels, suntan lotion, goggles, flippers, shades, or whatever beach accoutrements and attire they can think of. Beach tags are made and must be worn, lest a "mean ol' lifeguard" throws you off the beach. Sharks, planes trailing banners, and even a bather from the 1930's (our cook—who definitely made a splash when she modeled!) have been known to appear on this day.

As the last traces of Coppertone fade in my room, I think about how grateful I am to be in a school that truly celebrates children and reading.

✻ January 29

I told my class that today we were going to meet with Mrs. Alderfer's class (cheers!) and that we were going to read *Superfudge* in an hour (SILENCE!!). Then the whispers started. . . . "We can't do that! No way! Is she CRAZY?!!"

Well, maybe, but we wanted to try a cooperative reading activity we heard about called "A Book an Hour." After reading the first chapter aloud, we divided the kids into as many groups as there were chapters. Each group read one chapter; first to themselves, then quietly to each other. Next, they illustrated the beginning, middle, and end of the chapter on drawing paper (6" x 18"). When everyone finished, they began retelling the story, one chapter at a time. As each group presented their chapter, they placed their illustrations (now folded in a three-dimensional triangle) on top of the one below. The book was "read" in less than an hour (the fudge cookies eaten in less than two minutes!) and the illustrated "tower" grew as the story was retold.

I read the first draft of Greg's new story a few days ago. He worked on it "Oh, Ms. Swanson, for four hours!!" He had become "obsessed"; genuinely and personally committed to this piece. As I reread the work, I recognized many parallels to the plot and characters of *Weasel,* an historical fiction chapter book I had read to the class. Greg had thoroughly enjoyed the book and had responded often and enthusiastically to it in class discussions. How wonderful that he now emulated the author's style in his own work!

Today, during a sharing circle, another student recognized the similarities and wondered if that wasn't like "copying." It struck me that in the realm of the classroom, "copying" has acquired such a negative connotation when, in fact, it is often how we best learn—through modeling and observing, assimilating and replicating!

"When you visit some of the prominent museums in New York, for example, you might see students copying famous paintings. They do this because they learn so much from observing that closely, for that long, eventually becoming better painters," I offered.

"Yeah, and it's not like Greg took the same names and made the characters do the exact same thing," added Mara. "He just used them for ideas and made his own story."

The wind was back in Greg's sails, and the kids cited some other instances where "copying" was O.K.—like singing (K.T. recently sang in the Lip Sync program and tried very hard to sound like Whitney Houston!), sports, and even cartooning. Elena pointed out that she looked at the caricatures I did of the students and tried to draw eyes the same way.

I love when these "philosophical" discussions occur; it is exponentially more powerful when the kids themselves arrive at conclusions about how they interact with the world around them.

TEACHER AS LEARNER/TEACHER AS RESEARCHER

Audio and Video Recordings

Margie Coulter, a fourth-grade teacher in Billings, Montana, had been concerned for some time about the performance of one of her students—Leon Alvarez. Her field notes had indicated that Leon had difficulty participating in groups and that he was reticent to contribute information or attend to tasks designed and developed by the group. Margie suspected that part of Leon's difficulty was due to his lack of command of the English language and the attendant difficulties in articulating his ideas.

Margie's initial question—Why is Leon not a participating member of group work?—was a cause for concern. Margie decided that a videotaping of several group sessions would yield the necessary information she needed. She set up a video camera in one corner of the room (students were quite used to the camera) and filmed several small group sessions in which Leon was a member. In reviewing the tapes, Margie discovered that while Leon had some difficulty in expressing himself, it was equally apparent that the group members, who were practiced in cooperative learning, had not articulated the roles and responsibilities of each member in sufficient detail. In other words, Margie saw that Leon was just trying to "get along" without having the necessary instructions on how to perform in a group. It became apparent to Margie that "training sessions" on cooperative learning were needed periodically throughout the year for review purposes and to orient new students to this classroom process.

What Margie and other teachers have discovered is that audio and video recording of students can yield significant data that might be otherwise missed in casual observations or interviews. Of course, you will not want to record entire days or extended periods of instruction. By having a clear and concise question in mind, you will be able to designate a specific period of time to record information. Since you will undoubtedly collect more information than you will need, it is important to carefully analyze the data relevant to your initial question(s).

Here are some suggestions for making this research process profitable:

- Make sure students are comfortable with recording equipment in

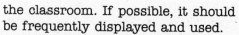

the classroom. If possible, it should be frequently displayed and used.

- If possible, allow students to record selected events in the classroom and to comment on the recordings.
- Let students know that the recordings are for the purpose of supplementing your observations and may be used as part of your overall assessment plan.
- Occasionally invite colleagues to view or listen to tapes and offer their insights and comments.
- Since reviewing audio- and videotapes is a time-consuming process, use them as a supplement to other research techniques.

Journal Reflections

Select one or more of the questions below that interest you and respond in your journal.

1. Cathy spends a great deal of instructional time helping her students "read like writers." What might be some of the advantages of this approach to language arts instruction? What activities or strategies will you use to promote this concept?

2. If possible, observe a group of youngsters in a classroom environment and the same group of children at recess or on the playground. In each situation, how much time do the children spend in listening activities? How much time is spent in speaking activities? What conclusions can you draw for your future classroom as a result of your observations?

3. Select a lesson from a science or social studies book. Using one or more of the ideas presented in this chapter, illustrate how you will help students develop and use their speaking and listening abilities within the context of that lesson.

4. Design your own question.
   - ✓ What is a question you have about the chapter?
   - ✓ How will you pursue the answer to that question?
   - ✓ Respond in your journal.

REFERENCES AND SUGGESTED READINGS

Bauer, C. *Handbook for Storytellers.* Chicago: American Library Association, 1977.

Block, C. C. *Teaching the Language Arts.* Boston: Allyn and Bacon, 1993.

Burley-Allen, M. *Listening: The Forgotten Skills.* New York: Wiley, 1982.

Cazden, C. B. "Classroom Discourse." In M. C. Wittrock, ed., *Handbook of Research on Teaching,* 3rd ed., 432–463. New York: Macmillan, 1986.

DeHaven, E. *Teaching the Language Arts.* Glenview, IL: Scott, Foresman, 1988.

Fredericks, A. D. *The Integrated Curriculum: Books for Reluctant Readers.* Englewood, CO: Teacher Ideas Press, 1992.

Fredericks, A. D. *Frantic Frogs and Other Frankly Fractured Folktales for Readers Theatre.* Englewood, CO: Teacher Ideas Press, 1993.

Funk, H., and Funk, G. "Guidelines for Developing Listening Skills." *The Reading Teacher* 42 (May 1989): 660–663.

Galda, L., Cullinan, B., and Strickland, D. *Language, Literacy and the Child.* Fort Worth, TX: Harcourt Brace, 1993.

Golub, J. Introduction. In J. Golub, ed., *Focus on Collaborative Learning* (Classroom Practices in Teaching English, 1988), 1–2. Urbana, IL: National Council of Teachers of English, 1988.

Heath, S. B. "Research Currents: A Lot of Talk About Nothing." *Language Arts* 60 (1983): 999–1007.

Kardash, C. A. M., and Wright, L. "Does Creative Drama Benefit Elementary School Students: A Meta-Analysis." *Youth Theatre Journal* (winter 1987): 11–18.

Kimmel, M. M., and Segel, E. *For Reading Aloud! A Guide to Sharing Books with Children.* New York: Delacorte, 1983.

Levesque, J. "ELVES: A Read-Aloud Strategy to Develop Listening Comprehension." *The Reading Teacher* 43 (October 1989): 93–94.

Loban, W. *Language Development: Kindergarten Through Grade Twelve.* Urbana, IL: National Council of Teachers of English, 1976.

Lundsteen, S. W. *Listening: Its Impact on Reading and the Other Language Arts,* rev. ed. Urbana, IL: National Council of Teachers of English, 1979.

Lundsteen, S. *Language Arts: A Problem-Solving Approach.* New York: Harper & Row, 1989.

Lytle, S. L., and Botel, M. *The Pennsylvania Framework for Reading, Writing, and Talking Across the Curriculum.* Harrisburg, PA: Pennsylvania Department of Education, 1990.

Mason, J., and Au, K. *Reading Instruction for Today.* Glenview, IL: Scott, Foresman, 1990.

Norton, D. *The Effective Teaching of Language Arts.* Columbus, OH: Merrill, 1989.

Pearson, P. D., and Fielding, L. "Research Update: Listening Comprehension." *Language Arts* 59 (September 1982): 617–29.

Sampson, M. R. *The Pursuit of Literacy: Early Reading and Writing.* Dubuque, IA: Kendall/Hunt, 1986.

Searfoss, L. "Integrated Language Arts: Is It Whole Language?" *California Reader* 22 (1989): 1–5.

Siks, G. *Drama with Children.* New York: Harper & Row, 1983.

Sims, R. "Reading Literature Aloud." In B. E. Cullinan and C. W. Carmichael, eds., *Literature and Young Children,* 108–119. Urbana, IL: National Council of Teachers of English, 1977.

Sloyer, S. *Readers Theatre: Story Dramatization in the Classroom.* Urbana, IL: National Council of Teachers of English, 1982.

Smith, F. "The Language Arts and the Learner's Mind." *Language Arts* 56 (1979): 118–125.

Stauffer, R. *Directing the Reading-Thinking Process.* New York: Harper & Row, 1975.

Stewig, J. W. *Informal Drama in the Elementary Language Arts Program.* New York: Teachers College Press, 1983.

Stother, D. "Practical Applications of Research on Listening." *Phi Delta Kappan* 68 (April 1987): 625–628.

Swanson, C. H. "Teachers as Listeners: An Exploration." Paper presented at the Seventh Annual Convention of the International Listening Association, Philadelphia, 1986.

Templeton, S. *Teaching the Integrated Language Arts.* Boston: Houghton Mifflin, 1991.

Tompkins, G. E., and Hoskisson, K. *Language Arts: Content and Teaching Strategies.* New York: Merrill, 1991.

Tompkins, G. E., Smith, P. L., and Friend, M. "Three Dimensions of Listening and Listening Instruction in the Elementary School." Paper presented at the Southwestern Educational Research Association Annual Meeting, Dallas, 1984.

Trelease, J. *The New Read-Aloud Handbook.* New York: Penguin, 1989.

Wagner, B. J. *Dorothy Heathcote: Drama as a Learning Medium.* Washington, DC: National Education Association, 1976.

Wagner, B. J. "Research Currents: Does Classroom Drama Affect the Arts of Language?" *Language Arts* 65 (1988): 46–55.

Wolvin, A. D., and Coakley, C. G. *Listening Instruction* (TRIP Booklet). Urbana, IL: ERIC Clearinghouse on Reading and Communication Skills and the Speech Communication Association, 1979.

Wolvin, A. D., and Coakley, C. G. *Listening,* 2nd ed. Dubuque, IA: William C. Brown, 1985.

CHAPTER 8

READING: PROCESS AND PRACTICE

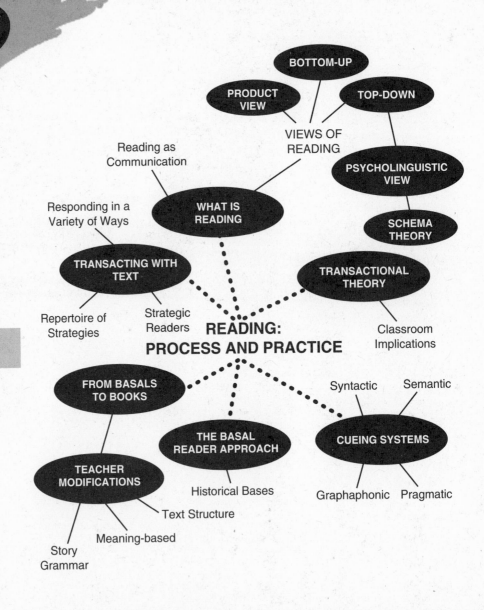

BOTTOM-UP

PRODUCT VIEW

TOP-DOWN

VIEWS OF READING

Reading as Communication

PSYCHOLINGUISTIC VIEW

Responding in a Variety of Ways

WHAT IS READING

SCHEMA THEORY

TRANSACTING WITH TEXT

TRANSACTIONAL THEORY

Repertoire of Strategies

Strategic Readers

Classroom Implications

READING: PROCESS AND PRACTICE

FROM BASALS TO BOOKS

Syntactic

Semantic

THE BASAL READER APPROACH

CUEING SYSTEMS

TEACHER MODIFICATIONS

Historical Bases

Graphaphonic

Pragmatic

Text Structure

Meaning-based

Story Grammar

What I Know: Pre-Chapter Journaling

How did you learn how to read? What were some of the things you remember doing in the classroom that contributed to your growth as a reader? What reading "event" do you remember most vividly? Take a few moments to record your memories.

Big Ideas

This chapter will offer:

1. Views on the nature of reading.
2. Reading as a process versus reading as a product.
3. Classroom implications of current views of literacy.
4. A historical and psychological perspective on basal reading programs.
5. Instructional modifications toward holistic practices.
6. The four cueing systems.
7. Reading strategies appropriate for prereading, during reading, and post-reading.
8. Text structure.
9. Story grammar.

WHAT IS READING?

The overriding message embedded throughout this book is that the definitions we ascribe to things guide our decision making and actions. The definitions we carry of the events in our lives flow from our experiences and, in turn, guide us toward new experiences that are in keeping with those definitions.

Children, too, interact with their worlds, based upon the understandings they make of their worlds and the definitions they ascribe to objects and events in their lives. Viewed from this perspective, then, the definitions that children ascribe to reading could be especially important to beginning teachers. Figure 8.1 re-

FIGURE 8.1

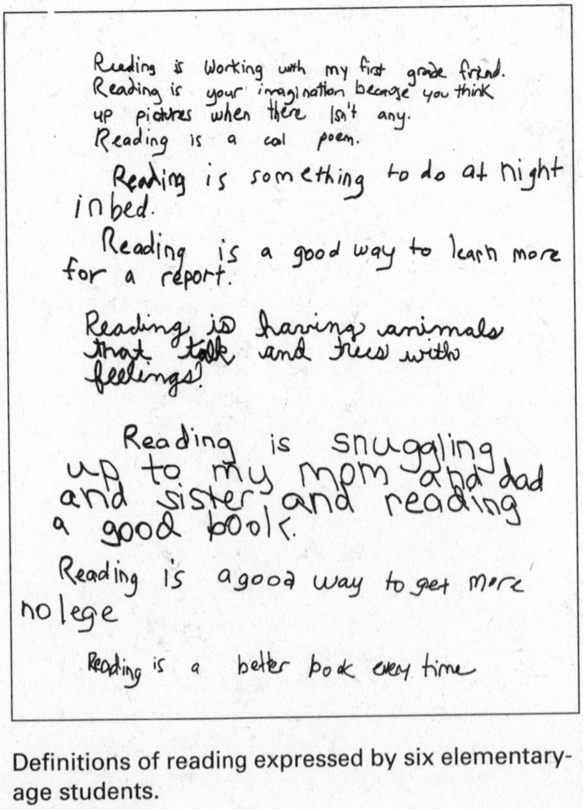

Reading is Working with my first grade friend.
Reading is your imagination because you think up pictures when there isn't any.
Reading is a cool poem.

Reading is something to do at night in bed.

Reading is a good way to learn more for a report.

Reading is having animals that talk and trees with feelings.

Reading is snuggaling up to my mom and dad and sister and reading a good book.

Reading is a good way to get more nolege

Reading is a better book every time

Definitions of reading expressed by six elementary-age students.

veals the responses of six children who were asked to respond to the question, "What is reading?"

Much can be deduced from the definitions of reading revealed by these six children. Not only do they reveal the understanding the children have acquired of reading, but implicit within these definitions are the classroom experiences that children have had with reading instruction. A closer examination of the first child's response in Figure 8.1 suggests that these youngsters have been exposed to a reading environment that encourages socialization during the reading process. We can extrapolate from this child's first response, *"Reading is working with my first grade friend,"* that this youngster has been in a first-grade classroom where children are permitted to relate to their peers about things they are reading. The second response, *"Reading is your imagination because you think up pictures when there isn't any,"* reveals that this student knows that readers' minds are active during reading. Reading is certainly more than reading stories: *"Reading is a cool poem."*

Each definition in Figure 8.1 reveals very personal and practical conceptions of reading, responses that tell us something about the experiences children have had with reading text.

Compare, for instance, the responses that another group of children—first- and second-grade students from Baltimore, MD, gave to the same question.

"Reading is the reading group you are in."
"Reading is sounding out the words."
"Reading is knowing all the words."
"Reading is knowing *lots* of words."
"Reading is getting all the answers right in your workbook."
"Reading is knowing all the sounds that letters make."
"Reading is getting a gold star and knowing you did everything right."

Qualitatively the answers provided by these youngsters differ substantially from those shown in Figure 8.1. The common element in this last set of responses is the *absence* of anything suggesting that reading is gaining *meaning* from what is being read or that it fills any personal needs for the reader. Rather, reading is something that is done primarily for someone else and that it has to do with "being correct," "reading lots of words," and "getting into a certain reading group." When children attach these kinds of notions to the act of reading, why would they want to add reading to the list of things they might want to voluntarily do in their spare time? The definitions children learn to ascribe to reading are the result of their day-to-day encounters with reading in the classroom. It is our job as teachers to create within students a lifelong zeal for reading, to teach them how to define reading in terms that are personally meaning to them.

READING AS COMMUNICATION

Reading is only one of the communication arts. Listening, speaking, reading, writing, and thinking do not occur in a vacuum. They are inexorably interwoven with one another as they work together to inform us about our world, while at the same time we use them to transform the worlds in which we live. When we ask elementary students to tell us what reading is, and when we receive responses that relate to being graded, grouped, and/or passed to the next grade, we conclude that these students have not acquired this notion of reading as communication. Yet, for most children, their worlds prior to entering school were filled with attempts at reading and writing as they strove to make contact with others.

Even the most casual observation of children in their "natural" (usually meaning "nonschool") environment will reveal that the majority of their actions are directed toward making meaningful connections with others. One of the most significant roles a teacher can play is to help children see how reading furthers their ability to communicate. When students are surrounded by language-rich environments, purposeful activity, and genuine opportunities for choice during reading-related activities, they will begin to regard reading as something in which they have a personal stake. Classrooms today are becoming environments where the communicative aspects of reading are prized, where children engage in a wide array of real encounters with language in all of its forms. Students write to one another to share information, they respond to each others writings to affirm something the other has accomplished. The writings of one child become opportunities for reading for another. Each of the language processes informs the other. It is in this sense of reciprocity that Tierney and Pearson (1983) note the need for children to "read like writers" and "write like readers."

Reading as communication is aided by balancing the use of the four language processes: listening, speaking, reading, and writing. Language develops best when authentic demands are placed on one's language resources. Classroom teachers can help by providing contexts and situations where students are continually challenged to use the four language processes for productive ends.

Researchers have reported on the link between children's definitions of reading and teachers' actions during reading instruction (Deford and Harste, 1982). Classroom practices often deter the development of a lifelong lover of reading, despite the best intentions of teachers. We are confident that no teacher ever deliberately set out to "turn off" youngsters to reading; yet the current state of reading in our country has been described as grim (Anderson et al., 1985). If it is true that the definitions teachers hold about reading direct their classroom decision making and the activities they select for children, then a closer examination of what actually constitutes reading would be helpful at this point.

An examination of the literature on reading instruction and a look at current classroom practices suggest that there are two somewhat opposing views of reading: the *word recognition view* and the *psycholinguistic view*.

THE WORD RECOGNITION VIEW OF READING

The word recognition view of reading places primary emphasis upon the *product* of reading. One of the simplest ways of determining this product view is to listen to students read. The value of this product usually centers around accuracy, precision, and correctness. Its purposes are usually established outside of the reader and the intended interpretation of text is usually judged by an authority figure. Basal readers, which have formed the basis for reading instruction for more than 50 years, have been guided by this point of view. This view of reading can be best illustrated by describing a reading conference taking place between a student and a teacher who embraces a word recognition or product-oriented view of reading:

Nine-year-old Karen is attempting to read the following passage from Stephen Kellogg's *The Mysterious Tadpole* to her teacher, David Lyons:

> *One day Mrs. Shelbert decided that Alphonse was not turning into an ordinary frog.*
>
> This is what Karen actually reads aloud: "*One day Mrs. Shelby. . .*"
>
> David: "That's Mrs. Shelbert."
>
> Karen continues to read, "*One day Mrs. Shelbert decided that Alphonso. . . .*"
>
> David: "What did we say the name of the frog was?"
>
> "Alphonse," replies Karen, and continues to read aloud. "*One day Mrs. Shelbert decided that Alphonse was not turning into a (silence) frog.*"
>
> David: "*Try to sound it out.*"
>
> Karen now attempting to sound it out: "*Or . . . Ordin . . . Ordina. . . . Ordina. . . . Ordinated. . . . frog. . . . Ordin. . . . Ordinary. . . . Ordinary frog.*"
>
> David: "Very good reading."

Throughout this brief reading conference, Karen's teacher had several choices to make. And with every choice made, some message was being conveyed to Karen about reading. It is thus that developing readers constantly draw conclusions about the nature of reading, based upon the choices teachers make. An analysis of the exchange between Karen and her teacher might lead the learner to several conclusions about the nature of reading and what constitutes a good reader:

1. The purpose for reading is to perform for an authority figure.
2. Being a good reader is being able to read with accuracy and precision.
3. The role of the teacher is to judge and correct reading behavior.
4. "Sounding out" is the way readers figure out words they do not know.
5. The way to please a teacher is to read all the words correctly and to make no errors.

The verbal responses teachers give to students thus carry lasting messages about reading; they establish certain definitions of reading and ultimately encourage selected reading behaviors in youngsters. The messages that Karen's teacher either intentionally or inadvertently delivered to her were consistent with a product-oriented view of reading.

Let's continue to process the exchange between Karen and her teacher to see what other hidden messages about reading may have been delivered in the original exchange and to obtain a clearer picture of how Karen's teacher views reading.

The Mysterious Tadpole was a book that Karen had selected for herself; she was engrossed in reading the book when her teacher requested that she come to the table at the back of the classroom to read aloud to her. Begun in this way, a logical conclusion for a young student to draw might be that reading is primarily about performing as opposed to an activity selected to further one's personal goals.

The first time Karen's oral reading deviated from the actual text occurred after she read only three words correctly. Notice the choice that David made in responding to her at this point. Instead of *"Mrs. Shelbert,"* Karen read *"Mrs. Shelby."* David immediately provided Karen with the actual name written in the text: *"That's Mrs. Shelbert."* Three words later, a similar response was given when Karen read *"Alphonso"* for *"Alphonse."* Here, David decided to prompt Karen with a question: "What did we say the name of the frog was?" To this Karen was able to correctly respond with *"Alphonse."*

Karen continued to read each word accurately until she came to the word "ordinary" in the sentence, *"One day Mrs. Shelbert decided that Alphonse was not turning into an ordinary frog."* When Karen came to this word, she responded with silence and continued on to read the next word that was familiar to her, "frog." At this point, David instructed Karen to sound out the word "ordinary." After several attempts at "sounding it out," Karen was finally able to unlock the word. Upon hearing Karen correctly complete the sentence, David responded with praise.

Although we can never be sure that the messages we deliver are those perceived by the learner, the likelihood is excellent that Karen received the following messages about how to become a successful reader in this classroom:

1. When reading, *any deviation* from the words that are actually in the text are *errors* and should be immediately corrected.
2. The teacher is the source of "right" and "wrong" of my reading performance.
3. My teacher is pleased with my reading when I read each word accurately and precisely.
4. When readers come to a word they don't know, they should STOP, and "sound it out."

How, then, does this verbal exchange between Karen and her teacher translate into a product-oriented view of reading? Throughout the reading conference, Karen's teacher focused upon the *product* of Karen's reading. Attention was placed upon correct pronunciation and precise verbal translation of the words written by the author. This approach supports a conception of reading that honors correct word calling as the primary feature in the complex act we call reading. It emphasizes the product of reading and diminishes other features such as personal involvement with the author, bringing personal meaning to the printed page, and pursuing an individual purpose for reading.

Implications of the Word Recognition View

An orientation that focuses upon product (over process) comes out of an industrial model of thinking about goods and services. While it may be useful in providing aid to the consumer in defining relative quality of goods and services and making wise consumer decisions, it does little to enlighten educators as to the nature of reading. A product, by its nature, is a definable entity. As such, it can be broken down into its component parts and can be reproduced by merely assembling the subcomponents, according to a particular quantity and sequence.

Attempts to apply a product orientation to reading has led educators to define reading as the end result of particular combinations of building blocks, referred to as *skills,* assembled according to a particular sequence, each one identifiable and necessary for the successful "manufacture" of the final product—i.e., "the reader." All of the possible building blocks or skills are referred to as the *scope* of the subparts comprising reading. The particular order in which each of the subparts, or skills, should be acquired in order to obtain the desired product is referred to as the *sequence.* Thus the logical evolution of a product view of reading is a scope and sequence of skills that make up the component parts and define what is termed "reading." The concept of an identifiable scope and sequence of subskills has formed the foundation for the reading materials utilized in schools for several decades. They have provided the basis for reading instruction in the form of materials known as *basal reading programs* (to be more formally described later in this chapter). Basal reading programs were designed to teach reading according to a systematic plan of skill acquisition, according to the particular scope and sequence that characterized basal programs.

Classroom Practices Associated with the Product or Word Recognition View

A product or word recognition view of reading supports the teaching of reading in two basic ways: (1) through the decoding of letters, and (2) through the recognition of whole words or groups of words. Though meaning is an eventual result of this process, those who hold these views believe that readers must first focus attention on the individual elements of reading involved with graphic symbols and the sounds that the graphic symbols represent. Belief in the proposition that reading in its initial stages requires automatic recognition of graphic symbols and their sounds, along with an ever-increasing repertoire of recognizable whole words implies that readers will follow a particular sequence when they engage in reading:

1. Look at print.
2. Transform print into recognizable sounds and arrangements of sounds.
3. Relate what has been recognized to experience.
4. Make the speech-print connection.
5. Acquire meaning of printed text through a series of accurate speech-print connections.

This sequence presents reading as a *Bottom-Up activity*, where the meaning of the text is ultimately acquired by beginning at the bottom (beginning with the individual letters) and systematically moving upward as words are combined to make sentences, sentences combined to make paragraphs, and eventually the author's intended meaning is acquired by the reader. This sequence is illustrated in Figure 8.2.

The role of the reader, according to this view, is that of receiver, and the reader's job is to receive the message intended by the author. Table 8.1 describes those teaching practices that are consistent with viewing reading as a function of word recognition and as a bottom-up activity.

The Limitations of a Product or Word Recognition View

When applied to the outcomes of business, a product view may permit consumers to act in informed and intelligent ways; when we attempt to apply the same kind of reductionist view to the complex act of reading, however, we discover some serious limitations.

Twenty years of research into the field of reading education reveals an analogy that depicts the act of reading to be closer to that of a symphony than to an assembly line, as is described in *Becoming a Nation of Readers:*

> Reading can be compared to the performance of a symphony orchestra. . . . Like the performance of a symphony, reading is a holistic act. In other words, while reading can be analyzed into subskills such as discriminating letters and identifying words, performing the subskills one at a time does not constitute reading. Reading can be said to take place only when the parts are put together in a smooth, integrated performance . . . success in reading comes from practice over long periods of time, like skill in playing musical instruments. Indeed, it is a lifelong endeavor. . . . As with a musical score, there may be more than one interpretation of a text. The interpretation depends upon the background of the reader, the purpose for reading, and the context in which reading occurs. (p. 7)

READING AS A PROCESS

Reading considered as a process runs counter to the notion that the act of reading is an end product, resulting from having been taught a vast array of subskills. Attempts by educators to organize the reading act into a series of discrete skills, each skill built upon the one preceding it, tends to

TABLE 8.1   Teaching Practices Consistent with Word-Recognition and the Bottom-Up View of Reading

- Teacher assigns text to be read.
- Teacher introduces story to students and motivates them to read the story.
- Teacher assigns students purposes for reading.
- Teacher divides the story up and directly guides students through the story parts.
- Teacher checks to see if students have acquired the meaning intended by the author—generally through questioning students on what they have read.
- Teacher emphasizes phonics instruction as a primary means to unlock unknown words.
- Teacher assigns workbook activities to give additional practice in word recognition and comprehension.
- Teachers obtain teaching objectives derived from skills that are contained in a scope and sequence of skills, associated with a commercial reading program, or mandated by the school district or individual school.
- Teaching often means children working independently and quietly during reading instruction.

deny the complexity of reading, contends proponents of a process view of reading. Current research supports the theory that readers sample from text and that they do not decode every word on the page. Such a conception of reading also fails to take into account the way that children naturally acquire literacy (Anderson, 1985).

Viewed as a process, reading is something that commences long before a child ever picks up a book (see Chapter 6). The precursors for reading

FIGURE 8.2   A Word Recognition View of Reading as a Bottom-Up Activity

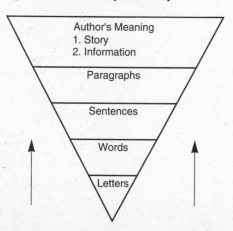

begin early (some conjecture that they begin in the womb!), and the process of becoming a competent reader evolves over a lifetime. As teachers, we are given the privilege of entering the lives of evolving readers at critical junctures. In this process we can serve as either enablers or obstacles. A look at a first-grade classroom may help you to begin the conceptualization of reading as a "process."

Mary Giard is a teacher of first graders, who is mentioned throughout this book because she embraces most of the beliefs and practices supported by current language arts research. Mary is a veteran teacher who did not begin her teaching career with young children. It was her concern for middle-school students, who were still struggling to make sense of reading, that encouraged her to make the shift to primary education. The student who best illustrates our thoughts about reading as a process is seven-year-old Nicole. Nicole comes from a home environment that can, at best, be described as fractured and, at worst, neglectful and intermittently abusive. She entered Mary's class with limited exposure to reading materials or reading events in her life. Her introduction to the world of story language and actual books was in kindergarten where she encountered a teacher who exuded passion for the sounds of language conveyed through good children's literature. Thus Nicole's natural curiosity about language and the world around her was given a focus—through the writings of others—by the time she entered Mary's first-grade classroom.

Mary Giard qualifies as an "enabler" in the most positive sense of the word—meaning she is a person who possesses the ability to further and positively support the natural inclinations and growth of others.

Mary and Nicole are seated beside one another at a round table, in the center of a semi-open space classroom, surrounded by other tables "inhabited" by 21 additional first graders engaged in a variety of reading and writing activities.

Nicole has requested a conference with Mary to share the book she has selected from their classroom collection: *Adam Draws Himself a Dragon* by Irina Korschunow. Nicole has requested a conference with Mary because there are a lot of words in this book that are presenting difficulty for her. The actual text that Nicole chooses to read for Mary is as follows:

> By now the little dragon had been with Adam for quite a while. He ate with Adam and he slept at the foot of his bed. He had learned many things— singing, dancing, turning somersaults, climbing trees. . . . (p. 17)

NICOLE: [Reading aloud to Mary.] *He had learned many things—singing, dancing.* [Stops here. Does not recognize the word.] I seen this word somewhere else. [Thumbs through parts of book previously read for the word she is stuck on.] I thought I seen it somewhere before. . . . [Thirty seconds transpire; Nicole continues to look for where she encountered the unknown word earlier in the book.] Right there! [Pointing to the word. Broad grin on her face as she looks up for Mary's approval.] Turns! [Continuing to read.] *He had learned many things—singing, dancing, turning somersaults, climbing trees. Now he wanted to learn to read.* [Looking up at Mary.] Is that ride or read?

MARY: You tell me.

NICOLE: *Read!* [Chuckling to herself, as though to say, "I knew that!"] *"Oh," said Adam. "Reading is browing . . . binging. . . . broring. . . . b.b.b., bahor. . . .* [Looking up at Mary.] "That doesn't work, does it?"

MARY: Try Plan B.

NICOLE: Hmmmmmm. [Looking upward toward ceiling in an attempt to recall some other way of figuring out the word.] I can break it up! [Divides word into parts with her fingers.]

MARY: If you want to break it up, you should be able to get it, because you know all the tricks.

NICOLE: *Bor . . . ing. Boring!* [Looks up at Mary with a very self-satisfied grin on her face.] Continues reading. *It takes a list. . . . list. . .* Is that word, "list"? [Looking up at Mary.]

MARY: What do you think?

NICOLE: [Continuing to read.] *At l . . . l . . . least!"*

MARY: That was a good decision.

NICOLE: What was?

MARY: To change it.

NICOLE: It took at least one hour to get through one peg.

MARY: [Laughing.] One what?

NICOLE: Peg.

MARY: What's that?

NICOLE: Peg. You know, peg. You know those things you use in a card game that you stick into holes.

MARY: Does that make sense? This isn't a game of cribbage they are talking about. [Chuckling again.] You read a what?

NICOLE: [Now in deep thought.] Peg!

MARY: Nicole, let's see if that makes sense. [Pointing to words and reading from text.] *It takes at least one hour to get through one . . .* [Stops reading here. Looks at Nicole to say a word that would make sense here.]

NICOLE: Peg. . . . Pog. [By this time a student working nearby comes over and looks at the text.]

OTHER CHILD: *Get through one part!*

NICOLE: Where's the "r"?

MARY: There is no "r." There is something else though that you aren't using, which when all else fails. . . . If you apply something

NICOLE: you know here, you ought to be able to figure it out.

NICOLE: [Looks back at text and attempts to "sound it out."] p . . . e . . . g . . . e.

MARY: It's one syllable.

NICOLE: *pege . . . pege.*

MARY: What does that "e" at the end of the word sometimes do to the vowel?

NICOLE: It's silent?

MARY: Yes; so what does it do to the "a"?

NICOLE: Makes it silent?

MARY: Nicole . . . [Chuckling.] . . . You are flipping me out! [Holds page between her fingers.] What is this?

NICOLE: Paper.

MARY: Nik-kiii. . . . Uggggggh. . . . [Now both Nicole and Mary are chuckling.] [Mary goes back and reads aloud to the point where Nicole is stuck on the word.] It takes one hour to get through one . . . [pauses; looks at Nicole.]

NICOLE: [The light dawns, and she smiles.] PAGE!

MARY: THANK YOU, Nicole. . . .!!!

[Very satisfied with herself now, Nicole proceeds to reread the page from the beginning. . . . perfectly. . . !]

FOR YOUR JOURNAL

Before you read further, REFLECT upon the exchange which just took place between Mary and Nicole. Notice the responses that Mary gave to Nicole. Write down what beliefs Mary has about young learners and what this scene says to you about reading as a process.

How did this exchange differ from the one between Karen and her teacher?

Let's take a look at what this scene reveals about reading, as well as this teacher's beliefs about reading. First, Mary views reading as a process. Each transaction Mary has with her students reveals important information as to where they are in the process of becoming self-sufficient, independent readers. Viewed as a process, Mary focuses upon students' strengths

and what they are discovering about reading, as well the diverse routes that individual students take in arriving there. Mary believes that students, as early as first grade, are adept at making decisions. They have been practicing their decision-making abilities on parents from approximately the age of two. Thus the cognitive structures are present in very young learners to make independent decisions. Mary sees herself as an important catalyst for conveying information about the reading process that will enable her students to make wise decisions regarding their reading behaviors. With each response, Mary is intentional about sending a very deliberate and direct message to her students:

> I believe in your intelligence and your ability to solve your own problems. I will be there to support you when you need me, and I will insist upon you employing what you know about figuring out unknown words and making meaning of what you are reading.

Did you notice that at no time throughout the exchange with Nicole did Mary provide answers where she knew that Nicole had the strategies to answer on her own? Despite Nicole's many attempts to get her teacher to "rescue" her, Mary remained consistent with the message she wanted Nicole to internalize: "You can do it!"

Glance back at Nicole's first attempt to engage Mary in making her decisions for her. When she looks up at Mary pleadingly and asks, "Is that ride or read?", Mary replies: "You tell me." Again, when she looks up at Mary after attempting to sound out the word "*boring*," Nicole says, "*That doesn't work, does it?*" To this Mary replies, "Try Plan B." Note where Nicole goes from there. She looks up at the ceiling, as though trying to think what other plan she has for figuring out an unknown word and says, "I can break it up!" Nicole then proceeds to divide the word into parts with her fingers.

As a process, the meaning of text unfolds as the reader interacts with the text in the kinds of strategic ways that Nicole demonstrated for us in this vignette. Notice the facilitative role that Mary played throughout the conference. Acting as facilitator to furthering Nicole's independence as a reader, we see her doing several things—and doing them *consistently:*

1. Mary encourages Nicole to employ the things she knows that competent readers do (referred to as *reading strategies*).
2. Mary consistently turns Nicole's requests for help into opportunities for Nicole to solve her own dilemmas.
3. Mary sits quietly and allows Nicole "think time."
4. Mary reflects back to Nicole the things that she is doing that are working for her. One of the ways she does this is by providing verbal labels for strategies she attempts, so that later when Nicole finds herself struggling on her own, she has the "inner language" to try things that may help her to solve her own problems.
5. Mary communicates, both verbally and nonverbally, that the purpose of the reading conference is not to read accurately for the teacher but to become more empowered as a reader.

How will you be able to realize your own power as a teacher and to remain excited about your profession? Mary Giard continues to cherish being a teacher after many years in the profession. The decisions she made during her exchange with Nicole mirrored the philosophy of a teacher who:

- Respects children
- Desires to support students in becoming strategic readers and writers.
- Engages students in reflection throughout every step of the process.
- Embraces a long-term goal of creating student independence.
- Believes that much of teaching occurs through invitational modeling.

- Knows that skillful "kid watching" reveals more than testing.
- Views children as natural seekers of meaning and knowledge.
- Regards teaching and assessment as synonymous.
- Knows that the language arts are learned when youngsters are authentically engaged in listening, speaking, reading, and writing throughout the day and across the curriculum.
- Regards her classroom as consisting of a community of learners, comprised of 24 teachers and learners.

THE PSYCHOLINGUISTIC VIEW OF READING

The psycholinguistic view of reading places greater emphasis upon the *process* rather than the *products* of reading. In the psycholinguistic model the reader is viewed as an active participant in the reading process who brings both background knowledge and knowledge of the language to the written page in an effort to construct meaning. There is no hierarchy of skills. Readers use three language cueing systems: (1) graphophonic, (2) syntactic, and (3) semantic. A fourth system will be discussed later in the chapter. The reader does not decode letter by letter but is encouraged to employ strategies to obtain meaning from the text (K. S. Goodman, 1982). The study of psycholinguistics has helped teachers realize that the act of reading is grounded in thought, language, and what we have personally experienced.

The psycholinguistic view of reading is no doubt a good depiction of the process you are engaging in as you read this section. A major determinant of how difficult or easy you find this chapter is the degree to which you are able to bring background knowledge to the information presented. Because each reader has a distinct background of experience and knowledge to impose upon the material presented in this book, no two readers will have *precisely* the same interpretation of what has been written.

As an accomplished and effective reader, you are probably unaware of actively constructing meaning as you move through each chapter. You are interchangeably, and often simultaneously, taking in minimal amounts of visual information and linking it to your prior knowledge, combining it with what you know about the English language, and making educated guesses about subsequent text material. This process is what led Ken Goodman to describe reading as a "psycholinguistic guessing game." Rather than viewing reading as a "bottom-up" activity, a psycholinguistic view emphasizes the ongoing interaction between what is in the mind of the reader and what is in the text. Conversely, then, this approach to making sense of what is in the written text is called a *top-down process*.

A Top-Down Process

A psycholinguistic perspective of reading views the flow of activity of the reader as originating at the top (information within the reader's mind) and resulting in a reciprocal, or interactive, action between what is in the reader's head and what is written on the actual page. A psycholinguistic view of reading is thus directly opposite to a word recognition perspective, which is a bottom-up process (Goodman and Burke, 1980).

A top-down approach to reading is meaning-driven. Meaning is not only the end product but the initiating event for reading to occur. Students encounter stories that they can relate to and are made increasingly meaningful through the deliberately planned verbal exchanges between teachers and students. Once children have been encouraged to bring their prior knowledge and experiences to the text and have become very familiar with a story, the teacher has created a vehicle from which the more abstract mechanical aspects (letters, punctuation, sentence structure, etc.) of reading can be understood. Isolated letters, and the sounds that those letters make, constitute the *least* meaningful encounter a child can have with a piece of text and should thus be dealt with by the teacher only *after* students have encountered the entire text in a meaningful way. Table 8.3 summarizes the teaching practices consistent with a psycholinguistic view of reading.

Psycholinguistics in Action

Let's look in on a classroom where we can observe psycholinguistic teaching practices in action. The classroom is that of Shadla Presley and her 24 second graders. Each day is characterized by authentic opportunities for children to listen, to read cooperatively and independently, and to express their ideas through talking and writing with their teacher and with one another. It is apparent upon entering Shadla's classroom that language and literature are important here. Reading materials of every size, shape, and description fill the room. Student-authored writings abound. They hang from the ceiling, they flow out of student folders, they line homemade bookshelves; they are bound within student-designed covers that make them durable enough for classmates to borrow and take home to share with family members. Children alternate working independently, in groups, as well as one-on-one with Shadla. Group sizes change fluidly according to the needs of students and the nature of the reading and writing projects in which youngsters are engaged.

It is 9:20 on Monday morning when we enter the classroom. As children complete their morning chores and check their shoe boxes to make certain that they have all of the materials necessary to carry out their day's work, they begin to gather on the rug around their teacher, who is seated on the author's hassock located in a corner of the room. She is holding an enlarged version of *The Grouchy Ladybug* by Eric Carle, and this signals to her students that as soon as they have taken care of their "housekeeping" duties, she is ready to read a book aloud to them. It is apparent from the scurry of activity in the classroom and the enthusiasm on the faces of the children, many

FIGURE 8.3   A Psycholinguistic or Top-Down View of Reading

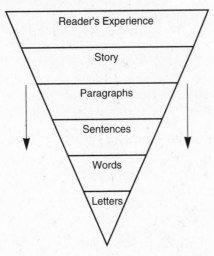

of whom are now seated cross-legged in front of their teacher, that this is a typical start to their academic day and that Shadla does not need to remind them where they should be. This is evidently something they look forward to each morning. After they are all assembled, Shadla begins by asking her students what time they arose that morning. The children offer various responses:

"My whole family overslept this morning because my mother forgot to set the alarm."

"I get up every school morning at the same time—seven o'clock. We all have a time to get up in our house so that we get to use the bathroom."

"Six o'clock. That is when my baby sister started yelling and woke us all up."

Each time a child shared what time he or she woke up that morning, Shadla offered a large, cardboard clock with movable hands, so that one of the students could show the rest of the class how the hands on the clock would look for the particular waking time of that classmate. Through this discussion, Shadla is preparing her students for the story she has selected to read to them this morning. She is activating background knowledge, which comes directly out of the youngsters' experiences and will give them a personal connection to Eric Carle's story of a grouchy lady bug who arises at 5:00 A.M. and appears to be looking for someone—anyone—to fight with.

Shadla joins the lively discussion in her classroom: "How many of you remember how you felt when you first woke up this morning?"

The most frequently given responses to this are "Sleepy," "Hungry," "Mad," "Happy," "Sick," and "I had to go to the bathroom." For future reference, Shadla records some of the responses on a large piece of chart paper attached to an easel located beside her. One youngster observes, after she has recorded "Sleepy," "Hungry," and "Happy," that it reminded him of the dwarfs in *Snow White and the Seven Dwarfs*. (This is the kind of spontaneous observation that occurs often in classrooms where there is broad definition of what constitutes literacy.)

TABLE 8.2   Teaching Practices Consistent with a Psycholinguistic Top-Down View of Reading

- Teacher begins with the sharing of a whole story, poem, or song.
- Teacher encourages students to make predictions, pose questions, and seek meaning rather than word recognition.
- Teacher uses all forms of communication to bring meaning to reading and actively involve students: listening, reading, writing, speaking, art, music, drama.
- Teacher tackles skills naturally from text as children reveal the need for them.
- Teacher encourages students to read aloud and silently in flexible groupings: partners, cooperative groups, interest groups, etc.
- Teacher uses a wide variety of reading materials.

Shadla had hoped that her children might use the word "grouchy" to describe how they woke up that morning. But now, Shadla seizes another opportunity, based upon one child's observation about *Snow White.* She asks, "If we were identifying the names of the seven dwarfs, who would we be missing? We have Happy and Sleepy. . . ."

"Sneezy!" exclaims one giggling youngster.

"Doc," offers another student.

"Wasn't there a one called Dumbo?" asks Jennifer.

"No. Dumbo was an elephant," replies Stephen. "You're thinking of Dopey."

"Oh, that's right. I remember now," responds Jennifer.

"We're missing one more that might be a synonym, or a feeling word that means the same as one that was used to describe how one of you felt when you woke up this morning," comments Shadla.

The children carefully examine the list of emotions that Shadla has recorded from their earlier contributions.

"When you think you know the name of the dwarf whose name is synonymous, or means the same, as one of the emotions you gave me to add to our list, quietly raise your hand, please."

One by one hands are raised. Shadla waits until everyone has had an opportunity to think her question through and asks students to say the word when she signals them. (Shadla does a great deal of whole-group instruction and has found that hand signals are helpful in enabling each of her students to have sufficient "think time" before responding.) At Shadla's signal, a chorus of voices chant in unison: "Grumpy!"

"Does anyone know another word that sounds like grumpy and means the same thing?"

"Grouchy!" shout the children.

"What does it mean to be grouchy?" asks Shadla.

"Mad," says Gretchen.

"Real, real angry, and nothing seems right," offers Jason.

"How many of you know what it's like to be grouchy?" All hands are raised. "Jason, you mentioned that when you feel grouchy that nothing seems right. Can you tell us what you meant by that, and is that different from being mad?"

"Well," responds Jason, "when I am mad, I am usually mad at something. Like I know what it is that made me mad. Sometimes when I'm feeling grouchy, I don't even know why but nothing seems right and I act like I'm mad."

"When was the last time that someone here felt grouchy, and what did it look like or sound like?" Shadla asks the class.

Seven-year-old Mariah rises from her chair, places her hand on her hip, and with a very animated pout says, "No! I don't want to!!" The class, as well as Shadla, are now laughing at this expert rendition of "Mariah the Grouch!"

"Well you know, the story I am going to read to you today is about someone who woke up feeling just like Mariah demonstrated for us and Jason described so clearly for us. The main character in our story today, authored by Eric Carle, just seemed to wake up wanting to take on the whole world for some reason. Have any of you ever felt like that or observed anyone else who seemed to feel that way?" Several hands go up. "Well I wonder if you, or they, learned a lesson like the one learned in today's story?"

For the first time, Shadla displays the cover of the book to the children. "Who can read for me the first two words of the title of Eric Carle's book?"

Dishon, reading aloud, says "*The Grouchy. . .*"

Shadla masks the remainder of the title. Encouraging her students to use the illustration on the cover as a clue to the remainder of the title, she asks, "Who thinks you can predict the rest of the title for this morning's book?"

"Spider!" squeal several students. "Lady Bug!" shout some others.

"We seem to have a difference of opinion, based upon the same clue. It may be that some of you aren't familiar with this little creature. But most likely, it's the illustration itself that might be throwing some of you off. Is this a *realistic* illustration?"

Students respond with a chorus of "No!"

"What does it mean when we say that something is not realistic?"

"It don't look like it's supposed to—just something like it."

"Well, let me tell you something I learned recently about spiders, and those of you who think the story today is going to be about a grouchy spider, try to use this information to decide. I learned that spiders belong to a group of small animals called "arachnids." The one thing that all arachnids have in common is that they have eight legs. Now, how many of you think that the title of our story is "The Grouchy Spider?"

Students are busy counting the legs of the critter on the cover and immediately begin responding with, "No. That's not a spider. It only has six legs." "It's a ladybug!"

"How many of you are certain that our story this morning is going to be about a Grouchy Ladybug?" All hands but six go up. This is a classroom where children seldom play "follow the leader" and go along with the majority when they are not certain of something. Shadla supports this independent decision making with her next response to the class.

"I'm glad to see that you are all thinking for yourselves this morning. When we are not sure of something, it helps us all to clarify our own thoughts. Is there anyone who is not certain what the main character of our story is, who would like to share with us why you think it might not be a ladybug?"

Shadla nods in the direction of Lionnel, who has his hand raised in response to her question: "I never seen a ladybug before," says Lionnel.

"Thank you, Lionnel. That supports something we have learned about reading, doesn't it? What is it that Lionnel just said that reminds us of something every good reader does before he or she begins to read a new story?"

Silence! Supplying students with another prompt (also referred to as "scaffolding"), Shadla suggests that if they look around the classroom, they might find a hint. Hanging from the ceiling are charts containing statements about what the students in Shadla's classroom have been learning about themselves as readers and about reading in general.

"I know; I know!" calls out Yolanda. "Before we begin to read something, we should ask ourselves what we already know about the topic. If we don't know anything about the topic, then we will have a hard time understanding what we are reading."

"Thank you, Yolanda. You have recalled something very important about getting meaning from what we read."

"Is there anyone else who is not sure that the grouchy little critter in our story is going to be a ladybug for the same reason as Lionnel?" The remainder of the hands go up.

"Does anyone recall the term we use here to describe what Lionnel and the others are missing?"

"Background knowledge?" says Tammy, with an air of doubt in her voice.

"Thumbs up if you agree with Tammy," says Shadla.

"Yeah! That's a big term to recall. What's the question good readers remember to ask themselves when they pick up a new book or reading selection? Nick. . . "

"Do I have the background knowledge to understand this story?" replies Nick.

"Right you are, Nick! Any other question that relates to this?"

"What do I already know about this topic," offers Christina.

"Wow! You guys sure know a lot about what it takes to be successful readers."

"Let's think now what good readers would do at this point to help themselves get ready to make sense of this story," suggests Shadla. "Take a minute to think about that and when I give you the signal, share your suggestion with the person nearest to you."

Following Shadla's signal, a buzz of voices offer ideas for what good readers do when they realize they do not have the background to understand a story.

"Let's list some of your ideas. What could we use as a heading for our list?"

"THINGS WE CAN DO TO HELP GET BACKGROUND KNOWLEDGE ABOUT LADYBUGS," suggests Joey.

The first item to go up on the list is: *Ask your friends who know about ladybugs.* (Students continue to generate additional ideas concerning background knowledge about ladybugs.)

Shadla's classroom thus presents us with an excellent glimpse of psycholinguistic principles and interdisciplinary teaching in practice. If we could shadow Shadla for the remainder of the day, we would see how she uses the shared experience of *The Grouchy Ladybug* to extend learning throughout the entire instructional day.

Psycholinguistics: Grounded in Language and Thought

By "observing" Shadla's approach to a shared book experience with her students, it should be evident that the core of a psycholinguistic view of reading instruction is the interplay of thought and language and the deliberate actions of teachers to continuously develop the thinking and language of students. Building a background of concepts through shared experiences is a cardinal element in psycholinguistic theory. Semantic webbing, oral and written discourse, and communication through art and drama are all vehicles for developing thoughts and language to express ideas, which together form the basis for reading comprehension.

Schemata and Reading

Schema provides readers with an organizational framework with which to make sense of what they are reading. Researchers also refer to schemata (plural for schema) as "cognitive frameworks" or "minitheories" (Rumelhart, 1981). As we read the words in a text, we call to mind schemata related to those words. Schemata are thus essential to gaining meaning from what is being read. Schemata can also be responsible for the misinterpretation of an author's intended meaning. Since schemata differ from individual to individual based upon the experiences that went into forming them, the individual interpretation of text will correspondingly differ as well. A passage from a story about a father coming home after a long day at work, for instance, will conjure up a very different picture in the mind of a child living in New York City and one living in the outback of Australia.

Evidence for the classroom implications of this can be demonstrated from the experience of Russell Kulinski during reading instruction in his fourth-grade classroom. The setting for the story his students had just completed took place inside a restaurant. When everyone had finished reading the story, Russell asked his students to recall the story for him. In the process of the retelling, one of his students recalled that as the characters in the story left the restaurant, one of them "punched out the waiter." Being puzzled by this, since he did not remember this occurring in the story, Russell asked his student to read him the passage where it stated that this had happened. The sentence the youngster read to his teacher went something like this:

> Before they left the restaurant, Fred tipped the waiter, said 'Good-bye' to his friend and hurried out into the street.

Although the youngster's interpretation of this passage was incorrect, in terms of the authors' intent, from the standpoint of the student, his interpretation made sense. In the course of this student's young life, he had never experienced dining in a restaurant where service was provided by waiters, who were subsequently given a tip for their good service. According to the schemata in this youngster's head, "tipping" the waiter, followed by the customer hurrying out of the restaurant, could reasonably be interpreted as having "slugged" the waiter. His experiences thus far had provided him with a schema whereby this interpretation made perfect sense.

The primary use readers make of schemata is to construct meanings as they read. From that perspective, then, the young student was doing what good readers do when they read. Competent readers make tentative selections of schemata they possess, as they move mentally through a passage and alter those choices, as required, during reading. In doing so, readers are actively involved with the text, by guessing or predicting what will happen before reading and reconciling what is going on in the story to what would make sense according to their schemata.

This teaching incident constituted a significant lesson for Russell Kulinski. From that point on, he carefully analyzed any reading material he assigned to students to determine if his students possessed the schemata for them to relate to the concepts contained in the assigned materials. It underscored for him, also, the interactive nature of reading.

Reading: An Interactive Process

The story of Russell Kulinski's student reveals the interactive facet of reading. According to interactive theory, readers begin with a hypothesis about the written text based on their prior knowledge while simultaneously processing the print (Reutzel and Cooter, 1992). Thus while Russell's student was processing the written text that was informing him that the character in the story tipped the waiter prior to leaving the restaurant (a bottom-up process), his previous experiences were influencing what he was receiving from the words stated in the text (a top-down process). Both "bottom-up" and "top-down" combined to produce this reader's unique interpretation of the reading passage. As readers interact with text, the balance constantly shifts between

what appears on the page and what is in the reader's head. As schemata for terms and concepts in the text diminish, the emphasis placed upon the features in the text increase. Thus interaction theory is a combinational theory. Readers are at varying times throughout the reading process both recipients and constructivists of meaning as they interact with written material. Readers, then, take on both active and passive roles during the reading process, according to interactive theory (Vacca et al., 1991) Reutzel and Cooter state it in this way: "If a reader possesses a great deal of prior knowledge about a given text, then she will be more likely to form hypotheses about the text and, thus use fewer text clues in reading. This is viewed as an active approach to reading. If a reader knows very little about a specific text, however, then the reader takes on a more passive role" (1992, p. 38).

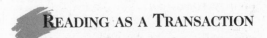

Reading as a Transaction

The work of Louise Rosenblatt (1978) has made considerable contributions to our understanding of the process of reading. She describes reading as a transaction between the text and the reader. According to Rosenblatt, a transactional view of reading expands beyond the notion of reading as being merely interactional. The key distinction between interactional and transactional theories of reading is related to context. Whereas interactional theory posits that either text or the reader predominates at various junctures in the reading process, transactional theory contends that both reader and text are transformed during the act of reading. Upon reading a text, the information is mixed with previously stored information in the mind of the reader, thus forever altering the exact message intended by the author for that particular reader. On the other hand, the schema that was previously held by the reader has undergone its own transformation as it is acted upon by the new information coming from the text.

The context in which reading occurs, according to Rosenblatt, cannot be separated from either the text or the reader. In addition to the schemata present in the minds of readers and the particular composition of the written material, contexts for reading include the purposes for reading. Thus if you are reading this portion of your text for the purpose of taking a test tomorrow, the transaction you are experiencing with it will probably be different than it would be if you were just perusing this chapter without a specific goal.

It is transactional theory that provides the underpinnings for the effective teaching of the integrated language arts. Whereas interactive theory allows for the separation of the text, the readers, and the context, transactional theory makes these three elements inseparable for purposes of instruction and measurement (Reutzel and Cooter, 1992). Among educators who view reading according to transactional theories, reading is seen as holistic in nature.

Classroom Implications of Transactional Theory

Transactional theory values the role of the reader in the reading process. As such, the reader must be part of an instructional environment that is both supportive and respectful of that role. Creating that environment—what we refer to as a literate environment—will be a significant element in the development of accomplished readers within your classroom. The following elements can serve as significant contributors to the establishment and maintenance of literate classroom environments (adapted from Cox and Zarrillo, 1993). These components, in concert, support a transactional view of reading instruction:

1. *A classroom overflowing with reading materials.* These should include a wealth of children's literature as well as a variety of other reading materials such as magazines, pamphlets, brochures, newspapers, and such. A classroom that places a high priority on reading is one in which there is access to lots and lots of reading materials.

2. *Appropriate reading material.* Children need reading material that is appropriate to their developing levels of reading maturity as well as to their interests. A classroom in which children are allowed to select material geared for their wide range of interests and abilities is a classroom that respects the individuality of growth and development.

3. *Writing tools.* When students have varied opportunities to write, they also have varied opportunities to enhance their reading development. Children thus need to be provided with pencils, pens, chalk, crayons, marking pens, and other writing instruments as part of their overall literacy growth.

4. *Somebody to read to students.* Usually this will be the classroom teacher, but do not discount the possibilities of other readers, too. These may include, but not be limited to, parents, grandparents, other students, older students, other teachers, visiting readers from the local community, or anyone else eager to share the magic of reading aloud to children.

5. *Adult helpers.* Adults provide a necessary support structure in the literacy development of children. Adults need to be available to answer questions, lend a needed hand, or offer encouragement throughout the day. The important consideration is that adults must be available to respond to the expressed needs of children throughout the learning process.

6. *A model of proficiency.* Teachers should be willing to model important and necessary reading behaviors for their students. By reading aloud to students, they can demonstrate the energy and enthusiasm that can result from a story well-told. By reading silently during portions of the day, they can model

the value of reading. By providing lots of books in the classroom, they can model the process of collecting a wide range of reading materials for pleasure or information. In short, children need models that they can observe and emulate throughout their literacy development.

7. *Literacy as a tool for learning.* One of the chief goals of reading instruction is the construction of meaning. When students are offered sincere and authentic opportunities to become aware of the power of print to convey comprehensible messages, then lifelong literacy skills are enhanced. Cox and Zarrillo (1993) have identified the fundamental question that teachers need to ask: Are children reading and writing to give and get meaning?

8. *Silent reading time.* Learning to read and having opportunities to practice the craft of reading are inexorably intertwined in a transactional classroom. Students need access to a wide range of literature and sustained opportunities to pursue that literature on a daily basis. Silent and sustained reading opportunities allow children to develop fully as accomplished and lifelong readers.

9. *A wide range of experiences.* Reading development is enhanced when children are provided with first-hand experiences with the world around them. We like the term "hands-on, minds-on" as a definer for the types of activities children should be exposed to throughout their educational experiences. The more opportunities students have to participate in direct experiences (via guest speakers, field trips, science experiments, playground excursions, etc.) the larger their schema and, hence, the better their abilities to read will become.

At this point it would be useful to revisit Brian Cambourne's eight conditions of language learning (from Chapter 1) and to relate them to the nine elements of a transactional classroom shown in Table 8.3.

The mere creation of a literate environment does not guarantee that each student in your classroom will grow up to become an accomplished reader. Not all of the elements described above are necessary for some children to become successful readers. Certainly, each child brings a set of aptitudes and attitudes that influence his or her development as a reader. However, the creation of a literate environment optimizes the conditions that can assist all children in learning to read and in reading to learn.

CUEING SYSTEMS

Whenever a reader is actively engaged in the act of reading, three types of cueing systems are occurring simultaneously: (1) *graphophonic* (sound/symbol relationships, (2) *syntactic* (the way language works in a text), and (3) the *semantic* (the meaning of language). (See Figure 8.4 on page 250.) These cueing systems are critical, interacting processes that influence how and with what degree of success we read. Competent readers readily employ each of the three cueing systems to obtain meaning from what they are reading. Let's take a closer look at each.

Graphophonics

When readers employ this cueing system in the act of reading, they are focusing on the individual symbols on the page (letters) and the sounds that are associated with the letters. Generally, the better the reader, the less he or she has to rely upon this cueing system. Overreliance upon the use of graphophonics promotes word-by-word reading, and the meaning of the text is often lost in the process of sounding out each and every sound element in the words. *Phonemes* are the sounds heard inside the head of the reader which relate to certain letters or letter combinations. Since one sound can be represented by two or more letters (graphs), good readers know that the number of sounds and the number of letters are not necessarily the same. The word "graph," for instance, contains five letters (graphs), but only three phonemes (distinct sounds): *gr/ + a/ + ph.*

Semantic Cues

When readers use semantic cues to determine an unknown word within a text, they are intuitively asking themselves, "What would make sense here?" For instance, if you were stuck on the following sentence because you did not immediately recognize the word represented by the blank, as a good reader, you would try on some word which would make sense to the rest of the sentence or passage:

> The army was issued _____ for only a two-week tour of duty. After that, they expected that they

would begin to lose some of their company if helicopters could not fly in to replenish their stock.

Did you guess food? Provisions? Ammunition? Using semantic cues alone, any of these words would be reasonable "guesses." With the inclusion of only one phonographic element, however, you will experience how knowledge of that element ensures confidence in your decision. In this case, the beginning grapheme is "p," making the word "provisions" the most likely candidate; and in this case, you would have been correct. Your word knowledge and the use of the words around the unknown word to suggest what would make sense there required that you employ semantics (or a meaning clue) to determine the unknown word.

Notice, that with the addition of the phonographic clue "p," you did not guess "punish," or "pretty," or "positively." By knowing that neither of these three words would have been likely candidates for the missing word reveals something

TABLE 8.3   Relationships Between Cambourne's Conditions of Language Learning and Elements of a Transactional Classroom

The Literate Classroom Environment	Cambourne's Conditions of Language Learning
1. Lots of books A classroom filled with literature	1. Immersion
2. Appropriate reading material Reading materials for various interests and abilities	2. Demonstration
3. Writing tools Pencils, crayons, word processors, and other instruments	3. Engagement
4. Somebody to read to children People sharing the joys of reading aloud	4. Expectation
5. Adult helpers Supporters of each child's literacy growth	5. Responsibility
6. A model of proficiency Students seeing how accomplished readers read	6. Employment
7. Literacy as a tool Children using reading to get meaning	7. Approximation
8. Silent reading time Opportunities to self-select and read without pressure	8. Feedback
9. A wide range of experiences Hands-on learning opportunities	

FIGURE 8.4 The Cueing Systems

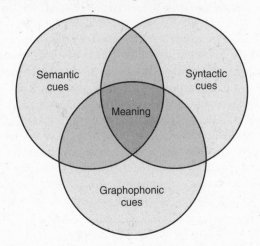

about your knowledge of English and what part of speech would be likely to be there. This understanding of the order that words go in is integral to the third cueing system.

Syntactic Cues Syntax refers to sentence grammar. Familiarity with the language reduces the guesswork that goes into predicting the type of word that would come next in a sentence. Syntactic cues are closely linked to semantic cues in that both seek to answer the question, "What would make sense here?" Syntax narrows the possible options to those which serve the same function as the unknown word—in other words, a noun for a noun, a verb for a verb, etc.

Finally, the cueing systems are supported by a reader's schematic system, which deals with the anticipations and assumptions a reader already has about a text. For example, as soon as a primary teacher begins storytime with the words "Once upon a time...", some children unconsciously, and sometimes not so unconsciously, will yell out, "Oh, this story is going to be a fairytale!" This is because the introductory line, "Once upon a time...", used in storytelling and bedtime read aloud, always signals a certain type of story. Something similar would occur if a person were to read, "Once upon a time..." at the

beginning of a newspaper article. "A most unusual way to begin a newstory," muses the reader. "I think I'll read on to find out more." In other words, the reader was not expecting to read that line. We have certain expectations as readers that we subconsciously expect as we begin reading particular magazines, newspapers, novels, etc.

In *Reading As Communication*, Frank May (1990) makes the following statement, which adds an informative perspective on the four cueing systems: *"Reading is not only an interaction between the schemas of the author and the reader; it is also an interaction among the four cueing systems—graphophonic, syntactic, semantic, and schematic"* (p. 78).

In other words, reading is an interweaving of cueing systems in differing amounts and differing degrees according to the nature of the material and the reader's "comfort level" with that material. There are, however, two most important points we would like to make at this juncture. The first is that there is no single way of teaching reading that will ensure that each child in your classroom will become an accomplished reader. The second is that reading is never separated from the other language arts in an integrated language arts program. We have made reading the primary focus of this chapter in order to examine a few of its salient features; in a classroom setting, however, the teaching of reading is woven into the simultaneous teaching of writing, listening, and speaking.

In order to better understand the distinctions of the whole language practices of the many teachers described throughout this book, let's examine the approach that has driven reading instruction in this country since the turn of the century—the basal reader approach.

THE BASAL READER APPROACH

The basal reader is a book that has been specifically designed to assist teachers in teaching children to read. The basal reader is just one component of a basal reading program, which consists of a complete package of teaching materials created to provide a roadmap for teachers to follow. Such a program includes all the accessories necessary to efficiently, economically, and effectively instruct young persons in becoming independent readers. Basal reading programs provide an entire reading curriculum and can include the following:

1. Student readers
2. Teacher's manuals
3. Student workbooks
4. Assessment and placement materials
5. Record-keeping folders
6. Sound filmstrips
7. Stories on audiotape
8. Ancillary book collections
9. Blackline for student seatwork
10. Blackline masters of letters to parents
11. Student journals
12. Computer management systems

In addition to the above offerings, publishing companies are making computer software and collections of notable children's literature available with the newer basal reading programs.

Basal readers traditionally have been built upon a word-centered or "bottom-up" view of reading. Controlled vocabulary, a system of carefully introducing new words starting with those in very frequent use, has been the central organizing strand in reading instruction. Basal programs have traditionally been predicated upon the assumption that whole word acquisition occurs through frequent, systematic repetition and is fixed in memory through a system of reinforcers (practice, skill sheets, workbooks, etc.)

The Basis for Basal Readers

Whether to use basal reading programs in their entirety, to use them selectively, or to abandon their usage entirely is a decision facing most teachers today, as the field of reading education experiences an unprecedented era of rethinking long-held notions and practices associated with reading instruction. As you visit classrooms during field experiences, you will observe teachers at all points along the philosphical and instructional continuum. Many find themselves somewhere in transition—from total reliance upon basal reading programs to a combinational approach of using basal readers along with trade books to a language arts block that is totally literature based.

An understanding of how basal reading programs came into existence can provide a backdrop for you to intelligently consider the role that basals will have in your teaching life. As with most events, the emergence of basals into the educational arena did not take place in isolation. Like any enduring phenomenon in our culture, the process was influenced by outside forces that prevented it from fading out of existence. Since the advent of the basal reader and its accompanying instructor's manual occurred some years ago, it can certainly be considered an enduring force within education. The fact that basal programs dominate reading instruction has been expressed in *Becoming a Nation of Readers: The Report of the Commission on Reading.*

> The observation that basal programs "drive" reading instruction is not to be taken lightly. These programs strongly influence how reading is taught in American schools and what students read. This influence is demonstrated by studies that have examined how time and instructional materials are used in classrooms. The estimates are that basal reading programs account for from 75 percent to 90 percent of what goes on during reading periods in elementary school classrooms. (p. 35)

THE STRUCTURE OF BASAL READERS

The basic structure of the teaching suggestions within the teacher's manuals accompanying basal readers is similar from publisher to publisher. Although the beliefs, emphases, and content may differ, the manuals follow a common five-step instructional sequence. We present here a brief description of each step, a summary of the beliefs that undergird each step, and the possible limitations associated with each step.

Step 1: Readiness/Preparation

a. Vocabulary Preteaching Because basals attempt to control for the introduction of new words, any words which are unfamiliar in the story are pretaught.

Underlying Beliefs Reading vocabulary is developed through a process of repetition. Students learn to read words by encountering them again and again. If there are words that have not been previously introduced, they should be pretaught so that students will not encounter difficulty with them in the story.

Limitations

1. Controlled vocabulary assumes that students have never encountered the new words before. If the basal reader is the only source of reading material that the learner is exposed to, then perhaps this would be a legitimate assumption. But since the goal of any good reading program is to immerse students in all kinds of reading materials, as well as to encourage parents to share books at home with their children, it is not possible for a teacher to know whether the "new words" in the story are familiar or unfamiliar to students.
2. If the goal of reading instruction is to create independence in students, then preteaching the "new word" in each of the basal stories robs students of opportunities to apply the three cueing systems (graphophonic, syntactic, semantic) in discovering words on their own. Instead, what this instructional approach is likely to do is foster dependence upon the teacher as the primary strategy for determining unfamiliar words in print.

b. Readiness for the Story

Underlying Beliefs It is the role of the teacher to motivate students and prepare them for reading the story. It is also the role of the teacher to establish a purpose for reading the story.

Limitations

1. The suggested readiness for the story often does not ask students to relate to the story theme. The script often has the teacher *telling*, not *eliciting*, background information from learners, which would activate previous knowledge that they can use to aid them in comprehending the story. (Use of background knowledge aids comprehension by enabling students to anticipate what is coming next; to hypothesize the outcome of the story; to make predictions.)
2. Establishing a purpose for reading is an essential prerequisite for effective comprehension, but teacher's manuals often provide only those purposes established by the publisher. A better role for the teacher to play here is to assist students in establishing their own purposes for reading a particular story or text.

Step 2: Guided Silent Reading

Students are stopped periodically throughout the story and asked questions to check their understanding.

Underlying Beliefs It is the role of the teacher to provide guidance during students' reading of a story and to monitor their comprehension.

Limitations

1. Breaking up the story in this way greatly impedes the ability of the reader to make sense of the whole passage and, instead, focuses the reader on isolated details.

2. Following this suggested procedure story after story can instill within learners the notion that the primary purpose of reading is to answer the teacher's questions correctly or that comprehension is only a process of remembering isolated details.

3. Often, the correct answers are provided for teachers, following the recommended questions they are to ask the students. By providing these answers, teachers are not encouraged to listen to the responses given by the student, they are instead merely programmed to listen for whether the answers are "correct" or "incorrect." When only those answers that conform to those provided by the publishers are accepted, student thinking is discouraged. In many cases, answers that deviate from those intended by the publishers can be equally as logical, given the reasoning applied to them by each reader.

4. This procedure creates an artificial reading situation. "Real" reading is not usually associated with being interrupted and questioned as readers move through a piece of written material. Again, it can encourage erroneous notions regarding what reading is. (This is why children, when asked how they feel about reading, say that they enjoy reading. Then, when they are asked if there is any subject in school that they don't like, they respond with, "Reading." We believe this is because they do not define what they do during reading instruction as "reading.")

Step 3: Skills Instruction

One or several new skills (determined by the scope and sequence of skills in the series) is to be introduced through direct teaching by means of a scripted lesson plan. Students are then given follow-up drill/reinforcement work to do at their seats.

Underlying Beliefs   Reading is the end product of the acquisition of a body of isolated skills, which are hierarchical and must be taught to all readers. The stories in the basal programs are, in fact, the vehicles used by basal authors to help teachers teach the skills of reading. Basal series distinguish themselves by the scope of the skills taught in their programs and the order in which the skills are taught.

Limitations

1. There is no research to defend any particular scope and sequence of skills that is necessary for all readers.

2. There is mounting evidence to suggest that skills taught in isolated fashion do not transfer to real reading.

3. There is much evidence to suggest that the workbook and worksheet page exercises are *not* worthwhile. Readers become effective readers by *reading*. Time spent filling in workbook pages is time not given to permitting children to read books and other "real" reading materials.

4. There is often little or no connection between the content in the workbooks and the passages read by students.

Step 4: Rereading the Story

Students are instructed to reread or read parts of the story on a day or two following the first, silent reading. Students are usually required to reread the story orally, and the reading is often performed in "Round Robin" fashion (students reading in order of seating arrangement, usually a paragraph or page at a time). Often the rereading step is combined with comprehension skill instruction.

Underlying Beliefs   To ensure success, the first reading of a story should be performed silently by students. Reading all or parts of the story aloud aids students in developing fluency in reading and permits the teacher to assess their progress in reading.

Limitations

1. Not every story is of sufficient depth or interest to students to warrant rereading.
2. The purposes for rereading are, again, teacher-established purposes and not based upon the expressed needs or interests of students.
3. There are more authentic and stimulating means of developing reading fluency (for example, through reader's theatre productions.)
4. Round Robin reading has been demonstrated to be one of the least effective techniques for helping children to more fully comprehend what they have read and contributes to behavior problems and boredom in students.

Step 5: Enrichment/Extension of Skills

The enrichment step is where readers can extend beyond the text and engage in activities that can add excitement and interest to reading. It is an opportunity to connect the contents of basal stories with other areas of the curriculum. It is also the step at which teachers can pull together students who require additional skill instruction or individual attention while others are engaged in enrichment and extension activities. Trade books can be used here. Accommodations can be made to meet the needs of students with special gifts and talents.

Limitations This vital step in the teaching process, which has the potential for getting kids really excited about reading and meeting the varied needs of students in the class, is most often left out in order to "cover the content." (Teachers who are required to follow a basal reading program and who desire to incorporate a more "whole language" approach in their classrooms report that they use this step in the basal structure to accommodate that desire.)

Moving from Basals to Books

A comparison of basal reading programs and reading instruction that flows from a philosophy of whole language reveals some similarities between the two. Both are concerned with the following:

Phonics
Knowledge of syntax
Word recognition
Spelling ability
Appreciation for literature
Skill in composition

It should be clear by this time, however, that a clear distinction exists philosophically with regard to how these should be acquired. More specifically, they differ in philosophy regarding certain points:

How children learn
Materials for reading instruction
The role of the teacher
Approaches to reading instruction
Methods for evaluating learning

As teachers reevaluate and rethink their beliefs about literacy development, the ways in which they utilize basal programs in their classrooms is changing for many; others have opted to use basal readers as simply another type of reading option for children in their classrooms. Still, others have decided to eliminate basals entirely from their reading programs and have replaced them with trade books of every type.

Whether basals are a primary, ancillary, or nonexistent feature of classroom reading instruction, teachers are approaching written text in a different manner.

NEW APPROACHES TO USING BASALS AND OTHER READING MATERIALS

As teachers strive to relate new research on language and literacy to existing practices in the language arts, they are making modifications to how they approach reading materials in the classrooms. Two areas in particular can provide sound starting points for teachers who want to move toward more holistic practices:

1. Meaning-based, Strategic Instruction
2. Story Grammar

Meaning-based, Strategic Instruction

The crux of the alterations that classroom teachers are making to reading materials, whether they be basal readers or trade books, is that meaning has become the central feature in the process of reading. And this emphasis upon meaning is central at each point in the reading process—i.e., Before, During, and After reading. Children are taught specific strategies to use *Before* reading a selection, *While* reading a selection, and *After* reading a selection to foster understanding of the text and a greater insight into reading as a process. A much greater emphasis is also given to the interrelatedness of reading and writing during "reading instruction." Children use literature as a springboard for topic ideas and as a model for their own writing.

Whether approaching stories from their basal readers or self-selected books from classroom collections, students are being guided by teachers to understand what it takes to become proficient readers. For instance, current practices in the teaching of reading help students to realize important techniques (Butler and Turbill, 1987):

- BEFORE reading, the proficient reader brings and uses knowledge:

  About the topic (semantic knowledge)

  About the language used (syntactic knowledge)

  About the sound-symbol system (graphophonic knowledge)

  About previous reading experiences

  About the presentation of the text

  About the purpose for the reading

  About the audience for the reading

- DURING reading, the proficient reader is engaged in:

  Draft reading

  Skimming and scanning

  Searching for sense

  Predicting outcomes

  Redefining and composing meaning

  Rereading

  Rereading parts as purpose is defined, clarified or changed

  Taking into account, where appropriate, an audience

  Discussing text, making notes

  Reading aloud to "hear" message

  Using writer's cues

  Using punctuation to assist meaning

  Using spelling conventions to assist meaning

- AFTER reading, the proficient reader:

  Responds in many ways—e.g., talking, doing, writing

  Reflects upon the reading

  Feels success

  Wants to read again

Story Grammar

Narratives tell a story. The organizational structure of a simple narrative consists of a situation that is introduced, developed, and resolved. The organizational pattern is referred to as *story grammar*. Just as sentence grammar provides a way of describing how a sentence is put together, story grammar helps to specify the basic parts of a story and how those parts tie together to form a well-constructed story. One of the major reasons for using trade books in the classroom is that the story grammar corresponds to the structure and flow of language that is familiar to children who have been read to prior to entering school. The artificial language that is viewed as a necessary component to commercial reading materials violate the principles of story grammar. Children who have heard stories read to them from the time they were young have acquired a story sense, which conditions them to anticipate certain things: that the story will take place in a particular setting or settings; that there will be a main character (often called the protaganist); that there will be one or more minor characters; and that there will be a conflict of some kind to resolve. Children whose backgrounds include listening to stories and making up their own stories from pictures within a book know that there will be one or more episodes that will occur before the resolution of the conflict is achieved. Although the labeling of these events differs from story grammar to story grammar, the following elements are generally included:

1. *A beginning or initiating event:* Either an idea or an action that sets further events into motion.
2. *Internal response (followed by a goal or problem):* The character's inner reaction to the initiating event, in which the character sets a goal or attempts to solve problem.
3. *Attempt(s):* The character's efforts to achieve the goal or alleviate the problem; several attempts may be evident in an episode.
4. *An outcome(s):* The success or failure of the character's attempt(s).
5. *Resolution:* The long-range consequence that evolves from the character's success or failure to achieve the goal or resolve the problem.
6. *A reaction:* An idea, emotion, or further event that expresses a character's feelings about success or failure to reach a goal or resolve a problem, or that relates the events in the story to some broader set of concerns.

(Adapted from Vacca, Vacca and Grove 1991.)

Many examples of good children's literature follow simple story grammar, as shown in Table 8.4. Young readers need a plethora of opportunities to engage with this simple organizational pattern.

One of the tools that authors use to manipulate the complexity of a story is by altering the story grammar. For example, a writer might use a flashback or flashforward variation of setting. Episodes may be placed out of sequence. Plots may be camouflaged or resolution made unpredictable, as in thrillers and adventure stories. It is important, then, that careful story selection be made during early attempts to encourage children to be conscious of story grammar contained in narratives.

Current practices of teaching reading subscribe to the notion that children are capable of becoming competent readers when teachers act as facilitators of the learning process. What we hope you will discover is that youngsters who are provided with a host of interactive and personally rewarding strategies throughout the reading program will be youngsters who become responsible learners and responsible readers. The teaching of reading implies that students must be *actively engaged* in the dynamics of reading as opposed to traditional practices in which the classroom teacher "takes charge" of each child's reading program. Indeed, your greatest challenge as a teacher of reading will be to assist your students in assuming competence and control for their reading "destinies." It is a challenge that is both exciting and dynamic.

TABLE 8.4 Examples of Simple Story Grammar

Setting	Episodes	Conflict	Resolution
It was a dreary Hallows Eve.	Jane approaches the king's castle.	She is spotted by the sentries.	The handsome prince tricks his father into freeing her.
At the birth of Hazel's brother, Billy, ...	Her pa predicted that he would grow up to be the worst monster in the world.	Everyone was so busy watching Billy live up to pa's prediction that no one noticed Hazel, and she wanted to be the worst monster in the world.	When Hazel said that she had given her brother Billy away, the family declared her the absolute worst monster in the world.

CATHY'S SWANSON'S JOURNAL

❧ February 8

Last year I found that letter writing can be a very useful way of testing or assessing. Somehow the idea of writing an essay telling "everything you know" about a subject throws students into a panic. But ask them to write a letter to me, a parent, or a friend and somehow the task becomes more manageable, more like conversation. This worked exceptionally well in fifth-grade American History studies; kids would write to each other as though they were one of the great explorers, or perhaps a drummer boy in the Confederate Army.

I wasn't sure if fourth graders could put themselves in another's place as comfortably as the older kids could, but I decided to try it out. We were studying the Northeast region. I told the kids that I did not live in this area but was considering relocating to the region. Their mission was to convince me to move here. What might draw me to this part of the country? What was the land like? The climate?

This format forced them to take all the "facts" they had memorized and assimilate the information, plus use persuasive language to do so. They also made a connection with what they personally knew about the region as residents of Pennsylvania. Writing with a purpose in the content areas works.

❧ February 9

Steph F. shocked me today! Josh had just finished reading his newest piece. Everyone responded, but told Josh they were feeling a bit confused about what he wanted help with. It was then that Steph, in one of those moments of great insight that leaves a teacher wondering "Are you secretly twenty-five in the costume of a nine-year old?!", suggested, "Maybe it would be good if you gave us something specific to listen for in your story."

After picking my chin up off the floor, I smiled at Steph (probably my most reluctant writer) and said, "Indeed, it would be. Thanks!"

❧ February 17

Managing Writing Workshop is still a challenge. I just don't feel I'm as efficient as I could be. The kids seem to have a good understanding of the steps of the process, and they do work well independently.

I keep short anecdotal notes (this isn't easy for me to keep up with) and we do have a "Status of the Class" chart posted on the wall. What I'm missing is working in those minilessons for small groups based on a common need to learn a particular skill.

I conference with the kids, but I feel I need something more tangible for *them* to keep and read over, other than their own notation of progress. This aspect of Writing Workshop seems to be a challenge to other teachers as well. Maybe someone has come up with a new idea. . . .

As part of our study of the regions, every student was required to give a presentation about one of the states. The following components were mandatory:

1. A written report
2. A speech
3. A visual aid of some sort

Beyond those three requirements, the choice was theirs. Travis made a video taped tour of Tennessee, Elena gave a "tour in the first person" as though she were actually from West Virginia. Two students taped interviews with their parents about their trips to the states. Julia came dressed as a Floridian might and pre-sented her speech as she lounged on her beach towel, surrounded by shells. Liz shared her family's collection of Native American art, skillfully displayed on a Hopi blanket.

One project that I really enjoyed was Steph H.'s presentation on Arkansas. After delivering her speech, she divided the class in half and proceeded to direct the "Steph version" of Family Feud. She asked good questions about her own presentation, had worked out all the rules of the game, and even handled the rewards in an equitable manner; all the players received at least one Jolly Rancher, the winners received two!

When the kids engage each other like this, I sit back and learn!

Yesterday, the kids announced they were bored with D.E.A.R. (another name for Sustained Silent Reading meaning Drop Everything And Read). "Let's think of something else to call it," they said.

"Fine with me," I responded. "Any suggestions?"

"How 'bout 'MOOSE'?" answered Josh after a few moments. He was trying to be funny, but the other kids took the challenge of finding something MOOSE might stand for. The final decision was:

M—Marvelous

O—Outrageous

O—Outstanding

S—Silent

E—Experience

And so, we now have MOOSE everyday!

TEACHER AS LEARNER/TEACHER AS RESEARCHER

Professional Resources

The concept of teacher as researcher has always, we believe, been at the heart of wonderful teaching. The term "teacher as researcher" merely gives a label to what good teachers have always done as they have earnestly attempted to meet the needs of every youngster in their classroom. Effective classroom teaching has "always" been synonymous with teacher reflection. Good teaching requires reflecting upon the outcomes of instruction, raising questions about improving what transpires in the classroom, and pursuing answers to ways of doing better. If differences exist, today, they revolve primarily around the accessibility of resources to teachers in pursuit of their own knowledge.

Support for classroom research comes in several forms. We share some with you here and encourage you to add to this listing so that when you begin to carry out research in your own classroom, you will have the assurance that you do not have to go it alone.

The first area of support comes in the form of other teachers, who like yourself are questing for knowledge that will translate into doing things more effectively in their classrooms. To get you started, you might want to begin by consulting a book that we think is a little gold mine for anyone who is contemplating taking that first step into classroom research: "The Art of Classroom Inquiry: A Handbook for Teacher-Researchers" (Portsmouth, NH: Heinemann) written by Ruth Shagoury Hubbard, of Lewis and Clark College, and Brenda Miller Power, of the University of Maine. Among the many great things that Hubbard and Power offer to the budding researcher is a list of teachers who were once where you are now and are willing to share with anyone the collective wisdom forged from many successful, as well as unsuccessful, attempts at conducting research in their classrooms. Another way to connect with teachers who share the same teaching interests as you is through electronic mail (e-mail) and electronic bulletin boards. With a little help from your local librarian, you could put yourself in touch with educators all over the world, who may have wonderful suggestions for how you can acquire the answers you are seeking. There are bulletin board networks on almost any subject of interest to an educator. There will undoubtedly be some area of interest to you.

For those of you who will be going into classrooms with absolutely no idea about where to begin or really what being a researcher in your own classroom means, the following selected sources from Hubbard and Power might be useful:

INTRODUCTIONS TO TEACHER RESEARCH

Bissex, G., and Bullock, R., eds. "Seeing for Ourselves: Case-Study Research by Teachers of Writing." Portsmouth, NH: Heinemann, 1987.

Mohr, M., and Maclean, M. "Working Together: A Guide for Teacher Researchers." Urbana, IL: National Council of Teachers of English, 1987.

Newkirk, T., ed. "Workshop 4: The Teacher as Researcher." Portsmouth, NH: Heinemann, 1992.

Patterson, L., and Short, K., eds. "Teachers are Researchers: Reflection in Action." Newark, DE: International Reading Association, 1994.

Rodduck, J., and Hopkins, D. "Research as a Basis for Teaching: Readings from the Work of Lawrence Stenhouse." Portsmouth, NH: Heinemann, 1985.

INDIVIDUAL TEACHER ACCOUNTS OF THEIR CLASSROOM RECORDS

Fisher, B. "Joyful Learning: A Whole Language Kindergarten." Portsmouth, NH: Heinemann, 1991.

BOOKS ABOUT CLASSROOM LIFE

Freedman, S. "Small Victories: The Real World of a Teacher, Her Students, and Their High School." New York: HarperCollins, 1990.

Perl, S., and Wilson, N. "Through Teachers' Eyes: Portraits of Writing Teachers at Work." Portsmouth, NH: Heinemann, 1986.

Journal Reflections

Select one or more of the questions below that interest you and respond in your journal.

1. At this point in Cathy Swanson's Journal, it seems as though she is able to infuse reading into many aspects of her curriculum. Based on what you have read so far, as well as the information in this chapter, how do you think Cathy's students might define the word reading?

2. How would you define the word reading? What does that word mean to you now? How is your definition different from a definition you may have had prior to reading this chapter?

3. How will you be able to integrate reading into all of the other areas of the elementary curriculum—science, math, social studies, etc? What procedures will you use that promote reading as a valuable part of every subject area?

4. Design your own question.
   ✓ What is a question you have about the chapter?
   ✓ How will you pursue the answer to that question?
   ✓ Respond in your journal.

REFERENCES AND SUGGESTED READINGS

Anderson, R., Hiebert, E., Scott, J., and Wilkinson, I. *Becoming a Nation of Readers: The Report of the Commission on Reading.* Campaign, IL: Center for the Study of Reading, 1985.

Becoming a Nation of Readers: The Report of the Commission on Reading. Prepared by R. C. Anderson et al. Washington: National Institute of Education, U.S. Department of Education, 1985.

"Before, During, After Reading Strategies." *Learning 92* 20, no. 8 (1992): pp. 31–46 Apr/May 1992.

Bettelheim, B., and Zelan, K. *On Learning to Read: The Child's Fascination with Meaning.* New York: Vintage Books, 1982.

Block, C. C. *Teaching the Language Arts: Expanding Thinking Through Student-Centered Instruction.* Boston: Allyn and Bacon, 1993.

Brazee, P. E. Handout. University of Maine (1985).

Burnett, F. H. *The Secret Garden.* Philadelphia: Lippincott, 1962.

Butler, A., and Turbill, J. *Towards a Reading-Writing Classroom.* Portsmouth, NH: Heinemann, 1987.

Carle, E. *The Grouchy Ladybug.* New York: Ty Crowell, 1977.

Clymer, T., and Venezky, R. L. *Ten Times Round.* Lexington, MA: Ginn, 1982.

Cox, C., and Zarillo, J. *Teaching Reading with Children's Literature.* New York: Merrill, 1993.

Cunningham, P. "Horizontal Reading." *The Reading Teacher* 21, no. 3 (1980): 31–34.

Davidson, J. L. ed. *Becoming a Nation of Readers* Urbana, IL: National Council of Teachers of English, 1988.

Deford, D., and Harste, J. C. "Child Language Research and Curriculum." *Language Arts* Vol. 59: 590–600, September 1982.

Durr, W. K., et al. *Moonbeams.* Boston: Houghton Mifflin, 1983.

Flesch, R. *Why Can't Johnny Read and What You Can Do About It.* New York: Harper and Row, 1985.

Frenald, G. M. *Remedial Techniques in Basic School Subjects.* New York: McGraw-Hill, 1943.

Goodman, K. S. *Language and Literacy: The Selected Writings of Kenneth S. Goodman,* F. V. Gollasch, ed. London: Routledge and Kegan Paul, 1982.

Goodman, K. S. *What's Whole in Whole Language.* Portsmouth, NH: Heinemann, 1986.

Goodman, K. S., et al. *Report Card on Basal Readers.* Katonah, NY: R.C. Owen, 1988.

Goodman, Y. M., and Burke, C. *Reading Strategies: Focus on Comprehension.* New York: Holt, Rinehart and Winston, 1980.

Grimm, J. *Snow White and the Seven Dwarfs.* New York: Farrar, Straus, and Giroux, 1972.

Harste, J. C., and Short K. G., with Carolyn Burke. *Creating Classrooms for Authors: The Reading-Writing Connection.* Portsmouth, NH: Heinemann, 1988.

Harste, J. C. "Understanding the Hypothesis, It's the Teacher That Makes the Difference: Part I." *Reading Horizons* 18: 32–43, fall 1977.

Hubbard, R. S., and Power, B. M. *The Art of Classroom Inquiry: A Handbook for Teacher-Researchers.* Portsmouth, NH: Heinemann, 1993.

Johnson, D. D., and Pearson, P. D. *Teaching Reading Vocabulary.* New York: Holt, Rinehart and Winston, 1984.

Johnson, T. D., and Louis, D. R. *Bringing It All Together.* Portsmouth, NH: Heinemann, 1990.

Keller, H. *Geraldine's Big Snow.* New York: Greenwillow Books, 1988.

Kellogg, S. *The Mysterious Tadpole.* New York: Dial Press, 1977.

Korschunow, I. *Adam Draws Himself a Dragon.* New York: Harper & Row, 1986.

Lapp, D., and Flood, J. *Teaching Reading to Every Child.* New York: Macmillan, 1978.

Lapp, D., and Flood, J. *Language/Reading Instruction for the Young Child.* New York: Macmillan, 1981.

Manzo, A. V. *Content Area Reading: A Heuristic Approach.* Columbus: Merrill, 1990.

May, F. B. *Reading as Communication: An Interactive Approach.* New York: Macmillan, 1990.

Mills, L. *The Rag Coat.* Boston: Little, Brown, 1991.

Munsch, R. *Love You Forever.* Willowdale Firefly Book, 1990.

Palincsar, A. S., and Brown, A. L. "Reciprocal Teaching of Comprehension-Fostering and Comprehension-Monitoring Activities." *Cognition and Instruction* (1984): 147–158.

Palincsar, A. S., and Brown, A. L. "Instruction for Self-Regulated Reading." In L. B. Resnick and L. E. Klopfer, eds., *Toward the Thinking Curriculum:*

Current Cognitive Research. Alexandria, VA: Association for Supervision and Curriculum Development, 1989.

Peregoy, S. F., and Boyle, O. F. *Reading, Writing, and Learning in ESL: A Resource Book for K-8 Teachers.* New York: Longman, 1993.

Reutzel, D. R., and Cooter, R. B. *Teaching Children to Read: From Basals to Books.* New York: Macmillan, 1992.

Rosenblatt, L. *The Reader, the Text, the Poem.* Carbondale, IL: Southern Illinois University Press, 1978.

Rumelhart, D. "Schemata: The Building Blocks of Cognition." In R. Spiro, B. Bruce, and W. Brewer, eds., *Theoretical Issues in Reading Comprehension.* Hillsdale, NJ: Laurence Erlbaum, 1981.

Samuels, S. J., and Farstrup, A. E. *What Research Has to Say About Reading Instruction,* 2nd ed. Newark, DE: International Reading Association, 1992.

Short, L. *Barren Land Showdown.* New York: Fawcett, 1981.

Smith, F. *Reading Without Nonsense.* New York: Teachers College, Columbia University, 1985.

Stauffer, R. G. *Directing the Reading-Thinking Process.* New York: Harper & Row, 1975.

Steig, W. *Caleb & Kate.* New York: Farrar, Straus, and Giroux, 1977.

Tierney, R. J., and Pearson, P. D. Toward a Composing Model of Reading. *Language Arts* 60 (5) (1983): 568–580.

Tierney, R., Readence, J. E., and Dishner, E. K. *Reading Strategies and Practices.* Boston: Allyn and Bacon, 1985.

Vacca, J., Vacca, R. T., and Gove, M. K. *Reading and Learning to Read,* 2nd ed. New York: HarperCollins, 1991.

Walker, B. J. *Diagnostic Teaching of Reading: Techniques for Instruction and Assessment,* 2nd ed. New York: Macmillan, 1992.

Walker, B. J., and Mohr, T. *The Effects of Self-Questioning on Reading Comprehension.* Paper presented at the Washington Organization for Reading Development Research Conference, Seattle, 1992.

Watson, C. J. "What Is a Whole Language Program?" *The Missouri Reader* 7, no. 1 (1982): 8–10.

West, N. "The Girl Who Couldn't Stop Reading." *Highlights for Children* (June 1989): pp 30–31.

"The Wired Bedroom." *Leadership News* (October 30, 1989): 79–85.

CHAPTER 9

DEVELOPING STRATEGIC READERS

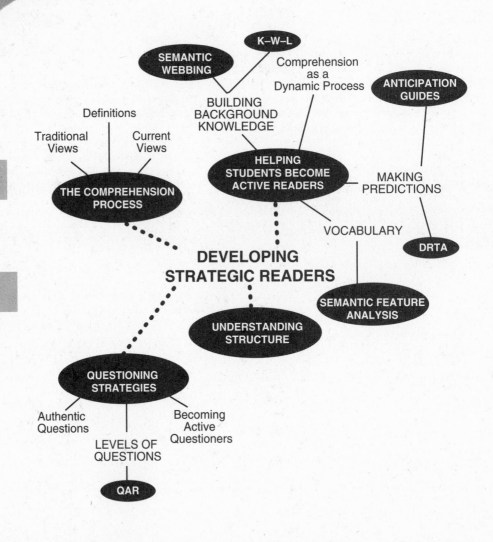

SEMANTIC WEBBING

K–W–L

Comprehension as a Dynamic Process

ANTICIPATION GUIDES

Definitions

Traditional Views

Current Views

BUILDING BACKGROUND KNOWLEDGE

THE COMPREHENSION PROCESS

HELPING STUDENTS BECOME ACTIVE READERS

MAKING PREDICTIONS

VOCABULARY

DRTA

DEVELOPING STRATEGIC READERS

SEMANTIC FEATURE ANALYSIS

UNDERSTANDING STRUCTURE

QUESTIONING STRATEGIES

Authentic Questions

Becoming Active Questioners

LEVELS OF QUESTIONS

QAR

What I Know: Pre-Chapter Journaling

How would you define the word *comprehension*? What does it mean to you as a literate adult? What do you think it means to a child who is learning to read? What do you think it would mean to the parents of that child? What might it mean to a child who is an avid reader? A child frustrated with reading? Select one of the questions above and jot down your response.

Big Ideas

This chapter will offer:

1. An examination of the differences between traditional and current practices of teaching reading.
2. A definition of comprehension.
3. Ways to help students become strategic readers.
4. A rationale for the importance of background knowledge to the development of reading comprehension.
5. Explanations for various questioning strategies appropriate in reading instruction.

Reading is a dynamic, ongoing transaction, much more than the decoding of symbols on a piece of paper. Reading is the interrelationship and interplay that take place between an interpreter (reader) and a producer (writer). It involves personalities, experiences, and affect, and it transcends the simple words on a page. In short, reading is a learning experience that moves beyond words and paragraphs and involves a complex interplay of cognitive, experiential, and affective abilities.

We like the term "transacting with text," for it implies that readers have a responsibility to text just as much as the author has a responsibility to potential readers. When we use the word *text*, we mean the reading students do in trade books or literature as well as from content area textbooks. That is to say, the reader brings to the text a mix of experiences, interpretations, and values that affect what will be taken away from a text (i.e., what will be read). In essence, reading to learn and learning to read occur simultaneously, each affecting the other in varying degrees. Or to state it another way, what readers bring to a text is just as important as what they take away from it.

The implications for teachers are many, a chief one being the fact that they must be able to help children appreciate reading as a constructive and meaningful process—a process that is ongoing, not static; engaging, not superficial; and personal, not pedantic. Helping students build personal structures for becoming competent readers is a constant challenge. We suggest that the teaching of reading within the context of the integrated language arts gives developing readers the framework they need to achieve high levels of reading competence.

Using a Varied Repertoire of Strategies

We consider reading to be a strategic activity—that is, readers must have a strategy about how they will approach and how they will interpret a piece of text. Of course, no two texts are entirely similar, and readers must thus make decisions about how one piece of text will be read as opposed to another. Readers will typically make these decisions based on the breadth and depth of their prior experiences and what they wish to get out of the text (pleasure, information, facts, etc.). For most readers, these choices will be unconscious ones, but they must be made if comprehension and appreciation are to be ensured.

What is unfortunate, however, is the fact that far too many students approach all reading tasks in much the same manner. They do not modify their style of reading, adjust their level of prior knowledge, or integrate new data with previous readings or experiences. It could be said that they do not "take charge" of their reading destinies, and that they often feel overpowered by certain reading tasks.

For too many students, reading is seen as the extraction of facts for artificial reasons, of being asked to "read the chapter and answer the questions at the end." Faced with that assignment in much of what they read (at least in school-based situations), children often assume that the "charge" is a universal one and should be used for all types of reading situations. In short, readers are asked to extract information deemed appropriate by the teacher and transfer that data into another form (a worksheet, test paper, or oral recitation). Or, to look at it another way, students read because they are told what to read and how to read it. In essence, there is no sense of ownership on the part of students.

In their review of the research on comprehension, Flood and Lapp (1991) make the case for a move away from a fragmented subskills approach, to a process and constructivist approach based on the more active role of the reader as a meaning-maker. The notion of instructional scaffolding (Vygotsky, 1979) is a way to understand how the teacher becomes a mentor to students. First, the teacher takes an active role in assisting children in an activity by providing them with examples and demonstrating the strategy to be learned. Later, the emphasis shifts to the student assuming responsibility for using the strategy. Teachers can apply the notion of scaffolding as they help children take a more active role with their reading.

As we discuss strategies for active comprehension, keep your students' capabilities in mind. On some occasions, students will need more examples or demonstrations of the strategy until they are able to demonstrate that they understand and can use it. As a teacher, you should provide support for readers but you should also help them become independent and strategic readers. For instance, students should be able to formulate their own purposes for reading and to monitor their own comprehension process—knowing when they do not understand something and knowing what to do about it.

This chapter investigates some ways to help students become strategic readers. The strategies described here can be applied to reading from literature (trade books) as well as from content area text books (in social studies, for example).

Most educators would agree that the most important thing about reading is comprehension. However, the route teachers take to help children understand what they read can be very different. Let's look at several classrooms to see reading programs in action.

Sally Parker has divided her fourth-grade children into three reading groups: a bottom group (the "Crows"), a middle group (the "Robins"), and a top group (the "Skylarks"). Each reading group uses a different level of the basal reader and meets with Sally for about 20 minutes. Although the stories are different in each level of the basal, Sally uses some common teaching procedures with each group. Let's take a look at the sequence of her instruction.

- Sally introduces new vocabulary for the story children will read. She helps to build back-ground for a story about the antics of a family's dog by asking several questions about the title and illustration on the first page of the story.

- Next, she gives students a purpose for silently reading the first few pages of the story by asking, "What makes this dog so funny?"

- They stop their reading and Sally poses the question again. One student answers, and the whole procedure is repeated again. Sally then asks what reactions the children in the story have to the dog's funny tricks. Students read the next few pages silently, stop their reading, and answer the question. This sequence of teacher questioning, reading silently, and responding to a question continues until the story is completed.

- The next day students take turns reading the story aloud.

- Sally then teaches the group several skills following the directions in the teacher's manual. Today she taught a comprehension skill of finding the main idea and a skill in decoding words with the vowel digraph ee.

- Students return to their seats to complete workbook pages on these skills and several other worksheets to reinforce a comprehension and decoding skill taught last week.

Now, let's look into Janet Forest's fourth-grade classroom. Janet has worked hard to establish a community of readers and writers in her classroom, including herself. She does not place her students in groups according to ability; all readers and writers in the classroom, including herself, help each other. They all have strengths and areas where they need to grow as readers and writers. During a block of time in the morning, students meet for a reader's workshop. Today some students are reading self-selected books from the school or class library. A literature circle of six children are sitting on the floor with Janet having a rather heated discussion over Natalie Babbit's *Tuck Everlasting* (1975). The children argue whether Winnie, a character in the story, should drink water from the spring that will give her eternal life. Janet is also a participant in this discussion. This is different from Sally who asked all the questions but did not participate in the discussion. Her questions from the basal manual were typically short fact type questions, not the kind that would have many different responses. In contrast, Janet deliberately asks more open-ended, thinking questions that will reflect how her students react to some of the "big issues" or themes in the book. Janet enjoys choosing books for children that have rich language and offer possibilities for challenging and interesting conversations. She does not believe that these kinds of books should be reserved for only her best readers. All students in her classroom read books that they select on their own and also meet in literature circles to discuss a book the group has read in common. Literature circles are fluid and change in terms of group composition throughout the year.

Children who are not reading a book are writing about their reactions and reflections to the chapters they have finished reading in their reading logs. (Reading logs will be discussed more extensively later in this chapter.) Another group of three students work on a play from a book they read together, while two other students are making a three-dimensional map of Abel's Island from a book of the same name by William Steig (1976). Janet spends considerable time talking with students about the many different activities they will be involved with during the workshop time.

The seemingly easy flow of children doing varied activities did not happen overnight in Janet's classroom. Her students had been in a third-grade classroom the year before that was much like Sally's. Students came into Janet's classroom with limited experiences working on their own; they were very dependent on the teacher establishing a routine for reading. Janet took a lot of time to model ways to work independently and to work as group members. The result was that Janet's teaching procedures remained congruent with her beliefs about literacy. Here are some of her thoughts:

- Children grow as readers by giving them generous blocks of time to read actual books.
- Children should see themselves as readers *and* writers. Janet plans ways for her students to respond to what they read by writing reactions to books in their reading logs. She also offers them choices about ways to respond to a book after they finish reading it. For example, students might make a shadow box or diorama depicting a favorite scene, design a poster advertising the book, or prepare a dramatization of a chapter from the book. Janet always requests that students "attach" some writing to a project. For instance, if children prepare a shadow box depicting a favorite scene, they must also write a description of that scene. (For more suggestions about responses to literature, see Chapter 10.)
- Children should be asked meaningful questions about plot, characters, setting, and theme. Janet begins such book conversations by asking students how they reacted to their reading. How did the book make you feel? What did you think of as you read the book? Have you read other books like this one? Janet also encourages students to ask their own questions about the book and to talk about what surprised them as they read, something they wondered about, etc.
- Teachers should be committed to bringing fine children's literature into the classroom and making reading truly come alive for their students. Janet is never bored by her book conversations with students, because the books chosen are excellent to read even as an adult! Janet has no greater joy than seeing her students truly engaged in what they are reading. Time passes so quickly that she sometimes literally has to ask students to carry over their book conversations to the next day.

Let's now look inside Jason Smith's fifth-grade classroom. Each student is reading silently, page by page, their eyes appearing to move from left to right and from the top to the bottom of each page. Several students return to a page they had previously read and then resume where they left off. Others seem animated as they read, several even chuckling over something they have read. Other students look fairly serious and thoughtful. What assumptions might you make about what is happening in Jason's class? All students appear to be on task and engaged with what they are reading. After all, no one seems to be gazing into space. Do you assume that they must also be comprehending what they read? From the behaviors described, this might be a fair assumption.

Let's explore this assumption. We have conducted the following "experiment" within the college classroom. First, we open a children's chapter book and begin reading silently, page by page, with little animation. We are simply reading silently in front of our audience. At this point, we stop and begin the second phase of the experiment. This time we open to a page and begin reading silently. However, this time we demonstrate more animated behaviors. We nod a lot, point to a paragraph as we read silently, and even chuckle over what we read. We stop our reading and ask our audience to judge whether they think we were comprehending during the first episode, during the second try, during both episodes, or not at all. What do you think? Usually in a class of about 25 students or so, the votes are almost evenly cast, with sometimes more students believing we were comprehending during the episode where we took on the behaviors of a reader engaged with print. These students were impressed with the outward signs of amusement over what we were reading—the nods, chuckles, and thoughtful looks. So as to not keep you in suspense any longer, we'll explain what we were doing.

We were not actually reading in any of the episodes. We were just acting, not doing anything related to the print on the page. What do these experiments tell you about the comprehension process?

- Comprehension is a covert, not an overt, process. This means that you cannot literally see a reader comprehending. You can only see the behaviors that would lead you to assume that comprehension is taking place. This is not to say that students will deliberately try to outwit you, but the fact remains that you cannot, obviously, see what is happening behind the eyes.

- Because comprehension is covert, a reader needs to respond in some way to what was read. The most common way in classrooms is through questioning procedures, a topic to be discussed in depth later in this chapter. Other ways include the discussion, writing, dramatization, and artwork.

- Readers comprehend text in an individual manner based on the "baggage" they bring to the text—their experiences with reading and their experiences in the world.

- As discussed in Chapter 8, the act of reading is an active experience of constructing meaning. Right from the start children seek to make sense of their world. When adults examine the scribbles a child makes on a piece of paper, they might be surprised to learn that it is a grocery list just like Dad makes before going shopping, a thank you letter to Aunt Jane, or the child's own rendition of a favorite bedtime story. Children believe that their writing makes sense and that they have a story to tell on paper. So, too, they expect that the black marks on pages in books will also make sense. Sometimes their expectations do not come true at the beginning of schooling. Reading becomes hard work, a tedious process of sounding out bits and pieces of language. It is thus crucial for teachers to encourage children to see that reading is a meaning-making process, that even if they cannot decode every word perfectly they can still construct meaning.

- To read is to comprehend. From an adult perspective, we cannot claim to be reading if we do not understand the material. For example, if we are reading IRS tax information, we will probably be successful at decoding or pronouncing every word on the page, but because of our lack of prior knowledge about tax laws, the language and concepts will be unfamiliar, almost sounding like a foreign language. Therefore, we simply decode the words on the page but do not actually read (or understand) the material.

Unfortunately, many children are placed in early reading programs that overemphasize decoding or word attack strategies and give comprehension a back seat. Such readers become good at "word-calling" but they have no idea whether what they have read is making sense. In other instances, children will become almost "paralyzed" in their efforts to correctly decode every word, and comprehension thus suffers. These children have not been given the message that comprehension is what matters in reading. For example, when some children come to a word that is not familiar, they will spend an inordinate amount of time trying to sound out the word. Fluent readers will use a more efficient strategy. When they come to a word they do not know, they will either skip the word and keep on reading, make a guess using their phonemic knowledge, or substitute a word that makes sense even though it may be different from what the text says. Fluent readers thus understand that reading is supposed to make sense and they have teachers who help them develop the most efficient strategies to enhance comprehension.

HOW HAVE OUR VIEWS ABOUT COMPREHENSION CHANGED?

Traditional Views

During the 1960s and 1970s, teachers relied on published materials based on the premise that if children learned to become good decoders, comprehension of the material would automatically

follow. For example, the prevailing view was that if children could say the words on the page then comprehension would take care of itself. What resulted was an overreliance on decoding skills.

Traditional theorists defined reading as a compilation of decoding and comprehension skills. During the past several decades, teachers used published materials to teach specific skills in comprehension (i.e., finding the main idea and supporting details) and decoding (word attack skills such as initial consonants, short and long vowels, etc.) rather than giving students time to actually read. There has been no evidence that spending time having students complete isolated skill exercises improves comprehension.

In past decades teachers also asked a preponderance of literal level or fact type questions. These kinds of questions did not challenge students to think in more complex and challenging kinds of ways. Later, teachers did begin to increase their use of questions on an inferential and critical level. However, in Durkin's studies of classrooms (1978–1979), teachers actually were "testing" comprehension, rather than teaching students to become better comprehenders. Durkin's work was significant in terms of challenging the status quo of many classrooms where workbooks designed to practice skills took the place of actual student-teacher interaction. Durkin observed that there was little actual teaching taking place. What was missing in the classrooms observed was more student and teacher interaction about how to comprehend in more powerful ways.

Current Views

Let's look at some current views on the subject of comprehension. Cooper (1993) defines it in the following way:

Comprehension is a strategic process by which readers construct or assign meaning to a text by using the clues in the text and their own prior knowledge. In the broad sense this is also a definition of reading, since reading is comprehending, or the construction of meaning. This meaning comes primarily from our own existing knowledge. (p. 12)

From our discussion of the work of the Goodmans and of Louise Rosenblatt, among many others, can you see how this kind of definition emerged for comprehension?

Current theory also supports the idea that comprehension and the construction of meaning refers to the reader's interaction with text. Prior knowledge influences a reader's understanding of what is read. Fluent readers also sample from text and do not always decode every word on the page. As stated in the journal *Teaching and Learning Literature with Children and Young Adults* (September/October 1992):

> Learning to read is a complex act. Decoding, blending, spelling, syllabication, etc., are important in getting there—but it is not being there. Being able to "look and say," to use phonics to get words pronounced, to use context-clues—all are useful in helping the child break the print barrier, but it is not yet reading. To become a real reader (to bring meaning to and take meaning from the printed page, to respond and react to an author's ideas, to appreciate the art of literature, to be able to discuss a book critically, all with simultaneity) takes a great deal more than being able to decode. Decoding is but one step on the long and winding road to real reading. (p. 24)

Helping Students Become Active and Strategic Readers

Building Background Knowledge

The reader, no matter how young or inexperienced, does bring a wealth of life experiences to text.

The more experiences a reader brings to the text, the better the comprehension. Teachers must be able to tap this prior knowledge and not make assumptions that readers have experience with the topic. In this next section, semantic webbing and

the K-W-L strategy will be described as ways to tap what students already know about a topic.

Semantic Webbing

Semantic webbing is a graphic display of students' words, ideas, and concepts in concert with textual words, ideas, and concepts. It helps student comprehend text by activating background knowledge, organizing new concepts, and discovering the relationships between the two. Its value lies in the fact that students are able to tap into their prior experiences, record those experiences in clusters or logical grouping patterns, and build upon those experiences by adding textual knowledge gleaned from their reading. Semantic webbing is appropriate as a prereading and/or postreading activity in all types of materials—fiction and nonfiction, narrative, and expository. In essence, semantic webbing allows students to focus on the relationships that can exist between the ideas they bring to and take away from the act of reading.

Let's look in on fifth-grade teacher Dave Lunden to see how he creates a semantic web with his students about the state of Maine.

Dave begins by asking students to pair off with each other and brainstorm a listing of everything they know about their state. Students can list words, phrases, and anything that comes to mind when they think of living in Maine.

Dave has thought a lot about the creation of this thematic unit and plans to help children explore different aspects of their state all year long in many different ways. However, he believes in designing the unit around the understandings his students already bring to the topic. Even though he has done a lot of planning about ways students might study about Maine, he does not believe in planning in a vacuum. He wants to know what students know—he may have students who already know a great deal—*and* he also wants to broaden their knowledge base. His intention is to design learning experiences that will challenge and enrich their understandings.

Dave next asks students to share their brainstorming list. He creates a web on the board that

FIGURE 9.1   First Draft Semantic Web of Maine

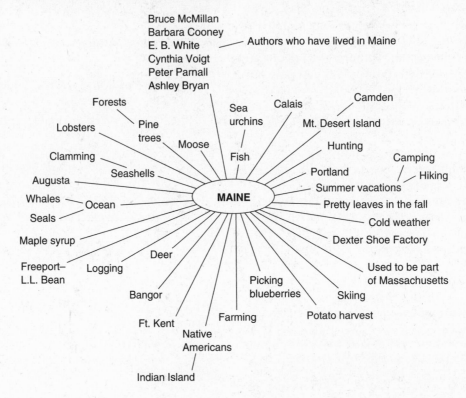

represents all of the students' responses, shown in Figure 9.1. He then asks students to look at all the words and phrases they have generated to see what items look similar in some way and to mark those items with colored chalk. He also asks students to explain their reasoning for grouping items. This gives Dave an opportunity to ask several questions to probe their experiences. For example, to find out more about their knowledge about cities and towns in Maine, Dave asks students to think about places they have visited and if they have friends and relatives who live in Maine. He is able to detect that students are unclear about whether Maine's state capital is Bangor or Portland—until they discover that it is in fact Augusta!

He asks the class if they are in agreement over the way items have been grouped. His next step is to ask for a title or label for each group. Figure 9.2 presents the semantic web that resulted after the grouping and labeling of items.

Now Dave has a much more informed view of what his students bring to the study of Maine. He didn't realize, for example, that students had so much knowledge about children's authors who lived in Maine. Now his planning will take into account what they bring to this thematic unit; the semantic web offers Dave a sense of direction. He will go back to the drawing board to see how his goals, objectives, and activities mesh with this new information. He also wants to find out what his students want to learn about their state. Dave believes that if students feel ownership over their learning, there will be more investment in the writing and reading they will do as part of their study.

Activating Prior Knowledge in an Eighth-Grade Social Studies Class Middle-school teacher Karen Ronaldi believes in fully immersing students in the study of history instead of just "covering" the material. She achieves this goal by going far beyond what the textbook offers by using her own materials. For example, in preparing a thematic unit on World War II, Karen gathers children's literature, videotapes, music, photographs, magazines, and newspaper advertisements from this time period.

Karen coordinates her planning of thematic units with the language arts teacher, Bill Cosgrove. Karen and Bill believe in a student-centered curriculum. However, they also believe that it is crucial for teachers to design a "blueprint" that includes the goals or "big ideas" (Routman, 1994) and several major focus areas or objectives to guide their planning. Although Karen and Bill are fully aware of their district's curriculum goals, they view their planning as a "blueprint" that they are fully willing to negotiate after collecting input from students. They envision the final written unit as one that combines their own goals and focus areas with those of their students. They decide that

several of the "big ideas" in the unit will be the following: to explore issues focusing on acceptance of differences and diversity in people, peer pressure to go along with the crowd, and survival during difficult times. (They are thinking specifically here of the persecution of the Jews and the internment camps for the Japanese in this country.) Framing these topics in terms of awareness and acceptance of diversity, peer pressure, and survival will help students to see what happened during World War II as being relevant to their own lives. In fact, they are prepared to extend the time period of a month for this unit if students are interested in pursuing these topics in terms of what is currently happening in the world (see Chapter 14, which focuses on thematic teaching).

Karen and Bill try to have a large number of books available for read alouds, student research, and other projects—from historical fiction, biography, and informational books to poetry about World War II. The social studies textbook becomes just *one* source of information out of many.

To acquire all the relevant material on the topic, Karen and Bill begin by gathering books already in their collections. They have a good

FIGURE 9.2 Second Draft of Semantic Web of Maine

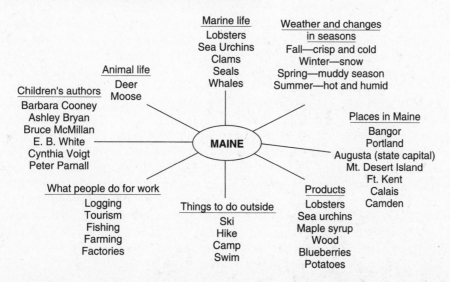

"starter collection" as they are avid readers and collectors of literature for children and adolescents. They also solicit the help of the school librarian and local bookstores to supplement what they already have and what students will find at local libraries and in their own collections.

At the start of the unit, they display an impressive array of material: student magazines, photos, music, videos, period clothes (borrowed from a variety of friends), books for children and adolescents written in the 1940s, and copies of newspaper articles. Later in the unit they plan to share a variety of foods from the 1940s mentioned in several of the trade books. They also create a classroom "jackdaw" collection. (The term *jackdaw* refers to a kind of crow that collects various objects for its nest.) The students' checklist for a jackdaw kit is presented in Figure 9.3.

Students are also invited to contribute materials from home for the jackdaw display. One student remarks that his grandfather has dozens of issues of *Life* magazine and *The Saturday Evening Post* from the 1940s that he might let him borrow. Another student says she has an old army uniform at home and some other memorabilia from the war. Karen and Bill will also investigate the availability of commercially prepared jackdaw kits for the study of this time period. These usually include collections of facsimile materials such as posters and a variety of documents housed in a large envelope. Jackdaw kits add an air of authenticity to the study of a particular time period. (The kits are available from Golden Owl/Jackdaw Publications, P.O. Box A03, Amawalk, NY 10501.)

From their previous work with thematic units, students are well aware that the materials, books, and projects they complete will represent the total picture of their work with a topic. In other words, Karen and Bill have left lots of room, both literally and figuratively, for student input and work produced throughout the unit. The classroom is, indeed, viewed as a learning com-

FIGURE 9.3   Checklist for a Jacdaw Kit

Theme: _____ World War II _____

Projected Dates of Instruction: _____ November _____ to _____ December _____

Literature
_____ Anne Frank: The Diary of a Young Girl by Anne Frank
_____ Journey to Topaz by Yoshiko Uchida
_____ North to Freedom by Anne Holm
_____ Number the Stars by Lois Lowry
_____ The Devil's Arithmetic by Jane Yolen
_____ The Island on Bird Street by Uri Olev
_____ The Upstairs Room by Johann Reiss

Clothing
_____ Uniforms
_____ Costumes
_____ Etc.

Nonprint
_____ Videos
_____ Films
_____ Music
_____ CD Rom

Artifacts
_____ Photos
_____ Newspapers
_____ Stamps
_____ Coins
_____ Other

FIGURE 9.4   Sample Parent Newsletter

Dear Family and Friends:

As we begin a new thematic unit, we'd like to ask for your help. Our eighth-grade class will be studying World War II. To help make the unit relevant to our students' lives, we intend to focus on several important "big ideas." These include:

- Exploring issues about the acceptance of differences and diversity in people
- Peer pressure to go along with the crowd
- Survival during difficult times

Do you have some experiences you might like to share with us about that time period? We'd love to have you, or someone you know, come to our class and share experiences. Do you have books on World War II? We want to gather as many resources from this time period as possible. Please check off any items from the list below that might interest you.

_____ Yes, I would like to come in and share experiences about this time period.

_____ I know someone who might be willing to share experiences or memorabilia from World War II.

_____ I have books to share.

_____ I have memorabilia such as music, newspapers, magazines, photos to share [circle the item(s)].

_____ I would be willing to help my child prepare a food representing this time period.

_____ Other? _____

Thank you for your continued support. We appreciate it!

Sincerely,

Karen Ronaldi (social studies)
Bill Cosgrove (language arts)

---

munity and not one where the teachers have done all the work to build an atmosphere.

In addition, Karen and Bill have sent a newsletter home inviting parents and extended family in as guest speakers and also asking for loans of World War II books and memorabilia (see Figure 9.4).

When this thematic unit is completed, Karen and Bill plan to place as many of the books as possible in the classroom library and will use a large cardboard garment box to "store" other materials for use in another year. Some teachers, unfortunately, put away books from a completed unit, when in fact students may want to return to some of the books they may not have read and to revisit old favorites.

The K-W-L Strategy

At the beginning of a thematic unit, Karen uses the K-W-L (what we know, what we want to find out, what we learned) strategy (Ogle, 1986), which is predicated on the belief that students construct their own meaning based on past experiences—books, films, people, museums, visits to other countries, etc. Because students rarely come to any topic with a "blank slate," it is up to the teacher to ask the kinds of questions that will tap student background about any topic. Sometimes one question will not be sufficient.

Karen initiates an expanded K-W-L strategy on large sheets of tablet paper tacked to a bulletin board. The expanded K-W-L chart depicted in Table 9.1 represents a beginning list of information on what students know, what they want to find out about World War II, and what they are learning. They will also work on two other aspects of the chart: what we still need to learn and where we can find information. They will leave out markers and encourage students to contribute to the chart on an ongoing basis. Karen and Bill want students to view them as lifelong learners, so they, too, will contribute to the chart during class time, and they will also spend time reading. They are not afraid to admit to students that they do not know everything about World War II.

Karen elicits information about what students know about the topic by simply asking, "What do you know about World War II?" She is surprised by how much they know but mentally notes several misconceptions. As the unit unfolds, some information will change on the chart, and the misconceptions will be corrected. Karen keeps a record of what was initially mentioned, so some of the ideas can be discussed again later. She also asks students to talk about how they obtained their information. Karen uses questions to elicit more from students:

> What do you know about what it was like to live in the 1940s? (Notice that Karen does not simply ask, "Do you know anything about living in the 1940s?", as that might elicit only a "yes" or "no" response from students.)
>
> What was the mood of our country like at this time?
>
> What famous people lived during the 1940s?
>
> Why were Jews put into concentration camps?

It was truly astonishing for Karen and Bill to find out how much knowledge their students brought to this topic from films, books they had read, and family stories. In fact, they also found out that several students seemed very well versed on the concentration camps since several of their relatives had survived them. They shuddered to think of the implications of not starting with the K-W-L strategy, if they had assumed that their students brought virtually nothing to this topic. Tapping what students bring to any topic demonstrates a valuing of their experiences.

This process also assists them in reassessing their goals, focus areas, and activities—some of which may be modified and others will be added since there is so much student interest in several topics. Students will refer to the K-W-L chart for possible topics to research, to write reports, and to prepare a product (such as a poster, model, or artwork). Again, they will also continue to add information to the chart on an ongoing basis.

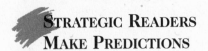

STRATEGIC READERS MAKE PREDICTIONS

Prior to reading a selection together, the teacher can play an active role in preparing students to either listen to a selection read aloud or before students read a selection for themselves. Meaningful questions and discussion prior to reading or listening activates prior knowledge and experiences students bring to the topic. Questions help to set purposes or reasons for reading. For example, fifth-grade teacher John Hayes has started a unit on the works of Katherine Paterson. One group has selected *Bridge to Terabithia* (1977) to read and discuss together. At the first group meeting, John prepares students to begin their reading of this novel by directing student attention to the title and cover of this book. He invites each member of the group to make predictions about what

they think it might be about. Several students think it will definitely be a fantasy story about a couple of kids who visit a strange land called "Terabithia." Another student comments on the cover and speculates that it will be about the way a relationship builds between a girl and boy. There are a few giggles about this response! Still another student remarks that she heard there was a death in the story and wonders whether it will be a sad story such as *A Taste of Blackberries* by Doris Buchanan Smith (1973), which she just finished reading. John asks students to keep their predictions in mind as they begin reading. Predictions are not made exclusively at the beginning of a

TABLE 9.1   Expanded K-W-L Chart

What We Know	What We Want to Find Out	What We Are Learning	What We Still Need to Learn	Where We Can Find Information
• The war took place in Europe.	• Who was president during World War II?	• Other groups were discriminated against, such as gypsies and other non-Aryan people.	• We want to learn more about the Japanese internment camps in the U.S.	• Nonfiction books • Biographies • Our textbook • Encyclopedias
• It was during the 1940s.	• What was happening in the U.S. during this time?	• People were brainwashed into thinking like Hitler.	• We want to learn why the U.S. didn't just go help the people in the concentration camps.	• Interviewing people in the community • Guest speakers
• There was a lot of prejudice against Jewish people.	• Why was there discrimination against Jews?		• How could so many people follow Hitler's beliefs?	• Internet
• Hitler was a Nazi.	• Who were the Nazis?			• CD Roms
• There were concentration camps that Hitler put the Jews in.	• What countries were involved?			• World Wide Web
• Only Jewish people were in the camps.	• Were Jews the only people put in concentration camps?			
• The concentration camps were horrible. Millions of people—young and old—died there.				

book but all the way through. A book having chapter titles often gives readers a springboard for their predictions.

This procedure—students making their own predictions about their reading—is far different from the directions in many reading manuals and commercially produced literature guides. These typically give the teacher a more active role than the students. The directions imply that it is always the teacher who sets the purposes for students as they read.

Sometimes it *is* appropriate for the teacher to suggest that students read for a particular purpose. However, doing this to the exclusion of students setting their own goals does not help the students become more active comprehenders. They begin to believe that having a purpose for reading is something that the teacher does during a reading lesson. When in reality, capable readers set goals and make predictions or hypotheses about what they set out to read all the time. Most of the time this is done on almost a subconscious level. Check this out the next time you begin to read something, then stop yourself. For example, if you take a break from your college textbooks and read a novel, your purpose might be to read for enjoyment. Other times, your purpose is to read a more informational text to find out how to repair or make something. Other times, you might read a textbook to prepare for an exam. You may have figured out the kinds of questions that are typically asked on an exam, so you read and study the information in a certain way, which might be different from class to class.

Students who become aware of purpose setting in reading also begin to vary their reading speed or rate. We need to talk to students more about what fluent readers do and to let them in on "reading secrets" such as adjusting reading rate or speed to the purpose for reading. By discussing aspects of reading behavior, it helps readers to tap into their own process and to talk about this metacognitive behavior. Asking students to make their own predictions helps them take ownership over their own comprehension process.

Let's now look at two strategies for helping students make predictions: the directed reading-thinking activity and the anticipation guide.

The Directed Reading-Thinking Activity

The directed reading-thinking activity (DRTA) is a comprehension strategy that assists students in formulating their own reasons for reading. These reasons are sometimes called predictions or hypotheses. As we have stated, teacher's manuals typically suggest that teachers state the purposes for reading a selection, not only in the basal reading manual but also in social studies and science manuals as well.

Eighth-grade teacher Karen Ronaldi uses this strategy often as it relates to selections that students read in common. Her social studies curriculum revolves around themes. Students read historical fiction, biography, poetry, informational books, and social studies oriented magazines such as *Cobblestone* and *Faces* to support their work on a theme. However, Karen uses the social studies text as one more source of information. The text also provides some "baseline" information for some of the themes her students will study throughout the school year. Students have begun a study of World War II. After some preliminary discussion, students read the information in the social studies text to provide some common background as well as to raise questions not addressed in the textbook. Karen approaches the reading by using a DRTA as a focus lesson to assist students in learning about making predictions and setting their goals as they read. She follows a series of distinct steps:

1. Based on the title of the chapter, Karen asks students to write down their predictions as to what they think the chapter will be about. By having students record their predictions, everyone in the group is involved.
2. As students call out their predictions, she writes them on the board.

3. After each prediction, she asks for a reason for making the prediction. She accepts all predictions without making any value judgments about them.
4. Karen asks students to begin reading the first section of the chapter.
5. After doing so, she asks students to return to their predictions to give evidence for their initial predictions. Some students are right on the mark, while others are not. This is to be expected if we assume that readers bring a host of varied experiences to a topic.
6. She then asks them to turn the next chapter heading into a question. Again, she asks students to record their predictions about what the next section will be about.
7. Students read and verify their new predictions and then complete their reading.
8. After a discussion of the chapter, Karen asks students to examine the strategy of making predictions and to what extent this helped them in their reading.

By asking students to reflect on their learning—a process known as metacognition—Karen helps students discuss the strategies she is teaching. She does not believe that it is enough to just walk students through a new strategy; instead she wants them to gain an understanding of the strategy from the inside out. She is convinced that these kinds of open discussions where students are given time to reflect upon a strategy, and then to openly and honestly accept their feedback, gives her valuable insights into the validity of her teaching and what she may do differently the next time. For example, some students said that making predictions was difficult because they have been used to relying on the teacher to tell them why they should read something. In other words, these students have built up a dependence upon the teacher, whom they expect to set purposes for reading. They never thought of doing it themselves, not even after Karen's focused lesson, without this follow-up discussion. Some students had teachers who told

them to read a chapter and answer the questions at the end of the chapter.

In summary, we need to reiterate the importance of some kind of follow-up discussion that invites students (even kindergartners!) to reflect upon their own learning process. We believe that these kinds of discussions help passive learners to become more active in their own learning.

The Anticipation Guide

The anticipation guide alerts students to some of the major concepts in textual material before it is read. Students have an opportunity to share ideas and opinions as well as activate their prior knowledge about a topic before they read about the subject. It is also a helpful technique for eliciting students' misconceptions about a subject and, as such, it can be used as a diagnostic tool by teachers to determine the breadth or extent of students' background knowledge. Students become actively involved in the dynamics of reading a specified selection because they have an opportunity to talk about the topic before reading about it. Motivation is enhanced and personal strategies for reading are developed. As a postreading activity it provides a way for students to blend background knowledge with textual knowledge. The following steps can be followed:

1. Read the story or selection and attempt to select the major concepts, ideas, or facts in the text. For example, in a selection on "weather" the following concepts could be identified:
   a. There are many different types of clouds.
   b. Different examples of severe weather include tornadoes, hurricanes, and thunderstorms.
   c. Precipitation occurs in the form of rain, snow, sleet, and hailstones.
   d. Many types of weather occur along "fronts."
2. Create five to ten statements (not questions) that reflect common misconceptions about

B O X
9.1

"WEATHER OR NOT"

Directions: Read the six sentences below. If you think a sentence is right, print "yes" on the line under the word "before." If you think a sentence is wrong, print "no" on the line under the word "before." *Note:* You will do the same exercise again *after* you read the selection.

Before   **After**

_____   _____   1. Hurricanes are the most destructive form of weather.
_____   _____   2. Precipitation is any type of moisture which falls from clouds.
_____   _____   3. Thunderstorms occur when a cold front meets and rises over a warm front.
_____   _____   4. There are five basic types of clouds.
_____   _____   5. Fog can be defined as a cloud on the ground.
_____   _____   6. Typhoons occur in the Pacific Ocean.

the subject, that are ambiguous, or are indicative of students' prior knowledge. Statements can be written on the chalkboard or photocopied and distributed. (Using the concepts for "weather" above, the statements indicated in Box 9.1 could be used.)

3. Give students plenty of opportunities to agree or disagree with each statement. Whole class or small group discussions would be appropriate. After discussions, allow each student to record a positive or negative response to each statement. Initiate discussions focusing on reasons for individual responses.

4. Direct students to read the text, keeping in mind the statements and their individual or group reactions to those statements.

5. After reading the selection, engage the class in a discussion on how the textual information may have changed their opinions. Provide students with an opportunity to record their reactions to each statement based upon what they read in the text. It is not important for a consensus to be reached or for students to agree with everything the author states. Rather, it is more important for students to engage in an active dialogue which allows them to react to the relationships between prior knowledge and current knowledge.

Anticipation guides are appropriate to use throughout the curriculum. The following steps might be followed for a science-related theme.

1. Choose a book to read aloud as a group.
2. Prepare statements (not questions!) related to important concepts about the topic.
3. Invite students to predict and anticipate responses to the statements prior to reading or listening to a story read aloud.
4. After the reading, ask students to look again at their responses by comparing and contrasting them with the actual text.

Anticipation guides are also appropriate for use with fiction material. Box 9.2 shows how the book *Today Was a Terrible Day* by Patricia Reilly Giff (New York: Viking, 1986) can be developed into an anticipation guide.

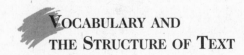

VOCABULARY AND THE STRUCTURE OF TEXT

There is no doubt that voracious readers constantly expand their vocabularies. In a similar manner, students of all ages expand their vocabularies when listening to stories read aloud. Vocabulary study that is tied to meaningful context is much more apt to be remembered and applied. You probably remember doing vocabulary exercises in which you were given a list of random words and then had to define each one and use it in a sentence. Typically, there was a vocabulary test on Friday. If you could memorize lists of words quickly, you probably scored well on these tests. But how long did you remember them? In what ways did you use them in your future writing? In other words, was there any carryover? Unfortunately, there was probably very little for the time and effort expended on this activity. The assignment of vocabulary words was just that—an assignment; there was very little actual teacher-student interaction or teaching apparent in this activity. Vocabulary study should not carry with it negative connotations, but it often does because of some past practices. What are alternatives to teaching vocabulary?

Let's return to John Hayes's fifth-grade class, where a literature group has been reading and talking about Katherine Paterson's *Bridge to Terabithia*. In order to study the author's choice of words in this book, John asked students to record interesting and challenging new words, phrases, or sentences that they encountered in their reading by noting them on stick-on tags as they read through the book. For example, as Janey read the first chapter, she listed the following words: despised, bragger, peculiar, drizzly, and delicately.

The next time the literature study group met, John asked students what words they encountered in their reading that were particularly challenging, new, or interesting. The group discussed at least one from each person's list in terms of its use within the context of the story. John participated in this activity as well. His contribution was "Sweating like a knock-kneed mule" (p. 5) and "Those girls could get out of work faster than grasshoppers could slip through your fingers" (p. 6).

After literature discussion that day, John reminded students to record at least two words in their writer's journal. These interesting words and phrases could be used in their writing. Students recorded the word within the context of a sentence to demonstrate an understanding of the definition. Next, they indicated how the word was used in the sentence—whether it was a noun, adjective, verb, or adverb—and they used a thesaurus to find any other words that could be used in the same way. John also asked students to commit to learning to spell at least five of these words as part of their spelling contract for the week. (Additional discussion of spelling contracts and strategies for spelling are found in Chapter 13.)

BOX 9.2

"A BAD HAIR DAY"

Directions: Read the five sentences below. If you think that what a sentence says is right, print "yes" on the line under the word "before." If you think a sentence is wrong, print "no" on the line under the word "before." Do the same thing for each sentence. *Note:* You will do the same exercise again *after* you read *Today Was a Terrible Day.*

Before	After	
_____	_____	1. You shouldn't be friends with people who get into trouble at school.
_____	_____	2. Kids who get into trouble at school don't like their teachers.
_____	_____	3. Teachers don't like kids who get into trouble at school.
_____	_____	4. Kids who get into trouble at school don't care what others think of them.
_____	_____	5. Kids who have trouble learning to read are dumb.

John uses this approach as one of many through the day to broaden his students' vocabulary. He feels that this approach has been successful because students have ownership over words. They have chosen the ones that are most meaningful to them. In addition, John may also point out words within the context of the story that children did not identify.

Specific guidelines for teaching vocabulary include the following:

1. Help students connect new vocabulary to what they already know.
2. Invite students to use new words in many different ways. Learning definitions is not enough. For example, encourage students to try out new words in their writing. Students can list new and interesting words in a writer's journal.
3. Ask students to identify interesting and challenging words from what the read, rather than identifying words out of context.

Semantic Feature Analysis

Semantic feature analysis is a powerful instructional tool that helps students to focus on important vocabulary words in a piece of text. This teaching strategy allows students to draw upon their backgrounds of information and arrange that data into a meaningful pattern. It assists students in determining the relationships that exist between words and how various features related to those words are intertwined. As such, it can serve as a very powerful prereading strategy.

The following steps can be used with this technique:

1. Select a reading selection that has a number of words that fall into a particular category. For example, a book on *mammals* might have words such as *monkeys, tigers, elephants,* *dogs, cats,* and *squirrels.* Another reading selection on *transportation* might have words such as *wagon, trains, bicycles, cars, skates,* and *horses.*
2. Have students prepare a sheet of graph paper by listing the words related to the selected category down the left-hand side of the sheet (see Figure 9.5).
3. Invite students to brainstorm for varying features of some of those items and then to write those features across the top of the grid.
4. Students can match the words with their features by placing a checkmark in the respective boxes.
5. Encourage students to discuss their decisions and confer with classmates about the identification of features for selected items.
6. After reading the selection, invite students to return to the original grid to modify or change original selections according to information contained within the text.

HELPING STUDENTS UNDERSTAND THE STRUCTURE OF WHAT THEY READ

Young children begin to develop a sense of how stories "work," or a story schema, through home and school experiences. They know that a story will have a beginning, a middle, and an end, and they can begin to predict what will come next in a story. They are, in effect, developing the elements of story grammar—how the parts of a story are tied together. As they talk about a story, they do not use the terminology of story grammar—plot, setting, character, theme, point of view, etc.—but they do use many of these elements in their oral and written retellings. If we define storytelling in its broadest sense, we see that we are always telling stories of one sort or another: "Guess what happened to me on the way to work today?", "You won't believe the dream I had last night!", "Supper won't be ready tonight because I caught the cat eating the fish from the counter!" It is in this way that stories begin to unfold.

Story mapping (Beck et al., 1979) is a useful strategy that can assist students at all grade levels to develop a heightened awareness of how stories work. The story map is a visual representation of the important elements of a story and can be graphically represented in a variety of ways. Vacca, Vacca, and Gove (1991) explain the strategy in this way:

> You can use story organization to plan instruction more effectively and to anticipate the problems students might have in following a specific story's action, especially if it lacks one or more story elements. Students, on the other hand, can build and use story schema to better understand what they read. The closer the match between the reader's story schema and the organization of a particular story, the greater the comprehension is likely to be. (p. 176)

Sixth-grade teacher Betty Robinson calls this procedure *plot diagramming.* Betty's students complete this diagram when they finish reading a self-selected book. Betty is able to detect whether students have an understanding of such concepts as the following:

Genre or type of book
Main characters
Setting
The "problem" needing resolution in the story
The climax or high point of the story
How the problem is resolved

FIGURE 9.5

Features →	Many Seeds	Few Seeds	Grows on Trees	Grows on Vines					
Banana									
Orange	✔		✔						
Strawberry									
Lemon									
Watermelon	✔			✔					
Grapes	✔			✔					

FIGURE 9.6

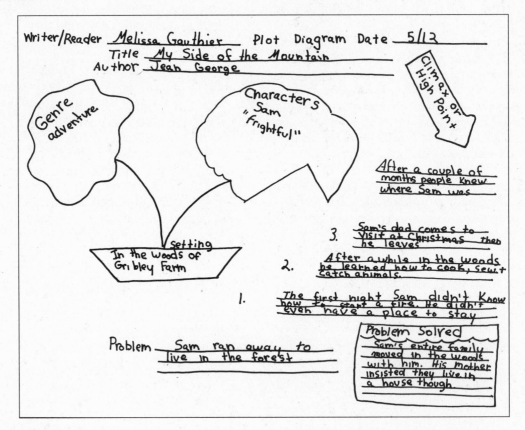

Writer/Reader _Melissa Gauthier_ Plot Diagram Date _5/13_
Title _My Side of the Mountain_
Author _Jean George_

Genre adventure

Characters Sam "Frightful"

Climax or High Point

After a couple of months people knew where Sam was

3. Sam's dad comes to visit at Christmas then he leaves

2. After awhile in the woods he learned how to cook, sew catch animals.

1. The first night Sam didn't know how to start a fire. He didn't even have a place to stay

Setting In the woods of Gribley Farm

Problem _Sam ran away to live in the forest_

Problem Solved
Sam's entire family moved in the woods with him. His mother insisted they live in a house though.

A plot diagram by one of Betty's students is shown in Figure 9.6.

QUESTIONING STRATEGIES

Authentic Questions

In some classrooms, it is the teacher who asks most of the questions. Many of these questions are of a factual nature, and the answers to them are right in the text and require more "regurgitation" than thinking. How many times were we tested in elementary school by answering questions that required little more than the memorization of facts? Someone once said that "facts are remembered as long as fish stays fresh on the kitchen counter." Researchers have been studying not only whether teachers should be asking all the questions but also the generally accepted practice of asking questions to tap comprehension. According to Allington and Weber (1993), "it is often the case that young children spend more time responding to questions during instructional sessions than they do reading." Although practices vary, many teachers ask most of the questions found in basal teacher's manuals.

Many researchers who study the reading process are advocating the development of more authentic questions, those that are actually derived from student interaction with text. From what we have discussed previously in this chapter, we know that a reader's transaction with text is personal and will be different with every student. Also there is an emphasis on helping students to become more active in asking their own questions about what they read.

As a first step in responding to these issues, let's look at ways to develop more authentic questions and ways to empower readers to become increasingly active in the comprehension process. Fifth-grade teacher John Hayes deals with these challenges by becoming actively involved as a reader in the literature circle. John regularly writes in his literature log, and he also becomes more actively involved as a reader in the circle through prompts such as, "When I was reading Chapter 2 from *Bridge to Terabithia,* it made me think of the summer a new kid moved into my neighborhood. Did you ever have the experience of learning to be friends with a new kid who moved to your neighborhood?" John finds that this kind of genuine reflection and puzzlement from his own reading leads to rich conversation. At other times, as an alternative to a prompt, John might enter the conversation with a statement rather than a question—for example, "It's often difficult to have a talent that others don't seem to appreciate"—and then to wait for student responses.

John's two approaches were at first confusing for students. They were not used to a teacher actually taking part in the discussion. They expected the teacher to quiz them on the reading by asking a variety of comprehension questions to find out if they had done the reading. John explained to students that it was important for his own growth as a reader to participate in the same kinds of ways that he asked students to reflect in their readings. He said their literature circle was similar to their writer's workshop, where he took time to do some of his own writing. Gradually, students felt more comfortable with these kinds of book conversations.

John is also a reader of professional literature. He felt very attuned with the ideas he found in Nancie Atwell's book, *In the Middle: Writing, Reading, and Learning with Adolescents* (1987). Atwell discusses the notion of book conversations

that seem like the talk occurring around the dining room table, much more natural and less contrived than classroom talk. John also liked the ideas he found in Peterson and Eed's book, *Grand Conversations: Literature Groups in Action* (1990). This book describes how teachers can begin to hold more authentic booktalk in the classroom—namely, grand conversations. Peterson and Eeds suggest that "genuine meaning, meaning over which readers have ownership, arises only if those readers are able to structure it themselves, through their own interpretations, in the light of their experiences and their intent." This suggests beginning with the kinds of questions that tap what children think and feel about a book, what they wondered about, and what they liked.

John also uses questions that Borders and Naylor suggest in *Children Talking About Books* (1993):

> What did you notice about the story?
> How did the story make you feel?
> What does the story remind you of in your own life?

He has also found Chamber's (1985) discussion of using open-ended questions invaluable. Chambers suggests using the phrase "tell me more about how you're thinking" rather than "why," which he claims "boxes-in" readers by putting them on the defensive. Although John has had to restrain himself from always asking "why" after a student response (which is not easy for a teacher!). He agrees with Chambers that by inviting students to offer additional comments about a specific response yields more in-depth conversations.

John has found that once students gain a sense of the rhythm of these conversations, they want to take turns leading the discussion. Because John prepares for each book conversation, even if a student plans to be the leader, he can still take an active role by posing questions that will guide students to think about the book in rich and more challenging ways. As Peterson and Eeds

(1990) suggest, questions can be designed that help children to "analyze, interpret, and seek out evidence for their positions." This process invites children to get back into the book, to revisit a passage or section to verify their response. As the conversation goes on, John sometimes finds questions and activities from published guides to be invaluable but he chooses these wisely, depending on what he feels will stretch and challenge his students.

You may be thinking that these ideas are all well and good for fifth graders or older students, but what about first and second graders? We respond with a resounding, "YES! Why not?" Mary Giard, a first-grade teacher, uses open-ended questions that require more than a yes or no response. The questions have worked so well that Mary is able to step out of the conversation, and students will carry on without her.

Using Three Levels of Questions

Teachers typically design questions at three levels of thinking: *literal, inferential,* and *evaluative. Literal-level questions* are low-level types of questions. Answers are found in the text, and students do not need to read "beyond the lines." These questions typically tap whether students understand the main idea or gist of the plot and some fundamental ideas of characters, setting, etc. *Inferential questions* are designed so that readers need to read "between the lines." At this level, questions should cause students to search for relationships between and among ideas and to draw conclusions about what they read. Students then need to return to the text for evidence. *Evaluative questions* are those in which students read "beyond the lines." These questions invite students to think about the relevance of their reading: "What would I do if I were in the same position as the character?" "What implications does this reading have for my life?"

As was previously discussed in this chapter, students have received far too much practice with literal-level questions, so much that national test results indicate that students have difficulty with higher-level questioning. It is our contention that literal-level questions have been used so much because of the following reasons: (1) For many years basal manuals were inundated with these lower-level questions. One second-grade teacher reported that she rarely got to the higher-level questions because the literal-level questions were the first ones suggested in the manual, and time always ran out before she was able to ask the higher-level questions; (2) Literal-level questions are easy to write, quick to answer (usually the talk is brief when factual questions are asked), and easy to grade for testing purposes. Sometimes there is a misconception that young children or slower progress readers of any age are capable of answering only literal-level questions. In our experience this is certainly not the case. Right from the beginning, children should experience conversation about books that is challenging and alive with wonder and stimulation. It is our speculation that older students who have been turned off to reading never experience reading and talking about a book in more authentic ways. They become bored with simpleminded, literal-level questioning.

The questions John creates for *Bridge to Terabithia* are designed as a result of conversations with students. He builds both upon their "agenda" (how they think, react, and feel toward the book) and ways he wants to challenge students in terms of thinking about particular literary characteristics, such as plot, character, point of view, theme, and style of writing. For his purposes, he sees little need to invent literal-level questions; his are designed for higher levels of thinking. Here are some examples of questions John has asked:

> Think about why the book is entitled *Bridge to Terabithia.* What is the significance of the bridge?
>
> Did Jesse grow and change during the story? In what ways?

What will Jesse's life be like after Leslie's death?

CHANGING ROLES—WAYS TO HELP STUDENTS BECOME STRATEGIC QUESTIONERS

The case has already been made that children learn early on that teachers are the questioners, and that they are the ones to give the answers to the questions. How can we help students become more active in the construction of their own meaning-making?

Reading Logs

John's students write in reading or literature logs, "tracking" their own "thought journeys" as they read. Most of what they will write in their logs will be reflections and feelings about what they are reading. At certain times, John will suggest specific questions or topics for their writing. John often varies the format for this exercise. He may ask students to dialogue in writing with another member of the literature group. Each student chooses a partner and writes in letter format on one side of the log; the partner responds on the other side. John responds to the log as well, along with a student partner.

It is important to keep in mind that, since such logs are first-draft writing, it is more appropriate to comment on the content of what is written than to focus on how it is written. Reminding students of all the mistakes they are making will almost ensure a lack of risk taking in writing. For example, why should students use an unusual word to describe a character's actions if they will be penalized for not knowing how to spell it?; it is safer to use a word they know how to spell. You might want to keep some notes of student strengths in the reading logs as well as particular aspects needing growth and refinement. These ar-

eas could become the topics for minilessons or focus lessons as part of a writer's workshop.

Students do significantly more writing about their reading if they are given opportunities to try reading or literature logs instead of worksheets or merely answering comprehension questions about the reading. Logs are much more authentic, with the results of such writing usually surprising the students themselves. They really do not know what they think about their reading until they have a chance to write about it, read what others have written, and then talk with each other. This is much more consistent with what "real" readers do and is not just another school assignment having little application to the world outside of the classroom.

We suggest that teachers maintain a log as well. By actually writing along with their students, teachers can demonstrate that this is an important activity. Such writing can provide the "fuel" for rich literary discussions when the group reconvenes to discuss what they have read and written.

Encouraging Students to Formulate Their Own Questions

Adam Cook's third-grade class is about to begin a read aloud of Chris Van Allsburg's *Jumanji*. Adam asks students what questions they have about the title of this book and the cover. The responses are varied. "Jumanji is a funny title," Tom says. "What is Jumanji?"

Linda chimes in, "What are those monkeys doing in that boy's living room?"

Tad asks, "Who are those boys on the cover? Why do they look so surprised?"

Adam invites other questions and then begins reading aloud. He then asks the children what they want to know more about and records their questions on chart paper. This strategy of the teacher's questions leading to students designing their own questions puts readers in the driver's seat. From the students' questions, Adam learns how students think about the story. This is a good example of the teacher beginning with the students' "agenda." There is an air of excitement and a willingness by many students to participate because all questions are welcome; no value judgements are made about who is right or wrong because students are not responding to the teacher's questions by giving answers. Their questions also serve as predictions and give students a real reason for listening to the story. There is an obvious investment in the process.

Adam also uses this procedure as he works with a small group reading Beverly Cleary's *Ramona Quimby, Age 8* (1981). He asks a few questions: What would you like to know about Ramona? What would you like to know about Ramona's family and where the story takes place? As Adam works through this process, he also asks students how these questions help them to understand what they read. This crucial step is often missing in teaching. We tend not to talk about the process with students. If we do not have students step out of the "picture," the assumption might be that students understand why we are using a particular strategy. In actuality, if we do not help them to think through a process and discuss it (tapping metacognitive behavior), we cannot expect to see transfer to what they do without the help of the teacher.

At the end of the discussion, Adam invites students to talk about the usefulness of posing questions as they read. He records responses from *each* student on chart paper, which is then posted on the wall. Getting a response from each member of the group takes a little more time, but Adam considers it a worthwhile process. If students do not have a ready response, Adam tells them that he will come back to them. When he does return to these students, it is quite acceptable for them to repeat a response someone else gave. This procedure in itself is different from the typical classroom scenario, where what usually happens is that only one or two students respond and that is the end of the discussion!

Discussions about process are crucial in Adam's class because he believes it is important for students to acquire a repertoire of strategies to help them become more powerful readers. By listening to each other, students begin to appreciate a diversity of responses. Becoming aware of a classmate's thoughts gives *all* students an opportunity to have their responses valued and may go a long way in informing each other about different strategies. Because this chart becomes a "public document" by posting it in the classroom, it also serves as a reminder of helpful strategies. This chart is depicted below.

What We Learned About Asking Our Own Questions About What We Read

- It was hard at first because I'm used to the teacher asking questions.
- Asking questions made me think more about what I was going to read.
- I like to think up the kind of questions Mr. Cook asks us. They're hard questions!

Question/Answer Relationships

Raphael's research (1986) into effective questioning strategies led to the development of question/answer relationships (QARs). This strategy helps students identify the nature of questions and can help them learn how to answer different types of questions. Explicit instruction is recommended to help students understand the nature of three different types of questions and what they demand of the reader in terms of response.

1. Text-based questions with the answers being found directly in the text ("*right there*").
2. Text-based questions that require the student to "*think and search*" for relevant information.
3. Questions that require a response that is found not directly in the text but in the mind of the reader ("*on my own*").

In order for students to determine question/answer relationships, the teacher needs to first take a more direct role in helping students to determine differences and then gradually to relinquish that control to students. Vacca, Vacca, and Gove (1991) claim that "through this strategy, readers become more sensitive to the different mental operations and text demands required by different questions."

Shelley Smith, a fourth-grade teacher, demonstrated the differences between these types of questions by distributing copies of the story, *The Clever Earthworm: An Animal Folktale from Vietnam* (Vo-Dinh, 1970). Since students were involved in a folktale unit, this story was a good choice to use as a focus lesson on QARs. She began the lesson by having a student read the title and asked another student to locate the country of Vietnam on the world map. Next, as an introduction to the story, a volunteer read the introductory quote at the top of the page. She asked students what questions they had about the story after reading the introductory passage. Next, Shelley read the story aloud as the children followed along on their copy. She then displayed an overhead transparency of three questions about the story:

1. Why did the man catch the earthworm? (*right there*)
2. How did the earthworm fool the fish? (*think and search*)
3. In what ways have you seen an animal or person use intelligence and cleverness to outwit another? (*on my own*)

Shelley displayed a chart with a description of the three types of questions and the phrases to remember them. She engaged students in a discussion of the differences between the questions listed on the overhead transparency. Next, she displayed three additional questions on the transparency and asked students to work in pairs to determine the question type and then to decide on a response to each. The following day, she repeated this procedure using another folktale to assess whether students understood the differences between the question types. As a teacher, you may find that additional work and explanation is needed before your students understand the differences between these three categories.

We believe that you will find QARs invaluable in helping students to think through the types of responses being asked of them. Teaching this procedure should not be considered an isolated activity but one that you continue to use all year in your work with thematic units and as part of literature circle activities. In order for students to become active meaning-makers, it is important that these strategies be added to your students' permanent repertoire of ways to become more powerful comprehenders.

We offer a final suggestion: It is beneficial for students to work through these strategies in pairs or small groups until they reach a point where they feel competent at using them independently. View your students as teachers, assisting each other by talking through these new strategies. Oftentimes, the conversations will benefit the entire classroom community and bring everyone to a richer and more dynamic understanding.

READING FOR PLEASURE

Research confirms that students who choose to read as a leisure activity outperform those who do not (Long and Henderson, 1973; Irving, 1980; Morrow, 1983). So, what is the link between choosing to read and comprehension? Students need opportunities to select what they want to read. Given this opportunity, many students will read more and demonstrate an overall gain in comprehension and attitudes toward reading. Thus students who are in classrooms that encourage reading both in school and at home, based on self-selection from a collection of high-quality trade books, become more powerful readers. These ideas are discussed throughout many of the chapters in this book because we believe that teachers who engage students of all ages in high-quality reading view literature as one of the most important features of an integrated literacy program.

CATHY SWANSON'S JOURNAL

❧ *March 2*

Although I've noted growth in many areas of the students' writing, getting them to revise/edit is like pulling teeth! I realize this is a tough thing to be motivated about; a thorough job in editing sometimes means another draft.

Everybody has a copy of the self-check list in their writing folders, and there are loose copies in the Writing Center if they'd prefer. I think what is difficult is to edit their own work and look for everything at once.

As a young writer, much less emphasis was placed on the content of my work. It was easier to notice when an ending mark was missing or a letter should have been capitalized because that is what was at-tended to by my teachers. Now, with developing fluency as a priority, our emphasis has been somewhat reversed.

Perhaps a successful strategy for next year would be to focus minilessons given in the beginning of the year on the skills most difficult for the children to incorporate automatically in first drafts—using paragraphs, for example. Had I spent more time modeling that initially, it would have been less of a "revising" struggle later.

By no means am I hoping for "perfect first drafts." That would contradict the value of process writing. But emphasizing some skills up front would buy more time for looking at writing as a craft later in the year.

❧ *March 5*

One writer in my class has really challenged me this year. His stories are inevitably about something violent or inappropriate. He really becomes engaged in and possessive of his stories, and I certainly don't want to extinguish his enthusiasm. I also feel these writings are cathartic; this boy needs that kind of safe vehicle for his anger.

When he shares his stories with the class, he doesn't seem to be aware of the response he gets (or doesn't get). He interjects words, phrases, and events that he expects will get a laugh but are not contributing to any sense of story. Someone once shared that his stories would be good except that he's trying too hard to make us laugh.

I try not to interfere too much with content—if I start giving too many ideas the kids begin to rely on me for that. I want them to value their own ideas. But in this case, I need to somehow model how his writing can evolve into something else without robbing him of the ownership of it. I need a positive way to help him accept the criticism and learn to see it on his own.

✤ March 8

It seems almost all kids love poetry. As we began to look at poetry, we shared our favorite poems and noted our poets.

Bill's hand shot up in the air. "Shel Silverstein! He's awesome!"

Chris told me Bill even knew what pages poems were found on in *Where the Sidewalk Ends*. I thought he was exaggerating until we were reading aloud from the collection one day.

"Read 'Sick' Ms. Swanson," requested Julia. Bill cited the page number. The same thing happened for the next five or six poems we selected!

"Can I do 'Sick' out loud tomorrow? I have it memorized," asked Bill.

"Sure, that would be great!" I answered.

This morning, Bill performed his beloved poem. He was sprawled on the floor with a blanket pulled up over his face. In "poem heaven," Bill was halfway through his recitation when our requests to uncover his face (so we could hear the words) finally broke through his trance! As he started over I thought, this poem may have been written by Shel, but it's Bill's now. He knows it, loves it, breathes it. That's poetry.

TEACHER AS LEARNER / TEACHER AS RESEARCHER

Determining What Data to Collect

You read about how to frame questions as a teacher/researcher in Chapter 1 and some data collection procedures in the chapters that followed. You may want to go back and review those sections before continuing.

Once you have framed a question, draft several subquestions that emerge from this central question. This process will help to sharpen and define your thinking and lead to the kinds of data you will need to collect. For example, fourth-grade teacher Suzanne Hall framed the following central question in her journal:

- In what ways do students in the literature circle group demonstrate their understanding of what they have read?

Her subquestions included the following:

- In what ways do students talk about what they have read together? In what ways does this talk change when I am part of the discussion group?
- In what ways do students write to demonstrate their understanding of what they have read?

- In what other ways do students respond to what they read?
- How do students go about making choices for responding to books?
- How does their decision making affect my role as a teacher?

By framing these subquestions, Suzanne now has a point of departure or a route to take in the collection of data. For example, Suzanne will design sociograms to provide information about how students interact during literature circle time. She will audiotape several book discussions, both with her as part of the group and during student-led discussions, to see if patterns of conversation emerge. Suzanne will also collect written responses to literature, as well as art or other kinds of responses to the books students read during literature circle time. She also plans to design questions to interview students about how they go about making choices for responding to literature. Suzanne believes that this process will not only help her to become better informed as to how students go about understanding what they read, but also how they make choices, and what her role is in this process.

Journal Reflections

Select one or more of the questions below that interest you and respond in your journal.

1. You have read Cathy's journal entries from the beginning of the school year to the middle of March. If you had an opportunity to write a letter to her students now, what would you like to say in that letter? Please feel free to comment on things you have learned about them as well as things you have learned about teaching language arts.

2. Interview several teachers concerning the comprehension strategies they have found to be most useful.

3. Interview students at two different grade levels (second grade and seventh grade, for example). Ask them to explain some of the reading strategies they use when they are reading. In other words, what do they do as readers that helps them understand what they read? Do you note any differences between students from different grade levels? How would you explain those differences?

4. Design your own question.
   ✓ What is a question you have about the chapter?
   ✓ How will you pursue the answer to that question?
   ✓ Respond in your journal.

REFERENCES AND SUGGESTED READINGS

Allington, R. L., and Weber, R. M. "Questioning Questions in Teaching and Learning from Texts." In B. K. Bretton, A. Woodward, and M. Binkley, eds. *Learning from Textbooks: Theory And Practice.* Hillsdale, NJ: Lawrence Erlbaum, 1993.

Andrews, N., and Salesi, R. *Extending Involvement with Special Books Using Whole Language Games.* Proceedings of the United Kingdom Reading Association Conference. New York: Macmillan, 1986.

Annis, L. F. "Student-Generated Paragraph Summaries and the Information-Processing Theory of Prose Learning." *Journal of Experimental Education* 54 (1985): 4–10.

Atwell, N. *In the Middle: Writing, Reading, and Learning with Adolescents.* Portsmouth, NH: Heinemann, 1987.

Bean, T. W., and Steenwyk, F. L. "The Effect of Three Forms of Summarization Instruction on Sixth Graders' Summary Writing and Comprehension." *Journal of Reading Behavior* 16 (1984): 297–306.

Beck, I. L., McKeown, M. G., McCaslin, E., and Burket, A. *Instructional Dimensions that May Affect Reading Comprehension: Examples of Two Commerces Reading Programs.* Pittsburgh: University of Pittsburgh Language Research and Development Center, 1979.

Bloom, B. *Taxonomy of Educational Objectives: Cognitive Domain.* New York: McKay, 1956.

Borders, S. G., and Naylor, A. P. *Children Talking Books.* Phoenix: Oryx Press, 1993.

Chambers, A. *Booktalk.* New York: Harper & Row, 1985.

Cooper, J. D. *Literacy: Helping Children Construct Meaning.* Boston: Houghton Mifflin, 1993.

Davis, F. B. "Research on Comprehension in Reading." *Reading Research Quarterly* 3 (1986): 499–545.

Durkin, D. "What Classroom Observations Reveal About Reading Comprehension Instruction." *Reading Research Quarterly,* 14 (1978–1979): 481–533.

Eeds, M. "What to Do When They Don't Understand What They Read." *The Reading Teacher* 34 (1981): 565–571.

Flood, J., and Lapp, D. "Reading Comprehension Instruction." In J. Flood, J. M. Jensen, D. Lapp, and J. R. Squire, eds. *Handbook of Research on Teaching the Language Arts.* New York: Macmillan, 1991.

Fredericks, A. *Whole Language and Literature: Creative Ideas for Your Classroom.* Medina, WA: Institute for Educational Development, 1992.

Fredericks, A. D., and Cheeseborough, D. L. *Science for All Children: Elementary School Methods.* New York: HarperCollins, 1993.

Gall, M. "Synthesis of Research on Teachers' Questions." *Educational Leadership* 42 (1989): 40–47.

Goodman, K. S. *Miscue Analysis: Application to Reading Instruction.* Urbana, IL: National Council of Teachers of English, 1973a.

Goodman, K. S. "Psycholinguistic Universals in the Reading Process." In F. Smith, ed., *Psycholinguistics and Reading.* New York: Holt, Rinehart and Winston, 1973b.

Goodman, K. S. "Basal Readers: A Call for Action." *Language Arts* 63 (1986a): 358–363.

Goodman, K. S. *What's Whole in Whole Language.* Toronto: Scholastic—TAB, 1986b.

Goodman, Y. M. "Kid-watching: An Alternative to Testing." *National Elementary Principals* 57 (1978): 41–45.

Goodman, Y. M. "The Roots of the Whole-Language Movement." *Elementary School Journal* 90 (1989): 113–127.

Hansen, J. "The Effect of Inference Training and Practice on Young Children's Reading Comprehension." *Reading Research Quarterly* 16 (1981): 391–417.

Hansen, J., and Hubbard, R. "Poor Readers Can Draw Inferences." *The Reading Teacher* 37 (1984): 586–589.

Hansen, J., and Pearson, P. D. "An Instructional Study: Improving the Inferential Comprehension of Good and Poor Fourth-Grade Readers." *Journal of Educational Psychology* 75 (1983): 821–829.

Irving, A. *Promoting Voluntary Reading for Children and Young People.* Paris: UNESCO, 1980.

Littlefair, A. "Reading and Writing Across the Curriculum." In C. Harrison and M. Coles, eds., *The Reading for Real Handbook.* New York: Routledge, 1992.

Long, H., and Henderson, E. H. "Children's Uses of Time: Some Personal and Social Correlates." *Elementary School Journal* 73 (1973): 193–199.

Manzo, A. V. "The Request Procedure." *Journal of Reading* 13 (1969): 123–126.

McNeil, J. D. *Reading Comprehension: New Directions for Classroom Practice,* 3rd ed. New York: Harper-Collins, 1992.

Morrow L. M. "Home and School Correlates of Early Interest in Literature." *Journal of Educational Research* 76 (1983): 221–230.

Nodelman, P. *The Pleasures of Children's Literature.* White Plains, NY: Longman, 1992.

Ogle, D. "K-W-L: A Teaching Model that Develops Active Reading of Expository Text." *The Reading Teacher* 39 (1986): 564–570.

Peterson, R., and Eeds, M. *Grand Conversations: Literature Groups in Action.* Toronto: Scholastic—TAB, 1990.

Raphael, T. "Teacher Question-Answer Relationships, Revisited." *The Reading Teacher* 39 (1986): 516–522.

Reutzel, D. R. "Reconciling Schema Theory and the Basal Reading Lesson." *The Reading Teacher* 39 (1985): 194–198.

Rhodes, L. K. "I Can Read! Predictable Books as Resources for Reading and Writing Instruction." *The Reading Teacher* 34 (1981): 314–318.

Rosenblatt, L. *Literature as Exploration,* 3rd ed. New York: Modern Language Association, 1976.

Routman, R. *Invitations: Changing as Teachers and Learners K-12.* Portsmouth, NH: Heinemann, 1994.

Spearitt, D. "Identification of Subskills in Reading Comprehensions by Maximum Likelihood Factor Analysis." *Reading Research Quarterly* 8 (1972): 92–111.

Teaching and Learning Literature with Children and Young Adults. Personalized Reading-Part I: First Principles (September/October, 1992): 23–28.

Vacca, J., Vacca, R., and Gove, M. *Reading and Learning to Read,* 2nd ed. New York: HarperCollins, 1991.

Vygotsky, L. S. *The Development of Higher Psychological Processes.* Cambridge: Harvard University Press, 1979.

CREATING LITERATURE-RICH CLASSROOMS

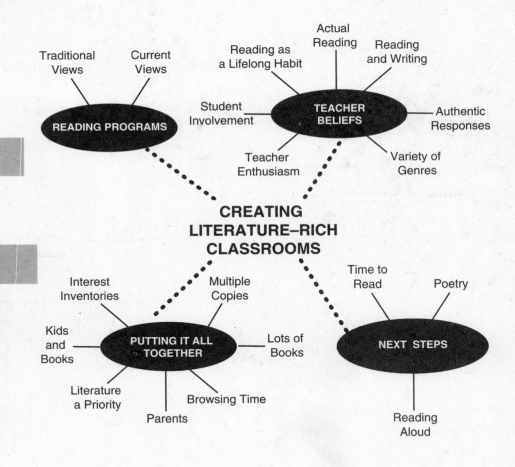

Traditional Views · Current Views

READING PROGRAMS

Reading as a Lifelong Habit · Actual Reading · Reading and Writing

Student Involvement

TEACHER BELIEFS

Authentic Responses

Teacher Enthusiasm · Variety of Genres

CREATING LITERATURE–RICH CLASSROOMS

Interest Inventories · Multiple Copies

Kids and Books

PUTTING IT ALL TOGETHER

Lots of Books

Literature a Priority · Parents · Browsing Time

Time to Read · Poetry

NEXT STEPS

Reading Aloud

Big Ideas

This chapter will offer:

1. The differences between traditional views of reading instruction and current views of reading instruction.

2. Important components of a literature-rich classroom.

3. Criteria teachers use to evaluate and select the best books for their classrooms.

4. Rationale for the value of reading aloud in elementary classrooms.

5. The ingredients for beginning and maintaining a literature-rich classroom.

What I Know: Pre-Chapter Journaling

What do you remember about the use of trade books or children's literature in the classroom when you were in the elementary grades? What were some of the most memorable books you read during that time?

As a child I felt that books were holy objects, to be caressed, rapturously sniffed, and devotedly provided for. I gave my life to them—I still do. I continue to do what I did as a child: dream of books, make books, and collect books.

(Maurice Sendak, p. 146)

How do we make books important to a child's life? How do we instill a love of books such as that felt by children's author Maurice Sendak? How do we ensure that books play a central role in our classrooms from the time children enter school until they leave?

We begin this chapter by describing some of the changes second-grade teacher Becky Allen made in her classroom as she made the transition from basal readers to incorporating more literature into her program. We begin with this teacher's story for several reasons. Teachers are becoming more enthusiastic about the possibilities of using literature in the classroom. In so doing they are rethinking the place of textbooks in the curriculum. As you work in schools, you may find yourself in classrooms where this transition is taking place. If you begin your own teaching career using a basal reader, it may be helpful to return to this chapter to review how several teachers made some powerful changes from a textbook orientation to the use of trade books or children's literature.

Becky Allen has some important decisions to make during the summer before she begins her twelfth year of teaching. She is enrolled in a master's degree program at a local university. Her coursework has prompted her to be more reflective about how she thinks about teaching reading and writing. When she was in college, she was taught to use a basal for reading instruction, and she feels that she has done a good job using it over the last 11 years of teaching second grade. She never really stopped to think about her beliefs on teaching the language arts; she just did what she thought was expected of her. Now, she is experiencing excitement over all the new practices she is hearing about in her coursework, but also a sense of apprehension about making changes.

Becky had a college junior working with her in the classroom, and the student, too, asked many questions about her reading program and the extent to which she uses children's literature in not just her reading program but across the curriculum. Becky had to admit that she used mostly textbooks for all of her program. She did routinely read aloud to students and had some books available for children to read when their workbook pages were completed. Now, she felt a sense that this was not enough. Becky has been reacquainted with the world of books and is excited about all the possibilities, but where should she start?

This scenario describing Becky's program is one that is constantly being repeated by teachers across the country. Teachers are becoming aware of so much evidence that points to the benefits of either replacing the basal reader with literature as the content of the reading program or, at least, supplementing use of the basal with literature. More and more elementary and middle school teachers are reading extensively and attending university courses, conferences, and workshops to learn about establishing literature-rich classrooms. They are reflecting more on their beliefs about what should happen in their classrooms in terms of reading, what the goals of a reading program should be, and ways that they can begin to take risks with their own learning in order to make changes in their classrooms.

This chapter will focus on ways that teachers can begin to make those changes and why those changes need to be made. Let's begin by looking at some current practices and what has typically happened in our classrooms in terms of reading programs.

Traditional Views

Traditional views of reading include the following:

- Typically in grades 1 through 6, there are reading groups based on ability levels (low, middle, and high).

- The basal reading textbook and accompanying workbooks provide the content of the reading material for students. The teacher uses a manual or teacher's guide to teach each selection.
- Students normally read the selection silently and, then, in round-robin fashion, they take turns reading aloud.
- The teacher asks comprehension questions about the story and teaches several skills, usually but not always related to the selection.
- Students return to their seats to complete workbook pages and, perhaps, additional worksheets with the intention of practicing the skills that were taught.
- Students who can quickly accomplish their assignment may be given time to read a "real" book from the library with the time that remains. Other students are assigned additional workbook pages, or they are asked to read short selections and to answer questions from the SRA kit or similar commercial material.
- The bulk of the "real" reading is expected to be done out of the classrooms. A book report is usually assigned as a result of this additional reading.

Current Views

Current views of reading include the following:

- More and more teachers at all grade levels are exploring ways for children to read from "real" books or trade books (rather than text-books) not just during reading time but within all subject areas.
- Teachers hold strong beliefs about the value of surrounding children with high quality literature and the power of children reading actual books instead of short snippets of stories. They believe that this is the best way for children to become readers.
- Teachers believe in establishing a classroom rich in the use of literature across the curriculum. They provide ample time for children to actually "get into" a book and read.
- They believe that in order for children to become good at reading, they need good books and lots of time to actually read in school.
- They believe that children can learn best about the world and have their questions answered, whether it be about the solar system, insects, prairie life, or dinosaurs, by reading books on the subject, not just an encyclopedia or textbooks.
- They believe that readers need guidance to help them become more skilled at reading. Teachers accomplish this through mini-lessons or lessons focused on certain aspects of reading. However, there is a good balance between this kind of work and time spent doing the "real" thing—actually reading.
- Teachers offer opportunities for children to respond to what they read in a variety of ways (art, drama, conversation, writing, cooking, related readings, etc.). They tend to avoid the use of the term "book report" because of the negative connotation many students hold. Also, many teachers believe that the book report format is not an adequate or authentic response to a book. Teachers see themselves as readers, too. They allocate a generous amount of time talking with (not to) students about what they are reading either individually or in small groups when students read a book in common.
- They believe that in order for students to become capable writers, it is necessary to talk about "real" books and "real" authors. Students need to discuss the craft of the writer, so discussions take on a different flavor, focusing on the author's style, choice of words, the way characters are developed in a story, how the setting was described, and so on. There is also an emphasis on talking about reactions to a book, journaling about what students are reading, and having more authentic conversations about books, rather than a question-and-answer cycle.

- There is an emphasis on strategic instruction rather than teaching a set of isolated skills.

When you were an elementary school student, did you experience a program based more on traditional views than on current ways of thinking about reading? Well, as we will discover here, more and more classrooms have a totally different look to them. They are literature-rich classrooms where high-quality children's books abound and where textbooks take a backseat. What are the distinctive characteristics of a literature-rich classroom?

1. Teachers are enthusiastic about books; they enjoy reading and demonstrate this joy in as many ways as possible; they know books and how to select the best ones.

2. Children in today's literacy-rich classrooms are feasting on a rich and varied selection of literature—from picture books, poetry, myths, folktales, and legends to fantasy, contemporary realistic fiction, historical fiction, informational books, and biography.

3. Teachers are seeing literature as the backbone of not only the reading program but of the entire curriculum. They are enthusiastic about ways to bring children and books together. In these classrooms, teachers use the basal reader as a supplementary text or an anthology. Or in some cases, teachers have abandoned the basal in order for students to self-select books that they would like to read on their own. Small discussion groups or literature circles meet to read a novel or picture book in common. For many students, this is their first opportunity to read an entire book in class rather than it being assigned as a book report to read outside of class.

4. Teachers read aloud to students on a daily basis from selections spanning the curriculum. For example, teachers may share poetry in science and historical fiction in social studies. Teachers introduce children to new books and provide lots of time to actually read.

5. In content areas such as science and social studies, students are moving beyond encyclopedias and textbooks and are using nonfiction children's books both as sources of information and as models for their writing. For example, in Betty Robinson's sixth-grade class, each student brainstorms a list of ten to 15 topics to be pursued. Topics range from the rain forest to learning more about AIDS. Students use webbing as a tool for brainstorming what they know about a topic and what questions they want to pursue. They learn how to summarize information and write it in a format that will be interesting. They follow the steps in the writing process such as drafting, conferencing, revising, and sharing their pieces with classmates.

6. Teachers form partnerships with the school and public librarians as sources for books and ways to enrich the entire curriculum using high-quality literature.

7. Teachers seek ways to extend each student's involvement with books outside of school through visits to the public library, obtaining library cards (don't assume that older children are familiar with the public library or already have library cards!), and making home–school links by planning ways for children to read at home.

It is easy to become overwhelmed if you visit literature-rich classrooms where books abound and are truly the "backbone" or supporting feature of the total curriculum. In such a classroom, you might make the following observations:

- Books are everywhere.
- The teacher is reading aloud to the whole class or a small group.
- Individual students are reading self-selected books, and small groups of students are reading the same novel.
- Students are responding to books they have read through drama, artwork, additional writing, etc.

- Other students are poring over several books to find answers to questions for a thematic unit on the Westward Movement or for some other topic.
- Both reading and writing are key elements in literature-rich classrooms.
- Teachers take some time to read everyday, too! They might choose right from the classroom library's selection. Children need to see adults as readers, engrossed in a book. Enthusiasm for books is evident.

IMPORTANT CONCEPTS IN ESTABLISHING LITERATURE-RICH CLASSROOMS

Lucille Wong, a kindergarten teacher, firmly believes that as soon as children enter school they need to be in an environment that will nurture them as readers. She believes that all her children are readers already! After all, all of them can read the sign that says "McDonald's" as well as the environmental print and contextualized messages found on cereal boxes, toothpaste tubes, soda bottles, soup cans, and cookie boxes.

Lucille is aware that many of her students do not come from print-rich environments at home; there are not many books or magazines available, children are not read to, and there are no visits to the public library. She views this as more of a challenge than a problem. She does exactly what she would do if children did come from print-rich home environments, but in ways to help children really appreciate the printed word.

Lucille is always excited about books and is very animated and vocal about them with students; in other words she goes out of her way to be obvious about her enthusiasm. She truly loves children's literature and cannot hold back her excitement. She does not want children to guess how she feels about books, and she does not want to tell them about how wonderful books are; she shows them in a variety of ways that reading is

the thing. She dashes in on a Monday morning with a book by Bruce McMillan, *Mary Had a Little Lamb* (1990). This is a great find because children in Lucille's class are already acquainted with many Bruce McMillan books. Lucille introduces this book the first thing in the morning. She gathers everyone on the floor. "Look what book I found at the library this weekend. Can anyone guess by looking at the cover who the author might be and what this book will be all about? I discovered this book by Bruce McMillan on the special display of books at the library this week-end. Did any of you visit the library on Saturday?" After Lucille read the book aloud and everyone talked about it, she talked with students about how she loves to discover books that are new to her and that one way to do this is by visiting the public library on the weekend. So, Lucille presents herself as an adult who reads as a leisure activity and one who visits the library. Since her class had a field trip to the library at the beginning of the school year, she always asks throughout the week if anyone visited the library, and she invites students to talk about or bring to class the books they borrowed. Since the children were so pleased with this version of "Mary Had a Little Lamb," Lucille decides to look for other versions of this rhyme to share.

Lucille always has a display of books that will probably be new to the children and ready for them to look at on Monday morning. She likes to start the day by having children browse through the new books or others in her well-stocked classroom library.

She introduces literature in many ways all morning, such as sharing stories and poetry aloud and using the flannel board to tell stories of familiar folktales such as *The Three Billy Goats Gruff* and *The Little Red Hen.* At the end of the morning, children leave with a poem in their heads that Lucille has shared right before the bell signaling the end of morning kindergarten.

Many children can also be seen leaving the classroom with a book bag. Several years ago, Lucille received some money from the school's parent-teacher organization to buy 30 book bags and $100 worth of books. In today's market $100 does not go too far for books, but Lucille was able to purchase some hardcover books as well as paperbacks. She supplemented these new books with those in the classroom library and one book bag for every child in the classroom.

Each book bag has a plastic-coated card attached to the bag listing the titles included in the bag. For example, one bag includes four popular books by author and illustrator Barbara Cooney. Another bag includes five books by Ezra Jack Keats; other bags might have a set of fairytales, or poetry, or *Ranger Rick* magazines, or dinosaur books. Every night children may opt to sign out a bag to take home. Children rotate the bags in order to experience a wide selection of books and then return to old favorites.

Lucille loves to watch children leave her room everyday with a bag of books to share with family members. She has received lots of positive feedback from parents about the bookbag program as well. As part of the sharing time in the morning, children volunteer to talk about favorite books they enjoyed the evening before and to make recommendations to other students. "Josh, you should really take out the bag of dinosaur books. You'd like the one about digging up dinosaurs; it's a wonderful book!"

Lucille has modeled this kind of book conversation about sharing and recommending books. In a short time, children begin to do the same. Several students also make recommendations for more book bags.

"Could you put together one on trains?"

"How about elephants? I love elephants?"

Lucille sees this as a wonderful sign, so takes out her marker and chart paper and records this information as suggestions for books. She then invites students to later record, on their own, other suggestions that might come to them. (Note that Lucille also treats her kindergartners as writers, as well!) One new student, Amy, approached her later and whispered, "Miss Wong, I don't know how to write, so I can't give any ideas." Lucille responded by saying, "Don't worry, Amy, you can

help me read your writing!" With this affirming message, Amy trotted off to the chart to write her book bag suggestion of "hoss," which got translated in grown-up spelling next to her entry (with Amy's approval!) of "horses."

Another way teachers can share their love of books is to spend some time actually reading when children are engaged in reading their own books. This behavior sends a strong message that the teacher is not just telling students to read, but that the teacher actually spends time doing this, too. Students also need to know that teachers are interested in expanding their own reading tastes. Aidan Chambers (1985), says that teachers are often "flat earth readers," reading only what is comfortable. He says that they need to become "intergalatic readers." For instance, if you only share fantasy or science fiction titles with children because that genre of reading is your favorite, you are not demonstrating to children that it is important to vary the literary diet. Be brave and try a recommended anthology of poetry or a book of nonfiction or even historical fiction. You might surprise yourself and find that you have a new favorite genre.

HOW TO EVALUATE AND SELECT THE BEST BOOKS

Let's begin with a review of genres of books for children and young adolescents:

- *Picture books:* Books in which the illustrations are integral to the story. Some picture books include only pictures, no words. These are called wordless picture books. Picture books include picture storybooks, ABC books, concept books, counting books, and Mother Goose books. Some picture books are highly sophisticated and are very appropriate for older readers.

- *Traditional literature:* Books that might be classified as folktales, fables, myths, and legends.

- *Fantasy:* Books that focus on modern fairy tales, fantasy stories about strange worlds, dolls, toys, animals, odd and curious characters, magic, and the supernatural. This genre also includes science fiction and high fantasy (stories about special powers and good overcoming evil)

- *Contemporary realistic fiction:* This genre includes stories about everyday happenings such as growing up, solving problems, families, and living in a multicultural society; also includes mysteries, animal stories, and stories about sports.

- *Poetry:* This genre includes different poetic forms such as limericks, haiku, ballads, free verse, as well as lyrical, narrative, and concrete poetry.

- *Historical fiction:* This genre focuses on events that have taken place in the past—prehistoric through more modern times.

- *Biography:* This genre includes complete biographies, partial biographies, simplified biographies, and autobiographies.

- *Informational books:* These include books that can be used across the curriculum in such areas as social studies, math, science, and the arts. The information presented is factual and is presented in a variety of formats: informational picture books, photo essay, chapter books, concept books, and fact books.

How do you decide what to include in your classroom library? Should you select animal stories, fantasy titles, stories about growing up, mysteries? The choices are endless when you consider all the genres to choose from. How do you go about making the best choices?

The following are a few ways to determine students reading interests:

- Know what books children enjoy at different ages and stages of their development.

- Take an interest inventory.

- Talk to students about their interests, hobbies, and what they enjoy doing in their spare time.

- Help children who have a difficult time selecting books by choosing several that will be of interest.

- Link writing interests with reading interests.

- Observe what books children choose during browsing time.

Sometimes students have not sampled from a wide array of literature so their preferences are quite narrow. You can thus play a powerful role in introducing children to books that they would not gravitate toward on their own. That is why it is important both to know your students and what they like and to know books. There is nothing quite so satisfying as being able to place the "right" book in the hands of a child who is ready for a new challenge. This approach requires a classroom library that offers a balance among the genres. You can't assume, for instance, that children will develop a love of poetry if you don't offer lots of poetry for them to "try on for size." Your enthusiasm for lots of different kinds of books coupled with having a wide variety of titles in the classroom will be a compelling "invitation" to read to your students.

One way to determine the reading tastes of your students is through interest inventories, which can be given at the beginning of the year as well as at midyear. Interest inventories might contain questions such as the following:

What kinds of books do you like to read?
What topics are you interested in exploring?
What is your favorite hobby?
What do you like to do in your spare time?

You may want to design your own inventory form using a variety of questions from several different sources to more closely match your needs. We believe that a child's interest in reading a particular book is a very strong motivator. That is why determining interests and allowing children to explore those interests is so important. You will find that the reading level of a book often plays a secondary role. Some trade books indicate a reading level (RL) and an interest level (IL). The reading level is usually determined by applying a readability formula to the text. The most common one is the Fry Readability Formula, which counts the number of words and sentences from three 100-word passages. The readability is determined by plotting the results of the computation on a graph. Readability formulas should be used with caution because they are not always accurate and can easily dissuade a child from even trying to read a book. So, consider interests as a starting place.

Some students may need your guidance in selecting an appropriate book. Simply inviting children to select a book to read from the classroom or school library can be overwhelming for some children, no matter what grade level. It is similar to going into a toy or candy store and not knowing how to make choices. Your careful kid-watching, coupled with information from interest inventories, will help you to determine what children may have the most problems identifying appropriate books. You might try narrowing the choices by choosing three to five books you determine that the child would like to read and could read. Meet with the child and share a little bit about each book. You might even ask the child to choose one book and to read a paragraph or two from it.

A real example highlighting the significance of a child's interest in a topic is the story of David, a fourth grader, who was tested as reading on the second-grade level. David was placed in a second-grade basal reader for his third- and fourth-grade years. On the playground during recess one day, he approached his teacher, Rosemary Collins, with an armful of books about the Civil War. David starting quizzing Rosemary about different battlegrounds. She admitted to not being able to answer David's questions. However, David was quick to answer each one of his own questions. Rosemary was amazed and asked David how he knew the answers. "Well, that's easy," he said. "I read about the battles in these books!" Rosemary was astonished to see that the books looked quite difficult, perhaps written for someone at a sixth-grade reading level or more! How could David read these difficult books when he was "tested" to read at only the second-grade level? Rosemary asked David to read several sections and sure enough, although he struggled a little, he was able to read and understand the content.

From that day on, David never was asked to read from a second-grade basal reader. With the help of the reading teacher, a program was designed for David so that he could read from self-selected books. At the time, a literature program was reserved for only the brightest fourth graders. But it took a child to prove the point. When given the opportunity to explore topics of interest, children will usually surprise us with what they can accomplish.

Another way to determine interests is to pay close attention to what children write about. If each child keeps a writing folder listing potential topics for writing, the teacher can quickly obtain a sense of topics of interest that could translate to the kinds of books to stock in the classroom library.

You can also use the time that children spend browsing through books on display in your classroom as well as in the library as a kid-watching opportunity. What books do children seem to gravitate toward? Talk to children in your class. Have everyone gather around you for a classroom meeting and talk about the kinds of books they would like to see more of in the classroom library. As a next step, invite children to find these types of books in the school library so they can be borrowed for classroom use.

INVOLVING STUDENTS IN ESTABLISHING AN ENVIRONMENT FOR READING

As a new teacher beginning your first year of teaching and entering your classroom for the first time, you may be shocked to find desks in neat rows on newly polished floors, the teacher's desk at the front of the class. Where are the book-shelves overflowing with beautiful new children's books? Reality sets in; the room you left behind in student teaching is just a distant memory. It is August and your task is at hand—how to organize for that first year of teaching and for that litera-ture-rich classroom you want so very much. This would be a good time to review your own beliefs about teaching and learning. In terms of estab-lishing an environment for literature, let your be-liefs guide you and begin thinking about ways to see students as collaborators in this venture.

Let's look in on Holly Avery, a new third-grade teacher. One of the first things Holly con-sidered beyond room arrangement of desks and tables was how to create a space for a classroom library. She felt that no matter how tightly cramped her classroom space was, she had to set up a comfortable nook for bookshelves, a rug, per-haps a rocking chair, and several other comfort-able chairs. Acquiring some old but durable furni-ture at garage sales and at home, Holly was convinced that these things would add a lot to the environment and, again, send a strong message that readers are welcome.

During college, Holly started collecting books for her future classroom library even though she was not sure what grade level she would ulti-mately teach. Holly knew that she would look for a position as a second- to fourth-grade teacher, which would mean that her future students' read-ing abilities and tastes would vary greatly. While in college, she also joined the Trumpet, Scholas-tic, and Troll Book Clubs through her professional courses. She found that this was an inexpensive ways to acquire books. Holly also requested books as gifts. She knew that if her parents and friends were aware that she wanted to start collecting books, she might receive some of the books she wanted as gifts.

If you are asking yourself the same questions that Holly asked—"If I don't know what grade level I want to teach, how can I begin collecting books?"—simply knowing whether you want to teach early primary, intermediate grades, or mid-dle school will give you considerable latitude in purchasing books. Remember that no matter what grade level you end up teaching, the range of reading levels and interests will usually be quite varied. For instance, some children in first grade will be ready for chapter books, and students in the intermediate grades and middle school can still be exposed to sophisticated and delightful picture books such as those by Chris Van Alls-burg, Mitsumasa Anno, Anthony Browne, and David Macaulay, among others.

Children of all ages are fascinated by their world, so your collection should also incorporate a sizable collection of nonfiction titles. Some of these are in picture book format, such as those by Seymour Simon. Poetry is often regrettably lack-ing from collections. Invest in several good an-thologies. The works of Shel Silverstein are some all-time favorites. Two "must-have" antholo-gies are *Where the Sidewalk Ends* and *A Light in the Attic*. Children also need to be exposed to other kinds of poetry as well. Some recommended col-lections include Arnold Adolf's *In for Winter, Out for Spring*; *American Sports Poems*, selected by R. R. Knudson and Mary Swenson; *Fresh Brats*, by X. J. Kennedy; *Anna's Garden Songs*, by Mary Q. Steele; *All the Small Poems*, by Valerie Worth; and *For Laughing Out Loud: Poems to Tickle Your Funny Bone*, selected by Jack Prelutsky.

Another excellent technique is to find books that children recommend to other children. You can do this by reading "Children's Choices," found every October in *The Reading Teacher* and "Young Adult Choices" found every November in the *Journal of Adolescent and Adult Literacy* from the International Reading Association. You can also look for "Outstanding Science Trade Books for Children" in the journal *Science and Children* and "Notable Children's Trade Books in the Field of Social Studies" in the journal *Social Education*. These lists are also jointly published by the Children's Book Council (CBC). These are helpful sources not only for you but also for children and parents. Think about ordering reprints or making copies for distribution at parent-teacher conference time.

Textbooks on teaching literature to children and adolescents can serve as helpful references. Some recommended titles include *Children's Literature in the Elementary School* (by Huck, Hepler and Hickman, 1993); *Through the Eyes of a Child* (by Donna Norton, 1991); *Essentials of Children's Literature* (by Lynch-Brown and Tomlinson, 1993); and *Literature and the Child* (by Cullinan and Galda, 1994).

Setting a Tone for Reading Enjoyment

At the beginning of the school year, Holly sets a tone for reading and books by establishing some classroom routines that will continue throughout the year. Her aim is to create a literature-rich environment that *all* children, regardless of ability, help to build. Here are some of the ways she does this.

Holly begins each morning meeting by gathering the children around her on the rug in the reading nook, where she reads a poem she has specifically chosen for that day. She takes time for "poetry breaks" all day but makes sure to both start and end the day with a poem. She goes into her classroom early in the morning to choose that day's poetry selections, which may be related to themes the class might be studying—the weather, a holiday, or something funny or joyful that will happen that day. In anticipation of providing a rich variety of poetry for her third graders, Holly has organized a file categorizing poetry for all kinds of "reasons and seasons" to keep at her desk. Such a file provides Holly with a great selection of poetry at her fingertips.

Organizing the Classroom Library During the summer, Holly thought a long while about how to organize her classroom library. She finally decided to ask her students to help organize *their* library. So at the beginning of the year, she invited students to take a lot of time to browse through all the books. When she assembled students on the rug, she asked them to talk about what they found. Were some authors and illustrators familiar? What titles would they like to read? What books looked interesting? What books looked like they would be fun to read?

Next, she asked for suggestions about how to organize the books in the classroom so that they would be easy to find. She recorded their suggestions on chart paper and asked the class to vote on the idea they liked best. Holly also asked them to establish categories of books: Poetry, books about sports, riddles, real people, olden times, made-up stories, chapter books, books about animals, and dinosaurs were just a few of the types mentioned. All the books were placed on tables, and teams of students began organizing them into categories for shelving. Labels were then prepared and taped to the shelves. New categories could be added as the year progressed and as children learned more about genres, there was much discussion of where to place books.

What did Holly learn from this process? It certainly would have been easier for her to organize the library over the summer, but she would not have learned so much about what her students knew about books, authors, illustrators, and types of books. She also would not have learned which children gravitated to the books and which seemed to drift off to other parts of the classroom. Her belief that it is important for children to help establish the reading community was communicated through this process. She also talked with children about the importance of being a community of readers, of everyone in class being a reader and this being just one of the in-class "family" projects they would *all* be involved with. This was truly a different experience for most of her students, as they were used to having everything done for them; they had not been participants in the process.

Sharing Favorite Books Holly also had a special time at the end of the week for everyone to gather on the rug to share with each other the books they had finished or were currently reading.

Holly also shared tidbits of books she really enjoyed. All readers, including Holly, who had completed books took a tracing of a footprint from the shoebox in the reading corner. (The children had decided on using footprints and had designed them!) Each reader recorded the bibliographic information about the book and a short annotation (Holly used the word "annotation" with her students!) describing the book and whether they would recommend it and why. Holly believed that it was important to contribute to the footprints as well, because she, too, was a reader in this group. Her contributions also provided models for the students' annotations and remarks about books.

The walls of the room were gradually covered with paths of footprints. Holly found that this was a good way to publicly display what each member of the classroom community had read without excessive competition—something she had thought long and hard about. She remembered seeing a bulletin board entitled "Rockets to the Moon" during one of her student teaching placements and didn't like the competition it engendered. Students had their own rocket on the bulletin board and elevated it each time a book was read until the rocket reached the "moon." Holly observed that many children—some of them the best readers in the class—never read long books because their rockets would take forever to leave the "earth."

Holly encouraged students to carefully mount and display their work, particularly their art and written responses to books they had read. She wanted to demonstrate that she truly valued their creativity and accomplishments. Unfortunately, children were used to having their work covered with teacher comments and a grade and then somewhat carelessly tacked to a bulletin board. Holly enlisted the talents of the art teacher to work with students in exploring various art media (beyond crayons) such as pastel chalk, watercolor, charcoal, and collage.

Sue Ross, a veteran sixth-grade teacher of ten years, only recently established a literature-based program in her classroom. She had previously re-

lied upon an anthology of stories for her students to read throughout the year. Through much reading, attending conferences, and soul-searching, Sue came to the conclusion that year after year her students just did not seem to be very excited about reading. They seemed bored by the stories in the anthology, and she, too, admitted to probably showing her boredom from the repetitious teaching she did from this text. Sue was very influenced by Nancie Atwell's *In the Middle: Writing, Reading, and Learning with Adolescents* (1987) and Linda Rief's *Seeking Diversity* (1992). Their ideas about reading and writing at the middle school level impressed Sue, and she tried to find ways to make these ideas work for her students. So, instead of trying to duplicate what Atwell and Rief had done in their classrooms, Sue developed her own modifications. We present some of them here:

1. With the help of her students, Sue decided to organize a classroom library stocked with books from her personal collection as well as many from the school library. She brought in some comfortable pillows to make the corner inviting to readers. Students designed posters advocating reading to decorate the corner. If reading was going to be a priority in this classroom, then Sue believed that the environment needed to reflect this.

2. Students were given time to browse and self-select books to read during the one-hour workshop time.

3. She held conferences with each child and maintained a record of what was read and the kind of response the student chose to complete after the book.

4. On Fridays, she planned to have students discuss how they went about making their self-selected choices.

5. Sue decided to incorporate thematic units on different genres of literature so that students would be exposed to many different types of literature (see Chapter 14).

6. Sue invited small groups of students to form a literature circle and read a book in common. This strategy meant that Sue and her students had to acquire multiple copies of books through book clubs and the library. She modeled the process of discussion during literature circles by using open-ended questions such as: "Tell me what do you think about this book"; "How does this story relate to your own lives?"; "What part did you like the best? The least?"

   She talked to students about the limitations of the usual kind of comprehension questions teachers ask about what students read. Pete, one of Sue's students, piped up and remarked, "Ya, I know those kinds of questions. Just a few students answer them like nobody else had an opinion!" Sue said she couldn't have said it better! She really wanted students to have a conversation about a book and not just a question-and-answer period.

7. Sue made the decision to read aloud every day so that students could hear quality literature. Books such as *Lyddie* by Katherine Paterson and *The True Confessions of Charlotte Doyle* by Avi became rich sources for minilessons at the beginning of the writing workshop. (See Chapter 11 for more information on minilessons.)

8. She has rediscovered the power of the picture book format. Initially, she dismissed picture books as being just for young children. However, her own enthusiasm for the illustrations (works of true art!) and the text became contagious among her students.

She discovered that these books became great examples for talking about plot, character, and point of view, etc. Her writers needed the "fuel" of well-written "real" books to fully appreciate the craft of the writer. This was the missing ingredient in her old program. She realized that she had reawakened the reading and writing "spark" in her students. Students wanted to write survival stories like Gary Paulsen and strange tales like those found in the picture books of Chris Van Allsburg and Anthony Browne. Her students found reading to be actually enjoyable, and she also was able to finally understand that all the values of literature she read about in textbooks (learning about the world, expanding horizons, learning about other cultures, etc.) were finally realized. And best of all, Sue's sixth graders actually seemed to enjoy coming to her class, which *they* renamed Reading and Writing Workshop.

Jack Jacobson is another teacher who has also discovered the power of using high-quality children's literature as the core of his science and social studies program. Jack's fourth graders learned about the moon, the sun, and the planets by reading Seymour Simon's books and about famous people in the books of Jean Fritz and Russell Freedman. They delighted in *Balloons and Other Poems* by Debra Chandra and *Rich Lizard and Other Poems* by Debra Chandra. They learned about Africa and how to make a *galimoto* from Karen Lynn Williams's picture book of the same name, and they became aware of the importance of learning how to write one's own name in the Egyptian story, *The Day of Ahmed's Secret* by Florence Parry Heide and Judith Heide Gilliland. Maybe the world isn't so big after all! Jack's children learned not only about the differences between and among cultures but also about the similarities.

Jack found that his students did not seem to be so excited about reading in general or about learning new things when he used textbooks as the core of his program in reading and the content areas. Textbooks, especially those in science and social studies, are typically fact based, and because of space and purpose do not focus on the human side of life. Now Jack's students read historical fiction, biographies, and other types of nonfiction. When Jack has students read from the science and social studies text, they are not content with only one chapter about a topic; they want to read and learn more.

Teachers who believe in the power of literature view its use in the classroom as the vehicle that will first and foremost foster a love for reading. We all know that to become proficient at anything—from skiing to swimming to cooking—we need time to actually engage in that activity. The same rule applies to developing proficiency in reading—and to going beyond that proficiency to become an avid reader "hooked on books" (Fader et al., 1976). Why is it that many children who learn to read never find the joy in reading? This can obviously occur for many reasons. One important consideration is just how much the environment and the teacher support every child as a growing reader.

Let's look again at Lucille Wong's kindergarten class. Like many early primary teachers, Lucille strongly believes that in their earliest years of schooling children should be surrounded by books. An attitude that prevailed for many years was that children had to first learn the skills of reading in order to learn how to read. This same notion also applied to learning how to write. From early on, students in these classrooms were inundated with a combination of skill drill in phonics, lots of worksheets practicing isolated skills, workbooks, and very short stories. The teacher probably read books aloud, but the children's own reading was usually limited to the kinds of exercises described above. Children did not personally interact with books until much later on—after they had mastered a predetermined number of skills. The research done over the last decade (Doake, 1988; Ferreiro and Teberosky, 1982; Galda, Pellegrini and Cox, 1989; Heath, 1983; Sulzby, 1982; Teale, 1984; and Teale and Sulzby, 1986) has had a far-reaching impact in terms of informing teachers of alternative ways to give children an early start with actual books and "real" or authentic reading experiences. (Practices related to emergent literacy are more fully discussed in Chapter 6.)

As a primary teacher, if you adopt this belief of early and continuous exposure to books, think of the messages you will be sending to your students: reading is a valuable and pleasurable ac-

tivity, and reading is something you can learn to do.

Remember also that students never outgrow this need for exposure to books. Students at the intermediate and middle-school levels should also be surrounded by a print-rich environment—books, magazines, newspapers, etc. Students who have been in programs offering too many textbook experiences and not enough exposure to actual literature often remark that they made it to fifth or sixth grade without ever reading a book! What a sad documentary on our educational system, but it can happen when teachers do not see the power of real books in the classroom. One sixth-grade teacher who abandoned the basal reader commented that her students, whose ability levels ranged from learning disabled to gifted, read over 100 books as a class from September through December!

As we've discussed in previous chapters, reading is a transactional process. It is one in which the reader brings many experiences to a book and, thus, a personal interpretation to the reading. You have probably experienced classes in which you had one interpretation of a reading, be it a novel or a poem, and the teacher had another, which usually became translated as the correct response. This often happens with the study of poetry, particularly in the higher grades. Studies indicate that students often begin to dislike poetry in the fourth grade because teachers do not care for poetry, and the study of poetry becomes just that—an analysis and dissection of a poem in order to figure out its "correct" meaning. We have all felt that frustration and anxiety, believing that we were not "getting it." One of the reasons for this is that teachers have adopted a different stance toward the reading of text. The meaning resided in the text, not in the reader. It is no wonder that students often felt frustrated with reading novels, poetry, or any other literature because of the feeling that they could not discover what the teacher was looking for in terms of a correct interpretation. That is one of the reasons why you will often see students looking to the teacher for verification of their understanding; they believe that if their interpretation does not match that of the teacher it will be considered wrong—not different, but wrong.

Rosenblatt's theories in *Literature as Exploration* (1976) slowly changed the way some teachers approached the teaching of literature. The reader plays a vital role in the interpretation of what is read. In other words, there is a dynamic relationship between reader and text, and there is value placed on what the reader brings to the text from past experiences. This is not to say that all meaning resides in the reader and that any way in which the reader interprets text is justified. Instead, the reader needs to keep returning to the text to test out interpretations. For example, does the reader's response make sense in light of what the text says? This kind of exchange within a group can lead to a lively discussion, which to an observer will look very different from a discussion in which the teacher merely asks comprehension questions and students take turns answering them. This scenario can be described as more of a question-and-answer period than a true discussion because everyone participates on an equal footing.

Sixth-grade teacher Richard Davidson read Rosenblatt's work and began to reconsider his literature program. Students in his class were reading from "real" books as the content of the reading program, but Richard found that his program mimicked a basal program in many ways. He often purchased lengthy guides to accompany the trade books he was using with students. These guides provided him with ready-to-use spirit masters of comprehension questions, vocabulary exercises, and fill-in-the-blank activities. At first, Richard felt comfortable using these materials because they represented a structured and organized routine, much like what he left behind with using the basal. However, from his reading of Rosenblatt's work, he discovered that the activities demanded that children read only from an *efferent stance*, meaning that they experienced

books only in an analytical way, instead of on an *aesthetic stance*, or personal level. He also discovered that most of the reading students do in school required an efferent stance. Richard realized that it was also important that students learn how to respond to literature on a more emotional level.

Richard decided to implement another way to approach his students' interactions with books. He found that rich conversation unfolded when he invited students to write to each other in a reading or literature log and recording their feelings and reactions to a story. He began this new plan using literature by sharing Yoshiko Uchida's *Journey to Topaz*, the story of a Japanese internment camp during World War II. He asked students to consider such questions as:

What surprised you as you listened to the story?
What part did you like the best?
What didn't you like?
What puzzled you about the story?
Did you see yourself in the story?

In order to experience this for himself, Richard also participated in the writing with a student partner. After the writing, students exchanged reading logs and responded to each other's writing, giving reactions, asking questions, etc. Volunteers then shared their writing aloud. This proved to be an excellent way for the classroom community to hear and appreciate the diversity of responses in the group. It was an eye-opening discovery process for students and for Richard to hear such a wide range of responses to the first several chapters of the book. The students also benefited from Richard participating in this activity. They began to appreciate that Richard, too, has personal reactions and that his voice is just one among many voices in their community of readers.

In the college classroom we, too, are always amazed to learn of students who have different interpretations to a book that we have used over many semesters. The responses are always different. Why is this the case? Every reader, depending on age and experiential level, brings the "baggage" of life experiences to reading. In fact, if we take the time to become conscious of our own process when we read, we will come to realize that we have an inner narrative dialogue going on simultaneously to our reading. For example, as we read or even listen to a book being read aloud, we might start thinking of the time we had a similar experience, or that we can identify with the setting of the story or time period in some unique way. Perhaps, we had a similar kind of friend or had the same kind of feelings about someone.

RESPONSE TO LITERATURE

What do you remember doing after reading a book when you were in elementary school? Most of us are very familiar with having to do written and oral book reports. In fact, when we ask our students about this, they typically refer to the activity as the "dreaded book report"—followed by lots of moans, groans, and sighs!

Sometimes a book report form was used. The form asked the reader to answer questions dealing with plot, character development, theme, and reactions to the book. Sometimes students were given only several lines to write their answers. Although this format is still alive in some classrooms, particularly at the intermediate grade levels and middle school, many teachers are becoming more aware of a transactional view of reading and its implications for a literature-rich classroom. These classrooms are becoming response-centered, which means that students are invited to respond to what they read in more authentic and meaningful ways. Teachers are expanding the opportunity to make books more meaningful by inviting students to choose from an array of choices—through drama activities, art-work, cooking, discussion, and writing in a variety

of ways. These response activities, or "enterprises" as Frank Smith (1988) refers to them, help to connect the reader with the text in a more intimate and memorable way.

Written Responses—Reading or Literature Logs

The reading or literature log is a valuable tool for teachers to determine the range of experiences, feelings, and thoughts the reading community has as a response to literature. Asking students to write, rather than simply discuss, means that everyone needs to participate. Writing will capture everyone's thoughts. The log—also called literature journal, dialogue journal, literary letter, gossip journal, and literature response journal—is a powerful way of uniting the reading community, including the teacher. This kind of activity values the experiences of the reader and, at the same time, says to students that what they have to say is important. It might not be the same thing the teacher wrote or said, but how can that be when we are all individuals and come from such a diverse set of circumstances?

The log can also be used simultaneously with other kinds of response activities. For example, through further discussion or writing responses, students will need to revisit the text to "test" out their reactions. Can they find enough evidence in the text, for example, to justify a response?

Many students at all grade levels are writing in response to literature. Fitterman-King (1988) describes this kind of writing as "a repository for wanderings and wonderings, speculations, questionings . . . a place to explore thoughts, discover reactions, let the mind ramble . . . a place to make room for the unexpected" (p. 5). Some teachers have students use a notebook, and others have students make their own notebooks using colored paper for the covers and filler paper. To help students get started with writing in a log, teachers can begin with their usual read-aloud time but tell students that they will be writing about their reactions to the story in their logs.

In a variation known as the *dialogue journal,* students use the literature-log format to correspond with a partner. In their notebook they divide the sheet lengthwise and, using a friendly letter format, they write to their partner about their reactions to a read aloud or a book read in common. It is best to introduce this format to the whole class after a read aloud, explaining that it is like having a conversation in writing. Again, the teacher should choose a partner or write to the class as a whole. After reading aloud, they begin their writing reactions of the story to their partner. After ten minutes or so, they swap their writing with their partner and then write back to their partner using the other half of the notebook paper. After this process, the teacher could invite students to share their writing or ask for nominations from the class. Each reader will probably have a slightly different (or very different!) reaction to the read aloud. This gives the teacher an opportunity to talk about how every reader, no matter what age, brings a different set of experiences (background knowledge) to a book. Therefore, it is expected that reactions will vary. In fact, it is crucial that teachers talk with students about this aspect of journal writing because some students are fearful of taking risks with their learning and their writing and might assume that there is one correct way to respond.

Yet another format for the literature log is the literary letter between student and teacher. Students write about the books they are reading in terms of their reactions to the story, characters, theme, etc. Sixth-grade teacher Betty Robinson uses the literary letter as a way for students to react daily to what they read.

If possible, read the first chapter from *Sarah, Plain and Tall* by Patricia MacLachlan. Set in the mid-1800s, the book follows the story of Sarah Wheaton, a woman living in Maine who answers an advertisement for a wife placed by a man in Ohio whose wife died, leaving him with two young children, Anna and Caleb.

After reading this chapter aloud to students, use an overhead transparency to write your own response. As you write on the transparency, talk out loud so that students hear your words as you write them. The conversation might go like this: "I can really identify with Sarah deciding whether she really wants to leave her home and move to another part of the country. It would be difficult to be far from all the things and people I love." You might also ask children for their input as you write. For example, you might say, "Tell me how you would feel answering such an advertisement."

This procedure involves students by giving them the opportunity to "hear" your thinking process in action. On the next day, you might choose another chapter and ask students to write their own reactions or do another whole group response, if needed.

You can also try some open-ended questions. For example, students might be offered a choice of several questions:

Which part did you like most?
Which part did you not like?
Which character interested you the most?
What did you notice about the story?
How did the story make you feel?
What does the story remind you of in your own life? (Borders and Naylor, 1993).

We recommend giving students the option of using one of several questions or simply writing their personal reactions. Most of the questions that we have offered work best for stories or narrative—usually from realistic fiction, fantasy, traditional literature, or historical fiction. These same questions also work with other genres, such as informational books, biography, and poetry. For example, if you chose an informational book, you might ask students the following questions: Was there anything that you wondered about? Was there anything that particularly interested you? Was there something special you learned from this book? At other times, depending upon your purpose, you might be more directive by designing questions focusing on specific literary characteristics. An example is shown in Box 10.1.

BOX 10.1

LITERARY CHARACTERISTICS

Literary Characteristic	Questioning Examples
PLOT	How does the author use flashbacks in this story? Book example: *Mrs. Frisby and the Rats of NIMH* by Robert O'Brien (fantasy)
CHARACTER	In what ways does the main character grow and change throughout the story? What would you say to the character if you met him or her? What would you do in the character's situation? Book example: *Missing May* by Cynthia Rylant (realistic fiction)
SETTING	In what way(s) does the author create an effective setting for this novel? Book example: *Number the Stars* by Lois Lowry (historical fiction)
THEME	What do you think the author was trying to say in this book? Book example: *Black and White* by David Macaulay (picture book)
STYLE	How did the choice of words make you feel? What point of view was used in the story? Book example: *Shabanu: Daughter of the Wind* by S. F. Staples (multicultural)

Note that these questions do not always have to be responded to in writing. They might be posed simply for oral discussion. We do find it helpful if students do some writing as a way to gather their thoughts before an oral discussion. However, any good thing can be overdone. Remember that responding in literature logs is just one way to respond to books. Also we have found that because more and more teachers are using journals or logs in their classroom, children may be familiar with the terms "journal," or "log." However, you will need to discuss your expectations as they may be very different from those of another teacher!

Other Ways to Respond to Literature Through Writing

Character Journals or Diaries In this type of written response, students write entries from the point of view of a character in the book. This is a wonderful way for students to get "inside the

character's head" and write from the character's point of view. If this is done using historical fiction, it challenges the student to revisit the book, as well as other books and materials to gain a better sense of the times. For example, writing entries from the point of view of Matt in *The Sign of the Beaver* by Elizabeth George Speare (1983) means that the words Matt uses in his entries have to be as authentic as possible. Modern lingo and slang, of course, would not have been part of Matt's vocabulary.

John Scieszka's comical books, *The True Story of the Three Little Pigs by A. Wolf* (1989) and *The Frog Price Continued* (1991), offer students a great opportunity to practice rewriting from a different point of view. Since these are picture books that will be enjoyed by any age group, students could use this format for their illustrated story.

Writing Prequels, New Beginnings, New Endings, and Sequels Another challenging written response is to suggest that one or two students try writing a story describing what happened before the first chapter (prequel). They might also write a new beginning, a new ending, or an additional ending chapter (sequel) to the book. Because these activities can prove to be very challenging, it is best for students to work on these responses with a partner.

Using Literature as a Model to Write New Stories, Poems, and Plays   Literature provides the "fuel" for writers of all ages. Encourage students to read and listen to books with the intention of a writer. For instance, many students enjoy the series of books by Lynne Reid Banks about a toy Indian who comes to life (*The Indian in the Cupboard,* 1981; *The Return of the Indian,* 1986; and *The Secret of the Indian,* 1989). Students might enjoy writing their own stories or episodes about model soldiers or other kinds of toys that come to life.

Cynthia Rylant's *Missing May* (1992), the Newbery Award–winning story about a girl in Appalachia who lives with her elderly aunt and uncle after the death of her parents, comes to grips with the meaning of death and the loss of someone dearly loved. Some students may take the opportunity to write a poem as a response to this book.

The more a teacher shares books through reading aloud and book talks and asks students to think about writing opportunities, the more this kind of response will happen naturally. We do not advocate that teachers demand that students write a new ending or episode, for example. However, the possibilities will be apparent with questions such as "What kinds of writing might you try as a response to the book I read aloud today?"

An invitation to write took the following form in a seventh-grade class: Students read lots of survival stories—*Hatchet* (1987), *The River* (1991), and *The Voyage of the Frog* (1989) all by Gary Paulsen; *Call It Courage* (1968) by Armstrong Sperry; *Julie of the Wolves* (1972), *My Side of the Mountain* (1959), and its sequel, *On the Far Side of the Mountain* (1990) all by Jean Craighead George; *Slake's Limbo* by Felice Holman (1974);

and *Monkey Island* (1991) by Paula Fox. The latter two books are about survival in the city, whereas the other titles deal with survival issues in the wilderness. The teacher asked such questions as What did you enjoy about these stories? What appealed to you about the writing style? What kinds of survival stories might you share with us? Since "survival stories" is a subgenre of contemporary realistic fiction, and the students in this particular seventh-grade class heard so many of them read aloud by the teacher, as well as on their own, it would be worthwhile for students to examine the craft of the writing through the eyes of being readers as well as writers.

Biographical information helps students to gain an understanding of how authors come up with ideas for their own writing. Sometimes ideas come from what they read, people they know, and things they have experienced themselves. The possibilities are endless. However, students need to know that ideas for their own pieces could come from the books they read in class and what you share aloud. It is not cheating to take an idea and mold it into one's own story!

Response Activities

We offer you several notes of caution. You should not view these suggestions as a laundry list of cute activities to do with books. We recommend that you start with what children make of a book. How do they think and feel about a book? Invite children to participate in the decision-making process of what seems to be a response suggestion that makes sense. Also it is not necessary to respond to each and every book read or shared aloud. Some books make such an emotional impact, that making a diorama or clay figure seems out of place and contrived. Trust a good book; be patient to see what emerges naturally from your conversations with children. Give students plenty of opportunities to make choices of response activities. Think about the books children read on their own and those you will read aloud. Consider the type and nature of responses. Keep in mind that some books are "quiet," thoughtful books and an immediate response does not make sense. However, as a response students might want to talk about their feelings.

Rather than giving students a long list of response suggestions to choose from, look through the list below and choose several writing responses, drama, and art activities. Students can make their initial selection from those. As students become familiar with different kinds of response activities, ask them to contribute their suggestions.

- Write a letter to a friend about the book.
- Keep a journal or diary entries from the point of view of one of the characters. Select a writing partner from class and exchange entries.
- Write a newspaper article about one of the characters.
- Write a fictional journal entry about a book character.
- Record part of a book on cassette tape for others in class to enjoy.
- Design and write newspaper articles about book events.
- Write a letter to a character or historical figure.
- Write a prequel or sequel to a book.
- Adapt a story into a news report or TV program.
- Write multiple endings for a story.
- Write interview questions for a character.
- Rewrite a portion of a story with students as major characters.
- Create a glossary or dictionary of important words in the story.
- Design word puzzles or crossword puzzles of events or characters.
- Write riddles about events or circumstances in a story.
- Design a "Question Box" containing questions and answers about specific stories or books.
- Print important phrases or quotations from the book on construction paper and post them throughout the room.

- Write a fictitious calendar of important story events.
- Pretend you're a story character and write a letter to someone in the class.
- Create a fictional biography of a book character.
- Write a travel guide to the story setting.
- Design a want ad for something in a book.
- Write a horoscope for a book character.
- Write a travel itinerary for characters.
- Create a scrapbook about important places, people, and events in the story.
- Create an original poem about a story event.
- Invent a coat of arms for a story character.
- Write a picture book (or wordless picture book) about a significant event.
- Conduct a debate or panel discussion about some of the main events in the story.
- Make a story map (see Chapter 9 for details).
- Create a time line of story events.
- Conduct a poll of other readers' reactions and graph the results.
- Create a budget to travel to the setting of a story.
- Turn part of a book into a series of cartoons.
- Create a political cartoon about a significant event.
- Illustrate portions of a book.
- Make an advertisement about the book or story.
- Draw illustrations of each character in a book and show the ways that characters change or develop throughout the story.
- Create a pop-up book about one historical event.
- Make puppets of historical figures.
- Draw or paint the outline of a story setting on the playground.
- Make masks for different characters.
- Create an original slide show.
- Make a papier-mâché head of a story character.
- Design a new book cover.
- Make a "flip book" about selected events.
- Create a collage from old magazines.

- Design an original flannel board.
- Create a commercial to get others to read the book.
- Paint a large wall poster.
- Design and create a diorama of a significant scene.
- Make "movie rolls" using shoeboxes, adding machine tape and pencils (as the "rollers").
- Design clay models of important characters.
- Create a salt map of a specific location.
- Write a radio show about a book.
- Act out events in a story and videotape them.
- Design costumes for characters in a story.
- Pantomime selected events in a story.
- Write an original play from a chapter or two.
- Create a song about a person or event.
- Give dramatic readings of a book.
- Dramatize a section of the book for another class.
- Produce a puppet show about part of a book.

Balance in the Literature Program

As previously discussed, students as well as teachers need to become "intergalactic readers" (Chambers, 1985). The field of children's literature is extensive, and students need to experience reading and listening to *all kinds* of literature. As teachers we need to work toward balance in the reading program, certainly encouraging self-selections but also providing new directions for group or class studies of other genres, such as historical fiction, which many students do not gravitate to on their own. Typically, contemporary realistic fiction is easier for students to read. They are reading about kids like themselves, solving problems that are much like their own. Again, this is very important for students, but they also need exposure to genres they might not naturally pursue on their own.

Fourth-grade teacher Nancy Healey found that her students read a lot of books. She was pleased about this, but realized that when she took an inventory of what her students were choosing on their own, they chose mostly contemporary realistic fiction novels. They loved books by Judy Blume, such as *Tales of a Fourth Grade Nothing* (1972), *Blubber* (1974), *Fudge-a-Mania* (1990), and *Superfudge* (1980). Instead of issuing dictates that her students could no longer read these kinds of books, she reflected on ways to bring balance into the literature program. One way Nancy achieved this balance was to prepare thematic units focusing on a particular genre each month. For example, in October students would begin brainstorming what they knew about poetry. In preparation, Nancy gathered dozens of volumes of poetry: some single poems in picture book format, anthologies of poetry, poetry by a single poet, and collections of poetry about one topic or theme. Students found that writing poetry was a lot easier because of the reading, sharing, and talking about poetry that took place in their group. Last year Nancy's students remarked that they had to write haiku and then some limericks, after having heard only a couple examples read aloud by the teacher. They had never even read any themselves.

In November, students read historical fiction that corresponded with their other thematic unit on colonial times in New England. In December, students read a variety of holiday books and started a unit on fairy tales. Nancy's strategy paid big dividends. Students became acquainted with different genres that increased their selecting power as they made individual choices. Also, Nancy never gave the impression that just because they would begin to explore a new genre that they would be all done with those genres studied before. They would continue their wide reading all year through. The topic of the month just gave their reading community an opportunity to join together in a concentrated exploration of a particular genre.

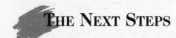 **THE NEXT STEPS**

Are you feeling anxious, thinking perhaps that you want to adopt some of the statements of teachers who believe in the power of literature? Perhaps when you were in elementary school, most of your reading instruction was from the basal reader, so the textbook model may be one that you are most aware of and comfortable using. You might be struggling with how to even begin incorporating literature in so many ways in your future classroom. Here are some good starting points.

As mentioned previously in the chapter, begin to build your own future classroom collection and consider your own literacy development by establishing the reading habit for yourself. Even if a children's literature and adolescent literature course may not be required in your undergraduate program, try to take one or both of these courses. Our recommendation would be to start with a children's literature course, as this course typically spans literature for the preschooler through eighth grade. Even if you are only interested in teaching at the middle school level (usually sixth through ninth grade), this would be an important course to take to experience reading picture books and traditional literature, for example. As stated earlier, these books can and should be incorporated into the middle school curriculum. Next, take an adolescent literature course that spans eighth grade through high school. At the middle school level, the literature for this age group will span the breadth of both children's and adolescent literature.

Educators have known the value of children reading and listening to good books for years. At present, though, more and more teachers are seeking ways to incorporate literature across the curriculum at all grade levels. In fact, many practicing teachers are returning to the college classroom for updated courses in children's literature, as well as attending conferences and workshops, and subscribing to professional journals and magazines that include book reviews and articles about ways to incorporate more literature. As an advocate of literature, you will probably spend more time at bookstores browsing through the children's section looking for new books to include in your growing collection, as well as writing "wish lists" of book titles for gift givers. Take

seriously the enthusiasm you have for books as an undergraduate student and carry this into your first year of teaching. Your students will undoubtedly remember you for helping to foster their own love of books!

If you started a book file as a student, keep adding to it when you begin teaching. It will serve as a handy reference. Begin to organize a system for keeping biographical information about authors and illustrators. When you locate valuable information about the authors and illustrators, duplicate this information and keep it in a file folder, which can be added to over the years. Organizing information in this way will save you time in the future.

READING ALOUD AS A STARTING PLACE

Do you remember being read to as a child at home and at school? Do you still have vivid memories of those special times when your teacher gathered the class on the floor to share some wonderful poetry, a picture book, or a new novel?

Reading aloud has historically been one important way that teachers have incorporated literature into their programs. However, for many years this practice occurred most often in the primary grades, so students in the intermediate grades often did not hear literature read aloud after third or fourth grade. Because more and more teachers have come to see the value of incorporating read alouds for a variety of purposes at all grade levels, even into the high school years, students are enjoying the pleasures of hearing high-quality literature read aloud sometimes as a daily part of the school day, not only during the language arts period.

Why has there been this change in attitude toward the use of read aloud? A few explanations might be offered:

- Exposure to hearing stories read aloud helps children to understand how stories "work," and that stories have a beginning, middle, and end.

- Children begin to develop preferences about authors and types of books and an understanding of the connections or similarities between and among books.
- Listening comprehension increases, as many children are able to comprehend stories that are written at a level beyond what they might be able to comprehend if reading the book independently.
- Hearing different types of literature brings the language of books alive to children. They enjoy the rhythm and rhyme of poetry, and they learn to appreciate how an author of nonfiction brings a topic such as insects, flight, or the story of the Civil War alive for listeners.
- With teacher guidance, students can also begin to see connections between their own writing and that which they hear come alive through the vehicle of an effective read aloud.
- Read alouds bring the class together as a community as everyone listens to the same book or selection being read aloud. Young children can participate in joining in on repetitive phases or lines. If a picture book is shared, the group can discuss the illustrations and how the pictures and text combine to form a harmonious whole. Students can also focus on the role of the illustrator and the media used in the book. Similar techniques may be applied in their own published works.
- Reading aloud is fun! The magic of literature comes alive for students of all ages. Hearing excellent literature read aloud, students will be transported to all corners of the universe and be introduced to heroes and heroines, and they will learn how others live, work, and play.

Beginning a Read-Aloud Program

Some helpful points teachers may want to consider as they plan for read alouds (Allen, Giard and Kristo, 1991) are described in Box 10.2. Several of the points will be discussed below.

First and foremost, plan on incorporating a read-aloud time at least once a day for all grade levels. Read alouds are usually scheduled during the language arts period of the day, but you might think about the value of sharing a poem or two during incidental times—just to appreciate the rhythm and rhyme, and the beauty of the images. Read a historical fiction novel every day during social studies or during a unit study and also try to incorporate a biography of a famous president or historical figure. Students of all ages enjoy Jean Fritz's short biographies in picture book format. They normally can be read aloud in a short amount of time. As a biographer, Jean Fritz has a special gift for bringing the past alive. Her extensive research even for a brief partial biography brings out some of the foibles and idiosyncrasies of some of our most notable figures in history in such titles as *And Then What Happened, Paul Revere?* (1973); *Can't You Make Them Behave, King George?* (1982); and *The Double Life of Pocahontas* (1983), to name only a few. The illustrations are humorous, and the writing style is engaging for even the most jaded reader. These titles are an especially good introduction to the genre of biography as well as a model for students writing their own autobiographies or reports about famous people.

How does Fritz draw in the reader or listener? What is unique about her writing style? Again, sharing high-quality historical fiction and biography is crucial if you expect students to research different questions or topics about a particular time period. Remember, students are often limited in the classroom to textbooks and encyclopedias, and they may not be aware of the great writing that exists in your classroom library or at the public library. This results in written reports that sound like textbooks or encyclopedia articles—since those texts have been their only models. It thus becomes crucial to provide students with writing that is enriching and powerful. Encourage students to research and write in Jean Fritz's style, to revisit her books to study her style, wording, and use of authentic historical information. As a next step, you may want to read aloud or ask students to read other books about a notable historical figure in order to compare and contrast information. Sometimes students will come to realize that some information or facts conflict from one book to another. This can lead to searching

BOX 10.2

READ ALOUD CHECKLIST

Classroom Environment

1. Have I arranged the seating so that all the pupils will be able to see and hear the story, the poem, and/or the illustrations?
2. Do I have a chartboard or paper available for noting repetitive lines, pupil comments, or extension activities?
3. Do I have a special place for read alouds so that the pupils can find the books and refer to them for information or for repeated readings?
4. Do I have a mechanism in place (predictable schedule, light, music, etc.) so that pupils will know that it is time for read aloud?
5. Have I established guidelines for read-aloud time? What should pupils be doing during this time?
6. Have I created an environment that allows and fosters active listening?

Teacher Preparation

1. Have I taken into account the age, needs, and interests of the group to whom I'm reading?
2. Have I read the text myself? Do I know the text well enough to share enthusiastically with the group?
3. Do I personally feel that this is a good story or poem or am I only reading it on someone's recommendation?
4. Do I need to practice reading the text?
5. Have I decided whether to read all or part of the story?
6. Have I internalized a method for knowing when to stop or give a break during the read aloud?
7. If I plan to read only a portion of the book, have I found several places that would be good stopping points?

8. Am I familiar with the sequence of events, characters, vocabulary, and concepts so that I can anticipate problem areas?
9. Have I highlighted words, settings, or situations for which pupils might need additional information? If so, have I done additional reading and/or research to help students with this information?
10. Have I looked at background information of the author, illustrator, or writing that might add to students' understanding and appreciation of the book?
11. How will I introduce the text?
12. How will I establish an appropriate mood for the story or poem?
13. How can I help the students to make connections between this text, author, or illustrator and other stories studied?
14. Do I have follow-up points in mind?
15. Have I considered ways for the pupils to extend this reading to make it memorable?
16. If this story or poem is part of a unit, how will I help pupils see this story as part of a larger picture?
17. If I am going to use this story or poem as a vehicle for discussing reading strategies, do I have a clear picture of how this text could be used for this purpose without sacrificing the enjoyment of the read aloud?
18. Have I chosen a time for read aloud that will be as free as possible from outside interruptions or distractions?

Source: Allen, Giard, Kristo. "Read Along, Prime Time Instruction." *The New England Reading Association Journal,* vol. 27, no. 1, 1991.

for more information. This contributes to the making of critical readers. In a nondogmatic or preachy way, you will be teaching the importance of investigating multiple sources for information and not taking one author's words as the ultimate truth. This kind of activity can start in the early grades and continue through all grade levels.

Time to Read

Several decades ago, a practice called sustained silent reading (SSR) emerged as a time when everyone in the entire school, including the principal, secretary, etc., would drop everything and read a book of their choice for 15 to 20 minutes during the same time every day. Unlike the usual reading time, students were not held accountable for what they read. They were not asked to complete worksheets or prove that they read in any way. The intent of SSR was to help instill the idea of reading for pleasure in school.

The basic idea was a good one, but in this case too many restrictions were placed on individual teachers and classrooms, such as everybody reading silently at their desks for a designated time. Some teachers grew impatient with students who could not decide upon a book or some other kind of reading material. Nowadays, the practice of SSR is still prevalent but under more relaxed and realistic conditions. In some classrooms, this time is called personal reading, DEAR time (Drop Everything And Read), or by some other designated acronym. In some classes it may last 15 minutes and in other classes for a much longer period of time. Some teachers do look at this time as a viable component of the reading period, and students do commit to reading an entire chapter book, for example. They conference with the teacher over the book and plan some kind of response to the book (i.e., writing a sequel, letter to the author, preparing a dramatic presentation, doing some artwork, etc.) to share with the class.

In other classes, teachers plan a block of time for students to freely browse through reading materials—be it picture books, children's magazines, newspapers, etc. The teacher, too, participates in this activity. In many classrooms you will even hear the low buzz of students buddy reading or reading to each other. Following this time of active reading, the teacher might also call the group together to share and recommend reading materials to each other. There are many ways to go about this endeavor, but it does flow back to the belief that it is important for students of all ages to self-select reading materials they really want to read and to have time to actually read. In fact, some students choose a book to read during this time to become part of a home reading program, where they commit to reading 20 to 30 minutes at home every night.

Strictly speaking, it is difficult to state how much time students should be given to read. In some ways it is easier to look at past practices when children were given precious little time to fully engage in a book. Reading time was just that, 20 minutes or so reading a short story from a basal reading text, and then, perhaps, a brief time in the afternoon reading from a social studies or science text—a kind of round robin or turn taking by reading a paragraph aloud. Again, the emphasis was on the skills of reading rather than becoming powerful readers by reading a lot. If students completed all the workbook pages, they were given more to do or other assignments. Sometimes reading a book was the last option after all assigned work was done. We probably all remember peers who struggled through all the written assignments and never had the luxury in the classroom to then go to a book. There was never any TIME! Slower progress readers read the very least in classrooms. It is unfortunate that reading a book was not the first option. It would be difficult to become an Olympic swimmer if you rarely get into the pool to really practice swimming. To become a powerful reader takes a lot of time actually reading and a teacher who will lead children to the good books and be a good coach along the way. Children need to read in different ways all day. They need to see that reading cuts across the curriculum, that reading (and writing) does not stop at the end of the language arts block in the morning. Students read to learn math, science, and social studies. They read from a variety of materials—textbooks, trade books, magazines, newspapers, and encyclopedias—to learn about the world.

Another way to immerse students in books is through theme studies that parallel social studies and science curriculum, as well as class topics of interest. Examples include a thematic unit on the Civil War, the seashore, whales, pioneer days, colonial times, explorers, dinosaurs, survival, and friendship. The possibilities are limitless and are discussed in detail in Chapter 14. Thematic units and genre studies can go on simultaneously. Teachers who design thematic units with children include lots of reading opportunities across as many genres as possible. For example, when studying the Civil War at the middle school level, students might read poetry, picture books, biography, historical fiction, and nonfiction about the Civil War.

PUTTING IT ALL TOGETHER

Let's summarize again the ingredients for a literature rich classroom:

1. Have lots of books and other kinds of reading material available for every grade level. Students will read more if books are readily available. Even if your school has a well-stocked library, it is still crucial to have many available right in the classroom. As stated previously, many books will be part of your collection, but supplement these with those you borrow from the school and local libraries. Another great way to acquire books is through bonus points your class will earn by purchasing books through clubs such as Scholastic and Trumpet, among others. Some teachers have joined forces to sponsor book fairs in their school, bake sales, and walk-a-thons to raise money for classroom books. Depending on how money is budgeted in your school, you might find that you have purchasing power to build the classroom library. Monies are also sometimes available via parent groups and state reading grants. It is worth pursuing these avenues in order to raise the level of concern and interest about the importance of literature in the classroom.

2. Make available multiple copies of books so that groups of three or four students can read and discuss a book in common. One word of caution though: Make sure you have read the books you want to purchase as multiple copies. Surprisingly, sometimes this is not done and multiple copies are left on the shelves not read.

3. Plan on having children complete an interest inventory early in the year and, again, midyear. Interest inventories are helpful in finding out the kinds of topics students are most interested in reading. These needs will change over time as students become enthusiastic about a variety of topics and authors, as well as illustrators. These interest inventories will also inform you as to what kinds of books children are most familiar with, as well as genres they may not have explored.

4. Celebrate literature all year long; make literature a priority in your classroom. For example, you might want to celebrate the birthday of one author or illustrator each month during the school year. This would be an event that students would look forward to each month and a kind of thread that would weave through the school year. Here are some steps for author/illustrator birthday celebrations:

   • Gather as many books as possible by the author or illustrator ahead of time. Let your school librarian and public librarian know who you are highlighting each month. They might be able to set aside books for you, as well as offer information about the author/illustrator.

   • Use biographical resources about authors and illustrators. Duplicate material from these sources to design a bulletin board. In many cases students could help with this. Also, write to the publisher for information about the person. Many times they will send informational packets, posters, etc. Make sure you do this ahead of time! Summer is a great time for this kind of preparation.

- During the month, have read-a-thon days or set aside time when students can indulge themselves in the author's or illustrator's works. Plan to share many of the books aloud. If many are chapter books, read snippets of them as a booktalk. Children will want to read these. If possible have multiple copies available.

- Invite children to write to the author or illustrator. Most authors and illustrators will write in return. Some teachers have also arranged conference calls to the author or illustrator. Call the publishing company for details.

- Invite many opportunities for response. Students will enjoy making posters advertising the books, bookmarks, shadow boxes, and murals depicting favorite scenes from the books. When the birthday is celebrated, children could dress as a favorite character from one of the author's books. Prepare a birthday cake. Use a sheet pan and precut the cake into as many pieces as needed. On individual slips of paper, type a question or something about one of the books shared during the month. Wrap the slip of paper around a toothpick. Insert one toothpick into each slice. When everyone has a piece of cake, ask children to unwrap the slip of paper, read what is on the slip of paper, and guess what book is being referred to. You may line up the books on the chalktray so that each child can go to the tray to pick the book.

- If you plan far enough in advance and monies are available, it might be possible to invite the author or illustrator to your school. If that becomes a reality, it is important that the whole school become involved. Children from every class need to be familiar with your visitor's works and to prepare lots of responses that can be posted around the school as a sign of welcome. (It would be quite embarassing to invite an author to speak to the whole school and discover that only one class knows anything about the person!)

5. Let the school, parents, and visitors know how important books are to the lives of your students. When others enter your classroom, do they see more literature than textbooks? Do they see lots of examples of art and writing responses to literature posted with pride in the classroom? Is there a cozy nook for reading? Read aloud everyday. Stretch your listeners by choosing books from a variety of genres. Celebrate books by having substantial time to not only read but to talk about books with your students.

6. Time to browse is also an important component in the literature-rich classroom, although its significance is sadly overlooked. Think how often you like to take the time to just scout bookstores or the library to see what is new. This does take time, but it is one of the most important times for children, too, to take a long look at just what is available. Some children know exactly what they are looking for and go right for that kind of book or to books by a favorite author or illustrator. One teacher did not see the importance of this and asked children to take the first book they took off the shelf of the library! Would we demand that of any adult? Browsing gives children an opportunity, at any age, to see just what is available to take home to read to parents and what they might want to read in class; it is time worth spending. You might even incorporate a time for children to re-

7. The most important ingredient is to have fun bringing children and good books together!

turn to the group circle after browsing to share their "finds" with each other. We would encourage teachers to do the same. (Remember the power of teacher modeling!)

CATHY SWANSON'S JOURNAL

❧ *March 16*

The problem facing Marty in the Newbery Award–winning book *Shiloh* is not an easy one. He has to choose between being honest with his parents and saving the life of a dog (acting on what he feels is right). Discussing Marty's dilemma led to a discussion about the idiom "standing at a fork in the road."

We read Robert Frost's poem, "The Road Not Taken." This poem was a bit tough for fourth graders, but we paraphrased and interpreted and eventually found ourselves in the midst of an interesting conversation about choices.

Later, the kids drew "a fork in the road" and then wrote about the two choices Marty had. Some came up with new choices that he could have had.

I missed my cue on this one; this was a perfect opportunity to show how a problem and its resolution are central to a story. I should have had them think of a problem (maybe one they've experienced) and work a story from there. Most of them still create a story sequentially rather than from a kernel or a central idea.

❧ *March 17*

As we read the first chapter of Phyllis Naylor's biography today, the kids noted many parallels between her real life and those of the characters in her novels. Aaah! This is modeling! They also noted parallels between her experiences as a young writer and what they are experiencing; she wrote little books, loved to read, and her parents admired and saved her early stories.

On the first page of their response log, the children drew a picture of the author and created a web around her, listing everything they know about her so far. This will be added to as we read the story.

I'm finding *How I Came to be a Writer* is a bit difficult for the class in terms of the reading level. I'm finishing the book as a read aloud, although the kids have copies to read along with me.

Since the kids seem most attuned to ideas about writing rather than all the details of her life, I picked out several parts of the book that could be seen as "advice" for writers. I gave a page number, and the kids scanned to see if they could find her "advice." We came up with a list of "Advice from a Writer." Part of the list follows:

- READ!
- Write about what you know best.

- Write often (daily).
- Write where you are comfortable.
- Read aloud to friends, to yourself.
- Get your first draft down on the paper; revisions will come more easily.
- Learn the basics of a story; have a main character that struggles with a problem and solves it.

We have the list posted in the room, and the kids put the list in their writing folders.

I was speaking with Sally last week about the idea that "less is more." We discussed how the fourth-grade curriculum is so packed; we need to somehow integrate more efficiently so that we have time to explore a few things in more depth.

Ruby suggested that we might create four integrated units, implementing one each marking period. The first period could be spent focusing on "learning to learn strategies." We could also use that quarter to tie in all the curriculum that doesn't easily fit anywhere else.

I loved the idea immediately. I know that had I taken more time with these strategies in the beginning of the year, I would have struggled with them less during the rest of the year. In particular, how to ask a question and what to ask would be a great strategy to teach right up front; the kids use the KWL strategy so often when doing research, and certainly when giving oneself a purpose for reading!

Several of us plan to work together on the idea this summer.

TEACHER AS LEARNER/TEACHER AS RESEARCHER

Teacher Self-Evaluation

Another way to grow as a professional is to develop techniques for self-evaluation. In this section, we will discuss several ways teachers can reflect on their own growth and development. It is common for administrators to ask teachers to evaluate their teaching. However, teachers can do this on a regular basis as a way to reflect upon their teaching.

One way to do this is to think through what you feel proud of accomplishing in your own teaching and what you see as challenges to your teaching. Note that we did not use the word "problem." If you view areas that need work as challenges, rather than problems, you may tend to take a more positive approach to the ways in which you work on these and feel good about yourself in the process. Work from these challenges to what your goals might be for the next three or four months. Supportive colleagues can help you move toward your goals, as can joining a literacy support group

such as TAWL (Teachers Applying Whole Language), and enrolling in courses and workshops.

You might also design a question-naire that you distribute to students asking them to give you written feed-back on different aspects of the class-room program. Or, have a suggestion box in your classroom. This provides another opportunity for informal writing, but suggestions might also be informative in terms of the ways children perceive what goes on in the classroom.

Interview students about the literacy program. For example, do they see themselves as readers and writers? What do they do best as readers and writers? What are they finding difficult about reading? About writing? How can you help them become better readers and writers? What is their favorite part of the day? Their least favorite? What would they tell next year's students about reading and writing in this classroom?

Journal Reflections

Select one or more of the questions below that interest you and respond in your journal.

1. From reading Cathy's journal entries so far, in what ways is her classroom one that is literature-rich?

2. Visit one or more teachers and ask them about their views on the use of children's literature within and throughout their language arts curriculum. What is going well for them? What challenges do they face?

3. This chapter presents children's literature as an important component of the language arts curriculum. Why would literature also be an important component of other parts of the elementary curriculum (in science or social studies, for example)?

4. Design your own question.
   ✓ What is a question you have about the chapter?
   ✓ How will you pursue the answer to that question?
   ✓ Respond in your journal.

REFERENCES AND SUGGESTED READINGS

Allen, J. S., Giard, M. H., and Kristo, J. V. "Read Aloud: Prime Time Instruction." *New England Reading Association Journal* 27 (1991): 2–13.

Anderson, R., Hiebert, E., Scott, J., and Wilkinson, I. *Becoming a Nation of Readers: The Report of the Commission on Reading.* Champaign, IL: Center for the Study of Reading, 1985.

Atwell, N. *In the Middle: Writing, Reading, and Learning with Adolescents.* Portsmouth, NH: Heinemann, 1987.

Bauer, C. F. *This Way to Books.* New York: H. W. Wilson, 1983.

Benedict, S., and Carlisle, L. *Beyond Words: Picture Books for Older Students.* Portsmouth, NH: Heinemann, 1992.

Booth, D. *Stories to Read Aloud.* Markham, Ontario: Pembroke, 1992.

Booth, D., and Moore, B. *Poems Please! Sharing Poetry with Children.* Markham, Ontario: Pembroke, 1988.

Borders, S. G., and Naylor, P. *Children Talking About Books.* Phoenix: Oryx Press, 1993.

Burton, B. *Tell Me Another: Storytelling and Reading Aloud at Home, at School, and in the Community.* Portsmouth, NH: Heinemann, 1986.

Butzow, C. M., and Butzow, J. W. *Science Through Children's Literature.* Englewood, CO: Teacher Ideas Press, 1989.

Carroll, F. C, and Meacham, M., eds. *More Exciting, Funny, Scary, Short, Different, and Sad Books Kids Like About Animals, Science, Sports, Families, Songs, and Other Things.* Chicago: American Library Association, 1992.

Chambers, A. *Booktalk.* New York: Harper & Row, 1985.

Children's Books of the Year. New York: The Child Study Children's Book Committee. (Annual)

Clark, M. M. *Young Fluent Readers.* Portsmouth, NH: Heinemann, 1976.

Coody, B. *Using Literature with Young Children,* 4th ed. Dubuque, IA: William C. Brown, 1992.

Cox, C., and Zarillo, J. *Teaching Reading with Children's Literature.* New York: Merrill, 1993.

Cullinan, B. *Literature and the Child,* 2nd ed. New York: Harcourt Brace Jovanovich, 1989.

Cullinan, B. E. *Invitation to Read: More Children's Literature in the Reading Program.* Newark, DE: International Reading Association, 1992.

Cullinan, B., and Galda, L. *Literature and the Child,* 3rd ed. New York: Harcourt Brace Jovanovich, 1994.

Denman, G. A. *When You've Made It on Your Own.* Portsmouth, NH: Heinemann, 1988.

Doake, D. *Reading Begins at Birth.* New York: Scholastic, 1988.

Durkin, D. *Children Who Read Early.* New York: Teachers College Press, 1966.

Fader, E., Duggins, Finn, and McNeil. *Hooked on Books.* New York: Berkeley, 1976.

Ferreiro, E., and Teberosky, A. *Literacy Before Schooling.* Portsmouth, NH: Heinemann, 1982.

Flitterman-King, S. "The Role of the Response Journal in Active Reading." *The Quarterly of the National Writing Project and the Center for the Study of Writing* 10, no. 3 (July 1988): 4–11.

Fredericks, A. D. *Whole Language and Literature: Creative Ideas for Your Classroom.* Medina, WA: Institute for Educational Development, 1992.

Fredericks, A. D. *Social Studies Through Children's Literature: An Integrated Approach.* Englewood, CO: Teacher Ideas Press, 1991.

Fredericks, A. D. *The Integrated Curriculum: Books for Reluctant Readers, Grades 2–5.* Englewood, CO: Teacher Ideas Press, 1992.

Galda, L., Pellegrini, A. D., and Cox, S. "A Short Term Longitudinal Study of Preschoolers Emergent Literacy." *Research in the Teaching of English* 23, no. 3 (October 1989): 292–309.

Gilbar, S., ed. *The Reader's Quotation Book: A Literary Companion.* New York: Penguin, 1991.

Griffiths, R., and Clyne, M. *Books You Can Count On: Linking Mathematics and Literature.* Albany, NY: Delmar Publishers, 1990.

Hancock, J., Hill, S., and Lynch, P. *Literature-Based Reading Programs at Work.* Portsmouth, NH: Heinemann, 1988.

Hancock, M. R. "Exploring and Extending Personal Response Through Literature Journals." *The Reading Teacher* 46, no. 6 (March, 1993): 466–474.

Heard, G. *For the Good of the Earth and Sun: Teaching Poetry.* Portsmouth, NH: Heinemann, 1989.

Hearne, B. *Choosing Books for Children.* New York: Delacorte Press, 1989.

Heath, S. "What No Bedtime Story Means: Narrative Skills at Home and School." *Language in Society* 11, no. 1 (March 1982): 49–76.

Heinig, R. B. *Improvisation with Favorite Tales: Integrating Drama into the Reading/Writing*

Classroom. Portsmouth, NH: Heinemann, 1992.

Holland, K. E., Hungerford, R. A., and Ernst, S. B. *Journeying: Children Responding to Literature.* Portsmouth, NH: Heinemann, 1993.

Huck, C., Hepler, S., and Hickman, J. *Children's Literature in the Elementary School,* 5th ed. New York: Harcourt Brace Jovanovich, 1993.

Hunt, L. C. "Effect of Self-Selection, Interest, and Motivation upon Independent Instructional and Frustration Levels." *The Reading Teacher* 24, no. 2 (1970): 146–151.

Hurst, C. O. *Once Upon a Time. . . . An Encyclopedia of Successfully Using Literature with Young Children.* Allen, TX: DLM, 1991.

Hurst, C. O. *Long Ago and Far Away . . . An Encyclopedia for Successfully Using Literature with Intermediate Readers.* Allen, TX: DLM, 1991.

Hurst, C. O., and Otis, R. *In Times Past: An Encyclopedia for Integrating US History with Literature in Grades 3–8.* New York: SRA-Macmillan/McGraw-Hill, 1993.

Jensen, J. M., and Roser, N.L., eds. *Adventuring with Books: A Booklist for Pre-K–Grade 6,* 10th ed. Urbana, IL: National Council of Teachers of English, 1993.

Johnson, T. D., and Louis, D. R. *Literacy Through Literature.* Portsmouth, NH: Heinemann, 1988.

Kobrin, B. *Eyeopeners! How to Choose and Use Children's Books About Real People, Places and Things.* New York: Penguin, 1988.

Koch, K. *Wishes, Lies, and Dreams: Teaching Children to Write Poetry.* New York: Random House, 1971.

Koch, K. *Rose, Where Did You Get That Red?* New York: Random House, 1973.

Lynch-Brown, C., and Tomlinson, C. *Essentials of Children's Literature.* Allyn & Bacon, 1996.

Mallan, K. *Children as Storytellers.* Portsmouth, NH: Heinemann, 1992.

McCaslin, N. *Creative Drama in the Classroom: And Beyond,* 6th ed. New York: Longman, 1996.

McClure, A., Harrison, P., and Reed, S. *Sunrises and Songs: Reading and Writing Poetry in an Elementary Classroom.* Portsmouth, NH: Heinemann, 1990.

McClure, A., and Kristo, J. V. *Inviting Children's Responses to Literature: Guides to 67 Notable Books.* Urbana, IL: National Council of Teachers English, 1994.

McCracken, R. A. "Initiating Sustained Silent Reading," *Journal of Reading* 14 (1971): 521–524, 582–583.

McCracken, R. A., and McCaricken, M. J. "Modeling Is the Key to Sustained Reading," *The Reading Teacher* 31 (1978): 406–408.

Mori, H., Cain, M., and Prosak-Beres, L., eds. *Collected Perspectives: Choosing and Using Books for the Classroom,* 2nd ed. Norwood, MA: Christopher-Gordon, 1992.

Norton, D. *Through the Eyes of a Child,* 3rd ed. New York: Merrill, 1991.

Peterson, R., and Eeds, M. *Grand Conversations: Literature Groups in Action.* New York: Scholastic, 1990.

Raphael, T. "Question-Answering Strategies for Children." *The Reading Teacher* 36, no. 2 (November 1982): 186–189.

Raphael, T. "Teaching Question-Answer Relationships, Revisited." *The Reading Teacher* 39, no. 6 (February 1986): 516–522.

Rief, L. *Seeking Diversity: Language Arts with Adolescents.* Portsmouth, NH: Heinemann, 1992.

Rosenblatt, L. *Literature as Exploration,* 3rd ed. New York: Modern Language Association, 1976.

Scher, A., and Verrall, C. *200+ Ideas for Drama.* Portsmouth, NH: Heinemann, 1992.

Shelton, H., ed. *Bibliography of Books for Children.* Wheaton, MD: Association for Childhood Education International, 1989.

Smith, F. *Joining the Literacy Club.* Portsmouth, NH: Heinemann, 1988.

Sulzby, E. "Children's Emergent Reading of Favorite Storybooks: A Developmental Study." *Reading Research Quarterly* 20, no. 4 (1985): 458–481.

Teale, W. H. "Reading to Your Children: Its Significance for Literacy Development." In H. Goelman, A. Oberg and F. Smith, eds. *Awakening to Literacy.* Portsmouth, NH: Heinemann, 1984.

Teale, W., and Sulzby, E., eds. *Emergent Literacy: Writing and Reading.* Norwood, NH: Ablex, 1986.

Trelease, J. *The New Read-Aloud Handbook,* rev. ed. New York: Penguin, 1989.

Trelease, J., ed. *Hey! Listen to This: Stories to Read Aloud.* New York: Penguin, 1992.

The Web, vol. 5, no. 2 (winter 1991). Ohio State University, Center for Language, Literature and Reading.

Webb, C. A., ed. *Your Reading: A Booklist for Junior High and Middle School,* 9th ed. Urbana, IL: National Council of Teachers of English, 1993.

Wells, G. *The Meaning Makers: Children Learning Language and Using Language to Learn.* Portsmouth, NH: Heinemann, 1986.

CHAPTER 11
INVITING STUDENTS TO BECOME WRITERS

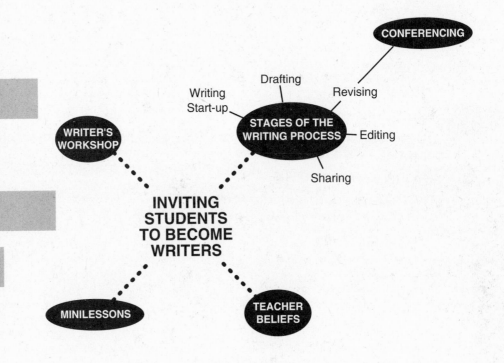

CONFERENCING

Drafting

Writing
Start-up

Revising

STAGES OF THE
WRITING PROCESS

Editing

Sharing

WRITER'S
WORKSHOP

INVITING
STUDENTS
TO BECOME
WRITERS

MINILESSONS

TEACHER
BELIEFS

What I Know: Pre-Chapter Journaling

What were some of the things your elementary teachers did when you were in school that contributed to or detracted from your enjoyment of writing?

Big Ideas

This chapter will offer:

1. The various stages of the writing process.
2. Ideas about how students can take an active role in their own writing.
3. The role of the teacher in the writing process.
4. The principles that stimulate engagement in writing.
5. The differences between traditional approaches and current practices in writing instruction.
6. Some of the beliefs held by teachers who are successful in promoting writing.

Does the following scenario sound at all familiar to you?

> Choose one of the following "story starters" and write your story. You'll need to submit it to me in 20 minutes. Please use your very best penmanship.
>
> It was a dark and stormy night when all of a sudden. . . .
>
> You have just won a million dollars. What will you do with the money?
>
> If you could be any animal you wanted to be, what would you choose?
>
> After giving the assignment, Mrs. McKillop returned to her desk and began grading some penmanship practice papers her fourth-grade students had completed earlier in the morning.

HOW WRITING PRACTICES IN TODAY'S CLASSROOMS HAVE CHANGED

Many teachers in today's classrooms are part of a vast discovery process, learning more about themselves as writers, reading books to children with an eye toward examining the craft of the writing, and creating a classroom environment that nurtures young writers. This is vastly different from past practice where writing was defined more on surface features, such as the neatness of penmanship and whether all the spelling and mechanical features were correct. "Creative writing" in traditional class settings usually meant that the teacher gave students a topic to write about and then retreated to her desk, leaving students totally on their own with their writing. There was little thought about how to help students become better writers. Workbook pages were assigned and grammar books were read, the hope being that this would improve writing.

And perhaps typical experiences such as the following also sound familiar:

- Lots of copying of text from the board
- Completing pages from a textbook or worksheets on word usage
- Endless penmanship practice
- Limited opportunities to actually write a story or another kind of writing such as poetry, journals, plays, or nonfiction pieces
- Topics for writing usually determined by teacher
- Little time to complete the writing
- The first draft was the final draft
- A focus on how the paper looked—neatness, correct spelling, and usage rather than on the content of the writing
- Writing was returned with a grade, red ink highlighting all of the "mistakes"

Unfortunately, when we ask college students today about their "writing history," their list of practices looks remarkably like ours from ages ago. Fortunately, though, some of our students are reporting positive writing experiences. These students experienced writing as a process during a time of day typically called writer's workshop. Just what are *writing as a process* and the *writing workshop?* We know from the groundbreaking research of Donald Graves (1983) that published authors work on a piece of writing that is important to them over time. Very rarely does an editor ask for a first draft of writing from an author! Sometimes writers have only a vague notion of a story they want to write. If they are writing a novel, perhaps, they have only a general idea of characters and actions. It is only when the actual writing begins that the author sees what emerges. That is why writing is a process of discovery for the writer; it is a process or a series of developments that unfold.

Let's use the analogy of a potter sitting at a wheel with a large lump of clay. The potter has an idea that the clay will become a beautifully crafted vase. However, the vase does not become a finished piece of work just like that. The potter goes through a process of refining the work, turning the wheel, adding and subtracting bits of clay. When a little pressure is added to one side, the clay begins to resemble a vase, but it is not a finished product yet. After more turns of the wheel, the lump of clay does evolve into a vase, which when glazed will be a work of art. The process of the potter took time, patience, and skill.

We know that in the real world of artists and writers the creative process takes time and that some days will be more productive than other days. We also know that to be really good at what they do takes practice: Professional potters and writers continuously work on their crafts because they know that they have to maintain some regularity to perfect their techniques.

All artists and writers—even those who have achieved professional status—need the support and encouragement of others in their field. They need mentors or teachers who guide them through the process of their creations. With that in mind, let's think about the role of classroom teachers in the writing process. Teachers in writing process classrooms are not passive; they are actively engaged with students from the start of writing to the final draft and sharing. As we discuss each stage of the process, we will also highlight the role teachers play to help support and encourage young writers.

So, what should we expect to happen in the classroom during the developmental process of writing? In the next section we list the stages of the writing process and then discuss each one in depth. Please note this warning before you go on: Even though we describe the writing process in stages, writing is not all that neat and tidy. Real writing gets messy. It is not a linear process that writers go through one stage at a time. Instead, writing is a recursive process—a process that involves multiple stages at any one time. You have probably experienced this as you have stared at a blank computer screen or sheet of paper and finally started writing. You begin crossing out words that do not suit you, or you delete a paragraph or two on your first draft. The message teachers try to relay to students is that their first draft probably will not be the last.

During writer's workshops, students experience a process similar to what actual writers go through—but, again, not usually in such a "neat" fashion. The term *writer's workshop* simply implies a time during the day when everyone, including the teacher, is actively involved with some aspect of the writing process. Usually the classroom is not absolutely quiet because the teacher might be in a corner of the classroom meeting or conferencing with a student over a writing draft. In another part of the room, there may be several students huddled around a table for an editing conference or putting the final touches on a piece of writing, such as correcting all the spelling errors. The environment of the classroom takes on the atmosphere of a studio where everyone is engaged in some aspect of the writing process. It is a supportive environment and one in which everything the writer needs is available.

Let's now take a look at each of the major stages of the writing process: (Major stages are highlighted in bold print.)

1. **Writing Start-Up**
2. **Drafting**
3. Revisiting the piece and receiving feedback
4. **Revising** and redrafting
5. Revisiting the piece and receiving feedback
6. Revising and redrafting
7. **Editing** the piece
8. Final draft
9. **Sharing** the final piece with others

WRITING START-UP: MINILESSONS

Lucy Calkins (1986) developed the idea of the writing minilesson and became popularized in Atwell's book, *In the Middle* (1987). A minilesson is a brief focused lesson that is usually done at the beginning of the writer's workshop, usually for the whole class but it could be conducted with a small group. The term minilesson has become so popular that many teachers use it to define a brief lesson that they might do with the class before reading or even science or social studies. Typically, the intent of the lesson is to help students with a specific problem, issue, or challenge to their writing. Teachers identify these areas of need by talking or conferencing with students about their writing. They also acquire topics for minilessons from being good kid-watchers—noticing, for example, that students are having a rough time identifying a topic to write about or that some students are struggling over a first draft because too much attention is devoted to spelling every word correctly.

Some common topics for minilessons might include the following:

Workshop materials and procedures—conferencing, writing folders, writing references such as different kinds of dictionaries and thesauruses

Writing different forms of letters—business letters, friendly letters

Using dialogue in writing

Writing interesting leads or beginnings

Poetry writing

Analyzing an author's style, leads, endings, etc., by using children's literature

Capitalization

Editing one's own writing

Coming up with topics for writing

The book *WRITE SOURCE 2000: A Guide to Writing, Thinking, and Learning* (1990) is an excellent resource for teachers and students alike. It contains information about different aspects of writing—from composing sentences, writing paragraphs, journal writing to technical concerns such as punctuation and spelling, etc. This book also includes a student almanac featuring maps, tables and lists, and historical documents. Many teachers find it a useful resource for developing minilessons.

The "writing start-up" phase of the writing process is sometimes also called pre-writing (Tompkins and Hoskisson, 1991) or topic selection. Students identify a topic for writing at this time. Of course, the topic is not completely thought out as is the notion in more traditional writing programs. Writers of all ages need to talk with each other during writing start-up, to try topics on for size.

There are several ways to help students during writing start-up. Let's take a look at how sixth-grade teacher Betty Robinson and fourth-grade teacher Beth Michaels go about helping students identify topics through minilessons. Betty begins the school year by arranging student desks in groups of four, with each desk already having a student's name on it. Betty knows something about the learning style and ability level of each of her students. Her aim is to form cooperative learning groups of mixed abilities and styles that will rotate about every six weeks. She wants to establish a spirit of collaboration right from the beginning of the year because writers need to help and support other writers in the classroom.

Betty also has a table displaying some of her favorite things, such as baskets she has made, her quilts, and books by her favorite poets. Above the table on a bulletin board she has photos of her children, pictures of her when she was young, and her wedding picture. She talks about all of her special things and begins a web on the board with "What We Know About Mrs. R." at the center of the web. Next, she invites students to brainstorm what they have learned already about her.

Her next step is to ask students to examine the web and to talk about potential topics *she* might write about in terms of *her* interests. The list includes the following topics:

- What it was like when she was in sixth grade
- A poem about her family

- Her quilting and basket-making
- Special times she has had with her family

This is an introduction to selecting potential writing topics. She distributes manila folders for students to begin webbing some aspects of their life, favorite things, hobbies, and special times, etc. Betty also invites students to sign up for a week they would like to bring in photos and things reflecting their lives, as she did.

What did Betty's students learn that morning about topic selection for their own writing? By bringing in personal things from her own life, Betty demonstrates not only a prewriting strategy, that of topic selection, but she shows herself as a human being, a person with a family and interests and hobbies outside of school.

Betty maintains her own writing folder, including her web. This folder will also serve as a place to store dated drafts of her writing, so she is also demonstrating herself as a writer. Students begin to web things about themselves and as a next step share these with each other. This serves as a "get acquainted" activity for students, as well as for Betty, who gets to learn more about her students. It also establishes the relevancy of the writer's workshop right from the first day of school.

Betty's beliefs about writing are clearly reflected in her practices:

- She believes that it is important to build a sense of classroom community, of which she is also a member.
- She believes that students need to work collaboratively and cooperatively. (This is especially helpful as students work on their writing, as well as on other projects.)
- She believes that students need to be engaged in the writing process right from the start of the school year.

After the initial webbing activity, she asks that students choose one of the topics from the web and begin to do some writing. The writing workshop begins in this classroom in an inviting manner, rather than with a lecture about the process. The workshop lasts about an hour, but this will vary with the age and experience of students. Betty gradually builds a list of steps in the writing process with students. In this way she also gets an indication of the knowledge of writing that students bring with them from their previous experiences. This list becomes one of the classroom documents that remains posted for students to refer to as they write. This list is depicted on the following page.

FIGURE 11.1

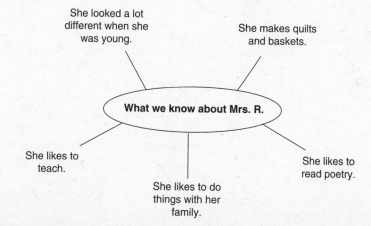

Steps in the Writer's Workshop in Betty Robinson's Sixth-Grade Class

1. *TS* (Topic search)
2. *D 1* (First draft or "sloppy copy")
3. *Conference with yourself* (Find a quiet corner and read your writing aloud. How does it sound?)
4. *D 2* (Second draft—skip lines, add or subtract writing)
5. *CC* (There are four conference corners around the room. Go to one with a writing friend and share your piece aloud.)

    Note: See typical conference questions for the writer and listener on page 347.

6. *D 3* (Third draft—use cut and paste and arrows to move text around on the page.)
7. *TC 1* (Teacher conference—discuss content)

    Note: At this point, students do not read their pieces to Betty. Instead, they *talk* about their writing in response to questions she asks such as: How is your writing going? What do you like the best about your piece? What problems are your having? Betty does not believe in taking over her students' writing. Her questioning leads children to take responsibility for it.

8. *D 4* (Fourth draft—Students add and delete content from their piece.)
9. *Self-Edit* (Students first edit their own work for misspellings, punctuation, capitalization, grammar and usage, etc., and then work with an editing partner to find anything additional to change.)
10. *TC 2* (Teacher conference, final editing)

    Note: Inside each student's writing folder is a list of writing tools (skills) students know and have demonstrated in their pieces and those skills that need work.

11. *FC* (Final copy, publishing)

Fourth-grade teacher Beth Michaels assembles her students on the rug for a minilesson at the beginning of the writing workshop time. When everyone is comfortably seated, Beth goes around the circle and individually asks students what they plan to write about and how they thought up their ideas. Beth records each writing topic on a piece of chart paper and labels the list "Writing Ideas." She posts this where all students can see it. This is extremely helpful to students as it generates other ideas for further writing. For example, Timmy says that he will be writing about seeing a deer and two fawns walking along the street as he passed by in the school bus. This idea gave Beth the opportunity to talk about other things students might see on the way to school. Maria and Ann both claim that they see the same old things on the way to school, but Beth says that it is important for writers to be observant all the time and that there can be a story "hiding" during some of our most common and ordinary days. Beth comments that she was stumped about what to write about, but now Timmy's topic of seeing the deer has given her an idea. She drives down a country road every day past an old one-room schoolhouse that is not used anymore. For her writing idea, she is going to imagine what life was like in the 1800s when children did attend this school. Beth decides that she will reread *Home Place* by Crescent Dragonwagon (1990), a story she read aloud last week. It is about a couple of people who take a walk in the woods and discover the foundation of an old house and begin thinking about who may have lived there in the past. By rereading this book, she says that she may be able to come up with some ideas for her story. Let's take a closer look at this scenario.

Beth's young writers already know that their teacher takes time during every workshop to do some of her own writing, usually ten minutes or so. However, Beth had not shown herself as a writer who also struggles sometimes about what she will write about next. She knew it was important for her students to actually know that topics do not suddenly appear for her. She modeled herself as a writer who found help from one of the other writers in class. Timmy had an idea to write about something he had seen on the way to school, so his idea generated a new writing topic for Beth.

Beth also demonstrated that there is a connection between what she reads and what she writes. She modeled this by saying that she wanted to reread the book *Home Place*. At this point Ronnie says, "Isn't that cheating? You're using Timmy's idea and some of the ideas in that book." Beth was expecting that response from somebody, and if it had not come up she would have it brought it up for discussion. She knows that her students did not have writer's workshop in third grade and did not have many opportunities to collaborate on class projects. They came to her class with the notion that it is cheating to take someone else's idea for writing or for another project. Beth's response is that writers are always searching for writing ideas everywhere. They sometimes use characters in their stories and model them after people they know. She also mentions that writers read a lot, too, and that ideas come from what others have written.

Beth decides that as part of tomorrow's minilesson she will show a videotape of one of her students' favorite authors, Lois Lowry. Beth has read many of Lowry's "Anastasia" books aloud to students: *Anastasia Krupnik* (1979), *Anastasia Again!* (1981), and *Anastasia at Your Service* (1982). These stories are full of humor, the challenges of growing up, and the importance of family life. In fact, Beth's students are begging her to read more Anastasia stories. By viewing a video tape about Lois Lowry, students will learn about how she gets some of her ideas.

Since so much interest is generated about Lois Lowry, Beth plans to make a display of some of her other books. She also plans to find biographical information about Lowry in reference sources such as *Something About the Author* and *The Junior Book of Authors* from the library. Beth wants to make a poster to display a photograph and some information about the author. This will pique the interest of her students.

Beth plans to incorporate additional minilessons when she shares more Anastasia stories.

For example, she will ask students to consider the following:

> What are ways Lowry describes Anastasia?
> What is it about Lowry's words that seem to pull us into wanting to listen to more of the story?
> How does she use dialogue in the story?
> How does she describe the setting of the story?

From these kind of questions, Beth wants her students to begin to look at the craft of the writer. She wants to help them read as writers.

Beth encourages her writers to look through everyones' list of topics to see what other topics are "hiding." She also has them web some of these additional ideas in their manila writing folders. In this webbing process students take one of the ideas listed and brainstorm other topics that can be generated from the main topic. The list of topics and sample webs are shown in Figure 11.2.

Reflections on Beth's Process Did you notice how Beth follows the lead of her students? She capitalizes upon an interest and goes with it. Her minilesson first focused on topic development. She was aware from her observations that some students were having a tough time figuring out what to write about next. She realized that only she knew everybody's topic. It was important to bring all her writers together to talk about the topic ideas but also to discuss how they thought up those ideas. In fact, she plans to post several pieces of tablet paper on the wall and label them, "How Writers Find Their Ideas." She will leave out several markers so that students can list their ideas. At the end of the week, the following ideas were listed:

> I webbed things that were scary—Sharon
> I'm writing a new chapter about Anastasia—Linda
> I want to write about when my mother was little—Ann

FIGURE 11.2

STEP 1:
TOPIC WEB

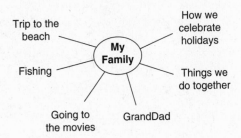

STEP 2:
SPECIFIC IDEAS
TO WRITE ABOUT

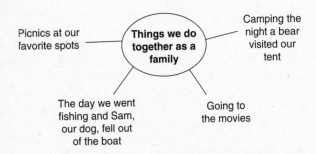

I'm writing my own book like Vera William's book, *A Chair for My Mother*—Paulette

I want to write about my favorite things to eat. But it might end up as a poem. I haven't decided yet—Dave

I am going to write my own little book of poems. (Dave's idea made me think of that.)—Ann

I want to do an almost wordless book you know like the book, *Tuesday* by David Wiesner—Randy

Paul Thompson helps his second graders arrive at topics by asking them, first, to come up with four or five topics or ideas as a class activity. Paul records each idea on the board: pets, family, funny things, scary things, and things we do after school. He then initiates a webbing process by asking students for at least four ideas about each topic they might like to suggest as writing topics. One of the webs is shown in Figure 11.3.

Paul next suggests that students choose one of the topics around the webs to write about if they are having trouble coming up with another idea. Paul will leave the tablet paper posted for a while so that students can refer to it.

WHAT ARE SOME OTHER WAYS TO GET WRITING GOING?

Tad Stone suggests to his sixth graders that if they are having a hard time coming up with a topic to just start writing. He modeled this for his students on the board. This is what he wrote:

Today is Thursday, and I just don't know what I'm going to write about. My brain is tired of thinking up ideas. I'd like to rest but I have to write. So what should I write about? It's almost Halloween, so let me think of that for a while. What do I remember as my scariest Halloween on record? Maybe I can write about that. How about a poem, a really scary poem about Halloween? I guess I'll read some scary poems and see if an idea comes up.

Tad's demonstration represents a technique called *free writing*. He remarked to his students that sometimes just by starting out as he did, a topic might emerge or might lead to another topic. It was a great opportunity for Tad to demonstrate that writing is a process of discovery—that he really had no plan to start writing about Halloween. He invited students to bounce ideas off of one another in a topic conference or to do some free writing to help generate possible writing ideas.

Fifth-grade teacher Toni Andrews invites her students to observe and talk about the world around them in the classroom. She asks them about what they are studying in their thematic units. Toni says that a topic for writer's workshop may lie "buried" there. Several students already have several ideas about writing poetry about the rain forest, and others want to write letters to businesses and governmental officials to persuade them to do more to save the rain forests.

Toni looks around the classroom and points to the pet rabbit. This rabbit is actually Toni's pet from home but it has become the class mascot. It does not take long before Joey remarks, "I know, I'd like to write stories like James Howe. Miss Andrews, you remember you read about that weird rabbit in *The Celery Stalks at Midnight* (1983) and *Howliday Inn* (1989)?" Sonia reminds everyone about all the great poetry Miss Andrews has in the classroom library. She says that she'd like to write a collection of color poems like O'Neill's *Hailstones and Halibut Bones* (1989).

Toni knows that sometimes good writing topics can be found right in the classroom, and just getting kids to look around them can generate lots of topics. She finds that one good idea from a student will "piggyback" onto someone else's good idea. Sonia's idea about what's available in the class library got Mike thinking about how he could write his version of *The Way Things Work* by David Macaulay (1988) by writing about how the farm machinery works on his family's farm. "After all," he said, "I'm an expert at that. Dad has shown me all kinds of neat stuff when he fixes a machine." This is a great project for Mike because he will use his talents as an artist to illustrate his book.

Toni has observed that some students, even at the fifth-grade level, like to draw first and then "attach" a story or some other form of writing to it, such as poetry. Toni was aware that young students often find the writing process too abstract and need to draw a picture first so they can "anchor" their writing to something. She has noticed this with some of her students who are particularly adept at drawing and will watch carefully that the drawing leads to some writing during workshop time.

It will sometimes seem easier to supply a topic to students who have a difficult time coming up with their own. Graves (1983) claims that for too many years students have been on "writer's welfare" because teachers have always given students topics to write about. If students are having difficulty finding a topic, then the teacher needs to work harder at helping this process along. Students who look to teachers for topics are those who have been in too many classes where they have been "fed" what to write about.

FIGURE 11.3

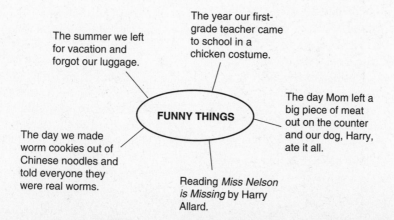

ACHIEVING BALANCE IN THE WRITING PROGRAM

Should students only write about their own self-selected topics? What if students want to write about violent things, like what they see on videos or television? Teachers need to assist and guide students throughout the writing process. Students can write on many different topics throughout the school day—on self-selected ones during writer's workshop and on more focused, topic-related ones in a thematic unit. For example, during a thematic unit of the colonial days in New England, students will have numerous opportunities to focus their writing on the topic of Colonial America. Students might write reports on some aspect of this time period, journal entries of what it was like to live during that time, diary entries, recipes, obituaries, newspaper columns, want ads, and the like.

A thematic unit (see Chapter 14) might also focus on a genre or type of children's literature (i.e., picture books, traditional literature, folktales, fables, legends, realistic fiction, historical fiction, poetry, nonfiction, biography, and fantasy). Students need lots of exposure to the writing within a genre of literature before they can be expected to do their own writing. One valuable way to do this is to read aloud examples of writing from a specific genre. For example, if students want to read biographies of famous people during Colonial America, a great choice would to be to read some of the following books by Jean Fritz:

And Then What Happened, Paul Revere?
Traitor: The Case of Benedict Arnold
What's the Big Idea, Ben Franklin?
Why Don't You Get a Horse, Sam Adams?
Will You Sign Here, John Hancock?

Many of Fritz's books are presented in short picture book format, but do not let appearances deceive you! Fritz is a master at historical research and uncovers the humor and foibles of our great historical leaders. These biographies are a treat to read (or listen to) whether you are nine or 90! Through sharing titles such as these aloud, the teacher can invite discussion about the craft of the writer:

How does Fritz begin her writing in such a way that captures the attention of the reader?
What kinds of information does she offer the reader?
What do we learn about the person from the illustrations?
Why are her books such fun?

Invite students to think about how they can write like Jean Fritz and make a person sound interesting. Share other titles about these great historical figures and have students compare and contrast the information in each. For example, other biographies of Benjamin Franklin include the following:

A Picture Book of Benjamin Franklin by David Adler, illustrated by John and Alexander Wallner
Benjamin Franklin by Ingri and Edgar Parin d'Aulaire
The Many Lives of Benjamin Franklin by Alika

Perhaps you wish to focus on poetry and want students to write some of their own. Here again you are giving a focus to the writing. You will also need to provide students with a lot of exposure to poetry and with discussions about the craft of the writing before they begin to write their own. Have a variety of poetry available for students to read aloud to each other: limericks, ballads, free verse, haiku, concrete poetry, etc. Children can make their own poetry anthologies or collections by copying their favorite selections, along with their own poetic creations. They can also illustrate the poetry and make a cover for their poetry collections.

Do you see in the examples above that students are still given a choice of what to write about, but within the limits of a unit or genre of literature? For example, not every student has to write about the same aspect of Colonial America, or the same historical figure. There are choices within limitations. It is important to bring this balance into the writing program so that children can experience a wide range of different forms of writing. This can be achieved through an integrated curriculum because students will be writing for different purposes and trying on different forms of writing throughout the day.

Audience, Purpose, and Form in Writing

Deciding on a topic also leads to more decisions: about the audience, purpose, and form of the writing. Let's look first at an *audience* for the writing. Most students are used to writing for one audience in school: the teacher. When other students also become the audience, writers must make different decisions about the form the writing will take. Will the writing also be for the principal, a pen pal, parents, or another audience?

Students next need to decide on the *purpose* of the writing. Is it to write to learn something new? Is it to entertain? Is the writing to be imaginative? Is it to be persuasive? Halliday's (1973) language functions offer a framework when considering purposes behind writing (see Table 11.1).

Writers also need to consider the *form* their writing will take. Will it be a play, the lyrics to a piece of music, poetry, a business letter, a report, an essay, an editorial? Audience and purpose will help to determine this. Writers also need to experience many different forms of writing, some of which may be incorporated into thematic units such as writing recipes, obituaries for historical or fictional characters, or a scripted dramatic presentation to illustrate a period in history or a scientific concept.

It is a good idea to establish a writer's corner or center where supplies are housed: different kinds of paper (lined, unlined, small, large, postcards, construction paper and oaktag to make greeting cards); all types and sizes of envelopes; pens, markers, pencils, charcoal, chalk; picture dictionaries, unabridged dictionaries, and junior and regular thesauruses, etc.

Inside a Writer's Workshop   Let's take a look at Betsy Lee's third-grade classroom during writer's workshop. Betsy is using the *status of the class procedure.* She stops at Jamie's desk and inquires about what his plans are for writer's workshop time this morning. Jamie responds, "I plan to work on a second draft of my piece on the flying turtles." They briefly chat about how the piece is going and what revisions Jamie is thinking of making. Betsy makes some notes on her clipboard and repeats this procedure with the next child.

The status of the class procedure is really a "mini-meeting" with each student. The same procedure has also worked well for Betsy during her reading block. Before children disband from the large group to read their books or to join a group reading the same book, she takes out her clipboard with another status of the class sheet. In fact, she has duplicated many copies of this form, which includes the names of all her students and the days of the week across the top and space for comments below. This technique works very well for Betsy. It helps her to keep track of what students will be doing, and also sends a message to students that they are responsible for accomplishing some specific work. Betsy recognizes that such writing is very personal to each child. She offers children choices all the way through the process from topic selection to revisions. Children in Betsy's room feel a sense of *ownership* over their writing. In fact, she does not write on their papers unless students say she can. She uses "stick-on tags" to write her comments on, or she writes them on the back of the child's paper. Even

TABLE 11.1

Language Function	Purpose	Form
Instrumental language	Writing for personal needs	Letter writing
Regulatory language	Writing to set limits	Rule writing
Interactional language	Writing to others for social reasons	Invitations and friendly letters
Personal language	Writing to make personal statements	Opinion letters to a newspaper, journal entries
Imaginative language	Writing that expresses creativity	Poems, songs, plays
Heuristic language	Writing to find answers	Interviews
Informative language	Writing to document learning	Reports

Source: Halliday, M. *Explorations in the Functions of Language* (1973).

visitors who come to this room can see there is an obvious sense of teacher respect for all children.

As the morning goes on, we see some children working individually on their writing, which varies from stories and poems to the beginnings of chapters books and plays. Several students conference with each other to brainstorm a listing of new topics for writing, while another group meets with Betsy to share their writing aloud and receive comments and compliments from those around the circle.

Reflections on Betsy Class Let's begin by listing some of the most obvious features in Betsy's classroom:

1. Betsy is *active* during writer's workshop.
2. She holds a status of the class conference with each student.
3. Each child appears to be at a different stage of the process.
4. Students conference with each other as well as with Betsy.
5. Students are working on many different forms of writing as well as writing for several different audiences: several work on a play for kindergartners from a favorite picture book, others are making their own poetry books to share with parents, and are writing stories and even books with chapters.

Even though children are busily working on a variety of things, there is a sense of organization and harmony in this room. Betsy's conversations with students show respect for each of her young writers. She wants them to have a sense that they are in the driver's seat. Betsy does not let students flounder. For example, she helps children who are having a difficult time deciding what to write about. She asks them to first identify several topics and then to try out one to see what works.

Betsy is helpful without being controlling. She sees remarkable progress when she offers children choices. Some of her young writers have never had to make decisions in school. The writing process finally gives them many opportunities to do this.

WRITING AND REVISING DRAFTS

After students identify a topic, they begin to work on their *first draft* of writing. At this stage, it is important to assure students that they are truly working on a first draft. They need not be concerned with spelling, neatness, grammar, etc. These might be considered the "cosmetics" of the writing process, which will become important only at a later point when students work toward a final draft. Again, even during the draft stage, writers need to take audience, function, and form of the writing into consideration. Preparing a wish-list of birthday presents for Mom and Dad is a little different from writing a letter to an author or a play script for other members of the class to perform. Students need to understand that the content of the piece is the most important aspect all the way through the writing process.

An important aspect of the drafting process is establishing a classroom atmosphere of *trust* and *support.* Writers need to know that they can take *risks,* try new ideas out, and share their writing with classmates and a teacher who will encourage them in their writing.

Students can practice writing several different leads or beginnings on the first drafts. An exciting, unique, or clever way to begin any piece will draw the reader in to read more. This is a good topic for a minilesson, which might focus around children's books with strong openings or leads. As part of a read aloud, teachers can direct attention to the way the author establishes the beginning of the writing. One strategy for students is to write several different leads to their piece and share it with peers to decide which one is the strongest. (Chapter 12 presents more information on the connection between what students read and what they write.)

While students are in the drafting stage, they should write "Draft," "Rough Draft," "Work in Progress," or "Sloppy Copy" at the top of the page and date it. Some teachers use a stamp marked "Rough Draft." These drafts are usually kept in the student's writing folder. If parents or other adults see these papers, the heading will alert them to the fact that these are indeed "works in progress."

Talk with students about some of the tools of the trade in terms of drafting—crossing-out material that is not needed in the writing, the use of arrows, and cut-and-paste methods. Keep in mind that more and more students are using word processors for their work, and that the techniques for revising drafts may vary.

If students in your class have a difficult time with drafting their writing or are finding the writer's workshop too overwhelming, try guiding students through the process by creating a group story. It can be a great way to help students through each stage of the writing process. Here are some specific steps to follow:

1. Have children identify a topic of interest to write about.
2. Invite as many students as possible to contribute a sentence or two for the first draft.
3. Read it aloud and have children help determine revisions in content. Use arrows and cross outs to indicate changes. Children will see that this first draft is indeed a "sloppy copy."
4. Rewrite the story and read it aloud. Make some mistakes in spelling, capitalization, and punctuation, etc.
5. If more changes in content are necessary, make them now.
6. Read the story slowly, asking students to focus on the mechanics—spelling, punctuation, capitalization, etc.
7. Have children come to the board to make corrections.
8. Decide on a title.
9. Type the story and post it for all to see. Add a strip of oaktag on top and write on it "Our Group Story."

The group story is a great strategy to ease children into the writing process, as they can actually witness the stages of topic development, drafting, editing, and sharing. It is also an excellent activity to introduce other kinds of writing, such as poetry, report writing, etc. Below are a first draft and final draft of a group story written by Mavis Norton's second-grade students.

First Draft

We sang songs on the bus. yesterday our class took a bus ride to the zoo It was a long rid from elm street school to the zoo? philip was sick so he didn't get to go.

gail forget her lunch. she got to buy a Hot Dog. Shes lucki.

We finally got there and saw a bunch of monkies a scary gorilla birds and 4 elephantz. We see an old lady feeding millions of pigeons. They was flying all over the place. We got to feed elephants Peanuts_We had a fun day and then we all went home.

Second Draft
Our Visit to the Zoo

Yesterday our class took a bus ride to the zoo. It was a long ride from Elm Street School, so we sang songs on the way. Poor Philip didn't go because he was sick.

When we finally arrived, we had lunch. Gail forgot her lunch, so she bought a hot dog. She's lucky!

We saw many monkeys, a scary gorilla, birds and four elephants. We even got to feed the elephants. We also saw an old woman feeding pigeons. The pigeons were flying all over the place. We had a fun time at the zoo!

Mavis learned many things from this group story. She observed that students have few problems coming up with writing topics. Her students also seem to enjoy writing and get started very quickly. From conferencing with students, however, she knows they need help in the areas of capitalization, punctuation, and paragraphing. As students dictated the story, Mavis purposely made errors in capitalization, punctuation, and omitted paragraphing.

Mavis asked the class to read the story together. Were they satisfied with the content of the piece? Tyler suggested adding the sentence, "We even got to feed the elephants peanuts." Other than that, everyone liked the story.

Next, Mavis asked students how they could make the piece better. Several students came up to the chart and underlined where capital letters, punctuation and spelling needed correcting. Then Mavis asked them to consider where the writing could be separated. It was a long story, and it all ran together. Jeff suggested that the first sentence belonged later in the story.

Mavis showed students how to use arrows to make changes on the piece without having to copy the story over for each draft and a symbol for where new thoughts could form another paragraph. Because paragraphing is new for most students, Mavis decided to do minilessons during the week using examples from children's literature.

CONFERENCING AND REVISING

Revision is often the most difficult stage in the writing process—especially for children. They want to finish as quickly as possible with a piece. Revision is also a messy stage. Arrows are used to move things around, words and phrases might be changed, entire paragraphs transformed or deleted or added. Rewriting a piece may occur because of a change in audience or a change in the form of the writing. By having students keep rough drafts and dating them, teachers can see growth in a child's writing. Another way to think of the revision process is as an opportunity to *revisit* a piece of writing. The feedback that peers and the teacher give the writer is in the form of compliments about the writing and suggestions to make the piece stronger. Sometimes students need to back away from their writing, to let it sit, and then revisit it in light of the comments about the piece.

A helpful way to get the revision process going is for students to commit to making some revisions based on the recommendations of others. If students have verbalized a plan, they are more likely to follow through with it. Revising is not a punishment; it is simply part of what makes for good writing, a natural stage that writers move through on their journey toward a polished piece.

Receiving feedback on drafts is crucial for writers. Usually this is done through *conferences*. There are many different kinds of conferences. One type of conference is held with oneself. This is an opportunity for writers to hear the writer's

FIGURE 11.4

FEEDBACK FORM

Writer: _____ **Listener:** _____

My partner's story: _____

This is what I heard: _____
_____
_____

My suggestions for the beginning are: _____
_____
_____

My suggestions for the ending are: _____
_____
_____

This is what I liked the best: _____
_____

This is my question for the author: _____
_____

My comment(s) about the story: _____
_____

voice, to hear their own words aloud. How does the writing sound when read aloud? Have you had the experience of reading your writing aloud and thinking that if only the teacher had heard the way you said your own words that he or she would have considered it a better piece?

Conferences also provide writers with the opportunity to read a piece aloud to at least one other person. By doing this, the writer does not surrender the writing over to someone but does get feedback from a person hearing the piece read aloud. This procedure "forces" the listener to focus on the *content* of the piece instead of the mechanical aspects of the writing—spelling, paragraphing, margins, penmanship, grammar, etc. Every conference should have a purpose. This will guide the kind of conversation and feedback the writer will receive. Figure 11.4 is a sample conference feedback form.

Sixth-grade teacher Betty Robinson and first-grade teacher Adele Ames both use a technique called the share circle in the same way. They ask for volunteers who want to share their writing. Most of the writing is at the draft stage so that these writers are looking for feedback from their peers. Perhaps six or seven volunteers sit in a circle on the rug. The other members of the class, including the teacher, sit in chairs in an outer circle. Both Adele and Betty have taught students the procedures for share circle. Let's take a look at how this goes with Betty's sixth graders.

Betty says, "Who would like to be share circle leader today?"

Vicky raises her hand. "Vicky." Betty says, "I turn the share circle over to you."

Vicky says, "Thank you. Who would like to start?"

David raises his hand. He reads his piece about going white water rafting and how there was almost a horrible accident because one older guy lost his balance and fell out of the raft. Everyone gasped, hanging on to each of David's words.

When David finishes, Vicky asks the other members of the inner share circle if anyone has comments or questions for David.

Yvonne askes a question about how people manage to stay in the raft anyway. She also wants to know if the guy had been fooling around.

David answers that question and several more.

Audrey is curious to know more about David's experiences white water rafting.

When the share circle finishes, David has to decide what revisions to make in order to answer some of the questions his classmates had about his piece.

Vicky asks what person would like to share next. The process continues until all students have a chance to share.

The role of the outside circle of students and the teacher is to listen and learn. They hear comments and questions about writing and learn of possible new topics for their own writing. No comments around the share circle are ever negative or humiliating to the writer. There is a feeling of acceptance and trust in Betty's classroom.

Even though we have given you an example of the conversation that goes on around share circle in Betty's classroom, just about the same kind of conversation goes on with Adele's first graders.

Share circle is a good example of two teachers, one at the first-grade level and one at the sixth-grade level, who have similar beliefs about the writing process and can use some of the same techniques. Adele's first graders are just beginning to learn to listen to each other and to make helpful comments and ask questions about each other's writing. Being able to listen, to ask questions, and to give helpful comments did not just happen for any of these students. Even Betty did not assume her sixth graders could do these things just because of their age. Both teachers modeled conferencing techniques with one student and small groups of students to demonstrate for the rest of the class the kind of conversation that takes place during conferencing. Figure 11.5 lists kinds of writing conferences.

EDITING

The editing phase of the writing process is best compared to putting the frosting on a cake. The content of the piece was the most important factor up until the time. Now the writer must look at surface features: correct spelling, usage, punctuation, capitalization, paragraphing, sentence structure, and other aspects that might be important for the final form.

Hints for the Editing Stage

Students need to be responsible for editing their own work, whether they are first graders

FIGURE 11.5   Kinds of Conferences

- *Status of the Class Conference:* The teacher briefly meets with each student to find out what the student will be working on and records this information on a daily status-of-the-class form.
- *Conference with Oneself:* To hear their own writing voices, students read their pieces aloud to themselves.
- *Topic Conference:* Students meet with each other to discuss and brainstorm topic possibilities. They can web or list ideas inside their writing folders and use this as a reference.
- *Content Conference:* Students conference with each other, a small group, and/or the teacher. At this point, the writers read their pieces to the others involved. During the content conference, the writer can ask the listener for advice on some aspect of the writing. For example:

  "I'm not sure my lead is exciting enough. Tell me whether it draws you in to want to hear more."
  "I'm having trouble with the flow of events; tell me if my story makes sense."

  As a result of such conferences, writers need to make choices about what they will do with the recommendations. They may choose one or two of the recommendations or none at all. A key responsibility that listeners have is to give compliments and make suggestions to the writer. Here are some samples:

  "I really enjoyed the part when you wrote about_____."
  "I learned about_____from your writing."
  "You have a great knack for making me feel as though I was right there. You sure gave a lot of rich details to describe the setting."
  "As I listened to your piece, I wondered about_____."

- *Editing Conference:* Students first edit or proofread their own writing. Next, they meet with another writer to check for corrections.

or eighth graders. One way to help them with this phase is to make an overhead transparency of a piece of student's work. (Get permission first from the student!) You can also use a piece from last year's class (with the student's name omitted) or one of your own pieces that you have worked on during writer's workshop. (Children will have a ball helping you find all the errors!) This is not the time to bring out the red pen! In fact, don't buy red pens; they send a message to students that their papers will be all marked up! Instead, demonstrate to students how you have to read carefully this time for the aspects of language that are important for the reader, such as spelling, grammar, and punctuation. Have students watch as you read the piece slowly and deliberately focus on each word. The process being demonstrated at this point is *proofreading*. The piece may be read several different times, each time focusing on a particular aspect. For example, the first reading may be for spelling, the second reading for punctuation, and so on. Using a marker on the overhead transparency will allow you to use a variety of proofreading marks to identify errors. With very young children—for example, with first graders—you might want them to focus on only one or two aspects, such as capitalization at the beginning of the sentence and appropriate punctuation at the end of the sentence. As students move through the grades, more can be added to the proofreading chart.

Helping children with the editorial stage is a perfect time for minilessons on grammar and usage skills, punctuation, and spelling. In fact, researchers such as Calkins (1986) and Graves (1983) advocate teaching mechanical functions of writing within the context of children's own writing rather than through workbook or practice pages. There seems to be more investment in learning these skills if children are using their own pieces that others will be reading.

After students have worked through their own pieces checking off each item on an editor's checklist, there are several options to consider. One option is that students move next to a "class editor" who goes through the piece following the same checklist. Both the writer and the "editor" then initial the paper, signaling to the teacher that the paper has been checked. Another option is for students to help each other edit their papers. If you do appoint an editor or have an editorial table with several editors, all children should have an opportunity to do this, not just the best students. The final check is made by the teacher, especially when the audience for the writing warrants this.

 SHARING

This is truly the high point of the writing process—sharing and celebrating all the hard work! Invite children to make their own books. Bookmaking does not have to be a complicated procedure. Book covers can be made from durable wallpaper remnants glued to cardboard.

In the classroom, have one chair designated as the "author's chair." It might be a comfortable rocking chair or a classroom chair that has been decorated with a special placard reading "author's chair." This might be the chair that you usually sit in to read aloud from published authors. When children are ready to share their writing, they can sign up for the author's chair.

As you read books aloud to children, point out the author information and talk about this as an important feature of a book. Work with students to create their own "About the Author" page for their books. Figure 11.6 presents a sample page by a fourth grader.

Children's books often include biographical information about the author. The following books include a page on the author:

Amelia Bedelia Helps Out by Peggy Parish
Ramona the Brave by Beverly Cleary
Runaway Ralph by Beverly Cleary
The Black Cauldron by Lloyd Alexander
The Mouse and the Motorcycle by Beverly Cleary
The Trumpet of the Swan by E. B. White

Students may also want to include a dedication page. Teachers might share some children's books that have interesting dedication pages, such as those listed below:

Old Yeller by Fred Gipson
The Lion, the Witch, and the Wardrobe by C. S. Lewis
Old Black Fly by Jim Aylesworth

Arrange for an *"author's tea,"* a special time to invite parents and other members of the community to help students celebrate their writing. Children can design the invitations. A program for the evening can be prepared by students, with teacher assistance, listing all the authors and the titles of their pieces. Those children who may not be ready to share, particularly very young children, could sit by you as you read the piece aloud to the group. Think about having several of these "teas" throughout the year so the audience gets a sense of growth and development in writing.

CHANGES IN WRITING PRACTICES

It is clear that classroom practices related to writing are gradually changing for many students.

FIGURE 11.6   Sample Author Page

Horses Are My Life!

                              About the Author
                                 by Mara

She has two parents and one brother. Mara was born on
May 3, 1983 and is now thirteen years old. In her spare time
she likes to read and ride horses. Her goal in life is to own a
horse.
     Mara has two dogs, one fish, one rabbit, one turtle, one
bird, and one guinea pig.
     Her favorite book series are THE BABYSITTER'S CLUB
and SWEET VALLEY TWINS.

Teachers are incorporating research on writing that has been done over the last 20 years. In summary, what are the changes we see taking place?

- Students are learning how to select their own topics for writing, instead of using topics predetermined by the teacher.
- More time is given to actually write and to experience writing as a process: students select topics, write a draft, receive feedback about the draft, revise and write additional drafts, share drafts, and work toward a final draft to share.
- The final written product is important but so is the process that writers go through to reach the final stages of revising, editing, and sharing the piece.
- Students conference and share writing with the classroom community of writers, not just the teacher.
- The mechanics of writing (spelling, neatness, grammar, etc.) are viewed as part of the final process, not at the beginning drafting stages.
- Students write every day or at least several times a week; writers need time to develop their craft.
- Students write for different audiences, not just the teacher.
- Students practice different forms of writing—journals, stories, poems, persuasive pieces, reports, plays, etc.
- Students feel ownership over what they write; their writing truly belongs to them. Some writing process teachers feel so strongly about this that they never write on a student's work. Instead they use "stick-on tags" for comments and reactions.
- Students feel empowered to take risks with their writing. They do not need to avoid a word if they do not know how to spell it, for example. They can use "bigger," more adult words because they know spelling will be tended to at a later draft of their writing.
- Students learn to operate in a workshop or studio atmosphere for writing, where every writer is usually at a different stage in the process.
- Teachers who use the writing process are not passive. They help students through each stage of the process without taking ownership of the child's writing. Teachers are also discovering more about their own writing process by spending time actually writing during workshop time and sharing their work and process with students.

What has contributed to the changes in the way we think about writing in the classroom? First of all, as educators, we sometimes tend to hold on to traditional practices long after they have proven to be ineffective. This has often been the case with writing instruction. Some teachers have felt that they need to abandon the teaching of the skills of writing in favor of just letting students write about their own topics. This is not the case at all with newer practices in writing instruction. Teachers actively help students through the writing process as we have discussed.

Over the last 20 years or so, researchers have explored how real writers go about their process. How do they arrive at topics? What is their process like as they progress from choosing a topic, to deciding on a form (a story, poem, song, play, etc.), to writing multiple drafts before the finished product? Donald Graves (1983, 1984, 1994), Lucy Calkins (1983, 1986, 1990), Nancy Atwell (1987), Donald Murray (1989), Tom Newkirk (1988), and others have been instrumental in exploring how children go about writing when freed from the constraints of traditional practices. Children in many classrooms—from kindergarten through high school—are selecting their own topics and choosing the form of writing and audience. They are also being given time to write multiple drafts, conference with each other, and share their writing. These practices have succeeded in changing the way we have traditionally viewed writing instruction.

Let's examine sample teacher beliefs about writing and how these beliefs may be implemented in the classroom. You will find that teachers who hold these beliefs may be first-grade teachers, third-grade teachers, or eighth-grade teachers. The belief statements coming from a whole language point of view are generic in terms of literally cutting across grade and age levels. What will be different will be how each teacher implements the beliefs.

Belief 1: *In today's classrooms teachers believe that writing is defined in a broader way that in traditional practice.* Traditional practices were defined in a narrow way with more of an emphasis on product than process. An emphasis on product rather than process meant that the student's goal was to write a story or another kind of text, such as a poem or report, that on the surface looked good—the paper was neatly written, margins and paragraphing were appropriate, and usage and spelling were correct. Students did not take risks with the content of their work, knowing that this behavior would not be rewarded. The content of the piece often took second place. Even if the content of the writing was given equal value, students did not have an opportunity to write and receive feedback on their work.

In today's classrooms the shift is on writing as a process. This means that writers of all ages now have an opportunity to go through a brainstorming process to identify a topic they would like to write about, write a rough draft, conference with a partner or group about their writing, make revisions, write additional drafts before going to final copy, and sharing their work. Many of these stages are what writers in the real world actually do. The demands that we have traditionally put on elementary school writers, such as to write on a given topic and to produce a final product in short order, would be disconcerting to the most capable adult writer.

The act of writing is also given a broader definition. Writing is viewed as a process of discovery.

You really don't know what you know until you write. Have you ever had the experience of writing a paper, report, letter, or whatever and being surprised about what you have created? Did you know ahead of time that you had something powerful to say? Did writing about a problem in a new way stimulate you to think in different ways? Writing can thus be looked upon as a form of self-expression, a way to help you look at the world in different ways. By helping students to see writing from this perspective, they, too, will grow to value written expression.

In Betty Robinson's sixth-grade classroom, students write for a host of reasons. They all participate in writer's workshop every morning but they all also keep about five different journals, each with its own purpose: to discuss math terminology in their own words; to explain science concepts; to make notes on their reactions to current events; to records topics, interesting words, and hints to remember when writing; and to record reactions and responses to their reading and new and interesting vocabulary. At first this seemed excessive to several observers. They assumed that students would resent keeping so many journals. Betty disagreed. She explained that at the beginning of the school year, she talked with students about writing being a process of discovering what we know. By asking students in her patient and reassuring way to write their reactions, reflections, or analysis in their journals on a regular basis, they came to view their journal writing as a natural part of every day.

One morning after several students reported on world events, Betty asked them to take out their current event journals and respond to how they thought the president should handle the situation. All students, including Betty, took ten minutes or so to record their reactions. After writing, volunteers shared their journal entries. It was incredible to hear the diversity in thinking among students. Betty also took this opportunity to invite students to discuss the impact of writing about current issues. Several students said they had felt confused about some of the issues until they began to write. Betty thus helped them to discover that writing can help sort out confusing issues. Billy, a usually quiet student, piped up and commented, "I bet that's why Mrs. Robinson has us do so much writing all day—so we can figure out what we're thinking!" Betty could not have said this better herself.

Another important aspect of the journal writing in Betty's class is that *all* students write in this classroom. Betty has a rich mix of high-ability students, as well as students who have been labeled learning disabled. As an observer, watching students during writing workshop and during journal writing, it is impossible to discriminate between the "haves" and the "have nots" in this room. Every student is expected to write, and every student is treated with respect for sharing. This is noteworthy because in so many heterogeneous classrooms, less would be expected from the lower ability students.

Belief 2: *Teachers believe that every child, no matter how young, is a writer and that writing is a developmental process that needs to be given time and nurturance to flourish and thrive.* Traditionally, we have thought that children grow into becoming writers. Certainly, when they enter kindergarten, we cannot consider them to be writers; they do not know how to hold a pencil correctly or how to form their letters. How could they possibly know how to write a story? Such comments are often heard from early primary teachers who view writing as an accumulation of skills: how to hold a pencil, forming letters correctly, being able to copy from the board, learning the correct spelling of a few words, and so on. When the teacher decides that all of these individual skills are in place, then the child is ready to begin writing, probably on a teacher-selected topic.

Again, this is an example of being clear as to how writing is defined. Is it narrowly defined? When a teacher remarks that a child is not a good writer, what is actually meant? For example, is the penmanship or spelling poor? Or does it mean that the content of the writing needs work, and if so, in what areas? If you believe that writing is more than an accumulation of isolated skills and that it is a demonstration of how writers think, then even as a primary teacher, you have to view writing stories, poems, etc., as what writing is really all about. The important skill work will develop both as the child works on pieces and through teacher guidance in the form of mini-lessons and conferencing.

We need to appreciate and value the early writing approximations of young children. The early scribblings, their attempts to form letters, drawings, etc., are the early stages of writing development. There is no special age or time when we can consider children ready to write, when we can actually label children as "writers." Writing, like other skills such as learning how to speak and talk, are developmental processes that take time, work, and guidance.

When teachers adopt the belief that every child is a writer, particularly right from the beginning of formal schooling, there is a change in attitude about what children are capable of doing and a new appreciation for their efforts as writers.

Teacher sensitivity to what children "bring" to the class in terms of attitudes toward writing is important. Let's take Amanda, our second grade teacher, as an example. Does she have background knowledge on the current class from previous teachers and files? If so, what is it? In what ways will she allow that information to influence her thinking about children? Sometimes information about specific children can be negative: "Susan will never learn how to write; she's lazy." "Mike isn't a good speller; he just doesn't apply himself. I've had all the children in that family, and they couldn't write or spell." Think about your reactions to such comments. That is why Amanda listens politely and sifts out the comments that might influence her in a negative way. She truly believes that there is a writer in every child (Amanda is not an idealistic new teacher; she has been teaching for 20 years!) and speculates that sometimes poor writers are the result of writing instruction that stifles rather than nurtures writers.

In order to communicate with students and their parents or caretakers before the start of school, Amanda sends them a newsletter about herself. She includes a second sheet and asks her students to write something about themselves to bring to class the first day of school. When all of these letters are gathered about each member of the class, Amanda assembles an "All About Our Class" booklet. She also tries to obtain a photo of each child at the beginning of the year to include in the booklet. Then at the end of the year, members of the class, again, write about themselves and include an end-of-the-year photo. It is fun for everyone to see the changes in writing and in the photos.

Amanda also organizes a picnic right before school starts that brings last year's students and her new students together. In fact, her "old" students help her with the schedule of events and preparation of foods. Remembering the fun they had with creating literature buffets, Amanda's veteran students solicit the help of family to cook dishes that go with children's books in some way. Each member of the class brings a food or drink and a book that goes along with it. For example, Janey made blueberry muffins to go with Robert McCloskey's *Blueberries for Sal* (1963) and Jamie brought chocolate "worm" cookies for *How to Eat Fried Worms* by Thomas Rockwell (1973). Last year's students also buddy up with a new second grader to share some of their favorite writing samples.

At the end of the year, Amanda also has her students write a letter to their third-grade teacher. In this letter they talk about some of their achievements as readers and writers and goals they wish to work on in third grade. The children also include copies of their favorite pieces. This activity communicates to next year's teacher about the kind of writing that was done the year before and demonstrates a child's growth from his or her own perspective. Naturally, Amanda briefs next year's teachers about these letters and the purposes behind them. She has found this to be a great strategy for communication, as well as nudging some

teachers along on their own risk taking to have children do more writing in their classrooms. Also encourage students to share what they know about the writing process with family members. A sample is shown in Figure 11.6. Amanda has found over time that the more writing students do, the more they want to do, and they begin to expect to continue to do much the same the following year.

WHAT ARE SOME WAYS TEACHERS CAN ENCOURAGE AND SUPPORT WRITING?

Writing does not have to be a hard and laborious process for young writers. Teachers have a choice as to how they approach their kindergartners' and first graders' initiation into writing. *We must add here that even though the following suggestions are important at the early primary grades, all of the points are equally important for teachers of writers at any age.*

- Be positive about what children can do; focus on strengths, not all the things they cannot yet do. Looking for perfection in writing (i.e., letters formed all correctly, all words correcting spelled, and neat penmanship, etc.) will only lead to disappointment and the notion that good writing equals correct mechanics. Figure 11.7 depicts a way to find out about how students view writing from Atwell's (1987) writing survey.
- Treat children not as "writers to be" but as writers in the present tense. Many children experience writing long before they enter formal schooling. Every time they take a pencil and pen and attempt to write a grocery list just like Dad's, scribble items down on a sheet of paper like the waitperson does at the restaurant, or create a story on paper that sounds just like "Goldilocks and the Three Bears," children are demonstrating that they are writers. Again, equate these early approximations with the first stages of learning to talk and to walk.

- Adopt the stance that you, too, are a writer within the classroom. Provide instances where children see you writing for many different purposes. Talk to them about the different reasons you write. This could easily lead into a class project where students list all the reasons they write.
- Parent communication is important at all grade levels. Depending on age and grade, the way in which this accomplished will be different, but the overall message is the same: Parent communication is crucial!
- If we accept the premise that writing is a life-long craft to be developed and nurtured, then we also need to accept the fact that students need to write daily and be provided with enough time and opportunity to develop the craft of their writing.

Belief 3: *Teachers believe in the importance of establishing an environment built on respect and trust for every writer.* What does a classroom environment look like that supports and encourages writers? Why is such an environment needed? Where does teaching the "basics" fit into this kind of classroom? What is the role of the teacher and students in such a classroom?

Imagine, if you will, the all too familiar classroom where students are always seated in rows, where collaboration among learners is not tolerated, and the teacher stands at the front of the class. Students normally do "their own work"; talking to one another is strictly taboo. For teachers who have adopted a process writing approach, it would be difficult to operate in such a restrained environment. Let's now look at what we would expect to see happening in a writer's workshop.

- A kind of "writer's buzz" can be heard, but not to the detriment of writers "at work." A totally silent classroom is virtually impossible in a writing classroom. In fact, many teachers have adopted the term *writer's workshop* to more accurately describe a group of writers literally at work (Atwell, 1987).
- Observers visiting a writing workshop at almost any grade level are likely to see the following: individuals at work on drafts, others discussing topics for future pieces; a small group conferencing over "working" drafts, still others working with each other editing their work; and students conferencing with the teacher over a play they are working on together.
- A writer's area has been established in the classroom, loaded with all kinds of paper, publishing materials, pens of all colors, markers, art supplies, different kinds of dictionaries, and several thesauruses—the supplies for a writer's toolbox! On the walls and hanging from the ceiling are a variety of word walls—lists of words on tablet paper that students can refer to as they write. One word wall might contain a list of commonly misspelled words, another might list synonyms for overused words such as "tired" "said," "happy," "sad," or "feeling words" or "interesting words." Word walls provide a great opportunity to move from brainstorming to using a thesaurus. Of course, children need to "test" out whether a different words might change the meaning of what they write.

Examples of word walls include the following:

- Instead of using "said" in your writing, try:

exclaimed

screeched

cried

commented

remarked

whispered

laughed

- Instead of using "happy" in your writing, try:

enthusiastic

joyful

delighted

overwhelmed

ecstatic

Word walls can also be generated when hearing good books read aloud. You can get such a discussion started by asking students to look at the kinds of words Mary Ann Hoberman uses so effectively in *The Cozy Book* (1982). Hoberman uses a poetic style to describe "everything cozy"—cozy sounds, cozy smells, cozy places, and cozy people, among other everyday things. Students can design their own word walls listing words that mean "cozy" to them.

- Why is it important to establish a climate of trust, support, and respect in the writer's workshop? What are some teacher behaviors that are important in establishing this kind of environment in the classroom? A climate of mutual trust is crucial at any age in order for students to take the risks necessary for growth and development as learners. In a classroom climate where the teacher is an agent of control and the structure is rigid, there is little room for growth. A sign displayed on one teacher's desk symbolizes this approach: "Do it because I said so; I'm the boss." This sends a message to students that there is little room for negotiation and risk taking. The freedom to try new things on for size is what learning is all about. In many whole language classrooms where the teacher does not feel threatened by students, there is a more welcoming and receptive atmosphere. This is not to say that the teacher has relinquished control over to students but rather that there is greater harmony as students and teachers work together rather than at odds with each other.

Betty Robinson welcomes her sixth graders in September by saying that she would like to establish an in-class family, one in which all members of the class community, including the teacher, work together to help and support each other throughout the school year. This is not something she merely says in passing the first day of school; it is a belief about the benefits of working with each other in a collaborative way that she demonstrates all year long. It was gratifying to observe this group of sixth graders, nervous because it was the first day of school, suddenly relax as they heard her words. Betty models this kind of attitude in all the ways she interacts with students and praises those who do the same.

A similar attitude was observed in a first-grade classroom where the teacher commented that there were really 25 teachers, not one teacher, in the room. The first graders looked a little surprised by the teacher's pronouncement, but gradually rose to the occasion as the teacher modeled behaviors that clearly demonstrated that children could work jointly on projects, that they could read to each other, conference over writing, etc. There is a different kind of spirit in these classrooms. There is an openness to showing the human side behind the title of "teacher," an acceptance and many demonstrations that the teacher is a student as well, a lifelong learner. How many of us thought that our teachers knew everything? Whole language teachers believe it is okay to admit to not knowing something. They do not brush off student questions, but rather work toward finding answers together. They do not talk "to" students; rather they talk "with" them. There is a distinctive climate in the classroom when you see whole language teachers in action. There is a sense of community, a spirit of learning, investigating, writing, and growing together.

COMING FULL CIRCLE

We began this chapter by looking at writing as a journey of discovery for the writer. As you reflect

FIGURE 11.6

254 Danielle Dr.
Harleyville Pa.
November 11

Dear Mom,

I'm going to tell you the steps of writing work shop.

First there is pre-write for the pre-wright you either draw a picture of your story or a web or a list.

Then you go onto drafting and that is when you write a rough copy

Then you go onto confrencing that is when you confrence with a partner and you and your partner have to fill these forms out and they are called feed beed back forms.

Then you go onto revising it is when you use arms add - remove - move - substitute.

Then you go onto editing you check for all spellings and then if you want to make sure the is a form it is a self check list then you confrence with a teacher.

Then you go onto publishing that is the big step you have to have all the right spellings and you have to copy the story all over again and then its a perfect story.

Sincerly,
Nikolaus D.

FIGURE 11.7   Writing Survey

WRITING SURVEY

Your Name *Alex Dunton*   Date *Oct. 5*

1. Are you a writer? *Yes*
   (If your answer is YES, answer question 2a. If your answer is
   NO, answer 2b)

2a. How did you learn to write? *I learned to wright
   by my mom and my dad also, I
   praticed wrighting*

2b. How do people learn to write?_____
   _____
   _____

3. Why do people write? *People wright because
   they need to learn and get a good education or collage.*

4. What do you think a good writer needs to do in order to write
   well?_____
   They need to pratice wrighting
   _____

5. How does your teacher decide which pieces of writing are the
   good ones? *She decieds by the kids,
   because we have a survey.*

6. In general, how do you feel about what you write? *I feel
   that what I wright is preety good.*
   _____

Source: Atwell, N. In the Middle: Reading, Writing, and Learning with Adolescents (Portsmouth, NH: Heinemann, 1987).

upon establishing a writer's workshop in your own classroom, what important points would you make about the following: your beliefs about the writing process; ways to establish a classroom atmosphere that supports and nurtures student writers, the teacher's role, and the student's role? Also consider the ways in which your beliefs about writing have changed as a result of reading about teachers who want to encourage children in their growth as writers.

Cathy Swanson's Journal

⁂ March 30

I tried something new to resolve my problem with writing workshop and recording progress notes for the kids to keep.

I inserted a sheet of lined composition paper into the front of their writing folders. My plans are to take home the folders of anyone who wants a teacher conference the next day as well as a few others. (I'll shoot for five or six each night.) That way, I can really concentrate on their writing, write a note to them on the composition paper, and date it. The next day, I'll meet with them and will be better prepared. It's just too distracting for me to read a piece during workshop.

I think this will also allow me to jot some minilessons that they could do independent of me. For example, I could write to John, "Which is the correct word for showing a location—*their* or *there?* When you're sure, explain the difference to two other people and have them initial your page."

I just have to keep trying. . . .

⁂ April 13

A sense of community is not important only among the children. Fostering a community spirit among the staff is vital as well.

Galen teaches this by example. Throughout the year, he has added postscripts of "Thanks so much for all you do," or "Keep up the great work!" to even the shortest memos that have been sent. He is always ready to listen to an idea and give meaningful feedback.

We were both enrolled in a graduate course entitled "Teacher as Researcher." This was my first graduate course and I was concerned about the paper I had to write. Galen had offered to read it, so I took him up on it and handed it to him at lunch. The next day it was in my mailbox with tiny stick-on tags everywhere! His comments were positive but straightforward. His input, and the willingness and excitement with which he shares it, exemplifies what community-builders do.

⁂ April 14

I'm not sure if the trends in whole language and the desire to use trade books spawned what seems like a flood of good children's books or vice versa, but I'm certainly excited about what I'm seeing on the shelves of the bookstores, and more importantly in the hands of children.

There seems to be a growing number of nonfiction collections that are just wonderful! Mike Venezia has written and illustrated a series of very readable and humorous biographies about artists, The lives and works of such masters as Rembrandt, da Vinci, Picasso, Renoir, and Monet are written with a perspective sensitive to the eyes of a child.

Reading about artists has been a good way to integrate the theme of our art gallery with biography as a genre. Our librarian pulled all the biographies in this series for us, and we spent several days reading through them.

It was interesting to note the responses the children had to the different styles and the preferences they established fairly quickly. Some were fascinated by Picasso's cubism, others thought his work looked like "little kids" had done it. (Venezia does have a great sense of humor—he drew a picture of Picasso and a "girlfriend" who had two noses, obviously Cubist in nature!)

Everyone chose an artist to research, then reread Venezia's book to pick out the most important events/things to note about their life. A "snapshot" biography, illustrating the artist and placing the events around the picture, served as a prewrite for their own biography.

In addition to learning about a new genre and becoming more knowledgeable about artists, the writers emulated Venezia's style. This was important in the battle against the ol' "read and regurgitate" method of encyclopedia research.

≈ April 15

Sometimes I feel very frustrated with our study of the U.S. regions. Although a few of the kids have traveled more extensively in the states than I have, most of them just don't have a frame of reference on which to build. They know about their own surroundings (PA), but "other places unlike our own" seem a bit abstract for them.

This being the case, it is sometimes difficult to determine what might be the most meaningful way for them to learn about our country. Literature is a given, though; when they get lost in a good book like *Shiloh,* they learn about the region in a more indirect fashion. (Most of the novels we've incorporated this year tie into the study of the regions.)

A few activities seem to be helping them to make sense of the knowledge they acquire: brochures created for the purpose of "selling" someone on the region, photo albums filled with pictures (children's illustrations in frames) and text that highlight the attributes of the region, and a chart that has remained visible throughout our studies.

We started with Pennsylvania because that's what we already knew about. We've been adding to the chart as we study each region, making comparisons as we go. The kids decided how the chart should be laid out, then embellished it with state abbreviations and illustrations in the column heading boxes.

REGIONS	CLIMATE	LANDFORMS	N.R./INDUSTRY	ATTRACTIONS
PENNSYLVANIA				
NORTHEAST				
SOUTHEAST				
MIDWEST				
SOUTHWEST				
ROCKIES				
PACIFIC NW				

≈ April 26

The first books came back from Miss Nelson's Publishing Company today. The kids were beside themselves!

I think there are close to 43 volunteers working in the company this year. They type, edit, and bind the children's work, resulting in beautiful hard-back books that the children truly cherish. Last I heard, the count of published pieces was approaching 350!

Included in these books are dedications to parents, friends, teachers, etc., and an "About the Author" page at the end of the book, complete with a school picture. A certificate of achievement, signed by the principal, is delivered with the finished book. It requires a lot of work on the part of all the volunteers, but if you could see the faces when their books are completed and in hand. . . .

TEACHER AS LEARNER / TEACHER AS RESEARCHER

Shadowing

"Sometimes teaching can feel so isolated. I'm in my classroom all day and only talk to my colleagues at lunch or after school," exclaimed fifth-grade teacher Margaret Dodge. Have you heard this comment before? Many teachers, even veteran ones such as Margaret, want more interaction with their colleagues for the purposes of learning and improving upon their own classroom practice. A useful technique for learning what it is like to be in someone else's shoes, so to speak, is to shadow that person for a period of time. Shadowing simply means that you, in a sense, follow in another person's footsteps. This technique offers teachers the opportunity to not only talk to another colleague but also to observe and participate in that teacher's classroom.

Arrange a period of time when it is possible to both observe and participate in the classroom of a colleague whose practices you admire. Let's imagine that it is a teacher who has a well-organized and successful writing workshop. If possible, arrive early to discuss the plan or routine of the writing workshop. Have a notebook with you to write your observations and questions. Try to observe as many aspects of classroom practice as possible. For example, how does the teacher begin the writing workshop? Do children follow a routine? What record-keeping procedures are used? Ask for copies. In what ways do children conference over their writing? Does the teacher use minilessons to teach writing strategies? What else goes on during this time? How do students make the transition from writing workshop to the next block of time? How is the remainder of the day organized? Also learn about writing workshop by becoming involved. Interact with children, ask if you can listen in on conferences, ask children questions about their writing, etc. At a convenient time, debrief with the teacher and share your observations, reflections, and questions. What did you learn? What are your next steps?

Journal Reflections

Select one or more of the questions below that interest you and respond in your journal.

1. Based upon Cathy's journal entries so far, how would you describe her approach to writing?

2. Observe and interview several first-grade students about their perceptions of writing. Ask one or more of the following questions: What kinds of writing activities do you do each day? What do you like/dislike about writing? What about writing is easy for you? What about writing is difficult for you? Based on their responses, your observations, and the information in this chapter, how would you help them grow as writers? Ask students at another grade level (preferably fourth grade or higher) the same questions. Compare the responses of first graders with those of students at a higher grade level. What similarities or differences do you note?

3. Why is it more important to focus on the processes of writing more than the products of writing? What might be some long-term effects of this approach?

4. Design your own question.
   ✓ What is a question you have about the chapter?
   ✓ How will you pursue the answer to that question?
   ✓ Respond in your journal.

REFERENCES AND SUGGESTED READINGS

Atwell, N. *In the Middle: Writing, Reading, and Learning with Adolescents.* Portsmouth, NH: Heinemann, 1987.

Calkins, L. *Lessons from a Child.* Portsmouth, NH: Heinemann, 1983.

Calkins, L. *The Art of Teaching Writing.* Portsmouth, NH: Heinemann, 1986.

Calkins, L. *Living Between the Lines.* Portsmouth, NH: Heinemann, 1990.

Fletcher, R. *What a Writer Needs.* Portsmouth, NH: Heinemann, 1992.

Frank, M. *If You're Trying to Teach Kids How to Write, You've Gotta Have This Book!* Nashville, TN: Incentive Publications, 1979.

Graves, D. *Writing: Teacher and Children at Work.* Portsmouth, NH: Heinemann, 1983.

Graves, D. *A Researcher Learns to Write.* Portsmouth, NH: Heinemann, 1984.

Graves, D. *A Fresh Look at Writing.* Portsmouth, NH: Heinemann, 1994.

Halliday, M. A. K. *Explorations in the Functions of Language.* London: Edward Arnold, 1973.

Hansen, J., Newkirk, T., and Graves, D. *Breaking Ground: Teachers Relate Reading and Writing in the Elementary School.* Portsmouth, NH: Heinemann, 1985.

Hubbard, R. *Authors of Pictures, Draughtsmen of Words.* Portsmouth, NH: Heinemann, 1989.

Murray, D. M. *Expecting the Unexpected: Teaching Myself—and Others—to Read and Write.* Portsmouth, NH: Heinemann, 1989.

Nathan, R., Temple, F., Juntunen, K., and Temple, C. *Classroom Strategies that Work: An Elementary Teacher's Guide to Process Writing.* Portsmouth, NH: Heinemann, 1988.

National Council of Teachers of English. *How to Help Your Child Become a Better Writer.* Urbana, IL: NCTE, 1985.

Newkirk, T., ed. *Understanding Writing: Ways of Observing, Learning and Teaching,* 2nd ed. Portsmouth, NH: Heinemann, 1988.

Parry, J. A., and Hornsby, D. *Write on: A Conference Approach to Writing.* Portsmouth, NH: Heinemann, (1988).

Parsons, L. *Writing in the Real Classroom.* Portsmouth, NH: Heinemann, 1991.

Preece, A., and Cowden, D. *Young Writers in the Making: Sharing the Process with Parents.* Portsmouth, NH: Heinemann, 1993.

Rief, L. *Seeking Diversity: Language Arts with Adolescents.* Portsmouth, NH: Heinemann, 1991.

Tompkins, G. *Teaching Writing: Balancing Process and Product.* New York: Merrill, 1990.

Tompkins, G., and Hoskisson, K. *Language Arts: Content and Teaching Strategies.* New York: Merrill, 1991.

Welde, J. *A Door Opens: Writing in Fifth Grade.* Portsmouth, NH: Heinemann, 1993.

WRITE SOURCE 2000: A Guide to Writing, Thinking, and Learning. Burlington, WI: Write Source, 1990.

CHAPTER 12

BUILDING READING/WRITING CONNECTIONS

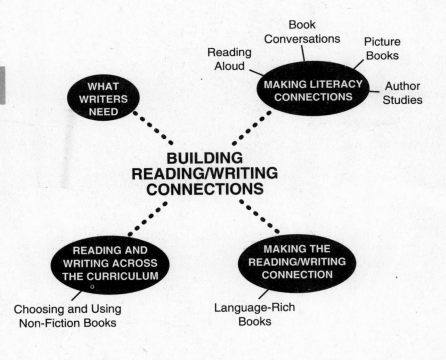

What I Know: Pre-Chapter Journaling

What is the most memorable children's book you read when you were young? Read it again. If you wrote a letter to the book's author, what would you like to say?

Big Ideas

This chapter will offer:

1. The importance of the reading/writing connection.
2. The various ways in which teachers can assist students in making literary connections.
3. The role of literature within and throughout the writing process.
4. Several ways in which teachers and students can celebrate literature.

To write well it is necessary to grow up hearing how other people have written well: to get into one's metabolism a sense of the grandeur, the playfulness and the plain narrative strength of the English language.

(Zinsser, 1990, pp. 17–18)

"With me," says Maurice Sendak, "everything begins with writing. No pictures at all; you don't want to be seduced by pictures because then you begin to write for pictures. Images come in language, language, language: in phrases, in verbal constructs, in poetry, whatever. I've never spent less than two years on the text of one of my picture books, even though each of them is approximately 380 words long. Only when the text is finished—when my editor thinks it's finished—do I begin the pictures."

(Zinsser, 1990, pp. 15–16)

Throughout many chapters of this book, we have referred to children's literature as the "backbone" of the curriculum from kindergarten through grade eight. The focus of this chapter is the role of literature in the lives of student writers. Research supports a reading and writing connection. Eckhoff (1983) and Deford (1981) found that children who read and listened to "real" books as part of their school program are substantially better writers than those students who do not read literature in school. The research of both Eckhoff and Deford on the kind of writing students do parallels what is emphasized in the reading program. Children who read from materials using highly controlled vocabulary (i.e., rat, fat, cat, mat, etc.) wrote stories that were similar in nature. Those who read primarily from basal readers also using a controlled vocabulary (i.e., Jack walked. Janet walked. Jack and Janet walked) wrote using the same tightly controlled kind of language. However, those students who read and listened to a wide variety of high quality children's literature wrote stories rich in language and used a variety of linguistic structures. They also see themselves as authors, as depicted in Figure 12.1. If we invite the authors of our children's favorite books to "teach" our young writers, then our students will write from what they know best—the highest quality literature experiences we can provide. In fact, the advice most authors give to writers is to READ and WRITE. It is clear that what improves writing is to write *and* to read. Sound simple? To make this a reality in classrooms is *not simple, but it is fun! The other key ingredient is the teacher.*

The following are guidelines that teachers at every grade level can use to help students become writers:

- Have high-quality children's literature available in the classroom. Work toward building a classroom library that includes the following kinds or genres of literature: picture books, traditional literature (i.e. myths, fables, folktales, and legends), fantasy, poetry, realistic fiction, historical fiction, biography, and nonfiction.
- Teach children the writing process. In the writing process, students determine their own topics to write about, write drafts, conference with others about their writing, revise, edit, and share their writing. (See Chapter 11 for an in-depth discussion of the writing process.)
- Help students make their own book selections for reading. Also form literature circles in which small groups of students read a book in common.
- Give students plenty of time to read and write. Readers need time to select books, to read, and to talk about what they read. Writers need time to select topics and develop their thoughts on paper. In some first grade classrooms, as well as in some later grades, teachers devote an entire morning to reading and writing workshop.
- Teachers need to demonstrate that they are readers and writers. They do this by actually reading and writing when children are involved in these activities. Children of all ages need to see that the teacher continues development as a reader and writer.

FIGURE 12.1

When I get older I want to become a great and famous children's author and write hundreds of books. I love to write!

I adore writing (writing is my favorite thing to do besides reading). The longest book I ever wrote was about 12 pages long. It was called My Puppy. Some other stories I wrote are Hansel & Gretel continued. It's about when they are married and have seperate familys.

Other stories I wrote are the Rabbit Under my shed. Its about a girl who finds a rabbit under her shed and they become real close.

I wrote about 15 stories. Actually, I never counted! Maybe More! Speaking of books, My favorite books are All the Roald Dahl books, There is a boy in the girls bathroom By Louis Shear, and Shiloh by Phyllis Reynolds Naylor. My favorite author is Roald Dahl. His books cheer me up.

written By
Caitlin
Patricia
Szewczak

• Teachers need to share their enthusiasm for books by reading aloud to children on a daily basis and planning ways that students can make connections between the writing of published books and their own writing.

Writing teacher Donna Skolnick offers these observations:

Five years ago I thought only in terms of story starters and book reports. But my own desire to write "like in a book" forced me to look more closely at the craft of the writer. Literature became my textbook: fine writing held lessons I wanted to learn. . . . This past year, while collaborating with teachers and conferring with writers, I searched for evidence that students, too, would grow as writers when they enjoyed fine literature. In observing writers at work, listening as they talked about their writing, and interviewing them, I found my answer. What children read and how they read do influence their writing. Peter, a student in Ann Shames's first grade, expressed it this way: "My own books are longer because I've heard more books and I learned how authors write and how they put in details, and I do the same thing." (1989, pp. 53–54)

What, then, are ways to bring children, their writing, and literature together in a dynamic way? How do teachers help students make connections between what they read and what they write? How do we help children "read as writers" and "write as readers"?

PLANT LITERARY SEEDS, WATER DAILY, AND LITERARY ROOTS WILL TAKE HOLD.

Bringing children and literature together in ways that literary roots will take hold is an enormously exciting and important role for teachers. The ingredients to produce a garden of budding student writers are teachers, the books they choose, and the kind of conversations teachers have with children about books and authors.

READING ALOUD AND BOOK CONVERSATIONS

One of the most important ways to bring children and books together is by sharing literature aloud. The talk about books following a read aloud is the dynamic link that helps students understand connections between the book and the writer. The discussion following reading aloud can also lead to students doing focused writing to practice using a literary technique (i.e., characterization, setting, etc.). Another option teachers frequently use following reading aloud is a minilesson (discussed in Chapter 11). In this case, the purpose of the minilesson is to discuss a particular technique used by the author. Students can use their own writing to explore possibilities of making their piece stronger by using the technique.

We will discuss both approaches to writing as a result of reading aloud: the focused writing experience and the use of children's own writing as the springboard to try new literary techniques "on for size." Let's begin by looking at some suggestions made by Stewig (1990, pp. 11–12) to help teachers and students begin the kind of book conversations that focus on the craft of the writer. Stewig recommends the following questions for very young children:

1. Which part of the story did you like best? Can you tell us why?
2. Which part was most exciting or interesting?
3. Which of the people in the story did you like best? Can you tell us why?

These questions are more complex:

1. Why do you think we don't like that character? What does he or she do that makes us feel that way?
2. Why do you think the story happened where the author made it happen?

3. That's an interesting word. Why do you think the author chose to use it instead of another one?

Stewig suggests the questions below for older students:

1. What do you notice about the differences in the language the characters speak?
2. How did the author convey the relationship between the characters without simply telling us?
3. What reasons might there be for the character to act that way?

Teachers of all grade levels can experiment with the above questions. Some younger students may be ready to respond to the more complex questions.

Stewig (1990, pp. 18–23) also recommends that teachers use a *focused lesson strategy*, which can be divided into six parts:

1. Sharing the material
2. Discussing the material
3. Presenting the writing problem
4. The writing task
5. Conferring about the draft, editing or redrafting, and sharing the composition
6. Sharing writing

Let's look at each step in detail.

Sharing the Material Choose a book to read aloud. Before reading, decide on how to introduce the book: something about the author, characters, setting, etc. It is often helpful for students to focus their listening on a certain aspect of the writing for the discussion to follow the read aloud. For example, your teacher might say, "As I read aloud today listen closely to how the author describes the characters in the story."

Discussing the Material After the read aloud, Stewig suggests posing questions that focus the discussion on a particular aspect of the writing (1990, p. 96). For example, if characterization is the focus, these questions might be asked:

Why did you like the character in the story? What things made him/her interesting to you?

Were there other things about the character that you wanted to know? What were they?

What details about the character did the author share with us that made him/her seem real (or imaginary, if that is the case)?

Did the character act the way you thought he/she would? Why or why not? If not, how did you think the character would have acted in the situation?

Did the way the character interacted with the other characters seem believable to you? Why or why not?

Stewig suggests that the above set of questions be asked of the writing students do, but we think they are good questions to ask after the read aloud as well.

Stewig suggests the following questions to examine the personality characteristics of characters (1990, p. 73):

What is the character like "inside"?

How does the character feel about things that happen in the story?

How does the character react to people, ideas, and events?

Presenting the Writing Problem In this step the focus of the writing is discussed. For example, to continue with the example of characterization here are several sample writing experiences.

We suggest that teachers begin with picture books—a fabulous source for student writers of all ages to learn a variety of techniques about writing. They are usually short, which means that teachers can share them during one read-aloud session. We'll discuss the use of picture books to teach about literary characteristics later in the chapter.

Third-grade teacher Janey Dickson noticed that in much of her students' writing characters were not described in very interesting ways. Janey decided to plan a focused writing experience by using a picture book. She chose *Annie Bananie,* written by Leah Komaiko and illustrated by Laura Cornell (1987), because she knew students would appreciate the humor and be able to identify with the characters.

Janey began by telling students to focus their listening on all the different ways the two friends in the story are described and why they are special to each other. Janey suggested that children could jot down these words or descriptions as she read aloud. Although this is a simple book, Janey knew it would be a challenge for students to think up words to describe the two friends, because the author tells more about what the girls do when they play together.

1. After reading aloud, Janey gave students the option to work in pairs.
2. She asked students to list all the ways the friends played together.
3. Next, she asked them to web all the ways to describe how the friends felt about each other and how they would describe some of the fun things they did together.

Janey's students have just started using their junior thesauruses to help find stronger describing words for their writing, so this was an opportune time for her to suggest finding synonyms for words to describe the characters. Figure 12.2 presents a web of words describing the two characters. Janey was delighted with the extensive web of describing words students brainstormed. She knew this kind of activity would also lead to using the thesaurus in more meaningful ways. Since students have not only described the characters in a rich way, they have also created a "web" of new words to use in their own stories. Janey plans

FIGURE 12.2 A Web of Describing Words for Two Friends

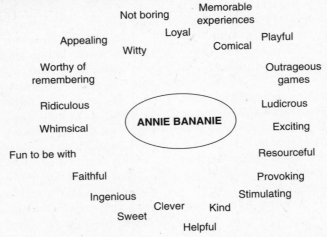

to leave the web posted on the wall for students to refer to as they write.

As a next step, Janey asked students if they noticed anything particular or special about the words the author used in the story. Janey showed students the text of the story on an overhead transparency.

"Oh, I know what's special about this story!" exclaimed Ronny. "The story is more like a poem. A lot of the words at the end of the lines rhyme. That's really neat!" At this point, students begged to read the "story poem" together. Following this, Janey asked students to come up and circle the rhyming words. This led Janey to Stewig's next step.

The Writing Task Janey invited students to write a story or poem, or to use another form of writing to describe a best friend or a friend they would like to have. She also gave students the option to write in pairs. She suggested that one way to start would be to list or web things they like to do with a friend and words to describe the kind of relationship they have with a friend, similar to what was done after reading *Annie Bananie*.

Conferring About the Draft, Editing or Redrafting, and Sharing the Composition Janey reminded students to conference with each other over their first draft. She uses a process approach to writing in her classroom, which includes the following:

Webbing is used to stimulate ideas for writing.
Writers conference with each other over drafts of writing (conferencing means that the writer shares the piece aloud in order to get feedback from a listener).
Using the feedback and questions generated by the conference (children learn to give only supportive feedback), writers choose recommendations they feel will make the writing stronger and revise their pieces.
Sometimes students write more than one draft and receive additional feedback from conferencing.
Writers edit their pieces first themselves, then edit with partners to "polish" the writing in terms of spelling, mechanics, and penmanship.
Each student shares writing with classmates.

Sharing Writing Children were intrigued with the humorous watercolor illustrations by Laura Cornell and came up with their own marvelously illustrated pieces. In fact, many of the children used watercolors to illustrate their writing. They wrote stories, poems, and even letters. (Janey encourages students to experiment with different forms of writing.) Students experimented with words to describe their friends in terms of physical appearance and personality characteristics, and fun things to do with a friend.

Tony and Bill, two students who are best friends in Janey's class, decided to write letters to each other describing their friendship.

Dear Tony:

You are the funnest friend a kid could ever have! I hope you never move away. I'd miss all the outrageous things we do together, like riding our bikes as fast as we can down the dirt road behind your house. You're such a daredevil. No one would believe some of the antics you try. Actually, you're more of a practical joker. Remember the time you left that plastic tarantula that had real hair all over it under Ms. Dickson's papers? When she lifted the papers I thought she was going to have a heart attack, but she was a good sport. (Lucky for you!). Anyway, I like how you make me laugh. You're good for me and are a loyal friend.

Your friend,
Billy (the kid)

Dear Billy:

I like to tease you. Sometimes you're so weird! (and definitely not boring). I don't know how I ever got a friend like you, but you better stay around. Nobody else thinks I'm so funny, especially Mom. She says I should be more like you. I mean you get good grades and study all the time and everything. How'd you get so smart, anyway??????????? You're still a good and faithful friend, anyway. You always like to do the things I like. Our best time was when we went camping with your dad and that big bear kept circling the tent. We weren't too scared were we! Anyways, we pretended not to be scared so your dad wouldn't panic. So, you better not move away, o.k.??????

From your best friend,
Y-not (I know Ms. Dickson doesn't like when I write my name backwards. But you like it!!!!!!!!!)

Janey's Next Steps Janey knows that learning how to describe characters in one story probably will not be enough to see some real differences in the ways students describe characters in their own pieces. Janey's students write every day from topics they select themselves, so there are many opportunities for students to work on character development. Janey wants to incorporate more challenging stories that depict strong characterization. She plans to have children choose several to read on their own, as well as several she will read aloud. During the next few weeks, Janey will plan minilessons using the books and the pieces that children are working on as the focal point. Instead of the more focused writing activity described above, the minilessons will help children examine their *own* pieces of writing for ways to describe characters in richer ways. Also, since children had so much fun thinking of words that describe, she also wants to introduce books in which authors use beautiful and rich language not only to describe characters but to write an interesting story.

Here is a list of books with strong characters that Janey gathered for her third-grade writers:

Ira Says Goodbye by Bernard Waber
Gertrude's Pocket by Miska Miles
Hey, What's Wrong with This One? by Maia Wojciechowska
Mirandy and Brother Wind by Patricia McKissack
Old Henry by Joan Blos
Secret Dreamer, Secret Dreams by Florence Parry Heide
The Stone-Faced Boy by Paula Fox

Janey also plans to use Ruth Heller's book, *Many Luscious Lollipops: A Book About Adjectives*. Ruth Heller has also written and illustrated other wonderful books that focus on parts of speech, among them *A Cache of Jewels and Other Collective Nouns* and *Kites Sail High: A Book About Verbs.*

These books are marvelous alternatives to using workbook pages to teach parts of speech.

Using Picture Books to Make the Writing Connection

We saw how Janey Dickson used a picture book to help students learn about describing characters. What are some other ways that picture books can be shared with student writers? Remember, picture books can be used with young children as well as with those in the intermediate and middle grades. You might also want to read *Beyond Words: Picture Books for Older Readers and Writers* (Benedict and Carlisle, 1992). A great source for book suggestions is *Using Picture Storybooks to Teach Literary Devices* (Hall, 1990). Hall states:

> Deceptively simple, picture storybooks have the advantage of teaching complex literary elements in an accessible format to students of all ages. Flashback, inference, and rich imagery occur in the art and text of the picture storybook as frequently as they occur in more mature fictional literature. Recognition of such devices on the part of any reader improves, at the least, comprehension of a book's message and may, at best, ultimately lead to enhanced reading pleasure and discriminating literary tastes, objectives which surely must find advocates among those working in the educational setting. (p. vi)

We would add to Hall's statements that picture books can be one of the "texts" teachers use to teach students about authors' writing techniques. Table 12.1 lists examples of picture books and the particular literary devices that they illustrate.

Student writers also benefit from talking about an author's way of organizing a story. Siu-Runyan (1996) offers this suggestion: "When one knows about various ways of organizing text, a student can more easily (1) choose an appropriate design to use when writing a piece, and (2) figure out what's happening in the story and thus use predicting strategies when reading. For this purpose, using picture books or short chapter books makes it easier for students to see the structure." Siu-Runyan identifies the following plot structures:

- Circle or turn-around plot: The story begins and ends at the same place.
- Story-within-a-story: There are two stories, one of them being the vehicle for telling the other.
- Flashback: A main character in the present tells a story about the past.
- Sequential: One event follows the other.
- Interlocking: The address for one response becomes the beginning for the next sentence.
- Question/answer: A question is asked followed by a response.
- Repeated refrain: A phrase is repeated throughout the story.
- Surprise ending: The end of the story is not the one expected.
- Patterns of three: There may be three characters, three tasks, or three things to overcome throughout the story.
- Familiar sequences: Stories are built around familiar sequences, such as months of the year, days of the week, holidays, etc.; stories capitalize on children's familiarity with sequences that are part of their daily lives.

Author Study

It is not only important to share great books with children, it is also crucial to share author infor-

TABLE 12.1 Picture Storybooks and Literary Devices

Literary Device	Sample Picture Storybooks
ALLITERATION: Repetition of a consonant sound at the beginning of words as well as within words.	*Chicken Little* by Steven Kellogg *The Rose in My Garden* by Arnold Lobel *The Voyage of the Ludgate Hill* by Nancy Willard
ATMOSPHERE: Mood developed through description of setting and details about the story.	*The Best Town in the World* by Bryd Baylor *The Man Who Could Call Down Owls* by Eve Bunting *The Green Lion of Zion Street* by Julia Fields *Rondo in C* by Paul Fleischman *Winter Barn* by Peter Parnall *Dakota Dugout* by Ann Turner
CARICATURE: Description of characters through the use of exaggeration.	*Fat Chance, Claude* by Joan Lowery Nixon *The Relatives Came* by Cynthia Rylant *Soup for Supper* by Phyllis Root
FLASHBACK: Technique used to take reader back in time.	*Miss Rumphius* by Barbara Cooney *Watch the Stars Come Out* by Riki Levinson *What's Under My Bed?* by James Stevenson *Why the Chicken Crossed the Road* by David Macaulay
FLASH-FORWARD: Technique used to take reader ahead in time.	*The Quilt Story* by Tony Johnston *Lost and Found* by Jill Paton Walsh
FORESHADOW: Technique that cues reader about upcoming action.	*Miss Nelson Has a Field Day* by Harry Allard *Annie and the Wild Animals* by Jan Brett *The Patchwork Quilt* by Valerie Flournoy *Hattie and the Fox* by Mem Fox *Knots on a Counting Rope* by Bill Martin and John Archambault
IMAGERY: Figurative description involving all the senses.	*There's More . . . Much More* by Sue Alexander *An Early American Christmas* by Tomie de Paola *Whale Song* by Tony Johnston *Apple Tree* by Peter Parnall *When I Was Young in the Mountains* by Cynthia Rylant
IRONY: Technique used to change the turn of events from what is expected to happen.	*The Dove's Letter* by Keith Baker *I Hear a Noise* by Diane Goode *I Wish I Were a Butterfly* by James Howe *The Very Worst Monster* by Pat Hutchins *Doctor De Sto* by William Steig
POINT OF VIEW: A device that establishes who is telling the story.	*Death of the Iron Horse* by Paul Goble *The Patchwork Cat* by William Mayne *The Snail's Spell* by Joanne Ryder *Rose Blanche* by Roberto Innocenti *Her Majesty, Aunt Essie* by Amy Shwartz
THEME: The main point or message of the story.	*Where the Forest Meets the Sea* by Jeannie Baker *Piggybook* by Anthony Browne *The Village of Round and Square Houses* by Ann Grifalconi *Blackberries in the Dark* by Mavis Jukes *The Wreck of the Zephyr* by Chris Van Allsburg *A Lion for Lewis* by Rosemary Wells

Source: Hall, S. *Using Picture Storybooks to Teach Literacy Devices: Recommended Books for Children and Adults* (Phoenix, AZ: Oryx Press, 1990).

mation as well. Have you ever met an author that you admired? Did you learn something interesting about the author's background, personality, and writing habits? Did you discover what influenced the author's writing? Did you read the author's works in a different way after learning this information? Even if you only read something about an author and see a photo, it does impact how you read and think about the author's works. The same holds true for children. They enjoy hearing about the life of an illustrator. It helps to shed new light on the writing and illustrations.

Here are some ways to "invite" authors and illustrators into the classroom.

Author/Illustrator Visit Write to the publisher of your students' favorite author or illustrator. The publisher usually has a publicist who works to arrange these visits. If the expense to invite an author or illustrator to your school is too expensive, talk to your principal about available funding sources. Also, if a local or regional reading group is holding a conference, find out if authors and illustrators will be a part of the conference. Perhaps, a visit can be arranged through that organization. You can also try to find out what children's authors and illustrators live in your state through your school or public librarian. Ask librarians and others for any listings they have of local authors and illustrators.

If a visit is scheduled, it is critical that all children are acquainted with the books by the author or illustrator. If possible, the school should try to obtain multiple copies of the books and share these with children. Invite students to make the books more memorable by responding to them through group discussions, writing, artwork, and drama. Acquaint children with the author or illustrator from references such as *Something About the Author*. If possible, have books by the author or illustrator available for purchase several days ahead of the visit for an autographing session.

Such preparations will enable students to appreciate the visit even more, as will the author or illustrator who sees responses to his or her books lining the school hallways. A great welcome will ensure a memorable visit! Have children write thank you notes as a follow-up to the visit.

If a visit is not possible, some teachers have good luck sending a list of children's questions and a blank cassette to an author or illustrator via the publisher. Some will respond on cassette and send it back to the classroom—which is almost like a personal phone call from a favorite author or illustrator!

Writing Letters Writing letters to authors and illustrators is often a favorite classroom activity. We suggest that you offer this as an activity children can do individually, or write a class letter if the enthusiasm is high for a particular author or illustrator. Always make sure the author or illustrator is still living by checking with the publisher for the most up to date information, or one of the sources listed below. It is also worthwhile to write to publishers directly. They are sometimes very generous in terms of sending biographical information, posters, and the like.

Biographical Sources Check your school, public, or university library for the following reference books. They contain fascinating and interesting information about authors and illustrators.

Behind the Covers: Interviews with Authors and Illustrators of Books for Children and Young Adults (1985)
Famous Children's Authors. Book 2. (1989)
Fifth Book of Junior Authors and Illustrators (1983)
Fourth Book of Junior Authors and Illustrators (1978)
More Junior Authors (1969)
Sixth Book of Junior Authors and Illustrators (1989)

Something About the Author (1990)
The Junior Book of Authors (1951)
Third Book of Junior Authors and Illustrators (1972)
Twentieth-Century Children's Writers, 3rd ed. (1989)

Start to build an author/illustrator file by duplicating information from these sources and storing the information in manila folders.

Another invaluable classroom resource is *Long Ago and Far Away: An Encyclopedia for Successfully Using Literature with Intermediate Readers* (Hurst, 1991) and *Once Upon a Time: An Encyclopedia for Successfully Using Literature with Young Readers* (Hurst, 1992). In the text for intermediate readers, Hurst includes a section profiling popular authors and illustrators. For example, did you know that Cynthia Voigt, who wrote *Homecoming* (1981), was inspired to write this novel after seeing a bunch of kids sitting in a car in a parking lot? She wondered what would happen if no one came back for them. Did you know that Chris Van Allsburg, the author and illustrator of *Jumanji* (1981), did not like board games when he was a child? Did you know that Gary Paulsen, author of *Dogsong* (1985), raced in the 1,049 mile Iditarod dogsled race three times? Paulsen experienced many hardships along the route—falling through ice, a moose attack, and being dragged by his pack of dogs. Cookie, his lead dog, is the only dog he ended up keeping as a pet. Hurst also offers teachers biographical information about 40 more authors and illustrators, information on thematic units focusing on books, and a "books at a glance" section, which includes a summary of a book, related books by the author, and response suggestions.

The following books present some authors' viewpoints—humorous and otherwise—about writing for children:

Lotus Seeds: Children, Pictures, and Books by Marcia Brown (1986)

Talent is Not Enough: Mollie Hunter on Writing for Children by Mollie Hunter (1976)
Worlds of Childhood: The Art and Craft of Writing for Children, edited by William Zinsser (1990). This volume includes essays by Jean Fritz, Maurice Sendak, Jill Krementz, Jack Prelutsky, Rosemary Wells, and Katherine Paterson.
Dear Mem Fox, I Have Read All Your Books Even the Pathetic Ones and Other Incidents in the Life of a Children's Book Author by Mem Fox (1992)
The Spying Heart by Katherine Paterson (1989)

Teachers will also find that children will enjoy the following author/illustrator biographies/autobiographies/memoirs:

A Girl from Yamhill: A Memoir by Beverly Cleary
Presenting William Sleator by James David and Hazel Davis
Self-Portrait: Trina Schart Hyman by Trina Schart Hyman
Stars Come Out Within by Jean Little
Starting from Home: A Writer's Beginnings by Milton Meltzer
The Art Lesson by Tomie de Paola
The Moon and I by Betsy Byars
The Pigman & Me by Paul Zindel
When I Was Nine by James Stevenson
Woodsong by Gary Paulsen

Fourth-grade teacher Cathy Swanson shared the book *How I Came to Be a Writer* by Phyllis Reynolds Naylor (1987). Naylor's books include *The Agony of Alice* (1985), *Alice in Rapture, Sort Of* (1989), *All but Alice* (1992), *Reluctantly Alice* (1991), and *Shiloh* (1991)—a Newbery Award–winning book.

Figure 12.3 presents a fourth grader's author web depicting some of the important points in Naylor's life. Another fourth grader wrote a list entitled "Advice From a Writer" and then summarized some of the chapters from the book (see Figure 12.4).

Several children made some other reading and writing connections using *Shiloh*. The story focuses on a dog named Shiloh, who is mistreated by Judd, his owner. Eleven-year-old Marty comes to the dog's rescue by hiding him from Judd. However, Marty faces the dilemma of whether hiding the dog to protect it is stealing. One child made a chart comparing Judd and Shiloh using similes. This is depicted below in Figure 12.5.

Figure 12.6 presents the work of two other students, a poem for "two voices" based on characteristics of Judd and Marty. These two young poets have been influenced by Paul Fleischman's poetry—*I Am Phoenix: Poems for Two Voices* (1985) and *Joyful Noise: Poems for Two Voices* (1988).

BOOK CHARACTERS WHO WRITE

School librarian Abigail Garthwait (1993) writes about books that help student writers consider various aspects of the writing process. She also includes questions, such as the following, for student writers to consider as they read books in which characters are writers:

Why does the main character write?
What does writing do for the character? How can you tell? Does it involve any character development?
How does the character's writing fit into the theme?
How does writing fit into the character's life? Is it as essential to that character as eat-

ing, sleeping, or breathing? Is it peripheral?
Can you make any generalizations about what type of character writes?
Is the writer seen as a stereotype (i.e., bookish, creative)?

MAKING THE READING/ WRITING CONNECTION

Betty Robinson, a veteran fifth- and sixth-grade teacher, incorporated writer's workshop in her classrooms years ago, having been influenced by the writings of Donald Graves (1983, 1989a, 1989b, 1990, 1991). She has been an advocate of incorporating literature throughout the curriculum and has seen the direct benefits of a reading writing connection over the years.

For example, Betty's students read many more books when given time to read in the classroom. She has also seen how becoming readers has improved their writing. Students are reading like writers and writing like readers. Literature provides the raw material for writers. Most adult writers would no doubt say that they are voracious readers who look at the written works of others in a different light.

Betty strategically helps her students see the links between what an effective writer does and their own writing. She does not leave this to chance; she makes wise choices about what to read aloud to students as one valuable vehicle to help students talk about what makes effective writing. Talking about the writer's craft after reading aloud helps students see that it was something the author did to make the writing so effective.

For example, when reading aloud *The True Confessions of Charlotte Doyle* by Avi (1990), Betty asks students to reflect on the *lead* or *beginning* of the book.

Not every 13-year-old girl is accused of murder, brought to trial, and found guilty. But I was just such a girl, and my story is worth relating even if it did happen years ago. (p. 1)

It is clear to Betty's students that this novel has a very strong lead: It literally pulls them in to want to find out more. Betty thus leads them into a discussion of why Avi's technique of drawing in an audience works, why they want to know more about why Charlotte, an eighteenth-century girl aboard a ship, is accused of committing murder.

FIGURE 12.3   A Fourth Grader's Web of Author Phyllis Reynolds Naylor's Life

FIGURE 12.4   A Fourth Grader's Summary of Author Phyllis Reynolds Naylor's Advice To Writers

Advice from a Writer

1. READ
2. Learn the basics of the story:
      Main characters that
         sruggles a problem and solves it

3. Don't make characters PREDICTABLE
4. Get your 1st draft on paper
         (revistions will come more easier)
5. Write about what you know best
6. Write down ideas! Brainstorm!
7. Keep it simple - have a cenral theme
8. Belive in your plot or no one else
      will either
9. Be accurate in reserch
10. Write often (Daily)
11. Write were you are comfortable
12. "Good enough" is NOT good enough
13. The first page is most difficult
      (but important because it sets the
            pace)
14. Read aloud to friends, to yourself
15. Make a peronal connection
16. Characters should change in some
      way

Betty asks students to consider what other ways Avi excited them. How did Avi "paint" a picture with his words about what Charlotte and the other characters on the ship were like? What was it like to leave England on a ship with no other females aboard? In what ways does Avi help readers to feel as though they are on the journey as well?

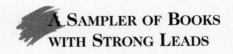

A SAMPLER OF BOOKS WITH STRONG LEADS

Alexander and the Terrible, Horrible, No Good, Very Bad Day by Judith Viorst
Charlotte's Web by E. B. White
Hatchet by Gary Paulsen

FIGURE 12.4 *Continued*

<u>Starting from Scratch</u>
Thes chapter means she's just getting started on writing she never dreamed she would become a writer.

a bubble Burst
First Phyllis sends away one of her stories to a church. Then a few days later she received a check of $4.67. Then she send away more of her stories so they could be put in childrens magazines. and every story came back. Then she sent more storie away, and again every storie came back exept one and in it's place she received a check for $60.00.

<u>A long Climb</u>
a long climb means it takes a long time to reach your goal. In this chapter it told that with many rejctions slips she slowly began selling stories to still more churches

Missing May by Cynthia Rylant
Queenie Peavy by R. Burch
Sarah, Plain and Tall by Patricia MacLachlan
The Best Christmas Pageant Ever by B. Robinson
The Indian in the Cupboard by Lynne Reid Banks
The True Confessions of Charlotte Doyle by Avi

Betty looks for novels where the *development of character* is a very strong feature. She asks students

to consider in what ways author Patricia MacLachlan writes about characters so that we identify with them and that we feel apart of their lives. Betty chooses MacLachlan's Newbery award–winning book, *Sarah, Plain and Tall* (1985). She presents students with a variety of questions. In what ways are the major characters developed throughout the story? How does MacLachlan use language to describe the characters in such a way that they remain memorable long after the book is finished? Since students are excited about MacLachlan's writ-

FIGURE 12.4 *Continued*

> The Things That Make Me Up
> I chapter four I noticed that
> Phyllis was told by a real poet
> to write about what you know
> best. And thats what you ussally
> tell us when we are stuck on
> something to write.
>
> From Paragraphs to Chapters
> In chapter 5, Phyllis made a
> mistake that many beginning
> book writers do. She sat down
> wrote a long list of every-
> thing exiting that could poss-
> obly happen at the ocean. When
> Phyllis ends her chapers, the last
> sentence ussally has to do with the
> title of the next chapter.

ing, Betty suggests that they read other titles by her, such as *Arthur, For the Very First Time* (1980); *Cassie Binegar* (1982); *The Facts and Fictions of Minna Pratt* (1988); *Unclaimed Treasures* (1984); and *Through Grandpa's Eyes* (1980).

A SAMPLER OF BOOKS WITH STRONG CHARACTERS

Call it Courage by Armstrong Sperry
Island of the Blue Dolphins by Scott O'Dell
Julie of the Wolves by Jean Craighead George
Missing May by Cynthia Rylant
The Door in the Wall by Marguerite de Angeli
The Pinballs by Betsy Byars

The Sign of the Beaver by Elizabeth George Speare
The Stone-Faced Boy by Paula Fox

Setting is usually a strong feature of historical fiction novels. Readers need to have a clear picture not only about where the story took place but also about the time period. Betty chooses such titles as *My Brother Sam is Dead* (1974) by James Lincoln Collier and Christopher Collier and the World War II novel, *Journey to Topaz* (1985) by Yoshiko Uchida. She also chooses historical fiction in picture book format. The titles she chooses are age-appropriate and quick to read. A favorite in this genre is Cynthia Rylant's *When I Was Young in the Mountains* (1982), a wonderful story about the author's childhood in the Appalachian Mountains. Diane Goode's illustrations, combined with

Rylant's writing style, make this book a memorable and rich source for discussion.

Betty also chooses from other types of books, in addition to historical fiction, where authors effectively use language to "paint" vivid and memorable settings. Some examples include *A Wizard of Earthsea* (1968) by Ursula LeGuin and the already familiar *Charlotte's Web* (1952) by E. B. White.

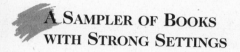

A SAMPLER OF BOOKS WITH STRONG SETTINGS

Anna, Grandpa, and the Big Storm by Carla Stevens
Charlotte's Web by E. B. White
Dogsong by Gary Paulsen
Lyddie by Katherine Paterson

On to Oregon! by Honore Morrow
One Morning in Maine by Robert McCloskey
Prairie Songs by Pam Conrad
Sarah, Plain and Tall by Patricia MacLachlan
Sounder by William Armstrong
The Witch of Blackbird Pond by Elizabeth George Speare
Time of Wonder by Robert McCloskey
When I Was Young in the Mountains by Cynthia Rylant

Other sources that Betty uses include books in which plots are strong and fast-moving. Natalie Babbitt's *The Eyes of the Amarylis* serves as a good model to discuss the author's use of figurative language. She also reads aloud several of Gary Paulen's books. One that is particularly successful is *Hatchet*, the story of a boy's survival in the Canadian wilderness after a plane crash. Sensing the enthusiasm of her listeners, she asks students

FIGURE 12.5

Jud is as mean as a bull

Shiloh is as nice as a cat

Jud is as gross as histabbcoo

Shiloh is as clean as a house cleaner

Jud is as dumb as his thumb

Shiloh is as smart as a fox

Jud is as ugly as a halloween mask

Shiloh is as hansom as a model

Jud is as evil as the devil

Shiloh is as good as an angel

They Both have their diffrenecs

FIGURE 12.6

Two Voices

Marty is as sweet as an angel	Judd is as mean as a wolf.
Marty is as brave as a bear.	And Judd is as evil as the devil
Marty is as caring as a mother.	Judd is as cruel as a child Killer
<u>I</u> <u>hate</u> <u>that</u> <u>Boy!</u>	<u>I</u> <u>hate</u> <u>that</u> <u>Judd!</u>

to discuss the effectiveness of Paulsen's wording, which makes this such an enjoyable story.

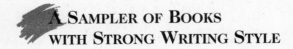

A SAMPLER OF BOOKS WITH STRONG WRITING STYLE

Anastasia Krupnik by Lois Lowry
Dicey's Song by Cynthia Voigt
Hatchet by Gary Paulsen
Incident at Hawk's Hill by Allan W. Eckert

Jacob Have I Loved by Katherine Paterson
The Cry of the Crow by Jean Craighead George
The Devil's Arithmetic by Jane Yolen
The Winter Room by Gary Paulsen
Tuck Everlasting by Natalie Babbitt

Betty's read-aloud sessions often evolve into the content of minilessons that will provide a focus for that morning's writer's workshop, which usually lasts about one hour everyday. It is a time for Betty's students to self-select topics, write drafts, conference with each over the drafts, revise, and edit to bring a piece to completion. She asks students to consider their own writing as a result of their discussion of a particular writer's strengths. Betty's role is that of a guide encouraging students to conference with each other about leads, character development, and setting, etc. In this way students can begin to view their strengths as writers and to see that what they read can have an influence on what they write. These students typically begin to read their own self-selected books with a more critical eye. They read beyond the plot level.

In conferencing with Mike, Betty learns that he wants to write his own survival story in the style of Gary Paulsen. Betty suggests that Mike begin by reading other kinds of survival stories such as *Lost on a Mountain in Maine* by Donn Fendler, *My Side of the Mountain* by Jean Craighead George, and the sequel *On the Far Side of the Mountain,* among others. In this way, Mike will see that other authors have written compelling survival stories and that in reading them he can not only enjoy the stories but begin to more critically examine each writer's unique style.

Betty tells her class that she has been keeping a journal since she was a child. She records memoirs, poetry she writes, and notes about writing. Megan, a student who loves to read and write, tells Betty that she decided to also keep a journal. Megan as well as other members of the class became interested in book characters who write—and those who keep journals and diaries.

Here is a sampler of books Betty gathered in which characters use journals or diaries.

A Book of Your Own: Keeping a Diary or Journal by Carla Stevens
A Gathering of Days: A New England Girls' Journal by Joan Blos
Dear Mr. Henshaw by Beverly Cleary
I, Columbus: My Journal—1492–3 by Peter Roop and Connie Roop
Nettie's Trip South by Ann Turner
Nothing But the Truth by Avi
The Burning Questions of Bingo Brown by Betsy Byars
The Death of Evening Star: The Diary of a Young New England Whaler by Leonard Fisher

FIGURE 12.7

Chapter on the Stranger

On a dark stormy night the rain was coming down in sheds. Slowly a tall dark figure made his way to the door of a stately home. He rang the bell, it echoed down the empty street. Again and again he rang the bell soon all that could be hear were the ecos of the bell..... at lenth a sour faced woman apeard. She said rudely," Who do ya think you are ringin that there bell at this cussed time o'night!"

"Ahem", the stranger replied.

"Oh, its you the master'll see ya ri' iss way sir."

"Thank you mam but I shant be needing any more assistence thank you," he replied sharply.

The Diary of Trilby Frost by Diane Glaster
The Island by Gary Paulsen
The Man Who Was Poe by Avi
The Private Worlds of Julia Redfern by Eleanor Cameron
The True Confessions of Charlotte Doyle by Avi

During reader's workshop, Megan decides to read *Oliver Twist* by Charles Dickens. During a reading conference midway through the book, Betty asked her why she chose this particular book. Megan's reply was, "I like how you talk about some of the great authors from long ago—like how you love Shakespeare, so I decided to find a really old book and read it, too!" An excerpt from a first draft written by Megan is presented in Figure 12.7.

Anyone familiar with the writing of Charles Dickens will see that Megan has tried to incorporate some features of his writing in her own piece. In fact, Betty said that when Megan read her chapters aloud during share circle, she had obviously rehearsed because she used a British accent! Everyone was intrigued and wanted to know what influenced Megan to write the story. This example, again, points to the strong influence reading has on what children write.

Another example of reading influencing writing can be seen in a story written by Molly, enti-

FIGURE 12.8

The Stinky Cheese Room By Molly Edwards as told to Cathy Edwards

When I was 2 years old I woke up earlier than my mom. I was always helping her with cleaning. That morning I thought I'd with vaccumm. I couldn't reach the chemcial cuboard to get the carpet fresh so I looked in the refrigerater. I open up the door and I saw a container that I had seen before. I took it out and sprinkled it all over the rug and furinture, the whole bottle. I didn't know what it was but when mom woke up she sure did. It was parmesan cheese. It stunk so bad she almost fainted. My mom thought there was a sweaty army in the living room. Then she realized it was parmesan cheese. My mom had to laugh! The bad thing was is that we had to vaccumm it up after she woke up. It was so bad we had to open the doors and windows.

The End!

Molly's writing, as influenced by hearing *The Stinky Cheese Man and Other Fairly Stupid Tales* read aloud.

tled "The Stinky Cheese Room" (see Figure 12.8). Molly decided to write this version after hearing Betty read *The Stinky Cheese Man and Other Fairly Stupid Tales* by Jon Scieszka (1992). The stories in this humorous book are parodies of some of our treasured folktales. Scieszka and illustrators Lane Smith and Steve Johnson are masters at creating the absurd in words and pictures. Betty's students also have enjoyed Scieszka's *The True Story of the Three Little Pigs by A. Wolf,* illustrated by Lane Smith (1989), and *The Frog Prince Continued,* illustrated by Steve Johnson (1991).

Betty offers this summary of what her students do in sixth grade: "These kids really amaze me. I read their writing and say, 'Wow!' They're saying such incredible things through their writing. I don't think this would happen without their rich experiences with literature!"

USING LANGUAGE-RICH BOOKS

Children in Priscilla Sawyer's second-grade class are avid readers and writers. At the beginning of the school year, Priscilla introduces writing journal responses to books by reading to the class and talking about ways students could write their reactions to books. Priscilla chooses language-rich books such as the following:

Brave Irene by William Steig
One Morning in Maine by Robert McCloskey
Owl Moon by Jane Yolen
Rosie's Walk by Pat Hutchins
Say It by Charlotte Zolotow
Swimmy by Leo Lionni
The Garden of Abdul Gasazi by Chris Van Allsburg
The Village of Round and Square Houses by Ann Grifalconi

Priscilla and the class came up with five questions to consider when they write journal responses:

1. What did you like or dislike about the book?
2. How did the book make you feel?
3. What did the book remind you of?
4. What did the book make you think about?
5. What did you think about the characters?

FIGURE 12.9

The Garden of Abdul G.

The book left me wondering and got me a little exited. Before the end I wondered how the dog would ever get back. I also wonded how the hat would ever get back And at the end when the dog and the hat are back I wondered if the dog was a duck at all.

FIGURE 12.10

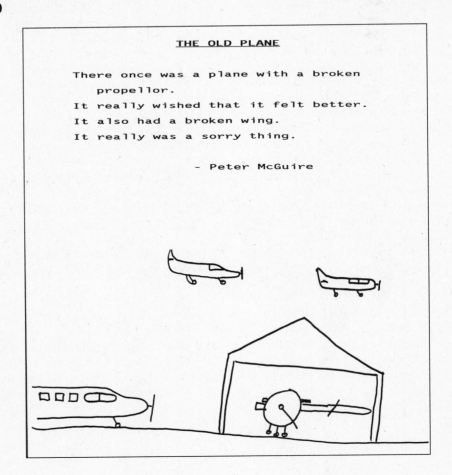

Figure 12.9 presents one journal entry by children in Priscilla's class who responded to the *Garden of Abdul Gasazi* by Chris Van Allsburg (1979).

Children in Priscilla's class also love to write poetry. Figure 12.10 illustrates the final copies of poetry children wrote after Priscilla read aloud *Flight*, written by Robert Burleigh and illustrated by Michael Wimmer (1991).

Adele Ames's first graders are hungry for all the literature she can provide. The "literary seeds" that Adele is planting with this group yield great and wonderful results.

Adele read aloud *Brown Bear, Brown Bear, What Do You See?* by Bill Martin Jr. and illustrated by Eric Carle (1983). The children then created their own version, entitled *Butterfly, Butterfly, What Do You See?*, which uses the same language pattern as the original version. Their "new" words are in parentheses.

Butterfly, Butterfly What Do You See?

Butterfly, butterfly what do you see?
I see a black caterpillar looking (spinning) at me?

FIGURE 12.10   *Continued*

FLIGHT

Flying eagles everywhere
Life is fun up here
I wish I was here too
Going going gone
Hot air balloons soaring slowly
Texas to Toronto

- Amy Freeman

Black caterpillar black caterpillar what do you see?
I see a green chrysalis looking (opening up) at me.

Green chrysalis green chrysalis what do you see?
I see a bluebird looking (making faces) at me.

Bluebird bluebird what do you see?
I see a yellow sun looking (shining) at me.

Yellow sun yellow sun what do you see?
I see a red ladybug looking (blinking) at me.

Red ladybug red ladybug what do you see?
I see an orange duck looking (quacking) at me.

Orange duck orange duck what do you see?
I see a purple rainbow looking (smiling) at me.

Purple rainbow purple rainbow what do you see?
I see a pink flower looking (growing) at me.

Pink flower pink flower what do you see?

I see YOU looking at me!

FIGURE 12.11

PROJECT LOG

Date: March 24

Action: Today we went to the library and I checked out a book called Anne Frank: Life In Hiding. It's by Joanna Hurwitz I also used the World Book Encycopedia

Reflection/Next step: I don't think that got that much done today because I came late (I was at mis Mayers).

Date: March 30

Action: Today I recorded all the information that I learned from the Anne Frank book and some of their dates

Reflection/Next step: I feel I got a lot of information Collected today. tomorrow I wanted to pick a Surtain subject.

READING AND WRITING ACROSS THE CURRICULUM

Reading and writing connections should not be limited to "language arts" time. Children need to read and write in different ways across all curricular areas. Cathy Swanson's fourth graders also read from a variety of genres and write research reports. The students keep logs and plans as records of their research process. Examples from Mara's work related to the Holocaust are included in Figures 12.11 through 12.14.

Students need to examine how authors of nonfiction books make their writing interesting and exciting. For example, sixth-grade teacher Betty Robinson chooses nonfiction titles with strong leads, interesting language, and unique formats. She helps students understand that writers need to capture their audience right from the start, no matter if they are writing a short story, a novel, or even nonfiction. For example, Betty chose Russell Freedman's *Lincoln: A Photobiography* (1987) to demonstrate how one author approaches the process of writing about someone's life. Initially, some students think that this kind of writing will be boring, but Betty surprises them as she reads the opening lines of Freedman's book:

> Abraham Lincoln wasn't the sort of man who could lose himself in a crowd. After all, he stood six feet four inches tall, and to top it off, he wore a high silk hat. (p. 1)

Betty also chooses other well-written nonfiction, sometimes in picture book format, to show students that nonfiction need not be dry or boring. Again, Betty is strategic in her decision making. Her students write research reports on self-selected topics—the rain forest, a famous inventor, the brain, dinosaurs, a favorite author such as Betsy Byars or Katherine Paterson, or anything else they are interested in pursuing. If Betty does not directly engage students in conversation about what makes examples of nonfiction writing successful, students may retreat to a writing style they are most familiar with in terms of nonfiction—encyclopedia and textbooks writing.

Betty knows she cannot just *tell* students to make their report writing lively and interesting; she has to *show* them what successful nonfiction writers do to capture a reader's attention. Betty accomplishes this by inviting students to follow a variety of routes.

They begin by examining the format of books. How are illustrations and photographs placed in the text? Does the author use some kind of interesting format in which to relay information? For example, the *Magic School Bus* series by Joanna Cole illustrates a clever technique. Even though these books are appropriate for younger readers, Betty likes to refer to them because of Cole's device of including a story within a story. The books revolve around a character named Mrs. Frizzle, a teacher who takes her students on various adventures—through the human body, the solar system, and the waterworks, etc. Throughout each adventure, Mrs. Frizzle's students learn valuable information about a particular topic.

Aliki also uses similar techniques in her dinosaur books, where readers feel as though they are walking through a museum to learn about dinosaurs. Patricia Lauber in her Newbery award–winning title, *The News About Dinosaurs* (1989), uses a format whereby one page provides readers with what used to be thought about dinosaurs, then the next page presents new findings.

A SAMPLER OF EXCELLENT NONFICTION WRITERS

AUTHOR	SAMPLE TITLES
Aliki	*Mummies Made in Egypt; Dinosaur Bones*
Vicki Cobb	*Why Can't You Unscramble an Egg? and Often Not Such Dumb Questions About Matter; For Your Own Protection: Stories Science Photos Tell*
Joanna Cole	*Magic School Bus* Series; *Large as Life Animals: In Beautiful Life-Size Paintings*
Russell Freedman	*Children of the Wild West; Immigrant Kids; Indian Chiefs*
Gail Gibbons	*The Milk Makers; New Road!; From Seed to Plant*
Joan Goodall	*The Story of an English Village; The Story of a Farm; The Story of a Castle*
Holling C. Holling	*Paddle to the Sea; Minn of the Mississippi*
Jill Krementz	*The Fun of Cooking; How it Feels to Fight for Your Life*
Kathryn Lasky	*Sugaring Time; Traces of Life: The Origins of Humankind*
Patricia Lauber	*Tales Mummies Tell; Volcano: The Eruption and Healing of Mt. St. Helens; The News About Dinosaurs; Summer of Fire: Yellowstone 1988*
David Macaulay	*Underground; Pyramid; Castle; The Way Things Work*
Milton Meltzer	*All Times, All Peoples: A World History of Slavery; The Black Americans; A History in Their Own Words*
Dorothy Hinshaw Patent	*Farm Animals; Spider Magic; Whales: Giants of the Deep; Gray Wolf, Red Wolf; Yellowstone Fires; Flames and Rebirth.*

How did Betty become acquainted with so many books? She obviously did not have all of these titles at her fingertips when she started teaching. However, because she valued the use of literature in her classroom and began to see the benefits right away in the first years of her teaching, she became committed to remaining updated on new titles and ways to incorporate books into the curriculum. Here are some of the ways she did that.

Betty subscribes to many professional publications and finds it is most efficient to receive them at home, where there is more of a likelihood of them being read. Full-time students can receive journals from such organizations as the International Reading Association and the National Council of Teachers of English at discounted rates.

Betty attends state and regional reading and language arts conferences and several national ones. These provide a vital opportunity to mix with like-minded professionals. As a student, find out how you can join local and state affiliates of the International Reading Association and the National Council of Teachers of English. Another opportunity is to find out whether there is a TAWL (Teachers Applying Whole Language) group in your area. TAWL groups have sprung up all over the country. Many of them hold informal meetings where, again, like-minded teachers and administrators can get together to talk about current practices in literacy.

Betty also attends workshops and conferences sponsored by the local university. She takes advantage of any opportunity to hear experts in the field of children's literature and other aspects of literacy learning. She also enjoys attending sessions where children's authors are speaking. It is a wonderful experience to actually see, in person, an author she admires. If it is possible, she also arranges to have students attend these sessions.

Betty has also established classroom sets of books that connect with each other in some way.

The survival story is one category she has focused on. As she has explored this topic, which is of so much interest to her students, she has discovered related books from other genres besides contemporary realistic fiction. For example, her collection includes historical fiction novels such as the World War II novel *The Devil's Arithmetic* by Jane Yolen and another of the same time period, *Number the Stars* by Lois Lowry. She also found Elizabeth George Speare's exciting novel of one boy's survival alone in the Maine woods of the 1700s, *The Sign of the Beaver*.

Other literature sets include books done by the same illustrator—Chris Van Allsburg, for example. Her students enjoy the magic Van Allsburg creates with his words and illustrations. Other sets include books about Maine (realistic fiction, historical fiction, nonfiction, and poetry titles related to living in Maine), dinosaurs, the rain forest, and friendship. It did take considerable time for Betty to acquire these books from her many sources—book clubs, bookstores, and libraries—but she feels the rewards are endless when she is able to place the right book in the hands of a student at just the right time.

Choosing Nonfiction Books

As children research areas of interest, it is important to make a wide variety of sources available, including books representing all genres—from picture books to poetry to nonfiction. Since nonfiction will be a primary source of information, use the following criteria to help with your selection process (adapted from Huck, Hepler and Hickman, 1993):

- Is the material current?
- Is the material substantiated by facts, or is it just the author's opinion?
- What are the author's qualifications to write such a book?

FIGURE 12.12

PROJECT PLAN

Name: Mara Shorr

Collaborators: ————————

Project Topic: Holocaust

What do I know about this topic:
- Over 1,000,000 jews were killed
- the war involved Hitler
- it took Place in or near Poland
- it was ment to torture the jews
- If the German soldiers found out that you
were jewish that would be the end for you.

What questions would I like to answer as I explore this topic?:

■ why did Hitler want to kill anybody?

■ what was it about the jews that made him kill them?

■ How did the "war" finally stop?

- Is the writing style lively; will it appeal to its intended audience?
- Is the information clearly organized and presented?
- In what ways does the book's format (i.e. use of graphics, photographs, illustrations, charts, reference information, etc.) contribute to the contents?

Australian teacher Jan Weis (1986) began to see the importance of weaving in reading and writing as students studied across subject areas, such as science and social studies.

Here is a partial list of reading, writing, and thinking activities she developed:

- Freewriting to record prior knowledge and learning outcomes and to share understandings.
- Brainstorming, listing, categorizing, and structuring information to show relationships among ideas.

FIGURE 12.13

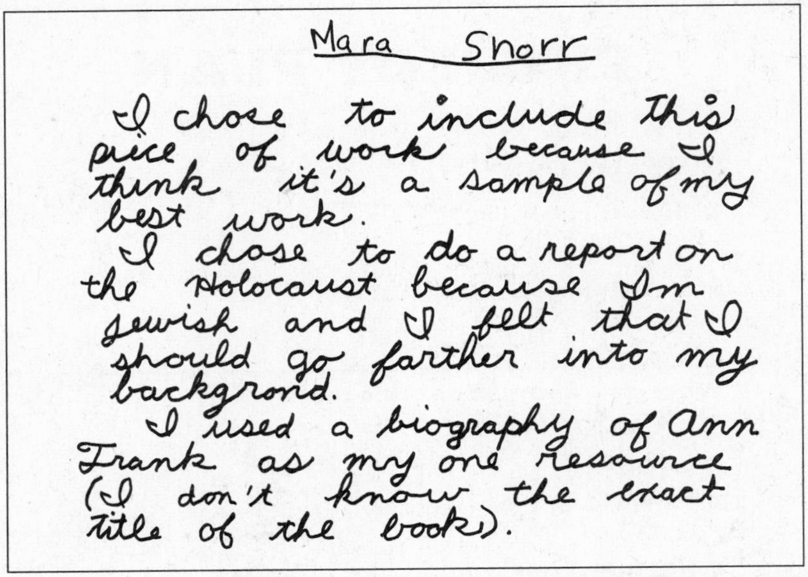

> Mara Snorr
>
> I chose to include this piece of work because I think it's a sample of my best work.
> I chose to do a report on the Holocaust because I'm Jewish and I felt that I should go farther into my backgrond.
> I used a biography of Ann Frank as my one resource (I don't know the exact title of the book).

- Challenging each other's thinking; questioning to clarify understanding.
- Abstracting main ideas and comparing them in small groups to negotiate a common set of key points.
- Recording ideas in small groups during discussion and sharing them across groups.
- Note-taking to show distinctions between main ideas and supporting details; summarizing ideas and justifying their inclusion or omission.
- Developing draft writing in response to information gleaned from text and discussion, for specific purposes and audiences, from various points of view and in forms appropriate to the occasion (p. 69).

Weis (1986) reflects her own learning process in this way:

> Whereas previously I had separated writing and reading in Language Arts from writing and reading in other subject areas, I came to appreciate their power to make thinking explicit and to extend learning beyond subject "boundaries." . . . What impressed me most was that both the children and I became more critical reviewers of our own knowledge, challenging not only what we found for ourselves, but also the very basis of how we knew what we thought we did know. (p. 80)

In summary, planting literary "seeds" by sharing, talking, and responding to good books will help strong literary roots to take hold, grow, and develop.

FIGURE 12.14

Hi! My name is Mara Shorr and I'm going to do my best to explain the Holocaust to you. The Holocaust was the "war" when Adolf Hitler tried to kill the Jews. Why did Hitler want to kill anybody? You see, Hitler tried to kill the Jews as part of his plans to conquer the world. Otherwise Adolf Hitler was a sick man with a cold heart.

the Holocaust started in 1933 and ended in 1945. In between these years over 6,000,000 Jews were killed. Many Jews hid in closets, rooms, basements, and anywhere else they could so that the Natzis (National Socialist German Workers Party) wouldn't find them. Jewish kids couldn't go to school. If Jews were found them and who ever was hiding them would be arrested and sent to a concentration camp.

Some Jews formed a secret group called a Resistance that bombed the German Buildings. Sometimes this kept other Jews from being arrested. Most shops at that time were forbidden to go into if you were Jewish.

CATHY SWANSON'S JOURNAL

April 28

Murphy's Law of Planning In a Whole Language Classroom:
What you planned to happen *won't*.
What you didn't plan to happen *will!*

So it seems at times! Today I planned to read Tomie de Paola's *Legend of the Indian Paintbrush* and talk about legends as a genre. I was excited about this lesson because I felt it integrated so many things: art, the study of the regions, our earlier study of flowers, writing, speaking, listening, and the value of contributing one's gift to a larger community. The kids would work in pairs to write their own legends about flowers indigenous to the southwestern U.S. whose names, I thought, would easily inspire legends. These included Knotweeds, Shooting Stars, Adder's Tongues, Rabbit Brushes, and Spider Flowers. Once the legends were written, we would record them on cassette tape and make a "buckskin canvas" out of torn paper stretched on a slick frame (similar to the canvas in the story).

Well, the kids enjoyed the story. A nice discussion followed. I read a legend I wrote to model how I listened to the story and emulated the style. Piece of cake, right? *Wrong!!*

Even those kids who usually have "blazing pencils" were struggling. After circulating for awhile and trying to help them get started, I realized this just wasn't working. We regrouped on the floor and discussed what was happening. Travis wanted to pick a different flower (originally, I had them pick a xeroxed picture of the flowers out of a bag). Others quickly agreed. We opted for a fresh start tomorrow.

❧ May 1

What I love most about Dr. Dugan's class, "Teacher as Researcher," is the opportunity to philosophize, to share, to learn from each other professionally. There are 11 of us enrolled this semester; a mix of elementary teachers, a secondary art teacher, an elementary counselor, and a reading specialist.

Although our research pursuits are varied, we are all fascinated by the questions raised and the journeys we have collectively taken to answer them. Brenda questioned the relationship between the language arts and visual learning. Bev wanted to see what happened when she became a committed journal-keeper and shared that experience with her students. Lynn observed the effect using a computer had on the early writing experiences of kindergartners. Sue (the counselor) wrote about her use of journals with students in denial. All the topics were truly interesting!

So often we tell our students to "share what you learned" with a peer; too seldom do we get to do that ourselves—at least on this level. This has been the most inspiring, reaffirming, thought-provoking experience; this kind of experience is of paramount importance.

❧ May 3

Today the first of the legends were presented! WOW! They were remarkable. I realize, in hindsight, that the kids were overwhelmed because the task I set before them had too many levels for them to handle all at once. When they broke it down into several smaller tasks (look at the appearance of the flower, decide how it got its name, decide on a character to deliver the story) they were able to soar! These decisions came about through purposeful conversation/negotiation.

We recorded several of the legends and did start the accompanying art project. At the end of the day, we listened to the tape again, noting that several pairs chose very different explanations for how the flowers got their names.

✦ May 6

Putting the new exhibits together has been a real learning experience! The best part has been all the storytelling that has been fostered. As the kids bring in the items selected for their exhibit, they want to share what they chose and why.

John picked a ceramic head his mother sculpted when she was in school. The face was "punched in," the result of his mom's reaction to an insensitive comment her art teacher made. She liked the piece better after she "reshaped" it, and the kids loved the story!

Josh brought in an admired sketchbook belonging to his cousin; Elena displayed a quilt sewn by her mother, an excellent craftsperson; Billy chose a print by Renoir, the same one that hangs on their living room wall and is the family favorite.

In addition to the pieces selected, everyone made a "minigallery" of family portraits that were displayed at the forefront of their exhibits. Brochures described the collections and told of the reasons the pieces were selected. In the center of the gallery, a table with flowers and a guest book solicited comments about their presentations.

The storytelling continued during open house as parents came in and admired each others' work. Bill received many compliments on his ceramic bear that dated back to his elementary school days. The theme for this exhibit fostered a much stronger sense of history, sense of family than I ever expected.

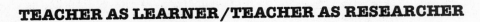

TEACHER AS LEARNER/TEACHER AS RESEARCHER

Observation Techniques

Imagine yourself at the end of a busy school day. The last group of students leave on the bus for the ride home. With a cup of coffee in hand, you decide to take a few well-deserved minutes for yourself. Reflecting on the day's events becomes a blur of activity. To help sort out all of the activity and reflect upon what went well and the challenges throughout the day, you open your journal and begin writing. As you muse over your notes, you begin to wonder what really took place and realize that you missed some of the special things your children mentioned to you that day. Now, what was it that Yolanda said about the book she brought from home? Jason and Paul really seemed to be making some progress during their writing conference, but you cannot recall their conversation because you were interrupted by a teacher coming in to ask you to take recess duty. Your journal notes reveal lots of gaps that might prove to be revealing about your teaching and the ways students interacted throughout the day. One way to help you organize and "size-up" the day is to make more deliberate observations of students at work (and

play). You can begin to do this by trying out some observational techniques.

Kidwatching (Goodman et al., 1989) is an informal way to document and make sense of student learning. Carry a clipboard around with you as you observe students working independently and in small groups. Jot down notes or anecdotal records as you make your observations. (See Chapters 4 and 6 for more information on notetaking procedures.) Try making your observations through the eyes of a child. Listen carefully to student comments. For instance, second-grade teacher Skip Andrews was surprised to overhear Samuel, a shy and reticent little boy, say that his mom had taken him to the library three Saturdays in a row! Skip assumed that Samuel did not have those kinds of opportunities at home. As a result of this careful listening, Skip planned to invite Samuel into the discussion at the end of the week about books he might recommend for others to read.

Skip also decided to look for any recurring patterns in what children do in reading and writing. These patterns might inform him as to what his students believe is important. For example, Skip began to see the writing Miranda did every day in a new light when he noted that her stories began with a decorated first letter, similar to the ones used in some of the fairytales Skip had been reading aloud with students. This behavior informed Skip that Miranda was making some important connections between her work and the literature read in class.

In addition to keeping informal observational notes, Skip also prepared classroom observational recording guides. One such guide lists each student's name, a space for the date, and then large blocks of space to record what happens during reading and writing conferences, as well as during other times of the day—for example, during math or recess. Skip also designed another form focusing on several behaviors he believes are important in literacy learning. Again, using

a form for each student, he divided the paper into four sections for each school quarter and identified the behaviors to be focused on during the school year:

1. Evidence that the student reads for meaning
2. Evidence that the student uses multiple resources for thematic unit work
3. Evidence that the student is trying different forms of writing
4. Evidence that the child contributes to class discussions.

Skip left enough space for recording observations on the form. Instead of relying on his memory, Skip now has designed several ways to record systematic observations of children to help keep him more informed of what actually happens as children grow as readers and writers in his classroom.

Journal Reflections

Select one or more of the questions below that interest you and respond in your journal.

1. Cathy's journal entries that are included in this chapter reveal some interesting observations about the reading/writing connection. What do you think was the most important "lesson" Cathy learned?

2. Visit and observe several classrooms. How is children's literature being used to promote writing? What are some activities teachers and students are participating in that enhance the reading/writing connection?

3. Think about the following statement: The more students have access to books, the more students will want to write. How would you react to this idea?

4. Design your own question.
   ✓ What is a question you have about the chapter?
   ✓ How will you pursue the answer to that question?
   ✓ Respond in your journal.

REFERENCES AND SUGGESTED READINGS

Atkinson, S., ed. *Mathematics with Reason.* Portsmouth, NH: Heinemann, 1992.

Atwell, N. "Writing and Reading from the Inside Out." In J. Hansen, T. Newkirk, and D. Graves, eds. *Breaking Sound: Teachers Relate Reading and Writing in the Elementary School.* Portsmouth, NH: Heinemann, 1985a.

Atwell, N. *Coming to Know: Writing to Learn in the Intermediate Grades.* Portsmouth, NH: Heinemann, 1989a.

Atwell, N. *Workshop I by and for Teachers: Writing and Literature.* Portsmouth, NH: Heinemann, 1989b.

Baker, A., and Baker, J. *Counting on a Small Planet: Activities for Environmental Mathematics.* Portsmouth, NH: Heinemann, 1991a.

Baker, A., and Baker, J. *Raps and Rhymes in Maths.* Portsmouth, NH: Heinemann, 1991b.

Baker, J., and Baker, A. *From Puzzles to Projects: Solving Problems All the Way.* Portsmouth, NH: Heinemann, 1993.

Benedict, S., and Carlisle, L. *Beyond Words: Picture Books for Older Readers and Writers.* Portsmouth, NH: Heinemann, 1992.

Bickmore-Brand, J. *Language in Mathematics.* Portsmouth, NH: Heinemann, 1993.

Brown, M. *Lotus Seeds: Children, Pictures, and Books,* 1992.

Burns, M. *Math and Literature (K–3).* Portsmouth, NH: Heinemann, 1992.

Calkins, L. *The Art of Teaching Writing.* Portsmouth, NH: Heinemann, 1986.

Countryman, J. *Writing to Learn Mathematics.* Portsmouth, NH: Heinemann, 1992.

Deford, D. "Literacy: Reading, Writing and Other Essentials," *Language Arts* 58, no. 6 (1981): 652–658.

Doris, E. *Doing What Scientists Do: Children Learn to Investigate Their World.* Portsmouth, NH: Heinemann, 1991.

Eckhoff, B. "How Reading Affects Children's Writing," *Language Arts,* 60, no. 6 (1983): 607–616.

Fox, M. *Dear Mem Fox, I Have Read All Your Books Even the Pathetic Ones and Other Incidents in the Life of a Children's Book Author.* San Diego, CA: Harcourt Brace Jovanovich, 1992.

Fredericks, A. D., and Cheesebrough, D. L. *Science for All Children: Elementary School Methods.* New York: HarperCollins, 1993.

Fredericks, A. D., Meinbach, A. M., and Rothlein, V. *Thematic Units: An Integrated Approach to Teaching Science and Social Studies.* New York: Harper-Collins, 1993.

Freeman, E. B., and Person, D. G., eds. *Using Nonfiction Trade Books in the Elementary Classroom: From Ants to Zeppelins.* Urbana, IL: National Council of Teachers of English, 1992.

Garthwait, A. "Helping to Make Reading-Writing Connections: Young Adult Characters and Their Authors Talk about the Craft of Writing," *New England Reading Association Journal,* 29 no. 2 (1993): 39–51.

Goodman, Y. M., Hood, W. J., and Goodman, K. S. *Organizing for Whole Language.* Portsmouth, NH: Heinemann, 1989.

Graves, D. *Writing: Teachers and Children at Work.* Portsmouth, NH: Heinemann, 1983.

Graves, D. H. *Experiment with Fiction: The Reading/Writing Teacher's Companion Series.* Portsmouth, NH: Heinemann, 1989a.

Graves, D. H. *Investigate Nonfiction: The Reading/Writing Teacher's Companion Series.* Portsmouth, NH: Heinemann, 1989b.

Graves, D. H. *Build a Literate Classroom: The Reading/Writing Teacher's Companion Series.* Portsmouth, NH: Heinemann, 1991.

Graves, D. J. *Discover Your Own Literacy: The Reading/Writing Teacher's Companion Series.* Portsmouth, NH: Heinemann, 1990.

Griffiths, R., and Clyne, M. *Books You Can Count On: Linking Mathematics and Literature.* Portsmouth, NH: Heinemann, 1991.

Hall, S. *Using Picture Storybooks to Teach Literary Devices.* Phoenix: Oryx Press, 1990.

Harlen, W. *Developing Science in the Primary Classroom.* Portsmouth, NH: Heinemann, 1990.

Harwayne, S. *Lasting Impressions: Weaving Literature into the Writing Workshop.* Portsmouth, NH: Heinemann, 1992.

Heller, M. F. *Reading-Writing Connections: From Theory to Practice.* White Plains, NY: Longman, 1991.

Huck, C., Hepler, S., and Hickman, J. *Children's Literature in the Elementary School,* 5th ed. New York: Harcourt Brace Jovanovich, 1993.

Hunter, M. *Talent is Not Enough: Mollie Hunter on Writing for Children.* New York: Harper, 1976.

Hurst, C. O. *Long Ago and Far Away . . . An Encyclopedia for Successfully Using Literature with Intermediate Readers.* Allen, TX: DLM, 1991.

Hurst, C. O. *Once Upon A Time . . . An Encyclopedia for Successfully Using Literature with Young Children.* Blacklick, OH: SRA, 1992.

Hurst, C. O. *In Times Past . . . An Encyclopedia for Integrating U.S. History with Literature in Grades 3–8.* New York: SRA (Macmillan/McGraw Hill), 1993.

Jett-Simpson, M., ed. *Adventuring with Books: A Booklist for Pre-K–Grade 6,* 9th ed. Urbana, IL: National Council of Teachers of English, 1989.

Johnson, P. *Literacy Through the Book Arts.* Portsmouth, NH: Heinemann, 1989.

Jorgesen, K. L. *History Workshop: Reconstructing the Past with Elementary Students.* Portsmouth, NH: Heinemann, 1993.

Karelitz, E. B. *The Author's Chair and Beyond: Language and Literacy in a Primary Classroom.* Portsmouth, NH: Heinemann, 1993.

Knight L. M., and Payne, P. *Literature-Based Social Studies: Children's Books and Activities to Enrich the K–5 Curriculum.* Phoenix: Oryx Press, 1991.

Kobrin, B. *Eyeopeners! How to Choose and Use Children's Books About Real People, Places and Things.* New York: Penguin, 1988.

McClure, A. A., and Kristo, J. V., eds. *Books that Invite Talk, Wonder, and Play.* Urbana, IL: National Council of Teachers of English, 1996.

Mills, E. "Children's Literature and Teaching Written Composition," *Elementary Teacher* (1994): 971–973.

Parker, R. E. *Mathematical Power: Lessons from a Classroom.* Portsmouth, NH: Heinemann, 1993.

Pigdon, K., and Woolley, M., eds. *The Big Picture: Integrating Children's Learning.* Portsmouth, NH: Heinemann, 1993.

Radencich, M. C. "Do Basal Characters Read and Write in Their Daily Lives?" *Elementary School Journal,* (1987): 467–474.

Routman, R. *Invitations: Changing Teachers and Learners K–12.* Portsmouth, NH: Heinemann, 1991.

Saul, W., and Jagusch, S. A., eds. *Vital Connections: Children, Science, and Books.* Portsmouth, NH: Heinemann, 1992.

Saul, W., Reardon, J., Schmidt, A., Pearce, C., Blackwood, D., and Bird, M. D. *Science Workshop: A Whole Language Approach.* Portsmouth, NH: Heinemann, 1993.

Scott, J., ed. *Science and Language Links: Classroom Implications.* Portsmouth, NH: Heinemann, 1993.

Siu-Runyan, Y. "Connecting, Writing, Talk, and Literature." In A. McClure and J. Kristo, eds. *Books that Invite Talk, Wonder and Play.* Urbana, IL: National Council of Teachers of English, 1996.

Smith, F. *Joining the Literacy Club: Further Essays into Education.* Portsmouth, NH: Heinemann, 1988.

Stewart-Dore, N., ed. *Writing and Reading to Learn.* Portsmouth, NH: Heinemann, 1986.

Skolnick, D. "When Literature and Writing Meet." In N. Atwell, ed. *Workshop 1 By and For Teachers: Writing and Literature.* Portsmouth, NH: Heinemann, 1989.

Stewig, J. W. *Read to Write: Using Children's Literature as a Springboard for Teaching Writing,* 3rd ed. Katonah, NY: Richard C. Owen, 1990.

Stoessiger, R., and Edmunds, J. *Natural Learning and Mathematics.* Portsmouth, NH: Heinemann, 1992.

Tunnell, M. O., and Ammon, R., eds. *The Story of Ourselves: Teaching History Through Children's Literature.* Portsmouth, NH: Heinemann, 1992.

Whitin, D. J., and Wilden, S. *Read Any Good Math Lately?* Portsmouth, NH: Heinemann, 1992.

Wilson, L. *An Integrated Approach to Learning.* Portsmouth, NH: Heinemann, 1993.

Zinsser, W., ed. *World of Childhood: The Art and Craft of Writing for Children.* Boston: Houghton Mifflin, 1990.

CHAPTER 13 WRITER'S TOOLBOX

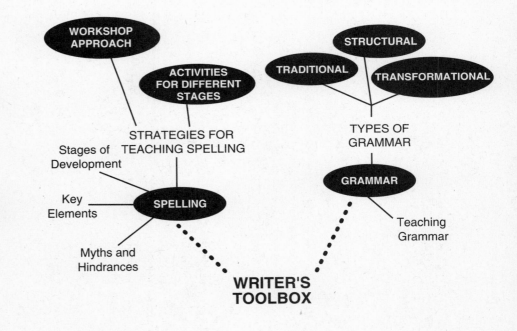

WORKSHOP APPROACH

ACTIVITIES FOR DIFFERENT STAGES

STRUCTURAL

TRADITIONAL

TRANSFORMATIONAL

STRATEGIES FOR TEACHING SPELLING

TYPES OF GRAMMAR

Stages of Development

Key Elements

SPELLING

GRAMMAR

Teaching Grammar

Myths and Hindrances

WRITER'S TOOLBOX

What I Know: Pre-Chapter Journaling

Take a few moments and think back to your years in elementary school—specifically the times you spent learning how to spell. What did your teachers do that *encouraged* or *discouraged* your development as a speller?

Big Ideas

This chapter will offer:

1. The principles of an effective spelling program.
2. Common spelling errors in students' writing.
3. The stages of spelling development.
4. Several approaches to the teaching of spelling in an integrated language arts program.
5. The three basic types of grammar used in the elementary classroom.
6. Effective strategies and techniques for teaching grammar within the integrated language arts curriculum.

A visitor to Cathy Stetter's fourth-grade classroom is amazed to discover the incredible amount of sharing and small group work taking place. Students are working on various drafts of their journal entries, proofreading each other's works, and engaging in a variety of discussions. Cathy explains that this sense of cooperation pervades all aspects of her classroom and helps to ensure that a "community of learners" is being created and supported.

Eric and Angela are in one corner of the room going over the second draft of Eric's writing assignment on "helicopters in war." Eric has personally chosen this topic because he enjoys anything having to do with helicopters, and also because his mother was an Army nurse in Vietnam and has had a lot of experience with helicopters. Angela listens carefully as Eric reads his draft and notes some of the words he uses. Occasionally, she will write some notes on a journal page that she will share with Eric upon completion of the story.

Martin, Twan, and Cecilia are working together in another part of the room transferring words from a master list to a "graffiti wall" (a sheet of newsprint hung along one wall of the classroom upon which students record thoughts, random ideas, or various word lists). The three classmates are creating a semantic web of words that begin with selected consonant blends. The words they use come from a sampling of journal entries contributed by other students in the class. Columns of words that begin with *bl-, cl-, dr-, cr-,* and *tr-* are written on the newsprint.

Carol, Peter, and Lucinda are also working together in another part of the room. They are putting together a minidictionary of words that might be found in books about the weather (e.g., barometer, anemometer, cold front, stratocumulus, hurricane). For each word, they are providing an illustration or picture, several selected sentences (which have also been contributed by members of the class), and alternative spellings for each word. The dictionary will eventually become part of a larger collection of dictionaries maintained in the classroom.

Other students in the class are reading silently to themselves, sharing a new piece of children's literature with a friend, or doing some independent writing in their personal journals. The energy level is subdued, but every student in the room is engaged in at least one language arts-related activity.

To the casual observer, Cathy's class may appear to be a hodgepodge of assorted activities and projects. To Cathy, however, this is part of her spelling program. It is obvious that Cathy's conception of spelling is quite different from that of her colleague down the hall who administers a pretest to his students on Monday, a practice spelling test on Wednesday, and a final test on Friday. The students in that classroom are asked to write each of their misspelled words ten times prior to the Wednesday test, and ten times more prior to the Friday posttest—activities they do for ten minutes each day.

Cathy, on the other hand, takes quite a different approach to spelling. She believes that spelling instruction, if it is to be effective and of practical use to students, must come from authentic activities—activities that encourage students to use spelling in realistic ways and realistic settings. Providing her students with a standardized list of spelling words from a commercial publisher goes against Cathy's philosophy of helping her students master words that are important to them and which grow out of their personal writing experiences. "Spelling should be taught within the context of writing; children learn how to spell through writing," states Cathy. "Copying down a word several times may be counterproductive to a child's spelling achievement, particularly since many traditional spelling lists contain words students may never see or use again."

Cathy is part of a growing legion of teachers who recognize that spelling, along with grammar, must be treated as essential elements of

FOR YOUR JOURNAL

Below is a short quiz (adapted from Gentry, 1987) to record in your journal. For each statement indicate whether you agree with it (TRUE) or disagree with it (FALSE). For those statements you feel strongly about, circle your response.

_____ Every student must learn how to spell.
_____ Students who cannot spell are ignorant.
_____ Spelling is supposed to be difficult.
_____ Spelling errors should not be tolerated on any piece of written work.
_____ Good teachers reduce marks on written assignments for poor spelling.
_____ Good spellers memorize lots of information.

_____ Good spellers memorize lots of spelling rules.
_____ To become good spellers, students need to do lots of spelling book exercises and drills.
_____ The most important thing about spelling is to master the weekly spelling test.
_____ Good teachers always correct their students' spelling.

Please compare your responses with those of another student in your class. How similar were the two of you in your responses? How different?

---

the entire language arts curriculum—not as isolated subjects to be "taught" for 15 to 20 minutes each day. Students' proficiency in spelling and grammar grow when they are provided with authentic opportunities to use those skills in meaningful and relevant contexts. Cathy will tell you that the divorce of spelling and grammar from each other and the other language arts is both impractical as well as unproductive. Cathy wants her students to understand that spelling and grammar are tools for writing, aids in communicating with other people, and instruments that facilitate comprehension. In fact, Cathy will also tell you that she does not teach spelling and grammar for a set period of time each day; instead, she facilitates students' spelling and grammar development throughout the entire day.

Let's take a closer look at the writer's tools of spelling and grammar and how they can be taught in your classroom.

SPELLING

How did you mark each of the statements in Box 13.1? Are they all true, all false, or did you have a combination of true and false responses? Interestingly enough, all of the above statements are myths about spelling instruction. These are beliefs that have been passed down from generation to generation and from teacher to teacher. They have been around ever since the first spelling test was created and are still extant today. Unfortunately, these beliefs tend to get in the way of meaningful and successful spelling instruction. They have become part of the conventional wisdom that may actually prevent normal spelling development (Gentry, 1987).

Are you a good speller? Are you a poor speller? How did you learn how to spell when you were in elementary school? It seems reasonable to expect that if you went to a traditional elementary school you learned how to spell (or how not to spell) in a way that was not all that dissimilar from many other students in your class. For most of us, spelling was treated as a separate subject—a subject divorced from the other subjects in the curriculum. Usually, there was a separate spelling book or workbook in which we supposedly learned a new set of spelling words each week (usually 20) and upon which we were also tested each week. Typically, spelling was taught in the following sequence:

1. A pretest of 20 words was administered to the entire class on Monday. The words on the test usually followed some sort of phonemic principle (e.g., words with double consonants, words ending with a silent e, words beginning with the prefix pre). The tests were returned by the teacher with a grade based on the number of words (out of 20) that were spelled correctly.

2. The words missed on the pretest would become the practice words for the week. The missed words would be recorded in folders or notebooks and usually written over and over again. The emphasis was on memorizing the "rule" for the week's words or simply memorizing the words themselves.

3. A practice test would be given on Wednesday or Thursday. This would indicate to students how well they were learning the "rule" or the pattern for the words selected for that week. Sometimes students would have to write any missed words several more times in their notebooks—again, the emphasis being on memorization of the words in isolation.

4. A final test on the 20 words would be given on Friday. (We're not clear why Friday has traditionally been designated as the unofficial "spelling day.") This score would indicate how well students had mastered the words for the week or had internalized the designated "rule."

5. The following Monday, spelling competency on a whole new set of 20 words would be tested. Words learned (or not learned) the following week would typically not be tested or utilized in succeeding weeks. The object was to add to the student's storehouse of memorized spelling words, but not necessarily to be able to use them in other language arts contexts.

We must admit that we have some difficulties with this tradition, with this method of teaching spelling. Here are some of our reasons:

1. The words used for each week's spelling list are provided by a published spelling series. Those words may or may not relate to any words necessary for writing or speaking activities in the classroom.

2. It is expected that all students will master all the words. In other words, each and every student in the classroom, without respect for his or her ability, interests, or needs is provided with an identical spelling list and required to master it.

3. The emphasis is on the simple memorization of words. Words are presented in isolated lists, and the primary objective is to memorize as many as possible by the end of the week in order to successfully "pass the test."

4. There is no carryover from one week to another. After 20 words have been presented (and supposedly learned), they may not be presented again. The emphasis is on mastering each spelling list independently of every other spelling list.

5. There is little or no attempt made to integrate the spelling words into writing activities in succeeding days or weeks. This reemphasizes the fact that spelling is presented as separate and isolated from the other aspects of language arts. It is a subject unto itself,

rather than one inexorably tied into the others.

6. For students, this traditional method of teaching spelling "labels" them as either "good" spellers or "poor" spellers; there are no gradations of developing spelling ability. Instead the ability to memorize patterns or lists of words is the sole determinate of which end of the "spelling continuum" each student stands.

What becomes clear from past practices and our own experiences as classroom teachers is that there is no single way to teach spelling. If all we do is present our students with a list to memorize, then we are demonstrating to all our students that there is only one way to teach (and one way to learn) spelling. As all teachers know, real classrooms are filled with youngsters of varying abilities, interests, and needs. To present all of those students with a singular approach to spelling (or any subject, for that matter) may rob several students of learning opportunities tailored to their individual learning styles. In other words, one size does *not* fit all.

Gentry and Gillet (1993) have provided a set of 12 key elements that will help teachers design and develop a spelling plan that can address the needs of *all* students in any classroom. Their guidelines are presented in the box on pages 408 and 409.

THE STAGES OF SPELLING DEVELOPMENT

Children tend to go through distinct stages as they learn how to spell. This does not imply, however, that all children go through all the stages at the same pace or spend an equal amount of time at each stage. What it does imply is that youngsters' spelling ability is individualistic and typically sequential. It also implies that not all children will need the same type of spelling instruction at the same time. Providing the same list of words to all the students in the class at the same time and in the same way obviates a developmental model of spelling instruction.

Gentry (1987) has delineated five stages of spelling development. Each stage represents the cognitive structures youngsters use as they move toward conventional spelling. Also implied in these stages is the fact that different strategies are necessary to help youngsters progress along the "spelling continuum" and upon which appropriate spelling skills might be developed. Each stage, with its attendant strategies, is a necessary prerequisite for a succeeding stage, but at varying levels of intensity for each youngster. Table 13.1 on page 410 presents the five stages of spelling.

Let's take a look at each of the five stages in greater detail.

Stage 1: Precommunicative Spelling This represents the child's earliest attempts at associating the sounds of language with the graphemes of language. Children at this stage do not know that letters represent sounds; rather they are beginning to realize that language can be depicted in more than one way. The child creates a message that cannot be "deciphered" by anyone else. Precommunicative spelling may consist of letters, half-letters, or no letters at all; pictographs or other scribblings may make up part of the message. The "writing" may move from left to right, right to left, top to bottom, or bottom to top depending on the inclinations of the child. The alphabetic principle that relates certain letters to certain sounds in any language has not yet been discovered. Typically, children up to the age of five are engaged in precommunicative spelling.

Indicators (Approximate Age Range: 3–5)

- The child frequently uses a variety of uppercase and lowercase letters, with uppercase letters predominating.

KEY ELEMENTS FOR A SUCCESSFUL SPELLING PROGRAM

1. *Treat spelling as a complex process.* It is important to keep in mind that spelling is much more complex than having students all memorize the same list of words each week. So too, is it important to keep in mind that the complexity of spelling means that learning to spell is not an incidental process, but rather one that demands a systematic and planned sequence of activities and strategies. Spelling is an integral part of, not tangential to, all the language arts.

2. *Help students meet all four demands of expert spelling.* When students learn how to spell they utilize a combination of phonetic, semantic, historical, and visual demands. In doing so, spelling moves beyond simple memorization or words into a multifaceted element of all the language arts.

3. *Treat spelling as a developmental process.* As we implied earlier, a child is neither a "good" speller or a "bad" speller. Spelling ability occurs developmentally from general ideas and concepts to more specific ones. Sometimes, children must "invent" some new structures or "rules" that provide a temporary bridge between standard rules of spelling.

4. *Individualize spelling.* Spelling instruction works best when it is individualized and tailored to the interests and abilities of each student in the class. Giving the whole class the same set of spelling words implies that each student needs to master the identical set of words.

5. *Integrate spelling in all subject areas.* Isolating spelling from the context of reading and writing in other subject areas may provide youngsters with a distorted view of spelling as an isolated subject.

6. *Take advantage of invented spelling as an opportunity for learning.* Children may create their own rules for spelling or even create their own interpretations of how certain words are spelled. This does not indicate that they do not know how to spell or are not learning how to spell. Rather, it suggests that these new words (often referred to as "invented spellings") are temporary crutches that allow youngsters to continue to maintain comprehension of a written piece of work (for example).

7. *Think of whole language and spelling instruction as being compatible.* One of the concepts you learned early in this text was the fact that whole language does not mean that children do not learn necessary language skills. Rather, when those skills are presented in a meaningful

---

- The child may have a limited repertoire of letters to represent sounds and may "invent" new letters or symbols for various sounds or words.
- The child may demonstrate some knowledge of the alphabet, although in a very limited form.
- The child may have some knowledge of left-to-right writing, although other directional formats are also used.
- The child's writing may include other symbols such as numbers, pictographs, illustrations, and the like.
- The child may repeat certain "letters" or symbols many times and may use the same symbol or letter for many different things.

Stage 2: The Semiphonetic Stage   At this stage, children begin using specific letters to represent specific sounds. For the most part, the words children create are short and indicate the exclusion of many letters, frequently vowels. For example, *WK* may represent *work; DG* may represent *dog;* and *BTR* may represent *brother.* This is the stage at which the alphabetic principle begins to emerge—that is, that alphabetic letters represent sounds. Obviously, children are not able to make all the letters for all the sounds, thus their spelling

context (as opposed to isolated lists), then learning is more realistic and useful. So too, with spelling—which can be effectively taught within the context of any whole language program.

8. *Use instructional resources for teaching spelling.* The success of a good spelling program rests on being able to provide students with a plethora of instructional strategies, activities, and procedures that will allow for a multifaceted approach to spelling instruction.

9. *Educate parents and solicit their help.* Parents are a significant and potent force in the integrated language arts program. Traditionally, the effectiveness of a teacher and the caliber of instruction are often gauged on students' spelling abilities. It is not unusual for parents (and the public) to believe that if students do not know how to spell, then the teacher is ineffectual or incompetent. Employing parents as allies in a spelling program can be a significant element in its eventual success.

10. *Pay attention to commonly used words.* High-frequency words—those words that children tend to use over and over again—are appropriate for study in any spelling program. Mastery of

those words helps youngsters form a necessary foundation for mastery of less commonly used or more difficult words, throughout the grades.

11. *Remember that spellers must also be readers and writers.* We are sure that by this point in the book you know that reading and writing are supportive of each other and that these two language arts are equally supportive of each child's developing spelling ability. When students are immersed in a host of reading and process writing activities, then spelling ability improves significantly. In other words, when spelling is presented as an element of reading and writing, youngsters begin to see its importance throughout the entire language arts curriculum.

12. *Teach proofreading and spelling consciousness.* One of the tasks before you as a teacher will be to help students take responsibility for their own learning as well as to develop a sense of pride in the work they do. Providing students with proofreading and editing skills gives them tools that they will be able to use long after they leave your classroom.

Source: Adapted from Gentry and Gillet (1993).

---

will be representative of the most rudimentary development of these skills. In other words, this is a critical evolutionary stage in which children enter into a realization that there are specific representations of specific sounds.

Indicators (Approximate Age Range: 5–6)

- The child begins to recognize the relationship between the sounds of language and their alphabetic representations.
- The child uses an abbreviated form of writing in which certain letters may represent a combination of several different sounds.
- The child uses initial consonants to represent entire words or major segments of words.
- The child begins to recognize the left-to-right arrangement of letters in the English language.
- The child begins to achieve some mastery of the formation of certain letters.
- The child begins to use letter-name strategies to spell selected words.

Stage 3: The Phonetic Stage Children's development of sound-letter representations becomes

TABLE 13.1   Samples of Leslie's Invented Spellings: The Five Stages

Stage	Leslie's Writing	Translation	Age
1. Precommunicative	EOIIVELIOE NEMLIEDN MDRMNE	(Story describing a picture of a flock of butterflies)	3 years, 3 months
2. Semiphonetic (from captions supplied by student)	ALD GIZ HMT DPD	allowed girls Humpty Dumpty	5 years, 11 months
3. Phonetic	TAS AS E PACHRR FER MOM	This is a picture for Mom.	6 years, 3 months
	I HEP UOU LEK TAS PACHERR EV DNL DEK AND DASY DEC	I hope you like this picture of Donald Duck and Daisy Duck.	
4. Transitional	WONES A PON a time we BOTE a LITTLE kitten. You NO how THAY are WHIN THERE little— THERE RASCULES! This one LUVES to CLLIME trees and SRCACH PEPPLE. HE is a MENE RASCULE.		7 years
5. Conventional	When I went to the zoo, I saw lions. They were sleeping. There were two of them. They were big and HARY.		7 years, 9 months

Source: Adapted from Gentry and Gillet (1993). Used by permission.

more refined at this stage. Usually, children begin including some vowels in their spelled words, although there is still a predominant emphasis on the use of consonants. Children will be doing quite a bit more writing at this stage (note the approximate age range) including lists, letters, notes, diary and journal entries, and other compositions. Children at this stage will be more cognizant of the sounds of language and will use or develop an orthographic system that represents some, if not all, of the sounds they hear in words (Gentry and Gillet, 1993). While the choice of letters and letter combinations may not conform to recognized practices, they are, nonetheless, recorded in a logical and systematic way for children. Although many words may not be spelled correctly, they can be deciphered using familiar graphophonemic principles.

Indicators (Approximate Age Range: 6–7)
- The child begins to recognize the segmentation of words—that words can be divided into syllables.
- The child shows some mastery of sound-letter correspondence for most of the surface features in words.
- The child is usually dependent upon the sounds of letters in selecting orthographic representations.
- The child develops specific spellings for regular phonemic forms such as *T* for *-ed* (*stopt/stopped*), *R* for *-ir-* (*brd/bird*), or *D* for *-tt-* (*bodl/bottle*).

Stage 4: The Transitional Stage At this stage of spelling development, children begin to use recognized spellings of familiar words, although they may still encounter some difficulties with irregular words. Gentry and Gillet (1993) indicate that this stage may be the most critical and certainly the most important milestone in the young child's progression to being an accomplished speller. It is at this stage that children learn that spelling represents not only the sounds of language but also what language looks like in printed form. Children have been typically exposed to many different variations of language over extended periods of time (e.g., reading aloud, storytelling, process writing) and these exposures have offered varied opportunities to see the "correctness" of recognized spellings. This is also the stage at which children begin to assimilate conventional spellings for familiar words; consequently, more emphasis on spelling practice is advocated during these years. So too do children begin relying more on morphological information

and visual clues while decreasing their reliance on phonological information.

Indicators (Approximate Age Range: 7–8)
- The child begins to adhere to the basic conventions of English orthography (e.g., a vowel sound in every syllable, the use of vowel digraphs such as *ee, ei, ai* instead of single vowels, the ending of some words in silent letters).
- Vocabulary size increases and the child uses a higher percentage of correctly spelled words.
- The child begins to recognize the correct spelling of many words by sight.
- The child may use alternate forms for spelling the same word.
- The child may use all of the letters of a word in its spelling but may occasionally reverse some of the letters.
- Common letter patterns appear in the child's spelling.

Stage 5: The Conventional Stage At this stage of spelling development, children are able to spell many words correctly, but this does not imply that they are able to spell all words correctly. Most of the basic principles of English orthography have been mastered, and it is at this point that children are ready for formal spelling instruction (Gentry, 1987). While children have mastered many words appropriate for their age and grade level, they still need instruction and familiarity with irregularly spelled words. Children are now able to "play with" many different spellings of the same word to determine if it "looks right."

It is at this stage that formal spelling instruction should take place. The implication is that the previous four stages are supported by incidental teaching. In other words, children begin to learn spelling principles and patterns early in their lives not through a simple memorization of lists of words but rather by using words of their own selection in a variety of reading, writing, speaking, and listening formats. In other words, exposing children to a variety of language modes helps them develop the personal strategies that will eventually form the foundation upon which more formalized spelling instruction can take place.

Indicators (Approximate Age Range: 8–13)

- The child learns the irregular spellings of many new words.
- The child has accumulated a large storehouse of properly spelled words.
- The child is able to demonstrate an awareness of word structure (e.g., syllabication, contractions, affixes, homonyms, and compound words).
- The child is able to test alternative spelling of a single word through trial and error measures.
- The child begins to achieve mastery of morphological structures such as consonant and vowel alternations.
- The child has learned many of the basic rules of the English orthographic system.

What is evident from this description of the stages of spelling development is that youngsters develop competence in a continuous and systematic fashion. What is equally evident is that providing formalized spelling lessons (e.g., memorizing a list of 20 spelling words) while students are in one or more of the early stages of their spelling development may be counterproductive to their spelling achievement. *When formal spelling instruction (e.g., memorizing words) begins before children have reached the fifth stage, their natural development is interrupted* (Tompkins and Hoskisson, 1991) [emphasis added]. In other words, formal instruction in spelling before children are ready for such instruction may delay spelling competence.

What surfaces from our discussions of spelling is the need to immerse youngsters in a variety of languaging activities—particularly in the early grades. Exposure to and familiarity with language in different activities helps children learn the uses and spellings of language. You need to be aware of the stage(s) of spelling your students are in (obviously, not every student in your classroom will be at the same stage of spelling development at the same time) and provide instruction accordingly. Memorizing words while children are progressing through the early stages of spelling development can be detrimental to their growth as accomplished spellers. It is more important that you deemphasize standardized spelling practices and instead invite children to examine, experiment with, and explore the variety of ways in which they can "play with language." Correctness at the early stages of spelling growth is of less importance than a feeling of "comfortableness of expression" in using language.

ANALYZING SPELLING DEVELOPMENT

Knowing at what stage of spelling development a child is in is essential to providing that child with the appropriate type of spelling instruction. As a teacher, it is important for you to be aware of the varied stages of spelling development within your classroom in order to establish a spelling program responsive to the individual needs of each student. For example, it would be inappropriate to assume that all children in your second-grade classroom are at identical levels of spelling proficiency. It is quite reasonable to expect to find children at different levels of spelling achievement and needing different types of spelling instruction. In other words, it would be most inappropriate to provide all the students in a second-grade classroom with random lists of spelling words to memorize for a weekly spelling test each Friday morning. The implication is that when you know the stage(s) of spelling development represented by students in your classroom, you will be able to offer appropriate instruction tailored to their individual learning needs.

The Developmental Spelling Test, presented in the box on page 414, is designed to assist teachers in determining the specific stages of development at which each of the students in their class performs (Gentry and Gillet, 1993). By analyzing children's spelling, the teacher is able to pinpoint the level of spelling proficiency and provide instruction designed to move specific youngsters to the next level (and beyond) of spelling development. The advantages of the developmental spelling test are as follows:

It is quick and easy to administer.
It is quick and easy to evaluate.
It is standardized for all youngsters.
It provides results comparable to longer and more complicated measures of spelling proficiency.
It is a simple and uncomplicated analysis of ten common spelling words.

The focus of the Developmental Spelling Test is to determine what percentage of words a child spells at the precommunicative, semiphonetic, phonetic, transitional, and conventional stages. If a youngster spells a majority of words at a particular stage, then it is that stage that would be considered the child's developmental level of spelling.

After you have administered the test to a child, it is necessary to look at each of the words the child spells in order to determine that child's appropriate developmental spelling stage. At this point, it is necessary to assign each spelling the child makes to a specific stage (although there may well be words that could fall into more than one category or are so undecipherable that they cannot be assigned to any category). The stage at which most of the child's words fall is probably the stage of spelling development for that child.

Table 13.2 indicates some sample spellings and where they might be placed in terms of children's developmental spelling stage(s). Obviously, this table is not designed to represent *all* of the spellings children may indicate on the developmental spelling test, but it does demonstrate a representative spelling type for each stage and how those types would be categorized according to the parameters of the five stages.

Let's now take a look at two spelling samples from two youngsters—one in first grade, the other in third grade.

Ben—First Grade

The Developmental Spelling Test was given to Ben, a first-grade student, in October. His test results are represented in Figure 13.1. While it is not necessary to analyze the ten words individually, it should be clearly evident that Ben is in the precommunicative stage of spelling. All of his words are represented by a series of random letters—most of which are not represented by letter sounds in the dictated words. The number of letters in each word that Ben spelled frequently has no relationship to the number of letters in each word. (Note that Ben uses 14 random letters to spell the word "human.")

Ben's teacher recognizes that Ben and his classmates need to be exposed to words in a host of authentic settings. She provides them with daily opportunities to write about things that interest them, in the form of notes to parents, a letter to a friend, a summary of a favorite story and the like. For each student, she then selects one or more misspelled words and words with the student to record the word(s) in a portfolio and use the misspelled words in a variety of other writing activities. Ben's teacher knows that most of her students are also at the precommunicative stage and that having them memorize a list of 20 or so words each week as part of a spelling lesson would not be in keeping with their stages of spelling development—in fact, it would be counterproductive to their spelling achievement. Instead, by selecting words in contextual frameworks (natural writing activities) Ben's teacher is helping her students gain familiarity with words in many different situations. The emphasis is on the utility of words, not the short-term memorization of words. (Additional

Source: Gentry and Gillet (1993). Used by permission.

THE DEVELOPMENTAL SPELLING TEST

Directions: Administer the following list of words to children in kindergarten and grades 1 and 2. Call out each word, read the sentence that follows the word, and call out the word again. It may be necessary to explain to children that some words are difficult to spell, but you are asking them to do their best on the test. Explain that words will not be graded right or wrong, that you are simply trying to determine the ways in which children spell certain words. Invite children to invent spelling for words they do not know. Whenever possible, make youngsters feel comfortable and relaxed about the test—perhaps even approaching it in a gamelike fashion.

1. monster — The boy was eaten by a monster.
2. united — You live in the United States.
3. dress — The girl wore a new dress.
4. bottom — A big fish lives at the bottom of the lake.
5. hiked — We hiked to the top of the mountain.
6. human — Miss Piggy is not a human.
7. eagle — An eagle is a powerful bird.
8. closed — The little girl closed the door.
9. bumped — The car bumped into the bus.
10. type — Type the letter on the typewriter.

ideas for spelling activities for precommunicative spellers will be presented later in this chapter.)

Michael—Third Grade

Michael is a third-grade student in the same school as Ben. Michael was also given the Developmental Spelling Test in October (see Figure 13.2). An analysis of Michael's invented spellings is presented in the box on page 417.

The following percentages are revealed in Michael's Developmental Spelling Test.

    0 percent–Precommunicative
    20 percent–Semiphonetic
    40 percent–Phonetic

TABLE 13.2 Possible Test Responses

Word	Precommunicative	Semiphonetic	Phonetic	Transitional	Conventional
monster	random letters	MTR	MOSTR	MONSTUR	monster
united	random letters	U	UNITD	YOUNIGHTED	united
dress	random letters	JRS	JRAS	DRES	dress
bottom	random letters	BT	BODM	BOTTUM	bottom
hiked	random letters	H	HIKT	HICKED	hiked
human	random letters	UM	HUMN	HUMUN	human
eagle	random letters	EL	EGL	EGUL	eagle
closed	random letters	KD	KLOSD	CLOSSED	closed
bumped	random letters	B	BOPT	BUMPPED	bumped
type	random letters	TP	TIP	TIPE	type

Source: Adapted from Gentry (1987).

FIGURE 13.1

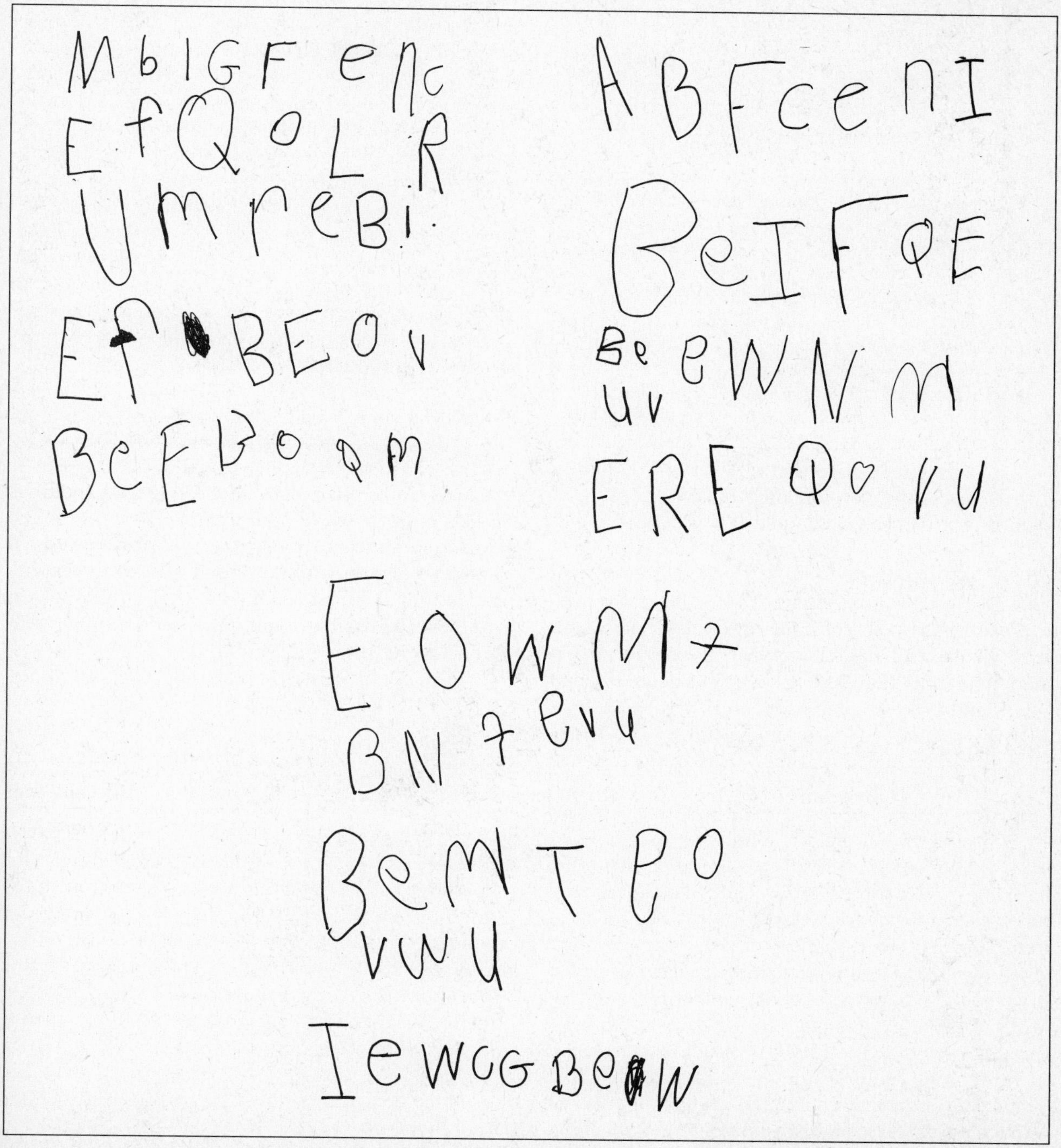

FIGURE 13.2 Michael's Spelling Test

```
1. monstr
2. unide
3. druse
4. bombomdom
5. hikt
6. humem
7. eggle
8. Clods Clodoes cholods
9. bumbed
10. tlpe
```

30 percent–Transitional
0 percent–Conventional
10 percent–Unclassifiable

These results indicate that Michael can be identified as a *phonetic speller* who occasionally uses some transitional spelling strategies. Although Michael is a third-grade student, his developmental spelling ability is below his expected level. What makes this even more interesting is how Michael's teacher presents spelling to the class. Each Monday, Michael and his classmates receive a pretest of 20 spelling words from a commercial publisher. They have a midweek practice test and an end-of-the week final spelling test on those 20 words. The words Michael misses on the Monday morning pretest must be written five times each on a separate sheet of paper in preparation for the midweek test. Words misspelled on that test are again spelled five times on another sheet of paper in preparation for the Friday morning test. In other words, in Michael's classroom spelling is "taught" by giving students a predetermined list of words and asking them to memorize that list.

Unfortunately for Michael, this practice is in opposition to his developmental stage of spelling.

As we indicated earlier in this section, children who are in the early stages of spelling development (precommunicative–phonetic) are actually harmed when traditional spelling assignments (e.g., memorization of a list of preselected spelling words) are used as the method of instruction. Indeed, Michael has completed two years (first and second grade) of nothing but weekly spelling lists and is beginning third grade with similar lists of words. As you might expect, spelling for Michael is a constant struggle and a constant frustration—simply because the method of instruction does not match his stage of development; indeed, it may be counterproductive to helping Michael achieve a satisfactory level of spelling competence throughout his school years.

What becomes clear is the need to strike a match between youngsters' stages of spelling development and appropriate spelling instruction. In the following section we present strategies to consider in developing a spelling program that is in line with the developmental needs of students. This compendium should not be looked upon as a random collection of activities but rather as elements in a systematic instructional program that is developmentally appropriate and responsive to the needs of individual children.

STRATEGIES FOR TEACHING SPELLING

It is important to remember that in an integrated language arts program, spelling is viewed not as a separate subject but rather as a natural and integrated part of the entire language arts program. As such, it is related to and supported by each of the language arts. When providing spelling instruction for your students, it is a good idea to ensure that spelling is perceived by youngsters as a normal element of all their language arts activities. When divorced from those activities, children may get an unnatural or unrealistic view of what spelling is all about.

By the same token, spelling is natural when it grows out of the other language arts. Separated from reading, writing, speaking, and listening, it becomes something to master rather than something to use in the utility of all the language arts. In other words, children do not become spelling proficient; rather spelling is part of a long-term developmental process just as reading, writing, listening, and speaking are also interrelated elements of a long-term process.

Children need to understand that spelling words and reading words (and speaking, writing, and listening to words) are all related functions. Thus when children recognize the utility of words in several different contexts, they are being provided with a strong foundation for the authentic use as well as the correct spelling of those words. To illustrate, when children are read to on a frequent basis, they hear words in action and begin to understand how words are used to convey actions. Also, when children are provided with regular opportunities to write, they have regular opportunities to use words in various contexts. In fact, research suggests that spelling is best

---

BOX 13.4   MICHAEL'S DEVELOPMENTAL SPELLING TEST

Michael's spelling test is displayed in Figure 13.2.

1. **monstr** (*monster*). Michael begins with *mon,* which is a conventional spelling of the first syllable of the word. However, *str* is a phoentic spelling since it does not contain any vowel. In this case (as in similar ones) it would be appropriate to select the lower of the two levels; thus this word is classified as phonetic.
2. **unide** (*united*). Here Michael has correctly written the first three letters of the word, but he has failed to use conventional spelling for the ending. This word is classified as phonetic.
3. **druse** (*dress*). Michael has determined the initial consonant blend for the word, but he was unable to represent the appropriate medial phonetic sound or the ending. Again, this spelling represents two levels of development; thus the word is classified as semiphonetic.
4. **bomdom** (*bottom*). This word is not spelled as it sounds, although Michael is able to identify the initial and terminal sounds. This word is classified as semiphonetic.
5. **hikt** (*hiked*). Michael has been able to represent all the sounds in this word, although he misspells the ending. The word is classified as phonetic.
6. **humem** (*human*). Michael is well on his way to spelling this word in a transitional manner; that is, until he reaches the end of the word. The first part of the word can be classified as conventional, while the second half is semiphonetic. Since there is such a gap (between the conventional spelling and semiphonetic spelling), this word is classified as phonetic.
7. **eggle** (*eagle*). Michael is able to represent all the sounds in this word, although in an unconventional spelling pattern. Note that he is able to represent the ending with a sophisticated *-le* pattern. This word is classified as transitional.
8. **cholods** (*closed*). Notice how Michael tries to spell this word in three different ways. Although he has many of the correct phonetic patterns, he is not quite sure how to arrange them in the proper order. This word is difficult to classify; thus this one is rated as unclassifiable.
9. **bumbed** (*bumped*). Michael has difficulty with the *mp* blend in this word, although he is able to represent all the phonetic elements. This word is classified as transitional.
10. **tipe** (*type*). Michael is able to represent all the phonetic elements of the word in their correct order. His substitution of *i* for *y* is very common. This word is classified as transitional.

learned through writing (Tompkins and Hoskisson, 1991). It should be evident that an integrated language arts program is supportive of the spelling development and achievement of all students.

A Workshop Approach to Teaching Spelling

One of the designs many teachers throughout the country have used effectively in teaching reading and writing is known as "the workshop approach" (Atwell, 1987). The emphasis in this approach is to focus on the individual needs of children and to help them take responsibility for their own learning. If you look back at Cambourne's conditions of literacy learning that we presented in Chapter 1, you will note that those conditions can be used to form the structure for an effective spelling program. The workshop approach, which we have modified in terms of a structure for spelling instruction, is illustrated below. Note how it embraces the tenets of literacy learning and offers youngsters an integrative approach to spelling instruction. The results of the workshop approach to spelling can be summarized as follows:

1. Students self-select most, if not all, of their own individual spelling words. (This is appropriate even for kindergartners and first-graders.)
2. Students can work collaboratively with other students, sharing their spelling words and assisting each other in learning personal words.
3. Students can spend a majority of their instructional time using words in meaningful contexts, rather than memorizing words in order to get a high score on a weekly spelling test.
4. Students develop the skills and information they need in order to become accomplished spellers through short, direct, and focused lessons rather than long or infrequent ones. The implication is that spelling is something that can be addressed throughout every day.

5. Students can each keep track of their spelling work by self-monitoring and maintaining their own personal records. This places an emphasis on the development of individual responsibilities for spelling achievement.
6. Students can receive feedback not only from their teacher but also from their classmates, friends, peers, and parents. Again, learning to spell can be a collaborative effort.

What you will notice about the six elements above is a move away from some of the more traditional practices associated with spelling instruction. Here the emphasis is on student self-responsibility instead of constant teacher direction. This shift, while seemingly slight, can have a major impact on the development of accomplished spellers, just as it has a positive effect on the development of accomplished readers and writers. Most significant is the fact that as a teacher, you will be assuming a different role than did your teachers. Yours will be one of support, time organization, and facilitating than it is of direct instruction. In short, the student is put at the heart of the spelling program instead of the spelling program serving as the focal point for all students.

Gentry and Gillet (1993) provide a basic plan that can be used to help students achieve appropriate levels of spelling mastery. This plan assumes that time can and will be devoted each day to spelling instruction, not necessarily as a series of isolated lessons but rather as inherent components of an overall language arts curriculum. Again, the object is not to "force" all students through the same activities with the same list of words. Rather, the design is for students to master spelling appropriate to their individual levels of spelling development. A "generic" spelling plan might be structured as follows:

- *Monday:* Students are encouraged to select a personal list of words to be used as spelling words for the week. These words will typically come from the daily writing activities they do during the course of the week or may include words found to be interesting by students. Younger students or less able spellers may wish to select no more than five words per week; older or more accomplished spellers may wish to work on nine or ten words per week. (*Note:* The use of a list of 20 commercially preselected spelling words each week is counterproductive to a workshop approach.)

- *Tuesday, Wednesday, Thursday:* A variety of workshop activities are provided for youngsters in the class. These activities, described in the following section, are tailored for individuals and not intended to be used by all students at the same time. As such, the activities chosen for a specific child are developmentally appropriate for that child (as a result of the Developmental Spelling Test, for example). The teacher's primary responsibility is to facilitate students' progress through individually selected activities.

- *Friday:* Each student is offered a test for the words he or she has worked on during the week. Tests may be administered individually to students or students may test each other. As results are tabulated, students may wish to enter their spelling words in a portfolio or spelling log to be shared with other students, administrators, or parents. Words not mastered one week may be carried over into another week for additional work.

The activities that follow are suggestions for authentic spelling work tailored to the developmental stages of students (Gentry and Gillet, 1993; Tompkins and Hoskisson, 1991; Routman, 1991; Wilde, 1992; and Phenix and Scott-Dunne, 1991). Quite obviously, you would not assign all youngsters all of the activities within a single category just as you would not want to use any single activity over and over again. The implication is that your role as a teacher of spelling changes from one of "director" to one of "facilitator." In other words, your main responsibility is to *guide* children through the stages of spelling development, rather than demanding their memorization of a "foreign" list of barely usable words.

Activities for Precommunicative and Semiphonetic Spellers

Children at this stage of spelling development are those who are just beginning to discover the alphabetic principle—that the sounds of the English language are represented by letters. While the letters they may choose to represent those letters may bear little or no resemblance to the actual letters in words, this is an attempt by these youngsters to transfer their knowledge of language from an oral stage to a written stage.

These students need to be exposed to a variety of activities that demonstrate the relationships between sounds and letters, the fact that words are represented by written symbols, that words have beginnings and endings, and that certain letters have certain sounds. Their spelling development is influenced to a great extent by constant exposure to books, literature, and reading. Reading aloud to precommunicative spellers provides the foundation they need to become comfortable with the oral and written expression of languaging skills. So too, do these youngsters need lots of free writing time. This writing may be in any form—drawings, illustrations, finger painting, scribbling, and the like—that will facilitate that important transfer from oral language to written language. In short, surrounding precommunicative and semiphonetic spellers with loads of language in other dimensions facilitates their development as strong spellers.

- *Picture sorts.* Obtain commercial cards that have pictures of common objects illustrated on them. Have students sort the cards into groups—each group composed of objects that begin with the same letter of the alphabet. Later, show children a single card and ask them to select other cards each of which begins with the same letter.

- *Word sorts.* Purchase word cards from a commercial vendor. Ask children to sort the cards into groups—each group of words beginning with the same letter. Later, invite children to place a word card on their desks and look through magazines and newspapers for other words that begin with the same letter as the word card. Students can cut out the words (or their accompanying illustrations) to paste on sheets of construction paper to form collages.
- *People letters.* Write a letter of the alphabet on the chalkboard. Ask one or more students to arrange themselves on the floor of the classroom in the shape of that letter (i.e., one student in a curved shape could represent the letter *C;* two students laying on the floor perpendicular to each other would represent the letter *T;* three students could lay on the floor in the shape of the letter *N*). Stand on a stepladder and take a photograph of each "student letter." When the photos are developed, arrange them on the bulletin board. Ask students to look through magazines to select words beginning with specific "people letters."
- *Sentence combinations.* Select a sentence from a favorite big book or story. Print the sentence on a strip of oaktag and show it to the students. With a pair of scissors cut apart each word and hand each word to a separate student. Invite students to come to the front of the classroom and place their word cards on the tray of the chalkboard in the same order as in the original sentence. Later, you may wish to invite students to each take one of the words and create an original sentence containing that word to be printed in a class journal.
- *Personal dictionaries.* Invite students to create their own personal dictionaries of favorite words, special words, difficult words, or just "Words I Like." Have children add to their individual dictionaries throughout the year and share them with each other. An al-

ternative strategy would be to provide each child with an inexpensive file box (or cardboard shoe box) in which to keep collections of words (each printed on a separate index card).

Activities for Semiphonetic and Phonetic Spellers

Semiphonetic and phonetic spellers are those children who are dependent on the sounds of language in helping them determine the spelling of unfamiliar words. At this stage, word recognition skills and spelling ability develop in tandem; thus these children should have regular and frequent exposure to lots of reading materials and time to utilize those materials in comfortable instructional settings. The following are some selected activities appropriate for assisting spellers at this stage of development:

- *Picture packs.* Ask students to cut favorite pictures from a magazine or newspaper, and then to paste these pictures on separate index cards. Each student's index cards can be placed inside a cellophane sandwich bag. Invite youngsters to look through other magazines and newspapers locating words, each of which begins with the sound of the word represented by a picture in the bag. Students may wish to make this a long-term activity collecting words and pictures and filing them all in a master file.
- *Word collage.* Have students form groups, with each group responsible for collecting words (from books, magazines, letters, journals, etc.) that share a common element (words beginning with a consonant, words with an *r* sound, words ending in *-ing,* words with a silent *e*). Each collection of words can be pasted onto a sheet of oaktag to complete a collage.
- *Word frames.* Provide students with word frames such as the following:

t_ _d

m_ _t

r_ _d

c_ _e

Invite students to complete the word frames to create as many words as possible. Encourage students to create their own word frames to share with their classmates or to post on the bulletin board as part of a "Daily Challenge."

- *Guess my rhyme.* Occasionally make up riddles such as the following: "I'm a word that begins with an s- and rhymes with *pink.* What am I?" "I'm a word that starts like *jump* and rhymes with *back.*" You may wish to have a "Riddle of the Day" for students to solve as they arrive in the morning or are waiting for the busses to take them home at the end of the day.

- *Letters to word.* Provide each child with a file folder that has been folded up from the bottom and stapled to create a pocket. Print letters of the alphabet on separate index cards and distribute those cards to students in the class. Invite students to contribute a word that you can write on the chalkboard. Have students select the appropriate letters from their collection and place them in the file folder pockets to correctly spell the designated word. Students can then hold up their individual pockets for sharing and checking. Continue with other student-selected words.

- *Edible letters.* Spread a small amount of whipped cream on a tabletop or desk. Trace a series of letters or a word into the whipped cream and invite students to move their finger through the tracing to tactilely spell selected words. Students can lick their fingers after each tracing, if desired.

- *Revealing words.* Select an appropriate big book to share with the class. (A book with predictable text is particularly appropriate.) Cover selected words in the text with small stick-on tags. As you read the story to the class, invite students to determine the word(s) that are covered based on context. You may wish to focus on selected spelling patterns (e.g., words with double consonants, words ending in *-ing,* words beginning with a consonant blend). The words can be posted on a large wall chart and added to when other books are shared in this manner.

- *Word of the day.* Each day call out a commonly misspelled word or a favorite word selected by students. (Each student can, on a rotating basis, be the "word selector" of the day.) Students are encouraged to look for the selected word in their writing or reading activities and use it in conversations with classmates as much as possible.

- *Word wall.* Students write words they have learned how to spell throughout the week on a large sheet of newsprint that has been posted along one wall of the classroom. Additional sheets of newsprint can be added to the wall throughout the year. This serves as a visual reminder of the number of words students have learned during the school year as well as a resource for students during selected writing activities. The word wall can also serve as a source of words for various spelling games (e.g., a variation of "Wheel of Fortune," Bingo, crossword puzzles).

Activities for Transitional and Conventional Spellers

At this stage of development, students have begun to master the sound-letter components of words. The focus now is on assisting children in recognizing word structures and components such as affixes, root words, and syllables (Gentry and Gillet, 1993). The following activities can assist youngsters in mastering those skills:

- *Word of the day.* Invite students to select a word from one individual's writing or a book being shared in class. That word is posted over the chalkboard, and students are encouraged to search for the word in their reading and writing. Sentences in which the word is located are rewritten on a large sheet of newsprint and posted along one wall of the classroom.

- *Half and half.* Introduce students to compound words by posting a base word over the chalkboard (*hand,* for example). Invite students to brainstorm for as many compound words as possible that use that base word (e.g., *handsome, handwriting, handiwork*). Later, students may wish to create their own special collections, notebooks, or dictionaries of compound words.
- *Word sorts.* As in the previous sections, word sorts can be used to help students focus on the elements or components of words. Students can collect words that contain an identified affix, pattern, or root word. Word cards can be prepared and spread out on a large table. Invite students to notice commonalities and comparisons between and among various word families.
- *Spelling journal.* Encourage each student to create and maintain a spelling journal. The journal can contain one or more of the following (according to student or teacher decisions):

A personal collection of words that are hard to spell.

Thoughts, feelings, and emotions about spelling ability or spelling progress.

Rules or word patterns the student has learned or is attempting to master.

A special mnemonic device the student has discovered that assists in the spelling of troublesome words.

"Demon words," or words that frequently give the student a great deal of difficulty while writing.

Interesting facts about words (their origins or various uses) or quotations that use words in unusual or interesting ways.

Reflections on conferences with the teacher—what was discussed, how the student felt about the conference, or how the student plans to use the information to improve spelling ability.

A record of the student's successes in spelling or learning to spell particularly difficult words.

It should be obvious that spelling can be and should be a natural extension of the writing process. Giving students a list of words to memorize each week separates spelling from the context of writing. As a result, students begin to see writing and spelling as two independent entities of the elementary curriculum. However, our experience has been that when spelling emanates naturally from the other language arts then it achieves a sense of importance in students' lives. So too is the fact that spelling is an individual matter: Not all students need the same list of spelling words to master simply because not all students are at the same level of spelling development.

Our own classroom experiences and observations have proven to us that spelling in an integrated language arts program is more realistic, holistic, and meaningful for students than it would be in more traditional classrooms. The implication is that spelling should be naturally embedded in (and a natural extension of) the other language arts and not isolated from reading, writing, listening, and speaking.

GRAMMAR

What do you remember about grammar instruction when you were an elementary student? Do you recall an endless succession of workbook pages and dull homework assignments from an English textbook? Do you remember filling in a succession of skill sheets that had little meaning or little relevance to other parts of your language arts program? Or, do you remember having to memorize some meaningless rules so that you could pass a grammar test or exam? Indeed, for many of us, our instruction in grammar was certainly less than exciting and often incomprehensible. Indeed, thousands of teachers around the country are questioning some of the traditional assumptions about how and when grammar should be taught. This becomes particularly significant when you look at some of the recent research on grammar instruction. For example, consider the following:

- "The teaching of formal grammar was found to have a negligible or even harmful effect on the improvement of writing because it usually displaces some instruction and practice in actual composition" (NCTE, 1987).
- "Papers written by students who studied traditional grammar for two years had more errors than students who merely wrote daily instead of working on exercises in grammar textbooks" (Elbow, 1973; Linden and Whimbey, 1990).
- "To understand the rules of grammar, children must be able to think in abstract terms, a cognitive skill they fail to possess until age 11 or 12 or even later" (Farris, 1993).
- "Over the past 30 years, innumerable studies of the efficacy of teaching grammar as a separate subject have all led to the same conclusion: Grammar drill may teach children enough to pass a weekly test, but most of them rarely use what they 'learned' in those drills in their own speaking or writing" (Galda, Cullinan and Strickland, 1993).
- *"The study of traditional school grammar wastes students' and teachers' time* [emphasis added] *because it is not useful in that it does not truly describe language and how it works, and time spent on grammar teaching and practice takes time away from actual language use"* (Galda, Cullinan and Strickland, 1993).

This research does not necessarily suggest that teachers should abandon grammar instruction altogether. What it does imply is a need to rethink the ways in which grammar instruction can become a natural and normal part of the languaging activities of children. Weaver (1979) makes a distinction between the formal or more traditional ways of teaching grammar, and the development of students' intuitive sense of grammar through informal instruction. We would like to emphasize that when children are surrounded by language in all its forms, they begin to develop an intuitive sense of grammar simply because they have opportunities to "see" how grammar works in a variety of contexts. In fact, the more language youngsters are exposed to during their formative years, the more they will begin to integrate and become familiar with the structures and principles of language. That learning frequently is incidental and informal and certainly has more of an impact on children's use and appreciation of grammar principles than does any series of workbook pages or formal skill lessons.

TYPES OF GRAMMAR

No doubt, when you think of grammar, you think of a series of workbook exercises in which you had to circle nouns, verbs, adjectives, adverbs, and the like in a series of sentences. It is probably safe to say that your recollections of those activities are less than favorable, that you see little relationship between the ability to identify verbs and an improvement in your writing or speaking skills.

Unfortunately, that notion of grammar instruction persists today, despite the new research and new ideas about the role of grammar instruction discussed in the preceding section. What remains, however, is the fact that there are three different types of grammar: (1) traditional, (2) structural, and (3) transformational. The way in which you include grammar as an element of your integrated language arts program will be dependent upon an understanding of these grammars and how they relate to one another. Let's look at each in greater detail.

Traditional Grammar

Traditional grammar is the type we are all probably most familiar with. This is the grammar of parts of speech, parts of sentences, and types of sentences. Traditional grammar has often been described as *prescriptive* in that it provides the rules necessary for socially correct usage.

Traditional grammar dates back to medieval times and is based primarily on Latin—a language many educators (past and present) considered the perfect language. Since many scholars perceived Latin to be the "noblest" language ever created, the logic was that if its rules were translated into the English language, then young students would be able to master to intricacies of language learning.

What we have discovered, however, is that the formal teaching of the rules of grammar have little or no effect on children's mastery of language. Too often, exercises designed to "train" students to recognize and memorize nouns, adjectives, and compound-complex or imperative sentences have little if any carryover effect in teaching writing competence. Unfortunately, these ideas about the "rules of grammar" persist today and unduly influence the teaching of language arts—particularly at the secondary level.

As further justification for the inefficiency of a traditional approach to grammar instruction, we offer the following conclusions:

> A knowledge of grammar does *not* in itself guarantee that even the serious-minded student will thereby become a master of correct English. One can know all about grammar and still make stupid blunders. . . . . Indeed, a *formal* study of grammar would certainly be an inefficient means by which to learn how to avoid errors. (Pence and Emery, 1963, pp. iv–v)

Such concentrated effort to learn rules and labels may make students adept at analyzing sentences, but it will have very little effect on students' ability to acquire better language habits or to use the language more skillfully. (Nessel, Jones, and Dixon, 1989, p. 290)

We do not suggest that you should forget grammar entirely; rather, we want to make you aware of the traditional ways in which grammar has been presented in the past and balance that with some integrated language arts activities and strategies that will help students use grammar in its proper context.

Structural Grammar

Structural grammar is concerned with the ways in which English is used. As such it is *descriptive* (whereas traditional grammar was *prescriptive*). Providing students with exposure to structural grammar helps them understand subtle differences in the meaning of our language as it is used. According to this theory, words are categorized into their functions—with some words having more than one function (the word *run,* for example can serve as both a verb and a noun depending on how it is used in a sentence).

Grammarians have determined that there are seven basic sentence patterns that can help students learn the function and structure of sentence elements. These are illustrated in Table 13.3.

As before, we are not suggesting that your grammar instruction be confined to lists of sentence patterns for students to underline, circle, and memorize. Rather, we wish to show you how to present to students some of the elements of the English language in meaningful contexts.

One of the ways in which you can help your students appreciate (not memorize) structural elements is to provide them with some of their favorite books and invite them to select one or more of their favorite sentences. These sentences can then be written on strips of paper and posted on the chalkboard or bulletin board. Encourage students to analyze the sentences and explain why they were memorable. Later, students may wish to rewrite or rearrange the words in the sentences in order to change the meaning. For example, the following sentence was selected by students in Marty Hemple's first-grade classroom as a memorable one from the book *I Know an Old Lady* by Rose Bonne:

I know an old lady who swallowed a spider that wriggled and wriggled and tickled inside her.

Marty's students decided that this was a good sentence because it was actually "a lot of smaller sentences put together":

I know an old lady.
The lady swallowed a spider.
The spider wriggled and wriggled.
The spider tickled inside her.

The students then decided that the smaller sentences could be rearranged into several new sentences, such as:

An old lady I know.
We know an old lady.

The old lady is known by lots of people.

The students discovered that although there were several ways to write the sentences, the way it was done in the book had the most impact.

Transformational Grammar

The third type of grammar is known as *transformational grammar*. This type of grammar is less concerned with the description of sentence types than it is with what goes on in the language user's head that allows him or her to generate sentences or combine sentences into new patterns. Two key concepts are involved in transformational grammar: *deep structure*—what a sentence means and how that meaning can be conveyed—and *surface structure*—the form (spoken or written) used to communicate the deep structure. The simple idea behind transformational grammar is that a simple declarative sentence (i.e., "The lion sleeps.") can be transformed to generate new sentences:

The lion, his belly filled, sleeps in the reeds near the river.

TABLE 13.3   Seven Basic Sentence Patterns

Pattern	Description	Sample Sentence
1. N-V	Subject (noun) and intransitive verb with no complements	Grasshoppers hopped.
2. N-V-N	Subject, transitive verb, and direct object	The grasshopper chewed the twig.
3. N-LV-N	Subject, linking verb, and complement	Grasshoppers are insects.
4. N-LV-Adj	Subject, linking verb, and predicate adjective	Grasshoppers are careful.
5. N-V-N-N	Subject, transitive verb, indirect object, and direct object	Grasshoppers give babies food.
6. N-V-N-N	Subject, transitive verb, direct object, and objective complement	Grasshoppers make babies hunters.
7. N-V-N-Adj	Subject, transitive verb, direct object, and objective complement	Grasshoppers keep babies satisfied.

TABLE 13.4 Transformation of Sentences

Transformation	Description	Sample Sentence
Simple Transformations		
1. Negative	*Not* or *n't* and auxiliary verb inserted	Lions roar. Lions don't roar.
2. Yes/no question	Subject and auxiliary verb switched	The lion stalked the jungle? Did the lion stalk the jungle?
3. *Wh-* question	*Wh-* word *(who, what, which, when, where, why)* or *how,* and auxiliary verb inserted	Lions roar. Why do lions roar?
4. Imperative	*You* becomes the subject	Lions give cubs meat. Give cubs meat.
5. There	*There* and auxiliary verb inserted	Lions are cautious. There are cautious lions.
6. Passive	Subject and direct object switched and the main verb changed to past participle form	Lions make cubs hunters. Cubs are made hunters by lions.
Complex Transformations		
1. Joining	Two sentences joined using conjunctions such as *and, but, or*	Lions roar. Tigers roar. Lions and tigers roar.
2. Embedding	Two (or more) sentences combined by embedding one into the other	Lions are animals. Lions are cautious. Lions are cautious animals.

The old and mangy lion sleeps in the sunlight undisturbed by the playful cubs nearby.

The hungry lion walks among the acacia trees looking for scraps; but finding none, sleeps in the cool of the river bank.

Transformational grammar activities help youngsters realize that there are a variety of ways in which sentences can be created, expanded, and elaborated in their writing and speaking. Obviously, the examples used above would probably not find their way into the speech patterns of an average third-grade student; but those same third-grade students can begin "playing with" language in unique and creative ways. In so doing, they begin learning about important grammatical principles—not through a process of memorization but rather through a "hands-on" process of creation and expansion. Table 13.4 illustrates the eight basic types of sentence transformations.

The current emphasis on transformational grammar has produced a number of strategies for teachers to use in helping youngsters appreciate the role of this form in all their language arts. One of the most promising is sentence combining, wherein students focus on sentence construction as they analyze, combine, select, rearrange, elaborate, organize, refocus, and edit their writing (Strong, 1986). Sentence combining is a process of manipulating sentences. This may make those sentences longer (although not always), while it may also improve students' writing and use of language. Sentence combining allows students to experiment with different combinations and varied creative approaches to sentence construction. It is important to keep in mind, however, that students may see sentence combining as nothing more than "busywork" instead of as an instructional writing strategy. Weaver (1979) cautions that "sentence combining activities are only an adjunct to the writing program and the writing process and should never be used as substitutes for actual writing" (pp. 83–84). Implicit in this is that sentence combining be an authentic part of language (e.g., a teaching tool to be used with an individual student's journal; a focus on structures used in a children's book). It should never be used as an isolated part of language instruction.

To illustrate, the box below presents examples of two types of sentence transformations: (1) sentence joining and (2) sentence embedding.

Another effective strategy to help youngsters realize the transformations that can take place within and between sentences involves the use of literature. For these activities, you can invite students to select one or more of their favorite sentences from a familiar book. Each of these sentences can be written on individual strips of paper and posted over the chalkboard. Invite students to "break down" each of the designated sentences into simpler sentences.

For example, the following sentence from *A Frog Prince* by Alix Berenzy (New York: Holt,

1989) could be broken down into several simpler sentences:

> But the frog, quick as a wink, flicked out his tongue and caught the poor creature on the end of it. (p. 12)

1. The frog was quick.
2. The frog was quick as a wink.
3. The frog flicked out his tongue.
4. The frog caught the poor creature.
5. The frog caught the poor creature on the end of his tongue.

It is important to remember that when you are using sentences from children's literature for analysis, you should stress what effect the author was trying to have on the reader (Tompkins and Hoskisson, 1991). The intent is to have students understand how combining can modify or change the impact of a sentence in a variety of ways. The ultimate goal is to provide opportunities for students to combine and modify the sentences from their own writings to achieve higher levels of writing proficiency and an appreciation for grammar

BOX 13.5

EXAMPLES OF SENTENCE COMBINING

Sentence Joining

1. The dog is big.
1. The dog is mean.
1. The dog is big and mean.

2. Jacob caught a fish.
2. Kevin yelled across the lake.
2. When Jacob caught the fish, Kevin yelled across the lake.

3. Karen won the race.
3. Karen received the gold medal.
3. When Karen won the race, she was given the gold medal.

Sentence Embedding

1. The cat is hungry.
1. The cat is making lots of noise.
1. The cat who is hungry is making lots of noise.
1. The hungry cat is making lots of noise.

2. Russell plays tennis.
2. Russell is an athlete.
2. Russell, who is an athlete, plays tennis.
2. Russell, a tennis player, is a good athlete.

3. The gnu is strange.
3. The gnu is walking through the compound.
3. The gnu which is walking through the compound is strange.
3. The strange gnu is walking through the compound.

in realistic, authentic settings. Sentence combining can be a powerful instructional technique—but only when students perceive it as an aid to their own developing languaging skills, not as a series of required workbook exercises.

Strong (1986) suggests using the following guidelines when developing any type of sentence-combining activities:

1. Discuss purposes for sentence combining that include creating good sentences, becoming flexible in writing, and exploring ways to transform sentences.
2. Encourage students to try new patterns and to take risks with solutions to sentence-combining problems.
3. Provide a positive environment for risk taking by accepting various solutions; when marginal solutions are offered, refer them to the class for judgment.
4. Use context clues and oral prompts to help students understand how sentence combining functions.
5. After modeling how sentence-combining exercises function, place students in pairs to work through exercises orally.
6. When students are working in pairs, have one student act as scribe for the other, then reverse roles. Have students discuss problems and work out solutions.
7. Have pairs of students develop options for a sentence-combining activity and then agree on the best solution. Ask them to explain why they prefer particular sentences.
8. In round-robin combining, encourage students to listen closely and then give as many solutions to a sentence-combining cluster as they can. Ask students to vote on and discuss reasons for their choices.
9. Be specific in your praise of good sentences; tell students what you like about these sentences.
10. Welcome mistakes as opportunities for group problem solving and use mistakes as a basis for skill development in editing workshops.
11. Use transformations handed in by students for in-class workshops.
12. Assign an exercise for homework and then ask several students to put their work on ditto masters. Compare their versions in class.
13. Brainstorm with the class about how an exercise could be made more specific and detailed by adding additional information. Put these details between exercise sentences, or elaborate sentence-combining clusters and then compare results.
14. Have students write out solutions to various sentence-combining clusters on note cards. Shuffle the cards and ask students to rearrange them into a clear, coherent paragraph.
15. Use sentence combining as a springboard for journal writing. Have students do an exercise each day and then extend that exercise with sentences of their own.
16. Have students combine sentences in a lean, direct style. Contrast the effects of the active and passive voices.
17. Ask students to compare their style with that of professional writers. Rewrite a passage into separate sentences and ask students to recombine the individual sentences and then compare their versions with the original.
18. Analyze a sentence-combining exercise for tone, cohesion, method of development, and logical patterns.
19. Create original sentence-combining exercises focused on specific transformations, course content, or discourse patterns.
20. Emphasize transfer learning by drawing sentence-combining activities from student texts and literature being studied. Have students revise their writing with a focus on particular sentence-combining skills. Follow sentence-combining lessons with parallel writing tasks for application.

TEACHING GRAMMAR

As we mentioned earlier, you probably remember grammar instruction as nothing more than the

BOX
13.6

TEACHING SENTENCE TYPES

1. *Introduce the concept.* For example, invite students to select several different sentences from the book *Ming Lo Moves the Mountain* by Arnold Lobel (New York: Scholastic, 1982). Print each sentence on a separate strip of paper and post on the bulletin board. Encourage students to move the sentence strips into each of four different sentence types (declarative, interrogative, imperative, exclamatory). For example:

   Declarative: Ming Lo and his wife lived in a house at the bottom of a large mountain.
   Interrogative: "My dear wife," said Ming Lo, "how can one small man such as I move a large mountain such as this?"
   Imperative: "Go home, Ming Lo."
   Exclamatory: "We *must* find a way to move the mountain!"

2. *Provide additional information about the grammatical concept.* Review for students the four different types of sentences and reread the sentences on the sentence strips. Then invite students to write additional sentences about Ming Lo and his wife on separate strips of paper. Encourage students to place their new sentence strips in the correct categories along with the sentence strips from the book. Encourage students to note any similarities between the sentence strips within a category.

3. *Provide activities.* Invite students to work in teams of two or three. Encourage each team to prepare sentence strips using the names of students in the classroom. Sentences should include examples of each of the four sentence types. Provide opportunities for teams to share their strips with each other.

4. *Review major points.* As a class, prepare a notebook that displays different examples of sentence types. Invite students to highlight words in each sentence strip that may offer clues to its type. Later, students may wish to create an additional display of these clue words (by category).

5. *Locate examples in literature.* Provide students with other examples of books by Arnold Lobel (e.g., *Days with Frog and Toad, Mouse Tales, Mouse Soup, On Market Street, A Zoo for Mister Muster*). Invite them to work in pairs or teams to locate examples of each of the four sentence types in one or more of Lobel's books. These can be posted or recorded on individual sentence strips.

6. *Apply to own writing.* Invite each student to write an imaginary letter to Ming Lo using all the sentence types in the letters. The letters can be recorded in their journals and can be framed as letters of advice ("Dear Ming Lo") or as informational letters concerning the composition and creation of different mountain types (as part of a geology unit, for example). Students should be provided with opportunities to share their information with each other and with the class.

completion of workbook pages or skill sheets. Yet, as we have discovered, the most effective way of helping students understand and appreciate the role of grammar in their lives is to use (1) children's literature, and (2) students' own writing as focal points for grammar instruction. Workbook pages frequently seem meaningless to children, whereas books and personal writing provide an authentic atmosphere for the inculcation of grammar skills.

Tompkins and Hoskisson (1991) have developed a six-step process that can be used to teach grammar and replace the traditional workbooks and skill sheets. This series of steps is appropriate for use with instruction built upon literature or personal writings (see Box 13.6).

It is important to keep in mind that language arts or English textbooks are not necessary to teach grammatical concepts. Those concepts achieve a sense of authenticity when they are structured within literature or writing activities.

In this chapter we have shared the basic tools of writers: spelling and grammar. Although we present these elements in separate sections of the chapter, we wish to conclude by making a most important point. That is, the tools of writing must be integrated throughout the entire writing process in order to achieve authenticity and meaningfulness in the minds of students. Conducting a grammar lesson, for example, which is separate from the process approach to writing may give students an unrealistic portrait of language arts. Students may view language arts as nothing more than a collection of isolated skills taught in a disconnected sequence. Current practices demonstrate that when the tools of writing are inexorably intertwined into all aspects of the writing process, then student's appreciation for, and growth in, language arts escalates dramatically. We hope that our discussion of these tools will provide you with a wealth of opportunities for developing integrated lessons that involve, engage, and interest youngsters throughout the language arts and throughout the entire elementary curriculum.

CATHY SWANSON'S JOURNAL

✤ May 10

What did the electron say to the proton?" asked Josh. After several children offered good, but incorrect, responses, Josh revealed the answer. "Wow, I'm really attracted to you!"

"What did the hair say to the balloon?" asked Greg. "Don't give me any static!" The class roared.

"What kind of book rubs you the wrong way?" queried a third student. "Science friction, of course!" (I think this child's parent had more fun helping with homework than usual!!)

After brainstorming words relating to the study of electricity yesterday, I asked the kids to write three riddles or jokes about the subject. They were really anxious to share them this morning!

✤ May 12

One idea I had that I want to follow through on next year is to build a library of cassette tapes featuring parents reading picture books. I collected two this year: Matt's parents taped an adapted version of the classic *Treasure Island,* and K.T.'s mom read *Mr. Mumble* by Peter Catalonotto (this is one of Kate's favorite stories).

The kids love to hear the parents read, and taping a story is a good way for working parents to become involved in the classroom without actually being there.

❧ May 13

Several things were reinforced for me today as Mara presented her (outstanding) report on the Holocaust:

- *Expectations are exceeded when the task is meaningful to the child.* Mara was interested in learning about the Holocaust because of her Jewish heritage. She heard a survivor speak about this atrocity and she wanted to know more. She was engaged on a very deep level.
- *Peer interest is high when it is obvious that the learning is personal and meaningful.* The children listened more intently than I've ever seen, and the questions they asked Mara afterward reflected how much they learned. The discussion that followed lasted 30 minutes and was completely student-directed.
- *When students question, interact with, and respond to the world around them they become life-long learners.* What Mara taught herself and modeled for her peers is invaluable. She raised the curiosity of the other children, showed what power there is in learning, and exemplified how one might go about finding the answers to your questions.

❧ May 20

Today I experienced one of those moments that makes a teacher want to dance!

We were talking about the characters of John Gardiner's book, *Stone Fox,* when Billy made a wonderful, incredible comparison. He said that there were several similarities between Little Willy (*Stone Fox*) and Marty in *Shiloh.* Like Marty, Willy showed great love and respect for a dog. He also showed bravery against "a mean guy; Judd in *Shiloh,* and Stone Fox in this book. And, Ms. Swanson, both the bad guys turned out to be O.K. in the end."

"WOW!" I shrieked (and probably scared most of my class). "Bill, that is one terrific insight!" Bill's face regained its color and the corners of his mouth began to turn upward as he fought a smile. I immediately taped a "Great Thinker" award to his shirt; he giggled humbly.

Bill sometimes struggles with reading—but when the stories and characters are meaningful to him, he can make the connections that help him "learn to learn."

TEACHER AS LEARNER/TEACHER AS RESEARCHER

Technological Networking

Patrick Wynne is a second-grade teacher in a rural school district in northern Wisconsin. As a lifelong resident of the area, he values the wide open spaces and easy-going lifestyle of this part of the country. An avid outdoorsman, he only needs to step outside his door to experience the solitude and majesty of nature in all its pristine beauty.

But Patrick is equally aware that his self-imposed isolation could leave him out of the mainstream of the educational reforms taking place in suburban and urban schools through the state. So, too, is he aware that his students, who are growing up in an increasingly technological society, could be "left out in the cold" in regard to technology and its place in their lives.

In the last few years, Patrick (along with several of his colleagues) has discovered that the electronic age offers unique opportunities to expand his learning as well as that of his students. Through networks and electronic bulletin boards, Patrick is able to interact and collaborate with educators from throughout Wisconsin and across the country. Utilization of various telecommunications networks offers Patrick an enhanced access to ef-

fective classroom strategies and techniques, unique opportunities to discuss some of the latest educational developments with teachers from coast to coast, an opportunity to share classroom challenges and potential solutions, a means to learn about the latest in children's literature, and a way in which to conduct classroom research through the assistance of teachers, professors, and researchers from around the world.

What Patrick has discovered is that he is now part of an "electronic team" —engaged in collaborative work that seeks to address common concerns, probe significant classroom issues, and raise varied questions in a spirit of cooperation and support. He is no longer isolated, rather he is now part of a larger "community of learners."

In our discussions with Patrick he outlines the following benefits of this technological networking:

1. He is able to stay up-to-date with many of the latest innovations, discoveries, and research related to language arts instruction.
2. He can "connect" with fellow second-grade teachers in any part of

the country to "talk" about mutual concerns and explore potential solutions.

3. He has increased his access to educational resources. He has been able to utilize data bases, instructional software, and new instructional material without leaving his classroom.

4. He has been able to expand the parameters of his classroom research by "interfacing" with people in business, industry, and government, as well as a host of educational agencies.

5. He is able to share his expertise with teachers both near and far and participate in "team teaching" opportunities that benefit larger numbers of students.

6. His students have been able to expand their research horizons through collaborative efforts with other second-grade students from around the country. Additionally, his students have increased access to computing resources (machines and software), and electronic publications, as well as the electronic delivery of instructional materials.

7. Students' communication skills are enhanced when they get "on-line" with other students. They are able to practice and use their developing abilities in a supportive, non-threatening, and reinforcing arena.

Patrick's outreach efforts have provided him and his students with the services of teachers and students that might normally be unavailable in his rural environment. Networking has opened up the walls of his classroom and enhanced the learning opportunities for everyone (himself included). Most important is the fact that Patrick has discovered the impact technological networking can have on his continual quest for innovative answers to classroom issues. Equally important, Patrick has become an ardent supporter of the "Teacher as Learner/ Teacher as Researcher" model. As he states, "Networking has helped me and my students to 'connect' with the larger world and to investigate all the dynamics possible through collaborative investigations and mutual sharing. For me, it reinforces the value of being a co-learner alongside my students."

Journal Reflections

Select one or more of the questions below that interest you and respond in your journal.

1. Cathy's journal entry for May 13 reveals three very powerful observations. Using any of Cathy's other journal entries for this section (May 10, May 12, or May 20) what might be a powerful statement you would pose? How might you apply that statement to your own classroom?

2. Select a section from a piece of children's literature. Using some of the ideas presented in this chapter, design a grammar lesson that focuses on the parts of speech. You may wish to work with a classmate to design some appropriate activities.

3. Do you support an individualized spelling program——one in which each child has his or her own separate list of spelling words to master? What might be some of the challenges of an individualized program?

4. Design your own question.
   ✓ What is a question you have about the chapter?
   ✓ How will you pursue the answer to that question?
   ✓ Respond in your journal.

REFERENCES AND SUGGESTED READINGS

Atwell, N. *In the Middle: Writing, Reading, and Learning with Adolescents.* Upper Montclair, NJ: Boynton/Cook, 1987.

Barbe, W. B., Lucas, V. H., Wasylyk, T. M., Hackney, C. S., and Braun, L. A. *Zaner-Bloser Creative Growth in Handwriting (Grades K–8).* Columbus, OH: Zaner-Bloser, 1984.

Barchers, S. *Teaching Language Arts: An Integrated Approach.* St. Paul, MN: West Publishing, 1994.

Block, C. C. *Teaching the Language Arts: Expanding Thinking Through Student-Centered Instruction.* Boston: Allyn and Bacon, 1993.

Bonne, Rose. *I Know An Old Lady.* New York: Scholastic, 1961.

Booth, D. *Spelling Links.* Markham, Ontario: Pembroke Publishers, 1991.

Cooper, J. D. *Literacy: Helping Children Construct Meaning.* Boston: Houghton Mifflin, 1993.

Elbow, P. *Writing Without Teachers.* New York: Oxford University Press, 1973.

Fairchild, S. "Handwriting as a Language Art." In Carl Personke and Dale Johnson, eds., *Language Arts Instruction and Beginning Teaching.* Englewood Cliffs, NJ: Prentice Hall, 1987.

Farris, P. "Views and Other Views: Handwriting Instruction Should Not Become Extinct." *Language Arts* 68 (1991): 312–314.

Farris, P. *Language Arts: A Process Approach.* Dubuque, IA: Brown and Benchmark, 1993.

Fowler, G. "Developing Comprehension Skills in Primary Grades Through the Use of Story Frames." *The Reading Teacher* 36, no. 2 (1982): 176–179.

Galda, L., Cullinan, B., and Strickland, B. *Language, Literacy, and the Child.* Fort Worth, TX: Harcourt Brace, 1993.

Gentry, J. R. *Spel . . . is a Four Letter Word.* New York: Scholastic, 1987.

Gentry, J. R., and Gillet, J. *Teaching Kids to Spell.* Portsmouth, NH: Heinemann, 1993.

Graves, D. "Research Update: Handwriting Is for Writing." *Language Arts* 55 (March 1978): 393–399.

Graves, D. *Writing: Teachers and Children at Work.* Portsmouth, NH: Heinemann Educational Books, 1983.

Hennings, D. G. *Communication in Action: Teaching the Language Arts.* Boston: Houghton Mifflin, 1994.

Hillerich, R. L. *Teaching Children to Write, K–8: A Complete Guide to Developing Writing Skills.* Englewood Cliffs, NJ: Prentice Hall, 1985.

Howell, H. "Write on, You Sinistrals!" *Language Arts* 55 (October 1978): 852–856.

Kiester, J. B. *Caught 'Ya: Grammar with a Giggle.* Gainesville, FL: Maupin House Publishing, 1990.

Linden, M., and Whimbey, A. *Why Johnny Can't Write.* Hillsdale, NJ: Lawrence Erlbaum, 1990.

Nessel, D., Jones, M., and Dixon, C. *Thinking Through the Language Arts.* New York: Macmillan, 1989.

Norton, D. *The Effective Teaching of Language Arts.* Columbus, OH: Merrill, 1989.

Norton, D. *The Effective Teaching of Language Arts.* Columbus, OH: Macmillan, 1993.

Pence, R., and Emery, D. *A Grammar of Present-Day English.* New York: Macmillan, 1963.

Petty, W. T., Petty, D. C., and Salzer, R. T. (1994). *Experiences in Language: Tools and Techniques for Language Arts Methods.* Boston: Allyn and Bacon, 1994.

Phenix, J., and Scott-Dunne, D. *Spelling Instruction That Makes Sense.* Markham, Ontario: Pembroke Publishers, 1991.

Routman, R. *Invitations: Changing as Teachers and Learners.* Portsmouth, NH: Heinemann, 1991.

Routman, R. "The Uses and Abuses of Invented Spelling." *Instructor Magazine* 102, no. 9 (May/June 1993).

Sitton, R. *Increasing Student Spelling Achievement: Not Just on Tests, but in Daily Writing Across the Curriculum.* Bellevue, WA: Bureau of Education and Research, 1991.

Stetter, K. *Integrated Spelling Curriculum for Fourth Grade.* Unpublished manuscript.

Strong, W. *Creative Approaches to Sentence Combining.* Urbana, IL: National Council of Teachers of English, 1986.

Templeton, S. *Teaching the Integrated Language Arts.* Boston: Houghton Mifflin, 1991.

Tompkins, G. E., and Hoskisson, K. *Language Arts: Content and Teaching Strategies.* New York: Macmillan, 1995.

Weaver, C. *Grammar for Teachers: Perspectives and Definitions.* Urbana, IL: National Council of Teachers of English, 1979.

Wilde, S. *You Kan Red This!* Portsmouth, NH: Heinemann, 1992.

PART

THREE

Extending
Learning
and Literacy

CHAPTER 14 TEACHING THEMATICALLY: INTEGRATING LANGUAGE ARTS ACROSS THE CURRICULUM

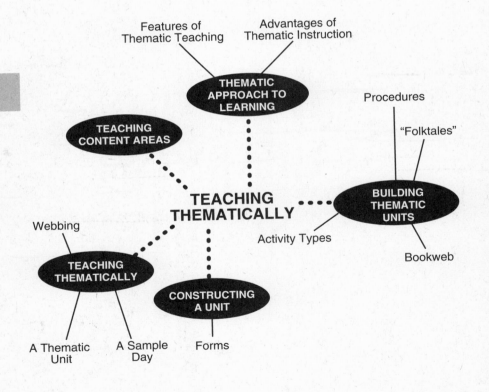

Features of Thematic Teaching

Advantages of Thematic Instruction

THEMATIC APPROACH TO LEARNING

TEACHING CONTENT AREAS

Procedures

"Folktales"

BUILDING THEMATIC UNITS

TEACHING THEMATICALLY

Activity Types

Bookweb

Webbing

TEACHING THEMATICALLY

CONSTRUCTING A UNIT

A Thematic Unit

A Sample Day

Forms

What I Know: Pre-Chapter Journaling

We invite you to think back to your years as an elementary student. What were some of the language arts activities, projects, or assignments you did as part of your study of other subjects (e.g., in science or social studies)?

Big Ideas

This chapter will offer:

1. The advantages of thematic units in integrating the elementary curriculum.
2. The steps necessary to create an effective and sustaining thematic unit.
3. Glimpses into classrooms in which thematic instruction is practiced.
4. The value of thematic teaching in establishing invitational classrooms.

This chapter describes the value of thematic teaching and provides you with a guide to developing thematic units that will challenge students, arouse their curiosity, and promote a broad understanding of concepts and ideas in all the subject areas. Thematic teaching provides practical opportunities for integrating the language arts into all dimensions of the elementary curriculum, and thematic units provide a vehicle through which thematic teaching can be effected. In using thematic units, you can assist children in developing understanding that moves far beyond "lessons" in a textbook. Additionally, youngsters are offered practical opportunities to use their language in realistic and authentic endeavors. As a result, children have an array of opportunities to become active and enthusiastic learners.

THE THEMATIC APPROACH TO LEARNING

A thematic approach to learning is a combination of strategies, activities, children's literature, and materials used to expand a concept or idea. Thematic teaching is multidisciplinary and multidimensional; it has no boundaries and no limits. It is responsive to the interests, abilities, needs, and input of children and supports their developing aptitudes and attitudes. In essence, a thematic approach to learning offers students a realistic arena within which they can pursue information through all the language arts.

Thematic teaching is built on the idea that learning can be integrative and multifaceted. Children need to be provided with a host of opportunities to become actively involved in the dynamics of their own learning. In so doing, they will be able to draw positive relationships between what "happens" in the classroom and what is happening outside the classroom. Thematic teaching promotes learning as a sustaining and relevant venture.

Features of Thematic Teaching

Thematic instruction provides multiple opportunities for students to engage in decision making and critical thinking. It offers a host of meaningful learning opportunities tailored to their needs and interests. Children are given the chance to make important choices about what they are learning as well as how they wish to go about learning that data. Most important is the fact that thematic instruction provides youngsters with hands-on learning opportunities in dealing with real-life issues and problems. The entire curriculum is interrelated and integrated to involve students in a multiplicity of learning opportunities and ventures.

Incorporated into well-designed and well-defined thematic explorations are the following important features—features that not only provide structure for a thematic unit (the instrument used to teach thematically) but also give purpose and direction for all students:

- Activities are utilized in which students are able to use all of their sensory modalities—taste, touch, hearing, seeing, and smelling.
- Lessons are created that build upon the background knowledge and prior experiences of students, giving them a firm foundation upon which learning can grow.
- A respect for and celebration of the cultural heritage, language differences, and varied socioeconomic backgrounds of students and their families is maintained.
- A value for the involvement of the community and the home as significant elements in the scholastic enhancement of students is promoted.
- Learning opportunities tied into children's interests, needs, and abilities rather than the dictates of a teacher's manual or curriculum guide are emphasized.
- A recognition of the social requisites of learning is featured. That is, students can share and discover with each other in a mutually supportive environment; one that is cooperative, rather than competitive.

BOX 14.1   ADVANTAGES OF THEMATIC TEACHING (FOR STUDENTS)

- Focuses on the *processes* of learning more than the *products* of learning.
- Breaks down the "artificial barriers" that often exist between areas of the curriculum and provides an integrative approach to learning.
- Provides a child-centered curriculum tailored to the interests, needs, and abilities . . . of children and set up to encourage children to make their own decisions and assume a measure of responsibility for learning.
- Stimulates self-directed discovery and investigation in and outside of the classroom.
- Assists youngsters in developing relationships between ideas and concepts enhancing appreciation and comprehension.
- Offers realistic opportunities for children to build upon individual backgrounds of information in developing new knowledge.
- Respects the individual cultural backgrounds, home experiences, and interest levels of children.

- Stimulates the creation of important concepts through first-hand experiences and self-initiated discoveries.
- Encourages and supports students in their efforts to take risks.
- Develops the self-direction and independence of students through a variety of learning activities and opportunities.
- Helps students understand the "why" of activities and events instead of just the "what."
- Encourages students to make approximations of learning, rather than to focus on the absolutes of learning.
- Give children ample time and opportunity to investigate topics thoroughly and to engage in reflective inquiry.

Source: Meinbach, A., Rothlein, L., and Fredericks, A. *The Complete Guide to Thematic Units: Creating the Integrated Curriculum* (Norwood, MA: Christopher-Gordon Publishers, 1995). Used by permission.

- The need for affective, social, physical, and emotional growth as tangents of cognitive growth is highlighted continuously.
- Creating a hands-on, minds-on environment in which active student involvement in learning is supported and celebrated is paramount.

Thematic instruction allows you to expand important concepts and issues. For example, if your students have a great deal of interest in environmental issues, the development of an appropriate thematic unit allows them to explore this topic in greater detail than would be possible if you relied solely on the textbook for all the necessary information. Thematic instruction also provides you with multiple opportunities to combine the skills, attitudes, and varying knowledge levels of your students with the resources,

information, and literature-related data available in and outside your classroom. In short, thematic teaching integrates many resources, all areas of the elementary curriculum, all the language arts, and the interests of your students into a meaningful and balanced approach to learning. Above all, thematic instruction demonstrates the varied relationships that exist between the integrated language arts and other aspects of the elementary curriculum in a positive and non-threatening format.

Advantages of Thematic Instruction

As you might imagine, thematic instruction offers many advantages for both teachers and students. Boxes 14.1 and 14.2 synthesize some of these advantages.

ADVANTAGES OF THEMATIC TEACHING (FOR TEACHERS)

- There is more time available for instructional purposes. Material does not have to be crammed into artificial time periods but can be extended across the curriculum and across the day.
- The connections that can and do exist between subjects, topics, and themes can be logically and naturally developed. Teachers can demonstrate relationships and assist students in comprehending those relationships.
- Learning can be demonstrated as a continuous activity—one that is not restricted by textbook designs, time barriers, or even the four walls of the classroom. Teachers can help students extend learning opportunities into many aspects of their personal lives.
- Teachers are able to relinquish "control" of the curriculum and assist students in assuming a sense of "ownership" for their individual learning destinies.
- Teachers are free to help students look at a problem, situation, or topic from a variety of viewpoints, rather than the "right way" frequently demonstrated in a teacher's manual or curriculum guide.
- The development of a "community of learners" is facilitated and enhanced through thematic teaching. There is less emphasis on competition and more emphasis on collaboration and cooperation.

- Opportunities for the teacher to model appropriate learning behaviors in a supportive and encouraging environment is enhanced.
- Assessment is more holistic, authentic, and meaningful and provides a more accurate picture of students' progress and development.
- Authentic use of all the language arts (reading, writing, listening, and speaking) is encouraged throughout all curricular areas.
- There is more emphasis on *teaching* students; less emphasis on *telling* students.
- Teachers are provided with an abundance of opportunities for integrating children's literature into all aspects of the curriculum and of the day.
- Teachers can promote problem solving, creative thinking, and critical thinking processes within all aspects of a topic.
- Teachers can promote and support children's individual autonomy and self-direction, offering students control over their learning.
- Teachers are also engaged as learners throughout the development and implementation of a thematic unit.

Source: A. Meinbach, L. Rothlein, and A. Fredericks, *The Complete Guide to Thematic Units: Creating the Integrated Curriculum.* (Norwood, MA: Christopher-Gordon Publishers, 1995). Used by permission.

BUILDING THEMATIC UNITS

Thematic units are built on the idea that learning can be integrative and multifaceted. As stated earlier, children can be provided with a host of opportunities to become actively involved in the dynamics of their own learning, to draw positive relationships between what happens in the classroom and what can or is happening outside the classroom. As such, a *thematic unit*—a concept surrounded by literature—promotes learning as a sustaining and relevant venture.

We wish to state at this point that a thematic unit is not simply a random collection of assorted activities. The effectiveness of thematic teaching rests on a structure (the thematic unit) built upon a specific topic, an assembly of major generalizations and/or principles, selected key concepts and materials, authentic activities and projects, and a distinctive arrangement of those activities.

Kucer (1993) has outlined a series of procedures that can assist teachers in the development of thematic units. His steps, outlined in Box 14.3 on page 444 offer guidelines that can be beneficial in structuring units. In addition, this sequence of six stages provides organization for the implementation and integration of thematic units across the entire elementary curriculum.

To illustrate the evolution and utilization of thematic units in action, let's look at the route followed by Lauren Saks. Lauren teaches fourth grade at Willow Valley Elementary School, where she has worked for the past nine years. She subscribes to journals such as *The Reading Teacher* and *Teaching K–8* and has a growing array of professional books in her library. Over the past several years, she has become increasingly aware of the impact and power of thematic teaching and has read everything she can find on the subject. She has also attended the annual conference of the Colorado Council of the International Reading Association four times during her teaching career—attending many sessions on thematic teaching. At each conference, she has taken advantage of the opportunities to talk with other teachers from throughout the state and solicit their ideas about thematic units. As a result of her "networking" and readings, Lauren gained some valuable insights and perspectives that built upon the basic principles of language arts instruction presented in the methods classes she took in college.

It quickly became apparent to Lauren that thematic teaching offered learning opportunities for her students that moved far beyond the dictates of a teacher's manual or the dry outline of a curriculum guide. Lauren became aware of the "power" of thematic teaching to involve students in their own self-initiated discoveries and participate in collaborative learning ventures. The more Lauren read about thematic units, the more excited she became about their utility for her classroom.

One year, in preparation for a thematic unit on folktales, Lauren sat down to craft a basic outline for the unit. (She knew that the unit would be "filled out" with the background knowledge, questions, and interests of her students.) Using the six stages outlined in Box 14.3, Lauren selected specific elements as follows:

1. Identification of a theme topic: Folktales
2. Identification of major generalizations and/or principles;

   Folktales are an important part of every culture.

   Common themes are evident in different folktales.

   Folktales have common characteristics related to plot, style, setting, and characterization

3. Key concepts:

   Good and evil

   Intelligence and bravery

   Caring and cleverness

   greed and kindness

4. Gathering of thematic materials (*literature selections*):

   Ransome, A. (1968). *The Fool of the World and the Flying Ship.* New York: Farrar, Straus and Giroux, 1968. (Russian folktale)

   Aardema, V. *Why Mosquitoes Buzz in People's Ears.* New York: Dial, 1975. (African folktale)

   Perrault, C. *Cinderella.* New York: Scribner's, 1954. (French folktale)

   Mayer, M. *East of the Sun and West of the Moon.* New York: Macmillan, (1980). (Norwegian folktale)

5. Generation of various activities: (Several activities were brainstormed through a process known as "bookwebbing," discussed below.)
6. Arranging thematic materials and activities: (After students engaged in selected bookwebbing activities, Lauren arranged the suggestions into a workable format that included simple/concrete activities, complex/abstract activities, general/specific activities, familiar/unfamiliar, and collaborative/independent activities.)

BOX 14.3

PROCEDURES FOR THEMATIC UNIT DEVELOPMENT

1. Identification of a theme topic.
   a. The topic is relevant and of interest to the students.
   b. The topic is relevant and of interest to the teacher.
   c. The topic is significant; it is important to know about.
2. Identification of major generalizations and/or principles (three to five usually work best) upon which the thematic unit will be based.
   a. The generalizations and/or principles are significant; they are important to know about.
   b. The generalizations and/or principles focus on "big" ideas rather than on minor concepts, facts, or details.
   c. The generalizations and/or principles are interrelated.
3. Identification of key concepts that support the generalizations and/or principles.
   a. Each concept is related to several generalizations and/or principles.
   b. The concepts are critical to understanding the generalizations and/or principles.
4. Gathering of thematic materials.
   a. The materials focus on the same set of generalizations and/or principles.
   b. Materials include different subject fields: science, social studies, literature.
   c. Materials include narratives, expositions, dramas, poems.
   d. Materials include different resources: books, magazines, newspapers, filmstrips, records/audiotapes, movies/videotapes.
   e. Materials represent a range of literacy and thinking abilities.
   f. Materials represent the home as well as the school culture and language.
5. Brainstorming and generation of various activities related to the theme topic, generalizations and/or principles, concepts, and materials.
   a. Activities are authentic in nature: linguistically, cognitively, developmentally, socioculturally.
   b. Activities engage students in the use of various communication systems (reading, writing, listening, speaking, art, music, mathematics, dance/movement) to learn about the generalizations and/or principles and concepts in the theme.
   c. Activities engage students in the use of various thinking processes from different disciplines (science, social science, literature) to learn about the generalizations and/or principles and concepts in the theme.
   d. Activities engage students in the use of various communication systems (reading, writing, listening, speaking, art, music, mathematics, dance/movement) for various purposes or functions.
   e. Activities are varied in nature.
   f. Activities engage students in both collaborative and independent work.
   g. Activities provide students with opportunities for problem solving, divergent thinking, risk taking, and choice (among activities as well as materials).
   h. Activities encourage students to take multiple perspectives toward various issues.
   i. Activities engage students in the generation of new meanings as well as in revisiting prior meanings; current and prior meanings are integrated and synthesized.
6. Arranging thematic materials and activities.
   a. There are opening activities that introduce students to the theme and closing activities that draw together and celebrate what has been learned and accomplished.
   b. Materials and activities are arranged around particular generalizations and/or principles and related concepts.
   c. Materials and activities are ordered from the most simple/concrete to the most complex/abstract.
   d. Materials and activities are ordered from the most general to the most specific.
   e. Materials and activities are ordered from the most familiar to the least familiar.
   f. Materials and activities are ordered from "hands on" to "hands off."
   g. Materials and activities are ordered from collaborative to independent.
   h. Throughout the thematic unit, activities require students to revisit prior meanings and to integrate them with current meanings.

Source: Kucer (1993). Used by permission.

Bookwebbing

Bookwebbing is a process in which a single example of children's <u>literature</u> serves as a "launching pad" for the creation of whole language activities. A variation of semantic webbing, bookwebbing surrounds a single piece of literature with all dimensions of the curriculum and with the integrated language arts. As bookwebs are created for additional pieces of literature, they are linked together through a common theme or topic to create a thematic unit (see below). The result is a <u>unit based on children's literature</u> and one that integrates learning through a multitude of options and possibilities.

To begin the process of bookwebbing, select a book that relates to a chapter in your text, an area of interest for students, or a topic of local concern. While it may not be possible to provide sufficient quantities of a book for every member of the class, it is possible to share the book in a host of presentation modes such as reading the book aloud to the entire class, recording the book on cassette tape for individuals or small groups to listen to during free time, or inviting a guest speaker in to share the book with a small group of students. Whichever presentation procedure you use, be sure to keep your enthusiasm and interest high—as you will want your students to do, too.

After the book-sharing process, <u>brainstorm with students</u> for curricular and language arts <u>ideas</u> that tie into the selected book. Providing students with an opportunity to brainstorm some ideas gives them a sense of "ownership" for activities selected later on. During this brainstorming process, work with students to develop a web on the chalkboard or on an oversized sheet of paper. This offers everyone an organizational plan from which elements or options for the final unit can be selected.

A "generic" web can be used as an outline or structure for the initiation and creation of a bookweb. You may wish to transfer this web onto an overhead transparency or a laminated sheet of poster board. As bookwebs are created for se-lected pieces of literature, students' ideas can be recorded with a washable marker and erased at a later date. This allows you to use the web over and over again.

As part of the design of the unit on folktales, Lauren read the book *East of the Sun and West of the Moon* to her students. Afterward, she and the students began to create a web of potential extending activities for the book—activities that would encompass several curricular areas and utilize all the language arts. The web Lauren and her students created is illustrated in Figure 14.1. The resultant activities they designed are outlined in Figure 14.2.

After the creation of the initial bookweb, Lauren began to craft some extending activities for several of the ideas suggested by the class. The final bookweb she created is summarized below. Note how Lauren took advantage of students' ideas to develop activities that were meaningful, holistic, and authentic for her students. Also, since these activities were built from student ideas, a sense of "ownership" was achieved that stimulated involvement and enhanced participa-

FIGURE 14.1 Bookwebbing

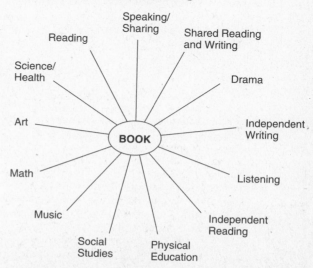

FIGURE 14.2 East of the Sun and West of the Moon

STUDENT IDEAS AND SUGGESTIONS

Questions We Have
Where do frogs live?
Where is Norway?
Where is east of the sun?

Science/Health
Study frogs
Frog life cycle
Real and fictitious animals
Weather data
Sun and Moon

What We Know
Story has a happy ending.
She will have some dangers.
There are a lot of
strange creatures.

Math
Currency rates
Distance traveled
Surveys ⟶ graphs
Categorization

Reading
Storytelling—folktales
Create folk tales
Time line of events
Language use
Other frog stories

Social Studies
Real and fictitious
    places
Forests
Vikings
Norway

Art
Troll palace
Trolls
Wind socks
Models

**Shared Reading
and Writing**
New adventures
Set in modern times

EAST OF THE SUN AND WEST OF THE MOON

Music
Folk songs
Wedding dance
Instruments

Independent Writing
Own folktale
News article
Modern version

Independent Reading
Read "The Frog Prince"
Read other versions

Physical Education
Obstacle course
"Leap Frog"

Speaking/Sharing
Take on character role
Interview character

Drama
Puppet play
Skit
Videotape

Listening
Reader's theatre
Tape recording

tion. Just as important was the fact that students were encouraged to make their own choices for activities and projects they wished to pursue. Student self-selection ensured high levels of involvement, motivation, and interest.

Reading/Language Arts

1. Invite students to contact the local public library and make arrangements for a storyteller to visit the classroom. Invite the story-

teller to share stories in the same genre as *East of the Sun and West of the Moon.*

2. To reinforce the process of how folktales are passed down from generation to generation, divide the class into several groups and invite each group to create its own original folktale. Encourage each group to tape-record their tale and preserve it in a special location. Several months later ask group members to recall the specifics of their folktale, then play the recording of their original story. Discuss the changes that occurred between the two tellings. Let students know that these changes are a normal and natural part of storytelling and give folktales their special flavor and design.

3. In a class discussion ask students to determine where important events took place. Invite students to record events on a time line to reinforce the sequential development of the story line. For example:

Maiden Frog Salamander Forest Fish Troll Marriage

4. Invite students to locate repetitious lines throughout the book. Examples include "Many weary miles" and "Do you know of a kingdom east of the sun and west of the moon?"

Science/Health

1. Students may wish to raise their own frogs. Kits can be obtained from Holcombs Educational Materials (3205 Harvard Ave., Cleveland, OH 44105, (800) 321-2543). Kit #998-0125H (currently priced at $14.95) includes a container, food, instructions, and a coupon for live tadpoles. A local teacher supply store may also have similar kits.

2. Show the video *Tadpoles and Frogs* (obtained through the National Geographic Society, Washington, DC, catalog no. 51218) to the class. Discuss the growth and development of frogs from tadpoles to adults.

3. Students might enjoy creating a list of all the real animals in the book and another list of all the fictitious animals. Encourage students to examine the list of fictitious animals to determine the real animals that would most closely resemble each fictitious one. For example: A gila monster or komodo dragon would be the real life equivalents of the giant salamander. Information can be charted and shared with the class in the form of an oral report, pictures, or a display.

4. Provide students with a copy of the Beaufort Wind Speed Chart (most science texts have one). Make arrangements to call a local weather station or the meteorologist at the local college on a daily basis to determine the average wind speed for the day. Invite students to record these speeds on a specially designed monthly calendar.

Art

1. Students may wish to build their own version of a troll palace. Encourage students to bring in recycled materials such as milk cartons, cereal boxes, tin cans, bottles, and loads of imagination. Glue, paint, string, and other art materials can be provided along with a scheduled period of time for completion of the project.

2. Students may enjoy creating trolls from homemade clay using the following recipe: Mix one cup of flour and ½ cup of salt. Add ⅓ cup of water, a little at a time. Squeeze the dough until it is smooth. Form into shapes, let air dry or bake at 225 degrees for 30 minutes. Paint with tempera paints. (*Note:* The recipe may have to be adjusted according to the number of students participating.)

3. Invite students to make their own wind socks. Form strips of construction paper into cylinders and attach colored streamers of tissue paper to the sides of the cylinders. Punch two holes in the cylinder, one on top and one on the bottom and insert a wooden dowel. (The cylinder should spin freely on the dowel.) Stick a pin through the dowel to serve as a resting place for the cylinder. Students may wish to go outside and hold their wind socks

in the wind or poke the dowels into the ground for a colorful display.

Math

1. Invite students to convert U.S. currency into Norwegian currency. (At this writing a Norwegian krone is worth 14 cents. Check with the local bank for current exchange rates.) Encourage students to determine how much a favorite fast food meal would cost in krones.
2. Students may wish to survey all the other students who have read this book. They can make lists of all the characters in the book and question others about who their favorite character is in the story. Encourage students to tabulate the results and present them in the form of bar graphs, pie charts, or line graphs.
3. Invite students to list all the animals in the book and categorize those animals from smallest to largest.

Music

1. Encourage students to learn the traditional folk song "A Frog Went a Courtin'" (one version can be found in "Go In and Out the Window," music arranged by Dan Fox [New York: Henry Holt and Co., 1987]). After students learn the song, they may wish to add some sound effects (frog and mouse sounds).
2. Students may choose to create a wedding dance. Children can stand in a circle, some with tambourines and recorders to provide background music. A piece of recorded classical music can also be used, too. (An example would be "Concerto for Harpsichord and Strings" by Johann Sebastian Bach.)
3. Students may wish to make their own recorders or flutes and invent an appropriate theme song for the book. Directions for making all sorts of musical instruments can be found in *Making Musical Things* by Ann Wiseman (New York: Scribner's, 1979).

Social Studies

1. In group discussions, invite students to list real places or things on earth that would resemble the fictitious places in the story. For example, Mountain of Ice could be the Antarctic, Father Forest could be Olympic National Forest, Great Fish of the Sea could be whales or manatees. Encourage students to form small groups and select one area to research. A display for each area can be set up in the classroom to include maps, drawings, photographs, pictures, stories, and facts.
2. To further appreciate "Father Forest," students may wish to contact the following organizations for materials and information regarding forests and forest conservation:

National Arbor Day Foundation, 100 Arbor Ave., Nebraska City, NE 68410

National Wildlife Federation, 1400 16th St. NW, Washington, DC 20036

Save America's Forests, 4 Library Court SE, Washington, DC 20003

Native Forest Action Council, PO Box 2176, Eugene, OR 97402

Lighthawk, PO Box 8163, Santa Fe, NM 87504

Information gathered from these organizations could be used as a bulletin board display or a classroom learning center.

3. Some students may be interested in researching the Vikings and their explorations. The information gathered can be presented to the class in the form of an oral report.

Physical Education

1. Students may enjoy engaging in an obstacle course relay race replicating the maiden's travels. For example: ice—carry ice cubes on spoons; swim—wiggle on mat to designated area; wind—blow a balloon along the floor; troll—beanbag toss at a picture of a troll.
2. Invite students to play a game of leapfrog over a designated course laid out on the playground.

Speaking

1. Selected students may wish to each assume the "identity" of one of the major characters in the book. Characters share their thoughts about their roles in the story.
2. One student assumes the identity of a character. Other students are invited to interview that character. Potential interview questions are brainstormed beforehand.

Drama

1. Invite small groups of students to each create their own puppet show based upon a selected scene from the story. Shows can be presented to members of the class or to other classes.
2. Encourage students to design a short skit of their favorite part of the story. Invite them to videotape the presentation and donate the completed video to the school library.

Listening

1. Invite students to create a reader's theatre version of the story for presentation to a lower grade.
2. Encourage small groups of students to plan and tape record the story. The finished tape can be added to the classroom tape library.

Shared Reading and Writing

1. Students may enjoy creating a series of new adventures for the princess. What will she do? Where will she travel? The ideas can be collected into a series of small booklets and shared with the class.
2. Encourage students to rewrite the story by setting it in modern times. What changes would need to be made in the setting, plot, and characters to make them more contemporary? How would the story unfold?

Independent Writing

1. Invite each student to create a folktale about an incident in his or her life. How could the folktale be embellished with fanciful characters and strange happenings?
2. Encourage students to each prepare a newspaper article about an incident or event from the story. These can be collected into a large newspaper for sharing with other classes.

Independent Reading

1. Read *The Frog Prince* by Jane White Canfield (New York: Harper, 1970). As a class discussion, invite students to list similarities and differences between the two stories. This will be done by using two semantic webs—one for each story. Details for each story will be listed on its appropriate semantic web.
2. Encourage students to check the library for other versions of this story. Included could be "East of the Sun and West of the Moon" in *Norwegian Folk Tales* by P. C. Asbjornsen and Jorgon E. Moe (New York: Viking, 1960), *East of the Sun and West of the Moon* by Kathleen and Michael Hague (San Diego: Harcourt Brace Jovanovich, 1980), or *East of the Sun and West of the Moon: A Play* by Nancy Willard (San Diego: Harcourt Brace Jovanovich, 1989).

Source: Adapted from Fredericks. A. *The Integrated Curriculum: Books for Reluctant Readers* (Englewood, CO: Teacher Ideas Press, 1992).

As a result of such brainstorming sessions, Lauren and her students were able to generate a host of creative whole language activities that expanded the book into every area of the curriculum and employed all of the language arts as vehicles for learning. Lauren then "employed" her students in whole class and small group brainstorming sessions for each of the other three folktale books—soliciting a variety of extending activities. Using the ideas and activities produced by the class, Lauren had the "raw data" she needed for the final design of her planned unit. What resulted was the initiation of a thematic unit constructed by students—a collection of "invitational" activities that ensured the eventual success of the thematic unit. While Lauren did not have to use all of the activities suggested by her students, she provided them with opportunities to contribute to the overall design of the final unit in personally meaningful ways.

CONSTRUCTING A THEMATIC UNIT

The construction of a thematic unit requires the consideration of a number of factors and elements. Its design, however, is flexible—allowing as it does for the utilization of a wide variety of literature and a wide array of background knowledge and interests on the part of students. While effective units will be built in concert with the students in your classroom, it is important to keep in mind that some structure is necessary in order to achieve a balance between what students desire and the overall needs of the language arts curriculum.

The figures that follow offer some planning guides for the development of thematic units.

- *Thematic Unit Plan Sheet* (Figure 14.3): This can be used as the initial planning guide for the development of a unit. It provides several opportunities for students to contribute their own ideas in concert with the principles and concepts you with to emphasize.
- *Activity Planning Guide* (Figure 14.4): These two forms permit you to develop holistic activities of different time limits as well as activities for various grouping strategies within your classroom. Again, it is not essential that every block be filled in; rather, it is more important that consideration be given to the different teaching strategies which can be included in the overall unit design.
- *Thematic Unit Materials and Resources Planning Form* (Figure 14.5): This planning guide will help in organizing the various materials and resources available for a selected unit. It will allow you to create activities based on a diversity of resources.

TEACHING THEMATICALLY

It had been a perfect weekend in Southern California. Warm weather and clear skies had sent thousands of people to the beaches, mountains, and desert to escape the congestion of Los Angeles and relax before returning to the cacophony of the work week. The fact that it was also a long weekend, with a national holiday on Monday, made the days off even that much more pleasant.

Isabel Ortiz and her family took the opportunity to visit her sister in Hermosa Beach and, as she said, "take a brief sabbatical from the classroom." It was to be a calm and quiet weekend with the requisite family barbecue, some books to read, and not a single paper to grade. Isabel has been a teacher in the Los Angeles area for 11 years. During that time she has taught fifth grade, first grade, and second grade. This year she was assigned to a fourth-grade class that, as her principal put it, "needed a ton of academic support." Always a positive thinker, Isabel saw this class as a unique challenge—a challenge she approached with vigor and enthusiasm.

The class, a wonderful collection of five different languages, a broad range of reading abilities, and 29 distinct personalities, was a true delight for Isabel. A strong believer in the integrated language arts, Isabel approached this class with lots of literature, lots of writing, and lots of love. As she would often admit to her colleagues in the faculty room at school, it was "a daily challenge and a daily joy" to be able to work with these youngsters, many of whom came from home environments that were less than supportive and certainly less than stable.

During the weekend, Isabel contemplated some of the activities and projects she would share with her students in the coming weeks. She had completed a series of lesson plans on the history of California, with a special emphasis on the Hispanic and Native American contributions to the art and architecture of the state. She wanted her students to appreciate their cultural heritage and its significance to the traditions of California. Isabel sat in her deck chair, looked out over the ocean, and smiled. She was pleased with her lessons and knew

FIGURE 14.3   Thematic Unit Plan Sheet

Topic: _____

Generalizations/Principles: _____
_____
_____
_____

Concepts: _____
_____
_____
_____

Materials: _____
_____
_____

Literature Resources: _____
_____
_____
_____
_____

Initiating Activity(ies): _____
_____
_____
_____
_____

General Activities: _____
_____
_____
_____
_____

Literature Specific Activities:
Book 1: _____
_____

Book 2: _____
_____

Book 3: _____
_____

Book 4: _____

Culminating Activity(ies): _____
_____
_____

Evaluation Techniques: _____
_____
_____

FIGURE 14.4 Activity Planning Guide

Note: The following two charts may be used to identify activities of different time lengths as well as those appropriate for various groupings of students. By including a variety of options for your students, you will be ensuring their sustained interest throughout the entire thematic unit.

Short-Term Projects (less than 1 day)	Mid-Term Projects (2–3 days)	Long-Term Projects (1 week or more)

Independent Activities	Small Group Activities	Large Group Activities	Whole Class Activities

it was going to be a good week. It was Sunday, January 16, 1994—blue skies, a warm sun, and the echoes of sea gulls were no harbinger to the events that were unfolding beneath her feet.

At 4:31 on the morning of January 17 it struck! A massive earthquake that shook everybody and everything in Southern California. Buildings collapsed, fires erupted, and gas mains ruptured all over the greater Los Angeles area. For hours, the entire region was in panic as rescue crews raced from one disaster to another, and police and firefighters were taxed to their limits and beyond. It was a horror movie in slow motion; a catastrophe that far exceeded the numbers recorded by the seismic instruments in distant laboratories. For many, it was the beginning of fear—and the beginning of an endless succession of nightmares.

In the days that followed, Isabel worried about her students—how they were coping, how they were surviving, and even where they were living. Her students all lived in the San Fernando Valley, all within 20 miles of the epicenter of the quake. For some, their apartments were reduced to a pile of crumbling concrete and broken sticks. For others, the structural damage was so great that their residences had to be condemned. Even Isabel's school had suffered several cracks and fissures and was closed for several days until the inspectors assured everyone that it was safe to reopen.

Isabel knew that when her students returned, the earthquake would be the continuing topic of conversation and thought for many days and weeks. She also knew that the personal events that touched each child's family would be all-consuming and mesmerizing—and would certainly be of far greater significance than long division, the parts of a flower, or the role of dairy farming to the nation's economy. The emotionality of the time—the fears and uncertainties students had to deal with every day after the earthquake—strained the patience and expertise of both teachers and counselors.

Isabel decided that one of the best ways she could assist her students in dealing with their immediate and long-term concerns was through a well-crafted thematic unit. Isabel believed that a thematic unit would help youngsters voice their opinions, share important information, research the causes and conditions that precipitated earthquakes and other natural disasters, and offer a vehicle through which students could better handle the daily trauma in their personal lives.

After several discussions with the class, Isabel invited students to brainstorm for the ideas, concepts, thoughts, and perceptions they had about earthquakes. Isabel also encouraged students to think about other natural disasters and their effects on the surface of the earth. (Isabel wanted to help her students understand that the earth is constantly changing, that those changes are natural ones, and that they each, in their own way, affect the humans who live on the surface of the earth.) By putting earthquakes into the broader perspective of "the changing earth," Isabel believed she could help students better comprehend and appreciate the earthquake they experienced

FIGURE 14.5 Thematic Unit Materials and Resources Planning Form

Topic: _____

Printed resources:	Student resources:
Audio/visual resources:	Literature selections:
Textbook selections:	
Neighborhood/family resources:	Guest speakers:
Artifact resources:	Field trip(s):

in the broader context of naturally occurring events.

The initial brainstorming session produced a flurry of ideas and facts—all of which Isabel recorded on the chalkboard. Students were amazed at the wide variety of experiences and breadth of background knowledge they shared about earthquakes in particular and earth changes in general. The <u>web was supplemented with children's literature</u> and additional concepts suggested by Isabel. The result of the brainstorming sessions is illustrated in Figure 14.6.

Isabel knew that the creation of a thematic unit—particularly this one—could have a powerful impact on her students. Because it was generated from the personal interests of her students, Isabel was able to design a wide range of extending activities that helped students master important concepts while, at the same time, deal with very real and personal issues. The three-week unit Isabel and her students created is presented in the following section. We invite you to discover the range of activities, the breadth of experiences, and the depth of subject matter around which this unit is constructed. Note,

FIGURE 14.6 "Earthquakes" Web

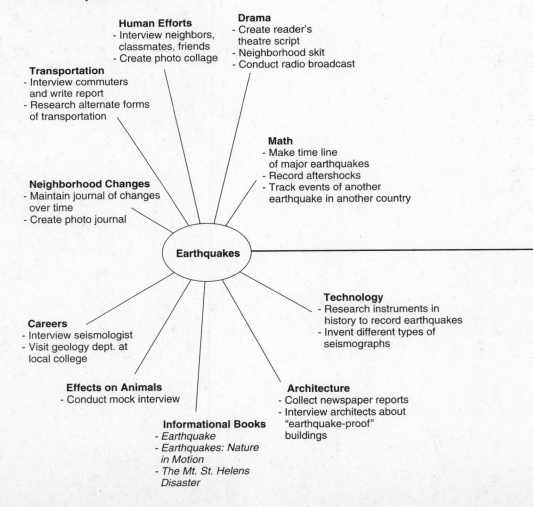

too, how the bookwebbing experience provided students with valuable input into literature-based activities. Most significant, however, is the fact that it was developed in a cooperative classroom atmosphere—Isabel and her students all contributed to its design and they all benefited from its cross-curricular orientation. What Isabel and her class did was to take advantage of a local event and local concerns to develop an integrated plan that underscored the importance of learning as something more than facts and figures extruded from a textbook.

As you might expect, students were involved in all the dynamics of the unit simply because it evolved from their own interests. The integrated language arts became the vehicle by which Isabel could "drive" her students to the furthest reaches of their imagination, interest, and creativity. In the process, she was able to systematically blend all subject areas into a unit that was dynamic, purposeful, and valuable. In essence, it was a unit of both direction and discovery.

FIGURE 14.6 *Continued*

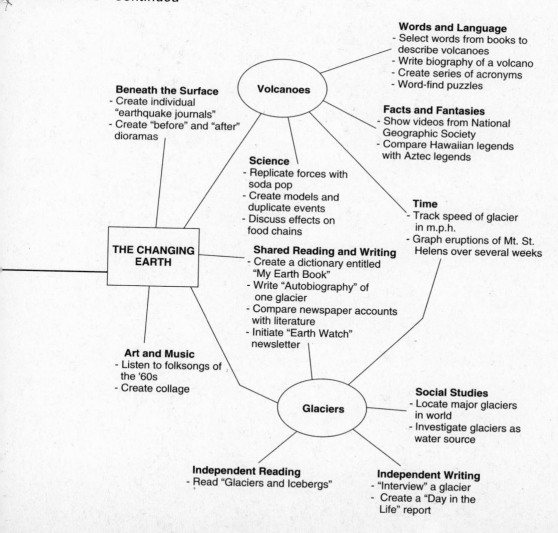

The Changing Earth

Generalizations/Principles

The surface of the earth is constantly changing.
Changes in the earth affect people living on the surface.
There are different types of forces that affect the earth.

Concepts

Earthquakes
Glaciers and icebergs
Volcanoes
Erosion (wind and water)

Materials

Primary Literature Selections

Lauber, P. *Volcano: The Eruption and Healing of Mt. St. Helens.* New York: Bradbury, 1986.

Radlauer, E., and Radlauer, R. *Earthquakes.* Chicago: Children's Press, 1987.

Rutland, J. *Exploring the Violent Earth.* New York: Warwick Press, 1980.

Simon, S. *Icebergs and Glaciers.* New York: Morrow, 1987.

Secondary Literature Selections

Aylesworth, T., and Aylesworth, V. *The Mount St. Helens Disaster: What We've Learned.* New York: Franklin Watts, 1983.

Bain, I. *Mountains and Earth Movements.* New York: Franklin Watts, 1984.

Bannon, J. *Sand Dunes.* Minneapolis, MN: Carolrhoda Books, 1989.

Brownstone, D. M., and Franck, I. M. *Natural Wonders of America.* New York: Atheneum, 1989.

Fodor, R. V. *Earth Fire! Volcanoes and Their Activity.* New York: Morrow, 1981.

McFall, C. *Wonders of Dust.* New York: Dodd, Mead, 1980.

McNulty, F. *How to Dig a Hole to the Other Side of the World.* New York: Harper & Row, 1979.

Navarra, J. *Earthquake!.* New York: Doubleday, 1980.

Nixon, H., and Nixon, J. *Earthquakes: Nature in Motion.* New York: Dodd, Mead, 1981.

Poynter, M. *Volcanoes: The Fiery Mountains.* New York: Messner, 1980.

Robin, G. *Glaciers and Ice Sheets.* San Diego: Harcourt Brace Jovanovich, 1984.

Simon, S. *Volcanoes.* New York: Morrow, 1988.

Taylor, G. J. *Volcanoes in Our Solar System.* New York: Dodd, Mead, 1983.

Resource Organizations

Alliance for Environmental Education
211 Wilson Blvd.
Arlington, VA 22201

American Forestry Association
PO Box 2000
Washington, DC 20010

Friends of the Earth
218 D. Street, SE
Washington, DC 20003

National Geographic Society
Educational Services
17th and M Streets, NW
Washington, DC 20036

Sierra Club
730 Polk Street
San Francisco, CA 94109

Audiovisual Selections (on Earthquakes)

The Forces of Nature (catalog no. C31012). Washington, DC, National Geographic Society (filmstrip).

Our Ever-Changing Earth (catalog no. C30730). Washington, DC, National Geographic Society (filmstrip).

Initiating Activity

Invite students to share their thoughts and feelings about the earthquake that occurred on January 17, 1994. How did they feel? What were some of the things they thought about during the earthquake and immediately afterward? Invite each student to record his or her thoughts in a personal journal. Students may elect to share their thoughts and feelings in small or large group settings. Encourage students to select one or more of the following activities to do by themselves or with one or more partners:

1. Create a "graffiti wall" that records personal feelings about the earthquake. Students may post a long sheet of newsprint on one wall of

the classroom and invite classmates and others to record their thoughts, feelings, and ideas about the earthquake.

2. Create a short skit about January 17, 1994. What events happened in their neighborhood? How did the local residents react to those events? Was there a memorable incident that happened nearby?

3. Create a mock news broadcast about the earthquake events specific to their neighborhood. Selected students can take on the roles of newscaster, interviewer, local citizens, and interested bystanders and recreate the events that occurred in their neighborhood.

4. Create a collage (using photos cut out of the newspaper or selected newsmagazines) that replicates the major events of the day. Encourage students to share their finished products with the class and arrange them into an appropriate display in the classroom (bulletin board, poster, collage, etc.). Students may wish to include appropriate captions for selected photos using ideas from their individual journals.

5. Interview adults concerning about their feelings and emotions as the earthquake was taking place. What did they do? How did they feel? How do the emotions expressed by adults differ from those recorded in students' journals? Students may wish to discuss any similarities or differences.

6. Use play houses and other models to create a make-believe town located on a fault line or assemble a town on a large sheet cake (see "Cakequake! An Earth-Shaking Experience" by Garry Hardy and Marvin Tolman in *Science and Children* vol. 29, no. 1 [September 1991]: 18–21).

7. Make a videotape of the effects of their earthquake.

Provide opportunities for students to share their products or results in a variety of interactive experiences. Discussion sessions are important in helping youngsters express their feelings (and fears) and receive communal support.

Activities Related to the Entire Thematic Unit

1. Invite students to look through the daily newspapers for articles regarding changes in the earth (volcanic eruptions, earthquakes, etc.). Encourage them to create a bulletin board to display the articles under the heading, "The Changing Earth."

2. Students create a dictionary booklet entitled, "My Earth Book," perhaps with a page for each letter of the alphabet. (For example: A = abyss; B = biosphere; C = chasm; D = dangerous.)

3. Share one or more videos from the following list. After viewing a selected film, invite students to create a review of the film to be included in an ongoing unit newspaper entitled *Earth Watch*.

   a. *This Changing Planet* (catalog no. 30352), available through National Geographic Society, Washington, DC. Explains how the earth is constantly changing its surface through weather, erosion, earthquakes, and volcanoes. After viewing this film, invite students to choose one of the ways described in the movie and draw an illustration regarding the event using appropriate captions.

   b. *The Violent Earth* (catalog no. 51234), available through National Geographic Society, Washington, DC. The video tours active volcanoes throughout the world. After viewing, encourage students to make a replica of a volcano from modeling clay or papier mâché. Students can model their volcanoes after one or more of those in the film.

   c. *The Johnstown Flood,* Johnstown Flood Museum Association, 1989; produced by Guggenheim Productions, Washington, DC. After viewing, students may wish to contact the Johnstown Flood Museum for further information (telephone (814) 539-1889). Data collected may be assembled into an appropriate display for one of the school's display cases.

4. Working in small groups, students create their own replica of a famous volcano. Encourage students to consult appropriate books in the school library for necessary information about their selected volcanoes. Students can prepare written statements that can be posted with their models.

5. Provide each student with an ice cube to rub over various sheets of sandpaper for several minutes. Encourage students to discuss any changes which occur on the surfaces of the sandpaper and to record their observations in an appropriate journal. Ask students to identify similarities between this activity and the forces a glacier might exert on the surface of the earth.

6. Invite students to maintain an "earthquake journal" that includes an ongoing chart of the Richter scale readings for the aftershocks occurring in the days and weeks following the main earthquake, photographs or illustrations of the damage observed in various neighborhoods, interviews with adults and other students, and lists of earthquake-related books located in the local library.

Primary Literature Selections

Title: *Earthquakes*
Authors: Ed and Ruth Radlauer
Bibliographic information: Children's Press, Chicago, 1987

Summary: This book contains information about earthquakes and how they affect our world. What causes earthquakes? How do earthquakes destroy the land? How do scientists measure and predict earthquakes?

1. Show the film *The Great San Francisco Earthquake,* produced by PBS Video (1988), or the video *Our Dynamic Earth,* produced by the National Geographic Society (catalog no. C51162). Discuss the similarities between the events portrayed in the film(s) and those that occurred in the Los Angeles area. Create a Venn diagram illustrating the similarities and differences.

2. Invite students to write their own newspaper article about the earthquake in Los Angeles. Afterward, students can form small groups and discuss their articles and how those pieces compare with the descriptions given in the book.

3. Construct a model of the different layers of the earth by painting a huge ball on a piece of poster board. The inside of the ball can be painted to represent the three layers of the earth: core, mantle, and crust. Students can wish to use a globe of the world to plot selected countries on their illustrations as well as the locations of some of the major earthquakes that have occurred during the past 50 years.

4. Students can work in small groups to research books about earthquakes. Each group then prepares a brief summary of their findings and presents their discoveries to the rest of the class. Groups can also prepare a fact book about their collected data and present their finished products to the school library.

5. Selected students can work in small groups to construct a simple model of a seismograph. Each group will need a ball of clay, a pencil, a string approximately one foot long, tape, and a white piece of paper. Tie the string to the eraser end of a pencil and punch the tip of the pencil through a clay ball until just the lead point is sticking out of the clay. A sheet of white paper is taped to a desk, then one group member stages an earthquake by shaking the desk while someone else holds the string steadily above the desk so that just the tip of the pencil is barely touching the paper as the seismograph records the waves of the "earthquake." Students can compare the recordings they obtain with those found in various library books.

6. Provide each group of students with a shallow pan of water and a marble. Each student drops the marble into the pan and then describes the ripples that are sent out. Ask students to compare the waves in their pans with those that might be sent out from the epicenter of an earthquake, or that might occur in the ocean. Students can record their observations in an appropriate journal.

Title: *Volcano: The Eruption and Healing of Mount St. Helens*

Author: Patricia Lauber

Bibliographic information: Bradbury Press, New York, 1986

Summary: The events leading up to and following the eruption of Mount St. Helens in Washington are described in rich detail. The author also describes how the surrounding environment began to rebuild itself.

1. Prior to reading the book with students, provide them with photographs of Mount St. Helens before the eruption. Invite students to imagine what the mountain must have looked like after the eruption and encourage them to each draw an illustration of how they think the mountain may have looked after the eruption. Later, students can compare their predictions with the actual photos in the book. What differences do they note?

2. Invite students to each imagine that they are a volcano and then to write biographical notes in their journals based on this perspective. Suggest some questions for them to answer: Why did they erupt? What did they feel prior to and following the eruption? What triggered the eruption? How did the eruption affect the environment in the immediate vicinity? Afterward, students can create an illustration of themselves (as volcanoes) to share with the class.

3. Invite students to research other books about volcanoes. Students may wish to choose a volcano (for example, Mt. Fuji) to compare with Mount St. Helens.

4. Small groups of students can write a fictional story about how they were affected when Mount St. Helens erupted. What were some of the effects of the eruption on their daily lives? How did they survive? What did they do afterward? Provide opportunities for students to share their creations with the class.

5. Demonstrate the gas pressure that builds up inside of volcanoes by shaking up a bottle of warm soda and then taking the cap off (use caution). Invite students to compare what they observed with the eruption of Mount St. Helens. Discuss how the soda compares with the magma of that volcano.

6. Divide the class into groups of "scientists" who will chart the specific eruptions of Mount St. Helens on a piece of poster board. Students can include the date of the eruption, what caused it, what type of eruption it was, and what the effects were. Invite each group to give a presentation of their findings.

7. Generate a class discussion on how the eruption of Mount St. Helens had an effect on the food chains for the surrounding area. Discuss specific aspects: How did the avalanches and mud slides affect the food chains? What are some of the ways that the vegetation was able to rejuvenate after the eruption? Why were some animals able to escape harm from the eruption? Individual journals can be used to record these discussions.

8. Invite students to compare the environment immediately following the eruption to the environment two years after the eruption. Students can take on the roles of news reporters and "interview" the plants and animals in the region about the processes they experienced during this transition phase.

Title: *Icebergs and Glaciers*

Author: Seymour Simon

Bibliographic information: William Morrow, New York, 1987

Summary: Using clear and concise language, the author explains how glaciers and icebergs are formed, how they move, and how they affect the earth. Color photographs are included throughout the text.

1. Set up a glacier experiment by putting pebbles, sand, and water into a paper cup. Freeze the cup. Ask students to predict what the ice will look like when it is frozen and to draw their predictions on the chalkboard or on paper. The next day, peel the cup away and observe the results. Compare the ice with the

predictions of the day before. Invite students to rub their "homemade glaciers" over portions of the school playground and to note any changes. Students can record their observations in a specially created journal.

2. Ask students to write a series of diary entries as if they were on an expedition to a new glacier. Have them record the location, observations, hazards, and discoveries during their imaginary journey. Later, encourage small groups of students to create a short skit about their respective travels.

3. Two to three students pretend to be glaciers that move by sliding. The rest of the class can be glaciers that move only by creeping. The sliding glaciers try to tag up with the creeping glaciers. Once tagged, the creeping glaciers must join the sliding glacier by holding on their back, forming a train. The object is to have the sliding glaciers hook up with all the creeping glaciers who are trying to avoid them. Afterward, discuss the similarities between this activity and that which occurs in nature.

4. Students create a series of "name poems" that describe glaciers by using each of the letters in the word *Glacier.* Example:

G laciologist

L arge

A laska

C old

I ce caps

E rosion

R ocks

5. Working in small groups, students can develop time lines about the rate of movement of glaciers. Students can make predictions about how far an "average" glacier might travel in one year, ten years, or 20 years. How long would a glacier need to travel across the school playground, the length of our city, or across the country? Encourage students to create appropriate charts and graphs.

Title: *Exploring the Violent Earth*
Author: Jonathan Rutland
Bibliographic information: Warwick Press, New York, 1980

Summary: The book deals with factual information on natural destroyers of the earth. Rutland explores volcanoes, earthquakes, tornadoes, floods, and more.

1. Students observe pictures of volcanoes and of the Grand Canyon. Discuss how the earth can change quickly or slowly. Students can then participate in a demonstration of how erosion shapes the land. Fill a one cake pan with dry loose soil; fill another cake pan with moist clay-like soil. Tip each pan at a 45-degree angle and ask a student to pour a container of water on the soil of each pan (at the top). Students then describe what is happening in each pan (students may wish to videotape these events). Invite students to record their observations in special journals.

2. Each student selects one of the topics from the book about the violent earth (volcano, flood, tornado, etc.) and then draws a picture of the event as if it were a photograph. Students then write about what is happening as if they took the photograph. Provide opportunities for students to share their respective illustrations.

3. Provide students with graph paper on which to make word-find puzzles using vocabulary words from the book. After making the puzzles, encourage students to trade their puzzles with each other for solving.

4. Students prepare a radio or television announcement of an expected natural disaster and how people should be prepared. Students can then write the announcement and record it on audiotape or videotape.

5. Working in small groups, students create a play about an impending disaster and how to be prepared. *The Family Survival Guide* by the Red Cross may be used as reference. Encourage students to share their plays with other classes.

6. Working in small groups, students research an actual disaster as reported in the newspaper or seen on television. Encourage students to keep an ongoing journal of the events and circumstances surrounding the disaster and to make regular reports to other members of the class.

7. Students create a time line from the events in the book and plot corresponding dates and disasters. Students can also plot the years between one particular type of natural disaster (i.e., floods in the United States) to determine if there are any consistencies. Provide opportunities for students to share their results.

Culmination

Students select one or more of the following activities and projects:

1. Preservice teachers from the local university will be invited to share specially prepared lessons on the changing earth. Additionally, students majoring in geology at the university will be invited to share their expertise with the class. Students can interview the college students.

2. Students initiate an "Earth Watch Newspaper"—a collection of stories about violent activities taking place on the earth's surface over a designated period of time. Periodic reports may be made to the class.

3. Individual students create an advertisement (written or oral) for a volcano. Class members describe the features that would be most necessary in the promotion (i.e., the sale) of an active volcano.

4. Students create a play or reader's theatre adaptation of a story concerning the steps that need to be taken in case of a natural disaster. Encourage students to consult with the local Red Cross center for information necessary in preparing the presentation.

5. Students create a puppet show on selected events that happened in their homes or neighborhoods during the earthquake of January 17, 1994. Class members can comment on the events portrayed in the puppet show and how they were similar to those that occurred in their own homes and neighborhoods.

6. Working in small groups, students create "before" and "after" dioramas of the local area prior to and immediately after the earthquake. Other groups of students can create "before" and "after" dioramas of selected volcano eruptions, floods, or other natural disasters as a result of their readings. Encourage students to discuss their feelings about these events.

7. Students create semantic webs of important information introduced in the unit and post the webs throughout the room. Encourage students to make two separate webs: "Natural Disasters" and "Disasters Created by Humans." Plan time to discuss any similarities or differences.

8. Small groups of students prepare tape recordings of selected books about natural disasters. The recorded tapes and the accompanying books can be set up in the school library in a special display on natural disasters.

The thematic unit Isabel and her students "built" offers a variety of authentic learning opportunities—opportunities fueled by an integrated approach to language arts. Students were able to experience the natural and normal connections that can and should exist between language arts and other subjects (science, for example).

A Sample Day   The following represents one day of the thematic unit Isabel shared with her students. She was able to take the events, projects, and activities designated for the entire thematic unit on the changing earth and select those appropriate for a single day (in this case, Day 3 of the unit). Again, note how Isabel and her students were able to utilize all of the language arts in an integrated fashion and explore all dimensions of the topic.

The unit was designed for three weeks of instruction. The initial portions of the unit revolved around the events of the earthquake on January 17. Later, elements of the unit were constructed to build upon that knowledge base and expand students' concept development into other forces that affect the surface of the earth. As a result, Isabel was able to begin the unit with an event familiar to her students and then enlarge their understandings through a series of interrelated activities and explorations.

Theme: The Changing Earth (Day 3)

- *8:30–8:50 Opening.* Students are animated as they enter the classroom, still buzzing about "The Big One" and the numerous aftershocks that have hit southern California in the past several days. Many youngsters are still expressing their fears about the events of recent weeks, and Isabel offers numerous opportunities for students to vent their worries and anxieties. She encourages students to chronicle their thoughts in personal journals as well as in a classroom diary that records thoughts of selected cooperative learning groups. One small group of students is transcribing the results of interviews conducted with other children in various neighborhoods. These will be shared with the class in succeeding days. A few children are reading quietly in scattered locations throughout the room.

- *8:50–9:15 Whole Class Sharing.* Isabel provides opportunities for students to discuss the events that have most affected their respective families. These are recorded on the chalkboard in the form of a large semantic web. The events shared are grouped into categories such as "Fears," "Neighborhood Dangers," "Transportation Problems," "Jobs and Work," "Richter Readings," and "Cracks, Creaks, and Crevices." Students are encouraged to form small groups to investigate an identified area of interest through interviews, related literature, and personal data gathering. Each group is invited to maintain a journal of their research—to be summarized and reported to the whole class.

- *9:15–9:45 Writing Process.* The following writing activities were selected by the class:

Facts on file: One group, consisting of Hernando, Carmella, Tran, and Lucy, goes to the school library to research various books for facts about earthquakes. They collect information about the location of major earthquakes around the globe as well as the damage done by each quake.

Journals: Several students have taken charge of monitoring the daily events reported in the local newspaper. These students are recording those events in their individual journals and are also comparing notes on their individual interpretations of those events.

Newspaper: Carlos, Manuel, Lupita, Michael, and Maria have designed a weekly newspaper that reports events that happen in and around the school. Each event is "assigned" a reporter and is developed into one or more articles. These have included an interview with a local building inspector, tips from the school counselor, and safety information from the local Red Cross center.

Interviews: A variety of students have initiated a series of interviews with parents and other community leaders in the neighborhood. The interviews have centered around the damage done to local apartment buildings, the effects on families and livelihoods, work done by emergency personnel, and a comparison of the fears of adults versus those of children.

- *9:45–10:30 Drama Time.* Students have been divided into four separate groups, each one assigned the task of developing a skit or play about the forces inside the earth. One group has decided to develop a reader's theatre presentation based on the book *Mountains and Earth Movements.* Another is creating a skit in which each person has taken on the role of a section of the earth (e.g., one student assumes the part of the earth's crust; another student is a tectonic plate). A third group of students has decided to initiate a daily newscast of the events of the day. Their mock TV station—KKID—presents a daily summary of important events to the entire school through a series of videotapes that are distributed to individual classrooms.

- *10:30–11:30 Required/Optional Activities.* The following optional activities were selected by the class:

Group 1: Students are composing a letter to the governor requesting that all school buildings in the state be built according to strict earthquake codes.

Group 2: Students telephone teachers and students in other schools throughout the Los Angeles area requesting information on the effects of the earthquake in their area. The resulting data will be collected in the form of several charts and graphs.

Group 3: Students have erected a "graffiti wall" outside the classroom and have invited students from other classes to record their thoughts and feelings about the earthquake of January 17. Later, these ideas will be reconstructed in the form of a semantic web to be displayed in the school cafeteria.

Group 4: After viewing the video *This Changing Planet* from the National Geographic Society, students are composing a book of adjectives and descriptive phrases that have been used to describe various earthquakes around the world. This list is combined with one generated by another group of students.

Group 5: Students have obtained the address of a colleague of Mrs. Ortiz who lives in Santa Clara, California. They have written to her requesting newspaper information and clippings from the *San Francisco Chronicle* about the earthquake that occurred in Northern California in October 1989. The data will be compared with information reported in the *Los Angeles*

Times concerning the January 17 earthquake.

- *11:30–12:00 Lunch.*
- *12:00–12:30 Sustained Silent Reading.* Students obtain books from the collection offered by Mrs. Ortiz and disperse throughout the room. Books selected include *Natural Wonders of America, How to Dig a Hole to the Other Side of the World, Earthquakes: Nature in Motion,* and *Mountains and Earth Movements.* Several groups of two and three students have formed to share their selected books in cooperative reading groups.
- *12:30–1:15 Teacher-Directed Activities.* Isabel decides to open the day's lesson with an Anticipation Guide. Using the book *Earthquakes* by Ed and Ruth Radlauer (Chicago: Children's Press, 1987), Isabel has created the following set of statements that are presented to students prior to the reading of the book:

BEFORE	AFTER	
———	———	1. Earthquakes happen all over the world.
———	———	2. More earthquakes happen in California than in any other state.
———	———	3. An earthquake is the most destructive natural disaster in the world.
———	———	4. Earthquakes always occur along tectonic plates.
———	———	5. Earthquakes are rare occurrences.

Students are provided with a duplicate copy of the Anticipation Guide and are invited to record "True" or "False" in the "before" column depending on their personal beliefs. The class discusses the responses made on individual Anticipation Guides. Agreements and disagreements are voiced and ideas are recorded on a special area of the chalkboard. Isabel invites students to make predictions about the book—each of which is also recorded on the chalkboard.

Isabel reads the book *Earthquakes* to the class. Prior to reading, she invites students to listen for statements or information that may confirm or modify their responses to the Anticipation Guide statements recorded earlier. She also stops periodically throughout the reading and invites students to change or alter their original predictions based on data in the book.

Students assemble in small groups and complete the "after" column of the Anticipation Guide (based on the information learned in the book, students record "True" or "False" in the space in front of each statement). Later, Isabel encourages students to share reasons for their responses and any changes they may have made in their original recordings. Isabel encourages students to confirm their ideas through additional reading in other pieces of literature.

- *1:15–1:35 Storytelling/Read-Aloud.* The students all gather on the large "Reading Rug" in the back of the classroom to listen to Mrs. Ortiz read the book *Exploring the Violent Earth* by Jonathan Rutland (New York: Warwick Press, 1980). Afterward, students discuss the violence of earthquakes in comparison with the violence of other natural disasters. (This discussion will form the basis for extended activities related to other natural changes on the surface of the earth—volcanoes, glaciers, and erosion.)

- *1:35–2:10 Art/Music.* The art teacher, Mr. Muñoz, has posted a large sheet of newsprint in the school cafeteria. Small groups of students have been invited to create a large mural of the events during and immediately after the earthquake of January 17. Mr. Muñoz has shared slides of Diego Rivera's murals that have been painted on public buildings throughout Mexico. He has suggested to students that the creation of an "Earthquake Mural" might be an appropriate testament to the events of the past few weeks.

- *2:10–2:40 Self-Selected Activities.* The following self-selected activities were selected by the class:

Group 1: A small group of students has created a series of word-find puzzles using words and phrases collected from recent issues of the *Los Angeles Times.* These will be assembled into a "Big Book" and donated to the school library.

Group 2: Students are constructing models of the three layers of the earth. Using tennis balls that have been cut in half, students are filling the halves with different colored layers of modeling clay. These will be displayed in the classroom with appropriate labels.

Group 3: Students are creating an ongoing time line of the major events related to the earthquake. Events are selected from those reported on local TV and radio stations as well as those have appeared in the newspaper.

Group 4: Students are writing letters to university students at UCLA requesting a personal visit. The college students are being invited to share data and information learned during a recent course—"The Geology of North America."

Group 5: Two small groups of students are each viewing the films *The Great San Francisco Earthquake* and *Our Dynamic Earth.* Later, reviews of the films will be written and shared with other members of the class.

- *2:40–3:00 Responding To Literature.* Students are completing the reading of the book *Earthquakes* by Seymour Simon. The class has been divided into three separate groups. The first group is discussing the similarities between the earthquakes mentioned in the book and the earthquake that just occurred in the Los Angeles area. A second group is developing a story map that outlines the major elements of the book in a graphic representation. The third group is summarizing the major points of the book in the form of a newspaper article to be included in the class newspaper—*Earth Watch.*

- *3:00–3:15 Daily Closure.* The class is divided into teams of three students each. The teams are invited to discuss some of the items they learned during the course of the day, items remaining for them to work on in the following days, and those items for which they would still like to obtain additional information. Each team's recorder shares some of the discussion with the entire class. Students are invited to share their ideas with parents upon their return home.
- *3:15 Dismissal.*

The creation and use of thematic units can add an exciting dimension to your entire classroom curriculum. Thematic teaching not only offers students unique opportunities to process and practice their developing language arts but also provides teachers with integrative strategies and activities that enhance learning in all curricular areas. In addition, students are assisted in drawing realistic parallels between classroom enterprises and events and circumstances outside the classroom. In short, thematic instruction can aid students in comprehending the relevancy of language arts instruction to their daily lives.

CATHY SWANSON'S JOURNAL

❧ June 2

Every year each class selects their favorite author. Although any work can be submitted for this honor, the kids usually submit their published books. The winners from each classroom are invited to attend the annual "Authors' Luncheon" held at a local restaurant. While the young writers feast on hamburgers, fries, and ice cream, a more "experienced" guest author speaks. This year our guest was Peter Catalonotto, author and illustrator of such books as *Dylan's Day Out* and *Mr. Mumble.*

The children then share their stories (or excerpts from them). The winning pieces this year included a heart-wrenching story of a mother's love, a complete history of the life of Spiderman, a humorous idle about Mrs. Kling in a clothing store, and a year-long diary of a girl who loves horses.

This last book was written by the favorite author in our class, Mara. There are many things to admire about this work. Mara's book, *Horses Are My Life,* is certainly about something very meaningful to her. The diary format, somewhat similar to Cleary's style in *Dear Mr. Henshaw,* was ambitious and challenging considering the entries covered the course of an entire year. Finally, Mara cleverly used the closings to reflect the mood of the entry for each day. We were very proud of her indeed!

When teachers are child-centered and supportive of each other, the result is a positive, enthusiastic atmosphere where the sky's the limit! I'm fortunate to be teaching in such an atmosphere.

Betty, our art teacher, is someone who engenders this attitude. She shares her supplies, her ideas, and her resources willingly. This has been a real gift to me, especially considering the nature of "our business" this year.

In our many discussions, Betty and I have expressed our mutual concern for the role art plays in education. Out of these discussions and this alliance have come some new goals, new ideas. One we are particularly excited about is "The Rumphius Club."

In Barbara Cooney's book, *Miss Rumphius,* a grandfather advises his beloved granddaughter (Miss Rumphius) to accomplish three things in her lifetime: to travel and explore the world, to live by the sea, and (most importantly) to somehow make the world a bit more beautiful. Miss Rumphius accomplishes all these things, making the world more beautiful by sowing lupine seeds that bloom the following Spring, painting the hillsides everywhere. It is this last accomplishment that reflects the goal of the Rumphius Club.

Our goal is to organize a collaboration of kids, parents, staff, and anyone else who would like be involved in perhaps four beautification projects per year. So many things would be naturally integrated into this experience: determining needs and planning, acquisition of resources, how best to implement each project, utilization of special skills and division of labor, the value of working toward a common goal, the sense of community, and finally, the sense of accomplishment and pride when the world is a more beautiful place thanks to the cooperative efforts of the club. (We may even leave a sign . . . The Rumphius Club was here!)

We plan on meeting this summer to get things together—I'm really looking forward to it!

We celebrated the end of our "Go For 2000 Pages" contest today with a pizza party! Matt far surpassed his goal by reading 5,138 pages since Christmas! His mother has told me it is not unusual for Matt to be up and reading at 5:30 a.m.

All the kids enjoyed working toward this goal, but the ones who benefited the most were the ones who didn't consider themselves to be readers before. I saw changes in attitude toward reading in quite a few children.

Steph, who came very near to reaching her goal, told me that she plans on keeping track of her pages this summer—even after she reaches her goal. She's going to tell me on the first day back to school!

Mrs. Cooper asked if she could come in to read a story to the class. She wanted to read a Chris Van Allsburg book; she knew he was a favorite author with many of the children. I was thrilled with the offer.

She arrived Wednesday with the book in one hand and popsicles in the other. She told the children she wanted to read this book as "motivation" for the start of their summer reading!

As she read the story, I watched the kids licking their popsicles, listening intently. I was sorry I didn't schedule more parents as guest readers; not only for the children's sake, but for mine . . . it's nice to be a part of the audience, listening with the kids, sharing our love for books from the same perspective.

Plan for next year . . . set up a schedule for guest readers in September so that we can enjoy this throughout the year!

TEACHER AS LEARNER/TEACHER AS RESEARCHER

A Community of Learners

Throughout this book, we have attempted to provide you with glimpses of classrooms around the country—from Idaho and California, to Pennsylvania and Florida, from Illinois and Arizona, to Maine and Tennessee. Our intent has been to provide you with insights into the teaching and learning process—insights that can be a significant part of the language arts education of children and the lifelong education of teachers. Our underlying theme with these vignettes is that we can learn from each other, support each other, and grow together as teachers.

We believe firmly that teaching and learning do not exist in a vacuum. It is not just one teacher and 25 students in a classroom (for example) that makes the educative process so exciting, so dynamic, and so fascinating. It is people working together—sharing ideas, making discoveries, and asking questions. Those people can be a small group of third graders wondering about the growth of monarch butterflies, or it can be a whole class of first graders investigating the geometric patterns formed with attribute blocks, or it can be an informal group of elementary teachers questioning the impact of journaling on the language growth of ESL students. Whatever the question and whatever the composition of the group, there is strength in numbers and direction in cooperation.

Your role as a teacher-researcher can be enhanced and supported when you engage others in your investigations. A community of learners—whether students or teachers—can work together in a supportive atmosphere to develop ideas, examine possibilities, and stimulate the accomplishment of realistic goals. As you begin asking questions or looking for answers, we suggest that you "employ" one or more colleagues in your quest. The support and encouragement of like-minded individuals can make the research process inspiring and dynamic. When you have the support of other professionals, you also have a firm foundation from which to launch new ideas, new strategies, and new questions.

Here are some ideas to consider in forming your own community of learners:

- Obtain the support and encouragement of your administrator. Ask that individual for time to gather a group of people together to discuss common concerns and develop new strategies.

- If possible, work with other teachers to develop a written plan of action for an in-service research group—one that will operate during regularly scheduled in-service days.
- Link up with teachers in other districts, near and far, using computer bulletin boards, modems, faxes, or the Internet.
- Plan meetings away from the school, too. Plan to meet in people's homes, a local restaurant, or the public library.
- Develop a common agenda that outlines goals, sets the expectations for contributions by the group's members, designates common questions for examination, and details how information will be shared with members and other colleagues on a regular basis.
- Keep the group informal but focused. The intent is to share issues, decide on ways to examine the designated questions, and improve instruction. A spirit of cooperation and consensus is necessary for the group's success.

We trust that this book not only has provided you with important information in your quest to become a successful teacher but that it has also stimulated some questions in your own mind about how and why kids become language users. We hope that we have provided answers to many of your questions, that you now have the tools to seek out responses and possibilities with your own students in your own classroom. We invite you to join with other teachers, both novice and experienced, who also have questions and concerns, and work with them in developing a community of learners that will support and strengthen the lifelong education of all its members.

Journal Reflections

Select one or more of the questions below that interest you and respond in your journal.

1. There are many "communities" working in Cathy's school. What are some of them and how did Cathy participate in their establishment or maintenance? How will these be maintained over time?

2. Work with a group of classmates to design a thematic unit plan sheet (see Figure 14.3) for one of the following topics: weather forecasting, Bill Peet books, the environment, Southwestern Native American customs, neighborhoods, creepy crawly critters, cars and trucks, women authors, or the night.

3. What would you consider to be your greatest challenges in constructing a thematic unit? How will you meet those challenges?

4. Design your own question.
   ✓ What is a question you have about the chapter?
   ✓ How will you pursue the answer to that question?
   ✓ Respond in your journal.

References and Suggested Readings

Amann, J. *Theme Teaching with Great Visual Resources.* Rosemont, NJ: Modern Learning Press, 1993.

Berry , C. F. and Mindes, G. *Planning a Theme-Based Curriculum: Goals, Themes, Activities, and Planning Guides for 4's and 5's.* Glenview, IL: Scott, Foresman, 1993.

Braddon, K. L., Hall, N. J., and Taylor, D. *Math Through Children's Literature.* Englewood, CO: Teacher Ideas Press, 1993.

Butzow, C. M., and Butzow, J. W. *Science Through Children's Literature: An Integrated Approach.* Englewood, CO: Teacher Ideas Press, 1989.

DeVito, A., and Krockover, G. *Creative Sciencing: A Practical Approach.* Boston: Little, Brown, 1976.

Fredericks, A. D. *Social Studies Through Children's Literature: An Integrated Approach.* Englewood, CO: Teacher Ideas Press, 1991.

Fredericks, A. D. *The Integrated Curriculum: Books for Reluctant Readers, Grades 2–5.* Englewood, CO: Teacher Ideas Press, 1992.

Fredericks, A. D., Meinbach, A. M., and Rothlein, L. *Thematic Units: An Integrated Approach to Teaching Science and Social Studies.* New York: Harper-Collins, 1993.

Gill, J. T., and Bear, D. "No Book, Whole Book, and Chapter DRTA." *Journal of Reading* 31 (February 1988): 444–449.

Kauchak, D., and Eggen, P. *Learning and Teaching Research-Based Methods.* Boston: Allyn and Bacon, 1989.

Kostelnik, M. J. et al. *Teaching Young Children Using Themes.* Glenview, IL: Scott, Foresman, 1991.

Kucer, S. B. "Procedures for Thematic Unit Development." Paper presented at the International Reading Association Annual Convention, San Antonio, April 1993.

Meinbach, A., Rothlein, L., and Fredericks, A. *The Complete Guide to Thematic Units: Creating the Integrated Curriculum.* Norwood, MA: Christopher-Gordon Publishers, 1995.

Pappas, C. C., Kiefer, B. Z., and Levstik, L. S. *An Integrated Language Perspective in the Elementary School.* White Plains, NY: Longman, 1990.

Epilogue

Dear Student:

By this time in your course you're probably wondering how you will be able to "put it all together." You've experienced a course in teaching the integrated language arts, and now you're concerned about how to begin and how you'll be able to continue and make it to the end of your first year of teaching. You've had opportunities to read Cathy Swanson's journal as she set sail through her second year of teaching, and you're speculating if you'll be just as successful.

We, too, experienced those same fears and trepidations when we began our teaching careers. We were just as worried, just as concerned, and just as dazzled by all we were expected to do . . . even before those first students set foot in our classrooms. Some of those initial days were humorous . . . some we'd just as soon forget! Yet, each and every one of those days, and each and every one of those students who "endured" our first year of teaching, are an important part of who we are now as teachers. Indeed, even as we complete the writing of this text, we still believe that our students have taught us more about teaching and learning than any textbook we ever had. We hope this text has given you a beginning and a foundation for your future . . . and that your future students also will be your guides along the way.

With that in mind we thought you might want to hear from two of our former college students as they took their first (tentative) steps into their initial year of teaching. We asked Pat and Mitzi to write to you and share their thoughts about their anticipations and expectations. We thought you might enjoy hearing from two first-year teachers who have taken our courses on teaching the integrated language arts and are trying to juggle all they know with all they are expected to teach. We think you'll find their words instructive as well as perceptive; but most of all, we hope you'll discover the same hope, energy, and possibilities for success in Pat and Mitzi's letters as we wish for you in your journey of discovery.

By the same token, we thought you might also enjoy reading one more piece from one of your instructors for this course—Cathy Swanson. Throughout this text you have journeyed with Cathy as she has discovered, contemplated, and considered the "learnings" that take place in the class-room—hers as well as those of her students. She, too, has been in your shoes—wondering how to bring it all together to become the best teacher pos-sible. So, she asked us if she could include a final letter and some final thoughts. We think you'll agree that her words are an inspiring way to end a textbook—particularly a text on teaching the integrated language arts.

Sincerely,

Tony, Bonnie, Jan

June 15

Dear Student:

As I listen to my students speak with great certainty as to what they will "absolutely, positively" be when they grow up, I smile, remembering. I was absolutely, positively going to be a musician, a writer, an artist, and a teacher; the "career of the week" depended on the success of my most recent piano lesson, or perhaps how good my new drawing was. In any event, to say I vacillated is an understatement.

As an adult, I have pursued what one Kutztown professor kindly called a "circuitous route" in becoming a teacher. After attending the University of Delaware for three years (with a major in "Changing Majors"), I returned home and entered the work force. Art store clerk, restaurant manager, and customer service representative for a computer company were only three of the titles I held during this time. It was not until I was hired as a painting instructor at the local Senior Citizens center that I realized (with true certainty this time!) what path my future would take, where I could make a difference in the world.

Watching these septegenarian students get excited about learning, work to change, and grow was more than fulfilling; it was addicting! I had been considering a return to college, and this was the impetus I needed to make a commitment. I entered Kutztown University as a part-time student in the fall of 1989 and finished with a vengeance by spring of 1991.

I was very fortunate in my undergraduate experience. Not only did I have some very supportive professors, but wonderful and caring cooperating teachers guiding my student teaching as well. (Thanks Sandy, Diane, and Kathleen!) I loved what I was doing! Little did I realize, at that time, that my education had truly just begun. . . .

Teaching is not an easy job. It take energy, commitment, TIME, resourcefulness, and patience. It also requires that you laugh at elementary humor (even upon hearing the same joke fifty times!), learn to decipher "magical spelling" (I used to know how to spell "their" until I taught fourth grade—now I have to resist spelling it "thier"), and juggle writing conferences and book projects in between remembering to go to the Just Say No assembly and sending Zachary to saxaphone lessons. But I would not—would "absolutely, positively" not—trade it for any other job in the world.

It has only been a bit more than three years since I was sitting where you might be now; worrying about resumes, scrambling for interviews, and trying to imagine what it would be like to actually have a class of your own. In thinking about the path I have travelled since that time, there are a few things I'd like to share that may be of benefit to you.

Regarding "getting in": keep trying!! Volunteer at a local school, get on sub lists—be known!! I happened to be in the right place at the right time (waitressing where my soon-to-be principal was having lunch; we had a preliminary interview over the Nectarine Genoise!), but it's not easy. If you really want to do it, you can't give up.

Regarding teaching: ahhh, where do I start? This will sound like a list from "All I Needed To Know I Learned in Kindergarten," but here goes . . .

Love children. Treat them as people who are simply at a different stage in life than you are. Accept differences, encourage strengths, help them find the tools to meet challenges. See your classroom as a family, the community that it is. Share yourself: your experiences, your own strengths, and weaknesses. Be a learner in school as well as in the outside world—modeling lifelong learning will accomplish far more than any well-planned lesson. Speaking of the outside, remember that it exists! Teaching, especially in light of the new directions education is taking, can be all-consuming. Take time for yourself, rejuvenate (somewhere my family is laughing right now . . .). And read, read, read.

You are at the beginning of an incredible journey. Children will teach you as much, if not more, than you will teach them. And they, indeed, make the world a much richer place. So will you. Best wishes!

Sincerely,

Cathy Swanson
Second-Year Teacher

July 18

Dear Fellow Student:

   With shaky knees, I listen to the voice on the other end of the telephone offering me a position as a fifth-grade teacher at a local elementary school. Sinking into a chair, I manage to squeak out a few words of acceptance, and complete the conversation without bursting into song or screaming, "YES! I did it!" As I hang up the phone, my mind is spinning. This is it—my big chance to hang up my Snoopy, put my wooden apple on my desk, and TEACH! It's the Fourth of July, Christmas, and New Year's Eve, wrapped up in one! I spend the next three hours laughing, jumping for joy, shouting, and spreading the news over the telephone. I want everyone to share my excitement!

   That was almost two months ago. It is now mid-July, and the euphoria is beginning to fade behind a cloud of self-doubt. I am entering the classroom as an elementary teacher for the first time! WOW! As a recent college graduate, I have been introduced to all the latest in educational research and theory. I live and breathe the whole language philosophy. After countless hours devoted to writing thematic units, my brain is geared to operate in a constant cross-curricular mode. I "know" that I have the ability to be an effective teacher. I should be bursting with knowledge and have all the answers, but I have nothing but questions!

   I feel like the director of a play, where all the actors have practiced their individual parts, but no one knows the entire story. Whole language, cooperative learning, hands-on science, portfolio assessment, classroom management, process writing, integrated curriculum, thematic units—these are the elements of my profession, but will I be able to put them all together to make the whole thing work in my classroom? Will my "story" make sense?

   In order to create a successful story for my classroom, I need to begin with the setting. Some of my specific concerns are: "What is the best way to arrange the desks?" "How should I organize supplies?" "How can I utilize bulletin board space?" "Where can I set up areas for reading and writing?" "What type of learning environment and classroom atmosphere do I want to establish?"

   Obviously, my first step should be a trip to the classroom, to take stock of available space, furniture, and supplies. Since my classroom is last on the list for summer carpet cleaning, I decided to draw a floor plan and cut out templates for desks, tables, etc. This allows me to try out a variety of classroom layouts, without moving the actual furniture, and provides a birds-eye view of traffic patterns. Mapping out the layout of the room also helps with decisions for utilizing wall space. For example, I would like to set up a science center near the sink. Thus, the bulletin board near this area will serve as a display for current science topics. I can use this map throughout the year to create new floor plans or new areas of study in the classroom.

I would like to establish an atmosphere of respect and trust in my classroom. To define my expectations for classroom behavior, I plan to introduce "Classroom C.P.R." This represents Cooperation, Pride in work and actions, and Respect for ourselves and others. I will display a poster, promoting this concept as a way to "keep our classroom alive and well." I also want to establish a learning environment that invites curiosity, asking questions, taking risks, and assuming responsibility. I hope to achieve this through lots of hands-on learning experiences, cooperative learning techniques, critical-thinking and problem-solving activities, and by assigning classroom jobs.

Characters are another important part of a story. "What can I do to learn more about my students before school begins?" "What level of work are they capable of?" "What are some of the individual needs, and how can I address those needs?" I already know that I will have approximately twenty-four students. I plan to talk with the fourth-grade teachers to learn more about the class as a whole. I can utilize individual student portfolios to assess progress and growth. Student cumulative folders can provide information on academic achievement, strengths, and needs.

To establish a positive relationship with my students before we meet face to face on the first day of school, I have decided to mail a brief note of introduction to each student at his/her home address. I will enclose an interest inventory to be completed by the student and returned to me before school begins.

It has also been very helpful to me to get to know some of the other "characters" involved in the school. I have attended several in-service workshops at my school during the past six weeks. This was a wonderful opportunity to meet and socialize with some of the teachers and staff that I will be working with throughout the year. I feel much more confident knowing that I already have a familiar support group to lean on as I plunge into uncharted waters.

Last, but not least, every good story needs a plot. "What will take place in my classroom?" This is perhaps the most difficult question for me to address. I know what I would like to see happening: a literature-rich environment. Students engaged in reading, writing, and listening and speaking activities across the curriculum. Creativity. Curiosity. Divergent thinking. Teamwork. Questioning minds. Sharing. And, of course—learning. My challenge at this point is to take the various aspects of the curriculum, make connections, or "build bridges" between the individual subject areas, and provide experiences that will make the learning meaningful to students. It always sounded so logical and well, simple—on paper. Now, I seem to spend a lot of time scratching my head and wondering, "How will I ever be able to do it?" As an education student, I truly enjoyed writing thematic units and integrating the subject areas. Just give me a topic, and the cross-curricular activities would flow from my brain faster than I could write them down. The situation is slightly different in the real world. For instance, I have a box filled with curriculum guides for each subject area, teacher manuals, and lists of learning outcomes. In college, my creativity knew no bounds. I could conjure up wonderful ideas and activities, without the restrictions or curriculum, materials, or time. All of a sudden, I am responsible for teaching an enormous amount of material in a limited amount of time, to an entire group of individuals who may or may not want to learn. I feel overwhelmed at the prospect of assuming such a role. After all, I alone will be held accountable for whatever learning takes place in my classroom. "What if I fail to cover the required material?" "What if my students fail to learn?" "How will I evaluate students and assign grades?" As you may have guessed, the plot remains a bit murky at this point. However, I am working on it.

You might be thinking, "Does this story have a happy ending?" The answer is . . . this story has no ending! This year will be the first chapter in the story of the life of a teacher, her school, and her students. At times it will be a mystery, a drama, a fairy tale, a comedy, or a love story. There may even be a few pages of horror or tragedy. It will be the product of many authors, written by myself, my colleagues, and an endless stream of students. I know that I will never run out of unanswered questions, self-doubts, worries, or uncertainties. But I am sure of one thing—it will always be an "adventure!"

Sincerely,

Pat Vanderberg
First-Year Teacher

August 4

Dear Fellow Student:

I write this letter to you with much excitement, but also with some concerns. I'm enthused to be entering my first year as a classroom teacher. Finally, I'll have my own classroom, my name on the door, my lesson plans in the book, and my responsibility for providing the best education possible for my students. But I'm also apprehensive.

I am confident I have received the best education and preparation available through my college courses; however, now comes the real learning experience. My whole language orientation will be evident as I am already picking out children's literature selections to use with units I will be teaching in reading, health, science, and social studies. I'm pouring over teacher magazines and journals looking for new ideas and new strategies. And I'm also "bugging" my former college professors for their thoughts and insights on how to develop a whole language curriculum. I'm confident, but concerned. Eager, but anxious. Prepared, but afraid. This has to be the most exciting time of my life—everything I've worked for and studied will be "put to the test" and it's up to me to make it happen.

Making thematic units and designing a truly integrative classroom environment "is" time consuming, but I think the effort will be worth it. In college, I just had to turn those projects in for a grade. Now, I will be "graded" by how well "my" students learn as a result of those ideas and strategies. This is where I am glad I have a mentor teacher. My mentor is eager to help me where necessary, but will not push her ideas on me. I know she will be a big help during my first, and most important, year of teaching.

Many of the projects I have planned include group work or cooperative learning. I have been trying to learn more about this because I believe even the experts are still learning. I plan to do some more research on my own this summer to determine the strategies that might work best for me. I plan to use a variety of different grouping plans according to the motivation, skills, and personality characteristics of my students. I want to make sure both gifted and at-risk students are equally supported and motivated in my classroom.

I'm also concerned about how I will be able to maintain discipline in my classroom. I have been doing as much reading as I can on the subject this summer. Fortunately, my district has planned a series of in-service workshops on discipline for the coming year. In the meantime, I have been able to devise a plan for my classroom that will emphasize good behavior and deter inappropriate behavior. I believe an interesting and involved classroom environment is still one of the best ways to maintain discipline, because students are able to invest in the process.

My summer has been filled with all sorts of journal and book readings, interviews with other teachers, conversations with former professors, and attendance at some in-service meetings and local conferences. While I learned a great deal in college, it seems as though being a good teacher means being a continual learner, too.

In closing, I would like to say that the feeling of obtaining my first teaching position is like no other feeling I have ever had. It is all my dreams come true! It makes all that hard work in college worthwhile. My advice to all prospective teachers is to "absorb" as much as you can while in college and to get lots of experiences with kids when you're not in class. Talk to lots of teachers, visit lots of classrooms, and read lots of books. You'll be a better candidate for a teaching position, a better teacher, and your future students will be better learners.

Sincerely,

Mitzi Karr
First-Year Teacher

APPENDIX A CHILDREN'S LITERATURE

Ackerman, K. *The Tin Heart.* New York: Atheneum, 1990.

Adams, E. B. *Korean Cinderella,* illustrated by Dong Ho Choi. Seoul, Korea: Seoul International Tourist Publishing, 1983.

Adler, D. *A Picture Book of Benjamin Franklin.* NY: Holiday, 1990.

Adoff, A. *All the Colors of the Race,* illustrated by J. Steptoe. New York: Lothrop, 1982.

Adoff, A. *Chocolate Dreams,* illustrated by T. MacCombie. New York: Lothrop, 1988.

Adoff, A. *In for Winter, Out for Spring,* illustrated by J. Pinkney. New York: Harcourt, 1991.

Adoff, A. *Malcolm X,* illustrated by J. Wilson. New York: Harper Trophy, 1988.

Adoff, A. *Sports Pages.* New York: J. B. Lippincott, 1986.

Ahlberg, J., and Ahlberg, A. *Each Peach Pear Plum.* New York: Viking, 1979.

Ahlberg, J., and Ahlberg, A. *The Jolly Postman.* Boston, MA: Little, 1986.

Alexander, L. *The Beggar Queen.* New York: Dutton, 1984.

Alexander, L. *The Black Cauldron.* New York: Holt, 1965.

Alexander, L. *The Book of Three.* New York: Holt, 1964.

Alexander, L. *The Wizard in the Tree,* illustrated by L. Kubinyi. New York: Dutton, 1975.

Alexander, L. *Westmark.* New York: Dutton, 1981.

Alexander, S. *There's More . . . Much More,* illustrated by P. Brewster. San Diego, CA: Harcourt Brace Jovanovich, Gulliver Books, 1987.

Aliki. *Dinosaur Bones.* New York: Crowell, 1988.

Aliki. *Feelings.* New York: Greenwillow, 1984.

Aliki. *The King's Day: Louis XIV of France.* New York: Crowell, 1989.

Aliki. *The Many Lives of Benjamin Franklin.* New York: Simon & Schuster Books for Young Readers, 1988.

Aliki. *Mummies Made in Egypt.* New York: Crowell, 1979.

Aliki. *My Feet.* New York: Crowell, 1990.

Aliki. *My Hands.* New York: Crowell, 1990.

Aliki. *The Story of Johnny Appleseed.* New York: Prentice Hall, 1987.

Allard, H. *Miss Nelson Has a Field Day,* illustrated by J. Marshall. Boston, MA: Houghton Mifflin, 1985.

Allard, H. *Miss Nelson Is Missing,* illustrated by J. Marshall. Boston, MA: Houghton Mifflin, 1977.

Allard, H. *The Stupids Have a Ball,* illustrated by J. Marshall. Boston, MA: Houghton Mifflin, 1977.

Allen, P. *Who Sank the Boat?* New York: Coward McCann, 1983.

Amon, A. *The Earth Is Sore: Native Americans on Nature.* New York: Atheneum, 1981.

Anno, M. *Anno's Britain.* New York: Philomel, 1982.

Armstrong, W. *Sounder,* illustrated by J. Barkley. New York: Harper, 1969.

Avi. *The Man Who Was Poe.* New York: Orchard, 1989.

Avi. *Nothing But the Truth.* New York: Orchard, 1991.

Avi. *The True Confessions of Charlotte Doyle.* New York: Orchard, 1990.

Aylesworth, J. *Old Black Fly.* NY: Holt, 1992

Babbitt, N. *The Eyes of the Amarylis.* New York: Farrar, Straus & Giroux, 1977.

Babbitt, N. *Tuck Everlasting.* New York: Farrar, Straus, 1975.

Baker, J. *Where the Forest Meets the Sea.* New York: Greenwillow, 1987.

Baker, K. *The Dove's Letter.* New York: Harcourt Brace Jovanovich, 1988.

Baker, O. *Where the Buffaloes Begin,* illustrated by S. Gammell. New York: Warne, 1981.

Bang, M. *The Grey Lady and the Strawberry Snatcher.* New York: Four Winds, 1980.

Bang, M. *Ten Nine Eight.* New York: Greenwillow, 1983.

Bang, M. *The Paper Crane.* New York: Greenwillow, 1985.

Banks, L. R. *The Indian in the Cupboard,* illustrated by B. Cole. New York: Doubleday, 1981.

Banks, L. R. *The Return of the Indian,* illustrated by W. Geldard. New York: Doubleday, 1986.

Banks, L. R. *The Secret of the Indian,* illustrated by T. Lewin. New York: Doubleday, 1989.

Baylor, B. *Everybody Needs a Rock,* illustrated by P. Parnall. New York: Scribner's, 1974.

Baylor, B. *I'm in Charge of Celebrations,* illustrated by P. Parnall. New York: Scribner's, 1986.

Baylor, B. *Your Own Best Secret Place,* illustrated by P. Parnall. New York: Scribner's, 1979.

Baylor, C. *The Best Town in the World,* illustrated by R. Himler. New York: Scribner's, 1982.

Beatty, P. *Be Ever Hopeful, Hannalee.* New York: Morrow, 1988.

Beatty, P. *Charley Skedaddle.* New York: Morrow, 1987.

Beatty, P. *Turn Homeward, Hannalee.* New York: Morrow, 1984.

Behn, H. *Crickets & Bullfrogs & Whispers of Thunder: Poems and Pictures by Harry Behn,* illustrated by H. Behn. New York: Harcourt, 1984.

Birdseye, T. *Tucker.* New York: Holiday House, 1990.

Blos, J. *A Gathering of Days: A New England Girl's Journal 1830–32.* New York: Scribner's, 1979.

Blos, J. *Old Henry,* illustrated by S. Gammell. New York: Morrow, 1987.

Blume, J. *Blubber.* New York: Bradbury, 1974.

Blume, J. *Fudge-a-Mania.* New York: Dutton, 1990.

Blume, J. *Superfudge.* New York: Dutton, 1980.

Blume, J. *Tales of a Fourth Grade Nothing,* illustrated by R. Doty. New York: Dutton, 1972.

Booth, D. *'Til All the Stars Have Fallen: A Collection of Poems for Children,* illustrated by K. M. Denton. Boston, MA: Little, Brown, 1989.

Booth, D. *Voices on the Wind: Poems for All Seasons.* New York: Morrow Jr. Books, 1990.

Bret, J. *Annie and the Wild Animals.* Boston, MA: Houghton Mifflin, 1985.

Bridgers, S. E. *All Together Now.* New York: Knopf, 1979.

Briggs, R. *The Snowman.* New York: Random, 1978.

Brooks, B. *The Moves Make the Man.* New York: Harper, 1984.

Broome, E. *Dr. Mr. Sprouts.* New York: Knopf, 1993.

Brown, M. *All Butterflies.* New York: Scribner's, 1974.

Brown, M. *Arthur's Eyes.* Boston, MA: Little, 1979.

Brown, M. *Arthur's Halloween.* Boston, MA: Little, 1983.

Brown, M. *Once a Mouse.* New York: Scribner's, 1961.

Brown, R. *A Dark Dark House.* New York: Dial, 1981.

Brown, R. *Ladybug, Ladybug.* New York: Dutton, 1988.

Browne, A. *Changes.* New York: Knopf, 1991.

Browne, A. *Piggybook.* New York: Knopf, 1986.

Browne, A. *The Tunnel.* New York: Knopf, 1990.

Bruce, H. Maud: *The Life of L. M. Montgomery.* New York: Seal Bantam, 1992.

Bunting, E. *The Man Who Could Call Down Owls,* illustrated by C. Mikolaycak. New York: Macmillan, 1987.

Burch, R. *Queenie Peavy.* New York: Viking Press, 1966.

Burkert, N. E. *Valentine and Orson.* New York: Farrar, 1989.

Burleigh, R. *Flight,* illustrated by M. Wimmer. New York: Philomel, 1991.

Burningham, J. *Come Away from the Water, Shirley.* New York: Harper, 1977.

Burningham, J. *Grandpa.* New York: Crown, 1985.

Burningham, J. *John Burningham's ABC.* New York: Crown, 1986.

Burningham, J. *Mr. Gumpy's Outing.* New York: Holt, 1971.

Burton, V. L. *The Little House.* Boston, MA: Houghton Mifflin, 1942.

Burton, V. L. *Mike Mulligan and His Steam Shovel.* Boston, MA: Houghton Mifflin, 1939.

Byars, B. *The Burning Questions of Bingo Brown.* New York: Viking, 1988.

Byars, B. *The Moon and I.* New York: Messer, 1992.

Byars, B. *The Pinballs.* New York: Harper, 1977.

Cameron, A. *The Most Beautiful Place in the World,* illustrated by T. B. Allen. New York: Knopf, 1988.

Cameron, E. *The Private Worlds of Julia Redfern.* New York: Dutton, 1988.

Carle, E. *Do You Want to Be My Friend?* New York: Harper, 1971.

Carle, E. *The Very Busy Spider.* New York: Philomel, 1984.

Carle, E. *The Very Hungry Caterpillar.* New York: Philomel, 1969.

Carle, E. *The Very Quiet Cricket.* New York: Philomel, 1990.

Carrick, C. *The Accident,* illustrated by D. Carrick. New York: Clarion, 1976.

Carrick, C. *The Foundling,* illustrated by D. Carrick. New York: Clarion, 1977.

Cendrars, B. *Shadow,* illustrated by M. Brown. New York: Scribner's, 1982.

Chandra, D. *Balloons and Other Poems,* illustrated by L. W. Bowman. New York: Farrar, Straus & Giroux, 1990.

Chandra, D. *Rich Lizard and Other Poems,* illustrated by L. Bowman. New York: Farrar, Straus & Giroux, 1993.

Chang, I. *A Separate Battle: Women and the Civil War.* New York: Lodestar, 1991.

Chesworth, M. *Rainy Day Dream.* New York: Farrar, Straus & Giroux, 1992.

Christian, M. B. *Grownin' Pains.* New York: Macmillan, 1985.

Ciardi, J. *I Met a Man,* illustrated by R. Osborn. Boston, MA: Houghton Mifflin, 1961.

Ciardi, J. *Mummy Took Cooking Lessons and Other Poems,* illustrated by M. Nacht. Boston, MA: Houghton Mifflin, 1990.

Clark, E. C. *I Never Saw a Purple Cow and Other Nonsense Rhymes.* Boston, MA: Little, Brown, 1990.

Cleary, B. *Beezus and Ramona.* New York: Morrow, 1955.

Cleary, B. *Dear Mr. Henshaw,* illustrated by P. O. Zelinsky. New York: Morrow, 1983.

Cleary, B. *A Girl from Yamhill: A Memoir.* New York: William Morrow, 1988.

Cleary, B. *The Mouse and the Motorcycle.* NY: Morrow, 1965.

Cleary, B. *Ramona Quimby, Age 8,* illustrated by A. Tiegreen. New York: Morrow, 1981.

Cleary, B. *Ramona the Brave.* NY: Morrow, 1975

Cleary, B. *Runaway Ralph.* NY: Morrow, 1970.

Cleary, B. *Strider,* illustrated by P. O. Zelinsky. New York: Morrow, 1991.

Climo, S. *The Egyptian Cinderella,* illustrated by R. Heller. New York: Crowell, 1989.

Cobb, V. *For Your Own Protection: Stories Science Photos Tell.* New York: Lothrop, 1989.

Cobb, V. *Why Can't You Unscramble an Egg? And Other Not Such Dumb Questions About Matter,* illustrated by T. Enik. New York: Lodestar, 1990.

Cole, J. *Large as Life Animals: In Beautiful Life-Size Paintings,* illustrated by K. Lilly. New York: Knopf, 1990.

Cole, J. *The Magic School Bus at the Waterworks,* illustrated by B. Degen. New York: Scholastic, 1988.

Cole, J. *The Magic School Bus Inside the Earth,* illustrated by B. Degen. New York: Scholastic, 1987.

Cole, J. *The Magic School Bus Inside the Human Body,* illustrated by B. Degen. New York: Scholastic, 1989.

Cole, J. *The Magic School Bus Lost in the Solar System,* illustrated by B. Degen. New York: Scholastic, 1990.

Cole, J., and Calmeson, S. *The Laugh Book: A New Treasury of Humor for Children,* illustrated by M. Hafner. New York: Doubleday, 1986.

Cole, J., and Calmeson, S. *Pat-a-Cake and Other Play Rhymes,* illustrated by A. Tiegreen. New York: Morrow, 1992.

Cole, W. *Poem Stew,* illustrated by K. A. Weinhaus. New York: Lippincott, 1981.

Cole, W. *A Zooful of Animals,* illustrated by L. Munsinger. Boston, MA: Houghton Mifflin, 1992.

Collier, J. L., and Calmenson, S. *The Laugh Book: A New Treasury of Humor for Children.* Garden City, NY: Doubleday, 1986.

Collier, J. L., and Collier, C. *My Brother Sam is Dead.* New York: Four Winds, 1974.

Conrad, P. *Prairie Songs,* illustrated by D. Zudeck. New York: Harper, 1985.

Cooney, B. *Chanticleer and the Fox.* New York: Crowell, 1958.

Cooney, B. *Island Boy.* New York: Viking, 1988.

Cooney, B. *Miss Rumphius.* New York: Viking, 1982.

Cooper, S. *The Dark is Rising,* illustrated by A. E. Cober. New York: Atheneum, 1973.

Cormier, R. *Fade.* New York: Delacorte, 1988.

Crews, D. *Bigmama's.* New York: Greenwillow, 1991.

Crews, D. *Freight Train.* New York: Greenwillow, 1978.

Cummings, P. *Talking with Artists.* New York: Bradbury, 1992.

Dahl, R. *Boy: Tales of Childhood.* New York: Farrar, Straus, 1984.

Dalgliesh, A. *The Courage of Sarah Noble,* illustrated by L. Weisgard. New York: Scribner's, 1954.

D'Aulaire, I., and D'Aulaire, E. P. *Benjamin Franklin.* NY: Zepher, 1987.

Davis, J. E., and Davis, H. K. *Presenting William Sleator.* New York: Twayne, 1992.

de Angeli, M. *The Door in the Wall.* New York: Doubleday, 1949.

de Paola, T. *The Art Lesson.* NY: Putnam, 1989.

de Paola, T. *An Early American Christmas,* illustrated by E. Young. New York: Putnam's, 1987.

de Paola, T. *Charlie Needs a Coak.* New York: Simon & Schuster, 1974.

de Paola, T. *The Comic Adventure of Old Mother Hubbard and Her Dog.* New York: Harcourt, 1981.

de Paola, T. *Nana Upstairs, Nana Downstairs.* New York: Penguin, 1978.

de Paola, T. *Pancakes for Breakfast.* New York: Harcourt, 1978.

de Paola, T. *Strega Nona.* New York: Prentice Hall, 1975.

de Paola, T., ed. *Tomie de Paola's Book of Poems.* New York: Putnam, 1988.

de Paola, T. *Tomie de Paola's Mother Goose.* New York: Putnam's, 1985.

de Paola, T. *Watch Out for Chicken Feet in Your Soup.* New York: Prentice Hall, 1974.

de Regniers, B. S., Moore, E., White, M. M., and Carr, J. *Sing a Song of Popcorn: Every Child's Book of Poems.* New York: Scholastic, 1988.

deAngeli, M. *Three Hannah!* Doubleday, 1949.

Deming, A. G. *Who is Tapping at My Window?* New York: Dutton, 1988.

Dewey, J. O. *Spiders Near and Far.* New York: Dutton, 1993.

Dickens, C. *Oliver Twist.* New York: Dodd Mead & Co, 1941.

Doherty, B. *Dear Nobody.* New York: Orchard Books, 1991.

Dorris, M. *Morning Girl.* New York: Hyperion Books for Children, 1992.

Dragonwagon, C. *Home Place.* NY: Macmillan, 1990.

Duncan, L. *Chapters: My Growth as a Writer.* Boston, MA: Little, Brown, 1982.

Eckert, A. W. *Incident at Hawk's Hill,* illustrated by J. Schoenherr. Boston, MA: Little, Brown, 1971.

Ehlert, L. *Feathers for Lunch.* New York: Harcourt, 1990.

Ehlert, L. *Fish Eyes.* New York: Harcourt, 1990.

Ehlert, L. *Moon Rope.* New York: Harcourt Brace Jovanovich, 1992.

Ehlert, L. *Red Leaf, Yellow Leaf.* New York: Harcourt Brace Jovanovich, 1991.

Ehrlich, A. *Cinderella,* illustrated by S. Jeffers. New York: Dial, 1985.

Ehrlich, A. *The Random House Book of Fairy Tales.* New York: Random, 1985.

Emberley, B. *Drummer Hoff,* illustrated by E. Emberley. New York: Prentice Hall, 1967.

Ernst, L. C. *Sam Johnson and the Blue Ribbon Quilt.* New York: Lothrop, 1983.

Evans, C. S. *Cinderella.* New York: Viking, 1972.

Farber, N. *Never Say Ugh to a Bug,* illustrated by J. Arnego. New York: Greenwillow, 1979.

Fendler, D. *Lost on a Mountain in Maine.* Somersworth, NH: New Hampshire Publishing Co., 1978.

Fields, J. *The Great Lion of Zion Street,* illustrated by J. Pinkney. New York: Margaret K. McElderry, 1988.

Fine, A. *The Book of the Banshee.* Boston, MA: Little, Brown, 1992.

Fisher, A. *Always Wondering,* illustrated by J. Sandin. New York: Harper, 1992.

Fisher, A. *Going Barefoot.* New York: Crowell, 1960.

Fisher, A. *Out in the Dark and Daylight.* New York: Harper & Row, 1980.

Fisher, A. *Rabbits, Rabbits,* illustrated by G. Niemann. New York: Harper, 1983.

Fisher, L. E. *The Death of Evening Star: The Diary of a Young New England Whaler.* New York: Doubleday, 1972.

Fitzhugh, L. *Harriet the Spy.* New York: Harper, 1964.

Flanders, M., and Swann, D. *The Hippopotamus Song,* illustrated by N. B. Westcott. Boston, MA: Little, Brown, 1991.

Fleischman, P. *I Am Phoenix: Poems for Two Voices,* illustrated by K. Nutt. New York: Harper, 1986.

Fleischman, P. *Joyful Noise: Poems for Two Voices,* illustrated by E. Beddows. New York: Harper, 1985.

Fleischman, P. *Rondo in C,* illustrated by J. Wentworth. New York: Harper & Row, 1988.

Fleischman, S. *The Whipping Boy,* illustrated by P. Sis. New York, NY: Greenwillow, 1986.

Fleming, A. *Hosannah the Home Run!* Boston, MA: Little, Brown, 1972.

Flournoy, V. *The Patchwork Quilt,* illustrated by J. Pinkney. New York: Dial, 1985.

Fox, M. *Hattie and the Fox,* illustrated by P. Mullins. New York: Bradbury, 1987.

Fox, M. *Koala Lou,* illustrated by P. Lofts. New York: Harcourt, 1989.

Fox, M. *Wilfred Gordon McDonald Partridge,* illustrated by J. Vivas. Brooklyn, New York: Karen/Miller, 1985.

Fox, P. *Monkey Island.* New York: Orchard, 1991.

Fox, P. *One-Eyed Cat.* New York: Bradbury, 1984.

Fox, P. *A Place Apart.* New York: Dutton, 1982.

Fox, P. *The Slave Dancer,* illustrated by E. Keith. New York: Bradbury, 1973.

Fox, P. *The Stone-Faced Boy,* illustrated by D. A. Mackay. New York: Bradbury, 1968.

Frank, A. *The Diary of a Young Girl.* NY: Doubleday, 1967.

Freedman, R. *Children of the Wild West.* New York: Clarion, 1983.

Freedman, R. *Immigrant Kids.* New York: Dutton, 1980.

Freedman, R. *Indian Chiefs.* New York: Holiday, 1987.

Freedman, R. *Lincoln: A Photobiography.* New York: Clarion, 1987.

Freeman, D. *Corduroy.* New York: Viking, 1968.

Freeman, D. *Dandelion.* New York: Viking, 1964.

Fritz, J. *And Then What Happened, Paul Revere?* illustrated by M. Tomes. New York: Coward, 1973.

Fritz, J. *Brady.* Penguin, 1987.

Fritz, J. *Can't You Make Them Behave, King George?,* illustrated by T. de Paola. New York: Coward, 1982.

Fritz, J. *China Homecoming.* New York: Putnam's, 1985.

Fritz, J. *The Double Life of Pocahontas.* New York: Putnam's, 1983.

Fritz, J. *The Great Little Madison.* New York: Putnam's, 1989.

Fritz, J. *Homesick: My Own Story,* illustrated by M. Tomes. New York: Putnam's, 1982.

Fritz, J. *Traitor: The Case of Benedict Arnold.* New York: Putnam's, 1981.

Fritz, J. *What's the Big Idea, Ben Franklin?,* illustrated by M. Tomes. New York: Coward, 1982.

Fritz, J. *Where Do You Think You're Going Christopher Columbus?,* illustrated by M. Tomes. New York: Putnam's, 1980.

Fritz, J. *Why Don't You Get a Horse, Sam Adams?* NY: Coward, 1982.

Fritz, J. *Will You Sign Here, John Hancock?* NY: Coward, 1982.

Gag, W. *Millions of Cats.* New York: Coward-McCann, 1928.

Galdone, P. *Cinderella.* New York: McGraw, 1978.

Galdone, P. *The Little Red Hen.* New York: Clarion, 1973.

Galdone, P. *The Three Bears.* New York: Clarion, 1972.

Galdone, P. *The Three Billy Goats Gruff.* New York: Clarion, 1981.

Gallaz, C. *Rose Blanche,* illustrated by R. Innocenti. Mankato, MN: Creative Education, 1985.

Gauch, P. L. *Thunder at Gettysburg,* illustrated by S. Gammell. New York: Putnam's, 1990.

Geisert, A. *Oink!* Boston, MA: Houghton Mifflin, 1991.

Geisert, A. *Pigs From A to Z.* Boston, MA: Houghton Mifflin, 1986.

George, J. C. *The Cry of the Crow.* New York: Harper, 1980.

George, J. C. *Julie of the Wolves,* illustrated by J. Schoenherr. New York: Harper, 1972.

George, J. C. *My Side of the Mountain.* New York: Dutton, 1959.

George, J. C. *On the Far Side of the Mountain.* New York: Dutton, 1990.

Geras, A. *My Grandmother's Stories: A Collection of Jewish Folk Tales,* illustrated by J. Jordan. New York: Knopf, 1990.

Gherman, B. *E. B. White: Some Writer!* New York: Atheneum, 1992.

Gibbons, G. *From Seed to Plant.* New York: Holiday, 1991.

Gibbons, G. *The Milk Makers.* New York: Macmillan, 1985.

Gibbons, G. *New Road!* New York: Trophy, 1987.

Gitson, F. *Old Yeller.* NY: Harper, 1956.

Goble, P. *Death of the Iron Horse.* New York: Bradbury, 1987.

Goble, P. *The Girl Who Loved Wild Horses.* New York: Bradbury, 1978.

Goble, P. *Her Seven Brothers.* New York: Bradbury, 1988.

Goble, P. *Iktomi and the Buffalo Skull.* New York: Orchard, 1991.

Goldstein, B. *Inner Chimes: Poems on Poetry,* illustrated by J. B. Zalben. Honesdale, PA: Wordsongs/Boyd Mills, 1992.

Goodall, J. *The Story of a Castle.* New York: McElderry, 1986.

Goodall, J. *The Story of a Farm.* New York: McElderry, 1989.

Goodall, J. *The Story of an English Village.* New York: McElderry, 1977.

Goode, D. *Cinderella.* New York: Knopf, 1988.

Goode, D. *I Hear a Noise.* New York: Dutton, 1988.

Greene, B. *The Summer of My German Soldier.* New York: Bantam, 1984.

Greene, C. *The Love Letters of J. Timothy Owen.* New York: Harper, 1986.

Greenfield, E. *Honey, I Love and Other Love Poems,* illustrated by L. and D. Dillon. New York: Harper & Row, 1978.

Greenfield, E. *Nathaniel Talking,* illustrated by J. S. Gilchrist. New York: Black Butterfly Children's Books, 1988.

Grifalconi, A. *Osa's Pride.* Boston, MA: Little, Brown, 1990.

Grifalconi, A. *The Village of Round and Square Houses.* Boston, MA: Little, Brown, 1986.

Gross, R. B. *What's On My Plate?,* illustrated by I. Seltzer. New York: Macmillan, 1990.

Guarino, D. *Is Your Mama a Llama?,* illustrated by S. Kellogg. New York: Scholastic, 1990.

Hale, S. J. *Mary Had a Little Lamb.* New York: Holiday House, 1984.

Haley, G. *A Story, A Story.* New York: Atheneum, 1970.

Hall, D. *Ox-Cart Man,* illustrated by B. Cooney. New York: Viking, 1979.

Hamilton, V. *Anthony Burns: The Defeat and Triumph of a Fugitive Slave.* New York: Knopf, 1988.

Hamilton, V. *The People Could Fly,* illustrated by L. and D. Dillon. New York: Knopf, 1985.

Hamilton, V. *W. E. B. DuBois.* New York: T. Y. Crowell, 1972.

Haviland, V. *The Talking Pot,* illustrated by M. Sweet. Boston, MA: Little, Brown, 1990.

Heese, K. *Letter from Rifka.* New York: Holt, 1992.

Heide, F. P., and Gilliland, J. H. *The Day of Ahmed's Secret,* illustrated by T. Lewin. New York: Lothrop, Lee and Shepard, 1990.

Heidi, F. P. *Secret Dreamer, Secret Dreams.* Philadelphia, PA: Lippincott, 1978.

Heller, R. *A Cache of Jewels and Other Collective Nouns.* New York: Scholastic, 1989.

Heller, R. *Kites Sail High: A Book About Verbs.* New York: Grosset & Dunlap, 1988.

Heller, R. *Many Luscious Lollipops: A Book About Adjectives.* New York: Grosset and Dunlap, 1989.

Higginson, W. J. *Wind in the Long Grass: A Collection of Haiku,* illustrated by S. Speidel. New York: Simon & Schuster, 1991.

Hill, E. *Nursery Rhyme Peek-a-Book.* New York: Price, Stern, 1982.

Hill, E. *Where's Spot?* New York: Putnam's, 1980.

Hinton, S. E. *The Outsiders.* New York: Dell, 1967.

Hoban, T. *Is it Red? Is it Yellow? Is it Blue?* New York: Greenwillow, 1978.

Hoban, T. *Shapes, Shapes, Shapes.* New York: Greenwillow, 1986.

Hoban, T. *What Is It?* New York: Greenwillow, 1985.

Hoberman, M. A. *The Cozy Book.* New York: Viking, 1982.

Hoberman, M. A. *A House Is a House for Me,* illustrated by B. Fraser. New York: Penguin, 1982.

Holl, K. D. *Perfect or Not, Here I Come.* New York: Troll, 1987.

Holling, C. H. *Minn of the Mississippi.* Boston, MA: Houghton Mifflin, 1951.

Holling, C. H. *Paddle to the Sea.* Boston, MA: Houghton Mifflin, 1941.

Holm, A. *North to Freedom.* NY: Harcourt, 1965.

Holman, F. *Slake's Limbo.* New York: Scribner's, 1974.

Hoobler, D., and Hoobler, T. *Next Stop, Freedom: The Story of a Slave Girl.* Englewood Cliffs, NJ: Silver Burdett, 1991.

Hooks, W. H. *The Ballad of Belle Dorcas,* illustrated by B. Pinkney. New York: Knopf, 1990.

Hooks, W. *Moss Gown,* illustrated by D. Carrick. New York: Clarion, 1987.

Hopkins, L. B. *Hey-How for Halloween!,* illustrated by J. McCaffrey. New York: Harcourt, 1974.

Hopkins, L. B. *The Sky Is Full of Song,* illustrated by D. Zimmer. New York: Harper, 1983.

Hopkins, L. B., ed. *The Sea is Calling Me,* illustrated by W. Gaffney-Kessell. New York: Harcourt, 1986.

Hopkins, L. B., ed. *Through Our Eyes: Poems and Pictures About Growing Up,* photography by J. Dunn. Boston, MA: Little, Brown, 1992.

Howe, J. *The Celery Stalks at Midnight.* NY: Atheneum, 1983.

Howe, J. *Howliday Inn.* NY: Atheneum, 1982.

Howe, J. *I Wish I Were a Butterfly,* illustrated by E. Younge. San Diego, CA: Harcourt Brace Jovanovich, Gulliver Books, 1987.

Huck, C. *Princess Furball,* illustrated by A. Lobel. New York: Greenwillow, 1989.

Huck, C., ed. *Secret Places,* illustrated by L. Barrett George. New York: Greenwillow, 1993.

Hughes, T. *Season Songs.* New York: Viking Press, 1975.

Hughes, T. *Under the North Star.* New York: Viking Press, 1981.

Hunt, I. *Across Five Aprils.* New York: Follett, 1964.

Hunt, I. *Up a Road Slowly.* New York: Follett, 1966.

Hurwitz, J. *Astrid Lindgren: Storyteller to the World,* illustrated by M. Dooling. New York: Viking, 1989.

Hutchins, P. *Changes, Changes.* New York: Macmillan, 1971.

Hutchins, P. *The Doorbell Rang.* New York: Greenwillow, 1986.

Hutchins, P. *1 Hunter.* New York: Greenwillow, 1982.

Hutchins, P. *Rosie's Walk.* New York: Macmillan, 1968.

Hutchins, P. *Titch.* New York: Macmillan, 1971.

Hutchins, P. *The Very Worst Monster.* New York: Greenwillow, 1985.

Hyman, T. S. *Little Red Riding Hood.* New York: Holiday, 1983.

Hyman, T. S. *Self-Portrait: Trina Schart Hyman.* New York: HarperCollins, 1989.

Hyman, T. S. *Snow White.* Boston, MA: Little, Brown, 1974.

Innocenti, R. *Cinderella.* Mankato, MN: Creative Education, 1983.

Itse, E. M. *Hey, Bug! and Other Poems About Little Things.* New York: American Heritage Press, 1972.

Ivemey, J. W. *Three Blind Mice,* illustrated by V. Chess. Boston, MA: Little, Brown, 1990.

Jacques, B. *Redwall,* illustrated by G. Chalk. New York: Philomel, 1986.

Janeczko, P. B. *The Delicious Day.* New York: Orchard, 1987.

Janeczko, P. *The Place My Words Are Looking For.* New York: Bradbury, 1990.

Johnston, N. *Louisa May: The World and Works of Louisa May Alcott.* New York: Winds Press, 1991.

Johnston, T. *The Quilt Story,* illustrated by T. de Paola. New York: Putnam, 1985.

Johnston, T. *Whale's Song.* NY: Putnam's, 1987.

Jones, C. *This Old Man.* Boston: Houghton Mifflin, 1988.

Joyce, W. *Dinosaur Bob and His Adventure with the Family Lazardo.* New York: Harper, 1988.

Joyce, W. *George Shrinks.* New York: Harper, 1985.

Jukes, M. *Blackberries in the Dark,* illustrated by T. Allen. New York: Knopf, 1985.

Karlin, B. *Cinderella,* illustrated by J. Marshall. Boston, MA: Little, Brown, 1989.

Keats, E. J. *Peter's Chair.* New York: Harper, 1967.

Keats, E. J. *The Snowy Day.* New York: Viking, 1962.

Keats, E. J. *Whistle for Willy.* New York: Viking, 1964.

Keith, H. *Rifles for Watie.* New York: Crowell, 1987.

Kellogg, S. *A Rose for Pinkerton.* New York: Dial, 1981.

Kellogg, S. *Can I Keep Him?* New York: Dial, 1971.

Kellogg, S. *Chicken Little.* New York: Morrow, 1985.

Kellogg, S. *Prehistoric Pinkerton.* New York: Dial, 1987.

Kennedy, X. J. *Brats,* illustrated by James Watts. New York: Atheneum, 1986.

Kennedy, X. J. *Fresh Brats,* illustrated by J. Watts. New York: Atheneum, 1990.

Kennedy, X. J. *Ghastlies, Goops & Pincushions,* illustrated by R. Barrett. New York: Atheneum, 1989.

Kerr, M. E. *Me Me Me Me Me: Not a Novel.* New York: Harper, 1983.

Knudson, R. R., and Swenson, M. *American Sports Poems.* New York: Orchard, 1988.

Komaiko, L. *Annie Bananie,* illustrated by L. Cornell. New York: Harper, 1987.

Kraus, R. *A Very Special House,* illustrated by M. Sendak. New York: Harper, 1953.

Kraus, R. *A Hole is to Dig,* illustrated by M. Sendak. New York: Harper, 1952.

Kraus, R. *The Carrot Seed,* illustrated by C. Johnson. New York: Harper, 1945.

Kraus, R. *Leo the Late Bloomer,* illustrated by J. Aruego. New York: Crowell, 1971.

Kraus, R. *Milton the Early Riser,* illustrated by J. Aruego and A. Dewey. New York: Windmill, 1972.

Krementz, J. *The Fun of Cooking.* New York: Knopf, 1985.

Krementz, J. *How it Feels to Fight for Your Life.* Boston, MA: Joy Street, 1989.

Kuskin, K. *Dogs & Dragons, Trees & Dreams: A Collection of Poems.* New York: Harper, 1980.

Kuskin, K. *Something Sleeping in the Hall.* Harper, 1985.

Langner, N. *Cinderella.* New York: Scholastic, 1972.

Larrick, N., ed. *The Merry-Go-Round Poetry Book,* illustrated by K. Gundersheheimer. New York: Delacorte, 1989.

Lasky, K. *Sugaring Time,* photographs by C. G. Knight. New York: Macmillan, 1983.

Lasky, K. *Traces of Life: The Origins of Humankind,* illustrated by W. Powell. New York: Morrow, 1989.

Lauber, P. *Living With Dinosaurs,* illustrated by D. Henderson. Bradbury Press, 1991.

Lauber, P. *The News About Dinosaurs.* New York: Bradbury, 1989.

Lauber, P. *Summer of Fire: Yellowstone 1988.* New York: Orchard, 1991.

Lauber, P. *Tales Mummies Tell.* New York: Crowell, 1985.

Lauber, P. *Volcano: The Eruption and Healing of Mt. St. Helens.* New York: Bradbury, 1986.

Lawson, R. *Ben and Me.* Boston, MA: Little, Brown, 1951.

Lawson, R. *Mr. Revere and I.* Boston, MA: Little, Brown, 1953.

Le Cain, E. *Cinderella or The Little Glass Slipper.* New York: Penguin Books, 1979.

L'Engle, M. *A Ring of Endless Light.* New York: Farrar, Straus, 1980.

L'Engle, M. *A Wrinkle in Time.* New York: Farrar, Straus, 1962.

Le Guin, U. *A Wizard of Earthsea,* illustrated by R. Robbins. New York: Parnassus, 1968.

Le Guin, U. *The Farthest Shore,* illustrated by G. Garraty. New York: Atheneum, 1972.

Le Guin, U. *Tehanu: The Last Book of Earthsea.* New York: Atheneum, 1990.

Le Guin, U. *The Tombs of Atuan,* illustrated by G. Garraty. New York: Atheneum, 1971.

Lear, E. *Of Pelicans and Pussycats,* illustrated by J. Newton. New York, Dial, 1990.

Lee, B. *Judy Blume's Story.* New York: Dillon, 1981.

LeGuin, R. *A Wizard of Earthsea.* New York: Parnassus, 1968.

Legum, M. R. *Mailbox Quailbox,* illustrated by R. Shetterly. New York: Atheneum, 1985.

Lent, B. *Bayberry Bluff.* Boston, MA: Houghton Mifflin, 1987.

Leontyne, P. *Aïda,* illustrated by L. and D. Dillon. New York: Harcourt, 1990.

Levinson, R. *Watch the Stars Come Out,* illustrated by D. Goode. New York: Dutton, 1985.

Lewis, C. S. *The Lion, the Witch, and the Wardrobe,* illustrated by M. Hague. New York: Macmillan, 1988.

Lindgren, A. *Pippi Longstocking,* translated by Florence Lambom. New York: Puffin Books, 1977.

Lionni, L. *Fish is Fish.* New York: Pantheon, 1970.

Lionni, L. *Frederick.* New York: Pantheon, 1967.

Lionni, L. *Swimmy.* New York: Pantheon, 1963.

Little, J. *Little, by Little: A Writer's Education.* New York: Viking, 1987.

Little, J. *Stars Come Out Within.* New York: Viking, 1990.

Livingston, M. C. *A Circle of Seasons,* illustrated by L. E. Fisher. New York: Holiday, 1982.

Livingston, M. C. *Callooh! Callay! Holiday Poems for Young Readers.* New York: Atheneum, 1978.

Livingston, M. C., ed. *Cat Poems,* illustrated by T. S. Hyman. New York: Holiday, 1987.

Livingston, M. C. *Christmas Poems,* illustrated by T. S. Hyman. New York: Holiday, 1985.

Livingston, M. C. *Easter Poems,* illustrated by J. Wallner. New York: Holiday, 1985.

Livingston, M. C. *I Like You, If You Like Me, Poems of Friendship.* New York: McElderry, 1987.

Livingston, M. C. *O Frabjous Day! Poetry for Holidays and Special Occasions.* New York: Atheneum, 1977.

Livingston, M. C. *Poems for Jewish Holidays,* illustrated by L. Bloom. New York: Holiday, 1986.

Livingston, M. C., ed. *Poems for Brothers, Poems for Sisters,* illustrated by J. Zallinger. New York: Holiday House, 1991.

Livingston, M. C. *Thanksgiving Poems,* illustrated by S. Gammell. New York: Holiday, 1985.

Livingston, M. C. *What a Wonderful Bird the Frog Are.* New York: Harcourt, 1973.

Lobel, A. *The Book of Pigericks.* New York: Harper & Row, 1983.

Lobel, A. *Days with Frog and Toad.* New York: Harper, 1979.

Lobel, A. *Fables.* New York: Harper, 1980.

Lobel, A. *Frog and Toad All Year.* New York: Harper, 1976.

Lobel, A. *Frog and Toad are Friends.* New York: Harper, 1970.

Lobel, A. *Frog and Toad Together.* New York: Harper, 1972.

Lobel, A. *The Rose in My Garden,* illustrated by A. Lobel. New York: Greenwillow, 1983.

Locker, T. *Where the River Begins.* New York: Dial, 1984.

Louie, A. L. *Yeh-Shen: A Cinderella Story from China,* illustrated by E. Young. New York: Philomel, 1982.

Low, A. *The Family Read-Aloud Holiday Treasury.* Boston, MA: Little, Brown, 1991.

Lowry, L. *Anastatia Again.* Boston: Houghton Mifflin, 1981.

Lowry, L. *Anastatia at Your Service.* Boston: Houghton Mifflin, 1982.

Lowry, L. *Anastasia Krupnik.* Boston: MA: Houghton Mifflin, 1979.

Lowry, L. *A Summer to Die,* illustrated by J. Oliver. Boston, MA: Houghton Mifflin, 1977.

Lowry, L. *Number the Stars.* Boston, MA: Houghton Mifflin, 1989.

Lyon, G. E. *Come a Tide,* illustrated by S. Gammell. New York: Orchard, 1990.

Lyons, M. E. *Letters from a Slave Girl.* New York: Scribner's, 1992.

Macaulay, D. *Black and White.* Boston: Houghton Mifflin, 1990.

Macaulay, D. *Castle.* Boston, MA: Houghton Mifflin, 1977.

Macaulay, D. *Pyramid.* Boston, MA: Houghton Mifflin, 1975.

Macaulay, D. *Underground.* Boston, MA: Houghton Mifflin, 1976.

Macaulay, D. *The Way Things Work.* Boston, MA: Houghton Mifflin, 1988.

Macaulay, D. *Why the Chicken Crossed the Road.* Boston, MA: Houghton Mifflin, 1987.

MacDonald, C. *The Lake at the End of the World.* New York: Dial Books for Young Readers, 1989.

MacLachlan, P. *Arthur, For the Very First Time.* New York: Harper & Row, 1980.

MacLachlan, P. *Cassie Binegar.* New York: Harper, 1982.

MacLachlan, P. *The Facts and Fictions of Minna Pratt.* New York. Harper, 1988.

MacLachlan, P. *Sarah, Plain and Tall.* New York: Harper, 1985.

MacLachlan, P. *Through Grandpa's Eyes.* New York: Harper, 1980.

MacLachlan, P. *Unclaimed Treasures.* New York: Harper, 1984.

MacMillan, B. *Mary Had a Little Lamb.* New York: Scholastic, 1990.

Marriott, J. *Letters to Lesley.* New York: Knopf, 1989.

Marshall, J. *George and Martha.* Boston, MA: Houghton Mifflin, 1972.

Marshall, J. *George and Martha Back in Town.* Boston, MA: Houghton Mifflin, 1984.

Marshall, J. *George and Martha Round and Round.* Boston, MA: Houghton Mifflin, 1988.

Martin, B., Jr. *Brown Bear, Brown Bear, What Do You See?,* illustrated by E. Carle. New York: Holt, 1983.

Martin, B., Jr., *Monday, Monday, I Like Monday.* New York: Holt, Rinehart and Winston, 1970.

Martin, B., Jr., and Archambault, J. *Chicka, Chicka Boom Boom,* illustrated by L. Ehlert. New York: Simon & Schuster, 1989.

Martin, B., Jr., and Archambault, J. *Knots on a Counting Rope,* illustrated by T. Rand. New York: Holt, 1987.

Martin, R. *A Storyteller's Story.* Katonah, NY: Richard C. Owens, 1992.

Mathis, S. B. *Red Dog: Blue Fly: Football Poems,* illustrated by J. S. Gilchrist. New York: Viking, 1991.

Mayer, M. *A Boy, A Dog, and A Frog.* New York: Dial, 1967.

Mayer, M. *There's A Nightmare in My Closet.* New York: Dial, 1968.

Mayne, W. *The Patchwork Cat,* illustrated by N. Bagley. New York: Knopf, 1981.

Mazer, N. F. *Dear Bill, Remember Me? And Other Stories.* New York: Dell, 1976.

Mazer, N. F. *I, Trissy.* New York: Dell, 1971.

McCloskey, R. *Blueberries for Sal.* New York: Viking, 1963.

McCloskey, R. *Make Way for Ducklings.* New York: Viking, 1941.

McCloskey, R. *One Morning in Maine.* New York: Viking, 1952.

McCloskey, R. *Time of Wonder.* New York: Viking, 1957.

McCord, D. *Everytime I Climb a Tree,* illustrated by M. Simont. Boston, MA: Little, Brown, 1967.

McCord, D. *One At a Time,* illustrated by H. B. Kane. Boston, MA: Little, Brown, 1977.

McCully, E. *First Snow.* New York: Harper, 1985.

McCully, E. *Picnic.* New York: Harper, 1984.

McCully, E. *School.* New York: Harper, 1987.

McKissack, P. *Mirandy and Brother Wind,* illustrated by J. Pinkney. New York: Knopf, 1988.

McMillan, B. *Counting Wildflowers.* New York: Lothrop, Lee & Shepard, 1986.

McMillan, B. *Here a Chick, There a Chick.* New York: Lothrop, Lee & Shepard, 1983.

McPhail, D. *Pig Pig Goes to Camp.* New York: Dutton, 1983.

McPhail, D. *Pig Pig Rides.* New York: Dutton, 1982.

Meigs, C. *Invincible Louisa,* Boston, MA: Little, 1933.

Melser, J., and Crowley, J. *In a Dark Dark Wood.* Auckland, New Zealand: Shortland Publications, 1980.

Meltzer, M. *All Times, All Peoples: A World History of Slavery.* New York: Harper & Row, 1980.

Meltzer, M. *Dorothea Lange: Life Through the Camera,* illustrated by D. Diamond. New York: Viking, 1985.

Meltzer, M. *The Black Americans: A History in Their Own Words.* New York: T. Y. Crowell, 1984.

Merriam, E. *Blackberry Ink,* illustrated by H. Wilhelm. New York: Morrow, 1985.

Merriam, E. *Fresh Paint,* illustrated by D. Frampton. New York: Macmillan, 1986.

Miles, M. *Gertrude's Pocket.* Boston, MA: Atlantic Little, Brown, 1970.

Miller, M. *Whose Shoes?* New York: Greenwillow, 1991.

Minarik, E. *A Kiss for Little Bear,* illustrated by M. Sendak. New York: Harper, 1968.

Minarik, E. *Father Bear Comes Home,* illustrated by M. Sendak. New York: Harper, 1959.

Minarik, E. *Little Bear's Visit.* New York: Harper, 1961.

Minarik, E. *Little Bear.* New York: Harper, 1957.

Minarik, M. *Little Bear's Friend.* New York: Harper, 1960.

Monjo, F. N. *Letters to Horseface: Young Mozart's Travels in Italy,* illustrated by D. Bolognese and E. Raphael. New York: Puffin, 1991.

Monjo, F. N. *Poor Richard in France,* illustrated by B. Turkle. New York: Dell, 1990.

Monjo, F. N. *The Drinking Gourd,* illustrated by F. Brenner. New York: Harper, 1970.

Montresor, B. *Cinderella: From the Opera by Gioacchino Rossini.* New York: Knopf, 1965.

Moore, L. *I'll Meet You at the Cucumbers,* illustrated by S. Woodring. New York: Atheneum, 1988.

Moore, L. *Six Dinner Sid.* New York: Simon & Schuster, 1991.

Moore, L. *Something New Begins: New and Selected Poems,* illustrated by Mary J. Dunton. New York: Atheneum, 1982.

Moore, L. *Sunflakes Poems for Children,* illustrated by J. Ormerod. New York: Clarion, 1992.

Morrison, L. *Sprints and Distances; Sports in Poetry and Poetry in Sport,* illustrated by C. Ross and J. Ross. New York: Crowell, 1965.

Morrow, H. *On to Oregon!,* illustrated by E. Shenton. New York: Morrow, 1954.

Murphy, J. *The Long Road to Gettysburg.* New York: Clarion, 1992.

Myers, W. D. *Scorpions.* New York: Harper, 1988.

Naylor, P. R. *The Agony of Alice.* New York: Atheneum, 1985.

Naylor, P. R. *Alice in Rapture, Sort Of.* New York: Atheneum, 1989.

Naylor, P. R. *All but Alice.* NY: Atheneum, 1992.

Naylor, P. R. *How I Came to Be a Writer.* New York: Atheneum, 1987

Naylor, P. R. *Reluctantly Alice.* New York: Atheneum, 1991.

Naylor, P. R. *Shiloh.* New York: Atheneum, 1991.

Ness, E. *Sam, Bangs, and Moonshine.* New York: Holt, 1966.

Nixon, J. L. *Fat Change, Claude,* illustrated by T. C. Pearson. New York: Viking Kestrel, 1987.

Noyes, A. *The Highwayman,* illustrated by C. Keeping. New York: Oxford University Press, 1981.

Nye, N. S. *This Same Sky: A Collection of Poems from Around the World.* New York: Four Winds, 1992.

O'Brien, R. *Mrs. Frisby and the Rats of NIMH,* illustrated by Z. Bernstein. New York: Atheneum, 1971.

O'Brien, R. C. *Z for Zachariah.* New York: Atheneum, 1975.

O'Connor, J. *Yours Till Niagara Falls, Abby,* illustrated by M. Apple. New York: Scholastic, 1991.

O'Dell, S. *Island of the Blue Dolphins.* Boston, MA: Houghton Mifflin, 1960.

O'Dell, S. *Sing Down the Moon.* Boston, MA: Houghton Mifflin, 1970.

O'Neill, M. *Hailstones and Halibut Bones,* illustrated by L. Weisgard. New York: Philomel, 1961.

Orlev, U. *The Island on Bird Street.* Boston: Houghton Mifflin, 1984.

Ormerod, J. *Moonlight.* New York: Lothrop, 1982.

Ormerod, J. *Sunshine.* New York: Lothrop, 1981.

Osborne, M. P. *American Tall Tales,* illustrated by M. McCurdy. New York: Knopf, 1991.

Oxenbury, H. "The Baby Board Books," *Dressing, Family, Friends. Playing, Working.* New York: Simon & Schuster, 1981.

Oxenbury, H. *The Helen Oxenbury Nursery Rhyme Book.* New York: Morrow, 1986.

Parish, P. *Amelia Bedelia Helps Out.* NY: Greenwillow, 1979.

Parnall, P. *Apple Tree.* New York: Macmillan, 1986.

Parnall, P. *Winter Barn.* New York: Macmillan, 1986.

Patent, D. H. *Farm Animals.* New York: Holiday House, 1984.

Patent, D. H. *Gray Wolf, Red Wolf,* photographs by W. Munoz. New York: Clarion, 1990.

Patent, D. H. *Spider Magic.* New York: Holiday House, 1982.

Patent, D. H. *Whales: Giants of the Deep.* New York: Holiday House, 1984.

Patent, D. H. *Yellowstone Fires: Flames and Rebirth,* photographs by W. Munoz and others. New York: Holiday, 1990.

Paterson, K. *Bridge to Terabithia,* illustrated by D. Diamond. New York: Crowell, 1977.

Paterson, K. *The Great Gilly Hopkins.* New York: Crowell, 1978.

Paterson, K. *Jacob Have I Loved.* New York: Harper, 1980.

Paterson, K. *Lyddie.* New York: Dutton, 1991.

Paterson, K. *The Spying Heart.* New York: Lodestar Books, Dutton, 1989.

Paulsen, G. *Dogsong.* New York: Bradbury, 1985.

Paulsen, G. *Hatchet.* New York: Bradbury, 1987.

Paulsen, G. *The Island.* New York: Orchard, 1988.

Paulsen, G. *The River.* New York: Delacorte, 1991.

Paulsen, G. *The Voyage of the Frog.* New York: Bradbury, 1989.

Paulsen, G. *The Winter Room.* New York: Orchard, 1989.

Paulsen, G. *Woodsong.* NY: Bradbury, 1990.

Peck, R. N. *A Day No Pigs Would Die.* New York: Knopf, 1972.

Peet, B. *Bill Peet: An Autobiography.* Boston, MA: Houghton Mifflin, 1989.

Peet, B. *Cyrus and the Unsinkable Sea Serpent.* Boston, MA: Houghton Mifflin, 1975.

Peet, B. *No Such Things.* Boston, MA: Houghton Mifflin, 1983.

Peet, B. *Wump World.* Boston, MA: Houghton Mifflin, 1970.

Perrault, C. *The Complete Fairy Tales of Charles Perrault,* illustrated by S. Holmes. New York: Clarion, 1993.

Pfeffer, S. *Dear Dad, Love Laurie.* New York: Scholastic, 1989.

Polacco, P. *The Keeping Quilt.* New York: Simon & Schuster, 1988.

Polacco, P. *Thundercake.* New York: Philomel, 1990.

Potter, B. *The Tale of Peter Rabbit.* New York: Warne, 1902.

Prelutsky, J. *Beneath a Blue Umbrella,* illustrated by G. Williams. New York: Greenwillow, 1990.

Prelutsky, J. *For Laughing Out Loud: Poems to Tickle Your Funnybone,* illustrated by M. Priceman. New York: Knopf, 1991.

Prelutsky, J. *It's Halloween,* illustrated by M. Hafner. New York: Greenwillow, 1977.

Prelutsky, J. *The New Kid on the Block,* illustrated by J. Stevenson. New York: Greenwillow, 1984.

Prelutsky, J. *The Random House Book of Poetry for Children,* illustrated by A. Lobel. New York: Random House, 1983.

Prelutsky, J. *Read-Aloud Rhymes for the Very Young,* illustrated by M. Brown. New York: Knopf, 1986.

Prelutsky, J. *Something BIG Has Been Here,* illustrated by J. Stevenson. New York: Greenwillow, 1990.

Pringle, L. *Bearman: Exploring the World of Black Bears,* photographs by L. Rogers. New York: Scribner's, 1989.

Pringle, L. *Living Treasure: Saving Earth's Threatened Biodiversity,* illustrated by I. Brady. New York: Morrow, 1991.

Pringle, L. *Wolfman: Exploring the World of Wolves.* New York: Scribner's, 1983.

Provensen, A., and Provensen, M. *The Glorious Flight Across the Channel with Lois Bleriot.* New York: Viking, 1983.

Provensen, A., and Provensen, M. *Shaker Lane.* New York: Viking, 1987.

Reeder, C. *Shades of Grey.* New York: Macmillan, 1989.

Reiss, J. *The Upstairs Room.* NY: Crowell, 1972.

Robertson, K. *Henry Reed, Inc.,* illustrated by R. McCloskey. New York: Viking, 1958.

Robinson, B. *The Best Christmas Pageant Ever,* illustrated by J. G. Brown. New York: Harper, 1972.

Rockwell, T. *How to Eat Fried Words.* New York: Watts, 1973.

Rodowsky, C. *P.S. Write Soon.* New York: Farrar, Straus Giroux, 1987.

Root, P., and Root, C., eds. *I, Columbus: My Journal—1492–3,* illustrated by P. E. Hanson. New York: Walker, 1990.

Root, P. *Soup for Supper,* illustrated by S. Truesdell. New York: Harper & Row, 1986.

Rosen, M. *We're Going on a Bear Hunt,* illustrated by H. Oxenbury. New York: Macmillan, 1989.

Rounds, G. *Three Little Pigs and the Big Bad Wolf.* New York: Holiday, 1992.

Ryden, H. *Wild Animals of Africa ABC.* New York: Lodestar Books, 1989.

Ryder, J. *The Snail's Spell,* illustrated by L. Cherry. New York: Frederick Warne, 1982.

Rylant, C. *A Solitary Blue.* New York: Atheneum, 1984.

Rylant, C. *Every Living Thing,* illustrated by S. D. Schindler. New York: Bradbury, 1985.

Rylant, C. *Henry and Mudge Take the Big Test,* illustrated by S. Stevenson. New York: Bradbury, 1991.

Rylant, C. *Henry and Mudge,* illustrated by S. Stevenson. New York: Macmillan, 1987.

Rylant, C. *Missing May.* New York: Orchard, 1992.

Rylant, C. *The Relatives Came,* illustrated by S. Gammell. New York: Bradbury, 1985.

Rylant, C. *When I Was Young in the Mountains,* illustrated by D. Goode. New York: Dutton, 1982.

Sachs, M. *A Summer's Lease.* New York: Dutton, 1979.

Sachs, M. *Dorrie's Book,* drawings by A. Sachs. New York: Avon, 1991.

San Souci, R. D. *The Talking Eggs,* illustrated by J. Pinkney. New York: Dial, 1989.

Sanderson, R. *The Enchanted Wood.* Boston, MA: Little, Brown, 1991.

Schulevitz, U. *One Monday Morning.* New York: Charles Scribner's Sons, 1962.

Schwartz, D. M. *How Much Is a Million?,* illustrated by S. Kellogg. New York: Lothrop, Lee & Shepard, 1985.

Scieszka, J. *The Frog Prince Continued,* illustrated by S. Johnson. New York: Viking, 1991.

Scieszka, J. *The Stinky Cheese Man and Other Fairly Stupid Tales,* illustrated by L. Smith. New York: Viking, 1992.

Scieszka, J. *The True Story of the Three Little Pigs by A. Wolf,* illustrated by Lane Smith. New York: Viking, 1989.

Selden, G. *The Cricket in Times Square,* illustrated by G. Williams. New York: Farrar, Straus & Giroux, 1981.

Selsam, M. E. *A First Look at Animals That Eat Other Animals.* New York: Walter & Co., 1990.

Selsam, M. E. *Egg to Chick,* illustrated by B. Wolff. New York: Harper Trophy, 1987.

Selsam, M. E., and Hunt, J. *A First Look at Seashells,* illustrated by H. Springer. New York: Walker, 1983.

Sendak, M. *Chicken Soup With Rice.* New York: Harper, 1962.

Sendak, M. *Hector Protector and as I Went Over the Water.* New York: Harper, 1990.

Sendak, M. *In the Night Kitchen.* New York: Harper, 1970.

Sendak, M. *Outside Over There.* New York: Harper, 1981.

Sendak, M. *Pierre.* New York: Harper, 1962.

Sendak, M. *Seven Little Monsters.* New York: Harper, 1977.

Sendak, M. *The Sign on Rosie's Door.* New York: Harper, 1960.

Sendak, M. *Where the Wild Things Are.* New York: Harper, 1963.

Seuss, Dr. *Horton Hatches the Egg.* New York: Random, 1940.

Seuss, Dr. *The Cat in the Hat.* New York: Random, 1957.

Shaw, C. G. *It Looked Like Spilt Milk.* New York: Harper & Row, 1947.

Shulevitz, U. *Dawn.* New York: Farrar, Straus, 1974.

Shulevitz, U. *Toddlecreek Post Office.* New York: Farrar, Straus, 1990.

Shwartz, A. *Her Majesty, Aunt Essie.* New York: Bradbury, 1984.

Siebert, D. *Heartland,* illustrated by W. Minor. New York: Crowell, 1989.

Siebert, D. *Sierra,* illustrated by W. Minor. New York: HarperCollins, 1991.

Silverstein, S. *A Light in the Attic.* New York: Harper, 1981.

Silverstein, S. *Where the Sidewalk Ends: Poems and Drawings.* New York: Harper, 1974.

Simon, S. *Einstein Anderson Sees Through the Invisible Man.* New York: Viking Press, 1983.

Simon, S. *Galaxies.* New York: Morrow, 1988.

Simon, S. *Neptune.* New York: Morrow, 1991.

Simon, S. *Soap Bubble Magic,* illustrated by S. Ormai. New York: Lothrop, 1985.

Singer, M. *Turtle in July,* illustrated by J. Pinkney. New York: Macmillan, 1989.

Slepian, J. *The Broccoli Tapes.* New York: Philomel, 1998.

Smith, D. *A Taste of Blackberries.* NY: Crowell, 1973.

Snyder, S. K. *Libby on Wednesday.* New York: Doubleday, 1990.

Sonnemark, L. A. *Something's Rotten in the State of Maryland.* New York: Scholastic, 1990.

Speare, E. G. *The Sign of the Beaver.* Boston: Houghton Mifflin, 1983.

Speare, E. G. *The Witch of Blackbird Pond.* Boston, MA: Houghton Mifflin, 1958.

Sperry, A. *Call it Courage.* New York: Macmillan, 1968.

Spinelli, J. *Maniac Magee.* Boston: Little, Brown, 1990.

Stamm, C. *Three Strong Women: A Tall Tale from Japan,* illustrated by J. and M. Tseng. New York: Viking Penguin, 1990.

Stanley, D. *Shaka: King of the Zulus.* New York: Morrow, 1988.

Stanley, D., and Vennema, P. *Bard of Avon: The Story of William Shakespeare,* illustrated by D. Stanley. New York: Morrow, 1992.

Stanley, D., and Vennema, P. *Good Queen Bess: The Story of Elizabeth the First of England,* illustrated by D. Stanley. New York: Four Winds, 1990.

Staples, S. F. *Shabanu: Daughter of the Wind.* New York: Knopf, 1989.

Steele, M. Q. *Anna's Garden Songs.* New York: Greenwillow, 1989.

Steig, W. *Abel's Island.* New York: Farrar, Straus & Giroux, 1976.

Steig, W. *The Amazing Bone.* New York: Farrar, Straus, 1976.

Steig, W. *Amos & Boris.* New York: Farrar, Straus, 1971.

Steig, W. *Brave Irene.* New York: Farrar, 1986.

Steig, W. *Doctor DeSoto.* New York: Farrar, Straus & Giroux, 1982.

Steig, W. *Sylvester and the Magic Pebble.* New York: Windmill, 1969.

Steptoe, J. *Mufaro's Beautiful Daughters: An African Tale.* New York: Lothrop, Lee & Shepard, 1987.

Stevens, C. *A Book of Your Own: Keeping a Diary or Journal.* New York: Clarion, 1993.

Stevens, C. *Anna, Grandpa, and the Big Storm,* illustrated by M. Tomes. Boston, MA: Houghton Mifflin, 1982.

Stevenson, J. *Could be Worse.* New York: Greenwillow, 1977.

Stevenson, J. *Higher On the Door.* New York: Greenwillow, 1987.

Stevenson, J. *What's Under My Bed?* New York: Greenwillow, 1983.

Stevenson, J. *When I Was Nine.* NY: Greenwillow, 1986.

Stevenson, J. *Worse Than Willy!* New York: Greenwillow, 1988.

Sussman, S., and James, R. *Lies (People Believe) About Animals,* photographs by F. Leavitt. Niles, IL: Albert Whitman, 1987.

Tafuri, N. *Have You Seen My Duckling?* New York: Greenwillow, 1984.

Tafuri, N. *Junglewalk.* New York: Greenwillow, 1988.

Taylor, M. *Roll of Thunder, Hear My Cry,* illustrated by J. Pinkney. New York: Dial, 1976.

Titherington, J. *Pumpkin Pumpkin.* New York: Greenwillow, 1986.

Turkle, B. *Deep in the Forest.* New York: Dutton, 1976.

Turner, A. *Dakota Dugout,* illustrated by R. Himler. New York: Macmillan, 1985.

Turner, A. *Nettie's Trip South,* illustrated by R. Himler. New York: Macmillan, 1987.

Uchida, U. *Invisible Thread.* New York: Messer, 1991.

Uchida, Y. *Journey to Topaz,* illustrated by D. Carrick. Berkeley, CA: Creative Arts Book Co., 1985.

Van Allsburg, C. *Ben's Dream.* Boston, MA: Houghton Mifflin, 1982.

Van Allsburg, C. *Jumanji.* Boston, MA: Houghton Mifflin, 1981.

Van Allsburg, C. *Just a Dream.* Boston, MA: Houghton Mifflin, 1990.

Van Allsburg, C. *The Garden of Abdul Gasazi.* Boston, MA: Houghton Mifflin, 1979.

Van Allsburg, C. *The Mysteries of Harris Burdick.* Boston, MA: Houghton Mifflin, 1984.

Van Allsburg, C. *The Polar Express.* Boston, MA: Houghton Mifflin, 1985.

Van Allsburg, C. *The Stranger.* Boston, MA: Houghton Mifflin, 1986.

Van Allsburg, C. *The Sweetest Fig.* Boston, MA: Houghton Mifflin, 1993.

Van Allsburg, C. *The Widow's Broom.* Boston, MA: Houghton Mifflin, 1992.

Van Allsburg, C. *The Wreck of the Zephyr.* Boston, MA: Houghton Mifflin, 1983.

Van Allsburg, C. *The Wretched Stone.* Boston, MA: Houghton Mifflin, 1991.

Van Allsburg, C. *The Z Was Zapped: A Play in Twenty-Six Acts.* Boston, MA: Houghton Mifflin, 1987.

Van Allsburg, C. *Two Bad Ants.* Boston, MA: Houghton Mifflin, 1988.

Van Laan, N. *Possum Come A-Knockin,* illustrated by G. Booth. New York: Knopf, 1990.

Van Raven, P. *Great Man's Secret.* New York: Scribner's, 1989.

Viorst, J. *Alexander and the Terrible, Horrible, No Good, Very Bad Day,* illustrated by R. Cruz. New York: Atheneum, 1972.

Vo-Dinh. *The Toad Is the Emperor's Uncle: Animal Folk Tales from Vietnam.* NY: Doubleday, 1970.

Voigt, C. *Dicey's Song.* New York: Atheneum, 1982.

Voigt, C. *Homecoming.* New York: Atheneum, 1981.

Waber, B. *Ira Says Goodbye.* Boston, MA: Houghton Mifflin, 1988.

Waber, B. *Ira Sleeps Over.* Boston, MA: Houghton Mifflin, 1972.

Waber, B. *Lyle, Lyle Crocodile.* Boston, MA: Houghton Mifflin, 1965.

Walsh, J. P. *Lost and Found,* illustrated by M. Ragner. London: André Deutsch, 1984.

Ward, C. *Cookie's Week,* illustrated by T. de Paola. New York: Putnam's, 1988.

Ward, L. *The Biggest Bear.* Boston, MA: Houghton Mifflin, 1952.

Webster, J. *Daddy-Long-Legs,* New York: Puffin Books, 1989.

Wells, R. *A Lion for Lewis.* New York: Dial, 1982.

Wells, R. *Noisy Nora.* New York: Dial, 1973.

Wells, R. *Shy Charles.* New York: Dial, 1988.

White, E. B. *Charlotte's Web,* illustrated by G. Williams. New York: Harper, 1952.

White, E. B. *The Trumpet of the Swans.* NY: Harper, 1970.

Whitney, T. *Vassilisa the Beautiful.* New York: Macmillan, 1970.

Wickstrom, S. K. *Wheels on the Bus: Raffi Songs to Read.* New York: Crown, 1988.

Wiesner, D. *Free Fall.* New York: Lothrop, Lee & Shepard Books, 1988.

Wiesner, D. *Hurricane.* New York: Clarion, 1990.

Wiesner, D. *Tuesday.* New York: Clarion, 1991.

Willard, N. *A Visit to William Blake's Inn: Poems for Innocent and Experienced Travelers,* illustrated by A. and M. Provensen. New York: Harcourt Brace Jovanovich, 1981.

Willard, N. *Beauty and the Beast,* illustrated by B. Moser. New York: Harcourt Brace Jovanovich, 1992.

Willard, N. *Pish, Posh, said Hieronymous Bosh,* illustrated by L. and D. Dillon. New York: Harcourt, 1991.

Willard, N. *The Voyage of the Ludgate Hill,* illustrated by A. and M. Provensen. New York: Harcourt Brace Jovanovich, 1987.

Williams, K. L. *Galimoto,* illustrated by C. Stock. New York: Lothrop, 1990.

Williams, S. *I Went Walking.* New York: Harcourt Brace Jovanovich, 1990.

Williams, V. B. *A Chair for My Mother.* New York: Greenwillow, 1982.

Williams, V. B. *Music, Music for Everyone.* New York: Greenwillow, 1984.

Wojciechowskia, M. *Hey, What's Wrong with This One?* New York: Harper & Row, 1969.

Wolff, A. *A Year of Birds.* New York: Dutton, 1984.

Wood, A. *Heckedy Peg,* illustrated by D. Wood. New York: Harcourt, 1987.

Wood, A. *The Napping House,* illustrated by D. Wood. New York: Harcourt, 1984.

Woodruff, E. *Dear Napoleon, I Know You're Dead, But,* drawings by N. and J. Woodruff. New York: Holiday, 1982.

Worth, V. *All the Small Poems,* illustrated by N. Babbitt. New York: Farrar, Straus, 1987.

Worth, V. *Small Poems Again,* illustrated by N. Babbitt. New York: Farrar, Straus, 1985.

Yabuuchi, M. *Whose Baby?* New York: Philomel, 1985.

Yabuuchi, M. *Whose Footprints?* New York: Philomel, 1985.

Yagawa, S. *The Crane Wife,* illustrated by S. Akaba (translated by K. Paterson). New York: Morrow, 1981.

Yates, E. *Amos Fortune, Free Man,* illustrated by N. Unwin. New York: Dutton, 1967.

Yep, L. *The Lost Garden.* Englewood Cliffs, NJ: Julian Messner, 1991.

Yolen, J. *A Letter from Phoenix Farm.* Katonah, NY: Richard C. Owen, 1992.

Yolen, J. *Bird Watch,* illustrated by T. Lewin. New York: Philomel, 1990.

Yolen, J. *The Devil's Arithmetic.* New York: Viking Penguin, 1990.

Yolen, J. *Owl Moon,* illustrated by J. Schoenherr. New York: Philomel, 1987.

Zilinsky, P. O. *Rumpelstiltskin.* New York: Dutton, 1986.

Zindel, P. *My Darling, My Hamburger.* New York: Harper, 1969.

Zindel, P. *The Pigman & Me.* New York: HarperCollins, 1991.

Zolotow, C. *Mr. Rabbit and the Lovely Present.* New York: Harper, 1962.

Zolotow, C. *Say It,* illustrated by J. Stevenson. New York: Greenwillow, 1980.

INDEX